Christian
Counseling Ethics

A Handbook for Psychologists, Therapists and Pastors

SECOND EDITION

EDITED BY
Randolph K. Sanders, Ph.D.

IVP Academic

An imprint of InterVarsity Press
Downers Grove, Illinois

InterVarsity Press
P.O. Box 1400, Downers Grove, IL 60515-1426
World Wide Web: www.ivpress.com
Email: email@ivpress.com

InterVarsity Press® is the book-publishing division of InterVarsity Christian Fellowship/USA®, a movement of students and faculty active on campus at hundreds of universities, colleges and schools of nursing in the United States of America, and a member movement of the International Fellowship of Evangelical Students. For information about local and regional activities, write Public Relations Dept., InterVarsity Christian Fellowship/USA, 6400 Schroeder Rd., P.O. Box 7895, Madison, WI 53707-7895, or visit the IVCF website at <www.intervarsity.org>.

Scripture quotations marked NIV are from the Holy Bible, New International Version®. NIV®. Copyright ©1973, 1978, 1984 by International Bible Society. Used by permission of Zondervan Publishing House. All rights reserved.

Scripture quotations marked NRSV are from the New Revised Standard Version of the Bible, copyright 1989 by the Division of Christian Education of the National Council of the Churches of Christ in the USA. Used by permission. All rights reserved.

While all stories in this book are true, some names and identifying information in this book have been changed to protect the privacy of the individuals involved.

Cover design by Cindy Kiple
Interior design by Beth Hagenberg
Images: abstract stream: © Ogphoto/iStockphoto

ISBN 978-0-8308-3994-0

Printed in the United States of America ∞

Library of Congress Cataloging-in-Publication Data

Christian counseling ethics : a handbook for psychologists, therapists and pastors / edited by Randolph K. Sanders, Ph.D.—Second Edition.

   pages cm
   Includes bibliographical references and index.
   ISBN 978-0-8308-3994-0 (pbk. : alk. paper)
   1. Pastoral counseling—Moral and ethical aspects. 2. Counselors—Professional ethics. I. Sanders, Randolph K., editor of compilation.
   BV4012.2.C516 2013
   241'.641—dc23

                                                                          2012045941

| **P** | 21 | 20 | 19 | 18 | 17 | 16 | 15 | 14 | 13 | 12 | 11 | 10 | 9 | 8 | 7 | 6 |
| **Y** | 29 | 28 | 27 | 26 | 25 | 24 | 23 | 22 | 21 | 20 | 19 | 18 | 17 | | | | |

Contents

1

Embracing Our Ethical Mandate

Randolph K. Sanders

As a newly graduated Ph.D., I was, like most new psychologists, concerned with finding my first full-time position in the field. I discussed jobs with supervisors, made phone calls and sent résumés.

One day, I received a call from the executive director of one of the Christian counseling centers to which I had sent my résumé. This man's agency was an established center, well known and well liked by many in the lay community.

After some preliminary discussion of my qualifications, I asked the director for more details about the programs at his center. "Just a minute," he replied. I could hear him rustling through some papers. "Take down these names and numbers," he said rather brusquely once he returned to the phone. I complied, but after taking down several listings, I felt myself becoming vaguely uncomfortable. "Dr. _____, exactly who are these people?" I asked.

"They're my clients," he replied. "I want you to call them, and they'll tell you what we do here and how they like what we do. If you like what you hear, you can call me back."

After pausing for a moment, and certainly not wanting to question an older, ostensibly wiser, colleague, I ventured rather carefully, "Ah, Dr. _____, I just wondered, have these clients given you permission to release their names and numbers?"

"Sure," he replied flippantly and with a lack of sincerity. And with a hint of sarcasm he asked, "Why is that so important to you?"

"Well," I began. "I was trained in the APA [American Psychological Association] Code of Ethics, which says . . ."

He cut me off abruptly. "APA Ethics Code? Well Dr. Sanders, that tells me something about you. We live by a higher standard of ethics here—Christian ethics—*not* APA ethics!"

"You know, Dr. Sanders," he continued, "I don't think we would need your services at our center after all. Goodbye!" And with that, he abruptly hung up the phone. Several years later, this man's counseling center closed after serious allegations of misconduct and improprieties arose.

Whatever the counseling director meant by Christian ethics as a higher form of ethics, it is clear that his concept of professional ethics was different from that which most therapists hold. The case illustrates the dangers of deciding, for whatever reason, to practice without benefit of the basic rules agreed on by most others in one's profession. By placing his counselees' rights to privacy and confidentiality below his desire to promote his counseling center, this counseling center director had placed them in a potentially embarrassing and possibly harmful position. Further, the case demonstrates rather dramatically why Christians should never presume that their faith perspective inoculates them against the ethical or moral failures that afflict others in society. Finally, the embarrassing closure of the man's counseling center several years later illustrates the far-reaching and harmful consequences that ethical or moral failures can have.

CHRISTIAN COUNSELING AND ETHICS

When Christians who are mental health professionals speak of Christian counseling, the conversation usually turns rather rapidly to matters of theology. Discussion often centers on the compatibility (or incompatibility) of various counseling interventions with accepted Christian tradition(s), or on what constitutes distinctively Christian interventions in counseling. To be sure, such questions are not just discussed among mental health professionals. They are also a topic of conversation among the clergy and others in positions of leadership in the wider Christian community. Much time and effort is spent theorizing, discussing, writing and arguing about these topics.

Concerns about the theological orthodoxy of Christian counseling are important. Yet as important as these concerns may be, this singleness of focus sometimes sidetracks professionals from attending to an equally valid concern: the ethical integrity of the Christian counseling profession in everyday praxis (practice).

Counseling and psychotherapy are deeply personal endeavors. When people come to counseling they are often immensely troubled and confused. In therapy they express feelings, concerns and secrets they might not feel comfortable sharing with anyone else, even personal confidantes, family or clergy. At times, the counseling room becomes an intimate interpersonal environment, even a sacred space. Life-changing experiences sometimes occur. I believe that God is deeply concerned about these encounters.

As professionals and as Christian people, we frequently have the opportunity to reflect the caring love and concern of God to the people we encounter in therapy. The empathic and deeply caring therapist, enriched with knowledge, wisdom and skill can touch lives and facilitate change. Our primary aspirational desires should be to do our best to help our clients and to make our actions pleasing to God. Our ongoing quest is to understand what God is calling us to be and to do (Jones, 1994) and to live in keeping with that calling personally and vocationally. We have a responsibility as people that God loves and redeems to reach out in agape love to others. Part of reaching out in love is endeavoring to practice ethically. For the clients who see us in counseling and the professionals who work with us daily, theological purity will make little difference if we do not practice with ethical integrity. It is at the point of practice that our clients best see our faith at work. Thus, good ethics are basic to good Christian counseling.

Whether the client (or the counselor) realizes it, I suspect that ethics are also of central importance to the average person who seeks out a Christian counselor. Clients want to know

- Will my therapist have the skills to help me?
- Will my therapist keep what I say confidential?
- Will I be able to trust my therapist to treat me with the same respect, care and attention the therapist would want for him- or herself?
- Will my therapist uphold moral values that I believe are important?

The purpose of this book is to create greater understanding regarding the kinds of ethical dilemmas that Christian practitioners face, help practitioners better understand and apply ethical rules and moral thinking to practice, and develop good decision-making strategies for navigating through ethical dilemmas and landmines.

ETHICAL ISSUES AND THE PROFESSIONAL CODES OF CONDUCT

Ethical dilemmas occur in mental health work. They are a given. Some are more common than others.

- A therapist is seeing an adolescent for therapy. After several sessions, the client reveals that he is taking drugs. Should the therapist tell the boy's parents?

- A psychologist teaches part-time at a college in addition to providing private practice services. A student at the college begins seeing her for therapy, but is not a student in any of her classes. A year later the student enrolls in one of her classes. What should she do?

- A therapist lives in a small town where there are few mental health professionals. A woman enters treatment for depression, but after several sessions, it becomes evident that she is suffering from an eating disorder also. The therapist has had no experience in treating eating disorders, but neither have any of the other therapists in the town, and the closest other referral is miles away. What should the therapist do?

- A therapist holds a Ph.D. in psychology but is licensed as a mental health counselor rather than a psychologist. The therapist tells clients at the Christian counseling center where he works that he is a psychologist. Has he acted unethically?

These are just a few of the many examples of the ethical issues and dilemmas that mental health professionals face. In response to these dilemmas, various entities have devised rules, codes and guidelines to help practitioners handle these problems. In addition to state and federal laws (Ohlschlager & Mosgofian, 1992), professional groups such as the American Psychological Association (2010), the American Association of Marriage and Family Therapists (2012), the American Counseling Association (2005), American Psychiatric Association (2006), National Association of Social

Workers (2008) and several other organizations maintain codes of ethical conduct that their members are sworn to live by.

Several religious groups have also developed codes or ethical guideline statements. The Christian Association for Psychological Studies (CAPS), a nonprofit organization comprising primarily mental health professionals and behavioral scientists, approved a statement of ethical guidelines in 1993 that its members are required to agree to. The latest rendition of that statement was approved in 2005 (CAPS, 2005). The American Association of Pastoral Counselors (AAPC) is a religiously pluralistic organization that credentials pastoral counselors. As Beck (1997) noted, "members are not just pastors who counsel; they are women and men who have carved out for themselves a distinct form of psychotherapy called pastoral counseling" (p. 315). This group first published an ethics code in 1991, with the latest version published in 2010. The American Association of Christian Counselors (AACC) addresses itself to "the entire 'community of care,' licensed professionals, pastors, and lay church members with little or no formal training" (AACC Mission, n.d.). The AACC published an ethics code in 2004 (AACC Code of Ethics, 2004) (see appendix 1 for information on codes of conduct of various groups). Many state boards also have rules of practice for all individuals licensed or certified by that board.

Underlying the ethics codes are philosophical bases for determining what constitutes ethical behavior. A number of these exist. For our purposes, I will point to at least two. One, the *deontological* approach, focuses on the essence of the act itself and defines some acts as good and others as bad. Defining what is good or bad might be based on the notion of the fundamental importance of respect for persons, a view that was advanced by Immanuel Kant. It might be based on convention(s) or on divine authority as revealed in Scripture or by religious tradition.

A *teleological* or *utilitarian* approach determines whether an act is ethical based on its outcome. If the action tends to create more good than harm, it is defined as ethical. We shall have more to say about these things later in this volume. However, I can say here that most mental health ethics codes as well as most interpretations of Christian ethics have elements of both deontological and teleological/utilitarian approaches embedded in them. For example, a Christian ethic refers to relevant Scripture for authority, but it also usually encourages adherents to follow "the spirit of the law," adapting principles to produce the greatest good or that which represents the most loving response to those concerned.

Most ethics codes include at least two levels of principles that they place on the clinician; aspirational ideals and mandatory obligations. *Aspirational ideals* are the ideal moral principles and overarching visions the ethical therapist should aspire to. It is recognized that the realities and the complex nature of life and of human beings make the realization of these aspirational ideals impossible to achieve perfectly. However, the ideals provide a lofty standard that therapists can aim for.

Kitchener (1984) identified five moral ideals that are foundational to many mental health codes: (1) autonomy, (2) nonmaleficence, (3) beneficence, (4) justice and (5) fidelity. One can see these ideals clearly embedded in the aspirational principles of the APA Code (2010).

Principle A: Beneficence and nonmaleficence. Following a mandate laid down originally in the Hippocratic Oath, the ethical therapist seeks to benefit clients and strives not to do things that would harm them. The therapist seeks to advance and refine his or her professional skills and generally avoids areas in which he or she is not knowledgeable. The therapist tries to be sensitive to and avoid those things that would harm the client. In unusual circumstances where harm is unavoidable, as when the therapist must break confidentiality to protect someone, the therapist does everything possible to minimize the harm.

Principle B: Fidelity and responsibility. Ethical therapists strive to be trustworthy. Clients should be able to trust that their therapists will do the best they can to uphold essential standards of clinical care and professional conduct. Therapists are sensitive to their responsibilities to the wider community and to society.

Principle C: Integrity. Therapists seek to be honest and consistent in the way they represent themselves and their professional activities. This is important when the therapist is involved in direct clinical service, but it is just as true when the therapist is engaged in research, teaching or in representing the profession and its knowledge base to the general public.

Principle D: Justice. Justice has to do with the therapist's responsibility to treat people fairly, to avoid prejudice and bias, and to be particularly sensitive to protecting the rights of the vulnerable among us.

Principle E: Respect for people's rights and dignity. This principle charges that therapists should seek to respect the worth of the people with whom they work, including the person's right "to privacy, confidentiality and self-determination" (APA, 2010). Again, the principle places special emphasis on remembering to respect the rights and dignity of those who are particularly vulnerable and whose ability to make autonomous decisions is compromised by physical, mental or other factors.

Many of these aspirational ideals are rooted at least in part in a Judeo-Christian tradition, though this may not always be self-evident. For Christians in the mental health professions, it may also be useful to consider some explicitly Christian ideals that seem pertinent to the ethical practice of psychotherapy and counseling. These principles may add further meaning and depth to the aspirational ideals set forth in the ethics codes. A number of these are set forth below.

1. Counseling as a calling. Historically in Western society many professions were at one time viewed as forms of ministry (Campbell, 1982). Many Christian therapists carry this tradition forward, experiencing their involvement in the work of counseling as a *calling*, and seeing their work not as a job but as a vocation of service.

2. Stewardship of talents. In addition to viewing counseling as a calling, a Christian perspective views one's talents, including professional talents, as a gift from God to be used in service to others (1 Pet 4:10). As such, the gift is a sacred trust, and the recipient is expected to prove faithful to that trust (1 Cor 4:2). Thus, in training and service the professional is called to the highest standards of preparation, competence and practice. In a real sense the work of counseling can be seen as an extension of Christ's healing ministry.

3. The comprehensive nature of the reign of God. "For Christians, the kingdom of God constitutes the primary ethical community" (Anderson, 1990, p. 204). The Christian faith makes the bold assertion that God's reign extends into all aspects of life (Christian Life Commission, 1981). This includes the professional life. God is as present with us in the therapy room as when we are at church. He is present when we make business decisions about our professional practice. He is concerned with the philosophies that inform our therapies and our ethical decisions.

This is a source of great comfort. It makes clear God's desire to be involved in our present realities, encouraging and supporting us, and it affirms God's care and love for us in the midst of the difficult, stressful decisions we face. It also confronts us with the fact that we cannot separate our faith from our vocation when it is convenient for us to do so. God challenges us to make our decisions with more than ourselves in mind. We must avoid the temptation to live as if God's standards are fine for ecclesiastical circles but impractical for the world of complicated client issues or the competitive world of the counseling business. To do so is to live as if our faith is impotent in the world we live in, and it leaves us open to hypocrisy in our thinking and our behavior.

4. *Humility*. Sin is a very real presence in our world (Rom 3:23). Generally forgotten in most professional codes, it is nevertheless an extremely important reality to which we are all prone (CAPS, 2005). Though traditional codes have done little to remind us of the presence of sin, psychology has certainly documented some of its characteristic patterns (McMinn, 2004). Attribution theory, for example, recognizes that human beings tend to make excuses and find extenuating circumstances for their own mistakes, while blaming other people for theirs. We readily take responsibility for success even when it isn't justified, but we tend to blame our failures on others (Myers, 1980). Rationalization, one of a number of psychodynamic defense mechanisms, illuminates our tendency to justify our unacceptable behaviors, attitudes and beliefs.

The reality of sin calls professionals to practice the art and science of therapy with humility. Ethical therapists remain vigilant to their own human limitations and avoid the notion that their professional standing, knowledge or their religious beliefs ever fully inoculate them from error.

5. *The image of God in humanity*. The Bible states that each person is created in the image of God (Gen 1:27). As such, human beings have a special quality, a uniqueness among creatures. The message of Scripture is that each person is of inestimable value to God, and by extension to us as therapists. These understandings undergird our responsibility to practice *beneficence* and *nonmaleficence* toward the people we serve (Kitchener, 1984), and a special obligation to respect the dignity and worth of our clients (APA, 2010, Principle E), no matter their condition or social standing. In

fact, in the narrative of the New Testament, Jesus Christ explicitly identifies himself with those who are weak or in need, and proclaims also that those who care for people like that have, in fact, cared for him (Mt 25:31-46).

As Christian mental health professionals, we are concerned about the dignity and needs of each individual, whether they are clients, colleagues, employees, students, research subjects or others we work with. A client is far more than a diagnostic label. An employee is more than a "hired hand." An employer is not just a boss. A professional colleague is not to be viewed solely as a competitor. All are people created in God's image. All are people of worth in God's eyes and in ours as well (Christian Life Commission, 1981).

6. *Autonomy.* Autonomy (Kitchener, 1984) refers to the therapist's responsibility to ensure clients' rights to make their own informed decisions and actions. Part of the task of the therapist is to help clients learn how to consider various options and make their own decisions. Obviously there are limits to this principle, as when the client is a child or is someone who is unable to make competent choices.

Though autonomy is a principle developed mostly out of the emergence of democratic societies, it is not without foundation in Christian thought, so long as by *autonomy* one means the ability to self-manage, self-control or self-discipline rather than to be self-willed (Tit 1:7-8). An important aspect of disciplined autonomy is recognizing how one's own actions affect others.

7. *Concern for community.* We are called to recognize the larger community in which we and those we counsel live (McCloughry, 1995). The New Testament emphasis on *koinōnia* (κοινωνία) fellowship illustrates God's concern with healthy community. Our counselees live as part of larger communities: nuclear family, extended family, church, neighborhood, God's world. Decisions that are made affect others as well as oneself. When a client ends a marriage, for example, it has repercussions that reach far beyond just the individual and the spouse. Children are affected, of course, but so are extended family, friends and associates. The therapist should be sensitive to the needs of the larger body in which the person lives (Eberlein, 1987, pp. 356-57), and though encouraging individual autonomy, should also assist the client in understanding how his or her behavior may or may not affect others. A sensitivity to community also has implications for the therapist. It implies that therapists should not practice in isolation but in the context of the larger community. This community provides support and accountability. For the professional, the wider community is both a source of sustenance and a group to which one is responsible (Reeck, 1982).

8. Covenantal relationships. The Old Testament concept of covenant is more than a contract. It establishes a trustworthy *relationship* between humankind and God. It forms the basis of the Old Testament ethic (Dumbrell, 1995). Likewise trust and *fidelity* are essential to the therapeutic relationship. Without them the relationship is unlikely to be beneficial. Trustworthiness encompasses keeping promises, being faithful and remaining loyal.

9. Concern for honesty. The ninth commandment says, "Thou shall not give false testimony," and with good reason. Lying destroys relationships, both individual and communal. Honesty and integrity are fundamental to good mental health practice. Clients have a right to expect it of us. Therapists who conduct themselves in this way set a tone of honesty and reasonableness for the therapeutic relationship, modeling these behaviors themselves and thus encouraging clients to do likewise. Being forthright is not the same as being brutally honest, however. Christian counselors are called to "speak the truth in love" (Eph 4:15), sharing information in a caring, understanding manner that reflects empathy for the listener.

10. Christian love. Love is the bedrock of the New Testament ethic (1 Cor 13). We are to love others with the love that God has bestowed upon us (2 Cor 1:3-7) and that is rooted in Christ's sacrifice for us. Jesus is our model of love in action (Smedes, 1983). In the context of therapy, it means that we are called to express a Christlike love toward those with whom we work.

Obviously the principle of love can be rationalized into a self-seeking focus. Therapists having affairs with clients frequently insist that they are in love. Nevertheless, the truth is that Christlike or *agapē* (ἀγάπη) love is love that is for the other's sake, both now and in the future.

11. Justice. Justice has to do with treating others fairly. It does not necessarily mean treating everyone exactly alike: "equals must be treated as equals and unequals must be treated in a way most beneficial to their own circumstances" (Gladding, Remley & Huber, 2000). Justice and love belong together, and in a sense, justice gives "backbone" to the concept of love (Tillich, cited in Field, 1995). Justice can also include trying to remedy unfair situations where they exist without creating greater harm.

In addition to aspirational ideals, codes of ethics also include what are called *mandatory obligations*. These are the rules and regulations that are sufficiently focused and specific to use as standards of practice, and that can be enforced when a clinician is judged to have broken them. We shall have much more to say about the content and application of these rules later in the book, but for now I can outline several of the fundamental obligations as follows:

- Competence—Are you qualified professionally and personally to provide the services you are offering (APA, 2010, Sect. 2.00)?

- Confidentiality—Do you understand the importance of holding information you receive in confidence? Do you recognize circumstances that could endanger your ability to be confidential? Do you know when it is appropriate to break a confidence (APA, 2010, Sect. 4.00)?

- Multiple relationships—Do you understand the potential problems in working with people in professional relationships at the same time you are relating to them in other contexts, such as at church, in business or at school? Most especially, do you understand why sexual intimacies with clients, students and so forth are always wrong and are clear examples of unethical multiple relationships (APA, 2010, Sects. 3.02, 3.05, 10.05-10.08)?

- Public statements—Do you avoid making deceptive, false or manipulative statements about the services, products or activities you provide? Do you avoid making public statements that cannot be supported by evidence? Do you discourage public relations people, book publishers and others who represent you from making inappropriate statements on your behalf (APA, 2010, Sect. 5.00)?

- Third-party requests for services—When a third party (a court, a parent, a business, a school, etc.) requests that you provide services for them (assessing an alleged criminal or victim, seeing a child, evaluating an employee or student, etc.), do you clarify with all parties the nature of the relationship with each of them? For example, if you assess an accused individual for the court, do you make sure the person understands that the information they give you will not be confidential and in addition, will be provided to the court (APA, 2010, Sects. 3.05, 3.07, 4.02)?

While the mandatory obligations are considered more specific and enforceable, it needs to be said that the wording of some of these rules acknowledges that in the real world of everyday practice individual judgment sometimes comes into play and that at times the clinician must formulate decisions based on a reasoned judgment rather than on a clear and unbending application of a rule. For example, when deciding whether to engage in a nonsexual multiple relationship, the APA code gives the clinician some latitude in estimating whether participating in the multiple relationship will help or harm the client.

These are some of the issues the codes and the law attempt to cover. We shall see in the chapters that follow how the various rules apply specifically to different issues and areas of mental health work. We shall also see that as important as the codes and the laws are, it is increasingly understood that they represent at best a foundation for the ethical practice of psychotherapy. They are absolutely necessary but insufficient in and of themselves for ethical practice.

RESPONSES TO CODES OF ETHICS

Confronted with a professional code of ethics, people respond in different ways. In some ways, their reactions mirror those of people confronted by an authority figure.

Some people largely resist the code of ethics. Faced with the constraints that ethical systems impose, they ignore the constraints and forge their own paths. In some cases, they carry on a passive-resistant relationship with ethical codes, verbally assenting to the codes while quietly disobeying them. Less commonly, they openly defy the rules. For these individuals, the codes represent restraints that stand in the way of their own self-serving motivations and impulses. These therapists often consciously or unconsciously use the therapeutic relationship as a place to meet their own personal needs and desires rather than to serve the best interests of the client. In the case that opened this chapter, one can only speculate about the personal reasons why a therapist who knew better would be willing to share so freely the names and addresses of "satisfied clients," showing little concern for the potential problems his hasty action might cause them. Disturbances in a therapist's character such as narcissism, impulsivity or sociopathy may all be underlying factors that affect the therapist's ethical thinking and result in his or her forging a path outside the parameters of the ethical code.

Others faced with the authority of ethical codes react with anxiety. For these people, ethical codes are to be feared. One is always in danger of making a mistake, and the person who fears the codes often worries about the gray areas in practicing psychology and ruminates excessively about risk management. As a result, anxious practitioners are sometimes less effective as therapists because they resist making any decision that might remotely be questioned ethically or legally. At times, in their failure to be decisive, they behave unethically anyway. For example, the anxious practitioner might delay acting to protect someone who had seriously discussed a plan to commit suicide, fearing that he or she might make a mistake and would be seen later as having violated the patient's rights.

Some therapists tend to avoid their ethical codes. When the codes are revised, they don't read them and seldom consult them for help when questions arise. Unlike therapists who feel themselves above the codes, the "avoider" is more phobic than rebellious and avoids the code in order to escape dealing with difficult issues. These individuals hope they will do the right thing, and they may feel guilty about not staying abreast with their field's ethical code, but when all is said, they do not consult the code because the gain in understanding hardly seems worth the discomfort in studying the code carefully.

Thankfully, most mental health professionals neither fear their ethical code nor rebel against it, but instead have a healthy respect for it. For these practitioners the code guides them and challenges them as they do their daily work, yet they don't deify the code. Such people recognize that there are gray areas that do not always fit the rules well and that part of behaving ethically is learning how to respond with ethical concern even when the rules are unclear or contradictory. Later in this chapter, we will discuss the means by which the Christian practitioner can approach this goal.

Yet even when there is basic respect for the ethics code, Koocher and Keith-Spiegel (2008, pp. 9-18) point out that there are still a number of reasons why a therapist might behave unethically. Inexperience and ignorance are common causes of unethical behavior in otherwise sincere professionals. Some counselors may be naive, believing that being a dedicated

Christian professional automatically insures against ethical problems. Still others act unethically because they have not anticipated a potential problem in advance. For example, a therapist may promise confidentiality to a couple in marriage counseling, but later finds him- or herself in a dilemma when the couple later divorces and one spouse wants to use the records from counseling in a child custody dispute. Or, as sometimes occurs when controversial treatment techniques are used, a therapist may not have been able to anticipate adequately the problems that might arise from using a controversial intervention. One must proceed with great care when considering unusual treatment techniques.

Therapists may encounter situations in which the possibility of behaving unethically was foreseen but was unavoidable. Or therapists can end up in situations in which they must choose between various less-than-fully-ethical responses. For example, if you the therapist receive a subpoena to release confidential information and do not have permission from the client to do so, you may find yourself in contempt of court if you do not release the information and guilty of a breach of confidentiality if you do. Finally, therapists may act unethically because there are no ethical guidelines or laws which precisely apply to the issue in question, or the guidelines or laws that do exist are ambiguous or conflict with each other. Haas, Malouf and Mayerson (1986), for example, collected data suggesting that despite awareness of ethics codes, it is not unusual for psychotherapists to disagree about the proper course of action in particular real-world, ethical situations.

CHRISTIAN MENTAL HEALTH CARE TODAY

Fortunately, most Christian therapists today are trained, service-oriented professionals who honestly try to behave ethically in their daily work. Most Christian practitioners hold advanced degrees in the helping disciplines. Many are state licensed and are bound by professional codes of ethics and state laws that regulate their practice in the community. Those who are state licensed seem at least as well-trained and sensitive to basic ethical obligations as their secular counterparts (Schneller, Swenson & Sanders, 2010).

Professional "Christian counseling" has become a major movement within the larger Christian community and has had an impact for good. Hurting people whose personal problems went largely unnoticed and uncared for in years past are now receiving hope and help, all in the context of caring Christian community. People who in the past would have been avoided, blamed or ostracized, even by the church, are now receiving understanding and intervention.

Yet, like any other widespread movement, ethical infractions are bound to occur at times, and as our earlier example illustrated, Christians are certainly not immune to ethical misconduct. Christian mental health professionals are confronted with all the same ethical dilemmas as their secular counterparts. Confidentiality, multiple relationships, competence and all the other fundamental issues of ethical practice will arise.

CULTURAL AND RELIGIOUS TRENDS

Christian practitioners also work in a larger cultural context, and for better or worse, are affected by cultural trends and values. For example, moral and ethical *relativism*, a position held by many, assumes that there are no universal standards, that what is right and wrong varies according to many factors including the situation, the culture and one's own personal point of view (MacKinnon, 2007).

The mental health professions have clearly been affected by this thinking. Indeed, perhaps due to the complex nature of people's problems and the gray areas which inevitably arise in practice, we are tempted to say that there are no absolutes, that all standards are relative. Once we have done that though, we run the risk of raising the exceptions to the rules to the same level as the rules themselves. For example, we might decide that because some parents abuse their children, traditional admonitions to respect and honor elders have little value for these times.

Absolutism, the position that there are no exceptions to moral rules or ethical principles and that rules are "context-independent" (MacKinnon, 2007), is another view prevalent in segments of the culture. In this view the rules or principles provide an answer for every situation (Pojman, 1995). Therapists who work in Christian settings sometimes find themselves confronted by ministers, board members or parishioners who hold to such a view. For example, consider the minister who believes that the marital contract is absolutely binding no matter the circumstances. He becomes incensed after he refers a married couple for counseling and finds out that the

Christian therapist has recommended at least a temporary separation because one of the spouses is abusing the other.

The emphasis on *individualism and the self* may also affect therapists' ethical decisions, particularly in Western culture. Popular culture teaches us that the healthy person takes care of him- or herself and his or her "needs" first, is independent, values personal happiness over obligation, is assertive, avoids stress and enjoys leisure. Where this emphasis on individualism is extreme, it brings with it a decreased emphasis on the importance of community, interpersonal connectedness, family and God. Martin Seligman, the eminent psychologist, has called this the "waning of the commons" (1990). As he put it

> The life committed to nothing larger than itself is a meager life indeed. Human beings require a context of meaning and hope. We used to have ample context, and when we encountered failure, we could pause and take our rest in that setting—our spiritual furniture—and revive our sense of who we were. I call the larger setting the commons. It consists of a belief in the nation, in God, in one's family, or in a purpose that transcends our lives. In the past quarter-century, events occurred that so weakened our commitment to larger entities as to leave us almost naked before the ordinary assaults of life. (p. 284)

Seligman, an expert on depression, believes that "a society that exalts the individual to the extent ours does will be riddled with depression" (p. 287). Such a society might be overrun by people who, in their emphasis on the self, ignore the personal and communal benefits of empathizing with others and behaving ethically toward their fellows. What purpose is there in following the rules if it's "every man or woman for him- or herself?"

For the therapist, the current cultural and to some extent the mental health emphasis on individualism raises deeper ethical questions about the proper goals of therapeutic intervention. Is treatment always and only about self-actualization and personal happiness? If so, does therapy then degenerate into a narcissistic exercise that idolizes the desires of the self (Vitz, 1994)?

Economic factors also affect ethical decision making. Prior to the 1980s, Christian psychotherapy was a helping profession provided by a relatively small number of practitioners, most of whom made a reasonable living, but often had to defend their work to a sometimes skeptical church community. In the 1980s that changed. Christian counseling was "in" and the market soon flooded with practitioners, authors and speakers. Most were sincere, but a few were attracted to the field by the promise of fame and fortune in this, the latest Christian fad. For the latter, the importance of truth in advertising, competency in counseling and interprofessional cooperation took a back seat to inflated claims, average standards of care and unbridled competition.

Now, new economic challenges are affecting the mental health community. With the advent of managed care, insurance companies are actively restricting access to health care in general and mental health care in particular. Insurance reimbursement for mental health care is decreasing. Nevertheless insurers demand more and more written justification for whatever care is provided. Ethical therapists find themselves with the dilemma of trying to provide optimal care for their clients, while dealing with increased overhead and administrative demands, and decreased reimbursement.

Religious factors also play a role in ethical decision making. During the latter part of the twentieth century, a period in which psychology gained great popularity, much of the emphasis in secular culture was on permissiveness and in the Christian church on grace. Much of this grace emphasis developed as a reaction to the legalism and prejudices all too prevalent during periods of church history. Consequently, the prevailing message of many within the church has been "God is love." Having seen the problems of rules without grace, many called for a return to a higher ethic based upon love (Stott, 1994).

Yet some who stress this emphasis on grace convince themselves that they are following a higher ethic of love when in fact they are ignoring basic rules of human conduct and interpreting Christian love to mean whatever fits their own sentiments and impulses, like the counselor in the vignette at the beginning of this chapter. Indeed, by ignoring the APA code, the counselor in that story had not lived above an inferior, secular code but had instead denied some fundamental rules of professional conduct and practice (the APA code) that were not at all inconsistent with a Christian ethic.

The shift of the Christian culture toward grace was a needed corrective to the legalism of previous days. However, as has been true from the beginnings of Christianity, there have always been those who would shift the balance of grace and law too far in one direction or the other with detrimental consequences on moral and ethical decision making.

THE CHRISTIAN MENTAL HEALTH PROFESSIONAL

Christian mental health professionals are confronted with all the same ethical dilemmas as their secular counterparts. Confidentiality, multiple relationships, competence and other fundamental issues of ethical practice will arise. Christian practitioners also work in the larger cultural context and for better or worse are affected by cultural trends and values.

The ethics codes that have been created by various secular professional guilds are fundamental rules of practice hammered out through years of common experience. For the most part, these codes are straightforward and place most of their emphasis on the patient's welfare. Recognizing that professional intervention can have negative as well as positive outcomes, the codes encourage practitioners to take all reasonable steps to "do no harm" to their patients (Fernhoff, 1993). As documents devised in a pluralistic culture, the codes usually avoid issues that would undoubtedly offend a particular cultural or religious group. In general, they represent the minimum that a licensed professional therapist should do to behave ethically and they do not frequently contradict a Christian ethic.

It is essential for every licensed professional to be familiar with the codes and laws that govern his or her own professional group. It is probably also wise for licensed therapists to be at least somewhat familiar with the codes of allied mental health professionals. For example, the APA Code is the oldest of the codes (Ford, 2006) and one of the most respected (Haas, 2000), and Cruse and Russell (1994) have suggested that nonpsychologists would do well to have at least some familiarity with its standards if for no other reason than they might someday face an opposing attorney in court who expects them to be familiar with it.

Though technically not held to the same standards as professional therapists, noncertified pastoral counselors and lay counselors have a responsibility to know as much as they can about the ethics of counseling. At a minimum they should be aware of common ethical pitfalls in counseling. In this way, they will be more likely to recognize potential problems and consult with supervisors, and know when to refer to others with more training.

Having asserted the importance of knowing and following the secular codes, Christian therapists must consider how these codes relate to the special kinds of ethical dilemmas they face because of the settings in which they work or the beliefs that they hold. Consider these examples.

- A young couple with two children comes to a Christian marriage counselor insisting at the outset that she help them negotiate an end to their marriage. What responsibility does the counselor have to the sanctity of the marriage and family as well as to the individuals involved?

- A pastor, who counsels regularly, questions whether or not to gain further formal training in counseling, knowing that in his state "religious counselors" are given an exemption from the strict training requirements facing other counselors.

- A Christian therapist works in a government agency. During the course of therapy with one client, material is revealed that suggests the client has serious concerns of a spiritual nature. Should the therapist talk about faith issues in the therapy despite the fact that he works for a nonpartisan, governmental agency?

- A licensed professional counselor joins the staff of a church as its minister of counseling. Soon after arriving, the senior pastor refers the church's youth minister for counseling. Is it appropriate for the counselor to provide therapy for the youth minister?

Beyond specific ethical dilemmas, Christians must also consider whether they are called to more than a mere practice of the "rules ethics" established by professional guilds. Surely those who live under grace are called to "mature in Christ" and develop higher-order decision-making abilities.

As Christians, we want to not only practice doing right but also being moral people. Morality is a state of *being* as much as it is *doing*. Ideally, if we are to truly follow a higher ethic, we must be growing in virtue as well as in principles (see Jordan & Meara, 1990, and Tjeltveit later in this volume for a discussion of virtue ethics and principle ethics). Character traits such as trustworthiness, wisdom, humility and integrity must have developed and be developing alongside knowledge of the rules of conduct. Otherwise, we run the risk of becoming legalistic, applying rules arbitrarily to situations where the spirit of the law—the internal law—might tell us to intervene more carefully. Conversely, we may rationalize away the rules we are called to uphold. Growing in virtue broadens the ability to see through to the essence of all good law: promoting justice and love (Smedes, 1983).

ETHICS AND SCRIPTURE

During his earthly ministry, Jesus frequently confronted prominent religious factions who had become excessively legalistic in their attempts to make the "letter" of religious law determinative in every situation. Jesus argued that these leaders had become so obsessed with the ceremonial law and with tradition that they had missed the essence of the law (Maston, 1964, p. 146). He summed up all law in a positive frame by asserting that the two greatest commandments were to love God with all one's being and to love one's neighbor as oneself (Mt 22:36-39).

Yet Jesus was not a libertarian in the theological sense of that term. He clearly stated that his mission on earth was not to abolish the Old Testament law but rather to fulfill it (Mt 5:17) "by bringing its essential teaching to its full development" (Maston, 1964, p. 147). To Jesus, the commandments were not rigid moralisms passed down from an outmoded civilization. They were basic truths for living and conduct that would be given new life and humanized in a pervasive ethic of love.

Jesus' ethic of love, far from being relativistic or anemic, sometimes went beyond the ethical legalisms of the day. For example, he argued that there was little advantage in following the letter of the law if one harbored such things as bitterness or lust or greed in one's heart (Mt 5:28). He called his followers to grow deeper in virtue.

The New Testament message proclaims a balance between grace and law. Nowhere is this balance better explained than in the book of Romans. Here Paul says that God's law functions to define what sin is and condemn the sinner (Rom 3:27-28). No one, no matter how good or how moral or how much he or she follows the rules, can or will measure up to the level of the divine. But God in his mercy provides a means for forgiveness and a way to peace and eternal relationship with him. It is through faith in God's Son, Jesus Christ, that people receive this gift of God (Rom 5:2). Followers of Christ do not live under law but under grace (Rom 6:14), which may be defined as the unmerited favor that God has bestowed on sinful humankind.

Paul does not stop here. He argues that through the sacrifice of Jesus

Christ on the cross and the assistance of the Holy Spirit, believers are empowered to fulfill the law and live righteous and loving lives (Rom 8:4; 13:8). They are free from the condemnation of the law yet free to keep the law in response to the loving grace of God and the ongoing care of his Spirit. The new covenant ushered in by Christ is one in which "the Holy Spirit writes God's law in our hearts" (Stott, 1994, p. 196).

Ideally, then, being a person of virtue follows naturally from a close, intimate relationship with God. Such a relationship, like all excellent relationships, must be marked by warmth, love, accountability and responsibility. The Bible is the unfolding drama of God's desire for this kind of relationship with his people. In the beginning he created man and woman in his image and desired fellowship with them. In the Old Testament he sought a covenantal relationship with his people that was much more than a mere contract; it was a deeply personal commitment one to the other. The New Testament reveals God's ultimate endeavor toward intimacy with humankind: God became human in the person of Jesus Christ and walked as a human being, with all the blood, sweat and tears that accompany that. While here, he became intimately familiar with people from all walks of life, not just the "good" people but the outcasts and the sinners as well. He was persecuted by those who did not understand him, and he experienced the hurts, anguish and negative emotions common to those who live in this world. He suffered a cruel and hideous death that he did not deserve.

The God of the Bible is not a distant figure, completely removed from his people. He is not a foreign figure who shouts impossible edicts from afar and then leaves his subjects alone to grapple with the pronouncements. In the Christian faith the rule of law takes place within the context of personal relationship, of covenant, of love. It is in this relationship of covenantal love that we are empowered to follow a Christian ethic.

To be sure, this is not an easy task. There can be no doubt that as leaders in the Christian community, Christian mental health professionals are called to a higher ethic. It is not out of context to argue that the qualities of the elder and overseer in the early church are some of the same qualities that Christian therapists should aspire to. These qualities enumerated by Paul in 1 Timothy 3:1-7 and Titus 1:5-9 include self-control, gentleness, temperance, respectability and avoiding greed.

ETHICS AND GOD'S CALL

The calling to be a Christian counselor is a high calling with exceptional expectations and responsibilities. Certainly it reflects a standard all should aspire to but none will fully attain (Rom 7:21-25). The good news is that the Christian process of being and becoming ethical is done in the context of supportive relationship—with God, the Holy Spirit and fellow Christians.

Earlier in this chapter we looked at the different responses that people have to ethics codes. Those who are fearful of the codes are often fearful of the code's power to "condemn" them, so they follow the codes legalistically in an effort to avoid judgment. In contrast, those who reject ethics codes sometimes take an antinomian position that the codes are of no value, and they rebel against these codes. Following Paul and assuming that the codes are in the main consistent with a Christian ethic, a Christian might face the codes secure in the grace of Christ, yet determined to fulfill the codes with God's help.

The message of Scripture is that God is with us at all times, but most especially in life's hard places, much in the same way a close personal friend is. He is there when we seek to help our clients in psychotherapy, when we struggle to teach others and when faced with tough ethical decisions. As a truly intimate friend, God is there to inspire, support and encourage us, and to hold us accountable and correct us. He walks with us and encourages us to embrace our ethical mandate.

Likewise the call to be ethical takes place best within the context of a Christian community in which we participate with other Christian people who are seeking as we are to fulfill God's will and ministry. Christianity takes place in *koinōnia* (κοινωνία), in close fellowship with one another. In fellowship with one another we benefit from the shared loved, support, wisdom, accountability and obligation to each other.

OUTLINE AND ACKNOWLEDGMENTS

The chapters that follow cover pertinent issues related to ethics and the Christian mental health professional. Chapter two reviews the fundamental relationship between Christian ethics and psychotherapy. Chapter three considers the issue of competence and what qualifies one to be a Christian mental health professional. The next chapter focuses on some of the essential rules common to most ethical codes and how they apply practically to the daily work of therapy. Chapters then address the issues of sexual misconduct and nonsexual multiple relationships.

The following chapters deal with some challenging issues in therapy. Included among the areas covered are issues unique to couples therapy and child therapy. We also take up the ethics of addressing spiritual or moral values issues in therapy. Specific client populations such as sexual minorities and clients with chronic conditions are considered. Cultural diversity issues in therapy are discussed as well as ethical issues related to psychotherapy as a business.

The next chapters address specific counseling settings and the ethical issues peculiar to them. The first chapter looks at the pastor as counselor, focusing not on professional pastoral counselors but rather on the typical parish minister. We consider the ethics of lay or paraprofessional counseling. Then we consider Christian mental health professionals who work in military or government agencies, university counseling centers, missionary care agencies and psychological first aid.

Finally, we consider current trends in teaching ethics to Christian mental health professionals and offer a model for ethical decision making. Appendix 1 includes some examples of ethics codes that are presently available, and appendix 2 contains examples of the types of consent and other forms that are used in counseling today.

The case studies in this book are representative of the kinds of cases faced by clinicians in practice. The cases are totally fictitious, are composites of a number of cases or have been altered to ensure anonymity and confidentiality. All names used for characters are fictitious, and any resemblance to persons living or dead is purely coincidental.

I am appreciative of the many colleagues who have helped in some way with the revision of this book. I am also thankful to those who have sponsored my continuing education workshops on ethical issues during the past several years as well as those individuals who have participated in the workshops and shared their experiences in dealing with ethical issues.

To act ethically can be difficult, to be ethical can be even more so. Our hope of approaching these ideals is found in God, who first loved us, who in his love encourages us to love others, and in the Holy Spirit and the community of friends who encourage us as we seek to live righteously in the world. God does not wish for us to run from his law in fear but to embrace and fulfill his law with confidence—confidence in our inestimable worth before him, in his power to be with us in the midst of Christian community and in his ultimate control of our destiny.

REFERENCES

American Association of Christian Counseling. (n.d.). AACC mission. Retrieved February 3, 2012, from http://www.aacc.net/about-us.

American Association of Christian Counseling. (2004). *AACC code of ethics.* Retrieved February 3, 2012, from http://aacc.net/wp-images/fammed/aacc_code _of_ethics.doc.

American Association of Marriage and Family Therapists. (2012). *AAMFT code of ethics.* (Available from AAMFT 1133 15th St., NW, Suite 300, Washington, DC 20005.)

American Association of Pastoral Counselors. (2010). *Code of ethics.* (Available from AAPC, 9504A Lee Highway, Fairfax, VA 22031-2303.)

American Counseling Association. (2005). *ACA code of ethics and standards of practice.* (Available from ACA, P.O. Box 531, Alexandria, VA.)

American Psychiatric Association (2006). *Principles of medical ethics with annotations especially applicable to psychiatry.* (Available from APA, 1400 K St. NW, Washington, DC 20005.)

American Psychological Association. (2010). *Ethical principles of psychologists and code of conduct.* Retrieved from www.apa.org/ethics/code/index.aspx.

American Psychological Association. (1995). Report of the ethics committee, 1994. *American Psychologist, 50,* 706-13.

Anderson, R. S. (1990). *Christians who counsel.* Grand Rapids: Zondervan.

Beck, J. R. (1997). Christian codes: Are they better? In R. K. Sanders, (Ed.), *Christian counseling ethics: A handbook for therapists, pastors and counselors* (pp. 313-25). Downers Grove, IL: InterVarsity Press.

Campbell, D. M. (1982). *Doctors, lawyers, ministers: Christian ethics in professional practice.* Nashville: Abingdon.

Christian Association for Psychological Studies. (2005). *Ethics statement of the Christian Association for Psychological Studies.* (Available from http://caps.net /about-us/statement-of-ethical-guidelines.)

Christian Life Commission. (1981). *Business ethics issues and answers series.* Dallas: Christian Life Commission, Baptist General Convention of Texas.

Cruse, R., & Russell, R. (1994, October). *Ethical thinking: New standards.* Paper presented at the Christian Association for Psychological Studies Southwest Regional Conference, Abilene, TX.

Dumbrell, W. J. (1995). Covenant. In D. J. Atkinson, D. H. Field, A. Holmes, and O. O'Donovan (Eds.), *New dictionary of Christian ethics and pastoral theology* (pp. 266-67). Downers Grove, IL: InterVarsity Press.

Eberlein, L. (1987). Introducing ethics to beginning psychologists: A problem-solving approach. *Professional Psychology: Research and Practice, 18,* 353-59.

Fernhoff, D. (1993). The valued therapist. In M. Goldberg (Ed.), *Against the grain* (pp. 55-77). Valley Forge, PA: Trinity Press.

Field, D. H. (1995). Love. In D. J. Atkinson, D. H. Field, A. Holmes, and O. O'Donovan (Eds.), *New dictionary of Christian ethics and pastoral theology* (pp. 9-15). Downers Grove, IL: InterVarsity Press.

Ford, G. G. (2006). *Ethical reasoning for mental health professionals.* Thousand Oaks, CA: Sage.

Gladding, S. T., Remley, T. P., and Huber, C. H. (2000). *Ethical, legal and professional issues in the practice of marriage and family therapy* (3rd ed.). Englewood Cliffs, NJ: Prentice-Hall.

Gottlieb, M. C. (1993). Avoiding exploitive dual relationships: A decision-making model. *Psychotherapy, 30,* 41-48.

Haas, L. J. (2000). Ethics in practice. In A. E. Kazdin (Ed.), *Encyclopedia of Psychology* (pp. 246-51). New York: Oxford.

Haas, L. J., Malouf, J. L., & Mayerson, N. H. (1986). Ethical dilemmas in psychological practice: Results of a national survey. *Professional Psychology: Research and Practice, 17,* 316-21.

Jones, D. C. (1994). *Biblical Christian Ethics.* Grand Rapids: Baker.

Jordan, A. E., & Meara, N. M. (1990). Ethics and the professional practice of psychologists: The role of virtues and principles. *Professional Psychology: Research and Practice, 21,* 107-14.

Kitchener, K. S. (1984). Intuition, critical evaluation and ethical principles: The foundations for ethical decisions in counseling psychology. *Counseling Psychologist, 12,* 43-55.

Koocher, G. P., & Keith-Spiegel, P. (2008). *Ethics in psychology and the mental health professions* (3rd ed.). New York: Oxford University Press.

Ladd, G. E. (1974). *A theology of the New Testament.* Grand Rapids: Eerdmans.

MacKinnon, B. (2007). *Ethics: Theory and contemporary issues* (5th ed.). Belmont, CA: Thomson-Wadsworth.

Maston, T. B. (1964). *Biblical ethics*. Cleveland: World Publishing.

McCloughry, R. K. (1995). Community ethics. In D. J. Atkinson, D. H. Field, A. Holmes, and O. O'Donovan (Eds.), *New dictionary of Christian ethics and pastoral theology* (pp. 108-15). Downers Grove, IL: InterVarsity Press.

McMinn, M. R. (2004). *Why sin matters*. Wheaton, IL: Tyndale House.

Miller, D. J. (1991). The necessity of principles in virtue ethics. *Professional Psychology: Research and Practice, 22*, 107.

Myers, D. G. (1981). *The inflated self: Human illusions and the biblical call to hope*. New York: Seabury.

National Association of Social Workers. (2008). *NASW code of ethics*. (Available from NASW, P.O. Box 431, Annapolis Junction, MD 20701.)

Ohlschlager, G., & Mosgofian, P. (1992). *Law for the Christian counselor*. Dallas: Word.

Pojman, L. P. (1995). *Ethics: Discovering right and wrong* (2nd ed.). Belmont, CA: Wadsworth.

Reeck, D. (1982). *Ethics for the professions: A Christian perspective*. Minneapolis: Augsburg.

Schneller, G. R., Swenson, J. E., & Sanders, R. K. (2010). Training for ethical dilemmas arising in Christian counseling: A survey of clinicians. *Journal of Psychology & Christianity, 29*, 343-53.

Seligman, M. E. P. (1990). *Learned optimism*. New York: Simon & Schuster.

Smedes, L. (1983). *Mere morality*. Grand Rapids: Eerdmans.

Stott, J. (1994). *Romans*. Downers Grove, IL: InterVarsity Press.

Vitz, P. C. (1994). *Psychology as religion: The cult of self-worship*. Grand Rapids: Eerdmans.

2

Psychotherapy and Christian Ethics

Alan C. Tjeltveit

Some schooled solely in secular psychotherapy might find the title of this chapter curious. Therapy, for them, is based solely on science. And Christian ethics is a neurotogenic (neurosis-producing) burden from which guilt- and anxiety-laden clients need liberation. That task being commonplace and well covered in most training programs, those therapists would expect a chapter that is brief, boring or both.

While recognizing the problem of legalistic abuses of Christian ethics, Christians committed to helping people overcome problems tend to view Christian ethics in a more positive light. But even Christian therapists occasionally see therapy and ethics as occupying entirely separate domains—between which dialogue is neither required nor desired.

In contrast, I contend that psychotherapy is a profoundly and pervasively ethical endeavor, and that Christian ethics both vigorously supports and sharply challenges the ethical positions represented (usually implicitly) in various forms of therapy. I also believe that Christian ethicists have much to learn from psychotherapists, and that Christian clients and therapists therefore need to engage—regularly and rigorously—in substantive reflection on the ethical dimensions of therapy. Only when Christians take Christian ethical perspectives very seriously can we understand—and act on—the vitally important implications of Christian faith for psychotherapy that is conducted in full accord with the gospel.

Lurking in the background of this chapter and book is the question of the distinctiveness of psychotherapy as understood and practiced by Christians. Is therapy with a Christian therapist really different from therapy with a person who is not a Christian? Christian therapists of good will and undisputed competence diverge—at times sharply—regarding how to answer this question. Some emphasize the uniqueness of Christian therapy; others stress the essential equivalence of therapy provided by Christian and non-Christian practitioners. Some of this disagreement stems, perhaps, from focusing on different presenting problems and different client populations (see Worthington, 1988, 1993b). Christian ethics is more obviously relevant, and Christian therapy more likely distinctive, when Christian clients are involved and ethical issues in therapy are overt and controverted. However, Christian ethics may also be relevant, albeit nondistinctively, in cases involving subtle and noncontroversial ethical issues. For example, when a Christian provides behavior therapy for a snake phobia to a non-Christian in a secular setting, that intervention may be behaviorally indistinguishable from the intervention of a non-Christian therapist.

By way of contrast, consider this vivid case:

Brad, a middle-aged midlevel manager who attends a local Baptist church on a semiregular basis, sees a therapist at the insistence of his son, a psychology major at a nearby college. The son has discovered that Brad is sexually involved with Jennifer, the 20-year-old daughter of one of Brad's coworkers. Both families attend the same church. Brad is ambivalent about whether there is really a problem, explaining that his wife, Carol, has been an invalid for several years and has been unable to maintain an active sexual relationship. Brad says he thinks Carol may even know "on some level" about his relationship with Jennifer and be secretly relieved that she no longer has to engage in an activity she's never seemed to enjoy.

Although he says he sometimes feels a twinge of guilt about his behavior, he brightens when talking about Jennifer: "This relationship makes me very happy. And Jenny tells me she's very happy too. That's what it's all about, isn't it—being happy? Surely God wants that for us." Brad adds that he thinks therapy "wouldn't hurt," because he wants to figure out a way to get his son to be more accepting of his relationship with Jennifer and doesn't know how to do that. "It's not like I'm planning to do anything drastic, like get a divorce," Brad adds. "I stand by my word; a promise is a promise. And Jenny knows about the situation. I've never made any false promises to her. She likes my wife very much."

About this case Christian ethics has much to say.

ETHICS AND CHRISTIAN ETHICS: TERMS WITH MULTIPLE MEANINGS

A lively discussion would likely ensue if a group were asked to provide an ethical analysis of this case or to analyze it from the perspective of Christian ethics. The discourse might involve several distinguishable dimensions of the case. Although each dimension may legitimately be called *ethical*, the variety of uses of the term may result in confusion. To minimize such confusion, and to make clear the full spectrum of ethical aspects of therapy, the following dimensions of ethics will be distinguished and discussed in turn: professional ethics, the context and content of ethics, ethical theory, and social ethics, public policy and consensus. Some of the implications of Christian ethics for psychotherapy across that spectrum of uses of *ethics* will also be addressed.

Professional ethics. Mention the word *ethics* to many psychotherapists and their thoughts turn immediately to codes of professional ethics (e.g., American Psychiatric Association, 2009; American Psychological Association, 2002; National Association of Social Workers, 1999; see appendix 1); that is, to ethical principles set down by various professional groups and "based on the goals, objectives, and fundamental values of the profession" (Bennett, 1994, p. 124). A violation of these principles may result in expulsion from a professional association.

Suppose, for instance, that Brad's therapist is a Christian psychologist who works at a public counseling center and did not state at the outset of therapy that she is an explicitly Christian therapist. She asks in the first session, "Have you thought about the moral issues here?" And when Brad arrives at his second session, he finds—to his surprise—that his pastor is waiting there for him, fully briefed about his affair with Jennifer and insisting that Brad repent and immediately end the affair or be expelled from the church. The psychologist would, of course, be in grave trouble with a psychological association ethics committee, which would point to her violation of Brad's confidentiality and failure to obtain informed consent about the type of distinctively Christian therapy being provided.

Christians who publicly declare themselves to be mental health professionals should, for reasons of honesty and integrity, and for other substantive reasons, abide by the appropriate professional code of ethics. Such codes do sometimes limit the actions of professionals, including behaviors Christians may otherwise appropriately exhibit. Recruiting a pastor to confront a friend about his immoral behavior wouldn't be considered unethical, but recruiting a pastor about a client's behavior without the client's consent would be. Overt evangelism in the therapeutic relationship is likewise proscribed by codes of professional ethics but is encouraged or obligatory for the Christian in other relationships.

The relationship between Christian ethics and professional ethics is complex (see Reeck, 1982). Some assert that the two perspectives are rivals, and so assert something like "Christians need to decide whether their allegiance lies with the world or with Christ. If allegiance to Christ means trouble with a professional ethics committee, so be it. Christians should not be conformed to the world." Christian therapists holding this perspective are unlikely to join a professional association or seek licensure.

Others see professional and Christian ethics as partially or fully compatible, because (1) Christian ethics provides a rationale for the professional standards, (2) the two are logically equivalent (the eighth commandment, for instance, forbids bearing false witness, as do codes of professional ethics) or (3) codes of professional ethics exhaust what Christian ethics has to say about ethics in therapy. Some advocates of the last position hold something like this viewpoint: "Christian ethics and professional ethics are functionally identical because the only obligation Christian ethics places on the therapist as therapist is conformity with professional ideals. The good Christian therapist is the therapist whose behavior is consistent with professional codes of ethics and standards. Accordingly, any claim that there are ethical obligations and ideals for therapy that are distinctively Christian is suspect." Christians assuming compatibility between Christian ethics and professional ethics would likely join the ethics committee in viewing the behavior of Brad's therapist as unethical.

Still others argue that—given careful thinking, creativity and a deep respect for both professional ethics and Christian ethics—codes of professional ethics give ample room for the expression of Christian positions in therapy, assuming Christian professionals behave in certain prescribed ways. Constraints are placed on the therapist, but not absolute constraints. A therapist can, for instance, communicate values in therapy in ways that uphold client freedom (not eliminating or reducing the freedom of clients to choose their own values, not imposing values on clients, not being judgmental or moralistic, and not propagandizing), provide clients with adequate information about the particular therapeutic approach employed (including its Christian distinctiveness, if any), honor the therapeutic contract, and limit practice to areas in which he or she is competent (Tjeltveit, 1999).

In addition, the American Association of Christian Counselors (AACC Law and Ethics Committee, 2004), the American Association of Pastoral Counselors (1994), and the Christian Association for Psychological Studies (2005) have promulgated codes of ethics that permit the *integration* of the content of professional ethics codes with Christian ethics.

Engaging with professional ethics will create for some Christians an experience like that of entering into a foreign land. Indeed, the process of becoming a professional has been likened to becoming a member of a new culture (Gottlieb, Handelsman & Knapp, 2008; Handelsman, Gottlieb & Knapp, 2005). Ways of resolving ethical issues and a belief in particular ethical ideals and obligations may seem natural in one culture but might be considered strange, or even wrong, in another. Christian counselors and psychotherapists may respond to this clash of ethical cultures in a variety of ways: Transferring one's moral allegiance solely to professional codes of ethics, rejecting professional ethics in favor of some separatistic understanding of Christian ethics, becoming confused and marginalized in relationship to both ethical traditions, or integrating Christian and professional ethics. Those adopting the integration solution, Handelsman et al. (2005) assert, "adopt the ethical values of psychology while understanding and maintaining their own value tradition" (p. 60).

One's understanding of the proper relationship of Christian ethics and professional ethics depends, of course, on one's approach to Christian ethics. I contend that Christian ethics is usually, but not always, consistent with standards of professional ethics. A Christian ethic that is exhausted by professional ethics is, at best, profoundly impoverished. However, Christian ethics undergirds professional ethics, so a therapist engaged in professionally ethical behavior (e.g., upholding client confidentiality) is engaged in fully Christian behavior. Although Christian ethics does sometimes limit the Christian's behavior, careful thinking and responsible professional behavior (especially centered around informed consent) will usually, though not always, result in a satisfactory resolution of dilemmas arising from conflicts between professional and Christian ethics.

Those engaged in education about professional ethics are increasingly recognizing the inadequacy of relying solely on codes of professional ethics to ensure adequate ethical practice, and especially optimal ethical practice (Anderson & Handelsman, 2010; Handelsman, Knapp & Gottlieb, 2009; Pope, Sonne & Green, 2006; Tjeltveit & Gottlieb, 2010). It's not enough to know what a professional code of ethics says. One must also be able to make ethical decisions (especially in cases where a code doesn't provide direct guidance and in dilemmas where ethical standards or principles conflict with one another, or appear to do so), so developing a mastery of an ethical decision-making model (e.g., Kitchener, 2000; Knapp & VandeCreek, 2006; and Koocher & Keith–Spiegel, 2008) may be very important. In addition, professionals need to pay careful attention to their emotions, character traits, motivations and social networks, especially in relation to individual personality dynamics and vulnerabilities. We must identify and draw on deep ethical sources—intellectual, psychological and spiritual—to nourish our ethical actions and lives (Tjeltveit, 1999). Professionals also need to establish ethical habits, develop ongoing relationship with honest consultants who are willing to challenge and confront us if we go astray, and work continually at identifying areas of weaknesses, eliminating those weaknesses, and establishing ethical strengths.

Christian counselors need to be especially wary of ways in which sin and unresolved psychological issues can sometimes lead to a pridefulness that blinds us to our own limitations and shortcomings, and can prevent us from recognizing ethical problems, our need to follow ethical principles intended to promote client well-being and protect their rights, our capacity for self-deception, and our need to consult with and be accountable to others. Our spiritual lives must be nourished if we aspire to optimal ethical practice. Actions that would not stand scrutiny both from one's congregational leaders *and* from professional association ethics committees should be eschewed. We need friends, spiritual mentors and colleagues who inspire us to move beyond practices that could be characterized as adequate to those characterized by excellence.

ETHICS IN CONTEXT AND AS CONTENT: STANDARDS, OBLIGATIONS, IDEALS, DECISIONS AND VIRTUES

In a sense of the term that moves well beyond professional ethics, *ethics* can also be understood as specific ideals or behavioral prescriptions that are either applicable to people in general or obligatory for Christians in particular. Ethics pertains to decisions, behaviors and personal qualities having to do with what is good, right, obligatory or virtuous. For example, people with different ethical perspectives might make the following assertions: "Thou shalt not commit adultery"; "Brad should be more aware of his own feelings and desires, and of the reality that his marriage is failing"; "It would be good for Brad to keep his marital promise to remain faithful to his wife"; "Brad would be healthier if he dropped his guilt-inducing Christian standards, ended his failed marriage and got into a more fulfilling partnership"; and "Brad lacks integrity, but his son is a courageous and loving young man." Rules for living, morality, behavioral prescriptions and ideal or authentic ways of being human are all aspects of ethics, broadly construed. Ethics in this sense can be understood as *content.*

Depending on one's perspective, the content of Christian ethics (e.g., "Thou shalt not commit adultery" for Brad, and "Thou shalt not bear false witness" for the therapist, who, by self-declaration as a psychologist, promised to uphold client confidentiality) will be more or less distinctive. Some hold that Christian ethics is based solely on reason and so is no different from other ethical perspectives. But others stress the authority of the Bible or Christian tradition, and assert that Christian ethics often provides distinctive answers to ethical questions.

But Christian ethics has to do with far more than just the content of particular principles. To content must be added context. Every session of psychotherapy, every moment of human life, must be seen in the context of creation, fall, redemption and eschaton. Human beings are created by God, have sinned, were redeemed though the death and resurrection of Christ, and are heirs of the promise of his coming again in glory. As forgiven children of God, we are free in Christ, saved by grace through faith. As such, we strive to "lead lives worthy of the Lord, fully pleasing to him" (Col 1:10 NRSV). God works in us, transforming us into his image and likeness. To sever ethics from this context, to proclaim law without gospel (however their relation is understood; cf. Forde, 1969; Fuller, 1980) is to irrevocably alter Christian faith and abandon truly Christian ethics. The contextual uniqueness is vital. An intellectual analysis of the abstract ethical principle "Thou shalt not commit adultery" is quite different when we add context: "The Lord your God expresses his love to you, his child, you for whom Jesus died, by saying, 'Thou shalt not commit adultery.'"

Christians striving to make ethical decisions must take context into consideration when making judgments, but should not be relativistic. It is usually necessary to balance flexibility and firmness in addressing ethical issues, avoiding both legalism and antinomianism. Christians should be pastoral at some times and prophetic at others, with therapeutic relationships almost always emphasizing the pastoral.

This emphasis on the context of Christian ethics means practically that psychotherapy can never be seen simply as a relationship between therapist and client. Rather, therapeutic relationships occur, always, in the midst of relationships among client, therapist, the families of each, the church (in local and global manifestations, as both the visible and invisible body of Christ) and God. Christian ethics is thus inextricably systemic; to understand therapy requires an understanding not just of the client's family but also of the system embracing the client, the client's family, the therapist, the church and God.

But if Christian ethics needs to be understood within the context of holy history, it also has specific content. Both are important. Christians disagree, however, about what constitutes the domain of ethics. To understand the ethics-psychotherapy relationship comprehensively, I will discuss several additional distinctions about the meaning of *ethics* that are sometimes made, noting in each instance some possible implications related to Christian ethics.

Ethics and morality. *Ethics* and *morality* are sometimes contrasted and sometimes "used interchangeably" (Annas, 1992, p. 329). *Ethics* is used in both a narrower and a broader sense. When used in a narrower sense, it is solely concerned with morality and can be used interchangeably with *morality*. When used in a broader sense, as in this chapter, *ethics* connotes a focus both on the traditionally moral questions of "how we should live and what we should do" (Annas, 1992, p. 329) and on nonmoral questions of goodness and value. For example, happiness and mental health can be considered nonmoral goods, because we are under no obligation to be happy or mentally healthy (and so we don't usually label as immoral the person who is unhappy or mentally ill simply because the person is unhappy or mentally ill). Ethics, broadly defined, includes both moral issues (e.g., "You should be faithful to your wife") and nonmoral issues (e.g., "It would be good for you to be happy").

Although rarely employing the term *moral*, codes of professional ethics, in their focus on professional obligations, tend to use *ethics* in the narrower sense. For instance, a therapist who sleeps with a client or violates confidentiality would be considered unethical, but the therapist who is unhappy or not fully self-actualized would not (unless, of course, those problems hurt clients, in which case harm to clients would be the problem rather than unhappiness or incomplete self-actualization per se). In other words, however much it may be good to be happy or self-actualized, a therapist is under no professional obligation to be so.

A similar distinction is sometimes made between Christian ethics, which focuses on obligation and morality, and the Christian life, which is a lifestyle motivated and lived by faith in Christ. The latter includes worship and prayer, for instance, which are considered good but are not generally considered "moral" issues. Most would tend not to label "immoral" or "unethical" a Christian who fails to pray, worship or "love the Lord your God with all your heart, and with all your soul, and with all your mind, and with all your strength" (Mk 12:30 NRSV). But if prayer and worship aren't moral issues, they do pertain to the Christian life, to the "good life" as understood in the Christian faith, and thus warrant careful reflection.

I use the word *ethics* in this chapter's title to refer both to nonmoral goods (like mental health, happiness, prayer and worship) and to moral issues (like adultery and the professional obligation to maintain client confidentiality). I prefer this broader usage of *ethics* because moral and non-

moral issues are not always easily separable and are often deeply intertwined in both therapy and Christian faith. To return to the example of
Brad: if a therapist thinks Brad's personal happiness (meaning the nonmoral good of experiencing happiness in the here and now) is the ultimate
good for him and no moral considerations are applicable, the outcome of
therapy is likely to be different than if a therapist thinks that the happiness
that comes from a right relationship with God is the ultimate human good
and that Brad has a moral obligation to remain faithful to his wife. In
general, I think it preferable to use an intellectual perspective that embraces
all of life and permits a consideration of both goodness and obligation.
Moral and nonmoral should be distinguished, of course, while still recognizing their frequent inseparability. Similarly, Christian ethics and the
Christian life may need to be distinguished, but both require the careful
attention of Christian therapists and clients.

  Ethical principles regulating behavior, virtue or both. Another distinction regarding the meaning of ethics has to do with whether ethics is
primarily concerned with (1) ethical principles, for instance, justice or autonomy (e.g., "Human beings should be just in their dealings with others" or
"No one should infringe on the autonomy of another human being"), or (2)
virtue, the optimal character of persons (e.g., "The ideal person is courageous, self-aware, loving and wise"). Of course, both may also be emphasized. Although ethicists have long emphasized principles, philosophers
and psychologists have recently turned to virtue or character as a critical
aspect of ethics (Fowers, 2005; MacIntyre, 1984; Oakley & Cocking, 2001;
Peterson & Seligman, 2004; Tjeltveit & Fowers, 2003). Christian ethicists, of
course, address virtues (e.g., Dell'Olio, 2003; Kotva, 1996; Lee, 1998) as well
as ethical principles, the former sometimes under the heading of sanctification. The concept of virtue has also been applied to psychotherapy and
the lives of mental health professionals (Cohen & Cohen, 1999; Doherty,
1995; Radden & Sadler, 2008; Tjeltveit, 1999).

  Virtues, as they pertain to psychotherapy relationships, have to do with
those relatively stable moral qualities that characterize persons. Psychotherapy either builds up or tears down client virtues. Therapists likewise
possess, or fail to possess, certain virtues. Doherty (1995), for instance,
points to three ideal therapist virtues: courage, caring and wisdom. Psycho-

therapists who posses the virtue of caring, for instance, routinely exhibit certain emotions, motivations and attitudes with their clients, in pursuit of the good end of client well-being. They don't need to think about the principle of beneficence and then rationally determine how it logically applies in a particular instance before implementing a particular course of action; caring has become second nature to them; being caring is part of who they are. Situational influences can, of course, alter caring—the wrong client on the wrong day can temporarily strip even the most virtuous therapist of concern for a client. And social psychologists have documented the powerful influence that situations can have on behavior (e.g., Zimbardo, 2007). However, openness to the full range of scientific evidence, as well as to Scripture, points to the existence of something like virtues. Indeed, one reason certain therapists have excellent reputations is the virtues they regularly exhibit. Combining both strands of empirical evidence, many psychologists have turned to an interactionist perspective, in which character and situation interact to produce behavior. Accordingly, in addition to attending to their character, Christian psychotherapists need to take responsibility for the situations they put themselves and their clients in. When therapist, client or both are attracted to one another, for instance, it is risky practice for therapists (however virtuous) to schedule a late-night appointment that creates the situation of their being alone together in a counseling suite.

The specific virtues espoused by Christians have been discussed extensively. Theistic perspectives on virtues have been examined in relationship to psychology (e.g., Kaplan & Schwartz, 2006; Roberts, 2007; Worthington & Berry, 2005) and to psychotherapy (e.g., Dueck & Reimer, 2003; Moncher, 2001; Moncher & Titus, 2009; Tan, 2006). Tan, for instance, contrasted Peterson and Seligman's (2004) empirically derived approach to virtues with a Christian approach, in which virtues are (in part) identified through careful study of the Bible and produced through the Holy Spirit. Love (for God and neighbor) is surely a virtue that is relatively stable, that people possess to varying degrees, and that Christians should possess. It is not, however, a topic to which researchers in general have devoted much attention. The role this virtue plays, and should play, in the character of Christian counselors and clients, and how to provoke others to (properly boundaried) love is a topic worthy of considerable attention.

To varying degrees, therapists' ideas about therapy goals and optimal outcomes are informed by their ethical convictions; those ideas thus have ethical dimensions (Tjeltveit, 2006). Whatever a therapist's intent, therapy may result in a client's adopting, abandoning or reprioritizing ethical principles, or in changes in the quality of a client's character. So to limit ethics to a discussion of principles would clearly pass over some of the other key ethical dimensions of psychotherapy (cf. Jordan & Meara, 1990; Weiner, 1993). The Christian concerned about the ethical dimensions of therapy should thus carefully consider both principles and virtues.

Whether a therapist thinks principles or virtues are more important may depend in part on his or her theoretical orientation. Cognitively oriented therapy may produce greater change in a client's ethical principles, while virtue ethics may be more pertinent in understanding psychodynamic therapy (seeking character transformation) and humanistic therapy (stressing the emergence of a self-actualized person). Those with theological perspectives that focus on correct ethical answers and proper behavior may emphasize principles, but those whose perspectives stress the whole person, emotions, spiritual formation, sanctification and the motivations for actions will likely emphasize virtues.

The influence of the therapist's ethical convictions can be subtle. For example, Taylor (1989) has argued convincingly that any notion of identity (arguably related to notions of character and virtue) includes some standard of goodness to which an individual compares himself or herself. For example, if Brad's identity were that of a "man's man" (as exemplified in *Playboy* magazine), the standards of "goodness" by which he would evaluate himself (e.g., sexual prowess) would be very different than if his identity were that of a "good father" or "faithful, loving husband" (as exemplified by God's relationships with his children and the church). To the extent that therapy produces an altered identity, it may also produce an altered sense of what is good and best in life. Change resulting from psychotherapy can thus be both psychological and ethical.

If different therapists were asked, What kind of person would Brad ideally become in therapy? they might propose a variety of answers: self-aware, able to communicate well, a faithful marital partner, guilt-free, spontaneous, one who loves God above all or a person who makes meeting his own personal needs his first priority in life. From the perspective of Christian ethics, it is vitally important which of those virtues Brad chooses, especially if one of those character traits becomes the guiding vision that shapes his behavior, identity and life.

Minimal obligation versus ideals. Some prefer to limit ethics to indisputable moral obligations, to minimal ethical principles about which there is widespread societal or rational agreement, and to conflicts between such obligations and principles. For others, ethics also encompasses ideals, that is, optimal states, behaviors or personal qualities to which persons may aspire. The American Psychological Association (2002) ethics code, for instance, distinguishes between obligatory ethical standards, which are *"enforceable* rules for conduct," and desirable ideals set forth in the Preamble and General Principles, which articulate *"aspirational* goals to guide psychologists toward the highest ideals of psychology" (p. 1061, emphasis added). For instance, the code states that psychologists "have a primary *obligation* . . . to protect confidential information" (Standard 4.01, p. 1066, emphasis added) but should *aspire* "to benefit those with whom they work" (Principle A: Beneficence and Nonmaleficence, p. 1062).

The same distinction applies to clients. Many psychologists, if pushed, would hold that certain obligations are universally applicable. Even Carl Rogers, who argued that exhibiting unconditional positive regard for clients is fundamental to good therapy, would likely have become somewhat conditional had his client, Brad, announced his intent to rapidly hasten the demise of his invalid wife, who wanted to continue living. And Bergin (1985) reported that, when eminent psychotherapy researcher Sol Garfield was asked "whether he believed there are [moral] absolutes," Garfield stated that "he believed in 'moderation in all things,' with the exception of fidelity, which he said he considered absolute" (p. 110). Setting forth such ideals, whether moral or nonmoral, is controversial, though I think all therapists hold some sort of (often implicit) aspirational psychological ideals.

Ethics, even when focused on minimal ethical obligations, has often tended to focus on ethical dilemmas, on conflicts between indisputable moral obligations. Much attention is devoted to clarifying and resolving such conflicts.

Ethical dilemmas do arise in therapy (Koocher & Keith-Spiegel, 2008;

Pope & Vetter, 1992). Therapists wrestle with situations in which honoring one ethical standard (like upholding confidentiality) may result in violating another (for instance, if a therapist upholds the confidentiality of a client who announces the intent to kill person A, the client is then free to kill person A; the therapist would have violated the ethical principle of nonmaleficence, of doing no harm; American Psychological Association, 2002). In the example of Brad, his therapist could argue that she invited Brad's pastor to the second therapy session because—when faced with the dilemma of a conflict between (1) upholding confidentiality and (2) saving Brad's soul, plus furthering his moral and spiritual well-being and ensuring the integrity of his family—the latter trumped the former.

Although addressing ethical dilemmas is important, an exclusive focus on minimal obligations or on conflicts between minimal obligations falls far short of addressing all of the ethical issues in therapy. Indeed, the ideals therapists and clients bring to a therapeutic relationship represent one of the most important ethical aspects of psychology. Questions of ideals arise most pointedly when treatment goals are formulated (Tjeltveit, 2006). What is the ideal life (the optimal behavior, character and lifestyle to which a Christian should aspire) for a particular Christian client? For all clients? What is the ideal life for Brad and his therapist?

The aspirational goals of psychotherapy are often discussed under the rubric *mental health*, a term that, ironically, rarely receives careful scrutiny by mental health professionals. Providing a simple, universally accepted definition of mental health has proven difficult (Jahoda, 1958; Keyes, 2005), and a variety of approaches to understanding the values associated with it have been pursued (Browning & Cooper, 2004; Consoli & Williams, 1999; Gellis, Huh, Lee & Kim, 2003; Howard, McMinn, Bissell, Faries & VanMeter, 2000; Kelly, 1990; Kubacki & Chase, 1998; Richardson, Fowers & Guignon, 1999; Tjeltveit, 1999; Walsh, 1995). Consensus beyond the superficial remains elusive. This is partly because mental health is a value-laden, hybrid term that combines the normative and the factual (Wakefield, 1992).

At its simplest, mental health means freedom from mental illness. The desirability of that ideal is indisputable, and there is nothing distinctive about a Christian seeking it. However, when mental health is viewed as a positive, ideal state, a goal toward which therapists strive to move people, divergences emerge. The value-laden character of psychotherapy (Barnes & Murdin, 2001; Doherty, 1995; Richardson et al., 1999; Tjeltveit, 1999) is relevant here. To the extent that therapy affects client values, the ethics-laden nature of concepts of mental health means that therapeutic approaches differ substantially. Christian ethics supports some understandings of mental health and challenges others. The aspirational ideals of mental health are thus different for some Christian therapists and clients. Indeed, it may be the case that, of all the ways in which therapy is tied to ethics, Christian ethics may provide the most distinctive perspective when addressing therapy ideals.

Mental health, however defined, is one good end toward which clients may aspire. Brad's mental health and happiness are indisputably good; other things being equal, we would presumably want him more, rather than less, happy and healthy. But other good ends exist as well, such as his personal integrity, his promise keeping and the quality of his relationship with God, his family and the Christian community. One vital task is to evaluate the relative merits of all those goods, to determine what is ideal or optimal for him, to clarify his highest good. Is his mental health more important than his relationship with God? Although many therapists—Christian and non-Christian—consider such a question to be beyond the scope of their expertise or calling, the therapy they provide often reflects their de facto balancing of goods, obligations and virtues. And so in working with Brad, his therapist would likely weigh the goodness of mental health against other goods and against moral obligations like marital fidelity.

Christian therapists cannot be indifferent to the direction in which Brad and others move in therapy, cannot be neutral about the ideals that shape and direct it. Removal of distress, however good and valuable, cannot be equated with optimal human functioning. Some argue that a Christian counselor should strive to help clients reach not merely the minimal goal of decreased suffering but deeper, more ultimate goals that reflect the highest ideals of the Christian life. Such goals would be distinctively Christian. For example, a Christian therapist, articulating an aspirational ethic, might set as a treatment goal for all clients what the Shorter Catechism of the Westminster Confession says is the optimal goal for human beings: our "chief end is to glorify God and to enjoy Him forever" (Westminster Divines, 1648, 1745, p. 369).

More often, therapists emphasize limited behavioral treatment goals, like reduced depression. Indeed, some assert that it is precisely the focus on mental health alone (and not the pursuit of more ambitious moral and spiritual goals in addition to better psychological functioning) that distinguishes psychotherapy from other forms of human transformation. Clearly, therapists set goals at different levels. Herron, Javier, Primavera and Schultz (1994) distinguish between "three levels of mental health—necessity, improvement, and potentiality" (p. 106), noting that current trends in health care funding limit financial assistance to the first level.

Even therapists who argue for therapy's role in helping clients achieve their potential, however, often exclude moral and spiritual dimensions of human potential. Those limitations, set by therapists themselves, may stem in part from genuine modesty about therapeutic efficacy, in part from an unwarranted assumption that "everyone knows" the goal of psychotherapy, in part from a focus on therapy process rather than on the ultimate goals of therapy, in part from a recognition of the limited function a therapist serves, and in part from a radical skepticism about the possibility of having any but subjective or conative grounds for selecting more ultimate treatment goals. Regarding the latter, MacIntyre (1984) argues that many believe "questions of ends are questions of values, and on values reason is silent; conflict between rival values cannot be rationally settled. Instead one must simply choose" (p. 26).

Nevertheless, therapists often have more fundamental underlying treatment goals (cf. Browning & Cooper, 2004; Jones & Butman, 2011) that implicitly shape their relationships with clients. Different therapists may well reduce Brad's distress (mental health at the level of necessity), but each would do so by moving Brad away from his symptoms and toward a variety of "ideal" directions. These underlying visions of optimal humanity can and should be analyzed from an ethical perspective.

The extent to which Christian therapists and clients can and should include the full range of Christian ideals in the goals they establish is a thorny and divisive issue. The Christian mental health professional cannot maintain either extreme position. Strict neutrality regarding Christian moral obligations and ideals is neither possible nor desirable. However, mental health professionals must limit their actions to the realm of their expertise—

mental health—and are thus not free to focus on the Christian life of clients in the way pastors and friends can. So the issue is not *whether* Christian ethics enters therapy but *how* it enters. Specifically, how intentional should Christian therapists and clients be in formulating therapy goals in relationship to Christian ideals? For the Christian therapist this issue is made more complex by the fact that many clients enter therapy deeply disturbed and confused. They know they want to suffer less but are unclear about what they want in terms of ideals and personal qualities they would like to develop. This can provide an opportunity for Christian therapists, but also potential peril. To avoid the peril, Christian mental health professionals need to act in concord with professional ethics and provide therapy fully informed by Christian ethics only when clients give their full, free and informed consent.

ETHICAL THEORY

In the academic realm, ethicists often use the term *ethics* to refer to ethical theory. Philosophers and others concerned with ethical theory strive to clarify the meanings of the concepts employed in moral discourse in order to determine whether it is meaningful to talk about goodness, virtue and moral obligation (or whether all moral judgments are relative), to establish the basis of goodness and moral obligation, to set forth ethical principles by which we can decide what is right or good, to obtain ethical knowledge and so forth.

Christians often give distinctive answers to questions of ethical theory (e.g., Davis, 2004; Hauerwas & Wells, 2004; Hays, 1996; Meilaender & Werpehowski, 2005; Reuschling, 2008; Stassen & Gushee, 2003; Wells & Quash, 2010), distinctive sometimes in relationship to their society at large and sometimes in relationship to other Christians. When seeking to set ethical standards, some Christians focus on God's commands (as found in Scripture and church tradition), some on reason, some on the relationship of persons to God, and some on a combination of these approaches (Long, 1967, 1982). Wells and Quash (2010) categorize Christian ethics in another way, differentiating among ethical strands that are relevant for everyone, for the excluded and for the church. Ethical *theories* held by Christians and non-Christians can diverge even when there is

agreement on a particular ethical standard or virtue, like that psychotherapists should uphold client confidentiality. But most Christians would
agree that ethical questions are best addressed in the context of a Christian
worldview. "What should I do?" is a very different question for a person
called by grace through Christ to be a just, loving child of God than it is
for a person who believes that the world consists entirely of physical
matter and that ethical questions are meaningless.

Ethical theory applies to psychotherapy in different ways. It may serve as
the source of therapeutic goals. Christian and non-Christian psychotherapists might agree that it would be good for Brad to end his present arrangement with Jennifer, and perhaps even that his infidelity is immoral,
but might do so for different reasons. One therapist may object to the relationship solely because it is inconsistent with his or her vision of mental
health for Brad. Another may agree that Brad's relationship with Jennifer is
not mentally healthy but may also consider the affair to be immoral—
promises are obligatory because of the damage to society if they are not
kept. Still another therapist might add that the affair is immoral because it
violates the clear command of God in the Ten Commandments or because
the clear thrust of Scripture is in support of marriage. Of course, many psychologists never state their underlying ethical theories clearly, and some
deny that they even hold such theories. Fortunately, Christian mental health
professionals wishing to evaluate the ethical theories of psychotherapeutic
approaches, including those that are implicit, can benefit from the substantial critical attention those theories have received in recent years (e.g.,
Browning, 2006; Browning & Cooper, 2004; Dueck & Reimer, 2009; Jones
& Butman, 2011; Richardson et al., 1999; Tjeltveit, 1999, 2007).

Another way in which ethical theory applies to psychotherapy is with
regard to clients' own ethical theories, which may (and perhaps sometimes
should) be altered over the course of a therapeutic relationship. Brad, for
instance, appears to hold a rather unreflective hedonistic ethical theory—
"Living the good life means doing what makes me happy"—in contrast to
the richer hedonism of the Westminster Confession—"enjoy [God] forever"
(cf. Piper, 1986, 1991). But some therapists may convert clients from a
Christian ethical theory to Brad's brand of hedonism and label the result
"mental health."

SOCIAL ETHICS, PUBLIC POLICY AND CONSENSUS

Given the deep, unresolved tensions in society over ethical theory, the content of specific ethical principles and the deeply ethical nature of therapy, the task of determining how society should regard therapy, and especially its ethical dimensions, is daunting. At present, society clearly sanctions therapy in its role of reducing the suffering associated with mental illness. But other ethical questions remain, having to do with ethics in the sense of social ethics: Which ethical position (or positions) is consistent with the socially sanctioned activity of psychotherapy? What is the proper role of therapy in society?

Adequately addressing these questions requires Christians to participate in the general societal debate regarding a public philosophy for psychotherapy (cf. Browning & Evison, 1991; Drane, 1991; Michels, 1991). Assuming that full societal agreement about the ethical dimensions of psychotherapy is unlikely in the foreseeable future, all who have a stake in therapy, including Christians, need to participate (Stiles, Shapiro & Barkham, 1993). Christians can contribute to this discussion by affirming on theological grounds the positive contributions of mental health professionals in general, while also arguing that the rights of religious persons seeking to provide and receive effective therapy that is consistent with their faith traditions should be upheld.

Some propose that we solve the problem of religious pluralism by erecting a "wall of separation" between religion (and, for many, ethics and morality) and the rest of life, including therapy. As a solution to the problem of the value-laden nature of therapy, this supposedly solves the problem of pluralism by ensuring that religious ethical perspectives don't inappropriately insinuate themselves (or insinuate themselves at all) into a publicly funded therapeutic relationship. The problem with this solution, despite its merits when applied in the arena of government, is that faith, ethics and therapy all have to do with deeply personal matters, matters that don't neatly fall into the categories created by psychotherapists and social planners. Expecting clients and therapists to be neutral about religious matters in therapy seems neither realistic nor desirable.

A much better solution to the question of the proper role of therapy in society includes a recognition that therapy can be understood on several different levels. Neimeyer (1993), for instance, distinguishes between four levels of therapy, in order of increasing abstractness: strategies and techniques (e.g., interpretations in psychoanalysis), clinical theory (e.g., the role of transference in psychoanalysis), formal theory (e.g., Freud's theory of the ego, id and superego), and metatheory ("assumptions about the nature of human existence, plasticity and the locus of change," p. 143, that are not generally empirically testable). He suggests that consensus may be most easily attained in the middle levels. Societal consensus about the role of ethics in therapy is also probably most achievable at an intermediate level of abstraction. Achieving ethical consensus about the goodness of freedom from disabling and deeply distressing psychological disorders, for instance, does not seem difficult. Such an ethical assertion falls somewhere between specific ethical assertions (e.g., "Thou shalt not commit adultery") and very general ethical assertions (e.g., "Reason and reason alone is the appropriate basis for ethical principles"). But there is not yet social consensus about either specific techniques or about ethical theory, nor is one likely to develop soon.

A public philosophy that assumes certain intermediate-level goals (e.g., reduced psychological symptoms) and permits a wide range of general and specific ethical assertions in support of those goals may be optimal. Distinctively Christian forms of therapy, and forms of therapy distinctive to other religious and philosophical traditions, would be supported so long as the consensual goals are met, permitting a genuine pluralism in society as a whole (Tjeltveit, 1996). Societal sanction would thus be given to therapy that uses a vision of humanity that is fully informed by Christian ethics (or Buddhist, Jewish or Wiccan ethics), so long as the therapist is clear about the philosophy and goals, clients are fully informed about them and the intermediate-level goals society agrees on are pursued and reached. Adopting this sort of public philosophy would, of course, require that Christians acknowledge the legitimacy of forms of effective therapy that are based, in part, on other religious/spiritual perspectives and are desired by other therapists and clients, ensuring that they have the same level of autonomy and distinctiveness we want for ourselves.

Johnson (1993) and Worthington (1993a) pointed out almost two decades ago that Christians had made too little progress in documenting the efficacy of Christian approaches to psychotherapy. Unfortunately, that situation has not changed substantially. Research needs to focus both on the effectiveness of Christian approaches to psychotherapy, as judged by traditional standards of therapy outcome, and on distinctively Christian standards—to evaluate whether Christian counseling produces outcomes (in addition to improved psychological functioning) that Christians see as desirable. Until that research is conducted, justifying distinctively Christian psychotherapy to society will be far more difficult than it need be.

CONCLUSION

To understand and practice therapy as Christians, we need to draw upon the best Christian ethical traditions and the best approaches to psychotherapy theory, research and practice. To take seriously the implications of Christian ethics for psychotherapy requires rigorous reflection on the full range of ethical dimensions of therapy—including professional ethics, the content of Christian ethics, the context of Christian ethics, both moral and nonmoral factors, both ethical principles and virtues, both minimal obligations and ideals, both specific ethical assertions and underlying ethical theory, and the proper role of religion and psychotherapy in society. We also need to devote ourselves to who we are, to our character, virtues, spirituality, emotions, motivations, relationships and communities. In all those ways, then, we need to wrestle with the distinctiveness of psychotherapy and Christian ethics in full harmony.

REFERENCES

AACC Law and Ethics Committee. (2004). *AACC code of ethics.* Forest, VA: American Association of Christian Counselors.

American Association of Pastoral Counselors. (1994). *Code of ethics.* Fairfax, VA: American Association of Pastoral Counselors.

American Psychiatric Association. (2009). *The principles of medical ethics with annotations especially applicable to psychiatry.* Arlington, VA: American Psychiatric Association.

American Psychological Association. (2002). Ethical principles of psychologists and code of conduct. *American Psychologist, 57,* 1060-73. Also available (with 2010 amendments) from www.apa.org/ethics/code/index.aspx.

Anderson, S. K., & Handelsman, M. M. (2010). *Ethics for psychotherapists and counselors: A proactive approach.* Malden, MA: Wiley-Blackwell.

Annas, J. (1992). Ethics and morality. In L. C. Becker & C. B. Becker (Eds.), *Encyclopedia of ethics*, vol. 1. New York: Garland.

Barnes, F. P., & Murdin, L. (2001). *Values and ethics in the practice of psychotherapy and counseling.* Buckingham, UK: Open University Press.

Bennett, T. S. (1994). Professional ethics. In R. J. Corsini (Ed.), *Encyclopedia of psychology* (2nd ed., vol. 3). New York: John Wiley.

Bergin, A. E. (1985). Proposed values for guiding and evaluating counseling and psychotherapy. *Counseling and Values, 29,* 99-116.

Browning, D. S. (2006). *Christian ethics and the moral psychologies.* Grand Rapids: Eerdmans.

Browning, D. S., & Cooper, T. D. (2004). *Religious thought and the modern psychologies: A critical conversation in the theology of culture* (2nd ed.). Minneapolis: Fortress.

Browning, D. S., & Evison, I. S. (Eds.). (1991). *Does psychiatry need a public philosophy?* Chicago: Nelson-Hall.

Christian Association for Psychological Studies. (2005). *Ethics statement of the Christian association for psychological studies.* Batavia, IL: Christian Association for Psychological Studies.

Cohen, E. D., & Cohen, G. S. (1999). *The virtuous therapist: Ethical practice of counseling and psychotherapy.* Belmont, CA: Brooks/Cole Wadsworth.

Consoli, A., & Williams, L. (1999). Commonalities in values among mental health counselors. *Counseling and Values, 43,* 106-15.

Davis, J. J. (2004). *Evangelical ethics: Issues facing the church today* (3rd ed.). Phillipsburg, NJ: Presbyterian & Reformed.

Dell'Olio, A. J. (2003). *Foundations of moral selfhood: Aquinas on divine goodness and the connection of the virtues.* New York: Peter Lang.

Doherty, W. J. (1995). *Soul searching: Why psychotherapy must promote moral responsibility.* New York: Basic Books/HarperCollins.

Drane, J. (1991). Doctors as priests: Providing a social ethics for a secular culture. In D. S. Browning & I. S. Evison (Eds.). *Does psychiatry need a public philosophy?* (pp. 40-60). Chicago: Nelson-Hall.

Dueck, A., & Reimer, K. (2003). Retrieving the virtues in psychotherapy: Thick and thin discourse. *American Behavioral Scientist, 47,* 427-41.

Dueck, A., & Reimer, K. (2009). *A peaceable psychology: Christian therapy in a world of many cultures.* Grand Rapids: Brazos.

Forde, G. O. (1969). *The law-gospel debate: An interpretation of its historical development.* Minneapolis: Augsburg.

Fowers, B. J. (2005). *Virtue and psychology: Pursuing excellence in ordinary practices.* Washington, DC: American Psychological Association.

Fuller, D. P. (1980). *Gospel and law: contrast or continuum? The hermeneutics of dispensationalism and covenant theology.* Grand Rapids: Eerdmans.

Gellis, Z. D., Huh, N. S., Lee, S., & Kim, J. (2003). Mental health attitudes among Caucasian-American and Korean counseling students. *Community Mental Health Journal, 39,* 213-24.

Gottlieb, M. C., Handelsman, M. M., & Knapp, S. (2008). Some principles for ethics education: Implementing the acculturation model. *Training and Education in Professional Psychology, 2,* 123-28.

Handelsman, M. M., Gottlieb, M. C., & Knapp, S. (2005). Acculturation as a framework for training ethical psychologists. *Professional Psychology: Research and Practice, 36,* 59-65.

Handelsman, M. M., Knapp, S., & Gottlieb, M. C. (2009). Positive ethics: Themes and variations. In C. R. Snyder & S. J. Lopez (Eds.), *Oxford handbook of positive psychology* (2nd ed.) (pp. 105-13). New York: Oxford University Press.

Hauerwas, S., & Wells, S. (Eds.). (2004). *The Blackwell companion to Christian ethics.* Malden, MA: Blackwell.

Hays, R. B. (1996). *The moral vision of the New Testament: Community, cross, new creation.* San Francisco: HarperSanFrancisco.

Herron, W. G., Javier, R. A., Primavera, L. H., & Schultz, C. L. (1994). The cost of psychotherapy. *Professional Psychology: Research and Practice, 25,* 106-10.

Howard, N. C., McMinn, M. R., Bissell, L. D., Faries, S. R., & VanMeter, J. B. (2000). Spiritual directors and clinical psychologists: A comparison of mental health and spiritual values. *Journal of Psychology & Theology, 28,* 308-20.

Jahoda, M. (1958). *Current concepts of positive mental health.* New York: Basic.

Johnson, W. B. (1993). Outcome research and religious psychotherapies: Where are we and where are we going? *Journal of Psychology and Theology, 21,* 297-308.

Jones, S. L., & Butman, R. E. (2011). *Modern psychotherapies: A comprehensive Christian appraisal* (2nd ed.). Downers Grove, IL: InterVarsity Press.

Jordan, A. E., & Meara, N. M. (1990). Ethics and the professional practice of psychologists: The role of virtues and principles. *Professional Psychology: Research and Practice, 21,* 107-14.

Kaplan, K. J., & Schwartz, M. B. (2006). *The seven habits of the good life: How the biblical virtues free us from the seven deadly sins.* Lanham, MD: Rowman & Littlefield.

Kelly, T. A. (1990). The role of values in psychotherapy: A critical review of process and outcome effects. *Clinical Psychology Review, 10,* 171-86.

Keyes, C. L. M. (2005). Mental illness and/or mental health? Investigating axioms of the complete state model of health. *Journal of Consulting and Clinical Psychology, 73,* 539-48.

Kitchener, K. S. (2000). *Foundations of ethical practice, research, and teaching in psychology.* Mahwah, NJ: Lawrence Erlbaum.

Knapp, S., & VandeCreek, L. (2003). *A guide to the 2002 revision of the American Psychological Association's ethics code.* Sarasota, FL: Professional Resource Press.

Koocher, G. P., & Keith-Spiegel, P. (2008). *Ethics in psychology and the mental health professions: Standards and cases* (3rd ed.). New York: Oxford University Press.

Kotva, J. J., Jr. (1996). *The Christian case for virtue ethics.* Washington, DC: Georgetown University Press.

Kubacki, S. R., & Chase, M. (1998). Comparing values and methods in psychodynamic and cognitive-behavioral therapy: Commonalities and differences. *Journal of Psychotherapy Integration, 8,* 1-25.

Lee, C. (1998). *Beyond family values: A call to Christian virtue.* Downers Grove, IL: InterVarsity Press.

Long, E. L., Jr. (1967). *A survey of Christian ethics.* New York: Oxford University Press.

Long, E. L., Jr. (1982). *A recent survey of Christian ethics.* New York: Oxford University Press.

MacIntyre, A. (1984). *After virtue: A study in moral theory.* (Rev. ed.). Notre Dame, IN: University of Notre Dame Press.

Meilaender, G., & Werpehowski, W. (Eds.). (2005). *The Oxford handbook of theological ethics.* Oxford, UK: Oxford University Press.

Michels, R. (1991). Psychiatry: Where medicine, psychology and ethics meet. In D. S. Browning and I. S. Evison (Eds.), *Does psychiatry need a public philosophy?* (pp. 61-73). Chicago: Nelson-Hall.

Moncher, F. J. (2001). A psychotherapy of virtue: Reflections on St. Thomas Aquinas' theology of moral virtue. *Journal of Psychology and Christianity, 20,* 332-42.

Moncher, F. J., & Titus, C. S. (2009). Foundations for a psychotherapy of virtue: An integrated Catholic perspective. *Journal of Psychology and Christianity, 28,* 22-35.

National Association of Social Workers. (1999). *Code of ethics of the National Association of Social Workers.* Washington, DC: Author.

Neimeyer, R. A. (1993). Constructivism and the problem of psychotherapy integration. *Journal of Psychotherapy Integration, 3,* 133-57.

Oakley, J., & Cocking, D. (2001). *Virtue ethics and professional roles.* Cambridge, UK: Cambridge University Press.

Peterson, C., & Seligman, M. E. P. (2004). *Character strengths and virtues: A handbook and classification*. New York: Oxford University Press.

Piper, J. (1986). *Desiring God: Meditations of a Christian hedonist*. Portland, OR: Multnomah Press.

Piper, J. (1991). *The pleasures of God*. Portland, OR: Multnomah Press.

Pope, K. S., & Vetter, V. (1992). Ethical dilemmas encountered by members of the American Psychological Association: A national survey. *American Psychologist, 47,* 397-411.

Pope, K. S., Sonne, J. L., & Green, B. (2006). *What therapists don't talk about and why: Understanding taboos that hurt us and our clients*. Washington, DC: American Psychological Association.

Radden, J., & Sadler, J. (2008). Character virtues in psychiatric practice. *Harvard Review of Psychiatry, 16,* 373-80.

Reeck, D. (1982). *Ethics for the professions: A Christian perspective*. Minneapolis: Augsburg.

Reuschling, W. C. (2008). *Reviving evangelical ethics: The promises and pitfalls of classic models of morality*. Grand Rapids: Brazos Press.

Richardson, F. C., Fowers, B. J., & Guignon, C. B. *Re-envisioning psychology: Moral dimensions of theory and practice*. San Francisco: Jossey-Bass.

Roberts, R. (2007). *Spiritual emotions: A psychology of Christian virtues*. Grand Rapids: Eerdmans.

Stassen, G., & Gushee, D. (2003). *Kingdom ethics: Following Jesus in contemporary context*. Downers Grove, IL: InterVarsity Press.

Stiles, W. B., Shapiro, D. A., & Barkham, M. (1993). Research directions for psychotherapy integration. In J. C. Norcross (Ed.), Research directions for psychotherapy integration: A roundtable. *Journal of Psychotherapy Integration, 3,* 91-131.

Tan, S. (2006). Applied positive psychology: Putting positive psychology into practice. *Journal of Psychology and Christianity, 25,* 68-73.

Taylor, C. (1989). *Sources of the self: The making of the modern identity*. Cambridge, MA: Harvard University Press.

Tjeltveit, A. C. (1996). Aptly addressing values in societal contracts about psychotherapy professionals: Professional, Christian and societal responsibilities. In P. J. Verhagen and G. Glas. Zoetermeer (Eds.), *Psyche and faith: Beyond professionalism* (pp. 119-37). The Netherlands: Boekencentrum.

Tjeltveit, A. C. (1999). *Ethics and values in psychotherapy*. London: Routledge.

Tjeltveit, A. C. (2006). To what ends? Psychotherapy goals and outcomes, the good life, and the principle of beneficence. *Psychotherapy: Theory, Research, Practice, Training, 43,* 186-200.

Tjeltveit, A. C. (2007). The psychotherapist as Christian ethicist: Theology applied to practice. In D. H. Stevenson, B. E. Eck, and P. C. Hill (Eds.), *Psychology and Christianity integration: Seminal works that shaped the movement* (pp. 268-76). Batavia, IL: Christian Association for Psychological Studies.

Tjeltveit, A. C., & Fowers, B. F. (Eds.). (2003). Explorations of human excellence in behavioral science: Rediscovering virtue in scholarship, teaching, and practice [special issue]. *American Behavioral Scientist, 47*(4).

Tjeltveit, A. C., & Gottlieb, M. C. (2010). Avoiding the road to ethical hell: Overcoming vulnerabilities and developing resilience. *Psychotherapy: Theory, Research, Practice, Training, 47,* 98–110.

Wakefield, J. C. (1992). Disorder as harmful dysfunction: A conceptual critique of *DSM-III-R*'s definition of mental disorder. *Psychological Review, 99,* 232-47.

Walsh, R. A. (1995). The study of values in psychotherapy: A critique and call for an alternative method. *Psychotherapy Research, 5,* 313-26.

Weiner, N. O. (1993). *The harmony of the soul: Mental health and moral virtue reconsidered.* Albany: State University of New York Press.

Wells, S., & Quash, B. (2010). *Introducing Christian ethics.* Malden, MA: Wiley-Blackwell.

Westminster Divines. (1648, 1745). The shorter catechism agreed upon by the assembly of divines of Westminster with the assistance of the commissions from the Church of Scotland. In *A compendium of the Westminster Confession of Faith and the Shorter and Longer Catechism.* Philadelphia: Benjamin Franklin. Pp. 367-410.

Worthington, E. L., & Berry, J. W. (2005). Virtues, vices, and character education. In W. R. Miller and H. D. Delaney (Eds.), *Judeo-Christian perspectives on psychology: Human nature, motivation and change* (pp. 145-64). Washington, DC: American Psychological Association.

Worthington, E. L., Jr. (1988). Understanding the values of religious clients: A model and its application to counseling. *Journal of Counseling Psychology, 35,* 166-74.

Worthington, E. L., Jr. (1993a). Critical issues in the study of psychotherapy and religious values. In E. L. Worthington, Jr. (Ed.), *Psychotherapy and religious values* (pp. 17-26). Grand Rapids: Baker.

Worthington, E. L., Jr. (1993b). Psychotherapy and religious values: An update. In E. L. Worthington Jr. (Ed.), *Psychotherapy and religious values* (pp. 127-44). Grand Rapids: Baker.

Zimbardo, P. G. (2007). *The Lucifer effect: Understanding how good people turn evil.* New York: Random.

3

Qualifications of the Christian Mental Health Professional

Richard E. Butman

One of the most interesting discussions in any standard text on ethical and legal issues in the helping professions is the section that develops the concept of professional competence (e.g., Corey, Corey & Callanan, 2011; Keith-Spiegel & Koocher, 2008). The assumption is usually made that a client's welfare is directly affected by whether or not the mental health professional knows his or her limitations and weaknesses, as well as his or her strengths and skills. In other words, *competence* is usually defined as some combination of clinical expertise, high levels of self-awareness and interpersonal effectiveness (cf. Corey & Corey, 2011). Obviously, the ability to explore one's motives and relationships insightfully is a skill that is hard to teach, difficult to assess and impossible to perfect. Yet few skills are more central to effective ethical and legal functioning as a mental health professional (cf. Keith-Spiegel & Koocher, 2008). Perhaps in no other profession does the behavior and personality of the professional make such a significant and potentially lasting impact on the client, or such a direct contribution to the eventual success and satisfaction of the change agent (Meier, 2008).

Every Christian mental health professional operates either implicitly or explicitly with a set of assumptions about what makes people "tick" (i.e., a working model of personality), a sense for how people get "messed up" in life (i.e., a working model of psychopathology) and convictions about how they best heal or grow in that process (i.e., a working model of psychotherapy). These assumptions have the potential to guide our attempts to accurately assess, effectively treat or even seek to prevent the "calamities of the soul" (cf. Yarhouse, Butman & McRay, 2005, chap. 1). That our consistent beliefs and behaviors should deeply inform our efforts to help or heal others should reflect not only our desire to be perceived as competent—but a reflection of the depth of our character and the absolute integrity of our work. Simply put—the issue is less "mere ethical compliance"—and more accurately a deep understanding of what it means to image God in all aspects of our work (cf. Jones & Butman, 2011, chap. 12). Surely, great measures of honesty and humility—and a profound respect for the basic dignity and worth of all human beings—should be tangible evidence of such a commitment in word and deed.

"Know thyself" is certainly a challenge for any Christian mental health professional, but it must be coupled with genuine wisdom and humanness (cf. Evans, 1989). Further, the Christian mental health professional is called to serve God and his church, and to imagine the Father in all his or her professional work (cf. Jones & Butman, 2011, chap. 12). These "lofty concerns" vie with more mundane and often preoccupying matters like intense competition for the mental health dollar, widespread interdisciplinary conflict over "turf" or financial security for business, self and/or families. Consequently, it becomes terribly tempting to "shrink from self-knowledge" and largely avoid the difficult challenge of thinking clearly about a truly Christian understanding of persons and their suffering (Anderson, 1990; Benner, 1983; Oden, 1984; Tidball, 1986).

This chapter will explore the challenge of defining *competence* for the Christian mental health professional. The implications are enormous, not only for training, licensing and credentialing issues, but for the challenge of maintaining excellence through continuing education, supervision and spiritual growth (cf. Collins, 1991). It seems imperative that this should also include some form of group accountability for true Christian distinctiveness and integrity beyond the maintenance of professional welfare only. Perhaps this would prompt the entire Christian counseling movement to move beyond its scientific infancy and current credibility problems, and move toward more responsible statements in the market place and mass media (cf. Butman, 1993). The discussion will be limited, by necessity, to professional applications for certified or licensed counselors, marriage and family therapists, psychiatrists, psychiatric nurses, psychologists and social workers. This in no way should be interpreted to diminish the importance of lay and paraprofessional counselors (see Tan elsewhere in this volume) or the tremendous example of the great tradition of pastoral care throughout the centuries (cf. Clesch & Jaekle, 1975; Holifield, 1983; and see Blackburn elsewhere in this volume). Recent work by McMinn and Campbell (2007), McMinn and Meek (1996), or Yarhouse, Butman and McRay (2005) would be especially helpful for applications in these areas.

Competence in the helping professions is difficult to define and even harder to assess. Standards and credentials in the mental health disciplines vary, and much controversy surrounds any attempt to discuss boundaries of competence and limitations of technique. Fortunately, each of the major professional associations (see appendix 1) has made an attempt to do so in their respective professional codes of ethics. The Christian Association for Psychological Studies (CAPS, 2005) has also published a statement on professional ethics (available at www.caps.net). Consider the relevant section on "Competence" in the "Ethics Statement of the Christian Association for Psychological Studies":

2.1 Limits of Competence

a. CAPS members do not provide services, including therapy, teaching, or research, unless they have appropriate educational background, additional training, supervised experience, consultation, study, or professional experience.

b. CAPS members are sensitive to the unique needs of special populations and assure that they have relevant training.

c. CAPS members seek appropriate additional training when planning to engage in the provision of services that are new to them. In emerging areas of practice or research, CAPS members take reasonable steps to ensure their competence and minimize the risk of harm to others.

2.2 Continuing Education

CAPS members pursue continuing education and training opportunities in order to maintain their competence.

2.3 Personal Difficulties

CAPS members refrain from professional activities that might be compromised by personal problems and conflicts.

In examining this document and guidelines from the major mental health professions, a number of conclusions are inescapable. First, it is not always clear how the professional should determine the boundaries of his or her competence. Obviously, advanced degrees alone don't confer, nor does the process of credentialing or licensing necessarily guarantee, specific clinical skills and sensitivities. Second, groups of individuals that work in existing structures charged with the responsibilities of detecting and then adjudicating incompetent professional behaviors (e.g., state licensing or certification boards, third-party payer quality assurance programs, professional standards review committees, professional associations, etc.) often have great difficulty in applying existing criteria to specific complaints against mental health professionals. Third, expulsion from professional associations—or even the loss of certification and/or licensure—haven't always served as deterrents against unethical behaviors. It is not surprising, then, that there has been a proliferation of litigation in situations (including the setting of the church) where alleged harm has been done (cf. Ohlschlager, 1991). Fourth, the codes can't "make" the practitioner accept existing practice criteria, review and carefully study the results of treatment outcome data, consult with more experienced practitioners, learn new skills and pursue appropriate levels of training. For example, knowing when to make a referral or learning how to make one that is most helpful to the client is a highly refined skill that presumes an existing network of colleagues that are willing to work in a collaborative manner. The sad reality is that professional licensure and credentialing are less than adequate indicators of an ongoing and continuing commitment to excellence. Professional codes of ethics don't necessarily "prompt" a practitioner to utilize peer review or consultation groups, participate in continuing education, take advantage of supervision or stay alive as a person and as a professional (Corey & Corey, 2011).

At a minimalist level, then, *competence* implies a recognition of one's strengths and weaknesses, and the humility to pursue further consultation, training and supervision throughout one's professional career. It includes the willingness not to allow others to assume that one has training or experience one does not have. Those who would do specialized forms of therapy or testing should be certain they have the skills and ongoing training necessary to offer these services. Honest and sobering self-appraisal likewise requires wisdom and discernment, capacities that are probably best developed in the context of some type of accountability group. We should not expect academic and practical preparation to guarantee competence, nor should we leave it to the judgments of professional licensing or credentialing bodies only. Since ethical codes tend to be too general in nature and give too few specifics to permit an easy identification of incompetent practice (cf. Keith-Spiegel & Koocher, 2008), the challenge remains of developing a consensus about those qualities that embody a commitment to excellence beyond formal education and credentials only.

Peterson and Bry (1980), in one of the few quality studies on the subject, discovered that four factors emerged in their analysis that consistently differentiated "incompetent" and "outstanding" student-clinicians toward the end of a doctoral training program. These were "professional responsibility," "interpersonal warmth," "intelligence" and "experience." These factors are strikingly similar to those reported by McLemore (1982) in a more anecdotal account of an unusually gifted Christian mental health professional. According to McLemore (pp. 171-72), this psychologist was "genuinely loving," "not afraid to care" and "communicated integrity." He goes on to say that "her core beliefs were manifestly Christian . . . in accord with the infrastructure of life." Further, "there was nothing that smacked of 'religion in the service of defenses,' of trying to avoid distressing thoughts and feelings by clinging to empty religious language. . . . My awareness of her faith on many occasions nourished my own." Yet it was a fifth quality, which he described as her "clear professional competence" that was most impressive:

> On the surface, there seems to be nothing particularly Christian about this. Many unbelieving practitioners are competent; in fact, I know a good number of avowed agnostic therapists to whom I would rather refer clients than to some of the Christian professionals I know. However, if God is the Source of all good, regardless of who does it, there is something Christian about competence after all. Moreover, I strongly believe that her Christian

love for people is largely what has motivated her to develop her clinical expertise. (p. 172)

A more recent discussion of similar themes can be found in an outstanding resource by the same author (McLemore, 2006).

In summary, then, *competence* in professional practice might best be understood as a cluster of virtues (cf. Roberts, 1993) or even as a process of character formation (cf. Holmes, 1992). At the most basic level, interpersonal skills and sensitivities must be coupled with clinical expertise. It is probably beyond the scope of any licensing or credentialing body, or even professional association, to define these qualities. It is not surprising, then, that admission committees have difficulty in always recognizing potential, or that training programs struggle in defining these criteria, or that professional associations are unclear about how best to encourage members to maintain and develop a commitment to excellence in their work. Such findings seem entirely consistent with recent themes raised in the helpful literature on effective coping and resilience in the helping professions and beyond (e.g., Anderson, 2000; Norcross & Guy, 2007; Pargament, 1997). Those who appear to cope well are deeply connected in meaningful relationships (i.e., social support), have a clear sense of efficacy (i.e., they are strongly committed to developing their gifts and talents), and stay sharply focused on what gives them meaning and purpose in life. On a more personal level, they are not seen by others as arrogant, isolated or fiercely independent (McLemore, 2003). They are always open and receptive to feedback (strong peer accountability), are deeply engaged in healthy relationships (strong community) and committed to an ongoing process of mutual discernment. In short, they care deeply about the maintenance of their mental, emotional, physical and spiritual well-being (Bilezikian, 1997)—be that in their families and immediate social networks—or their faith-based communities (i.e., local church).

We have already explored some of the reasons why it is difficult for professional mental health associations or licensing and credentialing organizations to define and evaluate clinical competence. Yet additional challenges face the Christian mental health professional who is willing to engage in much needed honest and sobering self-appraisal in the context of a discerning and wise accountability group. As is clearly stated in section 2.0 in the CAPS code he or she should "pursue continuing education and training opportunities in order to maintain their competence" (www.caps.net). To me, that also implies a never-ending process of accountability, consultation and supervision. Toward those desirable end goals, a number of guidelines will be offered for the expressed purpose of fostering a dialogue between committed Christian clinicians and the communities they are a part of. I think it is beyond the scope and purpose of the Bible to directly address the issue of competence as it applies to Christian mental health professionals (cf. Jones & Butman, 2011). Yet certain themes beyond clinical expertise and interpersonal warmth alone seem highly relevant to the discussion. These guidelines no doubt reflect some of my biases and convictions. (I am a licensed clinical psychologist with formal theological training who has worked in a Christian liberal arts and graduate school setting for more than three decades.) From that perspective, I have been able to observe clinicians who not only seem to be "surviving"—but "thriving"—and I have also seen individuals who have made tragic choices that have harmed themselves and others. With due regard for those who lapse because of burnout, compassion fatigue or personal losses, those who do well seem to be deeply insatiably curious about people, problems and process—whereas those who get "stuck" often seem to care far more about power, prestige or profit (cf. Foster, 1985). Succinctly put, arrogance and isolation can be synergistic when it comes to moral lapses and failures (cf. Norcross & Guy, 2007).

TEN GUIDELINES FOR IMPROVING THE
COMPETENCE OF CHRISTIAN CLINICIANS

1. We should encourage rigorous training in one of the major mental health disciplines. Specifically, I believe this should include formal education through at least the master's level at a regionally accredited college or university. In certain disciplines, specialized degrees and extensive clinical training are required (e.g., MSW plus practicum for social work, Ph.D. or Psy.D. plus internship for clinical or counseling psychology, M.D. plus residency for psychiatry). I share Levicoff's concern (1993) about the "chaff" that all too often accompanies the "wheat" in the burgeoning Christian counseling movement. Since at least forty of the fifty states have some kind of credentialing legislation in place, "that range from voluntary title acts to mandatory practice acts" (p. 58), it behooves us to take seriously the prerequisite education and training necessary to be even considered as a candidate for the appropriate credentials and licensure required for professional practice in any given state.

I share Noll's anguish (1994) about the "anti-intellectual" attitudes evident far too often in some conservative Christian circles. I would be greatly encouraged by a more engaging mindset, one that would be open and receptive to God's truth in all of the academic disciplines (e.g., Browning, 1987; Collins, 1989; Holmes, 1977). In my particular discipline I am deeply convinced that there is much in the theoretical and applied scholarly literature that bears directly on the many activities of the Christian mental health professional (cf. Jones & Butman, 2011; Yarhouse, Butman & McRay, 2005).

All systems of psychological thought have their points of compatibility and incompatibility with Christian systems of thought. I think it is a mistake to assume that the Bible declares itself to be sufficient to meet all human needs (cf. Bobgan & Bobgan, 1987, p. 11), or that it is sufficient to study the Holy Scriptures alone in order to equip oneself to become the servant of God (cf. Adams, 1979, p. 46). At the most basic level, such a position runs the risk of denying "general revelation" or "common grace" (i.e., all truth is God's truth). Consequently, I am deeply troubled by the widespread distrust of the mental health disciplines and the tendency for some Christians to "shoot their wounded" (cf. Carlson, 1994). Granted, the ultimate task of the Christian mental health professional is the "interrelating of Christian belief and practice with the best of contemporary scholarship and professional standards" in his or her particular discipline (Inform, 1994). Succinctly put, we can't establish or maintain true Christian distinctiveness as mental health professionals unless we are conversant in the major theories, paradigms, values and culture of our chosen mental health discipline. How this could be done apart from an extended residence at a high quality academic setting is beyond my comprehension. Only in a residential setting is there opportunity for the regular dialogue and discussion that is so essential for integrative learning. Only in a residential setting can close community form and modeling and mentorship take place. Only in a residential setting can the student be regularly held accountable by peers and professors. I believe the sacrifice is "worth it" and potentially an expression of the good Christian stewardship of our time, talents and resources. I seriously doubt that this can occur apart from live interaction in an "in-vivo" setting.

No doubt certain programs and institutions are better than others, and choices about which discipline to pursue are seldom easy. We need to help "the next generation" make wise and informed decisions about whether or not to pursue the helping professions, and give them the kind of practical information that can help them get the most out of their education and training (cf. the initial chapters in Corey & Corey, 2008). For those of us who have already made our choices and commitments, we must fully realize that our responsibilities for educating ourselves must transcend the confines of either educational and training settings (i.e., learning is a never-ending process). For those of us who serve in academic and clinical training settings, it is imperative that we give careful attention to how we select students, how best to train and supervise students, the curriculum we offer, and the criteria for certification and graduation (cf. Corey, Corey & Callahan, 2011). The qualifications of mental health professionals reflect, in no small measure, the academic milieus in which they were shaped, the training and supervisory experiences they were exposed to, and the modeling they directly observed (cf. Guy, 1986). This process of "imprinting" probably places certain limits on the potential for an individual's further capacity for personal and professional growth, one vital expression of a commitment to excellence.

2. We should encourage exposure to diversity in the initial training and beyond. This includes but is not limited to contemporary models of multicultural psychotherapy. Traditional approaches to people-helping are not always applicable in the cross-cultural context. Ours is a pluralistic culture that demands the ability to be "uncommonly decent" —the capacity to be "civil" without being entirely relativistic, and the capacity to be "convicted" without being overly dogmatic and rigid (cf. Mouw, 1992). We need to develop a kind of humility and openness that allows us to see the essential humanity of all persons. Arrogance and inflexibility about our theories, paradigms and values will certainly impair our ability to relate with others whose experiences can be vastly different than our own. We live in a society in which there is far too much intolerance and unnecessary conflict surrounding issues of racial or ethnic identification, age, socioeconomic status, religious affiliation or gender.

Ideally, professional preparation would include coursework and training experiences that would stress issues of diversity, and licensed and credentialed professionals would actively pursue the kind of continuing education and supervision that would challenge and stretch them in these areas. Hopefully, this would bring a heightened awareness of those who have been marginalized and wounded by living in nonpluralistic society (cf. concluding chapters in Corey, Corey & Callanan, 2011), or "silenced" by ethnocentric and culture-bound attitudes and behaviors (Van Leeuwen et al., 1993). "Exposure to diversity" should also include exposure to a variety of different client populations such as the chronically mentally ill and other client groups who are marginalized in society because of their mental illness and its byproducts (low socioeconomic status, poor socialization, lack of educational opportunity, etc.).

A respect for diversity should also be reflected in one's primary theoretical allegiances. A strong argument can be made for responsible eclecticism or "theoretical integrationism" in clinical practice (cf., Jones & Butman, 2011, chap. 11). There is no warrant for theoretical exclusivism in training, supervision or practice. The demands of most contemporary mental health settings necessitate flexibility and "epistemic humility," a willingness to learn much about (and from) those being served. "Know thyself" must be coupled with an equally strong desire to get to know others, including those whose experiences are very different than our own (Palmer, 1993).

Our culture seems to be in the midst of tremendous change and flux. As I reflect back on the changes that have occurred in my lifetime, never has it been more important—or more challenging—to be a world citizen and a world Christian. I applaud the work of groups like Capetown 2010 (the Lausanne Conference—cf. www.capetown2010.com) that struggle deeply with what it means to promote strategies that truly foster reconciliation and transformation. Competent Christian mental health professionals must acutely be aware of how world events are affecting the lives of their clients. Learning to more fully understand the contexts and situations in which they conduct their daily lives has perhaps never been so important in our work.

3. We should encourage a commitment to careful supervision and regular consultation for all Christian mental health professionals and students. This is a requirement in nearly every practicum and training setting, although the quality and quantity of that supervision and consultation varies widely. When it is good, the recipient can learn much about ethical issues associated with carrying out professional roles and responsibilities, the need to maintain clear boundaries between those roles, and the potential dangers of dual relationships (cf. Corey, Corey & Callanan, 2011). In that context, self-awareness of strengths and weaknesses and insights about the helper in the healing process can develop. Ideally, it can be a catalyst for self-exploration and growth, and a context for both modeling and mentorship. If personal problems arise in the personal life of the psychotherapist, it becomes easier to know how best to proceed with a referral to another professional for assistance. If one has the opportunity to recognize the limitations of one's technical expertise, he or she is more likely to make a timely referral to another mental health professional.

Careful supervision and regular consultation should last far beyond the formal requirements of a practicum or training setting. Becoming certified or licensed should not somehow signal the end for the need of this kind of intimate, one to one accountability. Exposure to a variety of styles or orientations is potentially useful, and a combination of individual and group involvement is the ideal. It is difficult for me to see how this kind of regular feedback, and the opportunity to hone clinical skills, could be perceived as unnecessary or irrelevant to the complex and often confusing tasks of the Christian mental health professional.

Granted, high-quality supervision beyond credentialing and licensure can be expensive and time-consuming. When coupled with a commitment to continuing education and training, I believe it has the potential to be a most worthwhile investment and a very tangible expression of a continuing commitment to excellence. Indeed, it may speak deeply to whether or not we aim toward the achievement of greater measures of wholeness and holiness, and to be the best that we can be (cf. Malony, 1994).

I suspect in the very near future that effective clinical supervision will insist on actual data (e.g., audiotapes or videotapes) rather than rely on the selective self-report of the supervisee. We are all prone to self-serving biases—and none of us are free from the temptations of image management. An excellent supervisor will keep us closely focused on the actual words of our clients—and our responses to them in word and deed. Ideally, some of the accountability might include total immersion—where the supervisor and supervisee actually work in collaboration—at the same time. I have a growing respect for the power of authentic and credible role modeling and dream of a day with this kind of supervision done in the most direct and intimate way.

4. We should encourage the pursuit of legitimate credentials and professional licensure. Mental health professionals usually recognize that most credentials and licenses are generic (i.e., they don't specify the problems or populations the practitioner is qualified to work with, nor do they indicate the nature of that individual's clinical expertise). In the majority of states, legislation has been enacted that presumably protects the public against untrained or potentially unqualified practitioners. The assumption is that those who are credentialed or licensed will only engage in psychotherapeutic tasks for which they have received specialized education and training. Fretz and Mills (1980) define licensure as "the statutory process by which an agency of the government, usually a state, grants permission to a person meeting predetermined qualifications to engage in a given occupation and/ or use a particular title and to perform specified functions" (p. 7). Certification, in contrast, pertains more directly to judgments made by members of a professional association about a particular individual's credentials (e.g., graduate education, supervised practice, internship or highly specialized postdoctoral training). The relationship between certification and/or licensure and clinical competence has not, unfortunately, been clearly documented (Keith-Spiegel & Koocher, 2008).

There are some strong arguments for and against professional licensing and credentialing. Corey, Corey, and Callanan (2011) assert that the main argument for certification or licensure is that it safeguards the consumer's welfare. In contrast, the main liability is that it is a self-serving process that limits competition and creates a union shop mentality.

No doubt there are competent counselors who are shut out because they are not certified or licensed, and this has the potential to produce adversarial rather than collaborative relationships (cf. Collins, 1991). In some Christian circles a strong argument is made that any biblically grounded Christian is "competent to counsel," a position that is critiqued and evaluated at length elsewhere (cf. Jones & Butman, 2011, chap. 1). A major concern about this position is the limited availability of any demonstrated (i.e., empirical) data beyond anecdotes and "case studies" to support this view. Advocates also seem unwilling to strive toward the development of a more inclusive and responsible eclecticism in theory or practice; nor does there seem to be a willingness to engage in discussions that could be characterized as evidencing a "convicted civility" (cf. Butman, 1993). In the interim the positions might be best viewed as a creedal assertion, a virtue statement that is difficult to confirm or refute (i.e., it needs to be put into the terms of a researchable hypothesis).

I am personally encouraged when faith-based groups like CAPS encourage their members not to hide behind the relative safety of a noncredentialed, church-based practice, assuming that they are somehow protected by separation of church and state. I share Ohlschlager's (1991) concern that by too loosely appealing to "church-state separation issues," one can avoid the more rigorous and demanding approach being advocated in this chapter for the Christian mental health professional. There are certainly delicate tensions for credentialing or licensing pastoral counselors, tensions fully appreciated by groups like the American Association of Pastoral Counselors or movements like Clinical Pastoral Education. I certainly have sympathy for positions that stress church-state separation. My bigger fear, however, is the temptation on the part of the counselor not to pursue additional education, experience or professional supervision, or the blatant disregard for any kind of peer review or system of accountability. I suspect that Ohlschlager (1991) is right when he argues that in the "grave new world" of Christian counseling, the threat of litigation may be the greater incentive for pursuing excellence, rather than a strong sense of personal or professional integrity that should undergird the desire to be competent in any services provided.

I seriously doubt whether the licensing or credentialing debate will be resolved in the near future. A bigger concern for me, however, is the attitude and belief on the part of a practitioner that he or she is somehow beyond the need to take these issues seriously, or is satisfied to settle for less than fully legitimate credentials. I share Levicoff's (1993) conviction that it is "better not to be certified at all than to be certified by a bogus organization that will reflect poorly on the counselor's professional reputation" (p. 58).

No doubt regulation can be a hassle—but I remain convinced that market forces alone should not drive the activities of Christian mental health professionals, since the risk of personal aggrandizement or the temptation to promote oneself in a self-serving manner is tremendous. Regulation, I firmly believe, is a much-needed potential corrective for these tendencies.

I believe an even more effective way to capture the "spirit and letter of the law" is to engage in professional disclosure. I would like to see Christian mental health professionals take the initiative by preparing an annual professional disclosure statement that would be submitted to regulatory boards—and perhaps even to a representative group of discerning peers, including members of their local churches (cf. Bernstein & Lecomte, 1981). Unlicensed or noncredentialed clinicians would be asked to demonstrate clinical skills that are clearly related to positive client outcomes (via audio, video or written transcripts). Licensed and credentialed clinicians might consider submitting evidence of their continuing commitment to academic and professional excellence, provide an updated and hopefully maturing statement of their philosophy of psychotherapeutic change and records of their attempts to measure client outcomes.

This idea is not particularly new. If follows logically from the practice of preparing informed consent documents for new and potential clients (see the chapter by Lukens and Sanders elsewhere in this volume, and the example in Collins, 1991, pp. 185-87). These documents provide clients with the information necessary for making intelligent decisions about whether or not to utilize the provider's services and what to expect from treatment.

I find it fascinating that nearly all of the international students I have worked with over the decades have been told by equivalent credentialing organizations in their government that they must bring some proof of their competency when returning home. I suspect the meaning of that credential might be quite different—but it does seem to respect the belief that some sort of minimalist expectation must be met. Even in so-called low-resourced countries in the global South and East, there appears to be the widespread recognition that nobody should just wing it.

In summary, the pursuit of legitimate credentials and professional licensure is to be commended, although it is not without its limitations. Beyond these regulatory considerations, it would be exemplary for Christian mental health professionals to develop the habit of offering annual professional disclosure statements and utilizing informed consent documents with all their clients. This type of accountability would most likely have a humbling and humanizing effect on the current practice of psychology. I have no doubt that recent changes in the delivery of human services and health care in the public and private sectors will have a similar impact. I also believe that these efforts would make the Christian mental health professional far more sensitive to the legal as well as ethical considerations that are involved in a variety of psychotherapeutic endeavors. This is no doubt a good thing since research by McMinn and Meek (1996) indicates that far too many Christian counselors somehow fail to see that all their actions are subject to the mechanisms of ethical restraint and regulation, whether they are credentialed, licensed or not. The freedom from these restraints is illusory if it leads to the disintegration of competence within the lay counseling and pastoral care movements (Richards, 1987). Indeed, clergy malpractice suits have become a painful reality in the past two decades (Malony, Needham & Southard, 1986). A cardinal rule of ministry is to do no harm.

5. We should encourage Christian mental health professionals to develop good treatment plans and use them as a basis for peer review. One very tangible expression of a commitment to excellence is the development of adequate treatment plans. It seems, at times, that Christian mental health professionals are too casual about their work and rather poorly focused (Collins, 1993). Careful assessment prior to intervention, and a willingness to evaluate the effectiveness of these efforts afterwards, should be marks of professionalism (McMinn, 1994). The inherent risks of "going with the flow" include the potential of becoming unreflective about problem identification, intervening in an unsystematic hodgepodge manner and being cavalier about engaging in the kind of outcome evaluation that has the potential to sharpen and refine clinical skills. This lack of focus can only lead to personal and professional isolation that contributes little to the legitimization of our collective efforts.

We have seen some profound shifts with reference to the need for documentation in managed care settings in this country in the past two decades (cf. Norcross, 2002; Nathan & Gorman, 1998). Long gone are the days when mental health professionals could keep informal notes on their work with their clients—most of which would never be read by anyone but themselves. Although few of us seem to enjoy these initial record-keeping efforts, I do think it helps us to be more sharply focused on what we are doing and why we are doing it. Perhaps it should be seen as a discipline that helps get us beyond our personal biases and theoretical preferences. I seriously doubt that the need for treatment planning and the measurement of goal attainment are likely to diminish in the near or distant future.

Networking on the basis of a shared commitment to develop effective treatment plans is one of the most effective means of building accountability and improving professional communication. It also provides impetus for continuing important discussions about the ethical and legal standards for Christian mental health professionals (e.g., What are you trying to accomplish? What are the identified problems? What are options for intervention? What does the available research evidence suggest about the differential effects of those strategies? How do you know that you were able to reach the stated goals and objectives of treatment?) Our approach to helping others should be flexible and responsive to the particulars of individuals in any given situation, as well as deeply informed by our understandings of how to intervene so as to enhance human welfare (Butman, 1993).

Christian mental health professionals should meet often with colleagues to exchange information as well as to ensure quality. Peer review in itself has the potential to encourage healthy self-regulation. I suspect that these groups do more to foster ethical practice than the major professional associations, certification and licensure boards, or any particular ethical code of conduct. Further, they may provide much-needed interpersonal and intellectual stimulation, absolutely essential for helping the clinician to stay alive as a person and professional. No doubt there will be debates about the criteria selected to determine the effectiveness of psychotherapeutic efforts or which approaches to treatment are most useful. I doubt, however, that there are more effective ways to ensure quality or to provide an opportunity for consultation about matters that most directly concern professionals (e.g., Should I terminate or refer this client? Is there evidence of serious psychopathology? Might there be a more effective approach? How best can I understand the reactions of my clients (or my own)?).

Recent research (Lewis, Greenburg & Hatich, 1988) indicated that about half of the psychologists in the sample belonged (23%) or had belonged (24%) to a peer-consultation group. Of the remainder, the majority (61%) would join a peer review group if it were available. Obviously, there is a "felt need" for the kind of challenge and support that can be found in such settings.

6. We should encourage regular participation in continuing education. Nearly four decades ago Dubin (1972) suggested that the half-life of a doctoral degree in psychology, as a measure of competence, was somewhere between ten to twelve years. If that is true, Koocher and Keith-Spiegel (2008) question how a professional whose career may span thirty years can possibly maintain competence without ongoing training. It seems essential for professional associations as well as regulation boards to require continuing education. It certainly seems unethical to be unaware of innovative methods, recent advances in theory and research, multicultural concerns or the host of professional resources available to Christian mental health professionals today.

Obviously, mandated continuing education is no guarantee that the clinician has actually incorporated the information. Corey, Corey, and Callahan (2011) have rightly observed that the mere attendance at conferences or workshops by no means implies there has been active engagement with the content presented—that is, has it really been internalized or incorporated into the clinician's actual practice? As an educator for more than three decades, it has become abundantly clear that an individual doesn't just "have" the truth (content) but that the truth must seize him or her at far deeper levels of awareness, understanding and comprehension.

The deeper value of education—be it mandated or voluntary—may be that it teaches the practitioner that he or she is not immune to mistakes. Experience alone does not guarantee clinical expertise. Christian mental health professionals need to strive for constant awareness of their limitations, recognize that these limitations may increase with the passage of time, and seek to develop constructive remedies maintaining professional capabilities. It may also help the practitioner to recognize the potential for burnout or exhaustion in certain professional activities and take action accordingly.

I have been encouraged by the increased access so many of us have to reliable and relevant information on the Internet. Let me give but two examples that I and my current and former students have come to appreciate. With reference to the exploding literature on trauma and recovery, I find the website of the Headington Institute in Pasadena to be very useful (www .headington-institute.org). With reference to broad information on the seemingly infinite varieties of psychopathology, I regularly utilize the site related to Internet Mental Health (www.mentalhealth.com). I am fully aware that we can't always go to cutting-edge conferences—or spend a small fortune on books and journals—but our professional associations can often help us to identify online resources where key addresses and papers can be accessed for a modest fee or even for free. When I network with student clinicians or seasoned professionals, it becomes readily apparent whether or not someone is current and informed about recent and relevant theory and research or merely surviving on the memories they have from graduate and professional training.

   7. We should encourage Christian mental health professionals to under-stand and use Scripture wisely. Any of the previous guidelines might be equally relevant to a discussion of the qualifications of generic mental health professionals. The challenge to Christian clinicians is more complex since they are called to be competent in two worlds, that is, the worlds of faith and professional practice (Jones & Butman, 2011). All our activities as practitioners should be grounded in, informed by and shaped by the prac-tices of the Christian faith (Inform, 1994). Not only do we need to be practitioner-scholars but adept in our understanding of the significant in-terface between mental health disciplines and Christian beliefs and practice. The ability to articulate that understanding is at the core of what it means to be truly distinctive as a Christian mental health professional (cf. Jones & Butman, 2011, esp. chaps. 11-22).

   The ethical behavior of Christian mental health professionals is ulti-mately grounded in obedience to the Word of God. Christian practitioners, whether they acknowledge it or not, are representatives of the church (An-derson, 1990). It seems imperative, then, that Christian clinicians have the ability to articulate the bases for their faith and lifestyle. Obviously, a certain amount of philosophical and theological sophistication is essential (cf. Evans, 1989; Holmes, 1977; Roberts, 1993). I would argue that Christian mental health professionals who are informed about the points of compatibility and incompatibility between their mental health discipline and the world of Christian thought are (1) more likely to be analytic and sophisticated in how they think about the many dimensions of the human condition, (2) able to clarify the core constructs of major psychotherapeutic approaches, and (3) more willing to strive for the goal of developing a responsible eclecticism in their clinical work.

A most essential discipline of the Protestant tradition is the personal study of the Bible (Smith, 1993). Through spending time reading and studying the Scriptures, we learn to listen to Christ's teaching on the importance of hearing his word and doing it. A good understanding of the Bible and theology has the potential to make our interventions complete and respectful of the fundamental commitments in life that are so central in American society and across the world. We are far more likely to see the implications of our faith in the clinical context and beyond. Potentially, we will come to see our work as a means of grace, thoroughly rooted in a theological as well as psychological foundation (cf. Anderson, 1990). As Malony (1994) has warned, we will be less likely to equate psychological wholeness (i.e., health) with spiritual maturity (i.e., holiness) or vice versa. A solid knowledge of Scripture is one aspect of what it means to be held accountable for Christian distinctiveness, and one expression of being more responsive to and centered on the will of God and the welfare of the church over and against our individual professional welfare (cf. Jones & Butman, 2011, chap. 11). Biblical literacy and a certain theological sophistication are essential competencies for the Christian mental health professions to cultivate (cf. Foster & Smith, 1993).

In the past three decades I have come to increasingly see the power of doing this study in collaboration—and with a representative group of fellow believers (cf. Bilezikian, 1991). I deeply appreciate studying God's Word in community so as to more accurately see its immediate relevance for my worldview and lifestyle. Those of us who care deeply about the consistency of our beliefs and behaviors (i.e., integrity) should recognize the synergistic power of integrating our experiences of worship, fellowship and service. I suspect that has much to do with what it means to bring all under the lordship of Jesus Christ (Anderson, 2000).

8. We should encourage Christian mental health professionals to de-

velop a strong link with a local church. The culture of professionalism can
be both a blessing and a burden for the Christian mental health professional, and a source of profound "ethical ambivalence." As Anderson (1990)
has noted, "professionals self-consciously embody and attempt to model
the higher ideals of the general society. . . . [They] want to be known for
their altruistic service, concern for all persons regardless of economic and
social status, and sacrifices made for the general good of society" (p. 202).
Yet it is the same culture that all too often provides the cues for values that
are "basically pragmatic, opportunistic, and entrepreneurial" (ibid.). The
potential risk for the Christian mental health professional, then, is that
survival in the marketplace replaces an idealistic and deeply Christian
value system as the modus operandi. In other words, kingdom ethics and
professional priorities clash.

To counter this tendency, it seems imperative for the Christian mental
health professional to establish a strong link with a local church. This is essential for several reasons. First, the church can serve as a source of support,
accountability and empowerment for the Christian mental health professional (Anderson, 1990, p. 209). Unless this link is strong, members can't
fulfill their calling, ministry or vocation (i.e., service to others as a form of
service to God). Christian clinicians must fully grasp the fact that the issues
they face daily in their offices are not just psychological concerns but
matters that have significant implications for promoting the kingdom of
God (e.g., How can we better help the church to become the church?). Such
a link can help promote a greater concern for the welfare and status of those
individuals who are marginalized in society, whereas the culture of professionalism tends to focus almost exclusively on the elite and powerful. Such
a link can serve as a source of community, whereas the culture of professionalism tends to be highly individualistic and rather isolated. Finally, the
local church can provide a context in which practitioners can reflect deeply
on their implicit or explicit goals and objectives for their clients, and
measure those against kingdom criteria for wholeness and holiness (cf.
Malony, 1994). Once again, consider the keen insights of Anderson (1990):

> Clinical problems . . . are related to a client's domestic, marital, family, and
> social structures. These networks of relationships contain moral, often reli-
> gious, and occasionally legal issues that impinge on the therapist's role. The

therapist's own values, convictions, religious beliefs, and commitments also influence this role. Probably no people in our society other than pastors and priests provide access to the core of life in all these areas as much as professional counselors. (p. 209)

Without that vital link between practitioner and parishioner there is a potential loss of genuine wisdom and humanness (cf. Evans, 1989), much needed social support and empowerment, and an ethical context for holistic healing beyond the confines of a very private office. The very outward discipline of service needs to be undergirded by the more corporate disciplines of confession, worship and celebration, and the more inward disciplines like prayer and meditation (cf. Foster, 1992; Foster & Smith, 1993). "Confessing Jesus Christ as Lord" was never intended to be a solitary pursuit (only). Linking arms with a local church is perhaps the most tangible and visible way to bring one's work under the lordship of Jesus Christ (Col 3:23).

I have heard much in the past decades about the need for Christian mental health professionals to develop clear boundaries with their fellow believers in the context of their local churches. Obviously, I can appreciate the concerns that are directly related to matters of privacy and confidentiality. What I do fear, however, is the temptation we all have to so compartmentalize our lives that we never allow the personal and professional roles to intersect. I know of a number of local churches in my community where significant numbers of Christian mental health professionals meet on a regular basis to explore shared concerns about the nature of their work and explore ways to do it in even more ethical, responsible and professional ways. When these individuals truly do life together, they find ways to challenge and support each other to do their work in an even more disciplined and reflective manner (cf. Jones & Butman, 2011; Yarhouse, Butman & McRay, 2005). We must be careful that we do not produce another generation of rugged individualists or isolated providers of services. None of us can do this work effectively alone, and never as well as we might if we don't rely heavily in the incredible resources, practices and traditions of the church (cf. Bilezikian, 1997).

9. We need to encourage Christian mental health professionals to become actively involved in a support group of Christians who are not therapists. Throughout this chapter I have called the Christian mental health professional to very high (but not inappropriate) standards. These "virtues" (cf. Roberts, 1993) are hardly qualities that can be cultivated and expressed by rugged individualists whose first allegiance is to the culture of professionalism. Qualities like compassion, servanthood, agape love, transparency, holiness, wisdom and humanness or integrity (cf. Jones & Butman, 2011, chap. 11) require an interpersonal context in which to develop outside of the consulting room. As suggested in the previous guidelines, the church, rather than the profession, should be the ultimate source of accountability, as well as the well-spring for healing and helping. The Christian mental health professional is not called to be merely compliant with ethical and professional codes, but challenged to develop a life of integrity, deeply transformed by the Spirit and empowered by the gospel.

To accomplish these lofty ideals, it is strongly recommended that the Christian mental health professional engage in regular and intentional dialogue with other believers who are not therapists. Not only is this important for intellectual stimulation but for interpersonal support as well. Professional peer review groups provide one essential form of accountability for the Christian mental health professional, and involvement in a local church provides another distinct type. Involvement in a support group of nontherapists is potentially an expression of courage and openness toward being held accountable for Christian distinctiveness and integrity (cf. Jones & Butman, 2011, chap. 12). Not only should these members ask the tough questions about our professional commitments and priorities, but they can challenge us to take our own spiritual formation seriously (cf. Smith, 1993). This type of substantive and formative feedback can get to the heart of what it means to be engaged in a distinctively Christian mode of counseling.

Ideally, this support group can provide a context for integrative growth for both the professional as well as nontherapist participants. The focus is not on the direct supervision of the professional's clinical cases. Indeed, this would be a clear violation of confidentiality. Rather, this network potentially provides "perspective, spiritual support, and a representation of the culture of the kingdom of God" (Anderson, p. 210). It is also perhaps one of the best antidotes for the professional burnout and exhaustion often felt by those who care deeply about the pain and agony of others, and feel called to bear some of those burdens, and help transform some of that pain (cf. chapters on "burnout" in Corey & Corey, 2011).

*10. **We should encourage Christian mental health professionals to commit themselves to the challenge of personal and spiritual growth**. Christian therapists, whether they acknowledge it or not, are representatives of the church and should image God in their work. If this is indeed true, then certain qualifications for Christian leaders ought to apply. Consider the challenging words of Titus 1:5-9:*

> I left you behind in Crete for this reason, so that you should put in order what remained to be done, and should appoint elders in every town, as I directed you: someone who is blameless, married only once, whose children are believers, not accused of debauchery and not rebellious. For a bishop, as God's steward, must be blameless; he must not be arrogant or quick-tempered or addicted to wine or violent or greedy for gain, but he must be hospitable, a lover of goodness, prudent, upright, devout, and self-controlled. He must have a firm grasp of the word that is trustworthy in accordance with the teaching, so that he may be able to preach with sound doctrine and to refute those who contradict it. (NRSV)

McMinn and Campbell (2007) respond to these challenging words in several ways. First, it seems clear that the Christian mental health professional should not be living in blatant sin. Granted, we are all broken and fallen persons—and none of us is "blameless" (cf. McLemore, 1982)—but a consistent pattern of clear disregard for God's command on a personal level raises fundamental questions about the nature of our Christian commitment. Second, it seems evident from the passage that our families and marriages should be spiritually and emotionally healthy (i.e., Are we willing to acknowledge our problems and seek appropriate help?). Finally, it seems clear that we need to be able to articulate the bases for our faith and lifestyle. Our holiness, then, is not merely a private matter; it should be an integrated expression of word and deed, cultivated in the context of peer review, a support group or in a local church.

The end goals of spiritual and psychological growth—holiness and wholeness—are absolute ideals, hopes to be aspired to (Malony, 1994). Quite frankly, life does not demand perfection in either of these areas: "You can exist without achieving either one. You can be well without being healthy.

You can be healthy without being whole. You can be moral without being religious. You can be religious without being holy" (Malony, p. 6). Indeed, these are ideals, hopes, aspirations, perhaps even utopias. Still, they are certainly not irrelevant to a ministry of caring and service. This is a well-developed theme in a powerful work by Benedict Groeschel (1992), a clinical psychologist who is also director of the Office of Spiritual Development of the Archdiocese of New York.

In the thirty plus years since I have left graduate school, I have increasingly seen the benefit of "help for the helper" (cf. chapters on self-care in Corey & Corey, 2011). The issue is not just the clinician's personal development. As McMinn and Meek (1996) have observed, personal distress commonly precedes unethical relationships. This is especially troubling since they also found that nonprofessional Christian counselors were generally less cautious about multiple-role relationships in counseling than Christian professionals (cf. McMinn & Campbell, 2007). It seems imperative, then, that we seek help—be it formal therapy or spiritual direction—when personal problems arise that could affect our work. Wholeness and holiness are goals we should take to heart and be the best that we can be. As Foster (1992) has noted, we desperately need deep people in the world today. Who we are and who we intend to become speaks volumes about our qualifications to be Christian mental health professionals. It is hard to imagine how we could help others if we haven't been willing to seek help ourselves.

SOME FINAL COMMENTS

These guidelines are given in the hope that they might prompt more discussion among the second and third generation of Christian mental health professionals. I seriously doubt that consensus will emerge on many of the themes raised in this chapter. Since the Christian counseling movement is hardly a monolithic enterprise, we should expect a plurality of voices in this much needed intentional dialogue.

I am encouraged by the fact that many of these issues are being raised in publications, professional associations and peer accountability groups. Currently, there are no legal restraints on the title "Christian mental health professional." Personally, I would advocate that we seek to establish some kind of clarity about the meaning of that title (i.e., greater standardization) if only to better educate ourselves and the public at large. Many of the abuses we see in the marketplace can be directly traced to the current ambiguity surrounding the title. In particular, it would be useful to be as concrete and specific as possible about the meaning of the phrase "clear professional competence." I would like to believe that it is always an expression of Christlike love that motivates the Christian mental health professional to develop his or her clinical expertise.

If we are serious about becoming effective imagers of God as therapists, we will resist the temptation to unreflectively "go with the flow." The times demand that Christian clinicians evidence greater measures of congruence, courage and commitment in their work. Our desire to be excellent in all that we do should motivate us to take seriously the challenge implicit in these guidelines, which I humbly admit are far easier to describe than to embody. Clearly, we are called to serve God and his church. No doubt we need to become more biblically and theologically grounded and informed in the interim. Further, we need to diligently pursue "additional education, experience, professional consultation and spiritual growth" in order to improve our competency (CAPS, 2005). Finally, we need to carefully avoid any appearance of personal aggrandizement when we represent ourselves to others. As Christian mental health professionals we realize that we are called to take our disciplines seriously and that this can be a very tangible expression of our compassion and service (cf. Noll, 1994).

I suspect we are a long way from developing standardized definitions for many of our key terms. This is unfortunate since it will directly affect the welfare of clients, and deeply influence the training, supervisory and credentialing processes. The issues can be complex and often confusing. If we continue to ask the right kind of questions and resist the temptation to "shrink from knowledge," there is the distinct possibility we will hear the words, "well done, thou good and faithful servant."

REFERENCES

Adams, J. (1979). *More than redemption: A theology of Christian counseling.* Phillipsburg, NJ: Presbyterian & Reformed.

Anderson, R. S. (1990). *Christians who counsel.* Grand Rapids: Zondervan.

Anderson, R. (2000). *Self care.* Pasadena, CA: Fuller Theological Seminary Press.

Benner, D. G. (1983). The incarnation as a metaphor for psychotherapy. *Journal of Psychology and Theology, 11,* 287-94.

Bernstein, B. L., & Lecomte, C. (1981). Licensure in psychology: Alternative directions. *Professional Psychology, 12,* 200-208.

Bilezikian, G. (1997). *Community 101.* Grand Rapids: Zondervan.

Bobgan, M., & Bobgan, D. (1979). *Psychoheresy: The psychological seduction of Christianity.* Santa Barbara, CA: Eastgate.

Browning, D. (1987). *Religious thought and the modern psychologies.* Philadelphia, PA: Fortress.

Butman, R. E. (1993). Where's the beef? Evaluating counseling trends. *Christian Counseling Today, 1,* 20-24.

Carlson, D. L. (1994). *Why do Christians shoot their wounded?* Downers Grove, IL: InterVarsity Press.

Christian Association for Psychological Studies. (2005). *Ethics statement of the Christian Association for Psychological Studies.* (Available from www.caps.net).

Clebsch, W., & Jaekle, C. (1975). *Pastoral care in historical perspective.* New York: Jason Aronson.

Collins, G. R. (1989). *Can you trust psychology?* Downers Grove, IL: InterVarsity Press.

Collins, G. R. (1991). *Excellence and ethics in counseling.* Waco, TX: Word.

Collins, G. R. (1993). Hot topics in Christian counseling. *Christian Counseling Today, 1,* 12-14.

Corey, G., Corey, M. S., & Callanan, P. (2011). *Issues and ethics in the helping professions* (8th ed.). Belmont, CA: Brooks/Cole.

Corey, M. S., & Corey, G. (2011). *Becoming a helper* (6th ed.). Belmont, CA: Brooks/Cole.

Dubin, S. S. (1972). Obsolescence of lifelong education: A choice for the professional. *American Psychologist, 27,* 486-98.

Evans, C. S. (1989). *Wisdom and humanness in psychology.* Grand Rapids: Zondervan.

Foster, J. R. (1992). *Prayer: Finding the heart's true home.* San Francisco: Harper-Collins.

Foster, R. (1985). *Money, sex and power.* New York: Harper & Row.

Foster, R. J., & Smith, J. B. (1993). *Devotional classics.* San Francisco: HarperCollins.

Fretz, B. R., & Mills, D. H. (1980). *Licensing and certification of psychologists and counselors.* San Francisco: Jossey-Bass.

Groeschel, B. J. (1992). *Spiritual passages: The psychology of spiritual development.* New York: Crossroads.

Guy, J. (1986). *The personal life of the psychotherapist.* New York: Wiley-Inter-science.

Holifield, B. (1983). *A history of pastoral care in America.* Nashville, TN: Abingdon.

Holmes, A. (1977). *All truth is God's truth.* Grand Rapids: Eerdmans.

Holmes, A. (1992). *Shaping character.* Grand Rapids: Eerdmans.

Inform. (1994). *The occasional bulletin of Wheaton College.* Wheaton, IL: Wheaton College.

Jones, S. L., & Butman, R. E. (2011). *Modern psychotherapies: A comprehensive Christian appraisal* (2nd ed.). Downers Grove, IL: InterVarsity Press.

Keith-Spiegel, P., & Koocher, G. P. (2008). *Ethics in psychology and the mental health professions: Standards and cases* (3rd ed.). New York: Oxford University Press.

Levicoff, S. (1993). In search of legitimate credentials. *Christian Counseling Today, 1*(4), 58.

Lewis, G. J., Greenburg, S. L., & Hatch, D. B. (1988). Peer consultation groups for psychologists in private practice: A national survey. *Professional Psychology Research and Practice, 19,* 81-86.

Malony, H. N. (1994). *Wholeness and holiness: Revisited.* Keynote address, Christian Association for Psychological Studies Annual Meeting, San Antonio, TX.

Malony, H. N., Needham, T. L., & Southard, S. (1986). *Clergy malpractice.* Philadelphia: Fortress.

McLemore, C. W. (1982). *The scandal of psychotherapy.* Wheaton, IL: Tyndale House.

McLemore, C. W. (2003). *Toxic relationships and how to change them.* Hoboken, NJ: Jossey-Bass.

McMinn, M., & Campbell, C. (2007). *Integrative psychotherapy.* Downers Grove, IL: InterVarsity Press.

McMinn, M., & Meek, K. (1996). Ethics among Christian counselors: A survey of beliefs and behaviors. *Journal of Psychology and Theology, 24,* 26-37.

Meier, S. (2008). *The elements of counseling* (6th ed.). Belmont, CA: Brooks/Cole.

Mouw, R. (1992). *Uncommon decency.* Downers Grove, IL: InterVarsity Press.

Nathan, P., & Gorman, J. (1998). *A guide to treatments that work.* New York: Oxford University Press.

Noll, M. (1994). *The scandal of the evangelical mind.* Grand Rapids: Eerdmans.

Norcross, J., & Guy, J. (2007). *Leaving it at the office.* New York: Guilford.

Norcross, J. (2002). *Psychotherapy relationships that work.* New York: Oxford University Press.

Oden, T. (1984). *Care of souls in the classic tradition.* Philadelphia: Fortress.

Ohlschlager, G. (1991). Liability in Christian counseling: Welcome to the grave new world. In G. R. Collins (Ed.), *Excellence and ethics in counseling* (pp. 41-74). Waco, TX: Word.

Palmer, P. J. (1993). *To know as we are known: Education as a spiritual journey.* San Francisco: HarperCollins.

Pargament, K. (1997). *The psychology of religion and coping.* New York: Guilford.

Peterson, D. R., & Bry, B. H. (1980). Dimensions of perceived competence in professional psychology. *Professional Psychology, 11,* 965-71.

Roberts, R. (1993). *Taking the word to heart.* Grand Rapids: Eerdmans.

Smith, J. B. (1993). *A spiritual formation workbook.* San Francisco: HarperCollins.

Tan, S. (1991). *Lay counseling: Equipping Christians for a helping ministry.* Grand Rapids: Zondervan.

Tidball, D. (1986). *Skilful shepherds: An introduction to pastoral theology.* Grand Rapids: Zondervan.

Van Leeuwen, M. S. (1993). *After Eden: Towards gender reconciliation.* Grand Rapids: Eerdmans.

Yarhouse, M., Butman, R., & McRay, B. (2005). *Modern psychopathologies: A comprehensive Christian appraisal.* Downers Grove, IL: InterVarsity Press.

4

Essential Elements for Ethical Counsel

Horace C. Lukens Jr. and
Randolph K. Sanders

Never before have counseling and psychotherapy services been so familiar to and so widely used by the American public with such sophistication, understanding and candor. In years past such services were often sought quietly and with a sense of embarrassment, shame and failure.

In order for the Christian therapist to excel professionally and spiritually, it is essential to identify, understand and apply appropriate guidelines and limits to the services being provided. Only through such a thorough examination and understanding of the relevant issues and a deliberate and careful application of these principles in clinical practice will we be confident of delivering services in a highly ethical manner, bringing healing to our clients and glory to God. This chapter attempts to identify and discuss some essential elements and issues that every Christian mental health professional and paraprofessional (lay counselor) needs to be aware of and to deal with in order to deliver competent and ethical counseling services.

There are many increasingly complex issues that confront the counselor and that require a clear understanding and careful handling with clients who are often in difficult or emergent circumstances. For example, informed consent laws have expanded far beyond their more simple origins and require thoughtful scrutiny and application. Standards for documentation are more detailed and complex than at one time.

These and other issues discussed in this chapter apply to credentialed mental health professionals, pastors who conduct counseling as part of their ministries, and church counseling centers that may have both professionals and lay counselors providing service. Other issues that are equally relevant to the topic of this chapter are addressed elsewhere in the book: the nature and extent of formal training, internship experiences, confidentiality in marriage and family therapy, and business ethics in counseling, to name several. While paraprofessionals may not have to comply with some of the regulations and policies required of the professionals—and, in fact, there will be differences among professional disciplines regarding regulations— awareness of and compliance with regulations is not only prudent but also assists in lowering liability exposure (Becker, 1987).

CONFIDENTIALITY

Confidentiality is crucial to an effective and trusting counseling relationship. Without it, most counseling relationships would never begin, and those that did would be unlikely to survive. Few ethical constraints within the field of counseling are as universally accepted as confidentiality. There are, however, important limits to confidentiality that must be recognized by the counselor and must also be reviewed with and understood by the client at the outset of counseling in order to adhere to proper legal and ethical requirements. Clients need to understand that counselors are obligated to comply with laws regarding disclosure. It is often helpful to advise clients when a request for information has been made even though the therapist may have some leeway regarding exactly what information is provided. Should a client discover such disclosure after the fact, the sense of betrayal and the erosion of trust is likely to be increased.

According to C. D. Stromberg and his colleagues (1988), who authored a handbook for psychologists covering the full range of legal issues encountered in practice, there are three concepts—privacy, confidentiality and privilege—that must be understood and distinguished. *Privacy*, the broadest of these concepts, refers to an "individual's right to be left alone and to decide the time, place, manner and extent of sharing oneself (one's thoughts, behavior or body) with others" (p. 371). The right of privacy grows out of the Fourth Amendment to the Constitution and is the foundation on which confidentiality and privilege are built.

Confidentiality is a professional and ethical term. It refers to the "quality of private information that is divulged with the implicit or explicit promise and the reasonable expectation that it will not be further disclosed except for the purpose for which it was provided" (p. 372).

Privilege, the narrowest of the concepts, is "a legal protection against being forced to break a promise or expectation of confidentiality in legal proceedings" (p. 372). While the concept of confidentiality is most familiar to counselors, it is important that counselors also have a working knowledge of privacy and privilege.

The "Ethical Principles of Psychologists and Code of Conduct" (APA, 2002) states that "psychologists have a primary obligation and take reasonable precautions to protect confidential information obtained through or stored in any medium, recognizing that the extent and limits of confidentiality may be regulated by law or established by institutional rules or professional or scientific relationship" (p. 1066). This principle, which has become a standard among other professional associations, fundamentally holds that all information about a client that is obtained in the course of a professional psychological relationship, including an initial contact such as a telephone call, should be viewed as confidential. It is not proper for psychologists or counselors to assume that clients understand the concepts and their implications. Rather, it is imperative that expectations about confidentiality and the possible exceptions be clarified with each client at the outset of the counseling relationship. Similar clarification of the scope and limits of confidentiality needs to occur with others with whom the psychologist will be working such as pastor, physician or attorney.

Federal and state laws also speak to the protection of client information. In 1996, Congress passed the Health Insurance Portability and Accountability Act (HIPAA). Among the provisions of this act were several measures designed to provide a uniform level of protection at the federal level for patient health information in practices that transmit information via electronic means. Some of the provisions were designed to provide a basic level of *privacy* for information in patient records. In particular, there was concern for the fact that in the age of managed care, insurers were seeking increasingly sensitive information about patients with little or no added protections for patients. HIPAA provided a means by which mental health professionals could give insurers basic information (with proper notification to clients) to justify payment of insurance claims without requiring the release of a client's most sensitive personal information. (How this is done in practice will be discussed in the section on *documentation* later in this chapter.) HIPAA also provided that in jurisdictions where state law was more stringent than HIPAA in the protection of client information, the state law would supersede HIPAA.

Another provision of HIPAA was to help better insure the *security* of client records, particularly in the modern age of personal computers, electronic record keeping and records transfer. For example, HIPAA requires that mental health institutions and practitioners have policies in place designed to decrease the chance of security breaches that would lead to the inappropriate release of client information.

In addition to an understanding of confidentiality, therapists need to have a clear understanding of the *exceptions* to the general rule of confidentiality. These may include (1) when the client consents in writing to disclosure, (2) when a law requires reporting of an event such as child abuse, (3) when there is a duty to warn or protect, (4) when reimbursement or other legal rules require disclosure, (5) when the client is deemed to waive confidentiality by bringing a lawsuit, or (6) in the case of an emergency. Therapists should be aware of the code of confidentiality mandated by their own professional organization. Equally important, every therapist must be familiar with state laws that govern confidentiality and privilege, and understand that laws can vary from state to state. In addition, professional rules and state laws occasionally disagree in what they require of therapists. In such a case it is incumbent on the professional to seek consultation and perhaps legal advice to determine the best course of action.

Written consent. When a client consents for information to be disclosed, it is essential that the client understand the information that will be provided, the individuals or entities to which it will be provided and the reasons for divulging such information. The best way to accomplish this is in a detailed yet clearly understood written release-of-information form. Adherence to federal and state law is essential when creating such a form. For instance, federal law requires that such releases include information about communicable diseases (including HIV) yet prohibits the use of the same information to criminally investigate or prosecute an alcohol- or drug-abuse patient. For more information about sample forms see appendix two, as well as forms provided by most professional associations, state licensing agencies and those found in Tan's volume (1991).

Duty to report. When state law requires that certain information about a client's circumstances or behavior be reported, the counselor is obligated to do so. In many states there are laws requiring reporting of child abuse, which typically includes sexual abuse, physical and even psychological abuse. Some states require the reporting of *suspected* child abuse and gross neglect of the child. These laws have complexities that vary from state to state.

Medicare and Medicaid laws. Federal and state laws that regulate health and welfare programs require access to client records in order to assure "program integrity." Typically, providers whose services are reimbursed by Medicare and Medicaid are required to furnish, upon request, the names and addresses of clients, the dates of service and a description of the services rendered (Stromberg et al., 1988). It should be recognized that there are occasions when such agencies request treatment records as part of their investigation.

Patient as litigant. When a client initiates litigation against a therapist, the client places his or her own mental status at issue and thereby is considered to have waived confidentiality rights as far as they relate to the issues of the case. At times clients may place their own mental status at issue without even realizing it. For instance, when a parent seeks custody of his or her child, and the parent's own mental competency is at issue, the court may direct the therapist to release confidential information because the issues at hand are the parent-child relationship and more specifically the welfare of the child.

Duty to warn or protect. Some of the most troublesome and complex issues counselors face have to do with managing the potentially or actually dangerous client. There is no evidence that even well-trained mental health professionals are able to make reliable predictions of future danger. Nevertheless, certain obligations have been imposed on counselors who are working with potentially dangerous clients. The "duty to protect," which has grown out of the *Tarasoff* decision, has triggered more discussion than perhaps any other legal issue in the mental health field. The landmark Tarasoff case litigated in California (*Tarasoff v. Board of Regents of the University of California*, 1976), ruled that when a therapist determines or should determine that a patient presents a serious, violent threat to another person, that therapist has an obligation to protect and warn the intended victim, and to notify others, including the police, against such danger.

Tarasoff is, however, not the only case focusing on the professional obligations of therapists. Therapists have also been held liable for issues such as a failure to diagnose accurately or to treat effectively in order to bring the client's violent tendencies under control.

While the *Tarasoff* decision has had significant impact on the evaluation and handling of the potentially dangerous client, Stromberg et al. (1988) note that there appears to be a judicial trend toward narrowing the ruling to apply it only to specifically articulated, credible threats to identifiable victims. Subsequent rulings have limited the duty to warn to revealing only information which is necessary to accomplish the intended purpose only to those who absolutely need to know (Stromberg et al., 1993).

Details of *Tarasoff*'s impact will not be reviewed. However, for our purposes here, it is very important to add that despite over three decades of discussion in classrooms, clinics and elsewhere, the implications of *Tarasoff* for the practicing therapist are still poorly understood. For example, a survey of psychologists in 2009 showed that most of them did not fully understand what their obligations were in duty to protect/warn situations (Pabian, Welfel & Beebe, 2009). The chief reason for that is that the *Tarasoff* decision, for all its notoriety, is a California decision and does not necessarily apply in the same way in all fifty states. The best advice to the practicing therapist who wishes to act prudently in duty to warn/protect situations is to become familiar with the laws (both coded laws and case law) in one's own state regarding these situations. Duties in these situations can vary widely from state to state, and in thirteen states there is no law that speaks to such issues.

It is also important to mention here circumstances where there is *imminent danger* that a patient will commit suicide. It is essential that every counselor know the fundamentals of assessing suicide risk and be prepared to disclose confidential information to protect suicidal patients from harming themselves (APA, 2002; CAPS, 2005). Depending on the limits of state law and the circumstances of each case, the therapist may have to contact law enforcement, emergency medical services, a responsible family member or some other party who is in a position to assist. Understand however that the information released in such a circumstance is limited to that which is necessary to remove the patient from harm's way.

Future criminal behavior. With the exception of reporting of child abuse, psychologists do not have an obligation to report to authorities when a client has committed a crime unless such activity suggests, by virtue of the duty-to-warn standards already noted, that future criminal behavior is likely to occur and future harm to a third party might be averted by reporting such information.

Emergencies. The courts have increasingly defined *emergency* narrowly with respect to reporting. That is, incidents in which the client's health is seriously or imminently at risk are viewed as appropriate for disclosure. For instance, an emergency-room physician might contact a therapist in an effort to determine the source of a client's delirious behavior. In such circumstances, it is probably appropriate for the therapist to disclose information pertinent to the client's care. The scope of the disclosure should, of course, be limited to that which is necessary.

Confidentiality with minors. When it comes to confidentiality and psychological care of minors, in most cases, all information shared by a minor child in treatment is accessible by the parents, and the parents are responsible for giving permission for disclosure to others of information regarding their child. At times this requirement is in conflict with effective treatment strategies: rapport and trust may be compromised if a child or adolescent knows that anything he or she might say in treatment could be conveyed to the child's parents. Thus it is important to establish with both parents and minors early in treatment what guidelines will be followed. Legal and ethical considerations must be delicately balanced here.

Group therapy. The unique setting of group therapy raises some different and difficult issues regarding confidentiality. The usual rule—when personal information is shared with third parties, the right to confidentiality is waived—must be modified due to the unique nature of group therapy. In this setting, part of the therapeutic process involves the sharing of personal information with other clients. Many courts have recognized this unique situation and consequently have upheld the client-counselor privilege if other individuals have participated in or facilitated the treatment process. Care must be taken, however, to ensure an accurate understanding of confidentiality among group members so that inadvertent violations do not occur. By using first names only and by discouraging socialization outside group, the risks of confidentiality violations can be reduced. A written contract and informed consent document with each member may also further stress the importance of confidentiality and clarify its limits.

Confidentiality and a deceased client. The limits of confidentiality continue to apply following the death of a client. If this were not so, clients would be reluctant to share personal information, knowing that there would be no protection from disclosure following their death. A number of states permit a legal representative of the client to continue to protect the confidentiality of the client's records from posthumous disclosure.

Responding to requests and subpoenas. The counselor faces a wide array of requests for access to client records, many of which come from individuals with little understanding of the therapeutic process and who have nontherapeutic goals. It is not unusual to discover that professionals such as physicians, pastors and even attorneys and other mental health professionals do not fully comprehend or appreciate the delicate nature of the therapeutic relationship. Consequently, counselors need to be prudent and cautious in responding to such requests. All requests should be in writing with the purpose of the request and the requested information clearly stated. Except in truly emergency circumstances the client must be consulted for a signed consent to the request. If the request is denied, then the counselor should adhere to the client's decision. If records are subpoenaed, the therapist should first determine if the subpoena is a valid, *court-ordered* subpoena. Furthermore, even if the subpoena is court-ordered, the therapist should consult with the client wherever possible to determine whether the client wishes to consent to release the record. If the client is unsure or refuses, he or she should be encouraged to consult his or her attorney about steps that may be taken to block such a release of records. If the court still orders that the records be made available, then the counselor must either produce the records or face contempt-of-court charges and possible imprisonment. In such an instance the counselor has taken the most conservative stance in protecting the confidentiality of the client-counselor relationship and the confidentiality of client records.

INFORMED CONSENT TO TREATMENT

The concept of informed consent as it applies to mental health circumstances is a relatively recent development. For years patients who assumed that their healthcare professional knew best deferred to that provider's judgment. Gradually the courts have recognized the importance of patients' rights and the need for greater equality in the doctor-patient relationship. Informed consent acknowledges the necessity of respect for the individuals, their autonomy and their privacy rights. Today courts require that informed consent be obtained from the client prior to disclosure, and not having it may be considered malpractice. It should be noted that a client can sue for being treated without consent, even if the treatment was competent in all other aspects.

There are at least four basic aspects that comprise informed consent (APA, 2002, sect. 3.10). First, the patient must be legally competent in order to consent to treatment. Second, all information regarding treatment that a reasonable person would want to consider should be presented to the client, including the nature of treatment, the potential benefits and risks, alternative treatments with their benefits and risks, and the benefits and risks of no treatment at all. Next, the client must understand this information. And finally, voluntary consent to the recommended treatment must be obtained and documented. In addition, counselors should discuss with clients as early as possible other relevant issues such as the anticipated length of treatment, fees and related financial policies, and the presence of a supervisor or student/intern (APA, 2002, sect. 10.01). Therapists should study their state board rules and professional codes of conduct carefully to ensure that they are providing all necessary information to clients.

Attorneys and others recommend that therapists use signed consent forms or contracts to provide essential information to clients and obtain their written consent to treatment. These forms should be provided at the outset of treatment or as near to the outset of treatment as possible. While signed consent forms are very important from the standpoint of risk management, there are admittedly times when their use may be somewhat awkward. If presented with poor timing and taste, they could make the establishment of rapport difficult. For example, for a client in crisis to spend most of his first session going over the therapeutic contract rather than receiving immediate assessment and intervention would be inappropriate. Unusual circumstances require special care. But overall, obtaining informed consent, preferably using a signed consent form, has become the standard in the field.

In addition to the general information suggested earlier, a number of specific items listed here should be provided to clients as a part of informed consent (Sanders, 2000; Texas State Board of Examiners of Psychologists [TSBEP], 1995). Appendix 2 also provides examples of how a written consent form might be organized.

1. Information about the services provided. In understandable language, explain something about your services and your philosophy of treatment. This may include information about the types of counseling you provide, your theoretical orientation and something about what clients can expect assessment and treatment to be like. Some information about alternative choices for treatment should be given: clients' rights to withdraw from treatment, and side-effects, stresses or strains that could occur as a by-product of treatment. If you offer Christian therapeutic services, you should provide some information about the nature of these services so that your clients will know how you apply Christian concepts in treatment. The primary purpose of these explanations is to give clients the opportunity to decide whether or not they want these concepts to be a part of their treatment. Providing this information is especially important if you offer Christian services and work in a center or practice that does not clearly advertise itself as offering Christian services.

If any of the services or techniques you provide would be considered experimental by a jury of your peers, it is important that the client be informed of the experimental nature of the treatment, the potential risks of treatment, alternative treatments available and the client's right to opt out of the treatment (APA, 2002, sect. 10.10b).

2. Goals of therapy and procedures to be used. What problems will you be treating in therapy, and what techniques will you use? Since each case is different, this information may not be included in a basic information form. However, it can be discussed early on in the therapeutic relationship, and the treatment plan and the client's consent to it can be documented in the chart. Since goals and procedures may change as therapy progresses, this topic will likely be revisited over the course of treatment, and the client should be encouraged to ask questions about goals and procedures as a part of therapy. Also included in this discussion could be some estimate of the frequency of sessions and length of treatment, albeit with some understanding that specific pronouncements may not always be possible early on in therapy or in every situation.

3. Financial issues. Clients should clearly understand the cost of services, when they will be expected to pay and the method of payment. How are insurance matters handled? Who is ultimately responsible for the bill? What is the policy for overdue accounts, and does the counselor reserve the right to use collection agencies?

4. Confidentiality. Clients must be told that therapy is confidential to the extent provided by law. They should understand that while confidentiality may be assumed in the majority of circumstances, there are exceptions. Admittedly, a focus on all the exceptions to confidentiality could raise worries for some clients. Notable exceptions to confidentiality have been presented earlier in this chapter. Other situation-specific issues might center around confidentiality in marriage and family cases (see chap. 7) or on child cases (see chap. 8). When insurance or managed care is involved, clients will need to sign and understand releases to permit information to be sent to third-party payers.

5. Qualifications. What are your qualifications, licensing, degrees and certification? It may be helpful to share where you received your academic as well as clinical training. If you are a trainee in supervision, the client needs to know that and who your supervisor is.

6. Other pertinent information. Other important information to be discussed may include how phone calls or emergencies are handled, what clients should do if they have a concern or complaint, and information about office hours. In any case, the information needed for informed consent depends somewhat on the nature of the counseling setting and the type of services provided.

One of the primary goals of informed consent is to prevent misunderstanding between client and therapist. Many of the complaints that come to a state licensing board have to do with miscommunication between therapist and client (TSBEP, 1995). While formal consent procedures should help keep serious miscommunication to a minimum, misunderstandings can and do occur in counseling relationships as they do in all relationships. Therapists who respond to misunderstandings with a spirit of concern and consideration, and who work closely with the client to deal with the issues and correct the misunderstanding, do much to restore, maintain and develop the trust factor so important to all successful therapy.

DOCUMENTATION

Proper documentation is essential for competent service. Many, if not most, state boards require that licensed professionals keep accurate records of evaluation and counseling services. In addition, professional guilds, counseling agencies and institutions have their own rules about documentation. Specific requirements regarding the content of records may vary from place to place, but records usually must include as a minimum, information about (1) the date and time of service, (2) the type of service rendered and by whom, (3) assessment and progress information, and (4) billing information. Of course, copies of all consent and release forms should be kept as well.

The Health Insurance Portability and Accountability Act (HIPAA) has also introduced national standards for record keeping that are designed to provide certain mental health records a greater level of privacy than others. HIPAA divides mental health records into two types. The first is called Protected Health Information (PHI). PHI "is information that relates to the past, present or future physical or mental health condition of an individual, the provision of health care to an individual, or the past, present or future payment for the provision of health care to the individual" (APA, n.d.).

In more specific terms, the PHI record includes basic information such as

- payment/billing information
- date of session and the session start/stop time
- modalities and frequencies of treatment furnished
- medications

- results of assessment or testing
- a summary of
  - symptoms
  - functional status
  - process to date
  - diagnosis
  - treatment plan
  - prognosis

The other type of mental health record provided for by HIPAA is called Psychotherapy Notes. Psychotherapy notes are "notes recorded in any medium by a mental health professional documenting or analyzing the contents of conversation during a private counseling session or a group, joint or family counseling session, and that are separated from the rest of the individual's medical record" (APA, n.d.). Psychotherapy notes are afforded a greater level of privacy protection by HIPAA. Thus, it may be assumed that, in general, psychotherapy notes include the most personal and detailed information and analysis about the counseling session. The intent of these HIPAA provisions are to protect a patient's most sensitive and personal comments and analysis from being divulged to insurance companies and other third parties while at the same time providing a means by which general information necessary to justify the authorization of service and the payment of claims is provided. In the event that a client's psychotherapy notes are to be released for some reason, the release of information form which the client signs must specifically mention that the release includes the release of psychotherapy notes.

Therapists frequently ask what is meant by keeping psychotherapy notes *separate* from the rest of the record. Unfortunately, the law does not specifically address this question. The most important thing is to maintain the psychotherapy notes in such a way that counseling clerical staff and professionals do not get confused about which documentation is PHI and which is psychotherapy notes, and inadvertently send out the wrong records to a third party. Some therapists maintain separation by using different colored papers to help differentiate the PHI from the psychotherapy notes, or they keep PHI and psychotherapy notes clearly partitioned in the client's chart.

Aside from meeting requirements, accurate records are necessary to help the therapist in the process of assessment, in devising and maintaining consistent treatment plans, and in recalling important therapeutic information. They can also serve a risk management function, allowing the therapist to document important information of an ethical or legal nature. As is sometimes said in the legal community, "If it isn't in writing, it didn't happen." Even negative findings should be documented as evidence that they were in fact evaluated. For example, if an evaluation showed there was no suicidal ideation, that should be noted. Good records are also helpful if the case is transferred to a new therapist at some point.

Documentation is not without its dilemmas, however. Therapists must realize that records, even psychotherapy notes, could at some point be seen by someone other than themselves. The trend in law has been to allow clients access to records of their treatment. Attempts by a therapist to withhold records from a client will be overturned except in the most unusual of circumstances, and withholding records could result in steps being taken to penalize or censure the therapist. What's more, therapists can never be sure that other parties such as attorneys, courts, insurers and other family members will not at some point see a record if the client either consents to it or if legal requirements demand it. The wise therapist should therefore document accurately but carefully, being sensitive to how what one says could be construed by others, including the patient and interested third parties.

Those who provide psychological assessment should also be aware that some state boards consider materials such as raw test data appropriate to release only to other professionals who have training in how to interpret them. The overriding concern in these situations is that misinterpretation, misunderstanding and misuse of records could occur the more available they become to others. For those interested in additional help in keeping accurate and careful records, Bennett et al. (1990, pp. 76-78) offer a useful checklist that encourages mindful consideration of various matters.

PRUDENT CHOICES IN TREATMENT SELECTION AND
THERAPIST-CLIENT RELATIONSHIPS

We speak often in the literature about *competence* as a fundamental principle of mental health ethics. By competence, we usually mean the need for therapists to have appropriate professional qualifications and training in the services that they provide. This is indeed important and is discussed in detail in chapter three. However, the ability to apply one's skills effectively with individual clients is of great importance also. The question is, how does the ethical therapist best go about doing this?

In recent years, driven by forces both inside and outside the profession, there has been a tremendous push toward developing evidence-based or empirically supported treatments (ESTs). In general, treatments that qualify as evidence-based are those which meet criteria for effectiveness based on empirical research. As one might expect, the current list of ESTs is heavily populated by behavioral or cognitive behavioral treatments, many of these of a short-term nature, and many using programmed manuals which control precisely the way in which treatment is conducted and the specific therapeutic principles taught.

There has been controversy about this methodology. In the first place, some question what qualifies as empirical research. Is it only a multisubject outcome study where variables can be rigidly controlled, or do qualitative research, single subject designs and case studies qualify also? Second, some argue that manual-based approaches force both therapist and client to conduct treatment in an almost robotic fashion that would often be unrealistic and ineffective in the real world of everyday psychotherapy practice. Others point to the fact that subject selection in these studies is so rigidly controlled that clients with co-morbid conditions (which many mental health patients have) are usually excluded from study (Westen & Morrison, 2001). Finally, others argue that these studies are of limited generalizability because the samples are so homogeneous that they frequently exclude ethnic minority groups or different age groups from the subject pool (Levant, 2003).

Not surprisingly, another line of research has developed which focuses on empirically supported therapy relationships (ESRs) (Norcross, 2002). In this line of research, the emphasis is on determining the elements that make for effective therapy relationships and how therapy can be customized to individual clients based on the nondiagnostic, personal characteristics of the client. This approach to research is supported by a review of the literature by Lambert and Barley (2002) which indicated that relationship factors and factors common to different therapies accounted for 30% of the variance in therapy outcomes, whereas specific therapy techniques accounted for only 15%. Additionally, expectancy factors (the belief that therapy would help) accounted for another 15% of the variance while patient qualities and extra therapeutic factors (such as the support of friends, clergy, reading, etc.) accounted for the other 40%. The accumulated evidence points to the notion that the person of the therapist, the nature of the therapy relationship and nondiagnostic patient characteristics and resources are incredibly important to the success of therapy (Norcross, 2001).

The Lambert and Barley (2002) figures should not be taken to mean that therapeutic techniques (or knowledge of psychopathology) are irrelevant to the success of therapy. Not only do techniques contribute in general to outcomes, they are more crucial in certain diagnostic situations (Lambert & Barley, 2002). For example, exposure techniques are important in treating specific phobias, and response prevention methodologies are important in treating the compulsive aspects of obsessive-compulsive disorder. Techniques are important to effective therapy but are clearly insufficient by themselves to affect meaningful change.

Returning to our original question, how does the ethical therapist best seek to display competence in everyday practice? The evidence would suggest that the ability to form good relationships with clients, and to adapt oneself and one's methods to the needs of the specific client are incredibly important. While these "good people skills" are absolutely necessary for developing good therapeutically effective relationships, they are not sufficient. The effective therapist must also have a scientific knowledge base about the nature of the conditions one treats. How can one form a genuine, empathic relationship with the client with an eating disorder (or anxiety, depression, cognitive impairment or a host of other disorders) if one does not have an understanding of the biopsychosocial intricacies of these conditions that he or she can use both to understand and educate the client? The therapist must also have a working knowledge of the therapeutic techniques that research has suggested are most effective with each condition. The therapist must have the ability to adapt these techniques to the needs of the specific client. Having the ability to help clients mobilize their own interpersonal and intrapersonal resources is also important to effective therapy. These extra-therapeutic factors are clearly important and the effective therapist will utilize his or her relational skills to facilitate the client in identifying and making use of these resources.

We must also admit that much remains to be known about what constitutes effective therapy. The empirically supported treatment and relationship literature has added a great deal to our knowledge base about what works, but much remains to be known.

However, as one admits the incomplete nature of our knowledge, both about effective clinical techniques and about effective clinical relationships, one must leave place for the role of clinical experience and wise judgment in making for effective, competent therapy. To be sure, an overreliance on clinical experience could result in therapists doing whatever feels right. But when properly understood, the wisdom of clinical experience is broad in scope and should develop out of one's training under those who have gone before, a commitment to lifelong education and consultation, and an appreciation for the accumulated wisdom of the profession as a whole. The *standard of care*, or those things a jury of one's peers would identify as the range of options and interventions in a particular case, should lead one to be *prudent* in the selection of treatments and in how one develops the therapeutic relationship.

Some would argue that the picture of clinical competence advanced here—one that emphasizes evidence-based relationships and techniques, as well as clinical experience, and appreciation for the standard of care put forth by the profession as a whole—leaves little room for innovation in the development of new and untested approaches to treatment. On the contrary, we believe that growth in knowledge and changes in the culture and the times require dedication to innovation as well. However, innovation should never take place in a vacuum. The ability of innovators to think critically and their willingness to expose their ideas to objective testing and peer review is the best way to advance knowledge. Some of the most questionable treatments in our field are developed by individuals who isolate themselves and their work from the critique of peers and others. For example, in Christian counseling this sometimes occurs when the individual develops an approach to treatment (or assessment, etc.) and promotes it as the one right Christian approach. The temptation to assume God's imprimatur for ideas untested or developed in isolation from the critique of others in the field can lead to denial about the shortcomings of the approach and at times to unethical or even harmful treatment.

Innovation is extremely important to the science and art of psychotherapy and assessment, but as in medicine and science, innovation needs to be carried out with sensitivity to established ethical principles and standards of critical thinking and peer review. Where ethical standards for a particular innovation do not exist, the development of standards should ideally take place in tandem with the development of the therapeutic innovation.

Teletherapy. To illustrate the ethics of dealing with emerging or innovative approaches to therapy and assessment, we could consider a number of different techniques, methodologies and technologies. We will however focus on one, teletherapy.

Advances in telecommunication have increased exponentially in recent years. Whereas previously such communication was largely limited to landline telephone, many people now have access to cell phones, fax, email, chat rooms and televideo communications.

Not surprisingly these forms of communication are now being used in mental health work. Therapists and clients use these methods to communicate with each other, but the modalities are also used for conducting supervision and interprofessional communication, and for sending information to third-party payers. A survey by the APA's Center for Workforce Studies found that practicing psychologists' use of email to communicate with clients more than tripled between 2000 and 2008 (Novotney, 2011). Practitioners' use of videoconferencing with clients was much less prevalent, but still increased from 2% to 10% during the same period.

Professional guilds and other concerned parties have been attempting to develop standards and guidelines for the use of electronic communication for therapy or assessment services. Reed, McLaughlin, and Milholland (2000) developed a set of ten principles for professional practice in telehealth. Their standards speak to issues of therapist competence, confidentiality, client safety and welfare, informed consent, documentation and other matters. They remain as a foundation for thinking about the ethics of e-therapy or teletherapy, as it is often called. The ACA also spoke quite specifically to the ethics of teletherapy in the 2005 revision of their ethics code (ACA, 2005, A.12), and they also published a freestanding set of ethical standards for Internet counseling (ACA, 1999). The APA ethics code (2002) speaks in a cursory way about electronic communication but the association did release a statement on services by telephone, teleconferencing and Internet in 1997 (APA, 1997), and the APA is currently in the process of developing additional guidelines.

Recent reviews of a number of peer-reviewed studies indicate that teletherapy is effective, at least in certain situations and certain kinds of treatment. Proponents argue that it reaches people who would never receive therapy otherwise. They point to clients in rural, underserved areas or who are in far-off military settings as examples. In addition, email and telephone therapy can be a useful adjunct to in-person therapy. For example, a therapist treating an anxiety-disordered client who fears going into large stores might hold a session by cell phone while the client is at a store. Dialectical behavior therapy, which utilizes a certain amount of client-therapist communication between sessions might use email as a means to reinforce or review therapeutic principles.

Having said this, much remains to be known about what types of services can be conducted successfully with electronic communication. Clearly, not all services would be equally appropriate. Providing smoking cessation treatment would not be the same as providing therapy for an eating disorder, which would be different from providing testing services. Each type of service must be evaluated separately for its own attendant risks as well as benefits, and some services, in part or in whole, will be found inappropriate for use in an electronic venue.

Despite increasing interest, use and research, we feel that teletherapy should still be seen as an emerging method in our field about which much remains to be known. As such, therapists should be mindful of ethical standards that recommend caution and competence when using clinical methods for which generally agreed upon standards of care do not exist (see APA, 2002, 2:01e).

The prudent therapist will consider many issues when deciding if and how to provide services electronically. First, the *competent* therapist will seek ongoing continuing education about the use of electronic communication as the field develops and more is known. Clearly, there are very real differences between the delivery of services face-to-face compared to that done electronically (Nowotney, 2011). For example, what types of diagnostic information does the therapist lose when he or she does not meet with the client personally and experience the client sitting in the same room? Will the client experience the kind of warm and empathic interpersonal relationship with the therapist for certain kinds of treatment such as grief therapy to be productive? What's more, not all teletherapies are "created equal." Televideo provides both therapist and client with a great deal more information about the characteristics of the other than does email. Therapists who assume that teletherapy is essentially no different from face-to-face intervention will surely be in danger of acting unethically.

Each therapist must also consider issues of *privacy* and *confidentiality* in teletherapy. Not only can confidentiality be breached on the therapist's end, but clients may leave confidential information exposed on their computer or may inadvertently send confidential information to unintended third parties. The therapist will need to develop informed consent documentation that the client will read and sign. At a minimum, this documentation should include the kinds of services the therapist provides electronically (as well as those not provided), the potential benefits and risks of assessment or therapy performed electronically, the way emergencies will be handled, and in the case of communications such as email that are not in real time, how long the client should expect to wait for a reply. There should be some type of disclaimer regarding the dangers and types of privacy breaches that can occur in electronic communication. Therapists must also make a reasonable attempt to investigate whether the specific electronic platform they plan to use for communication is compliant with HIPAA regulations and any applicable state laws.

Therapists must document all electronic communication with patients just as they do in face-to-face therapy. They must also understand that most teletherapy is not covered by insurance, and they must avoid any temptation to bill insurance as if it were a face-to-face session.

ENDING TREATMENT

When the therapeutic relationship must be *interrupted* or *terminated*, it is important to do so properly. Arrangements should be made for provision of services in the event of the therapist's absence due to illness, relocation or death, or as a result of the client's financial limitation or when insurance benefits have been exhausted (see the chapter on business ethics in mental health service). When the client no longer needs service, is not benefitting from service or is at risk of being harmed by continued service, termination of treatment and possible referral to an appropriate resource is appropriate.

Every counselor has experienced the dilemma of whether to refer a client to another professional. Sometimes the therapist-client mix is simply a mismatch. On other occasions issues such as age, sex of the therapist or personality style hamper the development of an effective therapeutic alliance. Limits in training and experience can also dictate the need for referral. A greater difficulty is encountered when there has been a positive treatment relationship but a poor response to treatment. Under such circumstances, appropriate referral is often clouded by issues such as the therapist's sense of failure, the therapist's positive or negative countertransference with the client, the therapist's reputation among his or her colleagues, or the therapist not wanting to acknowledge to the client that he or she has reached the limits of personal expertise. At times even financial and caseload pressures can cloud a therapist's objective evaluation of when to refer.

Ethical constraints and concern for the welfare of counselees require that counselors avoid the reality or the appearance of having *abandoned* a client. Abandonment can be avoided by carefully discussing the treatment plan with the client, providing thorough pretermination interventions, suggesting alternative service providers and taking any other reasonable steps to facilitate transfer of care to another provider if it is indicated (APA, 2002, Sects. 10.09-10.10). The sensitive therapist will realize that transfer or termination, though it may ultimately be in the client's best interest, can raise ambivalent or confusing feelings for some clients. A therapist's handling of such situations should be measured and compassionate. As much as possible, the therapist should avoid terminating the therapy when the client is in crisis. The therapist should be sensitive to the client's mental state and try to see the situation through the client's eyes as well as with respect for the ultimate best interest of the client. To the extent possible, the therapist should offer a compassionate rationale for the termination and should within reason be willing to dialogue with the client about it. When referring to another therapist, it may occasionally be best to offer a transitional period between therapists.

While sensitivity to the client's needs in the process of termination or referral is of greatest concern in most situations, there are cases in which the needs of the therapist take precedence. In recent years there have been an increasing number of cases in which clients have threatened, stalked, hurt or killed their counselors. Because of this, the APA Ethics Code now allows therapists to "terminate therapy when threatened or otherwise endangered by the client/patient or another person with whom the client/patient has a relationship (APA, 2002, sect. 10.10b; see also ACA, 2005, sect. A.11.c)." This needed addition to the code should help the therapist avoid being caught up in a dangerous situation and may also help protect the therapist from legal action should the threatening client decide to accuse him or her of abandonment at a later date (Sanders, 2005).

CONCLUSION

Counseling, and even more so Christian counseling, is accompanied by a host of complex and multifaceted issues and responsibilities. This chapter has considered several essential issues foundational to ethical counsel. Unless each of us as Christian counselors has a thorough understanding of these issues and those in the other chapters in this volume, practice them and hold one another lovingly accountable to the legal, ethical and professional issues and to God's basic truths, we will fall short of an authentic response to God's call on our lives. Let us each aspire to be thoroughly competent, professional and Christlike in all that we do. By this God will be glorified.

REFERENCES

American Counseling Association. (1999). *Ethical standards for internet online counseling*. Alexandria, VA: American Counseling Association.

American Counseling Association. (2005). *ACA code of ethics*. Alexandria, VA: American Counseling Association. Retrieved April 25, 2010, from www.counseling.org/Resources/CodeofEthics/TP/Home/CT2.aspx.

American Psychological Association. (1997). *APA statement concerning services by telephone, teleconferencing, and internet.* Washington, DC: American Psychological Association. Retrieved December 4, 2011, from www.apa.org/ethics/education/telephone-statement.aspx.

American Psychological Association. (2002). Ethical principles of psychologists and code of conduct. *American Psychologist, 57,* 1060-73. Also available (with 2010 amendments) from www.apa.org/ethics/code/index.aspx.

American Psychological Association. (n.d.). *HIPAA for psychologists* [Computer CD]. Washington, DC: American Psychological Association.

Becker, W. W. (1987). The paraprofessional counselor in the church: Legal and ethical considerations. *Journal of Psychology and Christianity, 6,* 78-82.

Bennett, B. E., Bryant, B. K., VandenBos, G. R., & Greenwood, A. (1990). *Professional liability and risk management.* Washington, DC: American Psychological Association.

Christian Association for Psychological Studies (2005). *Ethics statement of the Christian Association for Psychological Studies.* Batavia, IL: Christian Association for Psychological Studies. Retrieved April 27, 2010, from www.caps.net/index .php?option=com_content&view+article&id=253&Itemid=131.

Huber, C. H. (1994). *Ethical, legal, and professional issues in the practice of marriage and family therapy* (2nd ed.). New York: Macmillan.

Lambert, M. J., & Barley, D. E. (2002). Research summary on the therapeutic relationship and psychotherapy outcome. In J. C. Norcross (Ed.), *Psychotherapy relationships that work* (pp. 17-32). New York: Oxford.

Levant, R. F. (2003). The empirically validated treatments movement: A practitioner perspective. *Texas Psychologist, 54,* 18-21.

Norcross, J. C. (2001). Purposes, processes, and products of the Task Force on Empirically Supported Therapy Relationships. *Psychotherapy: Theory, Research, Practice, Training, 38,* 345-56.

Norcross, J. C. (Ed.). (2002). *Psychotherapy relationships that work.* New York: Oxford University Press.

Novotney, A. (2011, June). A new emphasis on telehealth. *Monitor on Psychology, 42,* 40-44.

Pabian, Y. L., Welfel, E., & Beebe, R. S. (2009). Psychologists' knowledge of their states' laws pertaining to Tarasoff-type situations. *Professional Psychology: Research & Practice, 40,* 8-14.

Reed, G. M., McLaughlin, C. J., & Milholland, K. (2000). Ten interdisciplinary principles for professional practice in telehealth: Implications for psychology. *Professional Psychology: Research & Practice, 31,* 170-78.

Sanders, R. K. (2000). Informed consent: Issues facing the Christian marriage and family therapist. *Marriage & Family: A Christian Journal, 3,* 25-38.

Sanders, R. K. (2005). Ethics codes: Monitoring the major changes. *Journal of Psychology & Christianity, 29,* 263-67.

Stromberg, C. D., Haggarty, D. J., Leibenluft, R. F., McMillian, M. H., Mishkin, B., Rubin, B. L., & Trilling, H. R. (1988). *The psychologist's legal handbook.* Washington, DC: Council for the National Register of Health Service Providers in Psychology.

Stromberg, C. D., Lindberg, D., Mishkin, B., & Baker, M. (1993). *The Psychologist's Legal Update: Privacy, Confidentiality and Privilege.* Washington, DC: The Council for the National Register of Health Service Providers in Psychology.

Tan, S.-Y. (1991). *Lay counseling: Equipping Christians for a helping ministry.* Grand Rapids: Zondervan.

Tarasoff v. Board of Regents of the U. of California, 551 P2d 334 (Cal. Sup. Ct. 1976).

Texas State Board of Examiners of Psychologists (TSBEP). (1995, Winter). Informed consent. *Newsletter,* pp. 11-12.

Westen, D., & Morrison, K. (2001). A multidimensional meta-analysis of treatments for depression, panic, and generalized anxiety disorder: An empirical examination of the status of empirically supported therapies. *Journal of Consulting & Clinical Psychology, 60,* 875-99.

5

Sexual Misconduct and the Abuse of Power

John F. Shackelford and
Randolph K. Sanders

As he approached Dr. Malpractice's door, Dr. Fairfax felt a gnawing discomfort in the pit of his stomach. Dr. Fairfax had arranged this meeting, but now a part of him wished to avoid what was to come. Taking a deep breath, he entered Malpractice's front door.

As he walked into the lobby and up to the desk, he was surprised at how nice Dr. Malpractice's office looked. Perhaps he thought a man accused of sexual misconduct by his colleagues would have a shabby office. But this office was neat and nicely appointed.

The secretary at the front desk acknowledged him and asked him to take a seat for just a moment. As he waited, he thought back over the reason he was here. Throughout the area in which they both worked, a persistent rumor had circulated that Dr. Malpractice had been romantically involved with one of his patients for a number of months. The rumor was so prevalent that several physicians had approached Fairfax in the last month wondering "what it would take" for the state board of examiners "to get involved."

Just now, Fairfax wondered why he had been the one to come. What if Malpractice became indignant and threw him out of his office? Still, Fairfax felt it was his responsibility to at least talk to Malpractice about the rumors. And besides, both he and Malpractice represented themselves as Christian therapists. *Surely,* Fairfax thought, *that makes me the person to talk to him.*

The door to the lobby swung open and there stood Malpractice. "Frank Fairfax, it's good to see you!" Malpractice exclaimed as he ushered him into his office. "I haven't seen you since the state convention a couple of years ago. What brings you over here to see me?"

"Well, I'm afraid what I have to talk about is rather unpleasant," Fairfax began. "You see there is a rumor about town that you are having a relationship with one of your patients. I would have discounted it, but I hear the rumor again and again, mostly from people who would have no reason to lie. I know how these rumors are, but I thought I should . . ."

Malpractice cut him off. "Well, the rumors are true," he said rather matter-of-factly. "A wonderful thing has happened to me in the last few months. God has brought a very special person into my life. I never planned to get involved with her, but this is different. We both feel the same way about each other. It just seems like we were led to be together. She had been a patient in a psychiatric hospital in the state where her parents live. She is from a very enmeshed family. It's fortunate for her that she moved back here and got in to see me when she got out of the hospital. The psychiatrist at the hospital diagnosed her as major depression with borderline personality, but I'm sure he was wrong about the diagnosis of personality disorder. She may have a few problematic traits. I guess anybody would who came from a family like that. But, you know, I've always thought that diagnostic categories label people and prevent us from seeing the richness of the unique individuals we counsel."

"But what about your wife, aren't the two of you still together?" Fairfax asked.

"Oh Frank, we have a marriage in name only. The relationship has been over for years. Don't get me wrong. I care for my wife, but it was hardly ever a marriage to begin with. By the letter of the law, I know we are still married, but I've come to learn that if one is ever going to live halfway abundantly, you have to live out the spirit of the law."

Malpractice talked on while Frank sat quietly on the couch. *How could a therapist be this far off center?* he thought to himself. *How could he miss so many obvious red flags? And what could have been done to prevent something like this from happening?*

INCIDENCE OF SEXUAL MISCONDUCT

How prevalent is sexual misconduct in the profession? Kardener, Fuller, and Mensh (1973) surveyed 114 male psychiatrists in Los Angeles and found that 10% admitted sexual contact with patients. Holroyd and Brodsky (1977) conducted a national survey of licensed doctoral-level psychologists with a return rate of 70%. They found that 5.5% of 347 male respondents and 0.6% of 310 female respondents had engaged in sexual intercourse with their patients. Eighty percent of the abusers admitted sexual contact with more than one patient. Bouhoutsos, Holroyd, Lerman, Forer, and Greenberg (1983) with 704 respondents, found a similar incidence with 4.8% of male therapists and 0.8% of female therapists.

The largest research study on therapist-patient sexual intimacy was done by Gartrell, Herman, Olarte, Feldstein, and Localio (1986) in which psychiatrists were surveyed nationwide. Questionnaires were sent to 5,574 psychiatrists with a 26% return. Similar to earlier studies, 6.4% acknowledged sexual intimacies with a patient. Eighty-seven percent of the victims were female with a mean age of 33. Genital contact was involved with 74% of these patients. The remaining patients reported sexual contact consisting of kissing, fondling or undressing.

Pope and Vetter (1991) surveyed 1,320 psychologists, with a 50% return rate, asking if they had treated a patient who reported sexual involvement with a prior therapist. Almost 50% of the psychologists had seen at least one such patient and some psychologists had treated several patients.

These studies document that a serious problem has existed in the mental health profession with a percentage of therapists who abuse their position of power and become sexually involved with their clients. Borys and Pope (1989) surveyed the three major mental health professional groups—psychiatrists, psychologists and social workers—and found no significant difference among the rates at which the various professionals acknowledged engaging in sex with their patients. What is of most concern is the problem of underreporting. Vinson (1987) has illustrated the potential magnitude of the problem with the following scenario: In 1982 there were 31,300 licensed psychotherapists in California, and if one projects that approximately 7% of the total, or 2,200 therapists, have sexually abused a patient, and some of those have abused several patients, then one could expect there to be roughly 6,000 patients who have been abused and psychologically damaged. In the same year, 1982, in California, records show that at least 12 but no more than 16 therapists were disciplined by their licensing boards.

Interestingly, some later surveys reveal only 1-2% of therapists reporting they have been sexually involved with a patient, which represents a marked decline (Borys & Pope, 1989; Gechtman, 1989; Pope, Tabachnick & Keith-Spiegel, 1987). Borys and Pope observe that this may represent a true decline in sexual involvement, or it may indicate a greater reluctance to report since such involvement is now recognized as a felony in many states.

A study of Christian counselors indicates that 2% admitted to having had sex with a client they were seeing in therapy. About 6% said they had been involved with a former client (see McMinn & Meek, 1996; 1997).

Jackson and Nuttall (2001) looked for a correlation between childhood sexual abuse and sexual boundary violations with clients. In their survey of 323 mental health professionals, 9% admitted to sexual activity with a client. Of those who had been sexually abused as children, 21% had sexual activity with a client (Jackson and Nuttall, 2001).

ETHICAL STANDARDS

The American Psychological Association's Code of Ethics (2002) states:

10.05 Sexual Intimacies with Current Therapy Clients/Patients

Psychologists do not engage in sexual intimacies with current therapy clients/patients.

10.06 Sexual Intimacies with Relatives or Significant Others of Current Therapy Clients/Patients

Psychologists do not engage in sexual intimacies with individuals they know to be close relatives, guardians, or significant others of current clients/patients.

Psychologists do not terminate therapy to circumvent this standard.

10.07 Therapy with Former Sexual Partners

Psychologists do not accept as therapy clients/patients persons with whom they have engaged in sexual intimacies.

10.08 Sexual Intimacies with Former Therapy Clients/Patients

(a) Psychologists do not engage in sexual intimacies with former clients/patients for at least two years after cessation or termination of therapy.

(b) Psychologists do not engage in sexual intimacies with former clients/patients even after a two-year interval except in the most unusual circumstances. Psychologists who engage in such activity after the two years following cessation or termination of therapy and of having no sexual contact with the former client/patient bear the burden of demonstrating that there has been no exploitation, in light of all relevant factors, including (1) the amount of time that has passed since therapy terminated; (2) the nature, duration, and intensity of the therapy; (3) the circumstances of termination; (4) the client's/patient's personal history; (5) the client's/patient's current mental status; (6) the likelihood of adverse impact on the client/patient; and (7) any statements or actions made by the therapist during the course of therapy suggesting or inviting the possibility of a post-termination sexual or romantic relationship with the client/patient. (See also Standard 3.05, Multiple Relationships.) (American Psychological Association, 2002)

The thinking behind the prohibition against sex with former patients was expressed by A. N. Brodsky in a 1983 paper given at the American Psychological Association annual meeting: "Father-daughter incest does not become acceptable one year after the daughter has left home. No matter how the therapy contract ends, the *imbalance of power* of the initial interactions can never be erased" (emphasis added).

PATIENTS ARE HARMED

Bouhoutsos et al. (1983) surveyed therapists who were treating patients who had sexual intimacy with a previous therapist. The therapists rated that 64% of the patients had experienced adverse effects, which included factors such as "increased depression, loss of motivation, impaired social adjustment, significant emotional disturbance, . . . increased drug or alcohol abuse" (p. 190). Eleven percent were hospitalized and 1% committed suicide. Therapists rated that 90% of patients had suffered at least some kind of negative effects. A later paper by Holroyd and Bouhoutsos (1985) revealed that the psychologists in the survey who claimed that their patients had not been harmed by previous intimacies had a 2.5 times greater incidence of patient sexual intimacies themselves.

Feldman-Summers and Jones (1984) took a different approach and collected their data by directly interviewing and testing patients. They found that women abused by their therapists had significantly more mistrust and anger toward men and their therapists than women who had not been sexually intimate with their therapists. These abused women also had significantly more symptoms one month post-therapy than the nonabused women. Another significant finding in their study was that the women with a prior history of childhood sexual abuse who were also involved with a married therapist suffered the greatest negative effects. Their previous wounds were compounded.

Pope and Sonne (1991), who have extensively researched the harm done by sexual intimacies with therapists, coined the diagnostic phrase "Therapist-Patient Sex Syndrome" to refer to the symptom picture of those who are victims of sexual misconduct. The symptoms include "ambivalence, guilt, emptiness, isolation, sexual confusion, impaired ability to trust, identity and boundary confusion, emotional lability, suppressed rage, increased suicidal risk, and cognitive dysfunction" (p. 175). They note similar symptoms in those suffering from rape, incest and other forms of child sexual abuse.

Solursh, Solursh and Williams (1993) summarize that the harmful effects of therapist-patient sexual intimacy for women patients include chronic distrust of therapy, increased sexual problems, anger at being exploited and lower self-esteem.

In a thought-provoking article, Baylis (1993) makes the point that it is impossible for a therapy patient who comes to treatment feeling vulnerable to give "consent" for sexual involvement with her doctor who is in a position of power. She argues that the components of consent are intentionality, substantial understanding, substantial voluntariness and autonomous authorization. Baylis concludes that "therapist-patient sexual relations are always non-consensual and inherently harmful . . . irrespective of who initiates the sexual contact" (p. 503).

PATIENTS MOST LIKELY TO BE ABUSED

In their book *Sexual Intimacy Between Therapists and Patients,* Pope and

Bouhoustsos (1986) describe from their clinical experience three categories of patients who have become sexually involved with their therapists: low-risk, middle-risk and high-risk.

1. The low-risk group. These patients have no history of prior hospitalizations and usually function on a high level with a history of stable, long-term relationships. What is distinctive about this group of sexually abused patients is that they had recently been highly stressed by a recent loss, such as a divorce or the recent death of a parent. The therapist took advantage of their temporary vulnerability.

2. The middle-risk group. This group of patients is seen as more dependent and needy, and they often receive a diagnosis of personality disorder. They have a history of relationship problems. Chesler (1972) interviewed eleven women and described them as feminine, intellectually insecure, economically limited and "frantically" attractive. They were sexually fearful as well as sexually compulsive with marked self-contempt. They were likely to blame themselves when they were mistreated by men.

Gorkin (1985) describes the masochistic female patient whose sexual fantasies and feelings toward their therapist take the tone of being injured or hurt by him. This particular patient frequently has a background of sexual excitement with a father or brother, which is also tinted with punishment or abuse. Despite this negative family relationship, it was often the only consistent relationship that provided attention. Belote (1974) found in a study of 25 women who had been sexually intimate with their therapist that most reported a negative relationship with their mothers and a close relationship with their fathers. Most of these women reported being attracted to relationships with older authority figures. Stone's (1980) research seemed to support her hypothesis that women who suffer from "severe anxious attachment" caused by separation-individuation failures are more vulnerable to becoming sexually involved with their therapist. The reason advanced is that they are trying to repair early ego damage and preserve the symbiotic relationship that helps them feel loved and complete.

3. The high-risk group. The following were identified as high risk.

Incest survivors. Pope and Bouhoutsos (1986) observe from their clinical experience that many of the high-risk patients have been incest victims. These authors write:

The usual incest victim has been involved . . . with a person in authority, either father or someone else, over a period of years and has had to keep the secret. She has learned to take the blame for what happened and has learned to exonerate the adult offender. The paternal role is fulfilled by the therapist with whom she is sexually involved. The therapist is assured of a pliable, often pathetically naive, needy patient who will not tell and who will not blame the therapist but who will frequently remain in the therapeutic relationship for years, paying for the damage and feeling guilty for causing the inevitable abuse and neglect by the therapist. . . . [S]uch women may find it almost impossible to admit . . . that victimization has occurred. (p. 53)

Thus the therapist, consciously or unconsciously, abuses his powerful parent role to inflict more damage on this most vulnerable type of patient, a patient who has been scripted for victimization.

Borderline personality disorder. Guntheil (1989) has written about the borderline personality and sexual intimacy in therapy. He makes the observation that the borderline may be a likely victim because the neurotic may have better perception and judgment than to succumb to sexual involvement and the psychotic patient may not be experienced as very attractive by the therapist. He further explains that the dynamics of the borderline, especially their neediness, their demandingness and their desire to be rescued and taken care of, can make it very difficult for the neophyte therapist to maintain boundaries. The therapist may fear that if he confronts and sets boundaries, he will be accused of rejecting them "as everyone else has."

SEXUAL MISCONDUCT AND THE ABUSE OF POWER

After reviewing the ethical code and the statistics indicating the prevalence of sexual misconduct, and particularly after examining the patient types most susceptible and the degree to which patients are harmed by sexual misconduct, one thing is abundantly clear. Sexual misconduct is an *abuse of therapist power.*

When people consult therapists, they most often do so in times of great personal vulnerability. They step into an office where they have never been, confused about painful issues they may not clearly understand, tell their innermost secrets to a person they hardly know, and, largely by faith, trust that the therapist will be able to help them. The therapist has a tremendous obligation to honor and respond appropriately to the patient's trust and avoid doing things that might harm the patient.

At least a few therapists relish the power they hold in the therapeutic relationship, using it to direct and perhaps manipulate the patient's life. These therapists may be the most dangerous. However, experience suggests that many therapists are naive about the degree of power they hold in some patients' lives and that this naiveté may also be problematic.

There may be several reasons why therapists are naive about the power they hold. Some therapists are trained to see themselves as "facilitators of change" rather than aggressive change agents. Perhaps therapists trained in this more passive approach fail to see the tremendous power that some patients project on them however client-centered these therapist's believe themselves to be.

Alternatively, some therapists may be blind to the power they hold because they have come to the realization that a number of patients in therapy do not change markedly despite all the "powerful" therapeutic techniques that therapists have at their disposal. Typically these practitioners are more experienced therapists who have realized that the therapeutic interventions they learned in graduate school do not always produce happy endings. Such therapists may conclude quite incorrectly that their power in the therapeutic relationship is much less than it really is.

Finally, some therapists may be naive to their power because of the ambivalence that various subgroups within the culture have had toward the mental health profession in the past. For example, Christian mental health professionals have sometimes had to defend the effectiveness of their work to portions of the Christian community that have viewed Christian counselors with skepticism. Perhaps therapists who have experienced this skepticism doubt the extent to which patients ascribe power to them. One has only to listen to Christian radio therapists, however, to realize that there is also a huge Christian public that is quite willing to follow without question the advice of radio counselors that they do not know and perhaps have never seen.

Some therapists may argue that viewing therapists as the ones who hold the power in the relationship is unfair and does not take into account the power and impact the patient has to effect the course of the therapeutic relationship. To be sure, therapy is not a one-way street, and the patient is never truly a passive participant. One of the things that makes therapy complicated, particularly for the young practitioner, is that therapy is not unilateral. A complicated interaction occurs between therapist and client in which the terms and process of therapy are negotiated and refined at each new turn.

If, at the third session, a woman client in despair becomes tearful and slides off the couch and on to the floor near her male therapist's chair, placing her hand on his arm, the therapist is left with a decision about how to respond. Among the extreme range of responses he could make: (1) He could sternly tell her that sitting on the floor is inappropriate and direct her to sit back on the couch; (2) he could wonder out loud about her despair and the possible reasons both therapeutic or counter-therapeutic, for her behavior; (3) he could express verbally his care and empathy for her deep despair, but say little about her sitting on the floor next to him or her touching him; (4) he could get down on the floor with her and embrace her while speaking warmly to her; or (5) he could act with some combination or variation on any of these responses. Though a therapist might rationalize a return embrace, arguing that it represents a genuine, caring response, responses of this kind clearly enter a danger zone that could set a collision course for blatant misconduct later.

The point is that however active patients may be in the direction of therapy, the burden falls upon therapists by virtue of their training and expertise to recognize and deal well with patient behaviors that could become counter-therapeutic. Indeed, the therapist is also responsible to recognize the thoughts and feelings within him- or herself that could become counter-therapeutic.

In the field of law, the term *fiduciary* is used to refer to those people in a society who are, because of special expertise or knowledge, typically accorded special authority by others. It is assumed that such people have special obligations to act in good faith toward those who put their trust in them (Feldman-Summers, 1987). Feldman-Summers has suggested that the mental health profession would do well to see itself as fitting the definition of a fiduciary and to understand that "even with the strongest feelings on the part of the client, sexual contact is unlikely to occur in the absence of a willing fiduciary" (Feldman-Summers, 1987, p. 203).

Diana Garland (Garland and Garland, 2007), dean of the School of Social Work at Baylor University, writes that the abuse of power is really an age-old problem. In the book *Flawed Families of the Bible: How God's Grace Works through Imperfect Relationships*, Garland uses the biblical story of David and Bathsheba to illustrate the abuse of power, in particular, sexual abuse. She argues that the gist of the biblical narrative is that the abuse was David's responsibility and that Bathsheba was essentially a victim of rape because of the power differential between her and David—she could not give consent.

OTHER TYPES OF ABUSE OF POWER

Sexual misconduct is not the only means by which therapists abuse their power. Any circumstance in which the therapist takes undue advantage of the patient or another person may be seen as an abuse of power.

In addition to sexual misconduct the APA Code describes a number of other circumstances that represent abuse of power. Like others, therapists can be guilty of sexual or other forms of harassment of patients, employees or other people. They can be guilty of discrimination toward people who are different from themselves. Therapists sometimes misuse their influence by allowing their name and professional standing to be used in an effort to endorse a commercial product whose clinical effectiveness is unknown. Therapists sometimes exploit persons over whom they have authority (American Psychological Association, 2002, 3.02, 3.01, 5.01, and 3.08).

In his book *Against Therapy*, Masson (1994) argues that all therapy is inherently abusive, no matter how altruistic it may appear. He believes that the very fact that therapists make their income from the emotional pain and suffering of others sets up an unavoidably unequal relationship that is certain to lead to problems. While some would agree that there are always dangers of abuse in therapeutic relationships, most would disagree that all therapy necessarily results in abuses of power.

Increasingly, however, writers are raising questions about the probability of abuse of power that may be inherent in certain forms of psychotherapy. For example, writers have expressed concern about the propensity for abuse in strategic therapy (Doherty, 1989; Solovey & Duncan, 1992) and hypnotherapy (Masson, 1994).

Doherty (1989) points out that strategic family therapists sometimes use deception in an effort to move families toward a desired end in the therapy. A therapist using a paradoxical intervention, for example, might prescribe that a "resistant" client do the opposite of what he really wanted the client to do, hoping that the client would then do the desired behavior. Or a therapist attempting to move a family to carry out a behavior might say that several other professionals recommended such an intervention when in fact the therapist had not consulted any other professionals. Proponents argue that such deception is appropriate when attempting to overcome blocks to progress, so long as the therapist is not purposefully trying to take advantage of the clients and the intervention is intended to lead the clients toward a therapeutic end (the ends justify the means).

Critics counter that deceiving clients, even if the client never becomes aware of the deception, "undermines one of the cornerstones of the therapist/client relationship—trustworthiness" (Doherty, 1989). Further, deception allows the therapist to exert power over someone who has voluntarily surrendered much of their power by revealing to the therapist their innermost feelings, thoughts and secrets.

Most of these critics would admit that not all clients come to therapy in such a passive, revealing way and that many clients do resist open, transparent therapeutic intervention even when ostensibly they claim they want change. Most would also agree that some "passive concealment" (Doherty, 1989) of therapist impressions and directions may be necessary if, in the therapist's best judgment, the client is not ready to deal with these impressions. Still, they would argue that frequent use of deception "in the patient's best interest" can set up a kind of paternalistic relationship between therapist and client in which therapists think they have the power to unilaterally decide what is best for clients.

Questions about hypnosis as a manipulative technique have been raised for years. The more obvious questions have to do with whether clients under hypnotherapy can be led to do things against their will. Traditionally hypnotherapists have argued that clients cannot be led to do things that they truly do not wish to do or that go against their values (King, 1990).

More complicated are the indirect approaches to hypnosis such as Erick-sonian hypnosis. In these approaches trance and suggestions are accomplished in much less obvious ways. For example, the therapist may paradoxically induce a trance by suggesting verbally that the patient might wish to fight the trance, but then making indirect suggestions and providing a therapeutic environment that subtly encourages the patient to go into a trance.

The power of hypnosis to manipulate will likely be debated for years to come. Surely some therapeutic approaches are more likely to be misused than others. But such arguments may miss the most important issue. Perhaps the greatest danger for abuse in hypnosis, strategic therapy or any other therapeutic technique for that matter lies not primarily in the therapeutic technique itself as in the person of the therapist and to some extent that of the client. We have already seen how some types of patients are more susceptible to sexual abuse than others. Surely there are some patients who are more open to abuse in hypnotherapy, and in all probability many of them are the same patients who are most open to sexual abuse. In the same way, as we will see, there are certain types of therapists who are more likely to abuse their patients sexually, and at least some of these may be the same types who would abuse their patients in hypnotherapy, strategic therapy or some other therapeutic modality.

THE ABUSING THERAPIST

Who are the therapists who are most likely to abuse patients sexually? In 1986 Pope, Keith-Spiegel, and Tabachnick surveyed 575 psychologists and found that 95% of the men and 76% of the women acknowledged having been sexually attracted to their patients, on occasion. While most therapists would consider feelings of sexual attraction to patients normal, acting on those feelings is recognized as harmful and an abuse of the therapist's power. Pope (1987) warns that the therapist who doesn't acknowledge and examine his sexual feelings toward patients "blocks its therapeutic potential and unleashes its destructive effects" (p. 150).

In an attempt to learn more about those who become sexually involved, Butler and Zelen (1977) performed a study that found therapists who sexually abuse had a mean age of 43.5 and that they were needy or lonely at the time that the sexual contact occurred. A number of these therapists had recently become separated or divorced. As a group, they were generally well-trained, private-practice clinicians.

Zelen (1985) concludes, "It might possibly be assumed that the therapists shifted the sources of gratification to their patients during these vulnerable or needy periods of time" (p. 182). He also observed that the therapists experienced few unrewarding or punishing consequences. Butler (1975) reported that 95% of therapists surveyed felt conflict and guilt about what they had done, yet most continued their sexual-acting out. Rationalization was frequently used, such as their desire to help the patient feel she was an attractive and desirable woman.

In 2003 Lamb, Catanzaro, and Moorman surveyed psychologists about sexual relationships with clients, supervisees and students. They found that 3.5% admitted to such a relationship, and they asked these psychologists to reflect on their experience. The most frequent occurrence was between a male psychologist and a female client, and was usually initiated after therapy. In a number of cases the therapy was discontinued so the sexual relationship could proceed. As found before, the violating psychologist was usually experiencing some stress or dissatisfaction in his personal life. Often, they appeared to rationalize that there would be no harm to the other party in proceeding with the relationship. The sexual relationship typically did not last very long and one-half said "that 'all and all' the relationship was not worth having."

CATEGORIES OF ABUSING THERAPISTS

Gabbard (1994) offers insights from his years of clinical practice at the Menninger Clinic, where he has treated a number of sexually abusing therapists. He offers the following broad categories of abusing therapists: (1) psychotic disorders, (2) predatory psychopathy and paraphilias, (3) lovesickness and (4) masochistic surrender.

1. Psychotic disorders. This is the smallest group and includes bipolar disorder, paranoid psychosis, schizophrenia and organic brain syndromes. These therapists usually require pharmacotherapy and often vocational counseling to steer them away from their careers as therapists.

2. Predatory psychopathy and paraphilias. Here Gabbard (1994) includes antisocial personalities and severe narcissistic personalities with antisocial features. Most of these offenders are male and have been involved with many female patients during their practice. They are refractory to rehabilitation and are highly skilled at manipulating the legal system to avoid consequences for their behavior. When caught, they often appear remorseful and claim they were in love with the patient. In reality, the patient is only an object for their gratification and their poor superego development keeps them from feeling true guilt or remorse.

3. Lovesickness. Gabbard (1994) sees most therapists who become sexually involved with their patients as being predatory or lovesick. Sixty-five percent of therapists who sexually abuse claim to be in love with their patient (Gartrell et al., 1986). These therapists have a strong need to be loved and idealized by the patient. They use the patient to boost their own self-esteem. Gabbard writes that the most frequent scenario is the middle-aged male therapist who, while in the midst of his marital or family crisis or loss, falls in love with his younger female patient. Such therapists often begin to share their own problems and needs, activating a role reversal which may lead to sexual involvement. Gabbard writes: "Both therapist and patient are refinding forbidden objects from the past, and the therapist colludes in an enactment rather than interpreting the unconscious wish to repeat past trauma, all under the guise of 'true love'" (p. 128).

Some of Gabbard's (1994) additional observations about therapist dynamics include:

- Therapist sees the patient's wish for maternal nurturance as a sexual overture.
- Belief that love is curative for the patient.
- Both patient and therapist have interlocking rescue fantasies.
- Sexual involvement as a manic defense against grieving at the end of therapy.
- Therapist feels this relationship is so special it's an exception to ethics.
- Validation of masculine identity.
- Female therapist who believes her love will settle down the "rowdy" man.
- Anger with patient's lack of progress leads them to cover over their anger with "love."

4. Masochistic surrender. Here Gabbard (1994) describes the therapist with masochistic tendencies who allows himself to be intimidated and controlled by the patient. The patient's increasing demands on the therapist have power because the therapist fears the patient will commit suicide if the various demands are not met. Oftentimes, setting limits to the patient feels sadistic on the part of the therapist. The therapist feels tormented, becomes angry, then feels guilty about being or showing some anger toward the patient. Out of this guilt the therapist may succumb to sexual demands. These therapists, unlike the lovesick, "are not in love with their patient and often feel they are being 'dragged down' by the patient" (p. 133). They often feel tremendous guilt after the sexual experience and some have turned themselves in to their licensing board.

Gorkin (1985) is another analyst who has written about the therapist's vulnerability to a demanding patient. He believes that the patient is really attempting to merge and form the symbiotic relationship with her therapist that she lacked with her mother. Such a sexualized relationship would bring instant utopia and dispense with the tough work of dealing with hostility and grief. When the patient realizes that the relationship is not permanent, she may be engulfed with rage and abandonment feelings so familiar from childhood.

Claman (1987) writes from the perspective of self-psychology about the therapist who did not have adequate mirroring during his early development. He has missed the experience of having the supportive and proud mother watch him and empathize with his excitement as he individuates. Kohut and Wolf (1977) write, "With mirror hunger as the underlying psychodynamic, the therapist falls in love with his mirroring self-object, rather than with the patient as a separate and individual person" (p. 414). He can't see the patient's idealization of him as a childlike or infantile need.

ANALYTIC/PSYCHODYNAMIC CONCEPT OF ENACTMENT

Plakun (1999), an analytic psychiatrist, applies the dynamic of enactment as a way of understanding and preventing sexual misconduct by the therapist. He defines enactment:

> One might think of enactment as a multistep process in which, first, there is the usual "reenactment" in the transference relationship on part of the patient's conflicted or traumatic past. . . . [T]he patient's associated unconscious

self experience is next disavowed and projected in to the therapist. Again, this is familiar terrain for dynamically oriented clinicians. Enactment begins to become a unique concept, though, when the therapist then participates unwittingly by projecting back into the patient reciprocal and complementary unconscious conflicted counter-transference material from the therapist's own life history. The therapist unwittingly colludes with the patient in a process of mutual and complementary projective identification organized around significant past events from the lives of both participants. (p. 286)

Plakun's view is the therapeutic relationship is complicated and rich with potential healing and potential pitfalls. To quote Plakun again:

The ideal technique in therapy is not even to avoid enactments—as if one could. In an endeavor as complex as psychotherapy, enactments that put therapist and patient on a slippery slope are as inevitable a part of the work as a slippery snow-covered slope is to the endeavor of skiing. In fact, in both situations the trick is to learn to use the dynamics of the slippery slope to help get to the bottom of things. (p. 287)

He recommends more education in graduate school/residency on sexual misconduct regardless of the theoretical orientation, since clinicians from analysts to cognitive behaviorists are vulnerable to mismanagement of enactments.

APPROPRIATE RESPONSES TO ALLEGED ABUSERS

What should a conscientious Christian mental health professional do when confronted with allegations that another therapist has been engaged in sexual misconduct? The case at the beginning of this chapter illustrates a situation in which rumors are present in the community at large. In that case Dr. Fairfax attempts to respond in a manner closely akin to the one laid down in Matthew 18:15-17. He approaches Dr. Malpractice one-to-one in an effort to present the rumor to him privately before taking other steps. As admirable as this approach is, it should be noted that in such a sensitive area attempts by a well-meaning fellow professional to confront personally can backfire if the alleged perpetrator becomes enraged and seeks revenge.

Moreover, most professionals probably become aware of alleged sexual misconduct not from rumors but from clients who report that they have been abused by previous therapists. In these cases Ford (2006, p. 280) asserts that the allegations are too serious to be dealt with on a one-to-one basis. According to him, the conscientious psychologist will do best to follow the prescriptions of section 1.05 of the APA code (2002) and section H.2.c. of the ACA code (2005), which recommend that the therapist should report the alleged "violation to an appropriate authority, such as a state licensing board or institutional authorities, . . . provided the reporting would not violate a client's confidentiality" (Ford, 2006, p .115).

Therapists should also understand that certain states have specific procedures to follow when a patient reports sexual misconduct by a previous therapist. In some states, therapists are required to report the incident to a particular state agency. In California, therapists are required to give the patient a copy of a state-published booklet titled *Professional Therapy Never Includes Sex* (available from www.bbs.ca.gov/pdf/publications/proftherapy .pdf). This booklet educates the patient about sexual misconduct and provides information about the reporting process.

The therapist whose client reports past sexual misconduct by another professional is faced sometimes with competing responsibilities. On the one hand the therapist needs to take the report seriously and respond in a manner consistent with the reporting standards in his or her jurisdiction. At the same time, the therapist must also focus on the therapeutic issues involved. Patients who have been abused by another therapist have been hurt, and the therapist who focuses only on reporting issues without being sensitive to the client's needs may inadvertently and unintentionally hurt the client again.

REHABILITATION OF ABUSING THERAPISTS

Pioneering work in the rehabilitation of abusing therapists at the Walk-In Counseling Center in Minneapolis has been described by Gartrell et al. (1988). Here therapists are assessed at the request of licensing boards or agencies. The therapist must fully acknowledge their sexual involvement and cooperate with the evaluation and treatment. They are usually quite motivated to do so in order to preserve their licenses and maintain their careers. Part of the assessment process is to interview the key people involved, if need be, such as the victim, supervisors, colleagues, employers or family members. After interviews and psychological testing, treatment recommendations are made. Therapists with sociopathic features may receive a recommendation to change careers. Others may receive practice restrictions such as no individual therapy with the opposite gender. It is usually up to the employer or agency to monitor the treatment plan and restrictions. If the therapist does not comply with the treatment plan or if the agency suspects the therapist may be in danger of abusing patients again, they must report him or her to their state licensing board or ethics committee.

Pope (1987) reviewed the literature searching for principles of therapy to treat abusing therapists and found nothing. He presents a hypothetical case of a therapist who comes for psychotherapy because of his strong attraction to a female patient. Pope encouraged the therapist to sign a "no sexual acting-out contract." He also assigned readings about the normalcy of sexual attraction and about the issue of sexual intimacy with patients.

Pope puts great emphasis on the therapist reading first-person accounts by victims of their abuse in therapy (Freeman and Roy, 1976; Plasil, 1985; Walker & Young, 1986). These accounts are sobering and helpful in preventing acting out. Pope also uses some conditioning "thought-stopping" techniques to deal with obsessive fantasies. Another part of the treatment is positive imagery or rehearsal on how to work effectively with the particular patient.

Pope (1989) believes rehabilitation should offer four procedures:

- *Establish a coordinator.* Separate from the therapist, an accountability person is needed who has access to all the information.

- *Distinguish between rehabilitative and therapeutic tasks.* There should be a rehabilitative specialist who focuses on issues of practice limits, professional attitudes and work setting. There should also be an individual therapist who works with the personal issues of the offending therapist.

- *Identify the appropriate professional to implement rehabilitation.* The coordinator or licensing board, which may be the same, should identify competent people for the two roles noted above. These two individuals should not have any prior professional, business or personal relationship with the offending therapist, and they must be knowledgeable about therapist-patient sexual involvements.

- *Evaluate the success of rehabilitation.* There should be another professional who can objectively evaluate the results of the rehabilitation. The rehabilitation specialist and the treating therapist should both submit reports to the coordinator for evaluation by an objective professional.

In 2007 Andrea Celenza wrote a wide-ranging book on sexual-boundary violations by therapists titled *Sexual Boundary Violations: Therapeutic, Supervisory, and Academic Contexts.* She writes that the abusing therapist makes the mistake of seeing the patient's transference as real. The erotic relationship sustains positive, idealizing feelings in the patient, which meets the narcissistic needs of the therapist. Coming from a psychoanalytic perspective and well-aware of the forensic issues, Celenza believes therapists who have committed sexual misconduct have been stereotyped as "bad therapists" worthy of banishment from the field. Aside from the psychopathic or sociopathic violators, she has treated many such therapists and believes most can be rehabilitated. She sees the typical offender as a middle-aged man with longstanding narcissistic vulnerabilities who has had a sexual involvement with one patient and is remorseful. They frequently have these precursors to their misconduct:

- intolerance of negative transference
- unresolved anger toward authority figures
- family history of covert but sanctioned boundary violations

Empathy training as part of the rehabilitation program for therapists guilty of sexual misconduct is addressed by Regehr and Glancy (2001). In addition to addressing the therapist's cognitive awareness of how their misconduct has hurt the client, Regehr and Glancy empathize with how the therapist feels victimized and devastated careerwise by being reported and disciplined. This empathy can help them understand better how the client has been victimized and damaged. They also focus on helping the therapist be more self-aware of their needs and feelings so they can manage their needs and feelings in appropriate ways in the future.

Celenza is an advocate for developing better ways for vulnerable therapists to get help or supervision without the fear of legal or board sanctions. As previously noted however, most ethics codes encourage reporting suspected offenders.

There is of course controversy in the field about whether offending therapists should ever be allowed to practice again. Those who favor terminating the therapist's privilege to practice argue that there is little data to support the efficacy of any rehabilitation program. They believe that the threat of recidivism is too great and potentially too harmful to the victims to ever allow an offending professional the right to provide services to hurting patients again (Layman & McNamara, 1997). Those who favor rehabilitation and ongoing supervision of offenders point to the fact that one unexpected outcome of stripping therapists of their licenses is that they sometimes surface again providing services to the public in some unregulated field such as life coaching or spiritual direction, and begin their pattern of abuse again with little or no recourse available to their victims.

Prevention

Strasburger, Jorgenson and Sutherland (1992) have written on prevention, stressing the point that certain types of nonsexual boundary violations almost always precede sexual contact. They list as examples the following: (1) scheduling a favorite patient as the last of the day so more time can be spent, (2) excessive telephone conversations with the patient, (3) extended sessions, (4) laxity with fees, (5) excessive self-disclosure, (6) meetings arranged outside the office, (7) asking the patient to perform work at the therapist's home or office, and (8) exchanging gifts. Any of these behaviors may cause detrimental effects on the therapy and they are warning signs of escalating boundary violations.

A number of other authors have offered suggestions for preventing therapist-patient sexual involvement:

1. Graduate schools could do a better job of screening therapist candidates if they are familiar with personalities prone to be offenders (Pope & Bouhoutsos, 1986).

2. Herlihy and Corey (1992) proposed that first-year graduate students be exposed to the topic of sexual relationships, followed by more emphasis in their ethics course, then further addressed in field placements and internships.

3. Graduate schools should have strict regulations about faculty and super-

visors not being romantically involved with students. Research has indicated that these students are more at risk of becoming sexually involved with a client later (Glaser & Thorpe, 1986).

4. Agencies and employers should strictly prohibit sexual intimacies of therapists with patients. They should evaluate "the risk factor" when hiring new therapists (Pope & Bouhoutsos, 1986).

5. Professional organizations should take an active role in educating members about the problem and informing them how to have their patients report past therapists who were sexually abusive. Such an organization might also develop a rehabilitation program for therapists (Pope & Bouhoutsos, 1986).

6. State consumer affairs departments could require therapists to display a sign that states that sexual contact is unethical and never a part of therapy (Bouhoutsos, 1985).

7. State licensing boards that have the responsibility for governing entry into the professions might begin requiring an oral ethics interview which covers the area of sexual intimacies between therapist and patient (Pope & Bouhoutsos, 1986).

8. Counselors need to utilize supervision or discussion with colleagues to help them reflect on ways they may be getting their needs met through their clients (Pope, Sonne & Holroyd, 1993).

CURRENT STATE OF SEXUAL ETHICS TRAINING

Housman and Stake (2008) report a recent study of graduate students' knowledge regarding sexual ethics. In it they found that

1. Seven percent did not know that sex with current clients is prohibited.

2. Thirty-four percent did not know that sex was still prohibited after transfer or termination of the client.

3. Sixty-eight percent did not know that sexual feelings for clients are normal and not unethical.

These results were disappointing since it was believed there had been more emphasis on sexual ethics training in recent years. The authors recommend supervision as the place where students can potentially learn more about boundary violations and how to handle their own sexual feelings toward clients. However, the survey also indicated that some supervisors didn't provide a supportive atmosphere that encouraged openness about sexual issues. The authors suggest that supervisors need to convey this kind of acceptance and yet model appropriate boundaries for their supervisees. They also recommended that directors of training programs need to see that students are exposed early to sexual ethics training and that the director should have a method to assess the effectiveness of such ethics training.

What was the training experience of clinicians who feel they were prepared to deal with sexual feelings in therapy? This was the focus of a study by Paxton, Lovett and Riggs (2001). After a survey to clinical faculty members, they summarized that those who had specific ethics coursework on dealing with sexual feelings in therapy and those who had supervisors who considered it normal for sexual attraction to surface during therapy felt best prepared to deal with this issue.

In a 2004 article Fisher examined the question of whether it might ever be appropriate or therapeutic for the therapist who has sexual feelings for a client to disclose those feelings to the client. Studies across mental health disciplines indicate that 70-90% of therapists admit to having had sexual feelings for at least one client. However, most studies on prevalence reveal that roughly 5-10% have ever disclosed such feelings to a client and that many therapists question the ethics of such sharing (Blanchard & Lichtenberg, 1998; McMinn & Meek, 1996; Nickell et al., 1995; Pope & Tabachnick, 1994; Pope et al., 1987; Stake & Oliver, 1991). According to case studies about therapists sharing their feelings of sexual attraction, clients reacted with horror, rage and disgust (Davies, 1994; Slavin et al., 1998).

While the APA ethics code does not have a specific rule against a therapists telling his or her client about sexual attraction, Fisher notes that other ethics principles are related: do no harm, sexual harassment, multiple relationships and informed consent. He addresses how each of these may be violated with this kind of therapist disclosure. Fisher's recommendations are summarized by saying that therapists need to be fully aware of the possible harm done by disclosing their sexual feelings for a client and should get supervision or therapy to avert hurting their clients or themselves.

CONCLUSION

This chapter has examined how counselors might abuse their power in the counseling relationship, and in particular has presented sexual misconduct as one very damaging abuse of power. It is alarming that many of those involved in sexual misconduct have been fully trained and licensed mental health professionals who knew better. Yet somehow the intellectual knowledge of simply knowing better did not prevent abuse of power when it was competing with strong emotional issues or character traits not adequately addressed by personal psychotherapy, spiritual growth and supervision. Both professional ethical standards and our Christian ethics direct the responsibility back to us as counselors to know ourselves, resolve our issues and become more aware of and responsible with the power and influence that we have.

REFERENCES

American Counseling Association. (2005). *Code of ethics*. Alexandria, VA: Author.

American Psychological Association. (2002). Ethical principles of psychologists and code of conduct. *American Psychologist, 57*, 1060-73. Also available (with 2010 amendments) from www.apa.org/ethics/code/index.aspx.

Baylis, F. (1993). Therapist-patient sexual contact: a non consensual, inherently harmful activity. *Canadian Journal of Psychiatry, 38*, 502-7.

Belote, B. (1974). *Sexual intimacy between female clients and male therapists: Masochistic sabotage*. Unpublished doctoral dissertation, California School of Professional Psychology, Berkeley.

Borys, D. S., & Pope, K. S. (1989). Dual relationships between therapists and client: a national survey of psychologists, psychiatrists, and social workers. *Professional Psychology: Research and Practice, 20*, 283-93.

Bouhoutsos, J. C. (1985). Therapist-client sexual involvement: A challenge for mental health professionals and educators. *American Journal of Ortho-psychiatry, 55*, 177-82.

Bouhoustsos, J. C., Holroyd, J., Lerman, H., Forer, B. R., & Greenberg, M. (1983). Sexual intimacy between psychotherapists and patients. *Professional Psychology: Research and Practice, 14*, 185-96.

Butler, S. (1975) *Sexual contact between therapists and patients*. Unpublished doctoral dissertation, California School of Professional Psychology, Los Angeles.

Butler, S., & Zelen, S. (1977). Sexual intimacies between psychotherapists and their patients. *Psychotherapy: Theory, Research, and Practice, 139*, 143-44.

Celenza, A. (1991). The misuse of countertransference love in sexual intimacies between therapists and patients. *Psychoanalytic Psychology, 8*, 501-9.

Celenza, A. (2007) *Sexual boundary violations: Therapeutic, supervisory, and academic contexts*. Lanham, MD: Rowman & Littlefield.

Chesler, P. (1972). *Women and madness*. New York: Avon Books.

Claman, J. M. (1987). Mirror hunger in the psychodynamics of sexually abusing therapists. *The American Journal of Psychoanalysis, 47*, 35-40.

Davies, J. M. (1994). Love in the afternoon, a relational reconsideration of desire and dread in the countertransference. *Psychoanalytic Dialogues, 4*, 153-70.

Doherty, W. J. (March/April, 1989). Unmasking family therapy. *Networker*, 35-39.

Feldman-Summers, S. (1987). Sexual contact in fiduciary relationships. In S. Fairbairn & G. Fairbairn (Eds.), *Psychology, ethics and change* (pp. 115-27). London: Routledge & Kegan Paul.

Feldman-Summers, S., & Jones, G. (1984). Psychological impacts of sexual contact between therapists, other health care professionals and their clients. *Journal of Consulting and Clinical Psychology, 52*, 1054-61.

Fisher, C. D. (2004). Ethical issues in therapy: Therapist self-disclosure of sexual feelings. *Ethics and Behavior, 14*, 105-21.

Freeman, L., & Roy, J. (1976). *Betrayal*. New York: Stein & Day.

Gabbard, G. O. (1994). Psychotherapists who transgress sexual boundaries with patients. *Bulletin of the Menninger Clinic, 58*, 124-35.

Garland, D. E., & Garland, D. R. (2007). *Flawed families of the Bible: How God's grace works through imperfect relationships*. Grand Rapids: Brazos Press.

Gartrell, N., Herman, J., Olarte, S., Feldstein, M., & Localio, R. (1986). Psychiatrist-patient sexual contact: Results of a national survey, I: Prevalence. *American Journal of Psychiatry, 143*, 1126-31.

Gartrell, N., Herman, J., Olarte, S., Feldstein, M., & Localio, R. (1988). Management and rehabilitation of sexually exploitive therapists. *Hospital & Community Psychiatry, 39*, 1070-74.

Gechtman, L. (1989). Sexual contact between social workers and their clients. In B. O. Gabbard (Ed.), *Sexual exploitation in professional relationships* (pp. 27-38). Washington, DC: American Psychiatric Press.

Glaser, R. D., & Thorpe, J. S. (1986). Unethical intimacy: A survey of sexual contact and advances between psychology educators and female graduate students. *American Psychologist, 41*, 43-51.

Gorkin, M. (1985). Varieties of sexualized countertransference. *Psychoanalytic Review, 72*, 424-40.

Gutheil, T. G. (1989). Borderline personality disorder, boundary violations, and patient-therapist sex: Medicolegal pitfall. *American Journal of Psychiatry, 146*, 597-602.

Herlihy, B., & Corey, G. (1992). *Dual relationships in counseling.* Alexandria, VA: American Association for Counseling & Development.

Hoffman, R. M. (1995). Sexual dual relationships in counseling: Confronting the issues. *Counseling and Values, 40*, 15.

Holroyd, J. C., & Bouhoutsos, J. C. (1985). Sources of bias in reporting sexual contact with patients. *Psychotherapy: Research and Practice, 16*, 701-9.

Holroyd, J. C., & Brodsky, A. M. (1977). Psychologists' attitudes and practices regarding erotic and non-erotic physical contact with patients. *American Psychologist, 32*, 843-49.

Housman, L. M., & Stake, J. E. (2008). The current state of sexual ethics training in clinical psychology: Issues of quantity, quality, and effectiveness. In D. N. Bersoff (Ed.), *Ethical conflicts in psychology* (4th ed.) (pp. 250-52). Washington, DC: American Psychological Association.

Jackson, H., & Nuttall, R. (Eds.). (2001). Innovative interventions in the practice of health [Special issue]. *Professional Psychology: Research and Practice, 32*(2).

Kardener, S. H., Fuller, M., & Mensh, I. N. (1973). A survey of physicians' attitudes and practices regarding erotic and non-erotic contact with patients. *American Journal of Psychiatry, 130*, 1077-81.

King, R. R. (1990). Hypnosis. In R. J. Hunter, H. N. Malony, L. O. Mills & J. Patton (Eds.), *Dictionary of pastoral care and counseling* (pp. 562-63). Nashville: Abingdon.

Kohut, H., & Wolf, E. S. (1977). The disorders of the self and their treatment. *International Journal of Psychoanalysis, 59*, 413-25.

Lamb, D. H., Catanzaro, J. J., & Moorman, A. S. (2003). Psychologists reflect on their sexual relationships with clients, supervisees, and students: Occurrence, impact, rationales, and collegial intervention. *Professional Psychology: Research, and Practice, 34*, 102-7.

Layman, M. J., & McNamara, J. R. (1997). Remediation for ethics violations: Focus on psychotherapists' sexual contact with clients. *Professional Psychology, 28*, 281-92.

Masson, J. M. (1994). *Against therapy.* Monroe, ME: Common Courage Press.

McMinn, M. R., & Meek, K. R. (1996). Ethics among Christian counselors: A survey of beliefs and behaviors. *Journal of Psychology and Theology, 24*, 26-37.

McMinn, M. R., & Meek, K. R. (1997). Training programs. In R. K. Sanders (Ed.), *Christian counseling ethics: A handbook for therapists, pastors and counselors* (pp. 277-96). Downers Grove, IL: InterVarsity Press.

Paxton, C., Lovett, J., & Riggs, M. L. (2001). The nature of professional training and perceptions of adequacy in dealing with the sexual feelings in psychotherapy: experiences of clinical faculty. *Ethics and Behavior, 11,* 175-89.

Plakun, E. M. (1999). Sexual misconduct and enactment. *The Journal of Psychotherapy Practice and Research, 8,* 284-91.

Plasil, E. (1985). *Therapist.* New York: St. Martin's/Marek.

Pope, K. S. (1987). Preventing therapist-patient sexual intimacy: Therapy for a therapist at risk. *Professional Psychology: Research and Practice, 18,* 624-28.

Pope, K. S. (1989). Therapists who become sexually intimate with a patient: Classifications, dynamics, recidivism, and rehabilitation. *The Independent Practitioner, 9,* 28-34.

Pope, K. S., & Bouhoutsos, J. C. (1986). *Sexual intimacy between therapists and patients.* New York: Praeger.

Pope, K. S., Keith-Spiegel, P., & Tabachnick, B. G. (1986). Sexual attraction to clients. *American Psychologist, 41,* 147-58.

Pope, K. S., & Sonne, J. L. (1991). Treating victims of therapist-patient sexual involvement. *Psychotherapy, 28,* 1174-87.

Pope, K. S., Sonne, J. L., & Holroyd, J. (1993). *Sexual feelings in psychotherapy: Explorations for therapists and therapists-in-training.* Washington, DC: American Psychological Association.

Pope, K. S., Tabachnick, B. G., & Keith-Spiegel, P. (1987). Ethics of practice: The beliefs and behaviors of psychologists as therapists. *American Psychologist, 42,* 993-1006.

Pope, K. S., & Vetter, V. A. (1991). Prior therapist-patient sexual involvement among patients seen by psychologists. *Psychotherapy, 28,* 429-38.

Regehr, C., & Glancy, G. (2001). Empathy and its influence on sexual misconduct. *Trauma Violence Abuse, 2,* 142-54.

Slavin, J. H., Rahmani, M., & Pollack, L. (1998). Reality and danger in psychoanalytic treatment. *Psychoanalytic Quarterly, 67,* 191-217.

Solovey, A. D., & Duncan, B. L. (1992). Ethics and strategic therapy: A proposed ethical direction. *Journal of Marital and Family Therapy, 18,* 53-61.

Solursh, D. S., Solursh, L. P., & Williams, N. R. (1993). Patient-therapist sex: "Just say no" isn't enough. *Medicine and Law, 12,* 431-38.

Stone, L. G. (1980). *A study of the relationships among anxious attachments, ego functioning, and female patients vulnerability to sexual involvement with their male psychotherapists.* Unpublished doctoral dissertation, California School of Professional Psychology, Los Angeles.

Vinson, J. S. (1987). Use of complaint procedures in cases of therapist-patient sexual contact. *Professional Psychology: Research and Practice, 18*, 159-64.

Walker, E., & Young, T. D. (1986). *A killing cure*. New York: Henry Holt.

Zelen, S. L. (1985). Sexualization of therapeutic relationships: The dual vulnerability of patient and therapist. *Psychotherapy, 22*, 178-85.

Zur, O. (2001). When crossing office boundaries and engaging in dual relationships are clinically beneficial and ethically sound. *Independent Practitioner, 21* , 96-100.

Case studies presented in this article are entirely fictitious. Names of characters are fictitious and any resemblance to persons living or dead is purely coincidental.

6

Nonsexual Multiple Relationships

Randolph K. Sanders

A therapist teaches as an adjunct professor at a university. On the first day of class, he is surprised to see one of his clients seated in the third row.

A psychologist sees a fellow church member for counseling.

A wealthy client is deeply appreciative for the help his therapist has given him. The client knows that the therapist is trying to raise the capital needed to start a group home for troubled young people. The client offers to donate the money needed for the project.

A therapist is seeing a couple for marital counseling and then begins seeing the couple's adolescent son for individual therapy.

A counselor begins seeing his girlfriend's sister in therapy.

Each of the above are examples of multiple relationships.

According to the APA "Code of Ethics" (2002),

A multiple relationship occurs when a psychologist is in a professional role with a person and (1) at the same time is in another role with the person, (2) at the same time is in a relationship with a person closely associated with or related to the person with whom the psychologist has the professional relationship, or (3) promises to enter into another relationship in the future with the person or a person closely associated with or related to the person. (p. 1065)

Whenever therapists find themselves relating to a client or a person closely associated with a client outside of therapy, they are engaging in a multiple relationship. Clearly, a sexual relationship with a client is an example of a multiple relationship. However, as the previous examples and countless others demonstrate, most multiple relationships are nonsexual in nature; what I refer to in this chapter as NSMRs, or more humorously, *close encounters of the* other *kind.* Therapists who do the following are all engaged in multiple relationships.

- provide therapy to a family member
- provide therapy for a relative or close friend of a client
- engage in business with a client
- engage socially with a client no matter how superficially
- sit on a committee or small group with a client
- interact with a client at the grocery store

As these examples suggest, the potential for engaging in, or at least being confronted with, a NSMR in the everyday practice of psychotherapy is really quite high, particularly in settings where people tend to see each other regularly.

All multiple relationships involve a mixing of roles or a *crossing* of boundaries. However, some multiple relationships involve a *violation* of boundaries or a loss of objectivity or effectiveness. The APA code (2002) instructs therapists to refrain

> from entering into a multiple relationship if the multiple relationship could *reasonably* be expected to impair the psychologist's *objectivity, competence or effectiveness* in performing his/her functions as a psychologist, or otherwise risks *exploitation or harm* to the person with whom the professional relationship exists. (p. 1065, emphasis added)

Will the therapist be *objective* if he provides therapy to one of his administrators, a board member or someone else who holds power over him? Will the therapist use all the therapeutic skills (*competence* and *effectiveness*) available to her in dealing with a conflictual issue in therapy if she knows she will be taking part in a four-day church retreat with the client next week?

Outside the question of how the NSMR will effect the therapist's ability to perform as a therapist, the ethics codes are also quite concerned with the ways in which some NSMRs can violate or harm the client. What if the therapist makes an agreement with a carpenter to provide therapy services for the carpenter in return for the carpenter building bookcases in the therapist's home, but when the work is not up to the therapist's expectations, the therapist asks the carpenter to replace the doors on the kitchen cabinets at no extra charge? Consider the therapist whose client is also a student in his or her class at the university. What if the therapist gives the client lower grades in the class because of negative things the client has revealed in therapy?

Note that the ethics code says that therapists should avoid NSMRs that could "reasonably" be expected to do harm or impair the therapist's judgment (APA, 2002, p. 1065). Presumably, the intent of the code makers is to leave the judgment about the rightness or wrongness of an NSMR in the hands of the therapist first, who it is assumed will rely on any or all of the resources at his or her disposal (i.e., ethics codes, experience and precedence, readings, training and education, consultation, supervision) to help in making the decision. Ultimately, if a complaint is filed against the therapist, the question of reasonability will be decided by a jury of the therapist's peers on the state board. All of this highlights the fact that therapists should do a regular review of ethical codes, reflect on individual cases and consult with other professionals when necessary.

NSMRs Not Always Forbidden

The current APA code indicates that NSMRs are not unethical per se. "Multiple relationships that would not *reasonably* be expected to cause impairment or risk exploitation or harm are not unethical" (APA, 2002, p. 1065, italics mine).

The American Counseling Association (ACA) code goes further and states that some NSMRs are "potentially beneficial." The ACA code requires that counselors carefully document (ahead of time, if possible) their rationale for engaging in the NSMR, and if "unintentional harm" occurs as a result of entering into the NSMR, the counselor must be able to show how he or she attempted to remedy the situation (ACA, 2005, A.5.d). These policies of greater acceptance toward engagement in some NSMRs represent the most explicit departure yet from the traditional training lore of the profession which, in the past, had generally discouraged if not forbade almost all NSMRs (Sanders, 2010).

There were various reasons behind this near-blanket opposition to involvement in NSMRs. Some who subscribed to a psychoanalytic therapeutic orientation opposed NSMRs on theoretical grounds (Gutheil & Gabbard, 1993). There should be clear and unwavering boundaries between analyst and client, and the idea of making the participants in the therapeutic alliance anything other than doctor and patient was not to be considered. As Gutheil and Gabbard (1993) point out, however, Sigmund Freud himself was not this rigid in setting boundaries, and was known to have given gifts to patients, sent postcards to patients and shared meals with a patient during a vacation. Moreover there are other therapeutic orientations that actually endorse crossing boundaries and engaging in NSMRs in certain situations (Zur, 2005). For example, cognitive behavior therapies for anxiety sometimes encourage the use of exposure or *in vivo* desensitization sessions that may require that the therapist accompany the client to the feared environment, which in many cases will be a public place.

Another professional line of lore advanced against engaging in NSMRs was the notion of the slippery slope. According to this position, therapists who engaged in nonsexual multiple relationships were at grave risk of proceeding down the slippery slope toward a sexual multiple relationship (Gutheil & Gabbard, 1993; Pope, 1990, p. 688). While not wrong in itself, the NSMR might inevitably lead to behavior clearly forbidden. However, a recent study casts doubt on this assumption, with evidence that therapists who took greater liberties in engaging in NSMRs were not more likely to violate other ethical standards (McCray, McMinn & Meek, 1998). Based on their review, Gottlieb and Younggren (2009) concluded that while slippery-slope situations do occur, they are uncommon.

Finally, some professionals have argued against NSMRs for risk-management reasons. These professionals have pointed out that attorneys and even professional colleagues on state boards sometimes seem unable or unwilling to see the distinction between a harmful NSMR and one that is not. Younggren and Gottlieb (2004) quote one mental health attorney who made the claim at a continuing education workshop that "all dual relationships in psychotherapy are unethical or at least run the risk of getting you in trouble with your licensing board." While this attorney's statement is not consistent with what ethical codes in the profession actually say, it is cause for concern that a member of the legal profession who claims to be an expert on such matters would make such a remark.

On the other side of the argument are those who make a case for the unavoidability of NSMRs in some cases or who aggressively assert the appropriateness, even positive therapeutic benefits, of multiple relationships in other situations. Regarding the former, it has long been recognized, even among those who usually oppose involvement in NSMRs, that rural therapists frequently cannot avoid involvement in NSMRs. Unlike many urban practitioners, therapists in rural areas frequently encounter clients in other contexts. Their children may be in the same grade at the one elementary school in town, or they may both be engaged in any one of numerous other community, religious, social, business or personal activities that bring people together. Not only is avoiding contact outside therapy often not realistic, but the options for referring to a different therapist are usually quite limited if not nonexistent (Campbell & Gordon, 2003; Hargrove, 1986; Schank & Skovholt, 1997).

In recent years an increasing number of psychotherapists are also speaking out about the unavoidability of NSMRs in settings other than rural ones (see Guthman & Sandberg, 2002; Johnson, Ralph & Johnson, 2005; Kesslen & Wahler, 2005; Kertesz, 2002, for example). Even if they live in cities or urban areas, some therapists serve smaller communities, enclaves or populations within the larger area and cannot avoid all NSMRs. Therapists who work in college or university counseling centers are fixtures on the campus and may encounter their clients in other settings on campus (see Hetzel et al. elsewhere in this volume). Military psychologists in combat zones may be embedded in close proximity to the troops they counsel (Johnson, Ralph & Johnson, 2005).

While the unavoidability of some NSMRs is one thing, there are growing numbers of professionals who argue that engaging in a NSMR can actually be good for therapy. Most well known among these proponents are Arnold Lazarus and Ofer Zur (2002). Zur (2000) describes the traditional prohibition against multiple relationships as "going too far in the right direction." He argues that people sometimes choose a particular therapist precisely because they do know that person, their values and what they stand for, and as a result, they trust them.

Consider, for example, a situation in which a Christian psychologist presents a three-session seminar on Christian parenting at his church. After the seminar, a fellow church member who attended the seminar calls requesting an appointment for help with job stress and anxiety. The psychologist initially tries to dissuade the prospective client, explaining to him about multiple relationships and the possible downsides of their attempting to work together. The prospective client responds by arguing that he is very conservative in his Christian beliefs, and that he has already tried several "secular" therapists in town and felt that their values were too disparate from his own. He indicates that based on attending the parenting seminar and the positive recommendation of several Christian friends, he is certain that he wishes to see the Christian psychologist. After deliberation, the psychologist agrees to see the client and is able to help the client with his anxiety and job stress. At the end of therapy the client expresses sincere appreciation that the psychologist agreed to work with him and says that for the first time in his life he feels good about himself because he has learned skills that help him come closer to following the biblical admonition to "be anxious for nothing" (Phil 4:6 NASB). For Zur, referring such clients out of hand is to risk not only alienating them but impeding them from getting the help they need. What's more, he argues that therapists who buy into rigid restrictions against NSMRs are also buying into a model of therapy that tends to isolate the therapist from the outside world, and actually increases the risk that the therapist might exploit or harm a client presumably in an effort to meet his or her personal needs.

Thus there have been and continue to be a wide range of opinions across the mental health profession about the appropriateness of engaging in NSMRs. For ultimate guidance, it is appropriate to appeal to the current ethics codes themselves, which clearly state that some NSMRs are ethical and others are not. Unfortunately, the stipulations of the ethics codes are sufficiently general that the decision to engage in all but the most obviously inappropriate situations is a judgment call on the part of the therapist.

Perhaps this should be understandable since as Keith-Spiegel and Koocher (1985) have pointed out, "it is probably impossible to create clear guidelines for psychologists with regard to dual-role relationships not involving sexual intimacy, since each situation presents unique features which must be considered" (p. 267).

THE PREVALENCE OF NSMRs IN ACTUAL PRACTICE

Whatever one believes about the appropriateness of engaging in NSMRs, the data reveal that in actual practice the occurrence of at least some types of NSMRs is not uncommon. In a study surveying the incidence of NSMRs in rural and urban settings, Helbok, Marinelli, and Walls (2006) found that while the incidence of NSMRs was certainly higher in rural areas, it was relatively frequent in urban areas as well, at least with regard to certain behaviors. For example, 29.5% of their rural sample and 18.4% of their urban sample had provided therapy to a client who they knew from being in the same social sphere. Moreover, 40.7% of their rural sample and 25.2% of their urban sample had provided therapy to a relative of an ongoing client.

CHRISTIAN SETTINGS

NSMRs also appear to be more common among therapists who work in Christian settings or who provide Christian therapy (McMinn & Meek, 1997; Sanders, Swenson & Schneller, 2011). A recent survey by Sanders, Schneller and Swenson (2011) found that among the licensed Christian therapists sampled, about 58% believed that it was generally appropriate to provide therapy to a member of one's church with whom one seldom had contact or to attend the same church as a client. Some 43% of the sample believed that it was appropriate to join the same community organization as a former client, and 21% believed that it was often appropriate to attend a client's special event, such as a wedding or graduation. The study found that therapists who worked in church-based settings were much more likely to engage in nonsexual multiple relationships than were Christian therapists who worked in other settings (private practices, university counseling centers, etc.).

Having said this, it is important to add that the survey sample, like a previous sample (Oordt, 1997), was aware of and sensitive to the dangers involved in some NSMRs. For example, the sample overwhelmingly avoided NSMRs that involved the mixing of business, commerce or finances with therapy, and the sample seemed to be able to differentiate between doing therapy with someone from their church that the therapist knows well, versus seeing someone from the church that the therapist rarely has any contact with (Sanders, Swenson & Schneller, 2011).

The fact that engagement in NSMRs is not uncommon among licensed Christian therapists should not be surprising when one considers that, like rural communities, religious communities are often close-knit enclaves where members of the communities' lives frequently intersect. Indeed, it can be argued that one of the strengths of religious communities is that, contrary to the individualistic cultures so prominent in Western cultures, religious communities generally value and encourage the close, personal support that comes from frequent interaction with others with similar values.

A Christian psychotherapist who is active in a particular church or denomination is likely to have clients who seek the therapist out precisely because he or she is a member of that order and shares the common worldview. To avoid doing therapy with all of these people because of multiple relationship concerns will undoubtedly be misunderstood by many prospective clients and might cause some to forgo needed therapy altogether.

Consider also the Christian therapist who serves on staff at a particular church, counseling the members of that church exclusively. Such a therapist, particularly if he or she is also a member of the church and considered part of the ministry, will likely have some type of multiple relationship, however slight, with nearly every client seen in the church (Sanders, Swenson & Schneller, 2011). Such church-based therapists are not unlike Navy psychologists who are embedded onboard large aircraft carriers and assigned to attend to the mental health needs of the crew (Johnson, Ralph & Johnson, 2005). Such therapists find that interactions with client crew members outside therapy are simply unavoidable.

This is not to say that Christian therapists do not struggle with ethical dilemmas brought on by practicing in such close quarters. Indeed in our survey the Christian therapists polled indicated that NSMRs represented the most frequent ethical dilemma they faced in practice. Almost twice as many respondents listed multiple relationships their most frequent ethical dilemma as compared to those who listed confidentiality (Sanders, Swenson & Schneller, 2011).

Consider these cases that illustrate the kinds of NSMR dilemmas that Christian therapists or therapists in Christian settings could encounter.

Case 1. A Christian therapist in private practice begins seeing a member of her church who is struggling with depression and unresolved hurts from childhood. Several weeks into therapy, the client begins attending a small Bible study group that the therapist also attends. Feeling quite safe in the therapist's presence at the Bible study, the client begins to treat the study as if it were a kind of group therapy, revealing much more of herself and her past than the other members, and triggering discomfort among the other study members. The client reacts with hurt and disgust at being "shunned" by the group members and "abandoned" by her therapist, who did not "do more" to come to her aid in the Bible study.

Case 1 illustrates how misunderstandings and hurt can sometimes take place when Christian therapists interact with their clients in different settings. This can be true whether the therapist is a private practitioner whose practice includes a focus on clients in a particular religious group with which he or she is affiliated, or perhaps even more so, if the therapist is employed in a church-based counseling center. Might the therapist in this case have avoided the negative outcome if at the next session after the client first attended the Bible study, she had discussed sensitively the possible pros and cons of the two of them attending the same study?

Case 2. A church hires a therapist as a staff counselor. There are no other therapists on staff. Several months into the position the therapist is approached by the pastor, who asks him to see his wife for "nervousness." Upon seeing the pastor's wife for an evaluation, the therapist finds that rather than an anxiety disorder, the pastor's wife appears to be suffering from major depression. Furthermore, she is very unhappy with the marriage and there seems to be abundant evidence that her depression erupted after the marriage turned increasingly rancorous.

Case 2 illustrates the fact that church-based therapists sometimes encounter NSMR dilemmas that pose real or potential conflicts between themselves and the sponsoring religious body or leadership over role expectations (Lukens, 1997). In this case the therapist is asked by his boss, the pastor, to see the pastor's wife in therapy. Therapists who seek employment in church-based counseling centers should obtain clarification in advance from their employers regarding role expectations, and seek to educate employers where necessary about role conflicts and the inherent dangers in some NSMRs.

NSMRs: SUMMARIZING WHAT WE KNOW

In review of what has been said thus far, we can say the following about the ethics of NSMRs. At one time, involvement in NSMRs was almost universally frowned upon by the profession, with the single exception of therapists working in rural settings. While engaging in multiple relationships remains controversial among some therapists, the profession as a whole is moving in the direction of accepting NSMRs as ethical so long as they do not exploit or harm the client, and that they do not impair the objectivity or effectiveness of the therapist. Moreover, there is increasing awareness that NSMRs can sometimes be advantageous to positive therapeutic outcomes. Recent renditions of ethics codes have done a good job of trying to codify these more recent understandings, but it must be understood that providing any more than general guidelines is difficult since there are so many different varieties of NSMR situations.

Accumulating survey research has confirmed that the incidence of NSMRs, despite previous proscriptions against them, are not that rare even in nonrural areas (Helbok, Marinelli & Walls, 2006). Perhaps because of the close-knit nature of devout religious communities, the incidence of NSMRs is particularly prevalent among Christian therapists, especially those who work in church-based settings (McMinn & Meek, 1996, 1997; Sanders, Swenson & Schneller, 2011).

All NSMRs represent a boundary crossing, but not all are boundary violations. As previous research (McCray, McMinn & Meek, 1998) has pointed out, NSMRs don't necessarily lead down the slippery slope toward sexual MRs.

Finally, a growing body of anecdotal evidence brings us to the conclusion that NSMRs should almost always be avoided in some situations, but that NSMRs can be quite beneficial to therapy in other situations (Zur, 2000).

The question that every therapist faces is how best to determine whether to enter into an NSMR with a client or not.

NSMRs: To Engage or Not to Engage

Over the years several models have been proposed for helping therapists decide whether to engage in a NSMR (Anderson & Kitchener, 1998; Gottlieb, 1993; Kitchener, 1988; Koocher & Keith-Spiegel, 2008; Younggren & Gottlieb, 2004). However, to declare that any model can provide hard and fast rules for any but the most obvious situations is unrealistic, since there are often many nuanced variables to consider.

Having said this, the responsible therapist will be clear about what NSMRs are, seek to accurately forecast situations in which NSMRs might arise, have a set of guidelines for deciding whether to engage in a NSMR, and strategies for dealing with unexpected or unavoidable NSMRs. In the passages that follow, I seek to provide self-assessment questions for therapists pondering whether to engage in a NSMR. However, prior to offering the questions, I will set forth several assumptions that underlie the self-assessment.

Assumptions

- All NSMRs represent a boundary *crossing* but not all are a boundary *violation.*

- NSMRs are not as uncommon as previously supposed, and most do not lead to ethical infractions.

- NSMRs should almost always be avoided in certain situations (e.g., business relationships) and with certain patient types (e.g., borderline patients).

- NSMRs that risk exploiting or harming a client are wrong (APA, 2002).

- Therapists should avoid NSMRs where there is good reason to believe that engaging in the NSMR will impair their objectivity, competence or effectiveness (APA, 2002).

- NSMRs can be quite beneficial to therapy in certain situations.

- Sometimes, managing an NSMR is more desirable than avoiding it altogether.

- Some NSMRs are unavoidable, and others emerge (or become more problematic) during the course of therapy.

- NSMRs that generate a board complaint are sometimes adjudicated with hindsight bias (i.e., that the board, knowing that the NSMR led to a problem, judges too quickly that the therapist should have seen it coming) or by board members who hold to a stricter prohibition against NSMRs than current ethical codes allow.

In some cases these assumptions are similar to those that lie behind other models for deciding whether to engage in a NSMR, but in other cases, they are different.

Self-Assessment Questions for Therapists Pondering Whether to Engage in or Continue in a NSMR

Client-Therapist Variables

- What is the client's diagnosis and life circumstances? For example, is this a borderline client (usually more risky) or a client seeking help with stress management (usually less risky)?

- Does the client appear to have the ability to recognize and maintain healthy boundaries?

- Are there reasons why you, the therapist, will have trouble maintaining healthy boundaries?

- What types of treatment are being provided or proposed? For example, intensive treatment (usually more risky) or brief intervention (usually less risky).

- How great is the power differential in the relationship? For example, the therapist who is also the client's professor or the therapist who is also the client's employer.

- Are you tempted to use whatever personal power you have to manipulate the client or use the relationship to satisfy selfish desires or personal needs?

- Will engaging in the NSMR exploit or harm the client (or the client's relationship with a family member or other associate)?

- Will engaging in the NSMR benefit the client or you, the therapist?
- Is there a risk the NSMR will make it difficult for you to be as effective in treatment or disrupt the therapeutic relationship?
- Will you be able to maintain confidentiality?

Therapist Objectivity/Consultation

- Have you engaged in a careful self-evaluation of your motives for engaging in the NSMR?
- Have you sought any consultation from an objective colleague?
- Have you thought about how a jury of your peers would likely view your decision to engage in the NSMR?

Informed Consent/Collaboration

- Have you engaged your client in a discussion of the present or emerging NSMR and helped him or her understand the issues involved?
- Understanding that you are ultimately the fiduciary in the relationship, have you offered the client the freedom to collaborate and discuss with you the pros and cons of engaging in the NSMR, and to be a part of the decision?

Documentation

- If you proceed with the NSMR, have you fully documented a client-oriented rationale for engaging in the NSMR?
- Have you documented the client's understanding of and agreement to engage in the NSMR?
- Have you documented any consultations with colleagues that you have sought?

Ongoing Vigilance and Collaboration

- NSMRs often arise during the course of therapy, as when the therapist realizes a client is the best friend of another client. Do you remain vigilant for NSMRs that may arise during the course of therapy? When NSMRs arise later in therapy, do you try to consider their magnitude in relationship to the client's needs and the overall status of the treatment process?

Client Satisfaction/Well-Being

- Do you try to keep the client's long-term satisfaction with the thera-peutic process and his or her ultimate well-being in mind when deciding whether to engage in the NSMR?

Not every one of these questions is equally relevant to all situations, but these are the kinds of questions that the conscientious therapist will keep in mind.

CONCLUSIONS

Deciding whether to engage in an NSMR is one of the more complex and at times perplexing ethical dilemmas that therapists face. For one thing, engaging in NSMRs can be beneficial to the therapeutic process in some instances and harmful in others, and it is sometimes difficult to tell which it will be prospectively. Ethics codes and guidelines provide general principles and are more sympathetic to NSMRs than they have been in the past, but they are clearly not up to the task of providing de-finitive recommendations, and state boards do not necessarily interpret rules and guidelines in the same way. Making the process more difficult is the fact that the therapist is not the only one who evaluates the appro-priateness or inappropriateness of the relationship. The client does also, and his or her evaluation may be disparate from that of the therapist (Pope & Keith-Spiegel, 2008). For example, consider the case I men-tioned earlier in which the therapist-professor gives a client-student a low grade in a class. Suppose that in fact the client-student has misinter-preted the therapist-professor's behavior as biased against him when in fact the client-student's poor grade is based on numerous incorrect an-swers on the final exam. Or consider the therapist and client who see one another on a deserted aisle of a grocery store late at night. The therapist gives a friendly hello and walks on, confident that there are "no worries" because no one else saw the interaction. The client, on the other hand, stands stiff and shaken in the aisle, embarrassed that the therapist has surprised him in this most public of places. Because of these and other fears, some therapists do their best to avoid all NSMRs for safety's sake. Yet in so doing, they bypass the opportunity to utilize selected NSMRs in a therapeutic way. What's more, if they live in a small close-knit community, avoiding all multiple relationships may involve isolating themselves from social relationships necessary to their own health and wellbeing (Helbok, Marinelli & Walls, 2006).

The research suggests that involvement in NSMRs is more common than some traditionalists in the field would like to imagine. Yet most licensed therapists appear to be conscientious and try to be sensitive when it comes to becoming involved in these relationships, and most NSMRs apparently do not lead to problems. Unfortunately, a minority of therapists become involved in harmful NSMRs, and sadly these same therapists often seem especially capable of rationalizing their behavior away (Koocher & Keith-Spiegel, 2008, p. 15).

The ethical Christian therapist understands the good that can come from some NSMRs but remains vigilant about the possible downsides, using self-assessments, such as the one illustrated in this chapter, and taking advantage of consultation when necessary or in doubt. Wherever possible, the therapist will seek to educate the client about multiple relationships when one is present or emerging, and collaborate together with the client to decide what is in the client's best interest. At times such an approach is not only appropriate ethically but also effective therapeutically. For example, a therapist who served on the personnel committee at a church was surprised to find a client she had been seeing for six months on a list of interviewees for the open bookkeeper's job at the church. At the next session she and the client discussed the issue and a plan was devised whereby the therapist could recuse herself from the interview process without raising question from other committee members. The client reported that she was deeply appreciative that her therapist would go out of her way to be sensitive to this issue, and after that, the client began to open up and make greater progress in her therapy. Of course the therapist must be mindful of the fact that there will be some clients who are not able to collaborate in this way because they are struggling with a serious Axis II or Axis I disorder.

Going forward, it is incumbent upon the mental health professions to do a better job of increasing understanding about the benefits as well as the liabilities of engaging in NSMRs. At the level of training, one hopes that graduate and internship training will move increasingly away from models that teach students to avoid or fear all NSMRs, and move toward a more nuanced view that helps students develop skills of discerning potentially helpful NSMRs from ones that are not. One way of doing this is to expose students early and often to real-world case studies that require them to forecast possible NSMR situations, reason carefully about the many variables that must be considered and make decisions in the safety of the classroom where they can learn from missteps (Barnett, Lazarus, Vasquez, Moorehead-Slaughter & Johnson, 2007). Christian programs that train students to work in church-based or faith-based counseling centers need to give special attention to these matters (Sanders, Swenson & Schneller, 2011; Schneller, Swenson & Sanders, 2010).

At the level of policy, it is hoped that professional bodies will take a more proactive stance toward ensuring that state boards, the legal profession and other adjudicatory bodies understand clearly the current rules regarding engaging in NSMRs and avoid perspectives that have been shown to be too rigid or outdated (Barnett in Barnett, Lazarus, Vasquez, Moorehead-Slaughter & Johnson, 2007). In evaluating cases against therapists involved in NSMRs, boards need to consider current rules, the client, the culture and setting in which the NSMR took place, and the therapist's rationale for engaging in the NSMR (Barnett, Lazarus, Vasquez, Moorehead-Slaughter & Johnson, 2007).

REFERENCES

American Counseling Association. (2005). *ACA code of ethics.* Alexandria, VA: American Counseling Association. Retrieved April 25, 2010, from http://coun seling.org/Resources/CodeOfEthics/TP/Home/CT2.aspx.

American Psychological Association. (2002). Ethical principles of psychologists and code of conduct. *American Psychologist, 57,* 1060-73. Also available (with 2010 amendments) from www.apa.org/ethics/code/index.aspx.

Anderson, S. K., & Kitchener, K. S. (1998). Nonsexual posttherapy relationships: A conceptual framework to assess ethical risks. *Professional Psychology: Research & Practice, 29,* 91-99.

Barnett, J. E., Lazarus, A. A., Vasquez, M. J. T., Moorehead-Slaughter, O., & Johnson, W. B. (2007). Boundary issues and multiple relationships: Fantasy and reality. *Professional Psychology: Research & Practice, 38,* 401-10.

Campbell, C. D., & Gordon, M. C. (2003). Acknowledging the inevitable: Understanding multiple relationships in rural practice. *Professional Psychology: Research & Practice, 34,* 430-34.

Gottlieb, M. C. (1993). Avoiding exploitative dual relationships: A decision-making model. *Psychotherapy, 30,* 41-48.

Gottlieb, M. C., & Younggren, J. N. (2009). Is there a slippery slope? Considerations regarding multiple relationships and risk management. *Professional Psychology: Research & Practice, 40,* 564-71.

Gutheil, T. G., & Gabbard, G. O. (1993). The concept of boundaries in clinical practice: Theoretical and risk-management dimensions. *American Journal of Psychiatry, 150,* 188-96.

Guthman, D., & Sandberg, K. A. (2002). Dual relationships in the deaf community: When dual relationships are unavoidable and essential. In A. A. Lazarus & O. Zur (Eds.), *Dual relationships and psychotherapy* (pp. 329-34). New York: Springer.

Hargrove, D. S. (1986). Ethical issues in rural mental health practice. *Professional Psychology: Research & Practice, 17,* 20-23.

Helbok, C. M., Marinelli, R. P., & Walls, R. T. (2006). National survey of ethical practices across rural and urban communities. *Professional Psychology: Research & Practice, 37,* 66-67.

Johnson, W. B., Ralph, J., & Johnson, S. J. (2005). Managing multiple roles in embedded environments: The case of aircraft carrier psychology. *Professional Psychology: Research & Practice, 36,* 73-81.

Keith-Spiegel, P., & Koocher, G. P. (1985). *Ethics in psychology: Professional standards and cases.* Hillsdale, NJ: Erlbaum.

Kertesz, R. (2002). Dual relationships in psychotherapy in Latin America. In A. A. Lazarus & O. Zur (Eds.), *Dual relationships and psychotherapy* (pp. 329-34). New York: Springer.

Kessler, L. E., & Waehler, C. A. (2005). Addressing multiple relationships between clients and therapists in lesbian, gay, bisexual and transgender communities. *Professional Psychology: Research & Practice, 36,* 66-72.

Kitchener, K. S. (1988). Dual role relationships: What makes them so problematic? *Journal of Counseling & Development, 67,* 217-21.

Koocher, G. P., & Keith-Spiegel, P. (2008). *Ethics in psychology and the mental health professions: Standards and cases* (3rd ed.). New York: Oxford University Press.

Lazarus, A. A., & Zur, O. (Eds.). (2002). *Dual relationships in psychotherapy.* New York: Springer.

Lukens, H. C. (1997). Essential elements for ethical counsel. In R. K. Sanders (Ed.),

Christian counseling ethics: A handbook for therapists, pastors and counselors (pp. 43-56). Downers Grove, IL: InterVarsity Press.

McMinn, M. R., & Meek, K. R. (1996). Ethics among Christian counselors: A survey of beliefs and behaviors. *Journal of Psychology & Theology, 24,* 26-37.

McMinn, M. R., & Meek, K. R. (1997). Training programs. In R. K. Sanders (Ed.), *Christian counseling ethics: A handbook for therapists, pastors and counselors* (pp. 277-96). Downers Grove, IL: InterVarsity Press.

McRay, B. W., McMinn, M. R., & Meek, K. R. (1998). Questioning the "slippery slope": Ethical beliefs and behaviors of private office-based and church-based therapists. *Counseling and Values, 42,* 142-52.

Oordt, M. S. (1997). The ethical behavior of Christian therapists. In R. K. Sanders (Ed.), *Christian counseling ethics: A handbook for therapists, pastors and counselors* (pp. 326-31). Downers Grove, IL: InterVarsity Press.

Pope, K. S. (1990). Therapist-patient sexual contact: Clinical, legal, and ethical implications. In E. A. Margenau (Ed.), *The encyclopedia handbook of private practice* (pp. 687-96). New York: Gardner Press.

Pope, K. S., & Keith-Spiegel, P. (2008). Dual relationships, multiple relationships, and boundary decisions. *Journal of Clinical Psychology, 64,* 638-52.

Pope, K. S., & Vetter, V. A. (1992). Ethical dilemmas encountered by members of the American Psychological Association: A national survey. *American Psychologist, 47,* 397-411.

Sanders, R. K. (2010). Ethics codes: Monitoring the major changes. *Journal of Psychology & Christianity, 29,* 263-67.

Sanders, R. K., Swenson, J. E., & Schneller, G. R. (2011). Beliefs and practices of Christian psychotherapists regarding non-sexual multiple relationships. *Journal of Psychology & Theology, 39,* 330-44.

Schank, J. A., & Skovholt, T. M. (1997). Dual-relationship dilemmas of rural and small-community psychologists. *Professional Psychology: Research & Practice, 28,* 44-49.

Schneller, G. R., Swenson, J. E., & Sanders, R. K. (2010). Training for ethical dilemmas arising in Christian counseling: A survey of clinicians. *Journal of Psychology & Christianity, 29,* 343-53.

Swenson, J. E., Schneller, G. R., & Sanders, R. K. (2009). Ethical issues in integrating Christian faith and psychotherapy: Beliefs and behaviors among CAPS members. *Journal of Psychology & Christianity, 28,* 302-14.

Younggren, J. N., & Gottlieb, M. C. (2004). Managing risk when contemplating multiple relationships. *Professional Psychology: Research & Practice, 35,* 255-60.

Zur, O. (2000). In celebration of dual relationships: How prohibition of non-sexual dual relationships increases the chance of exploitation and harm. *The Independent Practitioner, 20,* 97-100.

Zur, O. (January/February, 2005). Boundaries and dual relationships in therapy. *The National Psychologist, 14,* 12.

7

Ethics in Couples Therapy

Jennifer S. Ripley, Steven J. Sandage
and Everett L. Worthington Jr.

Couples therapy is full of complexities in ethics found nowhere else in mental health interventions. Issues of epistemology, values, diversity, family law and confidentiality are relevant to couples treatments, sometimes layered together interactively. Couples therapy may be even more complex than individual therapy because the couple comes to treatment to address the relationship—its quality and stability—with additional considerations of the two people (each with a different agenda) and of children who are in the care of the couple. The treatment modalities, assessments and goals of couples therapy are also affected by the dominant values of clinicians' adopted theories. Those necessary values are the context for our work and lives. Therefore, this chapter will focus on ethics in couples therapy with a particular focus on values as the context for couples therapy.

It is not unusual for the couples therapist to be faced with an ethical dilemma similar to this case: An African American couple, Jamal and LaShonda, requests therapy to help them deal with the coming out of their daughter as a lesbian. The couple was referred by a minister because the therapist occasionally attended the same church. Within the couple's relationship LaShonda would like to be more accepting of their daughter's sexual identity but doesn't have the decision-making power within the relationship. In fact the husband is rather controlling, and early in their relationship was a heavy drinker and abusive. The husband repeatedly attempts to triangulate with the male therapist with disparaging remarks about women, particularly lesbians. He assumes that the religious male therapist agrees. The wife finds the therapist's email address and sends a message that she's thinking about moving out and staying with their daughter to support her and remove herself from what she believes is an intolerable situation. She asks the therapist not to disclose that information because she's afraid that the husband might drink and become violent. The case is being billed to insurance with the husband as the identified patient due to his diagnosis of depression. The wife is also mildly depressed, but is not identified as the patient. The therapist has authorization from the insurance company to treat the husband's depression by marital and family therapy according to the most recently approved treatment plan. Each member of this relational system (including the daughter, the pastor and the insurance care manager) could have differing hopes and fears about the therapist's role in this case. Cases like this have layers of potential ethical dilemmas that create a veritable land mine of decision making for therapists, and which at times can lead to problems and even harm for any and all concerned. Principles of ethics are intended to guide the clinician in decision making, and for the Christian therapist these principles are embedded within a Christian worldview.

ETHICAL PRINCIPLES

Ethics is a philosophical, social and, for the Christian, theological endeavor. For many Christians, values are shaped primarily by their religious tradition, doctrines and social values learned in Christian community. There are at least three major approaches to ethics (Jost & Jost, 2009). The *consequentialist* (also referred to as teleological or utilitarian) approach examines costs and benefits to all parties, and it seeks to render ethical judgments on the basis of a judgment of optimized cost-benefit ratios. Ethical principles, ethical standards and case studies of ethical dilemmas are often used to practice consequentialist ethics. The *deontological* (Kantian) alternative, on the other hand, is one that seeks to do the right thing regardless of costs and benefits. It promotes doing one's ethical duty. *Virtue ethics* (Jost & Jost, 2009) has reemerged as another ethical framework in the helping professions by emphasizing the formation of moral character and the relational influence of the professional over and above moral decisions and duties.

Bloesch (1987) suggested a differentiation between philosophical and theological types of ethics. Philosophical ethics seeks to understand the good (i.e., the benefits vis-à-vis costs and the right thing to do) in light of the human plane; whereas, theological ethics looks to the divine revelation of God in human history. A Christian approach to professional therapy ethics can value the importance of wise ethical reasoning, faithfulness to ethical duties, and the formation of mature virtues.

CHRISTIAN MARRIAGE ETHICS

It is important to understand some basic themes that are a focus of a traditional Christian marriage ethic. These themes include covenants, suffering in marriage, marriage in church fellowship, and issues of equality and justice in Christian marriage.

Christian covenants. In Scripture and Christian tradition marriage covenants are thought to shape the nature and goals of the marriage relationship. A covenantal ethic is characterized by the priority of the family and especially the marriage in relationships. Those in the covenant marriage keep faith that a sacred covenant with their Creator has been built on oaths. God is believed to be the creator of the marriage and the sustainer of it. Originally, the covenant was a lifelong agreement ratified by blood—hence traditions that allow newly wedded couples to walk between blood relations of the bride and groom on each side of the aisle. Suffering is something that shapes character, and both parties give *all they can* for the good of the marriage. In contrast, modern contractual marriages are characterized by a quid pro quo relationship. Each party is expected to give their fair share in the relationship, receive positive rewards from the relationship and can terminate the contract if agreed upon actions or services are not being met. Contracts are justice-based human endeavors of agreed upon behaviors and exchanges of resources. Covenants are established by a Creator and agreed upon within the presence of the Creator and the community.

Suffering in marriage. "[T]hat I will keep you in sickness and in health and in whatever condition it will please the Lord to place you, and that I shall not exchange you for better or worse until the end" (Ritual from the Abbey of Barbeau, late fourteenth century, Stevenson, 1992). Christian tradition has emphasized perseverance of covenantal commitment through suffering, even in marriage. While the myth of Western romantic marriage is one of finding the perfect mate, falling in love and living happily ever after, the realities of relationships that may last decades are obvious. Offenses are common and sometimes severe. Health problems create strains and increased responsibility on the healthy partner. Children wander from the family and their faith. Each partner's individual faults annoy and confound the spouse. A Christian ethic must be strong enough to provide purpose and meaning to inherent suffering within the marriage. The ethic of suffering involves numerous aspirations:

- Sometimes there is an emphasis on joining in the suffering of Christ. (Rom 8:17; Phil 3:10; 1 Pet 4:13)

- Suffering is to develop character and hope. (Rom 5:3-4)

- Marriage can be a refining fire, testing the faith of both parties. (Prov 27:17)

Ultimately, a Christian marriage ethic supposes that both members trust in God "in whatever condition it will please the Lord to place you."

Marriage in church fellowship. Christian marriage has occurred within the fellowship of believers in all Christian traditions. Marriage is a sacrament in the Catholic and many Protestant churches, and a sacred vocation for Christians. Earlier in history, Christian couples sought approval from the parents of the couple and the priest before engagement. Those authorities were the agents of God on earth to young people. Seeking permission to many emphasized the responsibility of many parties creating and sustaining the new family. Modern churches often have programs aimed at promoting healthy marriages for couples within the fellowship. The couple has a reciprocal response to contribute to the congregation. Infant baptisms or dedications, Communions and family worship opportunities are illustrative of this. This embedded nature of the marriage relationship extends the ethic of marriage to consider the church fellowship, authorities and doctrines.

Equality and injustice in marriage. Historical Christian tradition has almost unilaterally assumed that women are led by men in the marriage relationship with inherent hierarchy. However, recent Christian scholarship has moved in the direction of equality by pointing out that injustice is intrinsic to hierarchy. A book edited by David Blankenhorn, Don Browning and Mary Stewart Van Leeuwen (2004) provides perspectives from Catholic, Protestant, feminist, Reformed and other traditions discussing the issue of equality in marriage. There is surprising consensus on the equal worth of males and females in marriage from all of the writers, which is a departure from early historic Christianity. The current debate centers around whether the marriage relationship should be considered to be a hierarchy with prescribed gender-determined roles or whether it should be characterized by mutual interdependence and have flexible and varied roles. Interpretations of Scripture and Christian teaching are the sources of authority in discussion of the debate. The issue is ultimately an ethical issue, not just a theological one, as Catholic author Daniel Mark Cere (2004) points out. Cere argues that while Christians differ on the ethic of hierarchy and equality in marriage, that essentially ethical (not scriptural) decisions tend to strongly prescribe one's interpretation of Scripture. Therefore careful study of the ethics of marriage is necessary for understanding various hermeneutics on the issues of justice and hierarchy in marriage.

A second emphasis in marriage relationships is a focus on clearly unjust circumstances such as domestic violence. The awareness of the Christian community of the existence of domestic violence inside and outside of the community has led to numerous academic discussions about the need for justice (Sokoloff & Pratt, 2005). In some tragic cases, we have even seen the religious language of "covenant" and "accepting all suffering is from God" used to control the freedom and silence the complaints of victims of abuse in Christian communities. Authors have argued that proper Christian ethics must include condemnation of domestic violence and community support for families with domestic violence (West, 2005). We argue that the development of a clear understanding of domestic violence is a necessary Christian marriage ethic.

Difficult decision making. Many difficult ethical decisions arise during therapy which are important factors for Christians doing couples therapy. These include practical moral issues such as our initial case—what to do about the coming out of a child as gay, lesbian, bisexual or transgendered. They also include issues such as whether and how to have input in abortion decisions, how to deal with recovery from an affair, disagreements over the content of religious beliefs and whether to become involved in decisions regarding elder care. The couples therapist can certainly deal with the communication, conflict resolution and forgiveness relating to such issues. The ethical issues center on how much influence over content of the decisions the couples therapist exerts or attempts to have.

Nonspecific Christian ethics. We would be remiss not to point out that most Christian ethics for relationships apply to the couples relationship. Ethics such as forgiveness of others besides the spouse, the value of children and infirm elders, the dignity of all people, peace, love and so many other general Christian ethics apply to Christian marriage and to the professional counseling situation.

PROFESSIONAL ETHICS

Christian therapists fulfill various professional roles and are members of various professional organizations. Psychologists, marriage and family therapists, counselors, pastoral counselors and social workers all have the opportunity to join professional organizations that have specific ethical codes of conduct. These secular ethical codes contain little that is objectionable to Christians. Most of the general principles or virtues that shape these codes, such as concern for others' welfare in the APA code, are highly consistent with Christian virtues. One study of the ethical practices of Christian psychologists found most reported being very consistent with the American Psychological Association's ethical code (Oordt, 1997).

A well-developed ethical guidelines statement for professional Christian therapists is the Christian Association of Psychological Studies (CAPS) "Statement of Ethical Guidelines" (CAPS, 2005). The American Association for Christian Counselors also developed a "Code of Ethics" that adds to the body of knowledge by including codes specific for lay counselors and ministers (AACC, 2004). The major differences from the secular ethical codes are the explicit statements about members' commitments to the Bible, the church, the family and to godly living. The CAPS Statement also emphasizes love as the motive for service.

This leads us to a practical question: How does one integrate biblical principles and virtues with professional principles and virtues in couples therapy?

INTEGRATIVE ETHICS

Ethics codes are typically principled guidelines for the complex ethical situations that marriage and family counselors face in the field and are based on consequentialist approaches to ethics. Consequentialist approaches emphasize the outcomes or consequences as the guiding principle for ethical decision making. Nevertheless it is not always clear how to apply either Christian or secular ethical codes to tough situations. Christian therapists may draw from at least three sources for help in ethical decision making. One source consists of Christian ethics derived from the Bible and the Christian tradition/community. Another source is made up of ethical principles from professional codes (i.e., APA, ACA, AAMFT, AASW, etc.). The third source is professional Christian organizations who have arrived at specific codes of ethics for Christian professional psychotherapists (i.e., AACC, CAPS). All sources of ethics are necessarily incomplete in their ability to speak to every ethical situation. Deciding ethical dilemmas may require that the Christian therapist consult ethical principles and standards, consider applicable case studies and review applicable scriptural principles that describe what is right according to religious traditions and hermeneutic principles (usually deontological ethics). Christian ethics will speak to some issues, such as adultery, that will not be a part of the secular professional codes. The professional codes may be explicit about things not clearly addressed in the Bible, like the use of current clients for testimonials in advertising or treatment of research subjects. There will obviously be some overlap and some issues not clearly addressed by either domain of ethical principles. The CAPS code and AACC code are attempts to bring these domains of ethical reflection together. But ethical principles arise out of an underlying ethical theory that provides the moral context of the entire therapy enterprise.

ISSUES ARISING FROM PROFESSIONAL PRACTICE

Several issues related to couples therapy merit special consideration. We will look at how four ethical principles influence some challenging ethical issues faced by couples therapists. These principles are competence, responsibility to clients, confidentiality and integrity. These principles are common to APA, ACA, NASW and the AAMFT Codes of Ethics (sometimes under a different name).

Competence. *Inadequate training.* Some therapists who try to provide family or couples therapy are trained in programs where they may have had little formal training in family therapy or couples therapy. Mental health codes emphasize that therapists should recognize the boundaries of their competence based on their education, training and supervision. Yet it is easy to go beyond one's level of competence as a therapist. Others are tempted to exceed their level of competence because of economic pressure to keep a full caseload. It should also be noted that there is still no consensus about the best ways to train therapists in family therapy modalities (Raimondi & Walters, 2004). This raises a question as to the uniformity and adequacy of training in marriage and couples therapy.

The general trend in training for therapists is competencies based on training (Chenail, 2009). This approach recommends that therapists without formal training in couples therapy should seek (1) continuing education specifically in couples therapy and (2) supervision from a supervisor with adequate credentials and training in couples therapy. For the Christian, such behavior should arise from a commitment to the virtue of honesty and to "devote themselves to doing what is good" (Tit 3:8 NIV) as well as adherence to a professional code of ethics.

Staying current. It is the responsibility of the therapist to keep abreast of changes in the research and practice of couples therapy. As part of one's continuing professional development, a therapist should pursue continuing education through workshops, courses or conferences on couples therapy. That is also a principle in the AAMFT code of ethics. Yet many professionals attend conferences and workshops that are easily available instead. In many cases, the presentations they attend, objectively speaking, do not systematically upgrade their specific competencies for treating the cases they see daily. For the Christian, responsible self-assessment of whether real competencies are being upgraded should be motivated by an active rejection of pride and expediency, and an enthusiastic embracing of humility and the desire for growth. Furthermore, ongoing clinical consultation and professional development can be viewed from a covenantal perspective as practicing within a community of colleagues to provide accountability and support.

Conflicting competency requirements. What happens if there is a conflict in the competency requirements of different fields? For example there are different expectations for the qualification of supervisor for couples therapists in the various professions. The AAMFT and ACA have developed specific and high standards for the supervisor role in their professions, generally exceeding the general expectations of master's degree entry-level couples therapists. Psychology as a field does not have specific standards for the supervisor role. Therefore, professionals who cross over may find themselves in an ethical dilemma. Generally, the license that one works under determines the standards one should follow, but clinicians should still consider whether they possess adequate training for the clinical task at hand.

Lack of specific knowledge. Ricky and Darchelle had a daughter who was assessed for ADHD. At that time they also discussed entering counseling with the same therapist (who specializes in child therapy) for issues of marital conflict. They both felt discouraged and ready to give up on sexual intimacy stemming from issues of sexual inadequacy that Ricky experienced due to childhood sexual abuse. The therapist worked with Ricky and Darchelle on communication and increasing general intimacy, which improved their relationship overall. But the sexual intimacy issues persisted.

A competent assessment of Ricky and Darchelle's problem would have indicated that the conflict difficulties were a result of the history of trauma and resulting sexual dysfunction. In this case, the therapist chose an intervention familiar to her rather than one appropriate to the presenting problem. A couples therapist could be expected to be familiar enough with sexual dysfunctions to make it part of assessment. A therapist should also know that some sexual problems are frequently treated successfully through medical or behavioral interventions. Any complexities may require a referral to a sex therapist or someone with specialized competency in sexual dysfunctions. In some communities no such specialized therapists exist, requiring that the practicing therapist disclose his or her level of competency to the couple, gain informed consent for treatment and seek the knowledge and training needed to treat the case adequately.

Not knowing the best treatments. Baucom headed a task force to determine which couples therapy treatments were empirically supported (Baucom et al., 1998). Four were deemed to be empirically supported. These included Integrative Behavioral Couple Therapy, Emotionally Focused

Couple Therapy, Insight-Oriented Couple Therapy, and Cognitive-Behavioral Couple Therapy. Increasingly, calls are issued that the ethical approach to treatment is to use empirically-supported treatments (EST). However, there are legitimate disagreements in this increasingly strident debate. Opponents of ESTs often argue that local data (in which a practitioner collects data on his, her or their local practices) are more important than data from controlled clinical trials, which are criticized as having little external validity. Proponents of ESTs counter that local data have little internal validity and are often little more than biased satisfaction surveys.

Whereas ESTs are established clinical science, there are a number of issues that question their usefulness in real practice. (1) They depend on accurate assessment. In the initial case with Jamal and LaShonda, Jamal's diagnosis (depression) may mask other important issues—substance abuse, violence, past sexual abuse and perhaps personality disorders. Treatment is predicated on Jamal being depressed and that being the disorder that is most in need of treatment. Combinations of disorders do not always have a specified prescribed EST. (2) The therapist might not have the EST treatment manual or have training and supervision in conducting the associated EST. (3) The therapist may be in an underserved community and be the only (or one of few) therapist, and may not be able to be competent in every EST appropriate for every diagnosis. Due to such practical limitations, the ethics of requiring or recommending ESTs is debatable—not a foregone conclusion. However, clinicians are responsible to remain abreast of future research and debate on the topic.

Responsibility to clients. Couples therapists have the responsibility of seeking to advance the welfare of their clients. This raises the pivotal question: Who *is* the client? Codes and professional writing on the topic vary as to whether the individuals or dyadic unit should be the priority in treatment. Unless the therapist thinks clearly about who the client is, treatment goals are likely to become muddled amid conflicting interests. Recall the case of Jamal and LaShonda. The therapist is seeing both Jamal and LaShonda even though only Jamal is diagnosed. There must be some responsibility to each. The decision about this may be complex and involve the couple's preferences for treatment, the expectations of the third-party payer, the existence of an identified patient with a diagnosis, and current research. Therapeutically, diagnosing one member of a couple system and not the other might be clinically accurate in certain cases but should also be considered carefully as it can also contribute to an imbalance of power in the relational system.

Diagnosis and insurance. Third-party payers generally do not reimburse for couples relational problem as a diagnosis, however mood disorders have a high correlation with relationship problems (Whisman & Uebelacker, 2006) and is often the diagnosis submitted for treatment. Therefore, improving the relationship is likely to improve the symptoms relevant to the diagnosis. Most research that has investigated the use of couples treatment for individual pathology has supported couples treatment as an effective modality, especially in treating depression that is tied up intimately with couple problems (Gupta, Coyne & Beach, 2005) and alcohol and drug abuse in couple relationships (Ripley, Cunion & Noble, 2005). Therefore, even if one client arrives in treatment with a diagnosis of depression and substance abuse, but the clients' problematic marriage is a major key to the maintenance of the disorders, then couples treatment focused on the improvement of the relationship may be the best primary treatment for the client. In contrast, a client with depression and substance abuse where their relationship is not a main key to the disorder may have couples treatment as an adjunctive intervention, but this adjunctive part of the intervention is not likely to be reimbursable by insurance.

Identified patient. The therapist's understanding of who the client is should be communicated early in counseling. The therapist might say, "It seems that the focus of your problems is with your relationship. I would like to work with you primarily to improve your relationship. I believe the relationship is the key to solving the problem most quickly. However, there are other kinds of counseling and foci we could take. Does a focus on the relationship sound good to you, or are you interested in counseling for something else?" Beyond that the therapist may need to clarify that the individuals in the counseling relationship would not be the priority in treatment goals and interventions, but the needs of the relationship would come first. Without this clarification, one or both partners may not agree with the focus of therapy being on improving the relationship, and misunderstanding can result. During a couples intake, the individuals might not ask direct questions about this but raise more general questions about whether treatment will include individual sessions.

Neutrality toward relationship health? Some people argue that couples therapists should remain more neutral, not presupposing that successful therapy should restore a more positive relationship. They say to the couple, "Therapy will determine whether you should continue or whether breaking up is the most beneficial course of action." We disagree. We would liken that reasoning to the individual therapist who counsels a depressed client by arguing that the therapist must remain neutral on suicide, merely because the client is ambivalent about working toward change. Rather, just as God generally prefers life to suicide, God also generally prefers that a marriage be transformed toward health versus ending in divorce. However, for a therapist to verbalize an opinion about whether a particular couple *should* stay married or get a divorce is to exert the power of undue influence on a potentially vulnerable client system. Therapists might feel some pressure to render an opinion if one or both partners ask about the viability of the marriage; however, the therapist can readily acknowledge that therapists are not reliably able to judge the likelihood of success or failure and that this is an important value question they (the clients) will need to resolve while inviting both to commit to the treatment plan for a set period of time. It is important for couples therapists to realize they are often being triangulated by one of the spouses who wants the therapist to say either that divorce is not a viable option or, conversely, that marital change is hopeless in their case.

Couples may need several sessions to decide whether they want to pursue couples therapy. Couples often enter therapy ambivalent about their goals for treatment. We recommend that Christian therapists ask whether both partners are willing to put off any decision toward breakup until after a good course of treatment has been completed. This may be more salient for married couples than for engaged or cohabiting couples who have not made marriage vows. However, matching the goals of treatment to the couple's view of their relationship is needed. If a breakup is inevitable, then therapy relevant to an amicable divorce would be the best course. Handled ethically and with wise therapist positioning, discussions about marital commitment versus divorce can be clinically useful and may uncover salient assumptions of one or both partners about relationships and personal values. Some couples may find their couples therapist to be their only "unbiased" dialogue partner on decisions that will change the course of their lives.

Integrity. Integrity is an explicit principle in all professional ethics codes. Integrity generally implies a commitment to honesty and fairness toward clients and other professionals. There are three key issues in couples therapy that relate to the principle of integrity.

Integrity is required in diagnosis. Because insurance generally does not pay for couples therapy unless it is clearly the treatment of choice for a diagnosis, therapists can be tempted to create a diagnosis (such as major depression) for the sake of reimbursement. Billing couples therapy sessions as individual sessions not only violates integrity but would be hard to characterize as anything but insurance fraud (Ohlschlager & Mosgofian, 1992).

Integrity is required for informed consent. Integrity requires an effort to inform clients about process, boundaries and goals of therapy. A Christian worldview will inform therapists' values about marriage in numerous ways. The description of integrity in the APA code requires psychologists to reflect on their own values and biases to determine how those values and biases may influence therapy. A couples therapist may have views about the permanence of marriage or roles within marriage that are divergent from those of the client. Potential clients may need more information about a therapist's values than merely the label "Christian" or "feminist" to decide whether to work with that therapist. If the therapist is engaging in "religious accommodative" therapy (Worthington & Sandage, 2002) then clients should be informed what that would involve in treatment. This can be especially complex for religiously heterogeneous couples or couples that differ in religious commitment. A good body of literature has now developed on accommodating religion in psychotherapy that applies to couples therapy as well (Stanley et al., 2001). Throughout the informed consent process, therapists should remain cognizant of the potential influence of their own beliefs and culture, and the potential for unduly influencing the client. They also should be knowledgeable about the beliefs and cultures of their clients.

Integrity is required for retention in treatment. Couples therapy has a high failure rate, some estimate as high as 50-90% of couples seeking treatment do not enter the "well-adjusted" range in their relationship as a result of treatment (Baucom, Shoham, Mueser, Daiuto & Stickle, 1998). Even with improved understanding of predictors of outcomes (Baucom, Atkins, Simpson & Christensen, 2009), couples therapy is challenging in most cases. It is common for couples therapists to feel as though their treatment is not effective with a couple even after a typical course of treatment has been engaged in with appropriate levels of professional consultation. The therapist with integrity will honestly address with the couple the therapist's assessment of a lack of change. Just like an oncologist would honestly talk with a cancer patient about not receiving the results hoped for due to treatments, psychotherapists should honestly talk with couples about whether continued treatment will improve their relationship. Options might include (1) referring to a therapist with a different approach or with more specialized expertise, (2) focusing in treatment on acceptance of the problems that exist in the relationship and developing the grace to live with the problems (Doss, Thum, Sevier, Atkins & Christensen, 2005), (3) simply ending treatment, or (4) reassessing whether individual treatment for one or both partners is a necessary precursor to couples therapy. In our clinical experience, we have noticed that beginning couples therapists frequently jump to option (4) in cases where further consultation or option (1) might be the best option.

Confidentiality. An essential part of being a therapist is protecting appropriate client confidentiality. It is widely understood that there are limitations to confidentiality. Confidentiality may be broken (1) if the client presents a clear and present danger to self or others, (2) if required by law, or (3) if the client waives the right to confidentiality. Physicians and mental health professionals are required to report child or elder abuse. The specific boundaries of confidentiality should be discussed with clients as part of the informed consent process. At times, another helping professional (e.g., therapist, psychiatrist or clergy) might be involved in a couples case and informally seek information from the couples therapist. Ethically, a written consent from the clients is usually needed to disclose information.

But what about individual confidentiality in couples therapy? Couples therapists often have sessions, parts of session or other communication with one partner. How should couples therapists handle secrets divulged by one partner that he or she does not want to tell his or her spouse? Recall the case outlines with Jamal and LaShonda. LaShonda sent an unsolicited email to the therapist confessing that she was considering moving and asking that the therapist not tell Jamal. Should the therapist tell Jamal, who is the client of record with the insurance company?

Couples therapists generally take one of three approaches to secrets:

1. All information is public information. This would mean telling the spouse everything.

2. All individually divulged information is private information. This would mean keeping secrets confidential.

3. Certain information divulged by one spouse may be withheld by the therapist from the partner, but confidentiality is not promised. This would make the therapist the arbitrator of what to share as public knowledge.

Whichever approach a therapist chooses should be agreed upon with the couple up front. We would try to meet with the couple conjointly as much as possible because this seems to be the most effective therapeutically and ethically (Kuo, 2009). It is also consistent with our definition of the relationship as being the client in couples therapy. If meeting or communicating with an individual, we thus prefer to tell the person to communicate as if the partner were present. We offer the only exception for issues relevant to safety or violence. We usually encourage the spouse to consider disclosing his or her "secret" to the spouse, perhaps within treatment. Clinicians can also consider creating a written document for the couple to sign that clarifies how individual confidences will be handled.

Infidelity. Infidelity presents a common dilemma to couples therapists. Butler, Harper and Seedall (2009) recommend that couples disclose infidelity as a relationship ethic and as an attachment issue. Disclosure provides the best possibility for relationship health and renewed attachment. Many couples have difficulties because they keep numerous secrets. Keeping secrets is usually a pattern that should be addressed in couples therapy. However, Ohlschlager and Mosgofian (1992) suggest that secrets be considered a process issue, as well as a legal or ethical issue. There may be situations where disclosure is not helpful.

Christian therapists may especially struggle with the ethics of treatment of couples with infidelity. Doctrinal teachings vary but many Christians consider a sexual affair as a legitimate reason that can justify a divorce (Instone-Brewer, 2007). However, most Christians would encourage willing married couples to reconcile after an affair. Therapists should be aware of their own doctrinal teachings surrounding affairs and divorce, but work within the goals and beliefs of the client on this sensitive issue. As with all clinical issues, it is important for therapists to reflect on their countertransference to limit the risk of becoming overly judgmental or excessively protective of one member of the couple system.

Privilege. Finally, we address the issue of privilege in couples treatment. Because the client holds privilege, the main issue is the definition of the client. States differ on how they handle client privilege. For example, in both Tennessee and New Jersey judges have ruled that therapists do not have to testify if one spouse objects. In Virginia, however, a judge ruled that a three-way conversation is public information. In this view, privilege does not exist and the therapist must testify. This highlights the importance of knowing state legal guidelines.

Issues Arising from Theological Interpretations

Divorce. *The value of marriage.* Marriage is an important theological construct for Christians. As discussed earlier, a covenantal interpretation of the marriage relationship rooted in Christian tradition influences the priority or value of marriage (Ripley & Worthington, 2002). This spiritual union of two people into one flesh points to the nature of God's covenant with us.

Couples therapists usually see relationships that are not characterized by intimacy or reciprocal giving and in which partners are often ambivalent (at best) about the permanence of the relationship. In a study of over one thousand marriage and family therapists, 61% claimed neutrality toward divorce, while 33% stated that they support preserving marriage and avoiding divorce (Wall, Needham, Browning & James, 1999). This often leads to the question of whether these relationships *should* be permanent. Is it ethical and moral, within a Christian framework that values marriage, for the therapist to focus on the positive side of partners' ambivalence even as partners are drawn to focus on their pain and distress? Is it ethical and moral *not* to bring up the positive? At what point does the therapist give up trying to help the couple salvage the marriage? What then?

Divorce is something every couples therapist faces and realistically cannot prohibit regardless of personal beliefs and values. Three main issues confront the Christian therapist. First, what is a biblical ethic on the permissibility of divorce? Second, how should a therapist handle his or her own values about divorce in the therapeutic process? Third, should a Christian therapist ever recommend divorce for a couple actively harming each other? An alternative might be to recommend permanent separation, although this is often a stepping stone to divorce. What if it becomes obvious to the therapist that improvement is likely not to be forthcoming and perhaps further deterioration seems inevitable? Professional ethics suggest that the responsible action is to disclose this to the couple and not continue to treat the couple, but the ethics within the Christian community often suggest it is not ethical nor moral to encourage a couple to divorce, and often stopping therapy would be considered to be encouraging divorce. The Christian couples therapist can feel pinned between different ethics from different communities. Fourth, what is the role of the Christian therapist in responding to a couple's decision to divorce? Does one agree? Does one then facilitate the couple's divorce?

Interpretations of divorce. Lewis Smedes discussed Christian marriage as multifaceted, a covenant of fidelity to a vow, a person, a community, a relationship and a calling (Smedes, 1987). The goal of marriage is a permanent covenant relationship that is total and exclusive (Balswick & Balswick, 2006). The reality of high rates of divorce have been difficult for the Christian church, and there is a continuum of beliefs about when divorce is allowable, from never to under certain circumstances like adultery to under the guidance of church leadership as in an annulment and finally to allowances in a variety of situations. More recent theological discussion (Nydam, 2005) has focused more on pastoral care responses to divorce instead of theological interpretations.

Therapists' own beliefs about divorce and experiences with divorce themselves or those close to them can influence the therapeutic situation. One might be tempted to be comforted by the idea that delineating ethical positions is not the main role of a therapist. The AAMFT code of ethics even says, "Therapists clearly advise the clients that they have the responsibility to make decisions regarding relationships such as . . . divorce, separation" (AAMFT, 2012, Principle 1.8).

However, this position, which tries to free the therapist from responsibility, is made murkier by virtually universal no-fault divorce laws. One of the two partners can make a unilateral and coercive decision to divorce in spite of any preference by the other spouse. Does a therapist bear any responsibility to identify coercion when it occurs? Margolin (1982) points out that client responsibility for decisions does not preclude influence from the therapist. It would be naive to suggest that clients are not influenced by therapist values. The main issue seems to be whether the therapist seeks to impose a view upon the client(s)—whether defined as the marriage or the individuals—in a manner that violates client autonomy. Principle D of the Ethical Principles and Psychologist's Code of Conduct (APA, 2002) states the importance of respect for people's rights and dignity. Autonomy and self-determination are two essential rights therapists are to respect.

Principle D of the Code of Conduct says of diversity issues, including religion, that "Psychologists try to eliminate the effect on their work of biases based on those factors, and they do not knowingly participate in or condone activities of others based upon such prejudices" (APA, 2002). If therapists' religious beliefs inevitably influence clients, then it would seem wise for the couples therapist to reflect upon what one's position is regarding divorce.

Ethical management of divorce issues. Couples therapists can clarify their role to the client. While a therapist can assist clients in considering ethical positions, particularly if the therapist is familiar with the religious tradition of the client, the therapist is not a professional theologian or ethicist. Therapists should show the humility to work within their competence and refer clients to religious professionals for more extensive theological reflection. Care should be taken to understand the client's expectations about the therapist's role, preferably at the outset of therapy.

Therapists can facilitate clients' understanding of their own values in light of the potential spiritual and psychological consequences of various decisions regarding divorce. Some clients who are serious about divorce may idealistically believe that divorce will resolve all of their problems. Therapists can (and ethically *should*) challenge such idealism supportively without interfering with client autonomy. Other clients might fear they cannot handle life postdivorce and stay married despite repeated patterns of abuse from a recalcitrant partner. In such cases, therapists can help clients toward empowerment whether they choose to remain in their relationship or not.

Christian therapists can carefully inform their clients of their own theological positions on divorce in a spirit of grace and humility. Many clients may wonder about the therapist's values without ever asking directly. This may not always be necessary, as some partners will manipulatively threaten divorce while in couples therapy even though they do not want nor intend to divorce. Therapists can overreact to this rather than recognizing the purpose behind the threats. In my (Ripley et al., 2010) experience in screening hundreds of couples for divorce intent, close to half indicate having considered and even discussing divorce with their spouse, but very few actually take any steps (i.e., consulting a lawyer, finding separate homes) toward separation or divorce within a year.

Christian therapists can deal pro-socially with divorce. They can work with pastors to educate congregations about divorce, to foster a climate of acceptance and forgiveness, and to encourage couples to seek counseling before problems get out of control. Therapists can also consult with churches in developing divorce recovery and other ministries that maximize therapeutic and spiritual healing. Christian communities should be characterized by an honest recognition of brokenness and offer ministries that are inclusive of a variety of relational situations. Singles and persons who are divorced are among those who sometimes feel marginalized and underrepresented in the marriage and family ministry offerings of churches.

Spouse abuse. *The ethical duty to recognize abuse.* Intimate partner violence (IPV) is a reality in all communities, including the Christian community. Studies have emphasized the need for awareness of IPV in religious communities (Cassidy-Shaw, 2002). While religious variables do not appear to predict lower IPV (Cunradi, Caetano & Schafer, 2002), other than frequent church attendance for men, there are still significant issues of IPV in the religious community. Many Christians allow belief in the permanence of marriage and the necessity of forgiving (Mt 6:12, 14-15) to shape a belief that an abused spouse should return and reconcile a marriage even if being abused. We believe that safety and respect for human dignity is paramount over return to an unsafe situation. Forgiveness may be granted and reconciliation attempted without placing a vulnerable client at physical risk. Therapists working with abuse victims who want to forgive their perpetrator might help them reflect wisely on healthy forms of forgiveness that include boundaries and appropriate levels of self-regard.

Therefore, it is the clinician's duty to assess and recognize abuse, positive and negative spiritual coping methods, religious community support structures (Copel, 2008) and spiritual vulnerabilities. Religious therapists should avoid interpreting Scripture in ways that are unsafe to victims of abuse or keep couples in victimizing situations.

The ethical duty to interpret Scriptures faithfully. Probably the most quoted verse in the case of spouse abuse is Malachi 2:16: "I hate divorce, says God . . ." (NIV 1984). Often pastors, therapists and friends sense the threat to the stability of the marriage when physical abuse becomes evident, and they react by trying to preserve the marriage by quoting this verse. Ironically, though, the second part of the verse is almost continually ignored: "and I hate a man covering himself with violence." Given the two statements within the same sentence, therapists (and clients) should engage in careful theological analysis prior to deciding which principle rates primacy.

The ethical duty to protect. The therapist has the ethical duty first to insure that his or her client comes to no harm and second to attempt to promote beneficence. This would suggest that the first approach to a couple in which (typically) the wife has been (or might reasonably be expected to be) harmed is to protect the abused partner through couples separation or even legal recourse. Rather than assume that the abusive behavior can be eliminated through promoting better communication, conflict resolution or intimacy, the therapist must deal directly with the physical threat. Only then should couples therapy seek to better the relationship.

Part of the duty to protect is for the therapist to be current in the research on violence. The current research on violence is emphasizing typologies of abusers that examine issues like "family only" batterers (men who harm their partner and sometimes children), or "antisocial" batterers (men at high risk for harming others in many situations) and their relative differential in danger for the family (Holtzworth-Munroe, Meehan, Herron,

Rehman & Stuart, 2000). Common couples violence (Johnson & Ferraro, 2000) is violence that usually is not injurious, may occur more by women than by men and may not require immediate separation. This type of violence is mild, has not led to harm, and is an ineffective method of problem solving and conflict. At the same time, it is important to not underestimate the psychological impact even of domestic violence that is not physically injurious. Moreover, therapists should remain cognizant of the possibility some clients will underreport abuse in their relationship. In contrast, antisocial batterers, sometimes called patriarchal terrorists, are characterized by bravado and controlling behaviors, often have personality disorder traits and may even have some brain damage. This type of abuser rarely stops their abuse in follow-up studies, and the chances of physical harm in those relationships is very high (Holtzworth-Munroe et al., 2000).

Definitions of marriage. The job of the Christian couples therapist is further complicated by the plethora of definitions of marriage that exist in our society. At one time there was essentially one common definition of marriage in the Western world, as created by God with that sacred union demonstrated by a religious ceremony. The twentieth century was a time when new definitions of marriage, shaped by social constructs, redefined by various groups within the Western cultures. Christians will face important issues with regard to the definition of marriage when counseling couples who cohabit or in the case of same-sex couples. With increased immigration and crosscultural consultation, Christian therapists may also face various definitions worldwide including polygamy, extreme patriarchy, arranged marriage or even forms of bride stealing. As with all forms of counseling, culturally competent practice is an essential dimension of ethical couples therapy. If a therapist is unfamiliar with a client's culture or ethnicity, professional consultation or referral should be considered.

For Christians who define marriage as one man with one woman who publicly commit themselves to the relationship for life and then begin to live together, the diversity of definitions of marriage or intimate relationships will present obvious difficulties. How should a Christian handle such couples? Christian therapists are likely to differ in their ethical decisions about these situations.

At the heart of the situation is a debate whether therapists can and should provide therapy that supports clients' main goals and morals if their own therapeutic goals and morals significantly differ from the clients' goals and morals. Consider this analogy: would a Christian therapist in a hospital counsel a client who values and wants to pursue suicide? What about a client desiring a change of careers from a safe job to one likely to put the client at risk for injury or illness? We argue that in all areas of life (intimate unions or otherwise) attempting to disregard one's own beliefs or values and adopt the client's beliefs creates an artificial environment that is not best for conducting psychotherapy. This may be on a continuum, from mild discrepancies that can be easily tolerated or even ignored, to major discrepancies that put a therapist in a position of helping a client toward a goal they personally think is not healthy or moral. Every therapist has his or her own sense of what makes for what Aristotle called eudemonia or a good life.

Autonomy is generally the principle of priority when it comes to clients' goals. While others in medical professions (e.g., doctors, nurses, pharmacists) may treat patients with widely discrepant value systems, psychotherapy is different than medical practice due to the intimate nature of the therapeutic relationship and the fact that the beliefs, values and attitudes of the client are the very stuff of the treatment. Therefore, we offer the following ethical principles:

- Therapists should work to increase their capacity in some areas where lack of experience (such as ethnicity or presenting issues) are the concern, but when moral issues are the concern, there are adjustments that therapists may not feel at liberty to make.

- In "gray areas" relevant to discrepancies of morals or beliefs the therapist should consult with colleagues and offer informed consent.

- For at least moderately functioning clients in settings with multiple options for clients, therapists can nonjudgmentally discuss that their own beliefs are different than the client's and how this might affect their work together. This allows the clients to decide whether they prefer to stay and work or to work with someone else.

- If a therapist cannot agree with the client's main goals of treatment to a degree that it feels disingenuous to do so, the best thing for the client is a natural and supportive referral to someone who can.

The complexity of these ethical considerations increase when we consider settings (e.g., prisons, hospitals, rural areas, military, EAPs, etc.) where clients may have more limited freedom to simply select another therapist. Therapists are wise to consider these dilemmas between values and service when considering the systems in which they can practice with integrity.

ISSUES ARISING FROM RESEARCH AND PRACTICE

The commitment of mental health professionals to the ethical principle of competence depends upon the belief that one is providing effective services. This means that counseling approaches must be evaluated to see whether the intended goals are accomplished. Some approaches to couples therapy may prove more effective with clients of a certain age, ethnicity, religious orientation or level of couple adjustment. Research can and must be done on Christian couples counseling, premarital counseling and marriage enrichment programs.

Couples counseling. Disorders. The research in couples counseling in general is supportive of the approach for general relationship problems (Baucom et al., 1998), substance abuse (Ripley, Cunion & Noble, 2005), depression and other mood disorders (Beach, Sandeen & O'Leary, 1990), and a host of individual and relationship issues. The general trend in the research is that couples therapy is a good alternative to many problems where the relationship is a large part of the presenting issue. Couples therapists can be assured that while the "failure" rate of couples counseling in general is high, it is significantly better than no treatment (Baucom et al., 1998).

Religious accommodative counseling. As far as religious accommodative counseling in general, while there isn't published research yet for Christian-accommodative couples treatments, there is support that it is at least equally effective as general therapy (Worthington & Sandage, 2002). There is a clinical trial study of religiously accommodative couples therapy that has been presented at conferences demonstrating equal efficacy to secular couples therapy (Leon, Ripley, Davis, Mazzio & Smith 2008; Ripley et al., 2010).

Promoting one theory as the best Christian theory. Scripture itself is silent about the technique of couples counseling and traditions of pastoral care for couples are diverse (Ahlskog & Sands, 2000). Christians may look to Scripture for general ideas about marriage and good relationships. It offers guidelines about love, marriage and helping others. However, we believe *justifying* a particular counseling or enrichment approach by using Scripture is inappropriate. Supporting one's stance as more or less consistent with Scripture is clearly desirable for Christians. However one should not claim scriptural approval of a particular counseling method. Instead, couples therapists should look to data in the natural realm (scientific and we believe to a lesser degree anecdotal or practice experience) for support and accommodate the spiritual needs of each individual client. This should be an ethical mandate, but it has seldom been discussed in ethics.

MARRIAGE ENRICHMENT, EDUCATION AND PREVENTION PROGRAMS

Many churches offer premarital or relationship enrichment programs. Some might even require it for couples marrying in their congregation. Jakubowski et al. (2004) reviewed the existing programs and found four programs to be rated as empirically supported: PREP, Relationship Enhancement, Couples Communication Program and Hope-focused Strategic Relationship Enrichment. All of these programs have been implemented in Christian settings, and PREP and Hope-focused approaches have explicitly Christian versions of the intervention.

An important ethical issue relevant to relationship enrichment, education and prevention is proper referral and exclusions. Troubled couples may become more frustrated by an enrichment program that glosses over serious issues in their marriage. There is even some empirical evidence that distressed couples may get worse from some marriage education programs (Doherty, Lester & Leigh, 1986). In this worst case scenario, highly troubled couples may begin to approach enrichment programs as though they were counseling and escalate their conflict without trained professionals to assist them in managing this process. If this becomes obvious to other couples, it might even interfere with the effectiveness of the entire program if conducted in a group format. Again, Christian therapists could help churches develop and evaluate marriage enrichment programs, assist with preliminary referrals within the church and educate church leaders on marriage interventions that are based on competent assessment and informed by research on effective programs.

SUMMARY

We have suggested an approach to ethics that integrates Christian and professional principles and identifies (as of 2010) current ethical issues in the treatment of marriage. We have also tried to remain true to Christian virtues and ethics passed on from Christian tradition and Scripture. A primary Christian virtue is humility, and this should lead those who follow Christ to remember the limitations of our knowledge. Grace, confession and forgiveness should always have a prominent place in Christian ethical reflection.

REFERENCES

Ahlskog, G., & Sands, H. (2000). *The guide to pastoral counseling and care*. Madison, CT: Psychosocial Press.

Alsdurf, J., & Alsdurf, P. (1989). *Battered into submission: The tragedy of wife abuse in the Christian home*. Downers Grove, IL: InterVarsity Press.

American Association for Christian Counselors. (2004). *AACC code of ethics*. Retrieved from www.aacc.net/about-us/code-of-ethics.

American Association for Marriage and Family Therapy. (2012). *AAMFT code of ethics*. Retrieved from www.aamft.org/imis15/content/legal_ethics/code_of_ethics.aspx.

American Psychological Association. (2002). *Ethical principles of psychologists and code of conduct*. Retrieved from www.apa.org/ethics/code/index.aspx.

Balswick, J. O., & Balswick, J. K. (2006). *A model for marriage: Covenant, grace, empowerment, and intimacy*. Downers Grove, IL: InterVarsity Press.

Baucom, B. R., Atkins, D. C., Simpson, L. E., & Christensen, A. (2009). Prediction of response to treatment in a randomized clinical trial of couple therapy: A 2-year follow up. *Journal of Consulting and Clinical Psychology, 77*, 160-73.

Baucom, D. H., Shoham, V., Mueser, K. T., Daiuto, A. D., & Stickle, T. R. (1998). Empirically supported couple and family interventions for marital distress and adult mental health problems. *Journal of Consulting and Clinical Psychology, 66*, 53-88.

Beach, S. R. H., Sandeen, E. E., & O'Leary, K. D. (1990). *Depression in marriage: A model for etiology and treatment*. New York: Guilford.

Blankenhorn, D., Browning, D., & Van Leeuwen, M. S. (2004). *Does Christianity teach male headship? The equal regards marriage and its critics*. Grand Rapids: Eerdmans.

Bloesch, D. G. (1987). *Freedom for obedience: Evangelical ethics for contemporary times.* San Francisco: Harper & Row.

Butler, M. H., Harper, J. M., & Seedall, R. B. (2009). Facilitated disclosure versus clinical accommodation of infidelity secrets: An early pivot point in couple therapy. *Journal of Marital and Family Therapy, 35,* 125-43.

Christian Association for Psychological Studies. (2007). *Ethical statement of the Christian Association for Psychological Studies.* Retrieved from http://caps.net/about-us/statement-of-ethical-guidelines.

Cassidy-Shaw, A. (2002). *Family abuse and the Bible: The scriptural perspective.* Binghamton, NY: Haworth Press.

Cere, D. M. (2004). Marriage, subordination and the development of Christian doctrine. In D. Blankenhorn, D. Browning & M. S. Van Leeuwen (Eds.), *Does Christianity teach male headship? The equal regards marriage and its critics.* Grand Rapids: Eerdmans.

Chenail, R. J. (2009). Learning marriage and family therapy in the time of competencies. *Journal of Systemic Therapies, 28,* 72-87.

Copel, L. C. (2008). The lived experience of women in abusive relationships who sought spiritual guidance. *Issues in Mental Health Nursing, 29,* 115-30.

Cunradi, C. B., Caetano, R., & Schafer, J. (2002). Religious affiliation, denominational homogamy, and intimate partner violence among U.S. Couples. *Journal for the Scientific Study of Religion, 41,* 139-51.

Dienhart, J. W. (1982). *A cognitive approach to the ethics of counseling psychology.* Washington, DC: University Press of America.

Doherty, W. J., Lester, M. E., & Leigh, G. K. (1986). Marriage Encounter weekends: Couples who win and couples who lose. *Journal of Marital and Family Therapy, 12,* 49-61.

Doss, B. D., Thum, Y. M., Sevier, M., Atkins, D. C., & Christensen, A. (2005). Improving relationships: Mechanisms of change in couple therapy. *Journal of Consulting and Clinical Psychology 73,* 624-33.

Gelles, R. (1982). Applying research on family violence to clinical practice. *Journal of Marriage and the Family, 44,* 9-20.

Gupta, M., Coyne, J. C., & Beach, S. R. H. (2003). Couple treatment for major depression: Critique of the literature and suggestions for some different directions. *Journal of Family Therapy, 25,* 317-46.

Holtzworth-Munroe, A., Meehan, J. C., Herron, K., Rehman, U., & Stuart, G. L. (2000). Do subtypes of maritally violent men continue to differ over time? *Journal of Consulting and Clinical Psychology, 71,* 728-40.

House, H. W. (Ed.). (1990). *Divorce and remarriage: Four Christian views*. Downers Grove, IL: InterVarsity Press.

Instone-Brewer, D. (2007). What God has joined. *Christianity Today, 51*, 26-29.

Jakubowski, S. F., Milne, E. P., Brunner, H., & Miller, R. B. (2004). A review of empirically supported marriage enrichment programs. *Family Relations, 53*, 528-36.

Johnson, M. P., & Ferraro, K. J. (2000). Research on domestic violence in the 1990's: Making distinctions. *Journal of Marriage and the Family, 62*, 948–63.

Jost, J. T., & Jost, L. J. (2009). Virtue ethics and the social psychology of character: Philosophical lessons from the person-situation debate. *Journal of Research in Personality, 43*, 253-54.

Kuo, F. C. (2009). Secrets or no secrets: Confidentiality in couple therapy. *The American Journal of Family Therapy, 37*, 351-54.

Leon, C., Ripley, J. S., Davis, W., Mazzio, L., & Smith, A. (2008, February). *Forgiveness in intimate relationships: The impact of hope focused couples therapy*. American Psychological Association Division 36 Midwinter Conference on Religion and Spirituality, Columbia, MD.

Lewis, K. N., & Epperson, D. L. (1991). Values, pretherapy information, and informed consent in Christian counseling. *Journal of Psychology and Christianity, 10*, 113-31.

Lewis, K. N., & Lewis, D. A. (1985). Pretherapy information, therapist influence, and value similarity: Impact on female clients' reactions. *Counseling and Values, 29*, 151-63.

Margolin, G. (1982). Ethical and legal considerations in marriage and family therapy. *American Psychologist, 38*, 840-50.

Markman, H. J., Resnick, M. J., Floyd, F. J., Stanley, S. M., & Clements, M. (1993). Preventing couples distress through communication and conflict management training: A four- and five-year follow-up. *Journal of Consulting and Clinical Psychology, 61*, 70-77.

Meylink, W. D., & Gorsuch, R. L. (1988). Relationship between clergy and psychologists: The empirical data. *Journal of Psychology and Christianity, 7*, 56-72.

Nydam, R. J. (2005). The messiness of marriage and the knottiness of divorce: A call for a higher theology and a tougher ethic. *Calvin Theological Journal, 40*, 211-26.

Ohlschlager, G., Mosgofian, P., & Collins, G. (1992). *Law for the Christian counselor*. Nashville, TN: Thomas Nelson.

Oordt, M. S. (1997). The ethical behavior of Christian therapists. In R. K. Sanders (Ed.), *Christian counseling ethics: A handbook for therapists, pastors and counselors*. Downers Grove, IL: InterVarsity Press.

Raimondi, N. M., & Walters, C. (2004). Training family therapists to work with children: Competence, relevance and interest ratings in the field of family therapy. *American Journal of Family Therapy, 32,* 225-37.

Ripley, J. S., Cunion, A., & Noble., N. (2005). Alcohol abuse in marriage and family: contexts and treatment considerations. *Alcoholism Treatment Quarterly, 24,* 171-84.

Ripley, J. S., & Worthington, E. L., Jr. (2002). Hope focused and forgiveness based group interventions to promote marital enrichment. *Journal of Counseling and Development, 80,* 452-63.

Ripley, J. S., Maclin, V. L., Pearce, E., Tomasulo, A., Smith, A., Rainwater, S., et al. (2010, August). *Religiously accommodative couples therapy: Process and outcome research.* Poster presentation at the annual meeting of the American Psychological Association, San Diego, CA.

Smedes, L. (1987). *The making and keeping of commitments: The Stob lectures.* Grand Rapids: CRC Publications.

Sokoloff, N., & Pratt, C. (2005). *Domestic violence at the margins: Readings on race, class gender and culture.* New Brunswick, NJ: Rutgers University Press.

Stanley, S. M., Markman, H. J., Prado, L. M., Olmos-Gallo, P. A., Tonelli, L., St. Peters, M., et al. (2001). Community-based premarital prevention: Clergy and lay leaders on the front lines. *Family Relations: Interdisciplinary Journal of Applied Family Studies, 50,* 67-76.

Stevenson, K. (1992). *Nuptial blessings: A study of Christian marriage rites.* Oxford, England: Oxford University Press.

Wall, J., Needham, T., Browning, D. S., & James, S. (1999). The ethics of relationality: The moral views of therapists engaged in marriage and family therapy. *Family Relations, 48,* 139-49.

West, T. C. (2005). Sustaining an ethic of resistance against domestic violence in black faith-based communities. In N. J. Sokoloff & C. Pratt (Ed.), *Domestic violence at the margins: Readings on race, class, gender, and culture* (pp. 340-49). New Brunswick, NJ: Rutgers University Press.

Whipple, V. (1987). Counseling battered women from fundamental churches. *Journal of Couples and Family Therapy, 13,* 251-58.

Whisman, M. A., & Uebelacker, L. A. (2006). Impairment and distress associated with relationship discord in a national sample of married or cohabitating adults. *Journal of Family Psychology, 20,* 369-77.

Worthington, E. L., Jr., & Sandage, S. J. (2002). Religion and spirituality. In J. C Norcross (Ed.), *Psychotherapy Relationships at Work: Therapist Contributions and Responsiveness to Patients* (pp. 383-99). New York: Oxford University Press.

8

The Child Client

Jeffrey S. Berryhill and Angela M. Sabates

According to the American Psychological Association (APA, 2009), over the last several decades child mental health problems have grown into a crisis in our nation and represent a significant public health concern. The APA estimates that approximately one out of every ten children or adolescents experiences a serious mental health disorder, and an additional 10% have mild to moderate problems. The Department of Health and Human Services (2009) reports that between 7.7 million and 12.8 million youth have diagnosable disorders. At present, at least 20% of children ages 8 to 17 receive mental health services in a given year (Kazdin, 2003). Although we do not have data for youth within the Christian community, they appear to experience a similar prevalence of child and adolescent problems.

Since the incidence of child and adolescent mental health problems has become so widespread, an awareness of the broad range of ethical issues related to treating youth has become a necessity for all clinicians. Even if a therapist does not directly see a child as a client, that therapist will be likely to at least help refer the child of a client to a colleague or see cases that involve younger members of a family. Therapists who work with couples should be well-versed in child ethical issues that might arise when parenting or family issues are addressed. Given the prevalence of cases involving children and adolescents, then, any therapist seeking to be well-informed regarding ethical issues needs to know as much as possible about ethical treatment of youth.

The ethical challenges one encounters when evaluating and treating children and adolescents are often quite complex. This complexity results from many factors, including specific developmental issues (e.g., the child's capacity to engage in and understand the purpose of treatment) and the legal vulnerabilities that are particular to children. In addition, controversies over issues such as children's rights and who is ultimately responsible for protecting children also complicate the application of ethical principles. Ethical treatment of children and adolescents is also challenging because youth with mental health problems are frequently involved with more than one agency or service system (e.g., school, social service agency and perhaps a church or youth group), and the therapist must often negotiate or coordinate information with some or all of them. And, as often happens, ethical dilemmas become more complex when it becomes apparent in working with a youth that the parents have significant pathology that must also be addressed.

One significant issue in working with youth has to do with specifying who is the identified client. Is it the minor child or the parent(s) or the entire family? The answer to this question is relevant for the specific ethical issues discussed in this chapter, although we will usually assume that the child is the client. Even when the child is the client, though, the parents usually have some applicable rights (i.e., with client records and informed consent), though they usually do not need protection to the same degree as do children.

Related to this, Salo (2006) notes another factor that makes working with children and adolescents ethically challenging. Specifically, Salo proposes that therapists who work with youth may often experience significant conflicts between what they consider to be their ethical or moral obligations and what the law dictates they must do. For example, while therapists are legally obligated to parents, they often feel ethically more responsible to their minor clients. This tension can result in difficulties when considering who the client is and how treatment should proceed.

Mannheim et al. (2002) likewise reflect on the difficulties inherent in the ethical issues involved in working with youth clients. The researchers conducted a survey of Minnesota child psychologists. On a seventy-six-item, Likert-type scale, respondents indicated whether they had engaged in a specific behavior and whether they considered it ethical. The respondents were more positive about practices such as accepting a hug or attending a client's event if the client is younger than if he or she is an older adolescent. Respondents also were more concerned about protecting adolescent's information compared to the information disclosed by younger children. These results indicate such a significant inconsistency in ethical perceptions regarding treatment of children that "there should be little wonder that the average practitioner can easily become confused or lack confidence when ethical choices emerge in day-to-day practice" (p. 27). The researchers suggest that complexities in dealing with children will likely remain a part of this work for years to come.

As noted previously, various licensing organizations have their own professional ethical codes, and these share in common the basic principles that guide ethical decision making while sometimes differing in specific applications of the codes. It is therefore essential that therapists consult the ethical guidelines observed by their particular discipline. For additional information, the reader is also encouraged to review the CAPS "Statement of Ethical Guidelines" (2005). For the purposes of this chapter, the specific ethical codes referred to will be the APA's (2002) "Ethical Principles of Psychologists and Code of Conduct" as well as the American Counseling Association's (ACA, 2005) "Code of Ethics."

As will become evident throughout this chapter, the individual ethical issues are interrelated. Thus, it is advisable for the therapist to consider the possible connections among the specific issues when working through ethical dilemmas. For example, those Christian therapists who see youth from their own church are more likely to contend with certain ethical challenges for those child clients, such as when a pastor or other church staff may want to obtain information about the child's treatment. In this way, the therapist is not only dealing with the issue of confidentiality but also with that of dual relationships.

Though there are obviously many different ethical issues related to treating youth, this chapter will first focus on informed consent, privacy and confidentiality, mandated reporting of child abuse and neglect, dual relationships, and record-keeping. In addition, a brief discussion regarding the ethical concern of diversity is presented, specifically as it relates to considering Christian families as a minority population in an increasingly secularized world. The possible difficulties inherent in parent-child differences with regard to values and life choices will be presented. Finally, there will be a discussion of the potential ethical issues related to collaboration with clergy, especially as such collaboration provides a good example of a treatment situation that incorporates several different potential ethical dilemmas. The authors of this chapter believe that some Christian counselors as well as lay counselors avoid treating children and adolescents because of the ethical and legal dilemmas that inevitably occur. But as the following discussions will demonstrate, knowledge of the important issues and willingness to work carefully through difficult situations can enable therapists and counselors to safely and ethically treat the young clients who very much need their help.

A word about terms in this chapter: Therapists today encounter many varied family and household configurations, and child clients may be under the care of a parent or parents, grandparents or other relatives, foster parents or other guardians, or a residential center or other agency. The therapist may work with a single child, sibling group, step-siblings or some combination of children or adolescents as well as biological or adopted parents or guardians or other family members or nonfamily persons. For the simplicity and economy of wording, we will generally speak of a single child or teen, and of parents as the caretakers of the child, but the information should be applicable on a broader scale.

INFORMED CONSENT

The ability to consent to treatment has been shown to have many beneficial effects, including a greater sense of autonomy and investment in the counseling process and a greater likelihood of continuing with the process even if difficult (Beahrs & Gutheli, 2001). As noted elsewhere in this text, the APA and ACA guidelines for informed consent for evaluation and therapy services include informing the clients as soon as possible about the nature and course of therapy, the fees, any possible involvement of third parties, HIPAA privacy rights and the limits of confidentiality. In addition, it assumes that the therapist has given sufficient opportunity for the client to have his or her questions answered. In cases where therapy is court ordered, the therapist also explains the implications of a mandated counseling process. But the ethics of informed consent become less clear when one is working with minors, who are not, except in extreme situations, legally permitted to give their own consent for treatment or otherwise refuse treatment they have been brought to and do not want. Thus, the therapist must be aware of who is able to give consent to treatment for the child and how to address consent with the child.

O'Donahue and Ferguson (2003) describe who is able to give informed consent for a child to receive treatment. First, in some cases, the older child/ adolescent may give informed consent for his or her own treatment without the parents' consent. But the circumstances under which this is permissible vary considerably by state and are generally reserved for emergency cases in which the child feels unsafe. A therapist should therefore be well-informed about state regulations regarding consent for treatment. Apart from these possible exceptions, and from situations where services are court-mandated and informed consent may not be a prerequisite for treatment (although it should still be obtained if at all possible), parents are the ones who generally give legal informed consent for the child's treatment. Note that since a minor client is not usually able to give legal consent, the therapist bears a greater responsibility to determine that the proposed treatment is in the client's best interests and to proceed or not proceed accordingly. Parental informed consent is usually straightforward with a single parent or guardian or when married parents agree to their minor's treatment, provided that the therapist also agrees that treatment is appropriate for the child in question. Where married biological or adoptive parents (i.e. those with legal standing as parents) disagree, the therapist should help the parents reach consensus on whether to initiate treatment prior to meeting with the child or teen.

Parental consent for treatment can become problematic in cases where the parents are separated or divorced. If a couple has joint custody and both agree to treatment, the therapist should ideally obtain consent from both parents for treating the child. This is particularly important because, as Thompson and Rudolph (1996) note, "the law generally supports parents who forbid counseling of their minor children, unless there are extenuating circumstances" (p. 509). Further, in the case of joint legal custody, either parent can legally demand an end to therapy for the minor child. In that case, the therapist could incur disciplinary action if he or she resists that parental demand without taking appropriate legal steps to obtain court authorization to continue the treatment.

Koocher (2008) notes that if the parents are separated or divorced and disagree about treatment, especially if they have joint custody, it is best (though often not possible) to meet with them together to resolve disagreement and obtain mutual informed consent. Where only one separated or divorced parent is bringing the child for treatment, it is wise for the therapist to request a copy of the custody agreement or divorce decree or a letter from the parent's attorney that verifies that parent's legal right to seek treatment for the child independently of the other parent. This is particularly important if the other parent does not know or does not approve of a course of treatment for the child. Of course the easiest way to avoid potential difficulties is simply to refuse to see children or adolescents unless both parents agree to treatment. But careful determination of parents' right to consent to the treatment and anticipation of potential problems will greatly reduce parental problems with consent as treatment proceeds and allow much-needed help for children in difficult family situations who might otherwise not receive care.

Even though a child or adolescent may not be able to give legal consent, the therapist should still give that child or adolescent as much information about the treatment process as is appropriate. An essential factor to consider is the developmental age of the child, especially with reference to his or her ability to understand the nature and purpose of the proposed therapy plan. Related to this, the APA specifies that the therapist must "use language that is reasonably understandable to that person." The ACA likewise states that "Counselors use clear and understandable language when discussing issues related to informed consent." There also may be family or other factors, such as a parental affair, job loss or financial hardship, or sexual abuse of a sibling or classmate, that are relevant to the purpose for treatment but not appropriate to share with younger clients. Again, the goal is for the therapist to provide a reasonable explanation, considering the person's "preferences and best interests," and to invite him or her to express any initial opinions or feelings (including fears) about participating in treatment or about the treatment process.

Another challenge to obtaining informed consent from a child or adolescent centers around the fact that in many cases the parents and child disagree about the nature of the presenting problems. Yeh & Weisz (2001), for example, found in a clinic sample that many parents and children did not even agree about what the referral problems were for which treatment was being sought. In fact, Yeh and Weisz found that fewer than half of the parent-child pairs agreed on even a single problem that needed intervention.

Another potential challenge with youth and informed consent is the reality that many initial sessions are held with families in which the child or adolescent was told little or nothing about treatment prior to arriving at the therapist's office. Often, the parents may have been unclear about how to tell the child about therapy, or perhaps the parents were concerned that if they had told the child, he or she would have resisted coming. In some instances children or adolescents accept the parents' strategy, but more often they feel deceived and are initially less inclined to consent to treatment. Therapists should be aware that children are often not included in their parent's decision to pursue treatment, and whenever possible they should help parents prepare the child for coming to therapy.

What if the child does not want treatment and therefore refuses to consent to treatment? Ford Sori and Hecker (2006) have reaffirmed the idea that the therapist should talk with the child openly about his or her feelings about participating in treatment and ideas about the goals being pursued. If a child is initially resistant to therapy, the therapist should show respect by acknowledging the child's feelings and perhaps by communicating an understanding that the child is being forced to cooperate. The therapist may then seek to enlist the child in the treatment process without resorting to coercion, such as by pointing out potential benefits of treatment. A therapist may tell the child, for example, that he or she has the freedom to tell parents when he or she thinks they are making unreasonable demands on the child, or that the child might have a better chance of being heard by the parents in the context of therapy. Therapists obviously must say only what they believe to be true, and must be careful not to cross the line between encouragement and manipulation.

Bear in mind that minors often are more opposed to treatment at the initial contact than later when they have learned about the process and had some time with the therapist. Adolescents are particularly likely to resist even coming to therapy at first; one of the authors sometimes asks older children and adolescents during the first session, "Are you here voluntarily or with your hands tied behind your back?" Remember also that an adolescent who is surly and uncommunicative while sitting with his or her mother may become surprisingly open to treatment once alone with the therapist.

In some situations where a child resists consenting to therapy, the therapist may also work with the parents to provide appropriate incentives or concessions for participating in therapy. Although parents certainly have the right to pursue treatment for their children, both within society and within God's established order, they may gain more therapeutic ground by respecting and negotiating with their children than by simply asserting their authority. One word of caution: parents sometimes can offer incentives that undermine the treatment process. In one case, a parent offered a resistant teen the remainder of the funds designated for therapy if treatment could be concluded earlier than planned. Not surprisingly, the teen quickly talked about the problem issues and pronounced himself cured after one session. It is thus a good idea for the therapist to help parents select incentives that appeal to the client and also support the therapeutic objectives. In these situations the therapist must be especially careful to avoid influence that is not in the client's best interest.

In extreme cases youths may be hospitalized against their will if they are in imminent danger of hurting themselves or another. It is important to be aware of differing state laws governing involuntary commitments to inpatient psychiatric hospitalization. Generally, parents have the legal right to commit a minor to inpatient care against the child's will and without a hearing (Carmichael, 2006). In the case of court-ordered treatment, even if the parents are not initially aware of the court order for their child's treatment, Lawrence and Kurpis (2000) note that it is advisable for the therapist to inform the parents of the child's treatment as soon as possible. To complicate matters, at times not only the youth but also one or both parents may be resistant to hospitalization. Again, in cases of imminent threat, the therapist has the right and sometimes the responsibility to begin the process of involuntary hospitalization, but if the parent is not in agreement the therapist should carefully document the reasons for the decision to pursue inpatient care.

One final issue related to informed consent has to do with the possibility of the need for medication. While most psychologists and other therapists do not prescribe medications, they often are in the role of suggesting an appropriate medical consultation to assess or confirm the need for medication and begin treatment accordingly. In such cases, a therapist may find that parents (and the child) are more reluctant to give their consent for this part of the treatment process. This issue can be an especially controversial one when it deals with youth, and some sectors of the Christian community are particularly opposed to psychiatric medications (though they sometimes are more open to nutritional supplements that purport to exert similar effects).

In order to prevent confusion about the boundaries of the therapist's treatment role, the therapist should make it clear that any decisions regarding medications will be made by the client and parent and by the prescribing physician. The therapist can often help the parent or the child work through reservations about medication as a treatment intervention, including possible concerns about medication side-effects, circumventing God's best plan for healing or engendering a self-perception of sickness. But it must be clear that the therapist is not deciding for the child or the family, and that consent for medication treatment is given to the treating physician.

PRIVACY AND CONFIDENTIALITY

As noted elsewhere in this text, the issue of confidentiality, or keeping a client's information, records and identity private, is a vital one for the counseling profession. Woody (1999), in fact, called confidentiality "the cornerstone of professionalism" (p. 607). Donner et al. (2008) note that therapy clients also have a keen sense of the importance of confidentiality. Violations of confidentiality lead to the perception of psychologists as less trustworthy (Merluzzi & Brischetto, 1983; as cited in Donner et al., 2008) and can of course lead to charges of unethical practice.

As with the ethical issue of informed consent, confidentiality can be challenging when working with youth. Many therapists and school counselors consider issues of confidentiality the most often experienced ethical dilemma (Bodenhorn, 2006; Pope & Vetter, 1992; Pope & Vasquez, 2007). Following are some of the factors that make confidentiality challenging in cases involving minors, along with suggestions for how to address these challenges.

First, the therapist bears primary responsibility for records and other information about a child client, even more so than with an adult client because the child cannot decide independently. The therapist must strive to manage the child's confidentiality in his or her best interests as well as in the best interests of the family, while considering carefully the wishes of the child, parents and other involved parties. For example, confidentiality usually must be violated in cases of suspected abuse or imminent harm to the client or to another person, or in cases where the court requires access to the records. But even then the therapist should try to do so in the way that best supports the minor client's welfare. More situations where the therapist must safeguard the child's interests are provided later in this section.

Next, minors are usually not afforded full confidentiality, partly because they do not bear full legal responsibility for themselves. The confidentiality rights of minors vary considerably. According to one source (Mitchell et al., 2002), minors under the age of twelve do not have confidentiality rights under the law, but depending on the jurisdiction, parents generally have legal control over confidentiality for nonemancipated children under the age of eighteen. There are often legal exceptions such as pregnancy or drug abuse, again depending on location, and therapists must know the state and local rules for confidentiality with minors in order to practice ethically.

When the child does not legally hold the privilege of confidentiality, that privilege is usually held by the parent or guardian unless otherwise specified by the court. Therapists often experience significant tension between the need to reasonably maintain the confidentiality of the child or adolescent client's records and the therapy process itself, and to provide enough information to the parents or other responsible parties for them to fulfill their own responsibilities for the child's well-being. So, on the one hand, the child or teen should feel safe about confiding in the therapist, and on the other hand, the therapist must be able to give parents enough information to help ensure effective treatment and support the welfare of the child client.

Remley and Herlihy (2007) note that younger children usually have less concern about privacy, "whereas teenagers often have a developmentally heightened desire for privacy from their parents" (p. 204). Remley and

Herlihy caution against assuming that children and teens are always concerned about privacy, and they point out that children may share information so that the counselor will carry that information to the parents.

The therapist must be aware that adolescents, especially older or more
mature ones, can be legally entitled to privacy in areas where their parents
might reasonably want to be informed. Some states, for example, allow
adolescents confidentiality for obtaining certain medical services (e.g., for
abortion). Even in situations where reporting information to parents
would be allowed but not required, a therapist may decide that parents
have the right to know something divulged during therapy. In those cases,
the therapist must be convinced that a more crucial issue than confidentiality is at stake. For example, while admission by a teenager that he or she
is using marijuana may not automatically warrant a report to a parent or
other appropriate adult, an admission of potentially self-injurious behavior
while smoking marijuana may well warrant such a report. Therapists
should be aware that they assume responsibility if they withhold information from parents if that information later results in injury to the child
or adolescent client. Such cases often involve the use of controlled sub-
stances by the child client (Remley & Herlihy, 2007). As is the case in all
therapy situations, the fundamental question is: What will best serve the
overall welfare of this client?

Ford Sori and Hecker (2006) suggest that when the therapist has to disclose information to the parents, the child be given several options, including
telling the parents him- or herself in the presence of the counselor, the counselor telling the parents in the presence of the child, the child waiting outside
the office while the conversation takes place. In any case, the counselor
should assure the minor client that he or she will be available to help the
family deal with the new information. Roberts and Dyer (2004) say that it is
also important to remember that even while parents can have access to their
child's records, there are many situations in which the therapist can and
should limit what information is released to the parents. One example would
be if the information would be harmful to the child if disclosed.

Many Christian parents will support a certain level of privacy for their
children with a therapist whom they respect, at least for encouraging
openness with the therapist, and many will trust the therapist to know when

to disclose information about their children. At the negative extreme, of course, some parents see therapy as a way to indirectly access information about their children, and they expect a direct report of what the child said or did during each session.

So how is this complex issue best handled? It is our recommendation, along with other writers on ethics (e.g., Lawrence & Kurpius, 2000; Ford Sori, 2006; Sparta & Koocher, 2008) that agreement on how to handle information disclosed during counseling be established as explicitly as possible during the first meeting and then as needed. This approach helps build mutual trust and clarifies expectations. If other persons will need or require access to information, releases can also be prepared. Thompson (1990) further suggests that all family members state their own understanding and expectations of confidentiality, toward the goal of achieving an agreement that can be acceptable to all. In some cases, the agreement might best be made into a written contract, especially where trust within the family is limited. When parents request a level of access that seems inappropriate to the therapist, he or she should discuss the matter with the parents (in private, if necessary) and attempt to reach a reasonable compromise.

The parents may have concerns that the therapist considers compelling, such as when certain behaviors have preceded self-injurious behaviors in the past. On the other hand, the parents may tend to violate the child's boundaries, and that tendency would need to be addressed. Or the parents may not understand that if they insist on knowing everything that is said the child or adolescent may resist the process, and therapeutic goals will not be accomplished. In any case, parental concerns for the child's well-being do not automatically eliminate the child's right to some privacy. Therapy should not be pursued unless an understanding between parent and therapist can be reached, otherwise difficulties are almost certain to arise.

In an effort to explore what factors therapists use when deciding to disclose risk-taking behavior of their adolescent clients to the parents, Sullivan et al. (2002) surveyed a group of therapists. Of the thirteen factors included, two key factors were, first, the "negative nature of the behavior factor," that is, the degree of risk to the client or others due to the behaviors. Second, therapists used the "maintaining-the-therapeutic-process factor." The authors suggest that this latter factor "may tempt therapists to refrain from

breaking confidentiality even in the presence of extremely dangerous behaviors" if doing so would disrupt the therapeutic relationship (p. 200).
Thus, Sullivan et al. suggest that therapists should consider ethical dilemmas
as a decision-making process rather than as a set of rules to follow. They
further suggest that therapists should document their decision-making
process in order to help avoid liability for the decisions made.

One issue related to confidentiality is especially important if a therapist
deals with a family who is a member of a church community. Ideally, the
client's church and church leaders are the extended spiritual family. As such,
they can provide a wealth of healing resources. In some cases the church
family provides more appropriate assistance to the child than does the
child's own family. Indeed, it is often within the church that family dysfunction is brought to light and confronted. Issues of confidentiality are
especially important when the church is intimately involved. For example,
there may be times when concerned pastoral staff might call the therapist to
request information regarding how the child is doing in therapy. These may
be sincere efforts on behalf of the child's well-being, but for the therapist
would represent ethical breaches of confidentiality, as church leaders have
no legal right to this information without a written release of information
by the legal holder of confidentiality. This is true even if the pastoral staff
member was the one who made the referral for treatment.

Pastors will sometimes assume that as spiritual leader of the church they
have the right to know what is being worked on in the counseling process,
what the therapist is trying to accomplish or what methods are being employed. While it is often appropriate for church leaders to learn about a
therapist's style or theology, it is a violation of confidentiality for the therapist to provide information about an individual without permission or
even indicate that the person is a client. In extreme cases, therapists have
been threatened with being "blacklisted" among local church pastors for not
divulging information about the child in question. When a pastor asks for a
report to a church leader when the child and his or her parents have not
given permission, this should be discussed with the family.

Thus, a child's right to privacy depends on a number of factors: the child's
age and maturity, the reason for referral, the source of the referral (e.g., with
court-ordered therapy confidentiality is essentially waived), state and local

regulations, the content of the therapy, parents' preferences, and the likelihood of risk resulting from behavior that was divulged in treatment. Minor children should generally be made aware of the limits of their privacy. Taking these factors into consideration, a therapist can manage the potential for misunderstandings and conflicts of interest regarding confidentiality, and be better able to determine how much information about the child's treatment should be related to the parents.

MANDATED REPORTING OF CHILD ABUSE AND NEGLECT

In cases where any therapist suspects that a minor client is being physically or sexually abused or otherwise neglected, there is both a legal and ethical mandate to report this to the appropriate authorities (e.g., Child Protective Services). As Carmichael (2006) notes, child abuse reporting is mandatory in all fifty states for those who are in professions (i.e., teachers, doctors, therapists, nurses, social workers) that provide direct services in the care and treatment of children. There are three common types of abuse reported. First, there is *emotional abuse*, which is often referred to as "psychological maltreatment" and is generally defined as a repeated pattern of behavior that conveys to children that they are worthless or unwanted. This may include serious threats of physical or psychological violence. This is often the hardest type of abuse for which to obtain evidence, as children and adolescents may out of fear deny that emotional abuse has occurred. In the absence of physical evidence, this can be a difficult case to prove. Bear in mind, however, that reasonable suspicion is all that is needed for a report to be mandated.

Physical abuse includes a specific physical harm to the child, as well as a substantial risk that a child will imminently suffer some form of physical harm. In this case, the child's parent(s) or caretaker(s) nonaccidentally inflict physical harm upon the child. This type of abuse is often the easiest to prove, given the greater likelihood of physical evidence (e.g., bruises, cuts, etc.). *Sexual abuse* generally refers to contacts between a child and an adult or other person significantly older or in a position of power or responsibility over the child. In this case the child is being sexually stimulated or used for sexual stimulation by the adult or other person.

Remley and Herlihy (2007) remind us that every state has its own statute for reporting abuse. Despite this, "many therapists do not do so because of confidentiality, fear of mishandling by authorities, fear of retaliation, or a desire not to betray the child's trust" (p. 213). Weinstein et al. (2001) note therapists' frequent concerns that reporting suspected abuse would be a breach of confidentiality and thus negatively affect the therapeutic relationship. Weinstein et al.'s research found that the quality of the relationship with the client prior to the report had the most significant effect on the eventual outcome of the report. They thus emphasize, as do other authors (e.g., Sternberg, Levine & Donech, 1997), the vital importance of establishing strong therapeutic relationships with clients in order to enhance the trust the client has of the therapist's motives for making reports to the authorities.

Remley and Herlihy (2007) insist that therapists should know the exact language of their state's statute for reporting abuse, including whether past abuse is reportable along with current abuse. Therapists should further note that the one reporting the abuse is only protected by law if the report is mandated by law and is also made in good faith. It is also essential to know to whom the report should be made, how soon the report needs to be made and whether it needs to be in writing or an oral report will suffice. In addition, given the significant rate of bullying in the schools, a therapist should be aware of any mandated reporting laws regarding violence in the schools. This includes threats of violence as well.

There are several steps that a therapist can follow to make sure that he or she is handling a suspected abuse situation ethically. First, know the state statutes and review them regularly. Second, consult with trusted supervisors or colleagues (taking care to protect client confidentiality) to help clarify the need to report and best manner for reporting, and document the consultation in your records. Third, when you are still not sure whether to report or how best to proceed with a report, contact the local child protection services or hotline and discuss the case informally with a caseworker prior to making a formal report. We have found that such a contact often helps make the decision clearer and also gives one a better sense of how the case will be handled by the authorities. These and any other decision-assisting steps should be documented to support the decision you make.

Although the handling of a child abuse report within the therapy process is beyond the scope of this chapter, it is important to remember that a mandated child abuse report must be made even when the therapist believes it will damage the therapeutic relationship or will not be handled in a way that best promotes the welfare of the child or family. It is often possible to talk in advance with the child or family about how the report will likely be pursued and to involve the parent in making the actual report in order to promote rapport with the child protection agency. A therapist could also serve as a contact with the church in cases where the church is involved in the process or when the abuse occurred in a church setting. In this latter case, a Christian therapist may be particularly helpful to a family or church in coping with the ensuing process. But if a report is required, ultimately the therapist has the responsibility to see that it is made or to make it personally, depending on state requirements.

MULTIPLE RELATIONSHIPS

As is evident from the discussion thus far, the professional relationship with a child and his or her family requires a significant amount of deliberate thought and planning on the part of the therapist. One area in which therapists must be careful is in maintaining clear and reasonable therapeutic boundaries in their professional relationships with clients. Christian therapists, who often participate in churches or other Christian entities, are especially likely to encounter clients in nonclinical settings. Maintaining clear boundaries has obvious advantages, including a greater likelihood of objectivity on the part of the therapist, and this helps the therapist avoid blurry dual or multiple relationships that could compromise his or her judgment. Clear boundaries also decrease the potential for client confusion about the therapist's role in his or her life.

The APA, ACA and NASW all offer specific guidelines regarding some types of dual relationships (e.g., sexual relationships between therapist and client). Yet, otherwise, there is much leeway for the therapist to decide what constitutes a potentially blurred relationship with a client. For example, the ACA "Code of Ethics" specifically notes that there are instances in which interactions with a client outside of the therapy context could be beneficial (e.g., attending a formal ceremony such as the wedding or graduation of a client). The APA "Code of Ethics" similarly notes, "Multiple relationships that would not reasonably be expected to cause impairment or risk exploitation or harm are not unethical" (1.17).

When working with youth, even more than with adults, it is imperative that the therapist engage in thoughtful deliberation about the possible motives and consequences for being involved in an ethically appropriate way in the child's or family's life outside of therapy. A therapist for a child or adolescent may wield considerable influence in some situations or may struggle to maintain sufficient rapport for therapy, so the impact of contact outside therapy must be carefully weighed along the client's or parent's wishes. What specific benefits might there be, for example, in attending an adolescent client's church confirmation or graduation? These benefits should be documented, along with any consultation sought about the matter. In some cases therapists have reported that by attending a client's graduation they were able to demonstrate appropriate genuine concern and nurturing toward the youth (e.g., Pope & Vetter, 1992). It should be clear to the therapist that the nontherapy contact would not undermine the *therapeutic* relationship, and preferably that the contact supports therapeutic objectives.

Another area in which potential multiple relationships can occur is when a Christian therapist sees youth who attend the same church as he or she does, or who are involved in the same children's group or youth group as the therapist or the therapist's child. Indeed, families sometimes choose to consult a therapist who is a member of their immediate faith community precisely because they want to work with someone who understands their spiritual practice and can incorporate it into the process of counseling. In such cases, a therapist should be especially deliberate about considering the relative benefits and potential drawbacks of seeing these clients, including possible role confusion, and discussing such benefits or drawbacks with the client and parents at the outset. For example, the therapist might consider whether knowledge of the child in a church context is helpful (e.g., providing opportunities for informal observations of the child that may appropriately assist in counseling). Conversely, perhaps the child or his or her parents in such contexts may try to cross therapeutic boundaries by having the expectation that the therapist will talk to them about counseling-related issues after a church service or discussing church matters during therapy. If so, clarifying the limits of the counseling relationship must be addressed frankly with the family, if possible at the beginning of therapy. Therapists who live in smaller or rural communities likely will encounter these ethical dilemmas with regard to dual relationships even more frequently.

It is important to note that, while the therapist is required to safeguard the client's rights and needs in this arena, therapists should also consider their own needs and preferences when deciding whether to see clients from their own faith community. A therapist who provides therapy to persons from his or her own church may for the clients' sake have less freedom to participate fully within that community; some therapists accordingly choose not to provide professional services to people in their own churches or ministries.

Koocher (2008) argues that "psychotherapy with children and adolescents constitutes a kind of forced multiple relationship" (p. 606). In other words, the therapist not only has a relationship with the child client but also to varying degrees with all the other people who may have been involved in getting the child in therapy, those who may be responsible to pay the therapy bill, those who may have outcome goals quite different from the child, and also those who may or may not have legal decision-making authority. It is thus imperative that the therapist clarify boundaries with each of these parties, first through the informed consent process and then as challenges arise.

On a different note, therapists may encounter a minor client in accidental or incidental ways (e.g., running into a client at the store or unexpectedly seeing a client at a party). Younger clients most often are quite open about such chance meetings, while some older minors may pretend not to notice or avoid contact. The therapist should generally follow the client's lead as to inadvertent contact and not initiate contact outside therapy unless previously agreed.

Thus, the issue of multiple relationships can present a challenge for those working with youth. Nevertheless, as noted throughout this discussion, therapists can make careful decisions that can help reduce the likelihood of misunderstandings regarding contact outside the therapy context. As with all other ethical dilemmas, the issue of multiple relationships ultimately has to do with the best interests of the client. A therapist who works with youth can make reasonable decisions regarding factors that might entail multiple relationships, including setting appropriate boundaries with clients and relevant others, and discerning when it is valid to have some ethical form of contact with the minor client outside of the therapy context.

Record Keeping

The ethical issues related to informed consent, confidentiality, mandated abuse reporting laws and multiple relationships all involve record keeping. As with other ethical issues, one must be aware that the ethical codes of one's profession may be in conflict with state or federal laws regarding record keeping, and it is thus important to know these and to follow whichever is either more stringent or predominant (federal laws generally take first priority). Not surprisingly, there are issues related to the record keeping for child and adolescent clients that differ from those related to adult clients. As a general practice, we encourage therapists to always remember that records kept under a minor client's name may be successfully obtained by a parent, attorney or court, regardless of the therapist's wishes, so records should be produced and maintained accordingly.

As to specific strategies for record keeping, Koocher (2008) offers a useful though potentially cumbersome strategy: he suggests that therapists who work with youth keep separate records of their meetings with the child and with others. So, for example, the notes regarding therapy with the child would remain separate from those of family sessions or notes of meetings with one or both parents, preferably by means of separate case records with separate informed consents. Koocher offers the example of a therapist who treats a child routinely and then meets individually with the child's divorced parents. Thus, when authorized to release the child's records, the therapist would not include material from meetings with one or both of the child's parents.

Separate records can help with limiting parents' access to records, and they can be especially helpful in divorce or custody situations or whenever records are likely to be demanded regardless of the therapist's or child's wishes. In divorce cases the therapist would keep a chart for the child or children and for each parent if both are involved in the counseling. We should add that the practice of keeping separate records for parents can also benefit them, in that it can help protect their information from being used in legal proceedings regarding child custody. We strongly recommend that any policies of this sort be communicated up front, especially in cases of divorce or possible contested custody. Koocher further states that if one of the parents asks for a copy of the child's records, regardless of whether separate records are maintained, the therapist should be aware that the notes from separate meetings with the other parent cannot ethically be included and usually are legally protected.

If a therapist works in an agency or group practice, he or she should personally handle records requests for minors or at least educate the support staff who file records or respond to requests for record releases to pay special attention to these restrictions. If a child's records are requested and the therapist believes it is not in the child's best interest to do so, the therapist should take appropriate steps to prevent the release. Such steps may include explaining the therapist's concerns to the requesting party or, if records are sought by subpoena or court order, the therapist must respond by producing the records or filing the proper court motions to quash the request. In the latter situation, it is advisable to seek legal consultation to help avoid becoming the target of further legal action.

The therapist, then, should take all reasonable steps to protect the minor client's records when appropriate but should do so prudently and within the prescribed procedures of relevant jurisdictions. Pay close attention to the details of a subpoena, as it often will seek any records that pertain to the client even if another family member's name is on the chart. Remember also that where separate records are not kept, the therapist is often legally as well as ethically required to redact information that is privileged to a parent or other person that is not the subject of the subpoena. Again, consultation with clinical colleagues or peers as well as with legal professionals is highly recommended.

DIVERSITY AND PARENT-CHILD DIFFERENCES

There are many issues unique to working with Christian families. One issue already noted earlier in this chapter involves working with youth whose church leaders do not exercise the same limits of confidentiality to which the therapist is bound. In this section we will discuss other unique situations that a therapist who works with Christian youth is likely to encounter and how these situations may be considered from an ethical standpoint. Specifically, we will discuss the issue of Christian families as an example of a culturally diverse (i.e., minority population) and the parent-child differences that can occur in matters of faith and resultant life style choices.

Therapists may not be accustomed to thinking about Christian families with whom they work as examples of a cultural minority. Typically, we think of racial and ethnic factors when considering diversity. But professional organizations such as the APA consider diversity to encompass a broad range of factors such as age, gender, disability, sexual preference, race and ethnicity. Of note, religion is also considered an important feature of diversity according to all the ethical codes. According to the APA, psychologists are required to "try to eliminate the effect on their work of biases based on those factors" and to "not knowingly participate in or condone activities of others based upon such prejudices" (Principle D). In sum, therapists are encouraged to be aware of their own potential biases and to make every effort to ensure that these do not adversely affect the treatment process. In cases where this is not possible, the therapist must refer the client to another competent professional.

When considering the ethical issue of diversity, it is helpful to consider many Christian youth to be members of a religious minority in an increasingly secularized society. This is true for several reasons. First, youth who are actively involved in a community of faith often seek to live by messages from that community or from their families regarding life choices that are significantly different than those that are prominent in the culture at large (see Jas 1:27). Such messages could relate to issues of moral character, sexual abstinence until marriage, abstinence from alcohol or drugs, appropriate choices for media or career choices. It is important for the therapist to be sensitive to such potentially conflicting messages and to the child's or adolescent's responses to those messages. Christian therapists are uniquely positioned to help young clients navigate between competing directives, provided they do not make unwarranted assumptions about what constitutes a morally appropriate response to the issues under consideration and also follow their discipline's ethical guidelines for diversity.

When considering the Christian family as an example of a cultural minority, it is also essential to remember that the child or adolescent client may have significant differences of opinion from the parents on issues related to faith itself as well as to lifestyle choices. For example, it is especially common for many adolescents to question the faith of their parents and to differ from them on issues such as what constitutes appropriate use of media, the role of sexuality in dating relationships, church attendance and sexual preference. Christian therapists quite commonly are sought out by parents because of their Christian worldview, but the children of those parents may embrace much more secularized stances about life practices. These differences can be likened to cultural differences experienced by parents who have emigrated to the United States and subsequently raised their children here.

Parents who bring the child to therapy often seek to enlist the therapist to support their spiritual and moral positions with the child. The therapist, regardless of his or her own convictions, should seek first to understand both the child and the parent, and also to clarify with them what the therapist's role will be regarding these issues. The therapist must be particularly alert to the possibility of coercion, even if the therapist is convinced of the rightness of a particular position.

As we have already stated, a child's or adolescent's rights on many issues must be particularly safeguarded when the parent and even the therapist disagrees with the client's stand on a particular issue. For some moral issues where the therapist cannot ethically take a side or where a more authoritative voice is needed, it may be appropriate to refer the family to a perceptive pastor or other clergy person for help with the issue. If the therapist finds that he or she will not be able to work with the child or family in a professionally ethical (or personally comfortable) way with an issue such as sexual preference or illegal activity, a sensitive referral to a different therapist is ethically necessary.

Therapists may also encounter children and teens from Christian families who have quite limited exposure to the broader culture because of their parents' desire to keep them "unstained by the world." This strategy can be quite effective, particularly with children who are very easily swayed in what the parents consider to be negative directions. At other times, the restrictions can create or aggravate clinical conditions. Some Christian parents, for example, significantly limit the amount and type of television shows or other media that their child may watch or play, and this can result in a child struggling with peer interaction. Parents may have their children "opt out" of sexual education programs because of the approach taken in the programs, but if not otherwise taught about sexuality those children may be at increased risk for being subjected to or unknowingly perpetrating inappropriate sexual activity.

From a diversity standpoint it is important that the therapist understands the parents' decisions within their religious community and address difficulties in a culturally sensitive and informed way. If the therapist can determine that the family is taking extreme measures within their faith community, a person in spiritual leadership may be an important resource for helping the family moderate its stances. Again, the Christian therapist must actively seek to understand the context for the client's or family's behaviors, and to respond in ways that are clinically appropriate and also ethically consistent with diversity guidelines for his or her professional discipline.

As suggested earlier, an important issue related to seeing Christian youth as a minority subculture is the fact that Christian therapists may not be aware that they have significant biases about the particular expression of faith that the family exercises. Remaining deliberately conscious of such possible biases can occur if a therapist is sensitive and aware of differences between his or her own views and that of the family in matters related to such factors as religious denomination, liberal versus conservative theology (or politics), charismatic or noncharismatic practices and so forth. Such differences can often lead to differences in expected therapy outcomes. In one case, for example, a Christian therapist was seeing an adolescent whose family belonged to a church that emphasized the miraculous healing power of God. This adolescent had been molested by her father. The mother insisted early in the therapy process that if her daughter "just forgave" her father, God would restore their relationship and the daughter would be healed emotionally. In this case the therapist was aware that she herself believed in the restorative power of forgiveness but that this would be a difficult process for the adolescent, who would likely benefit from longer-term therapy than the mother thought would be necessary.

In such a case, a therapist might feel that the mother's position is a simplistic one that does not acknowledge the painful process often involved in forgiveness. But in this case, being aware of this difference in perspective helped the therapist acknowledge the mother's conviction regarding the value of forgiveness and talk with her in a respectful and compassionate way regarding the ways God could use the process of therapy as a healing agent toward that end. This respectful response by the therapist encouraged the mother to talk in a later session regarding her own fears about the difficulty of the therapy process for the entire family and her fears about the possibility that her daughter might not ever be able to forgive her father. This is but one example of how diversity issues related to religion may be powerful forces in the counseling setting. And for this reason, therapists must remain, as the ethical codes suggest, consciously aware of their own theological biases and remain respectful of the client and family's perspective in order to practice ethically and, hopefully, to help maximize the effectiveness of the treatment process.

COLLABORATING WITH CLERGY: A SPECIFIC EXAMPLE OF ETHICAL CHALLENGES

As the previous discussions suggest, there is considerable overlap among the different specific ethical guidelines. Confidentiality issues, for example, are obviously related to those involving informed consent, record keeping and multiple relationships. One area in which a combination of specific ethical concerns may be involved is the process of collaborating with church leaders. In some cases, for example, it may be helpful to consult with a client's youth pastor or church leader to seek additional observations that may be of help in the therapeutic process. Though this is not specifically addressed in the APA or ACA code of ethics, it provides a good example of a therapeutic process that requires careful consideration of numerous specific ethical guidelines.

Collaboration with clergy is consistent with the APA's "Ethical Principles": "When indicated and professionally appropriate, psychologists cooperate with other professionals in order to serve their clients/patients effectively and appropriately" (3.09). Thus, when a young client's difficulties involve spiritual, religious or church-related issues, ethically appropriate care may call for the therapist to cooperate or collaborate with a trained clergy person or spiritual or church leader who has expertise or authority in those issues. Interestingly, no specific research on the ethical issues involved in such collaboration was available at the time of the writing of this chapter.

As noted earlier, clinicians who are Christians operate within the professional counseling world and are required to follow its practices and regulations. They often also operate within or at least interact with the Christian community, where counseling practices and regulations may be unclear or inconsistent and often are different or even in conflict with professional standards. It is thus necessary for therapists to safely navigate the differences between the professional and church worlds. For the sake of simplicity, in this discussion the word used for clergy will be *pastor*, though it is certainly acknowledged that numerous other such titles as *priest* and *minister* exist. The following discussion will focus on two specific areas of ethical challenges when working with clergy: confidentiality and multiple relationships.

In general, clergy and church workers are not required to safeguard information as carefully as therapists, and there is much variability in how they may handle confidential information about clients. Examples of potential problem situations include when a pastor refers a person for counseling without written consent from that person, or when client information provided to a pastor is divulged to other church staff members who may not treat it as confidentially as the therapist. In addition, a youth pastor may choose to share with a youth statements made by his or her therapist or may share information about the client that the client does not know is being shared. Furthermore, a church that is paying for counseling may assume access to information about the therapy.

Berryhill (2008), in collaboration with colleagues, suggests several strategies for managing confidentiality issues in these situations. First, it is important for the therapist to be very clear about the limits of confidentiality with the youth client, his or her parent(s), and with the pastor. This is especially true in cases of divorce or custody disputes, where the therapist should be careful to adhere to the limitations regarding which parent(s) has the legal right to information about the child's treatment. Second, written permission should be obtained before releasing information to anyone in the church setting, and the release should be specific about who is authorized to receive the information (e.g., pastor, secretary, elder, etc.). Third, the therapist should exercise particular caution in releasing written records to churches. For example, in an honest effort to be helpful, a youth leader may wish to see the psychological test report for one of his group members. But the youth leader must be informed that this is privileged information. Such situations suggest the necessity for the therapist to educate youth pastors and church leaders about confidentiality requirements observed by therapists.

As noted earlier, multiple relationships can be rather common when one serves clients within the Christian community. Recall that the APA's "Ethical Standards" require psychologists to avoid a multiple relationship when it "could reasonably be expected to impair the psychologist's objectivity, competence, or effectiveness in performing his or her functions . . . or otherwise risks exploitation or harm" to the client (3.05). There are several types of multiple relationships that can occur when therapists collaborate with pastors. For example, a therapist may need to discuss child or adolescent client referrals or progress with a pastor when the therapist also sees (or has seen) that pastor or a family member as a client, or when the pastor has provided pastoral care to the therapist. As another example, a therapist could consult with a pastor who is counseling with someone the therapist knows personally from church or elsewhere. Additionally, a therapist may be involved in ministry or other church leadership while also attempting to collaborate with that church's pastor regarding the case of a church member. These types of situations become more common the longer a therapist practices within a Christian community and the better he or she knows the ministry community.

Some helpful suggestions for dealing with multiple relationships when collaborating with pastors could include the following. First, be alert for multiple relationship situations and identify them to the client or pastor as appropriate. Second, extend trust judiciously as you collaborate, and learn which pastors use appropriate judgment in client situations. Third, benefit from colleagues' experiences in collaborating with pastors in your area. Fourth, be prepared to sensitively refer a youth client if appropriate when a multiple relationship appears or develops. Finally, consider choosing not to see people from your own church for therapy, especially if you are in a small community or you do not worship in a very large church.

A WORD ABOUT ETHICAL SELF-DEFENSE

Even when a therapist works to follow all of the ethical and professional guidelines, he or she may at some point face a professional complaint or lawsuit (Lawrence & Kurpius, 2000). Such an unwelcome experience may challenge one's commitment to serving children and families, especially when it results from the therapist's efforts to protect or support the welfare of a minor client. But the therapist must remember that being investigated or sued does not mean that a violation has taken place, nor does it mean that a conviction will be the outcome. Legal assistance is extremely valuable in such situations, and therapists must continue to follow ethical guidelines regarding records and confidentiality even in defending themselves before a court, licensing board or federal agency such as the HIPAA department.

Complaints against a therapist are usually brought by parents rather than the child client and sometimes by one parent in a divorce situation when therapy is ongoing. Even under such difficult conditions the therapist should remain focused on the welfare of the child or adolescent client. Consultation and support from professional colleagues, especially ones who have encountered similar challenges, can be invaluable at these times and can help the therapist proceed wisely as well as ethically.

CONCLUSION

As the discussions in this chapter make clear, treating children and adolescents can indeed be a complex and challenging process. In addition to the specific ethical concerns discussed, there are many others that are directly related to working with youth. For example, Lawrence and Kurpius (2000) note that the issue of *competence* is quite relevant, as licensing statutes offer little guidance and most regulatory authorities do not specify what particular skills are necessary for working with children and adolescents. For example, a therapist may be tempted to offer parenting advice to an adult client without having sufficient knowledge and experience with child development to have professional competence in doing so. In addition to issues related to competence, there are many other specific ethical concerns related to working with youth, such as the pastor collaboration challenges noted earlier. Taken together, these issues present a sobering look at the complexities of ethically dealing with child and adolescent clients and their families.

Despite the challenges that therapists face when working with youth and their families, we are convinced that it is possible to work ethically as well as effectively with this population. The key to addressing potential ethical concerns is to always keep the welfare of the client in mind and also to remember that resolving ethical dilemmas is most often a deliberate process that entails considering possible resolutions and their implications. In addition, consultation with colleagues is an important part of resolving ethical concerns. In fact, as noted throughout the chapter, there are instances in which no explicit ethical guideline is given, and therapists must then do their best to act in a way that other professionals would agree is in the best interests of the client.

Lawrence and Kurpius (2000, as cited in Carmichael, 2006) have made suggestions to help the therapist navigate the difficult arena of working with minors. These suggestions serve as a helpful summary of the sections of this chapter.

- Practice within the limits of your training, education and supervised expertise.

- Be completely familiar with what constitutes privilege and its limitations within your state.

- Develop a written informed consent that clarifies confidentiality for the child and the parents at the onset of therapy and that asks for the child and parents' (legal guardian's) cooperation. The document needs to be signed by all parties and dated prior to the first treatment session.

- Keep accurate and objective records of all therapy sessions.

- Secure malpractice insurance that will adequately cover cost in case of suit or investigation by a professional board or other regulatory agency (e.g., HIPAA).

- Confer with colleagues or legal counsel when unsure of the proper ethical or legal procedure.

Children and adolescents appear to have greater need for mental health services than ever before, and therapists who competently practice with youth and families in the Christian community are much needed. Although there are considerable ethical challenges for therapists who treat children and their families, it is also important for the reader to remember that Scripture in general and Christ specifically placed particular value on children (e.g., Ps 127: 3-5; Mt 18:2-6; Mk 10:13-14), and that great and life-changing good can be done when intervening in the life of a child. Serve them with caution, but serve them nonetheless.

REFERENCES

American Counseling Association. (2005). *Code of ethics.* Alexandria, VA: American Counseling Association.

American Psychological Association. (2002). Ethical principles of psychologists and code of conduct. *American Psychologist, 57,* 1060-73. Also available (with 2010 amendments) from www.apa.org/ethics/code/index.aspx.

American Psychological Association. (2009). Promoting awareness of children's mental health issues. Retrieved from www.apa.org/about/gr/issues/cyf/awareness .aspx.

Beahrs, J. O., & Gutheli, T. G. (2001). Informed consent in psychotherapy. *American Journal of Psychiatry, 158,* 4-10.

Berryhill, J. S. (2008). *Ethical challenges for therapists who collaborate with pastors.* Paper presented at Eastern Regional Conference of the Christian Association for Psychological Studies, November 15, 2008, Greencastle, PA.

Bodenhorn, N. (2006). Exploratory study of common and challenging ethical dilemmas experienced by professional school counselors. *Professional School Counseling, 10,* 195-202.

Carmichael, K. D. (2006). Legal and ethical issues in play therapy. *International Journal of Play Therapy, 15*(2), 83-99.

Donner, M. B., VandeCreek, L., Gonsiorek, J. C., & Fisher, C. B. (2008). Balancing confidentiality: Protecting privacy and protecting the public. *Professional Psychology: Research and Practice, 39*(3), 369-76.

Ford Sori, C., & Hecker, L. L. (2006). Ethical and legal considerations when counseling children and families. In C. Ford Sori (Ed.), *Engaging children in family therapy: Creative approaches to integrating theory and research in clinical practice* (pp. 159-76). New York: Routledge.

Kazdin, A. E. (2003). Psychotherapy for children and adolescents. *Annual Review of Psychology, 54,* 253-76.

Koocher, G. P. (2008). Ethical challenges in mental health services to children and families. *Journal of Clinical Psychology, 64*(5), 601-12.

Koocher, G. P. (n.d.). *Ethical issues in working with children and families.* (Power-Point slides). Retrieved from www.oup.com/us/ppt/pdr/ChilrenandFamilies.ppt.

Lawrence, G., & Kurpius, S. (2000). Legal and ethical issues involved when counseling minors in nonschool settings. *Journal of Counseling & Development, 78,* 130-36.

Mannheim, C. I., Sancillo, M., Phipps-Yonas, S., Brunnquell, D., Somers, P., Farseth, G., et al. (2002). Ethical ambiguities in the practice of child clinical psychology. *Professional Psychology: Research and Practice, 33,* 24-29.

Mitchell, C., Disque, J., & Robertson, P. (2002). When parents want to know: Responding to parental demands for confidential information. *Professional School Counseling, 6*(2), 156-62.

O'Donahue, W., & Ferguson, K. (2003). *Handbook of professional ethics for psychologists: Issues, questions, and controversies.* Thousand Oaks, CA: Sage.

Pope, K., & Vasquez, M. (2007). *Ethics in psychotherapy and counseling. A practical guide* (3rd ed.). San Francisco: Jossey-Bass.

Pope, K. S., & Vetter, V. A. (1992). Ethical dilemmas encountered by members of the American Psychological Association: A national survey. *American Psychologist, 47,* 397-411.

Remley, T. P., & Herlihy, B. (2007). *Ethical, legal, and professional issues in counseling.* Upper Saddle River, NJ: Pearson Education.

Salo, M. (2006). Counseling minor clients. In B. Herlihy & G. Corey (Eds.), *ACA ethical standards casebook* (6th ed., pp. 201-3). Alexandria, VA: American Counseling Association Press.

Sparta, S. N., & Koocher, G. P. (2006). *Forensic mental health assessment of children and adolescents.* New York: Oxford University Press.

Sternberg, K. L., Levinve, M., & Doneck, H. L. (1997). Effects of legally mandated child abuse reports on the therapeutic relationship: A survey of psychotherapists. *American Journal of Orthopsychiatry, 18,* 112-22.

Sullivan, J. R., Ramirez, E., Rae, W. A., Pena Razo, N., & George, C. A. (2002). Factors contributing to breaking confidentiality with adolescent clients: A survey of pediatric psychologists. *Professional Psychology: Research and Practice, 33*(4), 197-202. Washington, DC: American Psychological Association.

Weinstein, B., Levine, M., Kogan, N., Harkavy-Friedman, J., & Miller, J. (2001). Therapist reporting of suspected child abuse and maltreatment: Factors associated with outcome. *American Journal of Orthopsychiatry, 55*(2), 219-33.

Woody, R. H. (1999). Domestic violations of confidentiality. *Professional Psychology: Research and Practice, 30,* 607-10.

Yeh, M., & Weisz, J. R. (2001). Why are we here at the clinic? Parent-child (dis) agreement on referral problems. *Journal of Consulting and Clinical Psychology, 69,* 1018-25.

9

Addressing Spiritual and Value Issues in Therapy

Randolph K. Sanders

This chapter considers the ethics of two issues of considerable importance in therapy. One has to do with the spiritual concerns of the client; the other examines moral value dilemmas clients bring to therapy.

In keeping with the theme of the book, the chapter assumes that the reader is a Christian mental health professional in practice or in training. A chapter directed toward mental health professionals of other faith perspectives or of no faith in particular would have a different emphasis. Having said this, it is recognized that the population of the Christian mental health professionals is a rather heterogeneous group in itself. They come from a variety of Christian traditions, often believe quite differently about the same religious issues, have different philosophies of psychotherapy and vary in their opinions about how spiritual or value issues should be addressed in therapy. I attempt to be mindful of this in the chapter.

In addition, the chapter takes into account that the spiritual backgrounds of clients treated by Christian therapists can vary widely. While it is understood that some Christian mental health professionals work in quite insulated religious settings where virtually all the clients come from the same church or religious persuasion, many Christian therapists see clients from a variety of religious persuasions or no religious background.

SPIRITUALITY AND THE MENTAL HEALTH PROFESSIONS

In recent years the mental health professions at large have become very interested in spirituality. Numerous books and articles have appeared discussing the interface of psychotherapy and spirituality at a theoretical and at an applied/clinical level (Aten & Leach, 2008; McMinn, 2006; McMinn & Campbell, 2007; Miller, 1999; Pargament, 2007; Plante, 2009; Richards & Bergin, 2004, 2005; Shafranske, 2006; Sperry & Shafranske, 2005). Some writers focus on spirituality in its broadest context (i.e., the client's sense of the transcendent or the ultimate meaning in life), while others focus more on the interface of psychotherapy with a particular mode of spirituality (e.g., Christian counseling, etc.).

This relatively new interest in psychotherapy and spiritual matters by the mental health professions at large comes in response to needs long held by many clients but generally overlooked by the profession at large. In one study, 55% of clients surveyed indicated their desire to discuss religious or spiritual matters in therapy (Rose, Westefeld & Ansley, 2001). The authors of the study declared:

> Clearly, many clients, especially the highly spiritual, believe that religious and spiritual issues not only are acceptable and preferable for discussion in therapy, but also are important therapeutic factors, central to the formation of worldview and personality and impacting human behavior. (p. 69)

Some clients ask specifically for spiritual issues to be addressed, and others are disappointed if they are not. In addition, data suggest that even when spiritual issues are not addressed in therapy, clients sometimes find ways to integrate their own spiritual helps into treatment protocols (Rye et al., 2005; Sanders, 1980).

Gradually, the professional bodies that set policies and ethical standards have attempted to raise consciousness about the importance of religious/spiritual issues in therapy through official pronouncements. For example, the Diagnostic and Statistical Manual of the American Psychiatric Association, the accepted guide for clinicians for diagnosing problem areas that are a focus of treatment, added a new code in its fourth edition. This code, V62.89, is to "be used when the focus of clinical attention is a religious or spiritual problem" (American Psychiatric Association, 1994).

General Principle E of the ethics code of the American Psychological Association (APA), in its 2002 edition, added a new statement which reads in part,

> Psychologists respect the dignity and worth of all people, and the rights of individuals to . . . self-determination. . . . Psychologists are aware of and respect cultural, individual, and role differences, including those based on . . . religion . . . and consider these factors when working with members of such groups. Psychologists try to eliminate the effect on their work of biases based on those factors. (APA, 2002)

Moreover, in its "Guidelines for Providers of Psychological Services to Ethnic, Linguistic and Culturally Diverse Populations," the APA said that "Psychologists respect client's religious and spiritual beliefs and values, including attributions and taboos since they affect worldview, psychosocial functions and expressions of distress" (APA, 1993).

As the reader no doubt notices, much of this interest in spiritual matters by professional bodies is driven by appropriate concerns to respect client diversity, autonomy, dignity and worth in all areas, including religion. Sensitivity to and respect for the client's religious beliefs seems obvious to many modern readers, but this issue was largely ignored by professional bodies in the past, and we may legitimately ask why. Perhaps one answer can be found in studies indicating that in general, psychologists are less religious than the U.S. population as a whole (Beit-Hallahmi, 1977; Bergin & Jensen, 1990; Delaney, Miller & Bisonó, 2007; Hill et al., 2000; Ragan, Malony & Beit-Hallahmi, 1980). It is not unreasonable to think that therapists who are not particularly religious themselves would tend to overlook these matters in their clients. Unfortunately, in some cases, therapists have actually been guilty of denigrating clients' religious beliefs (Gonsiorek, Richards, Pargament & McMinn, 2009). Thankfully, and perhaps because professional bodies are urging members to be respectful of clients' beliefs, studies now indicate that clinicians are becoming aware that spiritual issues are relevant to treatment and that spiritual practices can be beneficial to mental health (Delaney, Miller & Bisonó, 2007; Frazier & Hansen, 2009; Hathaway, Scott & Garver, 2004).

Beyond respecting client religious beliefs, some professional bodies have gone further, highlighting the importance of gaining *competence* in evaluating and dealing with spiritual issues in therapy. The APA ethics code, for example, states that:

Where scientific or professional knowledge in the discipline of psychology establishes that an understanding of factors associated with . . . religion . . . is essential for effective implementation of their services, . . . psychologists have or obtain the training, experience, consultation, or supervision necessary to ensure the competence of their services, or they make appropriate referrals. (APA, 2002, Sect. 2.01 (b))

Thus, the APA urges therapists to gain competency in understanding and evaluating spiritual issues in therapy or, lacking these skills, to be able to refer to those who do. Unfortunately, early research suggests that despite these admonitions, few therapists are actually pursuing training in these skills (Frazier & Hansen, 2010). Christian therapists with the kinds of competencies I will describe shortly may be in a unique position to play a role in meeting these needs.

Before doing so, however, it is important to note that while mental health professional bodies as a whole have embraced the notion that spiritual matters are important and should be respected and assessed as part of psychotherapy, there is little agreement about how to intervene in these matters. Some professionals attempt to draw clear lines of demarcation between the interventions of mental health professionals and those of clergy or other religious leaders. They want to be sensitive to spiritual matters, but worry about issues of "competence, role confusion, integrity and respect" when mental health professionals are involved in directive spiritual intervention, and so they recommend great caution in crossing any boundaries (Saunders, Miller & Bright, 2010). Others believe that some directive spiritual interventions are appropriate, as for example when the therapist makes a method like rational emotive therapy more effective by presenting it within a spiritual framework acceptable to the religious client (Gonsiorek, Richards, Pargament & McMinn, 2009). Still others point out the difficulty of trying to clearly differentiate "spiritual" from "psychological" interventions (Pargament, 2007, 2009). McMinn, for example, notes that interventions such as forgiveness counseling were once thought of as solely religious practices, but now there is a large body of psychological research pointing to their effectiveness and they are frequently employed in secular as well as spiritual counseling (Gonsiorek, Richards, Pargament & McMinn, 2009). Moreover, he points to preliminary research suggesting that for Christian clients, the use of more directive spiritual interventions such as prayer can enhance the effectiveness of forgiveness interventions.

Those who encourage spiritual "sensitivity" but eschew any spiritual intervention do not fully take into account the fact that there are a number of professionals who have been trained in accredited mental health programs that teach students how to address spiritual matters in therapy. Moreover, they may not understand that if the mental health professions establish policies requiring therapists to avoid all directive spiritual interventions, it can be expected that many subpopulations of devoutly religious clients will resist accessing mental health care altogether.

Of course, an uncritical integration of spiritual with psychological interventions is also of concern. While as Pargament (2007, 2009) asserts there is most certainly overlap between spiritual matters and mental health matters, the two endeavors are not synonymous. The mental health professions place great emphasis on "psychological adjustment" while many from the world of religion place emphasis on what Malony (1982) calls "holiness."

And therapists who are so wedded to a particular spiritual approach to therapy that they are unable to appreciate points of positive therapeutic reference in the client's own spiritual journey are a concern. Of most concern are those who might be termed "stealth" mental health professionals: practitioners with mental health credentials who once they are credentialed, scuttle their mental health training and use their position to impose a particular approach to spirituality or religious practice on their clients.

MODELS FOR ADDRESSING SPIRITUAL ISSUES IN THERAPY

What is needed is a nuanced approach to spiritual intervention. Such an approach would respect the need many clients have for integrating spiritual matters in therapy, be mindful of potential problems or conflicts, and be sensitive to the fact that religious clients approach the psychological-spiritual interface in therapy in a wide variety of ways. Consequently, I suggest that rather than promoting just one standard, multiple approaches be considered. In the section below I describe three models that are illustrative of approaches currently being utilized by licensed Christian counseling professionals. The three models are not mutually exclusive, but may be seen as points along a continuum. Indeed, as we will see, persons who subscribe to one of the second two models must also subscribe to the first model in order for their approach to be ethically credible. The models reflect appreciation for the continuum of spiritual care advanced by Saunders, Miller and Bright (2010), but with significant contrast. I assume, for example, that each model may be more or less appropriate ethically depending on the circumstances, the client populations, the competencies of the therapist, the counseling setting and the methods by which the informed consent process is handled.

- Sensitivity-based model (SB). In this model, the Christian therapist is sensitive to and actively assesses the spiritual issues in the client's presentation. Respectful and situation-appropriate evaluation of spiritual issues is a part of the intake process, and the therapist is concerned with how spiritual issues relate to the problems the client presents for treatment. However, the therapist does not try to intervene in the spiritual matters directly beyond providing an accepting, empathic environment for exploring the issues. If the spiritual issues seem significant, the therapist considers referral to a religious leader acceptable to the client. The client's minister, pastoral counselor, chaplain, campus minister, spiritual director or other religious leader might be considered, provided the leader is sympathetic to mental health concerns and open to collaboration. The therapist's chief responsibilities are to continue to monitor the importance of spiritual issues in the therapeutic process and, with client authorization, to carry on consultation and coordination of care as needed with the religious leader. This model might be most appropriate for Christian therapists who lack competence in addressing the spiritual matters presented or who face institutional restrictions that limit their responding to spiritual matters.

- Integratively based model (IB). Like the SB model, the Christian therapist in the integratively based model is sensitive to and actively assesses the spiritual issues in the client's presentation in a respectful and situationally appropriate manner. If spiritual issues exist, however, a competently trained therapist may seek to address them utilizing methods that are consistent with the overall mental health treatment plan and that accommodate as much as possible to the unique set of spiritual perspectives and tools the client brings to therapy. In short, the trained therapist in this scenario attempts to integrate selected spiritual interventions as part of the psychological treatment plan and in a manner that is client centered. For example, a Christian client who is a member of a Bible church presents for therapy struggling with passivity in relationships. She wants help with boundary setting, but notes that she has trouble saying no to people because it seems to conflict with her belief that she should always "go the second mile" and "turn the other cheek." Following assessment the psychologist, with the client's consent and as part of a comprehensive treatment plan, institutes a cognitive behavioral assertiveness training intervention and integrates it with a scripturally based rationale for assertiveness (Sanders, 1980; Sanders & Malony, 1982). Or consider the client who comes to therapy struggling to manage stress and anxiety. Assessment reveals that the client has had a little experience with meditation and has found it somewhat helpful because, according to him, it seems to get him "in touch" with something bigger than himself. The integratively oriented therapist might encourage him to explore meditation in more depth, perhaps using selected readings that are psychologically sound and sensitive to the client's spiritual understandings.

- Doctrinally based model (DB). Again, like the SB model, the therapist is sensitive to and actively assesses the spiritual issues present in the client's presentation. However, in the doctrinally based model, the Christian therapist clearly starts from a particular religiously based perspective that underlies the entire approach to therapy. The therapist's doctrinal basis directs the way in which spiritual issues will be addressed. For example, a therapist might advertise that she provides biblically based counseling services that make use of cognitive therapy techniques. By this she means that she presumes a particular doctrine of biblical interpretation that she actively incorporates into the therapy and that informs the approach to cognitive therapy she utilizes. In another case a Christian marital therapist might require that all couples complete a Bible study guide that describes "God's plan for an intimate marriage," and use this study guide as a precursor to behaviorally oriented marital interventions.

I wish to reiterate that the three models are not mutually exclusive. The second two must have the sensitivity-based model embedded within them in order to be ethically credible. In addition, the models should be seen on a continuum, with some Christian therapists demonstrating elements of more than one model. Nevertheless, it is fair to assume that most Christian therapists today adopt a variation of one of these models as their predominant standard for practice.

In the material that follows, I will overview and then discuss in greater detail the ethical principles that come to the fore when one contemplates addressing spiritual issues in therapy. Then I will attempt to discuss how well (or how poorly) each of the models of care just discussed meets the standards advanced by those principles. As we will see, the models each have their place, but are more appropriate to some situations than others.

One ethical principle that comes into play when one considers the ethics of addressing spiritual matters in therapy is therapist *competence*. What kind of training and experience is needed for a therapist to competently address spiritual issues in therapy? What types of spiritual interventions are ethically and professionally appropriate?

A second principle involves client *self-determination* or *autonomy*. When addressing spiritual issues, how does one insure that the client's freedom of choice and right to self-determination are safeguarded in the process?

A third principle has to do with *fidelity* (Kitchener, 1984). The professional therapist in his or her role as a therapist has loyalties, responsibilities and obligations first to the client(s), of course, but also to the profession, to the institution where the professional works, to the wider community and, the Christian might add, to Christ and the kingdom of God (*basileia tou theou*).

The fourth principle is that of *beneficence* (Beauchamp & Childress, 1983). It is the therapist's job "to benefit those with whom they work and take care to do no harm" (APA, 2002, Principle A). How can one best benefit the client(s) when addressing spiritual issues?

COMPETENCE IN ADDRESSING SPIRITUAL ISSUES

Obviously therapist *competence* is a fundamental ethical concern when spiritual issues are addressed in therapy. Elsewhere in this volume Butman does a fine job of drawing up essential qualifications for those who hold themselves out as Christian counselors. For Christian therapists who would address spiritual issues in therapy competently I would add the following:

1. Christian therapists should have a segment of their training specifically oriented toward understanding and responding to spiritual issues in therapy. Such training might be taken in a traditional academic program such as a college, university or seminary that offers training specific to this form of counseling, or through internships or practicums where this spiritual counseling is offered. Training could also be developed over time through continuing education events sponsored by professional organizations such as the American Psychological Association (APA), the Christian Association for Psychological Studies (CAPS) or through supervised experiences and self-study.

2. Three essential elements of a training curriculum should be *self-awareness* training, basic techniques of *spiritual assessment*, and training in the use of *spiritually related interventions*.

- Self-awareness training incorporates at least three core competencies. First is the ability to articulate one's own spiritual/religious/moral frame of reference. The second is to understand the influence of one's cultural background, history and tradition on one's spirituality. The third is insight into one's own spiritual and religious biases, prejudices and gaps in knowledge.

- Regarding spiritual assessment, several writers have offered helpful approaches to this sensitive area (Cornish & Wade, 2010; Plante, 2009; Richards & Bergin, 2005; Saunders, Miller & Bright, 2010). In general, they recommend different kinds of general questions to aid the practitioner in assessing spiritual matters. These might include: How important is spirituality or religion in your daily life? Are you affiliated with a particular religious community? Has the problem for which you are seeking help affected your spiritual life? While the content of spiritual assessment is important, fully as important is the process of the assessment. As Richards noted, the competent therapist must "have the ability to create a spiritually safe and affirming therapeutic environment" if spiritual issues are to be assessed and dealt with (Gonsiorek, Richards, Pargament

& McMinn, 2009). In short, the therapist must be able to sensitively and caringly adapt the spiritual assessment to the client who is present and the needs which he or she brings into the room. It must be client-centered. In many ways, a dialogic spiritual assessment develops naturally from the initial session(s). Suppose that at the first session a very depressed client is describing the circumstances and life stressors that have led him to this point in his life. After empathically responding to his discouragements for a time, the therapist asks, "What keeps you going day by day?" After reflecting for a few moments the client replies, "Well I guess it would be my church," to which the therapist responds, "Well, tell me a little about your church and how it helps you." Thus begins a client-centered spiritual assessment. Consider also the client with marital problems who when asked during the initial interview her goals for therapy said, "I need to know if God will forgive me if I divorce my husband." Hearing this, the therapist could change course and inquire, "Well, tell me about your relationship with God," or to be more specific, "Tell me how you think God looks at situations like this." Approaches to spiritual assessment that begin with what the client is willing to share, and mirror the client's own religious language where possible, show respect and sensitivity for the client and take into account that client spirituality is a very individual and personal matter. They also allow the spiritual assessment to proceed naturally and decrease the chances of triggering defensiveness on the part of the client.

- As for spiritually related interventions, an essential curriculum would include training in *evidenced-based approaches* to spiritually oriented psychotherapy. Therapists who would practice ethically need to know and have an appreciation for therapeutic interventions for which there is empirical support. In order to do that, of course, therapists must have a foundational background in behavioral statistics and research methods. They must be able to read research studies critically and utilize findings prudently in their day-to-day therapeutic interventions. Admittedly, the volume of research on spiritually oriented therapies is lacking, but it is developing and reviews of outcome studies are beginning to appear (Richards & Worthington, 2010). In addition to an appreciation for evidence-based approaches, however, therapists need to stay abreast of the evolving *standard of care* for intervening in spiritual matters in therapy. The standard of care refers to the consensus guidelines that evolve within the mental health professions regarding what constitutes the minimum standard of prudent care relative to various clinical concerns. It is developed in the clinical literature and in the guideline statements that professional bodies issue from time to time.

3. Christian therapists should have training in the *beliefs of various churches/denominations*, and of *world religions* as well. Therapists who are Christians, particularly those who have not had training in religious matters at a seminary or university, may incorrectly assume that their own personal faith perspective makes them competent to counsel most Christian clients who come to see them. That is a myopic perspective that is fraught with potential pitfalls. Even those who have had seminary or higher education in religious studies have sometimes received that training in one tradition only. Thus, it is important for the therapist to find avenues for learning about other faith traditions. Ideally, such a curriculum would include some interpersonal interaction with leaders and laypeople from other traditions. Of course, it must be understood that individual clients do not necessarily believe or act in all ways like their religious tradition teaches. Not all Roman Catholics oppose abortion, and there are those who consider themselves born-again Christians who do not believe in the inerrancy of Scripture. Nevertheless, knowledge of world religions, denominations and church polity can give Christian therapists a broader perspective from which to work with people from a variety of traditions, and it can also help the therapist discern when clients are experiencing dissonance between their own beliefs and behaviors, and the norms and social customs taught by their religious tradition.

4. Christian therapists should develop consultative resource persons in the mental health field who have specific expertise in addressing spiritual issues in therapy. These consultants could provide help with cases in which the therapist lacks expertise and act as an objective resource when ethical dilemmas arise.

5. The competent Christian therapist will endeavor to build suitable clergy consultative and referral resources. Clergy, especially those with

some training in pastoral care or chaplaincy, can often provide assistance with spiritual matters that are beyond the therapist's level of competence. Moreover, it can sometimes be helpful to refer clients back to their pastor or spiritual leader for help with specific spiritual issues or questions that are outside the therapist's realm of expertise, or that are otherwise better dealt with by a religious leader within the person's faith tradition. As we have seen, an important part of being competent involves obtaining and maintaining the training necessary to address spiritual issues. Just as important is developing the judgment to recognize when one lacks knowledge in a particular area and needs to coordinate care with another professional or to refer the client outright to someone with stronger skills. Therapists commonly refer to physicians when physical problems may be at issue or when an evaluation for psychotropic medications is needed. Christian therapists also need to consider the importance of referring to religious professionals suitable to the client when the client's spiritual concerns are outside the therapist's knowledge and expertise.

Unfortunately, McMinn and his colleagues (McMinn, Chaddock, Edwards, Lim & Campbell, 1998) found that referral patterns between clergy and psychologists tend to be unidirectional with clergy doing most of the referring and not the other way around. Of course therapists must be prudent when they make referrals. Not all clergy have basic training in counseling and psychopathology, and some referrals can result in negative consequences. Moreover, consultation is not helpful in some situations, particularly when clients are uncomfortable with their religious leader knowing too much about their personal life. Having said this, there are instances where consultation as well as coordinated care between pastor or religious leader and therapist can be of significant benefit to the client. In cases where the client has a religiously based dissonance regarding a particular intervention, the religious leader may be able to reframe issues in such a way that the client is able to inculcate the therapeutic intervention more successfully. Conversely, the religious leader may be able to increase the understanding of the therapist if the therapist is calling for change that may run counter to a basic tenet of the person's faith.

CLIENT SELF-DETERMINATION—AUTONOMY

The autonomy of the client and his or her right to choose whether to participate in any type of therapy is a major tenet of the ethics codes of virtually all professional counseling bodies (APA, 2002, Principle E; ACA, 2005, sect. A). All therapists licensed by the state and/or sworn to obey the ethics codes of one of these professional bodies have agreed to this principle. This means that the ethical therapist will respect the right of the client to choose whether he or she wishes to make spiritual issues a point of discussion in the therapeutic process and will collaborate with the client when spiritual interventions are used. It most surely means that the therapist will not *impose* his or her spiritual beliefs on the client.

One way to help insure that clients' rights to autonomy and self-determination are safeguarded is to provide the client with appropriate *informed consent* relative to participating in spiritual interventions. Good informed consent consists of providing the client information about the nature of the spiritual intervention(s) proposed, and the right to accept or refuse the intervention(s). It may also include information about the potential benefits and risks of the intervention, and alternative means of accomplishing the therapeutic goals.

Informed consent is usually provided through some combination of printed information or disclosure, a written agreement signed by the client, and verbal discussion properly documented by the therapist. The therapist needs to consider several factors in determining what information should be included in the informed consent procedure. One is the counseling setting. Counseling centers explicitly affiliated with a specific denomination, church or religious group may carry with their name some information about the kind of counseling provided. On the other hand, a private practitioner listed in the phone book by name and profession only provides no clues to the prospective client about how spiritual matters might be handled.

Another factor has to do with the types of spiritual interventions the therapist offers. Tan (1996) speaks of *implicit* and *explicit* approaches to intervention. By implicit, he means that the therapist "does not openly, directly, or systematically use spiritual resources like prayer and Scripture or other sacred texts, in therapy" (Tan, 1996). The therapist might pray for his clients outside of therapy, but would not pray openly with a client in the session.

Explicit intervention is described as the open use of selected spiritual resources in the therapy. For example, in explicit intervention, the therapist might pray aloud with a client during a therapy session. All other things being equal, the therapist using explicit interventions has a greater responsibility to make sure clients are properly informed about the techniques that may be used. Sanders (2000) has provided several examples of how a therapist might introduce his use of implicit or explicit interventions in an informed consent document.

Another factor has to do with the perspective of individual clients. Some clients assume that counseling offered at a religiously affiliated counseling center will be explicitly religious in nature and may be surprised and disappointed if it is not. Others may assume that accepting counseling at such an agency will be no different than say, receiving health care at a denominationally affiliated medical hospital where the emphasis is placed on medical rehabilitation and there is no overt emphasis placed on religious matters. Therapists who work in church counseling centers that only see members of that particular church for counseling may feel safer about clients understanding and affirming the kinds of religious interventions offered. Even here, however, the therapist must be careful not to assume too much. For example, consider a counseling center sponsored by one of the large, evangelical "seeker" churches prevalent in the United States. Some clients, though members of the church, may be new to Christianity and not well-versed or in agreement with some of the doctrines of the church, nor understand how the beliefs and practices of the church impact the counseling process.

From an ethical perspective the least problematic situation is the one in which the client approaches the therapist of his or her own volition specifically requesting spiritual intervention. That is assuming of course that the spiritual intervention being requested is not mentally or physically harmful to the patient and does not run counter to other basic standards of mental health care.

Of the three models, the SB and IB models provide the greatest degree of autonomy and self-determination to the most clients. In these models clients, whatever their spiritual/religious backgrounds, have the latitude to collaborate in how spiritual matters will be handled in therapy. The DB model restricts the directions intervention can take to those that are considered doctrinally appropriate by the therapist or his or her sponsoring institution. At first glance, this approach might seem clearly objectionable and not in keeping with the aspirational goals of insuring client autonomy. There are surely cases where objections could be argued cogently. However, it must also be considered that there are clients who because of their religious backgrounds self-select this form of intervention and would be unhappy with and decline to participate in any other form of counseling less firmly attached to their doctrinal foundations. For these clients the DB model may actually show respect for their autonomy by providing them a way to obtain care within a doctrinal environment that is comfortable to them. Principle E of the APA Code (2002) urges psychologists to respect and give due consideration to individual differences including those based on religion, and the DB model offers a means of doing that in some situations.

Having said this, therapists who work under this model have an increased responsibility to insure that through brochures, disclosure statements and informed consent documents they provide adequate information about the doctrinal underpinnings and faith perspective of their counseling. The materials should explain how these understandings will effect the counseling process and should note the freedom of the client to accept or reject these approaches. They should make it clear that the therapist will do his or her best to refer the client to practitioners who use other methods if that is the client's desire. Further, the therapist must be able to give evidence that the client wanted this type of counseling.

Above all, licensed Christian therapists, whatever the model, must avoid imposing spiritual interventions on clients. Authoritarian interventions are not appropriate. While many clients have the ego strength to think critically about the directives given by a therapist, the therapist must recognize that some clients react to a therapist's directives with acquiescence, passivity and in some cases dependence.

Unlicensed pastoral counselors are in a somewhat different position. As ordained or licensed ministers, they are responsible to follow the standards of their own church or overseeing religious body and may not be subject to the same restrictions as professional therapists. Indeed counselees who seek out pastors for counseling usually anticipate that the counseling will be accompanied by certain theological and moral values.

FIDELITY AND RESPONSIBILITY

Professional ethics codes clearly point to the importance of fidelity to those with whom therapists work (APA, 2002, Principle B). First and foremost, this encompasses trustworthiness in fulfilling one's responsibilities to the client(s). However, the codes also stress the therapist's responsibility to other groups as well, such as the client's family and the community the client comes from. That community includes the client's church and spiritual commitments. In addition, therapists have obligations to the institutions where they work, the professional organizations and state boards that certify them, and to any third party payers that are helping to defray the cost of counseling. The Christian therapist also has a commitment to his or her faith. Sometimes, the therapist's obligations to these different parties are in harmony, but sometimes they are not.

Institutional commitments. When one considers addressing spiritual issues in therapy, the agency or institution one works for must be taken into account. These settings may have their own rules about such matters. Government-sponsored institutions such as state hospitals, public schools and the military may severely limit an employee therapist's ability to address such issues. Christian therapists who work in these settings sometimes chafe at the limitations placed on their ability to respond to patients' religious issues because they feel it runs counter to their faith calling. In Michigan, for example, a social worker was dismissed from his job as a mental health counselor at a county prison camp when he persisted in counseling inmates with Bible reading, prayer, addressing spiritual issues and casting out demons after being instructed by superiors not to do so (Bullis, 2001; Spratt v. County of Kent, 1985).

In order to understand the county's position, one must understand the larger issues at stake. The First Amendment to the Constitution states that "Congress shall make no law respecting an establishment of religion, or prohibiting the free exercise thereof." The Constitution's framers had seen the abuses perpetrated by the state churches in Europe. While there were certainly people in the colonies who would have preferred a state church, the supporters of the first amendment were an ironic mix of deists (such as Thomas Jefferson), revivalists (such as Roger Williams) and others who saw the dangers of the government's endorsement of any one religious group

(Brauer, 1974; Estep, 1990). They also saw the importance of freedom of conscience, ensuring that individuals had the right to make up their own minds in matters of faith. Thus, in the United States the government is forbidden from engaging in acts that could be construed as favoring one religion over another, or in prohibiting the free exercise of religion.

In everyday practice this means that individual citizens have the right to believe what they will and express those beliefs so long as their expression does not deleteriously infringe on the rights of others. However, individuals who are acting in their roles as representatives of the state do not have that right. Thus, for example, while public school students are free to bring a Bible to school, pray and share their beliefs with other students, a school psychologist is not free to recommend that a student client attend a particular church (mosque, synagogue, etc.).

Likewise, therapists who work for the state are forbidden from engaging in behaviors that appear to be preferential toward one religion. Evangelical Christian therapists in these institutions may find consolation in the fact that the same law that prevents them from utilizing direct Christian interventions in therapy also prevents therapists from other religious persuasions from doing so either. Nevertheless, these therapists are left with the problem of what to do about the many clients who bring spiritual issues with them to therapy. Some institutions address the problem by making available alternative resources through chaplains. In this way the institution seeks to handle the problem by establishing clear lines of demarcation between the roles of mental health professionals and religious professionals.

Therapists who work in government institutions can usually abide by both ethical principles and institutional regulations by employing the SB model of addressing spiritual issues in therapy. Institutional regulations should not prevent the therapist from being sensitive to spiritual issues in therapy and providing spiritual assessment so long as the assessment is conducted prudently with due respect for client sensitivities. Second, therapists who work in these settings should develop networking relationships with chaplains and other clergy available to these work settings, actively referring clients to competent clergy who can provide religious help appropriate to the needs of the specific client.

Case 1. Dr. Jenkins, a psychologist at the state hospital, was providing therapy for a man who was recompensating after an episode of psychosis that had included a number of religious delusions. The patient, who was an active member of a church, was troubled both spiritually and emotionally by a number of the things he had said and done while he was psychotic. With the patient's consent Dr. Jenkins assisted him in seeing the hospital chaplain, and Jenkins and the chaplain collaborated in helping him. The patient felt that this team effort helped him to sort out the conflicts he had in his mind about the things he said and did while psychotic. Before the client was released from the hospital, he also agreed to sign a release allowing the chaplain to speak with and make recommendations to the minister at the client's local church.

There are documented occasions when administrators of state institutions incorrectly interpret institutional regulations or the First Amendment such that therapists are prevented from being sensitive to client's spiritual concerns. When these situations occur, therapists must do the best they can to explain the nature of the conflict to those in leadership and seek a resolution that will meet client needs and allow the therapist to adhere to ethical standards (APA, 2002, sect. 1.03). The spirit of maintaining a separation between church and state in institutions is to protect the religious freedom of all, not to silence clients' religious concerns or prevent professionals from responding to client needs.

While some work settings limit the degree to which spiritual issues may be addressed, other settings applaud the practice. Increasing numbers of religious counseling centers follow either an IB or DB model, and see the integration of spiritual concepts into therapy as a central element in their mission. When this kind of therapy takes place with a willing client who has self-selected this form of treatment, and a competent therapist who has due respect for the autonomy of the client and provides the client with appropriate informed consent, there is usually little problem. However, ethical problems can occur in settings where the goals of the sponsoring religious institution conflict with the ethical standards of the mental health professional.

Case 2. One of the ministries of Faith Church was a counseling center staffed by a team of licensed professional therapists. The center welcomed clients from throughout the area, not just those who attended the church.

Informational brochures as well as informed consent documents clearly stated that counselors used the Bible as part of the counseling process and that counselees were free to request a referral elsewhere if they were not interested in counseling with this emphasis. What prospective clients were not told was that staff therapists were expected, as part of their duties, to actively seek to convert clients to Christianity if they were not already.

The church's undisclosed goal of converting clients through the counseling center is in conflict with the professional therapists' ethical imperative to respect the autonomy and right to self-determination of all clients. Where the goals of the sponsoring religious body conflict with the professional therapist's code of ethics, the therapist must explain the conflict to the sponsoring body and attempt to resolve the conflict in such a way that the therapist can remain true to the professional code. There might be some religiously sponsored institutions where a licensed professional could not work and still maintain a commitment to his or her professional code of ethics.

Before accepting employment in a religiously sponsored institution, it behooves Christian therapists to find out all they can about the mission, policies, rules and expectations of the institution that may impact the conduct of therapeutic and assessment services offered. Many problems can be avoided if both the institution and the therapist are clear with each other in advance of employment.

Case 3. A Christian therapist took a position at a church counseling center. After she had been on staff a week, the senior pastor mentioned that it was the pastoral staff's expectation that she would pass along to them the needs of the people she counseled so that staff could pray for each one. Even though the pastor did not ask for the names of the counselees, the therapist immediately realized that the staff would no doubt be able to discern the identities of some of the counselees based on the information she was being asked to divulge.

The intentions of the senior staff in this case may have been innocent and flowed out of their habits and training as ministers. Nevertheless, what they asked the therapist to do would have violated client confidentiality and would likely have affected the counseling center's ability to be effective therapeutically.

Commitments to professional bodies and licensing boards. When therapists become licensed, they agree to follow the ethical principles, standards and rules of practice handed down by the licensing entity or professional body. DB and IB model therapists must be able to show that the therapy provided is *mental health counseling* and meets the fundamental standards of care promulgated by the helping professions. Professional therapists can place themselves at risk when they introduce spiritual interventions that are quite foreign to the client or to methods not commonly accepted by the mental health profession. A complaint was filed against a psychologist in the state of Missouri for practicing contrary to acceptable professional standards when he allegedly counseled a client on demon possession (Lieb, 2003).

Counselors who are both licensed by the state and ordained by the church are in a complicated position relative to their commitments. If the counselor clearly holds him- or herself out to the public as a licensed counselor, then it is fair to assume that the counselor is acting primarily in that role and would be obligated to follow the code of ethics of that profession. However, matters become murky when the counselor presents him- or herself in more than one role, as when the pastor of a church tells his or her parishioners that he or she is also a licensed marriage and family therapist and is thus qualified to offer marriage counseling to the couples in the church. When ethical and legal problems arise in such cases, it is likely that they will be decided based on the circumstances of the specific case ("Texas supreme court backs pastor," 2007). A pastor who is also a licensed counselor would do well to make it clear in writing in what role he or she is providing services, and what this role means for matters such as confidentiality, privacy, payment for services and so forth.

The spiritual loyalties of the therapist. Many, if not most, Christian therapists see their work as more than a job or even as a profession, but as a vocation or calling. This call to service has spiritual roots. For some Christian therapists there is no incongruence between their work as a therapist and their Christian identity. The therapist assumes that if he or she provides psychotherapeutic services within the standards and values advanced by the profession, then the therapist has fulfilled his or her commitment to God as well. Not all therapists find the interface between their Christianity and their psychology so seamless. At the least they see differences in emphasis if not points of discrepancy between their commitments to the profession of psychotherapy and their commitments to God.

A good example of this is the evangelical therapist whose tradition teaches that a primary responsibility of all Christians is to "make disciples," that is, to share the gospel (good news) about Christ and bring others into the Christian faith. For many from this tradition, helping others come to a Christian faith is the highest form of love and is essential for salvation as well as for good health. Many of these traditions also subscribe to the "priesthood of the believer," by which they mean that all Christians, and not just professional clergy, are ministers and thus have a responsibility to help others come into the faith. This creates a situation in which all adherents feel called to evangelize.

Evangelical Christians from these traditions may experience dissonance between their sense of religious calling and their commitment to their profession. Frequently these Christians resolve this dissonance in one of two ways. First, they may gravitate toward working in settings that subscribe to a doctrinally based model of care (DB). Here they will likely work mostly with clients whose religious beliefs are already similar to their own. Others deal with the dissonance by coming to accept that while a focus on a client's mental health is not evangelism, it is a meaningful form of ministering that might indirectly have bearing on the client's relationship with God.

BENEFICENCE

Therapists "strive to benefit those with whom they work and take care to do no harm" (APA, 2002, Principle A). The aim of every therapist is to be helpful to those they serve (beneficence). And while we realize that in an imperfect world it is not always possible to be helpful to everyone, we will do our best to avoid hurting those in our care (nonmaleficence).

For many clients a spiritual dimension is intertwined with their understanding of their emotional suffering. This spiritual dimension is not easily separated from the psychological dimension, and it can be argued that attempts to draw clear distinctions are useful in theory but much less so in practice. As Pargament (2007, 2009) has said, the relationship between the spiritual and the psychological is inherently "messy."

The therapist who engages in "spiritually avoidant care" (Saunders, Miller

& Bright, 2010), or who personally rejects the spiritual dimension in the client is neglecting an important issue, and in some cases this will be harmful to the client. The models of care discussed earlier represent an attempt to intervene in a *beneficial* way with the spiritual concerns of clients in therapy. Each one has its strengths and weaknesses.

The SB method's strength is that it is strongly client-centered. The therapist is deeply respectful of the client's narrative and in a nonjudgmental manner attempts to understand how the client's spiritual perspective helps or hurts his or her attempts to respond to the presenting problems that led to seeking therapy. The weakness of the SB model is a relational one. At the end of the therapeutic "day," the therapist may end up referring the client to a religious professional for further spiritual help, and for some clients this may be less than beneficial to the therapeutic relationship and to ultimate outcomes, no matter how sensitive the therapist attempts to be in making the referral. To be sure, a referral is far to be preferred over attempting to address spiritual issues that the therapist is not competent to deal with, but it must be recognized that in the dichotomizing of care between the psychological and the spiritual, something of value can be lost, even if in some cases it cannot be helped.

The IB model is also strongly client centered. Here again, the therapist is deeply respectful of the client's spiritual narrative and perspective, and attempts to adapt an intervention to the client's needs. In the hands of a competent therapist who is conversant with the varieties of religious experience and trained in various spiritual "tools" for intervention, the effect can be quite beneficial. Both the spiritual assessment *and* the intervention focus intensely on helping the client using tools and extensions of tools that the client carries within him or herself. The question of beneficence relies greatly on the skill of the practitioner. Further, it should be noted that clients who come out of church traditions that vest power for interpreting spiritual matters in a few select leaders may see the integrative therapist as an interloper, and this could negatively affect the therapy.

The DB model, as described here, is sensitive to the client but begins with a strong doctrinal point of view that directs the entire therapeutic process. Clearly, such an approach would not be beneficial to many clients, and for some it would be inappropriate ethically. However, prospective clients who are adherents of the doctrine espoused by a specific DB model may be more likely to be benefitted by those kinds of therapists and would be unhappy with a therapist representing another model. Thus, one could argue that DB model therapists are uniquely beneficial to a subgroup of people who might reject all mental health care otherwise (see Tjeltveit, 1999, pp. 249-51 for a discussion of "finding place" for different ethical communities within psychotherapy).

Before leaving the topic of beneficence, it is important to note that attention to the twin ethical ideals of beneficence and client autonomy are not always without conflict. There are surely times when respecting the client's autonomy about a spiritual matter may not be beneficial to them. This may be true in situations where a client is holding to a particular religious belief that may be harmful to their mental health (see Knapp, Lemoncelli & VandeCreek, 2010, for a discussion of these types of cases). It can also be true in situations where the client is rejecting a previously held religious belief, and the rejection of this belief is potentially harmful to them. Therapists' interventions at these times must be sensitive, measured and prudent.

Moral Values in Psychotherapy

At one time much of the psychotherapeutic profession believed that therapy was a value-free endeavor. Patterning itself after the medical model, psychotherapy became a *treatment* for mental *illness*; the goal was to produce mental *health*. In the same way that differences in patient's or physician's moral values should not figure into the setting of the patient's broken leg, moral and value issues should be inconsequential in successfully *treating* a *diseased* psyche.

Nondirective approaches to therapy such as Rogers' client-centered therapy only bolstered the notion of value-free therapy by suggesting that even if issues of values did arise, the therapist could easily sidestep them and still facilitate successful outcomes by being a reflective other to the client. Under this approach, it was assumed that clients would naturally choose their own healthy (or good) path once they had experienced the freedom and nonjudgmental environment provided by the client-centered therapy.

In fact, the therapy process is inescapably value-laden. Unlike most medical procedures, psychotherapy usually includes questions of right and wrong, better or worse, and good or bad, in addition to questions about what constitutes good "mental health." Though they may not be conscious of it, and some therapists do not acknowledge it, clients frequently come to therapy with moral concerns. And therapists, whether they admit it or not, frequently dispense moral counsel, whether it is dispensed explicitly or implicitly. As Perry London noted years ago, "most clients come [to therapy] for simple cure, not knowing that they may take home moral counsel" (1986, p. 48).

A few examples will illustrate the kinds of moral and value concerns that clients raise in therapy.

- I'm depressed. My wife loves me, but I don't love her. We have three children. Should I get a divorce?

- Is it right to be assertive with my mother?

- I love my boyfriend. He wants sex. I think I want to wait. What should I do?

- I'm very anxious over whether to be completely truthful on my application for my family's health insurance. What should I do?

- I have four children and a chronically ill parent, and only a twenty-four-hour day. Do I take time to take care of me when I know it will have some negative effects on them?

Some therapists approach such questions by ignoring them or by trying to have as little influence on the client as possible. That does not make the questions any less real to the client. Often, the way the client answers those questions (with or without the therapist's help) has much to do with whether the client leaves therapy feeling better.

Some therapists address these questions using some variation of "values clarification" in which the client is encouraged to freely explore their values, recognize inconsistencies, resolve conflicts and determine a course that is "right for them." Such approaches are admirable. They are frequently helpful and in line with the aspirational ideal that the therapist should respect the client's autonomy and freedom to find their own path. However, some clients, left to their own desserts, consistently choose paths that most objective observers would agree are unhealthy. For these clients, their deeply embedded and intransigent propensity for making unhealthy choices is one of the things that brings them to therapy in the first place. In such cases, values clarification may not be enough.

Moreover, and with due respect for individualistic, self-enhancement approaches to therapy, a client's values do not exist in a vacuum. Clients, like other human beings, live in complex networks of relationships that include family, friends, community and culture. In addition to their own individual values, part of health and well-being involves learning to find a way to live effectively with others. Thus, as Bergin (1980, 1991) notes, the values of the patient's family, community and culture are a hidden third set of values present in any therapeutic encounter between client and therapist.

Some therapists deal with moral/value questions in therapy by implicitly or explicitly imposing their values on the client (Richards, Rector & Tjeltveit, 1999, pp. 136ff.). Ironically, therapists who earnestly believe that therapy is either value-free or that they can easily minimize the influence of values in therapy may actually be at greater risk of imposing their values on clients because they are largely unaware of the pervasive presence of values in the therapeutic milieu. Consider the recently divorced therapist who, because of his own recently failed marriage, neglects to determine a client's goals for his own struggling marriage and instead persists in talking about the "cold realities" of failing relationships and how counselees often find that they need to "break free." These kinds of incidents do happen and, unfortunately, not all clients are perceptive enough to catch the bias.

Of equal concern are therapists who have little reluctance to impose their values on clients, believing without question that they know what's best.

Case 4. A new client came to his initial session discouraged about his marriage and listing numerous examples of the discord that existed. As he described his situation, he mentioned that he had been thinking strongly about divorce. His Christian therapist spoke up. "God hates divorce," she said, quoting from the book of Malachi. Pulling a contract out of her desk, she urged the client to sign a pledge agreeing not to divorce his wife under any circumstance (unless she had committed adultery).

In many situations the influence of therapist values on the client is much more subtle than either of these examples. Consider the therapist who expresses empathy for a female client who says she has begun an affair after years in an emotionally abusive marriage, but then says nothing when she expresses guilt about cheating on her husband. Does this therapist's behavior tacitly communicate to the client that affairs are justified when there is emotional abuse? At the very least, does this therapist's behavior subtly tell the client that some troublesome topics in the client's life are suitable for therapeutic discussion and some are not? Or consider the evangelical therapist who reacts with visible discomfort or thinly veiled displeasure when his client tells him that she and her husband have an open marriage in which each have had other sexual partners.

Moral and value issues do matter in the therapeutic process. They add a measure of complexity to the therapeutic process that many therapists are not well prepared for. Nevertheless, dealing appropriately with value issues is an important and often overlooked part of successful therapy. We must do a better job of training therapists to recognize and respond sensitively and effectively to client value concerns. This can be accomplished in a number of ways.

HELPS FOR DEALING WITH CLIENT VALUE CONCERNS

Understanding one's own values. A fundamental starting place for dealing with moral and value issues in therapy is with the person of the therapist. Therapists need to become consciously aware of their own values and beliefs (Vachon & Agresti, 1992). In educational and training settings this can be encouraged by helping therapists do a thorough self-assessment exploring their own life narrative as it relates to value and moral issues. Training modules such as the one suggested by Anderson et al. in this volume can be helpful both to new and experienced therapists for understanding themselves. Therapists must also remain vigilant through the course of their careers as their beliefs and values develop. Personal experiences, successes and failures, multiple experiences with clients and life hardships can all lead to changes in the therapist's values and beliefs temporarily or over the long term, and these are matters that the wise therapist will work to stay abreast of, seeking to understand how these changes may affect him or her in the therapy room.

Respecting the client's perspective. The therapist must seek in an intentional manner to develop his or her understanding of and appreciation for the client's moral and value perspective. Even when the therapist disagrees with the client's value perspective, the therapist can empathize with the patient's perspective and diligently seek to understand how that perspective has evolved in the patient's intrapersonal and interpersonal life. The therapist should also be sensitive to places where a client's personal values seem to contradict one another, or present the client with competing claims regarding what constitutes right and wrong. Clients present these kinds of conflicts often and they are frequently accompanied by anxiety, indecisiveness or discouragement and depression. Assuming that the client's emotional condition is not too severely compromised at the time, a sensitive therapist can do much to aid the client in gaining greater insight into his or her moral perspective.

In addition to understanding the client's personal values, the sensitive therapist will also seek to understand and respect the values of the community the client comes from. The therapist will consider how these community or cultural values interact with the client's values, sometimes reinforcing them or, perhaps, contradicting them.

Therapist self-disclosure. Some writers recommend that therapists disclose their value orientation to potential clients as part of the informed-consent procedure at the beginning of therapy. It makes sense that a therapist provide some general information about his or her value orientation in informed consent materials, and that included in this information would be a statement that encouraged clients to inquire about matters they were concerned about. If the client mentioned other value-oriented issues during the intake process that were pertinent to the therapeutic process, the therapist might determine that it would be best to respond to these as well and would do so with carefully chosen comments, sensitive to the client's condition and the circumstances present at the time.

Having said this, in most cases it does not seem appropriate or therapeutic for a therapist to engage in lengthy or exhaustive discussions at the beginning of therapy about the therapist's value orientation, particularly when it has no relevance to the presenting problems or to the individual client (Ford, 2006). If the client is in therapy to learn how to manage panic attacks, for example, the therapist's beliefs about pre-marital sex are probably irrelevant, and if discussed, might actually disrupt the therapeutic process.

In situations where an unforeseen value conflict arises later, the therapist will have to handle it carefully with due respect for the sensitivities of the client. The therapist must remember that some clients see them as an authority figure, and may be sensitive to what they perceive as "judgment" toward them by the therapist.

Case 5. In Washington state a psychologist was disciplined by the state board after he told a client who had decided to end her pregnancy that he was personally opposed to abortion (Bartley, 1995). He had been seeing the client for three years before the matter came up. In the case the board faulted the psychologist not so much for stating his own values per se as for the abrupt way he did it, placing "his own needs to disclose his personal values about abortion before his client's needs to discuss the emotional impact of her decision."

What about situations where the institution that employs the therapist has a strict perspective on some value issue? For example, what if the therapist works for a Catholic counseling agency that expressly forbids its therapists from actively or passively supporting abortion? In such cases it is best for the institution to develop a written informational statement that describes its beliefs on key issues that might be of concern to a client. Such a statement should be provided to the client at the outset of therapy, and it may be important for it to be included in the informed consent.

Assisting clients who have value concerns. Client's moral value questions, such as those at the beginning of this section, present a definite challenge to the therapist. While a question about whether it is justified to be assertive with one's mother may appear simple to therapists who hold the value that everyone has a right to be assertive, the issues can be more complicated than that. One needs to know how the client understands the meaning of assertiveness: as something that connotes clear respectful communication between people or as something more closely akin to aggressiveness? One also has to understand the culture the client comes from. Does the client come from a culture in which keeping peace and respecting elders at all costs is prized?

In other words, responding to client value questions usually means exploring the client's questions and what lies behind them. It means helping clients verbalize the conflicted values that stand behind their questions. For example, with assistance, the overextended adult with four children and an ailing parent may determine that she is basically conflicted over two things that she perceives as good (taking care of her family and taking care of her health) and that are unfortunately competing with each other.

Or consider the depressed client who is trying to decide whether to continue an affair and possibly leave her difficult marriage, or maintain the marriage in order to focus her attention on assisting her son and daughter find their way through adolescence. In these types of situations the therapist tries to *collaborate* with the patient in a sensitive and prudent manner as they seek together to understand and sort out the client's value conflicts. In some circumstances where the client is too fragile psychologically, such as when the client is decompensating or is severely impaired emotionally, wisdom may dictate that the therapist forgo a discussion of the value conflicts until the client is more stable.

The preceding discussion covers effort to understand and clarify the value problem, and in some cases this may be all that is needed to facilitate the client in making an effective decision. But what about those situations in which the therapist becomes more directly involved in helping the client make a decision? Certainly there are some clients who for a variety of reasons need more direct intervention. But how far should the therapist go in influencing a client's decision?

Clearly therapist influence is an important part of therapy. Research indicates that clients perceive therapy as more effective when therapists influence the process by imparting their clinical expertise (McCarthy & Frieze, 1999). However, the same research indicates that when clients perceive the therapist's influence as *coercive* in nature, they view it as having a negative and perhaps harmful impact. Consider all the different words that might be used to describe a therapist's influence on therapy: "educative, advisory, healing, coercive, persuasive, transforming, emancipatory, actualizing, pastoral, priestly, prophetic, exhortative, judging, supportive, authoritative, corrective, and authoritarian" (Tjeltveit, 1999, p. 173). Outside of avoidance of value questions on the one hand and coercive authoritarianism on the other, which approach is best in any given situation? Unfortunately, there is no answer that neatly fits every situation. When there is a need for the therapist to become more than a "clarifier of values," it is appropriate for the therapist to "bring research findings and clinical insight to bear on the consequences of certain actions, particularly for vulnerable individuals" (Doherty, 1995, p. 44). In these situations the therapist is not coercing but informing, and that is part of the therapist's job both therapeutically and ethically. But this should always be done prudently and with respect. In most cases the therapist's influence regarding the client's moral value questions should take place in the context of an *open dialogue between two equals,* avoiding interactions that are "implicit or authoritarian" (Tjeltveit, 1999, p. 172).

Seeking consultation or supervision. Much like other complicated issues in psychotherapy, therapists can find themselves losing objectivity and thus their effectiveness when dealing with client's moral/value concerns or their own moral/value concerns. Here the input of a supervisor or consultant can be beneficial. Such a person can help the therapist review the case and the therapist's emotional as well as intellectual response to it. However, not just any supervisor or consultant will do. The consultant must be sensitive to and experienced in dealing with value issues in therapy in the way that I have outlined here.

Being prepared to caringly refer when necessary. In a few cases, where the client's and the therapist's value perspectives differ markedly and the therapist sees no way to collaborate with the client or the client with the therapist, it may be necessary for the therapist to refer the client to another therapist (Ford, 2006; Keith-Spiegel & Koocher, 2008; Odell & Stewart, 1993). Examples might include cases where the client wants assistance with moral behavior that runs so counter to the therapist's strongly held moral convictions that the therapist finds it impossible to work with the client. Trying to force the therapist to ignore strongly held moral convictions is not likely to be wise either for the therapist or for the client. As Tjeltveit (1999) points out, making a referral in such situations is clearly "consistent with the ethical principles of respect for client autonomy and beneficence" (p. 260). However, one caveat is in order. When referrals of this kind are made, it is still incumbent upon the therapist to be sensitive to the manner in which the referral is made. Referrals that are made hastily during a crisis point in therapy, when the client is decompensating or when there are no other competent providers in the catchment area are not helpful. Neither are referrals that are made with little attempt to offer a therapeutic and compassionate rationale for the referral, namely, that the therapist's primary motivation is to ensure that the client has an opportunity to meet his or her therapeutic goals.

Conclusion

Addressing spiritual or moral value issues in therapy adds another level of complexity to the therapeutic and ethical process. The effective Christian therapist realizes that it is ethical, appropriate and important to respond to such issues so long as it is done in a sensitive and prudent manner, being mindful of the unique circumstances of each client. The ethical therapist has good insight into his or her own values and beliefs and therapeutic competencies (or lack of competencies) relevant to these matters, and has a system of helps that aid him or her in working with clients and their spiritual and moral value concerns.

References

American Counseling Association. (2005). *Code of ethics.* Alexandria, VA: American Counseling Association.

American Psychiatric Association. (1994). *Diagnostic and statistical manual of mental disorders* (4th ed.). Washington, DC: American Psychiatric Association.

American Psychological Association. (1993). Guidelines for providers of psychological services to ethnic, linguistic, and culturally diverse populations. *American Psychologist, 48,* 45-47.

American Psychological Association. (2002). *Ethical principles of psychologists and code of conduct. American Psychologist, 57,* 1052-59. Also available (with 2010 amendments) from www.apa.org/ethics/code/index.aspx.

American Psychological Association. (n.d.). *APA guidelines for practitioners.* Retrieved July 24, 2011, from www.apa.org/practice/guidelines/index.aspx.

Associated Press. (2007, June 30). Texas supreme court backs pastor over his publicizing of affair. *New York Times.* Retrieved July 18, 2011, from www.nytimes.com/2007/06/30/us/30texas.html.

Aten, J. D., & Leach, M. M. (2008). *Spirituality and the psychotherapeutic process: A comprehensive resource from intake to termination.* Washington, DC: American Psychological Association.

Bartley, N. (1995, September 2). Therapist disciplined for remark on abortion. *Seattle Times.* Retrieved from http://community.seattletimes.nwsource.com/archive/?date=19950902&slug=2139432.

Beauchamp, T. L., & Childress, J. F. (1994). *Principles of biomedical ethics* (4th ed.). New York: Oxford University Press.

Beit-Hallahmi, B. (1977). The beliefs of psychologists and the psychology of religion. In H. N. Malony (Ed.), *Current perspectives in the psychology of religion*. Grand Rapids: Eerdmans.

Bergin, A. E., & Jensen, J. P. (1990). Religiosity and psychotherapists: A national survey. *Psychotherapy, 27,* 3-7.

Brauer, J. C. (1974). *Protestantism in America*. Philadelphia: Westminster.

Bullis, R. K. (2001). *Sacred calling, secular accountability: Law and ethics in complementary and spiritual counseling*. Philadelphia: Brunner-Routledge.

Delaney, H. D., Miller, W. R., & Bisonó, A. M. (2007). Religiosity and spirituality among psychologists: A survey of clinician members of the American Psychological Association. *Professional Psychology: Research and Practice, 38,* 538-46.

Doherty, W. J. (1995). *Soul searching: Why psychotherapy must promote moral responsibility*. New York: Basic Books/HarperCollins.

Estep, W. R. (1990). *Revolution within the revolution: The first amendment in historical context, 1612-1789*. Grand Rapids: Eerdmans.

Ford, G. G. (2006). *Ethical reasoning for mental health professionals*. Thousand Oaks, CA: Sage.

Frazier, R. E., & Hansen, N. D. (2009). Religious/spiritual psychotherapy behaviors: Do we do what we believe to be important? *Professional Psychology: Research and Practice, 40,* 81-87.

Hathaway, W. L., Scott, S. Y., & Garver, S. A. (2004). Assessing religious/spiritual functioning: A neglected domain in clinical practice? *Professional Psychology: Research and Practice, 35,* 97-104.

Hill, P. C., Pargament, K. I., Hood, R. W., Jr., McCullough, M. E., Swyers, J. P., Larson, D. B., & Zinnbauer, B. J. (2000). Conceptualizing religion and spirituality: Points of commonality, points of departure. *Journal for the Theory of Social Behaviour, 30,* 51-77.

Kitchener, K. S. (1984). Intuition, critical evaluation and ethical principles: The foundation for ethical decisions in counseling psychology. *The Counseling Psychologist, 12,* 43-55.

Knapp, S., Lemoncelli, J., & VandeCreek, L. (2010). Ethical responses when patients' religious beliefs appear to harm their well-being. *Professional Psychology: Research & Practice, 41,* 405-12.

Lieb, D. (2003, November 23). Psychologist faces complaint for discussing demons. *Southeast Missourian*. Retrieved July 16, 2010, from www.semissourian.com/story/125037.html.

London, P. (1986). *The modes and morals of psychotherapy* (2nd ed.). Washington, DC: Hemisphere.

Malony, H. N. (Ed.). (1983). *Wholeness and holiness: Readings in the psychology/ theology of mental health.* Grand Rapids: Baker.

McCarthy, W. C., & Frieze, I. H. (1999). Negative aspects of therapy: Client perceptions of therapists' social influence, burnout, and quality of care. *Journal of Social Issues, 55*, 33-50.

McMinn, M. R. (2006). *Christian counseling* [DVD in APA Psychotherapy Video Series]. Washington, DC: American Psychological Association.

McMinn, M. R., & Campbell, C. D. (2007). *Integrative psychotherapy: Toward a comprehensive Christian approach.* Downers Grove, IL: InterVarsity Press.

Miller, W. R. (Ed.). (1999). *Integrating spirituality into treatment.* Washington, DC: American Psychological Association.

Odell, M., & Stewart, S. P. (1993). Ethical issues associated with client values conversion and therapist value agendas in family therapy. *Family Relations, 42*, 128-33.

Pargament, K. I. (2007). *Spiritually integrated psychotherapy: Understanding and addressing the sacred.* New York: Guilford.

Pargament, K. I. (2009). The psychospiritual character of psychotherapy and the ethical complexities that follow. *Professional Psychology: Research & Practice, 41*, 391-93.

Plante, T. G. (2009). *Spiritual Practices in Psychotherapy.* Washington, DC: APA.

Ragan, C., Malony, H. N., & Beit-Hallahma, B. (1980). Psychologists and religion: Professional factors associated with personal beliefs. *Review of Religious Research, 21*, 208-17.

Richards, P. S., & Bergin, A. E. (Eds.). (2004). *Casebook for a spiritual strategy in counseling and psychotherapy.* Washington, DC: American Psychological Association.

Richards, P. S., & Bergin, A. E. (2005). *A spiritual strategy for counseling and psychotherapy* (2nd ed.). Washington, DC: American Psychological Association.

Rose, E. M., Westefeld, J. S., & Ansley, T. N. (2001). Spiritual issues in counseling: Clients' beliefs and preferences. *Journal of Counseling Psychology, 48*, 61-71.

Rye, M., Pargament, K. I., Wei, P., Yingling, D. W., Shogren, K. A., & Ito, M. (2005). Can group interventions facilitate forgiveness of an ex-spouse? A randomized clinical trial. *Journal of Consulting and Clinical Psychology, 73*, 880-92.

Sanders, R. K. (1980). *Short-term assertiveness training among a Christian population* (Doctoral dissertation, Graduate School of Psychology, Fuller Theological Seminary). *Dissertation Abstracts International, 41*, 2345-B.

Sanders, R. K. (2000). Informed consent: Issues facing the Christian marriage and family therapist. *Marriage & Family: A Christian Journal, 3*, 25-38.

Sanders, R. K., & Malony, H. N. (1982). A theological and psychological rationale for assertiveness training. *Journal of Psychology & Theology, 10*, 251-55.

Saunders, S. M., Miller, M. L., & Bright, M. M. (2010). Spiritually conscious psychological care. *Professional Psychology: Research and Practice, 41*, 355-62.

Shafranske, E. P. (Ed.). (1996). *Religion and the clinical practice of psychology.* Washington, DC: American Psychological Association.

Sperry, L., & Shafranske, E. P. (Eds.). (2005). *Spiritually oriented psychotherapy.* Washington, DC: American Psychological Association.

Spratt v. County of Kent, 621 F. Supp. 594, 1985. U. S. Dist. LEXIS 13988 (1985).

Tan, S.-Y. (1996). Religion in clinical practice: Implicit and explicit integration. In E. P. Shafranske (Ed.), *Religion and the clinical practice of psychology.* Washington, DC: American Psychological Association.

Tjeltveit, A. C. (1999). *Ethics and values in psychotherapy.* New York: Routledge.

Vachon, D. O., & Agresti, A. A. (1992). A training proposal to help mental health professionals clarify and manage implicit values in the counseling process. *Professional Psychology: Research and Practice, 6*, 509-14.

10

The Sexual Minority Client

Mark A. Yarhouse, Jill L. Kays
and Stanton L. Jones

This chapter focuses on the treatment of persons who are struggling with same-sex attractions or a homosexual orientation, or who are sorting out sexual identity questions or conflicts. We recognize, however, that many sexual minorities who enter therapy do not seek treatment for change of orientation or behavior, or because of sexual identity conflicts. Rather, they enter therapy for concerns related to mood disorders, anxiety disorders, sexual dysfunctions, interpersonal conflicts and so on. The question of the Christian's opportunity or responsibility to assist sexual minorities in these and other areas (and how that responsibility relates to existing ethical principles) is beyond the scope of this chapter. However, we urge Christian clinicians to consider and apply relevant ethical principles, especially those pertaining to competency and concern for others' welfare, and to critically evaluate their capacity to work effectively with sexual minorities who come for help for a variety of reasons.

The ethical considerations inherent in the care of sexual minorities who are either asking for help in changing sexual orientation or are in conflict about their sexual identity are concerns Christian practitioners may not have thought through explicitly and in a focused way. Although there is much diversity in training and education of Christian clinicians (spanning such fields as social work, pastoral care, counseling, clinical and counseling psychology, and marriage and family therapy), each mental health profession is guided by ethical principles that are generally equivalent in that each addresses issues of competence, integrity, client well-being and respect for client autonomy. We will frame our discussion of ethical issues for Christians working in the areas of homosexuality and sexual identity around these broad ethical concepts.

COMPETENCE

Competence refers to one's suitability for the profession, based on skills, attitudes, and knowledge (APA, 2006). Competence is critical in our effort to benefit our clients, avoid harm and provide the best treatment possible. There are general competencies that are critical to working in the field, as well as specific competencies needed to work with more focused clinical issues. The pursuit of defining, enhancing and measuring competence has been emphasized among mental health professions recently. In fact, the APA recently issued a task force that published a report on the topic in 2006, looking into how the profession can better assess competence (APA, 2006). As clinicians, we pursue competence through various avenues, including education, training and experience. Christian mental health professionals are held to the same standard of competence as others in the field, and what are considered necessary competencies seems to be ever evolving. Therefore, as Christians we should not only pursue the highest level of competence in our area of work but be a part of the developmental process of defining and measuring competence.

As Christian counselors reflect on their own competence to provide services to sexual minorities, it may be helpful to review what we know in terms of background information on homosexuality and sexual identity by summarizing research on prevalence, etiology, mental health correlates and whether sexual orientation can change (see Jones & Yarhouse, 2000; Jones & Kwee, 2005; Yarhouse & Kays, 2008; Yarhouse, 2010a).

Prevalence. The reader will note that we use the designation *sexual minority* in this chapter. We define *sexual minorities* as "individuals with same-sex attractions or behavior, regardless of self-identifications" (Diamond, 2007, p. 142). Some people will object to the use of the word because of the political connotations of using a designation that follows that of racial minorities and implies something about a fixed or immutable trait. We are neither choosing the designation nor resisting its use for those reasons;

rather, we are reminding the reader of the accuracy of the claim that those who experience same-sex attraction are numerically in the minority, representing about 6% of males and 4% of females (Laumann et al., 1994). Those who experience a sufficient amount of same-sex attraction such that they would say they have a homosexual orientation are about 2% of males and 1% of females. Interestingly, more surveys offer a range of prevalence estimates, perhaps due to conflating orientation and identity (see Egan, Edelman & Sherrill, 2008; Herbenick et al., 2010).

Etiology. Recent research on the etiology of homosexuality has almost exclusively focused on biological factors involved in sexual orientation. Studies have continued to examine similar theories as in the past, such as fraternal birth order and handedness (Blanchard & Lippa, 2007; Bogaert, 2007) and twin studies (Langström, Rahman, Carlstrom & Lichtenstein, 2008). While some new developments are seen by proponents as strengthening the biological explanations for sexual orientation—for instance research on genetic scanning (Mustanski et al., 2005) and research on brain symmetry and neural connections (Savic & Lindström, 2008)—biological factors remain *possible* contributing factors in *some* homosexuals that are neither necessary nor sufficient to account for homosexuality. Indeed, there continues to remain no conclusive evidence as to a single biological cause for homosexuality in all individuals (Jones & Kwee, 2005; Yarhouse & Kays, 2008), and the remarkably low level of orientation concordance in the Swedish identical twin study of only seven pairs concordant (both twins gay) out of 71 twin pairs (Langström et al, 2008) stands as stark evidence of the elusiveness of powerful unitary biological causal factors. Rather, the prevailing hypothesis is that there are multiple factors, both biological and environmental, that may contribute to homosexuality, and these vary in presence and strength from individual to individual. The APA (2008) recently summarized the current understanding of the etiology of homosexuality:

> There is no consensus among scientists about the exact reasons that an individual develops a heterosexual, bisexual, gay, or lesbian orientation. Although much research has examined the possible genetic, hormonal, developmental, social, and cultural influences on sexual orientation, no findings emerged that permit scientists to conclude that sexual orientation is determined by any particular factor or factors. Many think that nature and nurture both play

complex roles; most people experience little or no sense of choice about their sexual orientation. (From the resource Answers to Your Questions about Sexual Orientation and Homosexuality on the website of the APA; www.apa .org/topics/sorientation.html#whatcauses)

This is an accurate summary of the existing knowledge about etiology. Although the biological hypothesis continues to be forcefully advanced and consideration of potential environmental influences has been largely ignored, there remains no single influence. Rather, multiple factors probably contribute to homosexuality and these likely vary from person to person.

Mental health correlates. It is widely recognized in the field that those who identify as gay, lesbian or bisexual (GLB), often report greater risk for mood disorders, anxiety disorders, substance use disorders, suicidality, poor self-esteem and so on (e.g., Cochran, Sullivan & Mays, 2003; Cochran & Mays, 2007; Cochran, Mays, Alegria, Ortega & Takeuchi, 2007; Hughes, 2003; Lewis, Derlega, Griffin & Krowinski, 2003; Yelland & Tiggeman, 2003). Increased psychological distress, social stress and greater risk for HIV can also lead to other health concerns (see Cochran & Mays, 2007). Racial minorities who are also sexual minorities have a double minority status that is often thought of as placing them at even greater risk of psychological distress; however, recent research reports equal or slightly lower risk for psychological disorders (Cochran, Mays, Alegria, Ortega & Takeuch, 2007). Other culture norms can also affect rates of distress, such as decreased substance abuse rates among these populations.

In any case, there has been some disagreement in how to understand these differences. The leading interpretation among some in the gay community is that these differences reflect the stigma and minority stress tied to being gay, lesbian or bisexual in a heterosexual society. However, this theory does not seem to hold for all sexual minorities, as there does seem to be some variability among different sexual minority individuals and groups. Therefore, further research is needed to understand the complexity of the social stress experienced by sexual minorities and its relationship with their psychological functioning. In any case, clinicians should be familiar with these concerns and assess for these other mental and physical health concerns that may be more likely to be present among sexual minorities.

Change of sexual orientation. Attempts to change sexual orientation typically occur in one of two main approaches: professional therapy and paraprofessional/religious ministry contexts. There are many approaches to sexual reorientation cited in the literature, including behavioral interventions (e.g., Freeman & Meyer, 1975; Schwartz & Masters, 1984), aversion treatments (e.g., McConaghy, 1970; MacCulloch & Feldman, 1967), psychoanalysis (e.g., Hadfield, 1958; Hatterer, 1970), reparative therapy (Nicolosi, 1991), and group therapies from a variety of theoretical orientations (e.g., Birk, 1974; Pittman & DeYoung, 1971; Munzer, 1965; Truax & Tourney, 1971). Among the actual studies of change of orientation, the rates of positive outcomes have been about 30%, although what was counted as "positive outcomes" ranged considerably in these studies (e.g., decreased same-sex fantasy or behavior, increased opposite-sex fantasy or behavior, marriage and so on).

More recent survey research has produced results generally consistent with the extant data, including MacIntosh's (1994) survey of 1,215 analysts who reported working with homosexual clients, of whom 276 (23%) were said to have experienced a positive outcome. The survey published by Nicolosi, J., Byrd, A. D., and Potts, R. W. (2000) reported similar shifts following change efforts. The study by Spitzer (2003) also suggests that some people may experience change, and that even those who were not as far along as they would have liked still believed that therapy was worthwhile and valuable given their values and vision of quality of life (see also Schaeffer et al., 1999; 2000). Spitzer recently expressed regret as to how he interpreted the results and how other organizations have used those findings; he suggests the results speak to the experiences of those persons who believed they experienced a change of sexual orientation.

Critics are right to point out that many studies cited to support the effectiveness of professional change therapies and religion-based ministries suffer from poor methodologies, including small sample sizes, lack of clear definitions and consistency in measures of change or success, and use of therapist report and self-report of change (APA, 2009). However, poor methodologies do not disprove success; what is needed are prospective, longitudinal studies of those entering such change programs and greater consistency as to what constitutes success as well as whether there is a risk of harm.

Faith-based, paraprofessional approaches to change or healing of sexual orientation include ministries affiliated with Exodus International, ministries affiliated with Homosexuals Anonymous, and many other independent ministries. In all of these cases, ministries may vary considerably on how much emphasis they place on change or healing. Some may focus more on supporting chastity and personal sanctification, while others may focus on change of sexual orientation or healing.

In a more recent study we (Jones & Yarhouse, 2007; 2009) reported on an initial sample of ninety-eight people who attempted change of sexual orientation through involvement in an Exodus ministry. When asked after three years in that specific change effort to rate their identity (e.g., homosexual, heterosexual, bisexual, other—which combined "something else," "don't know," and any other uncategorizable responses), 45% reported *positive change* from homosexual, bisexual or other to heterosexual, or a change from homosexual to bisexual or other. Forty percent reported no change, meaning they rated their identity label (homosexual, heterosexual, bisexual) the same at the third assessment as they did at the first assessment. Eight people reported *negative change* and three reported *uncertain change*, for example, bisexual to "other."

When we looked at the different measures of sexual orientation, we reported an average decrease in same-sex attraction by participants. We also reported a more modest average increase in attraction to the opposite sex.

We also categorized participants based on what they shared about their change efforts. At the three year mark, 15% fell into the category of "Success: Conversion" (to heterosexuality), 23% landed in the category of "Success: Chastity" (or the "freedom to live chaste," helped by a reduction in same-sex attraction); and 29% of the participants were categorized as "Continuing Change Effort," which meant there was some reduction in attraction but not enough to describe themselves as having experienced success. In addition, 15% of participants were designated as having "No Response" to change effort; 4% as "Failure: Confused"; and 8% as "Failure: Gay Identity." The designations of failure were only with reference to the goals of the participants themselves in terms of being a part of Exodus to experience a change in attractions or orientation.

In 2009, we updated these results with those who would provide information after six to seven years. Of those sixty-three participants who remained in the study, the average gains made early on in a person's change attempt appeared to be sustained over time. Again, there were more average gains away from homosexuality (diminished same-sex attraction) than toward heterosexuality (increased opposite-sex attraction). We asked participants which category best described their experience in Exodus, and "Success: Conversion" (to heterosexuality) rose to 23% of the remaining sample, while "Success: Chastity" also increased to 30% of the sample.

These are important findings for those who are considering whether to participate in a similar change effort. However, it is important to understand that these changes do not, on average, reflect categorical changes from gay to straight. They reflect movement along a continuum of attraction, with more success being reported in diminished same-sex attraction that makes chastity less of a burden. For a smaller number of people, these changes also included increases in attraction to the opposite sex such that they thought of themselves as heterosexual, signaling too an important shift in not only sexual attraction but also sexual identity or a person's sense of self and whether or not he or she identifies as gay. Even in these cases, however, it should be noted that people reported some experiences of same-sex attraction. Perhaps most importantly, we believe the figures reported here are a very optimistic projection of the potential success of attempted sexual orientation change via religious ministry, because our sample—while in some meaningful way representative of highly motivated Christians seeking change—probably was slanted toward those more likely to succeed at the attempt.

CONTROVERSIES AND ISSUES

Competence is becoming a major focal point in ethical issues with sexual minorities. For example, in an attempt to address the matter of competence, the American Counseling Association ethics committee released a statement in 2006 in which counselors were reminded to respect client autonomy and the welfare of their clients, and to keep in mind the historical and sociocultural context in which requests for reorientation therapy were made. They were also informed that a counselor must be competent to provide reorientation therapy, but that no approved training in reorientation therapy exists (Whitman, Glosoff, Kocet & Tarvydas, 2006).

> Clients may ask for a specific treatment from a counseling professional because they have heard about it from either their religious community or from popular culture. An ethical counselor, however, only provides treatment that is scientifically indicated to be effective or has a theoretical framework supported by the profession. Otherwise, counselors inform clients that the treatment is "unproven" or "developing" and provide an explanation of the "potential risks and ethical considerations of using such techniques/procedures and take steps to protect clients from possible harm" (Standard C.6.e., "Scientific Bases for Treatment Modalities"). (Whitman et al., 2006)

It is certainly appropriate to inform clients about the empirical support for or against any particular approach taken in the course of counseling. What seems disingenuous is when certain interventions are identified as requiring this while many other "unproven" or "developing" therapy approaches continue to be offered with little reference to what is required from clinicians providing those services. To some it seems as though this area of service is receiving increased levels of scrutiny. This does not mean counselors should avoid being honest about the state of their knowledge in this area, but that this same standard should apply to all counseling services in terms of what evidence exists to support specific interventions.

The ACA also offered a recommendation to take extra responsibility when making a referral to insure that the person offering services practices ethically, an added suggestion that exceeds what is typically required of the mental health professional making a referral:

> Considering all the above deliberation, the ACA Ethics Committee strongly suggests that ethical professional counselors do not refer clients to someone who engages in conversion therapy or, if they do so, to proceed cautiously only when they are certain that the referral counselor fully informs clients of the unproven nature of the treatment and the potential risks and takes steps to minimize harm to clients. . . . This information also must be included in written informed consent material by those counselors who offer conversion therapy despite ACA's position and the Ethics Committee's statement in opposition to the treatment. To do otherwise violates the spirit and specifics of the ACA Code of Ethics.

Again, this heightened scrutiny is a cause for concern, and some counselors see this as more politically motivated than an expectation that is being applied consistently to all counselors.

THE MULTICULTURAL MOVEMENT AND
MULTICULTURAL COMPETENCE

A significant part of the discussion surrounding ethical practice and competence in working with sexual minority clients is related to the multicultural movement that has come to be a strong force in the fields of counseling and psychology. Multiculturalism places emphasis on understanding and appreciating clients' unique differences (e.g., age, gender, gender identity, race, ethnicity, culture, national origin, religion, sexual orientation, disability, language and SES), and allowing those differences and various contexts to inform both the therapist's conceptualization and treatment of the client (APA, 2009). Being multiculturally competent has become a pillar of what it means to be an ethical and competent clinician, motivating professionals to seek avenues through which they can gain knowledge and skills to work effectively with diverse clientele. According to this model and the areas of multiculturalism indicated by the APA (2002) and ACA (2005), clinicians are expected to be competent in working with sexual minorities. However, what this looks like specifically, including the skills and knowledge necessary, has not been precisely defined and is still evolving. Some may consider it to mean primarily using gay-affirmative therapy with clients, while others may broaden it to various aspects of sexuality, identity, behavior and more.

For Christian therapists the emphasis on multiculturalism has both its benefits and areas for possible concern. Obviously most Christian therapists would agree that being sensitive to and appreciative of others' differences and unique qualities is not only a good thing in general but a key component of counseling. After all, we expect the same sensitivity from others in respecting the Christian's religious beliefs and values. The multicultural movement has the ability to help people be more open minded, valuing and considerate of others, allowing the richness and complexity of individual cultural influences to inform our understanding and relating to one another. However, potential difficulties arise when there is no dialogue about what constitutes multicultural competence, and instead clinicians are given directives that may be coming from a specific and sometimes divergent perspective, creating value conflict.

One example of this is the trend toward competency scale development. Existing attempts to measure competence appear to preclude students or clinicians who hold conventionally religious beliefs or values about sexuality and sexual behavior (Yarhouse, 2008). Specifically, The Sexual Orientation Counselor Competency Scale (Bidell, 2005) distinguishes skills, attitudes and knowledge for working with sexual minorities. Bidell highlights the importance of attitudes for counselor competence. For example, one item is: "Personally, I think homosexuality is a mental disorder or a sin and can be treated through counseling or spiritual help" (p. 273). Another item on the counselor competency scale is: "I believe that LGB couples don't need special rights (domestic partner benefits, or the right to marry) because that would undermine normal and traditional family values" (Bidell, 2005, p. 273). Both items are problematic in that they conflate mental health concerns and moral concerns, or reach beyond mental and spiritual health issues and treatment into political views surrounding domestic partnership benefits (Yarhouse, 2008).

These kinds of emerging measures of competency attempt to define competence in working with sexual minorities as requiring values, beliefs and political views that may conflict with some Christians and may have little if anything to do with providing professional services.

So, what does this all mean for the Christian counselor? How can Christians be a part of the multicultural movement while not letting it result in the sacrifice of key moral values or generate value conflicts? One critical component is for Christians to be a part of the dialogue on multiculturalism and defining competence with various groups, including sexual minorities. Rather than pull away, Christians can bring an important voice to the discussion, one which reflects spiritual and religious values and ideals, and that can significantly add to the diversity of perspectives. However, this requires Christians to also be open minded and willing to engage in the discussions while not dismissing perspectives which may be different. Ultimately, Christians should strive to be a part of the movement toward multiculturalism, helping define competence and knowledge when possible.

In addition to the foregoing, Christian counselors should be increasingly aware of and sensitive to the meaning of a homosexual orientation, identity and behavior in the particular individuals we offer therapy to. For example, when we look at sexual identity it is helpful to understand how a person's sexual identity develops and synthesizes over time. Adults who have looked back on their experience with sexual identity development tend to report an initial awareness of attraction around ages 8-11, followed by same-sex behavior around ages 12-15. Behavior tends to precede labeling (as gay), which occurs at an average age of around 15-18. Disclosure to others occurs around age 17-19, while first same-sex relationships tend to occur at around 18-20 years of age (Dube & Savin-Williams, 1999).

In our work with Christian sexual minorities, we have seen similar age ranges: awareness of attraction (age 12-13); same-sex behavior (among those who engaged in it, age 16-17); initial attribution of being gay (age 17-18); labeling as gay (not as frequent, but when it happened, it was around ages 17-18); and first same-sex relationship (age 18-19) (Yarhouse, Stratton, Dean & Brooke, 2009). What was interesting is that very few Christian sexual minorities in this sample identified themselves as gay or pursued same-sex relationships. They seemed to value the Christian sexual ethic and refrain from sexual behavior, perhaps looking at other ways to think about themselves and their identity in addition to the fact that they were attracted to the same sex.

In our work comparing Christians who integrated their experiences of same-sex attraction into a gay identity and those who disidentified with a gay identity, we saw that the process of synthesizing an identity took even longer. Those who integrated their same-sex attractions into a gay identity indicated that identity synthesis occurred at an average age of about twenty-six, while those who disidentified with a gay identity reported identity synthesis at closer to age thirty-four (Yarhouse & Tan, 2004).

The very idea that some people integrate their attraction into a gay identity while others do not identify with a gay identity suggests there is something important going on with respect to attributions and meaning-making among sexual minorities. Most treat same-sex attractions as synonymous with a gay identity. They follow what has been referred to as a "gay script" that views homosexuality as central to who someone "really is" (Yarhouse, 2010a, p. 49). The emphasis is placed on discovering an identity that already resides within the sexual minority. Sexual attractions, then, are at the core of who that person is and sexual behavior is an expression of who they are. This script leads to a kind of sexual self-actualization of a gay identity.

We mentioned earlier that other sexual minorities do not form their identity around their sexual attractions. Rather, they follow a different script that relies on different attributions about what a person's sexual attractions signal about them. Among Christian clients, for example, they might attribute their attractions to the fall—as something that was not God's ideal for sexuality and sexual behavior.

In either case, clinicians can work with sexual minorities to live and identify themselves in ways that are consistent with their beliefs and values. They can seek a kind of congruence that comes with either lining up their beliefs and values with their identity and behavior (as can be seen among some who adopt a gay identity) or lining up their identity and behavior with their beliefs and values (as can be seen among some who do disidentify with a gay identity).

In any case, rather than focus on discovering who a person "really is," this sexual identity approach creates space in therapy for a person to decide whether or not to integrate his or her experiences of same-sex attraction into a gay identity.

We have introduced the reader to some of the issues facing clients who are distressed by their experience of same-sex attraction or who have a homosexual orientation. We have also looked at reorientation therapy, the concerns and criticisms of this approach, and the potential areas for Christian counselors to be familiar with when working with sexual minorities.

INTEGRITY AND CLIENT WELL-BEING

Competence is important in part because it helps ensure that the services counselors provide are offered with integrity and in a way that helps to protect the public from harmful clinical practices. The idea of integrity here is being honest about what we know and do not know about homosexuality. It is this knowledge base that helps inform clinical practice, which is why it is tied to competence and, ultimately, client well-being. Indeed, the idea of promoting client well-being is another central ethical principle in the ethical codes of the major mental health organizations. The idea is that mental health professionals are to benefit their clients and avoid doing harm to their clients.

However, there can sometimes be disagreement on what exactly is beneficial and what is harmful and how it is both defined and measured, even among Christians. One area where this conflict is especially salient is in the area of homosexuality, particularly in regards to reorientation therapy.

Reorientation therapy has as its goal change of sexual orientation from homosexual to heterosexual. It is sometimes also referred to as conversion therapy, a name that some reject because it can be confused with religious conversion rather than orientation change as such. Reparative therapy is a specific form of reorientation therapy that places emphasis on repairing a normal drive that has been essentially misdirected and taken the form of homosexuality in the life of the individual with a homosexual orientation.

The primary ethical questions that have been raised regarding change of orientation attempts are whether there is a professional or scientific basis for the services being provided, and whether the services provided are harmful to the client. We have just reviewed what we know about the professional or scientific basis. There is a disagreement about whether orientation can change, and some of that disagreement may be due to whether we are discussing categorical changes or whether we are discussing meaningful shifts along a continuum. The latter seem possible for some people, although it is difficult to say exactly how frequently that occurs. Categorical change is much less likely, if it occurs at all, but even these statements should be qualified because there is a need for better research on attempted change, particularly through involvement in professional therapy.

The other ethical concern is whether reorientation therapy or ministry-related change attempts are inherently harmful. When sexual minorities enter into therapy asking for help changing sexual orientation or behavior or navigating sexual identity conflicts, a concern that has been raised is about whether specific practices, such as change-of-orientation therapies or ministries intended to change orientation are harmful. The basis for the charge of harm has been largely anecdotal, derived from the growing phenomenon of "ex-ex-gays" or those who at one time indicated that they were in a change program of some kind (were attempting to become "ex-gay") but felt that they did not experience success in that change effort.

Such anecdotal accounts laid the foundation for studies of apparent harm. The most frequently cited study on the question of harm is the study by Shidlo and Schroeder (2002). The study itself has a number of methodological weaknesses, such as the use of convenience sampling and the potential for bias toward finding harm given the research design.

In our recent follow-up study of attempted change, we (Jones & Yarhouse, 2009, 2011) found that people were not reporting harm on average. → When there were average changes, it was in the direction of improved psychological functioning rather than harm among those continuing in the change attempt.

How might we account for reports of harm? It is difficult to say. It does not appear that the change attempt per se is the cause, but it could be the approach being used is the problem or the person providing the services or the expectations of the person seeking change or some other unknown variable.

In addition to the question of whether change attempts are intrinsically harmful, another fundamental question is how likely such change attempts are to produce positive results. This is also a difficult question to answer. A recent American Psychological Association (APA) task force background document, "Appropriate Therapeutic Responses to Sexual Orientation," discouraged psychologists from "promising or promoting" change of sexual orientation. The report concluded that there is "insufficient evidence" to support the efficacy of change efforts (APA, 2009).

We disagree with some of the conclusions of the task force report, as well as some of the decisions made in employing different standards in addressing the likelihood of change, the likelihood of harm and the evidence to support claims about homosexuality being a "positive variant of human sexual orientation" (APA, 2009, p. 119). However, we agree that Christians must be honest about the efficacy of change methods. The existing data on efficacy of change methods suggests that most homosexuals do not find a "cure" in reorientation programs. Many struggle all their lives with homosexual inclinations, self-hatred and guilt. Even in cases of reorientation or behavioral modification, many individuals are still tempted by lustful thoughts and homoerotic urges. To present treatment less realistically or to assume overly optimistic projections of outcome of current treatment procedures is to engage in ethically questionable practice.

In addition, many sexual minorities turn to Christian ministries for help. Directors of such programs should be careful to promote their programs accurately. Haldeman (1994) is correct in saying that Christian ministry programs have enormous power over many individuals. With power comes great responsibility. Perhaps such ministries should consider more realistic advertising that presents their ministries as supportive environments for sexual minorities struggling to curb homoerotic desires and behaviors, form an identity in Christ and work toward chastity steeped in sanctification and grace. In other words, if celibacy rather than reorientation is the realistic goal for most individuals who enter such programs, ministry leaders should advertise accordingly.

As one might suspect, sexual identity issues, including orientation concerns, is an area in which recognized standards for preparatory training to change sexual orientation or even to navigate sexual identity conflicts do not yet exist, either in secular or in Christian professional training programs. We do see guidelines and policies emerging for models that are largely "gay affirmative" (e.g., APA, 1997). The recent APA task force report background document also provided a rationale for affirmative (not gay-affirmative) approaches that are more client-centered and identity-focused. We will return to these shortly. For the time-being, how do we ensure the competence of our work and protect our sexual minority clients from harm?

Emerging affirmative approaches. We turn our attention now to what are referred to as emerging affirmative approaches to sexual minorities. *Affirmative* should be distinguished from *gay affirmative*, which we will discuss. Indeed, a longstanding concern has been the push for gay-affirmative therapy or gay-integrative therapy as the only acceptable form of counseling with sexual minority clients, including those who may be in conflict over their sexuality. Fortunately, more recent developments in the APA seem to favor a more client-centered direction, so long as the client is not requesting assistance with change of orientation.

The more recent APA (2009) task force report background document encouraged a client-centered, identity-focused approach to working with sexual minorities, which encourages clinicians to respect all aspects of the sexual minority's identity, including their religious values. This is referred to as an "affirmative" rather than "gay affirmative" model of care.

By *affirmative* the APA is moving away from an exclusively gay-affirmative approach and broadening the term to mean something that is more client-affirmative. APA (2009) describes their affirmative approach, stating:

> We define an affirmative approach as supportive of clients' identity development without a priori treatment goals for how clients identify or express their sexual orientations. Thus, a multiculturally competent affirmative approach aspires to understand the diverse personal and cultural influences on clients and enables clients to determine (a) the ultimate goals for their identity process; (b) the behavioral expression of their sexual orientation; (c) their public and private social roles; (d) their gender roles, identities, and expression; (e) the sex and gender of their partner; and (f) the forms of their relationships. (p. 14)

This definition of *affirmative* allows for a variety of values, beliefs and possible outcomes to be included in one's exploration of their sexual identity and orientation, while still encouraging a realistic consideration given to the reality of one's sexual attractions and the possibility of change. For the client that is in conflict over their identity, the APA (2009) encourages therapy to contain the following components: (1) acceptance and support which includes, (a) "unconditional positive regard and empathy for the client," (b) "openness to the client's perspective as a means to understanding their concerns," and (c) encouraging the client's development of a positive self-concept; (2) comprehensive assessment of the client's unique history and various social and cultural contexts, as well as the possible impact of stigma on the client's life; (3) teaching them active coping strategies, including behavioral, cognitive and emotional, to help them reduce the distress they experience; (4) encouraging and building up of multiple sources of social support; and (5) identity exploration and development (APA, 2009, p. 86). Identity exploration is described as "an active process of exploring and assessing one's identity and establishing a commitment to an integrated identity that addresses identity conflicts without an a priori treatment goal for how clients identify or live out their sexual orientation. The process may include a developmental process that includes periods of crisis, mourning, reevaluation, identity deconstruction, and growth" (APA, 2009, p. 86).

This process of accepting and affirming the client's unique experience and allowing him or her to work through an exploration of sexual identity in order achieve congruence and a positive self-concept without a previously established goal or outcome is where the "multicultural" and "affirmative" concepts are primarily demonstrated. This emphasis represents a shift in APA's approach in working with sexual minorities, specifically with those who are in conflict over their sexual identity. It reflects a movement toward the center of the spectrum between gay-affirmative versus reorientation therapy, and challenges both sides to follow them in the process. This direction encourages clinicians to be sensitive to sexual minorities from multiple backgrounds and values, including religious individuals who may experience conflict over their same-sex attractions. At the same time APA has presented an exceptionally pessimistic evaluation of the scientific evidence concerning sexual-orientation change efforts, their efficacy and the potential risk they pose to clients, and encouraging this as a foundation for appropriate therapeutic responses. The task force gave some examples of therapies that fit their client-centered model, including sexual identity therapy, which some may find to be a good fit as an alternative to models that emphasize change of orientation.

Sexual identity therapy. Sexual identity therapy (SIT) is a client-centered, identity-focused approach to the concerns raised by sexual minorities (Yarhouse, 2008). SIT focuses less on sexual orientation and more on sexual identity and congruence, so that persons are able to live and identify themselves in keeping with their beliefs and values.

In their discussion of a framework for providing SIT, Throckmorton and Yarhouse (2006) discuss the four stages of assessment, advanced informed consent, psychotherapy and sexual identity synthesis.

Assessment includes an extended discussion of the concerns the person is bringing to counseling. If the person is distressed by his or her experience of same-sex attraction or behavior, this too is assessed. It is important to consider intrinsic and extrinsic motivation for seeking services. When working with minors, it is imperative that counselors obtain assent for treatment from the minor as well as consent from the parent or guardian.

Advanced informed consent involves several steps given the contro-

versies in this area (Yarhouse, 1998). For example, it can be shared that homosexuality is not viewed as a mental illness by the major mental health
organizations. Advanced informed consent also includes a discussion of the
causes of homosexuality and the limits of the research in this area, as well
as professional interventions that are available (and that there are currently
no well-designed outcome studies of reorientation therapies, gay affirmative therapies or sexual identity therapy) and paraprofessional or ministry alternatives to professional therapy.

The therapy stage of the SIT framework involves helping clients reach
congruence, so that they live and identify themselves in ways that are consistent with their beliefs and values regardless of whether they experience
shifts in attractions or orientation. One way to do this (see Yarhouse, 2008,
for an extended discussion) is to distinguish between attractions, orientation and identity, so that a person can use more descriptive language (e.g.,
"I experience same-sex attraction") rather than an identity label (e.g., "I am
gay"). Clients can also look at the relative weight that they give to their
sexual attractions over other aspects of themselves as a person, such as their
gender identity, biological sex, behaviors, beliefs and values. In this approach the counselor joins the client on an attributional search for sexual
identity that has as its endpoint this experience of congruence, which is the
final stage of the SIT framework, sexual identity synthesis.

CLIENT AUTONOMY AND SELF-DETERMINATION

The major mental health organizations also promote and protect client autonomy and self-determination. One way to help ensure a sense of autonomy and self-determination in our clients is through informed consent.
Clients should be able to consider the options available to them and ultimately decide for themselves the direction their lives take.

Disclosure and informed consent is a principal task in our efforts to preserve integrity in the work that we do and respect the rights and dignity of
our clients. As Rosenfeld (2002) states, it is a critical part of protecting the
autonomy of our clients, making sure they have all of the information necessary to make a knowledgeable, voluntary and competent decision about
their treatment. The burden of providing the sufficient information to help
the client make the most informed decision possible rests with the clinician;

and therefore a thorough and systematic process of providing informed consent to the client is recommended (Rosenfeld). In regards to homosexuality and particularly those sorting through conflicts with their sexual identity this is especially important. Clients may have multiple influencing factors contributing to their distress and motivations for seeking treatment (e.g., family, religious values, past experiences, etc.) and the informed consent process can help the client sort through these pressures to make a more autonomous and informed decision about the course of treatment that is best for him or her.

Before the Christian counselor moves forward in therapy with a client in conflict over sexual identity, it is critical that the client has been informed of all possible options and consequences, so that he or she can make the most informed decision possible about treatment. We noted earlier that this is referred to as advanced informed consent. The recommended approach is to obtain written informed consent that educates the client about various key areas, including (1) current knowledge about the causes of homosexuality, (2) professional treatment options (including success rates and methods of obtaining efficacy rates), (3) paraprofessional ministry options (including success rates), (4) potential risks and benefits to treatment, and (5) potential outcomes with or without treatment (Yarhouse, 1998). In addition to giving this information to the client in writing, we recommend the therapist verbally review the information contained and any other relevant topics, and thoroughly address any questions or concerns before a client consents to therapy.

Here are some examples of suggested language (Yarhouse, 2010b) the clinician can use when discussing each of these different areas.

A place to begin would be with a general discussion about homosexuality and the possible causes of a homosexual orientation. A counselor might consider the following language:

CLINICIAN: Let me tell you at the outset that homosexuality is no longer viewed by the major mental health organizations, such as the American Psychological Association, as a mental illness. I understand, however, that you are here today because you are distressed by your experiences of same-sex attraction and that you have questions about how your experiences of same-sex attraction or orientation came about. There are several ideas about what causes a person to experience same-sex attraction or to later identify as homosexual or gay or lesbian. The bottom line is that scientists do not really know for certain why one person experiences same-sex attraction and another does not. The competing theories tend to fall into one of two camps. Do you remember the old "nature versus nurture" debate you probably discussed in school? Well, some say that same-sex attraction is due primarily to Nature, that biology—through genetics or exposure to prenatal hormones—contributes to same-sex attraction. Others say it is Nurture. People on this side of the debate tend to think that parent-child relationship contribute to experiences of same-sex attraction, or that being sexually abused as a child can contribute to same-sex desire later in life. These are theories, not facts. Let me go over some of the evidence for each, while making it clear that we really don't know for sure. There have been some studies of twins where it looked like identical twins were a lot more likely than fraternal twins to both be homosexual as adults. More recent research has suggested that the evidence for this theory isn't nearly as strong as we thought. Similarly, research on a marker on a chromosome was initially suggestive of a genetic marker for homosexuality, but follow-up research has not confirmed this, and in one case the researchers couldn't find the marker at all. But similar problems come up when we look at evidence for Nurture or the environment shaping our sexual identity. Research on parent-child relationships has been mixed and somewhat confusing. Some studies seem to support the theory, while others do not. Most experts today believe that both Nature and Nurture contribute to a person's experience of same-sex attraction. The specifics vary from person to person.

Part of the rationale in mentioning the current position of the major mental health organizations is that we feel that information should not be hidden from clients and should be made available by their counselor. At the same time, we want to acknowledge that sexual identity conflicts may still be a clinical problem for the person requesting counseling services. This might then lead to a discussion of professional treatment options:

> CLINICIAN: Let me talk to you now about professional treatments that are available to address same-sex attraction and behavior. The treatments with the most support for their effectiveness tend to address changing thoughts and behaviors so that people do not have as many or as intense same-sex thoughts or fantasies or engage in as much same-sex behavior. There have also been several studies published on addressing what some see as developmental needs from childhood that may have gone unmet in a person's relationship with his or her parents. These approaches have also been studied, but the research here has been criticized for not being as strong as research we do in other areas. That being said, when researchers survey people who are involved in these kinds of therapies, many of them say they are experiencing change of behavior and sometimes orientation, at least as far as they or their clinician are reporting. In any case, please note there are no well-designed outcome studies that address sexual identity concerns—whether reorientation, gay affirmative, or sexual identity approaches (including this one).

What is important here is to communicate the limitations in current research on outcomes in therapy. We want to avoid giving the false impression that there is the same quality and quantity of studies on therapy with sexual identity issues as there is for the treatment of depression or anxiety, for example.

In this context, we also recommend expanding the discussion about professional treatment options by also discussing paraprofessional ministry options. The following language may be helpful:

> CLINICIAN: I have just explained some of the professional treatments. Let me share with you information on paraprofessional approaches. These are most often religiously-affiliated support groups, for example, a Christian support group or a Jewish support group for people who are concerned about their experiences of same-sex attraction or behavior. There has been much less research to demon-

strate the effectiveness of these support groups or ministries, but when researchers survey people involved in these ministries, many people report experiencing success either with changing their behavior and working toward chastity or celibacy, or changing their sexual orientation, at least as they say they experience it. I should tell you that these studies are not meant to be studies of what is most people's experience, or what might be typical at a ministry, but the studies seem to be saying that some people report experiencing success. Some clinicians might see involvement in a ministry as an alternative to professional therapy or as an adjunct to the work being done in therapy, depending on your goals.

It has been suggested that the decrease in interest among major mental health organizations in providing services to sexual minorities who were distressed by their experience of same-sex attraction led in some ways to the growth of religion-based ministries. These ministries vary considerably in what they provide, how they provide it, what their goals are and so on.

At some point in advanced informed consent it is also important to review the possible risks and benefits of treatment. Here is language that may be helpful to the Christian counselor:

CLINICIAN: Another area I want to discuss with you are the possible benefits and risks of this program. I will work with you to help expand alternatives to what you are doing and experiencing today. In keeping with this model, you may experience greater emotional stability insofar as how you live and form your identity reflects the beliefs and values you hold about how you want to live. Of course, you may also decide to live out your values in ways that are difficult for you, and that may be hard for us to predict, but we can certainly discuss it throughout our work together. The risks are primarily financial and emotional. It is expensive to be in counseling, and you may have to pay for some or all of your counseling out of pocket. Emotional risks are tied to goals and expectations for counseling, which we will discuss in greater detail. But if you were working toward congruence—so that how you live and identify yourself is consistent with your beliefs and values—you might also hold out expectations about your sexuality, your attractions, your behaviors and so on. Those other expectations may or may not be met, and when we hold expectations that are not met, we can feel discouraged or frustrated in ways that we might not have anticipated.

It should be noted that this advanced informed consent is about addressing sexual identity issues in counseling and not informed consent to change of orientation therapy. Language and key concepts would have to be changed if a counselor were providing a different kind of therapy with a different set of treatment goals in view.

This is also when it is important to discuss the possible outcomes of treatment:

CLINICIAN: Since I just reviewed the possible benefits and risks of treatment, I want to go over the possible outcomes without treatment. Let's say as we are talking about options you decide you would rather not work on changing your thoughts, behaviors or attractions. It is difficult to predict what you might experience if you choose not to pursue counseling. Many people integrate their experiences of same-sex attraction into a gay, lesbian or bisexual identity and report having good relationships, gainful employment and so on. But the research suggests there are higher rates of depression, anxiety and other negative emotions as well as heightened risk of STDs among those who are gay and lesbian. So a therapy approach of some kind might be helpful, even if you decide this one is not the best fit for you. I also want to be clear that the studies showing elevations have sometimes been criticized for not being of a representative sample of gay and lesbian persons. In other words, the question is: Is there a typical gay or lesbian experience? Also some view higher rates of depression, anxiety, suicidality and so on as reflecting society's disapproval of homosexuality, and that if society were to change and be more accepting, the rates would even out. There also appear to be higher rates of relationship instability, especially among gay males. That is not to say that gay males cannot be in longstanding and monogamous relationships, but many are not, and at a higher rate than what we see among hetero-sexuals who try to be exclusive. Some argue that this is because there is nothing equivalent to marriage for gay and lesbian persons, so they lack social support for being stable. Others say that this reflects a difference among gay and lesbian persons, and that gay males in particular make a commitment to emotional faithfulness but not physical or sexual faithfulness. Again, let me say that there is no one experience that I can point to as the typical gay or lesbian experience, but I want you to be aware of some of the research in this area so you can make your own decision about where to go from here.

It is also recommended that therapists explain to their clients their specific approach and orientation toward therapy and how it may differ from other treatment options. Informing clients of one's worldview as a Christian and how this may influence the therapist's approach and perspective is an additional step in making sure clients are fully aware and informed of what they are consenting to.

Finally, as part of the discussion it is recommended that the therapist thoroughly explore clients' motivations for seeking therapy, their perceived understanding of the cause or source of their distress, expectations and goals for treatment, and any other relevant topics. Open-ended questions that allow the client to explain themselves objectively can be helpful in accessing this information, such as "What is it about your experiences that brings you in to see a clinician?" (Yarhouse, 2010b). This discussion should ideally occur at the onset of treatment, before the client even consents to treatment. Understanding why clients are distressed over their same-sex attractions, what is motivating them for treatment and what their expectations are can have a significant impact on the most ethical course of treatment the clinician should take. For example, some individuals may feel pressured from friends and family to "change," or they may be motivated by other external pressures (e.g., minority stress, prejudice, discrimination, etc.). In these examples there should be some red flags to the clinician that the client may not be in a place to make an informed and autonomous decision about what direction is best for them to take because they are being highly influenced by outside sources. In such a case the client may benefit more from therapy focused on helping the client explore his or her own thoughts and feelings about same-sex attractions, sources of distress and how the client wants to integrate his or her attractions into life (i.e., achieve congruence). Therefore, it is important that the therapist spend considerable time exploring these various topics and concerns before proceeding with therapy to ensure the client is making an autonomous and informed decision about the course of treatment.

This type of consideration and caution is necessary when dealing with a controversial issue in which multiple influences and stakeholders may be present. Taking the time to review the noted areas will ensure the clinician is practicing in the most ethical way and that the client will be able to be as informed as possible (Yarhouse, 2010b).

VALUE CONFLICTS AND REFERRALS

Related to the discussion of respecting client autonomy and self-determination is recognizing that counselors and clients may experience value conflicts in such a way that a referral is in the best interest of the client. It is widely understood that counselors will inevitably experience value conflicts with a client. A gay psychologist might work with a conservative Muslim; a feminist counselor might see an evangelical Christian woman in a complementarian marriage. Often such differences do not necessitate a referral. However, differences can be strong enough to warrant a referral when the differences might affect services in a way that could impact client well-being. This is usually more likely in cases in which political, religious or value issues are central to the presenting problem; in such cases, a referral is a real consideration, particularly if the limits of counselor competence have been reached, there is concern for counselor objectivity or there is risk of imposing values on the client (Tjeltveit, 1986).

For those who may experience significant value conflicts in the area of homosexuality or homosexual behavior, how should they proceed? It is important, first, to look at the source of the conflict. What is contributing to the conflict, and how does that connect with work counselors do with other clients where there may also be value conflicts that do not seem as severe? Is it moral concerns in general that are difficult for the counselor, or is it something specific to homosexuality? Counselors may find it helpful to consult with a more experienced colleague who can provide insight and support as the counselor tries to understand the conflict further.

In any case, precedent has suggested that making a referral in some cases may be the most appropriate course of action, particularly if it helps safeguard client welfare. However, recent events suggest that this existing precedent and course is being challenged.

A recent legal case dealing with this exact issue may provide a new perspective on the most ethical course of action. In the case of Julea Ward v. Eastern Michigan University, a graduate student was reportedly dismissed from a counseling program for not agreeing to go through a program to "remediate" her conventionally religious beliefs and values regarding same-sex behavior. According to news media (Coffman, 2009), Julea was in her training when she had a value conflict with a client because she felt she should not affirm his same-sex behavior. Her supervisor had her make a referral to another therapist who did not have the same value conflict, and Julea did so. Julea was then required to participate in a program that would address/remediate her Christian belief system. When she refused, she was dismissed from the counseling program and soon after the Alliance Defense Fund (ADF) filed suit (Coffman, 2009). The U.S. District Court granted a summary judgment in favor of the university citing among other things ACA "Code of Ethics" provisions against discrimination in providing services. Ms. Ward appealed the decision and recently the Court of Appeals reversed the decision in her favor, noting that in another section the ACA Code permits value-based referrals.

Several questions arise from this case. One question is, When are referrals appropriate? One of the more common reasons for making a referral is when a counselor does not feel he or she is competent to provide services. Competence is determined by education, training and supervised clinical experience, and mental health professionals are required to practice within the scope of their competence. So a referral is considered appropriate when a counselor who has no training in working with older adults, for example, refers an elderly client to someone who has that competence. But competence is not the only reason for referrals.

Are value conflicts a legitimate reason to consider a referral? Let's back up a moment and ask this: How are value conflicts generally handled in counseling? Counseling ethics textbooks recognize that value conflicts are inevitable in mental health practice (Corey & Corey, 2007). A politically liberal counselor will meet with a client with strong conservative views; a gay counselor will meet with an evangelical Christian client; a Catholic counselor will meet with a woman deciding on abortion; an atheist will meet with a devout Muslim. The question is, at what point does a counselor make a referral when a value conflict arises? As discussed previously, the major mental health organization's ethics codes each tend to stress being multiculturally competent and having respect for differences—these are often identified as differences due to age, gender, sexual orientation, religion, socioeconomic status and so on. Showing respect for these differences can mean different things in counseling, but it at least means being aware of how these factors impact clients and their presenting concerns. It often also means taking these factors into consideration in assessment, case conceptualization and treatment planning.

Generally speaking, ethics textbooks tend to look at whether a value conflict between a counselor and a client is significant enough to have a negative impact on their work together. If so, a referral is thought to be appropriate. According to the complaint filed by the ADF, the professor who chaired the hearing on Ward actually taught a course in which a textbook was assigned that indicates the appropriateness of making a referral when value conflicts arise—specifically citing the instance of value conflicts regarding homosexual behavior. The decision of the appeals court appears to recognize the making of referrals in cases where there is significant value conflict and there is danger of the therapist imposing his or her values on the client. It remains to be seen what the final outcome of this case will be, and so we currently lack clarity on the question of whether counselors should and can make referrals based on value conflicts. Until then, the ethical counselor should keep the client's best interest in mind when making a decision about whether to make a referral. If the therapist feels that proceeding in therapy with a sexual minority client will do more harm to the client than good, then a referral is likely a responsible course of action. However, this case is a good reminder that counselors should not be hasty in making such decisions and should proceed only after careful consideration and consultation.

Practice location. In order to reduce the chance of value conflicts arising in the first place, Christian counselors should give consideration to their location and scope of practice, and seek employment in such a place that is more congruent with their values and belief system. In other words, if a Christian counselor knows that value conflicts will prevent him or her from being able to effectively work with sexual minorities, the counselor might consider practices and job placements where the chances of receiving such a referral is less likely. This reduces much of the risk for value conflicts, which is best for both the therapist and the client. When counselors work in places that are less congruent, the chance for difficulties rises. A salient example of this was demonstrated in the legal case Bruff v. North Mississippi Health Service.

In this case Sandra Bruff, a licensed professional counselor with an Employment Assistance Program, asked her employer to accommodate her religious beliefs about not counseling a lesbian client on her same-sex relationship. After attempts to reconcile her complaint, Bruff was ultimately dismissed of her counseling duties and placed on leave (Hermann & Herlihy, 2006). Bruff filed a lawsuit against North Mississippi Health Service, claiming that according to Title VII of the Civil Rights Act of 1964 (as amended in 1972), the company had violated federal law by not accommodating her religious beliefs (Hermann & Herlihy). The jury initially awarded Bruff over two million dollars in damages; however, the ruling was reversed on appeal because the judge believed it would have been an undue hardship on her employer to accommodate Bruff's religious beliefs (Hermann & Herlihy).

There is a lot of important information in this case, and we appreciate the challenges Christian counselors face in trying to live out their convictions in a position like an EAP or other similar practice setting. It is challenging where to draw the line on the kinds of cases or issues a person feels he or she can work with, whether it is a matter of competence or a value conflict. And this extends far beyond mental health services, as Christians in the medical fields and in pharmacology and other areas are also facing these challenging questions.

According to Hermann and Herlihy (2006), one way to interpret the decision in this case is that an employer is not legally obligated to make accommodations with respect to referring a gay or lesbian client who is asking for counseling to address relationship issues. Limiting one's practice to only cases that do not reflect a conflict for the counselor was viewed as not sufficiently flexible for the demands of that particular type of position.

Many issues arise from this and other related cases. We should note that any time a Christian becomes licensed by the state to practice as a mental health professional, they enter into a fiduciary space characterized by trust. The public trusts that the licensed mental health professional will practice in keeping with the regulations of the state and the field of counseling or psychology or other profession. Christians weigh what it means to honor that obligation with questions they have about providing services in areas where value conflicts arise. So we want to help our professions understand and make provision for appropriate referrals in cases where referrals are warranted. We may also need to reflect on what it means to provide care to people who are different than us in important ways, including value conflicts, as these inevitably arise in our professional role. In most cases such value conflicts do not rise to the level of necessitating a referral; rather, counselors are trained to practice within the bounds of their competence and their known comfort level to reduce the risks of value conflicts (Herman & Herlily, 2006). We do well to learn how to counsel people whose values are different from our own. In the final analysis the primary concern for the licensed mental health professional is client welfare, and safeguarding that might necessitate an appropriate referral. To assist in minimizing value conflicts, a Christian counselor who anticipates values conflicts may decide it is best to practice in settings that are congruent with his or her own beliefs and values, and to advertise accordingly, identifying relevant information in therapist disclosure and informed consent forms (Herman & Herlily, 2006).

CONCLUSION

As Christian counselors reflect on their work with sexual minorities, they quickly realize that there are several ethical issues that are important to understand further. These include basic competence to work with sexual minorities, to understand some of the mental health considerations and to recognize the conflict that sometimes exists between religious and sexual identities. It is also important to understand the controversies surrounding change-of-orientation therapies, recent statements by the major mental health organizations and the empirical research in this controversial area. It may also be helpful to recognize emerging models of treatment that are more likely to be recognized by others as appropriate because they are more client-centered and identity-focused. Recent legal cases (such as the law in California making it illegal to provide sexual orientation change therapy to minors) are also beginning to shape the services that counselors provide. It is important that Christians remain active members of their profession, providing a voice in areas in which others may not fully appreciate the perspectives and considerations of those who draw more on a conventionally religious identity, beliefs and values.

REFERENCES

American Counseling Association. (2005). *ACA code of ethics.* Alexandria, VA: American Counseling Association.

American Psychological Association. (2008). *Answers to your questions: For a better understanding of sexual orientation and homosexuality.* Washington, DC: American Psychological Association.

American Psychological Association. (2002). *The ethical principles of psychologists and code of conduct.* Available (with 2010 amendments) from www.apa.org/ethics/code/index.aspx.

American Psychological Association. (1998). Resolution on appropriate therapeutic responses to sexual orientation. *American Psychologist, 53,* 934-35.

American Psychological Association. (2006). *APA task force on the assessment of competence in professional psychology: Final report.* Available at www.apa.org/ed/resources/competency-revised.pdf.

American Psychological Association. (2009). *Appropriate therapeutic responses to sexual orientation.* Available at www.apa.org/pi/lgbc/publications/therapeutic-response.pdf.

Bidell, M. P. (2005). The sexual orientation counselor competency scale: Assessing attitudes, skills, and knowledge of counselors working with lesbian, gay, and bisexual clients. *Counselor education and supervision, 44,* 267-79.

Birk, L. (1974). Group psychotherapy for men who are homosexual. *Journal of Sex & Marital Therapy, 1,* 29-52.

Blanchard, R., & Lippa, R. A. (2007). Birth order, sibling sex ratio, handedness, and sexual orientation of male and female participants in a BBC internet research project. *Archives of Sexual Behavior, 36,* 163-76.

Bogaert, A. F. (2007). Extreme right-handedness, older brothers, and sexual orientation in men. *Neuropsychology, 21,* 141-48.

Cochran, S. D., & Mays, V. M. (2007). Physical health complaints among lesbians, gay men, and bisexual and homosexually experienced heterosexual individuals: Results from the California Quality of Life Survey. *American Journal of Public Health, 97,* 2048-55.

Cochran, S. D., Mays, V. M., Alegria, M., Ortega, A. N., & Takeuchi, D. (2007). Mental health and substance use disorders among Latino and Asian American lesbian, gay, and bisexual adults. *Journal of Consulting and Clinical Psychology, 75,* 785-94.

Cochran, S. D., Sullivan, J. G., & Mays, V. M. (2003). Prevalence of mental disorders, psychological distress, and mental health services use among lesbian, gay, and bisexual adults in the United States. *Journal of Consulting and Clinical Psychology, 71,* 53-61.

Coffman, J. (2009, May). When conscience is criminalized. *Examiner.* Available online at www.examiner.com/article/coffman-when-consience-is-criminalized.

Corey, M. A., & Corey, G. (2007). *Becoming a helper* (5th ed.). Pacific Grove, CA: Brooks/Cole.

Diamond, L. M. (2007). A dynamical systems approach to the development and expression of female same-sex sexuality. *Perspectives on Psychological Science,* 2(2), 142-57.

Dube, E. M., & Savin-Williams, R. C. (1999). Sexual identity development among ethnic sexual-minority male youths. *Developmental Psychology, 35,* 1389-99.

Egan, P. J., Edelman, M. S., & Sherrill, K. (2008). *Findings from The Hunter College Poll of lesbians, gays, and bisexuals: New discoveries about identity, political attitudes, and civic engagement.* New York: City University of New York.

Freeman, W., & Meyer, R. G. (1975). A behavioral alteration of sexual preferences in the human male. *Behavior Therapy, 6,* 206-12.

Hadfield, J. A. (1958). The cure of homosexuality. *British Medical Journal, 14,* 1323-26.

Haldeman, D. C. (1994). The practice and ethics of sexual orientation conversion therapy. *Journal of Consulting and Clinical Psychology, 62,* 221-27.

Hatterer, L. (1970). *Changing homosexuality in the male: Treatment for men troubled by homosexuality.* New York: McGraw-Hill.

Herbenick, D., Reece, M., Schick, V., Sanders, S. A., Dodge, B., & Fortenberry, J. D. (2010). Sexual behavior in the United States: Results from a national probability sample of men and women ages 14-94. *Journal of Sexual Medicine, 7,* 255-65.

Hermann, M., & Herlihy, B. (2006). Legal and ethical implications of counseling homosexual clients. *Journal of Counseling and Development, 84,* 414-18.

Hughes, T. L. (2003). Lesbians' drinking patterns: Beyond the data. *Substance Use and Misuse, 38,* 1739-58.

Jones, S. L., & Kwee, A. W. (2005). Scientific research, homosexuality, and the church's moral debate: An update. *Journal of Psychology and Christianity, 24*(4), 304-16.

Jones, S. L., & Yarhouse, M. A. (2000). *Homosexuality: The use of scientific research in the church's moral debate.* Downers Grove, IL: InterVarsity Press.

Jones, S. L., & Yarhouse, M. A. (2007). *Ex-Gays? A longitudinal study of religiously mediated change in sexual orientation.* Downers Grove, IL: InterVarsity Press.

Jones. S. L., & Yarhouse, M. A. (2009, August). *Ex-gays? An extended longitudinal study of attempted religiously mediated change in sexual orientation.* In D. Byrd (Chair), *Sexual orientation and the faith tradition: A test of the Leona Tyler Principle.* Paper presented at the American Psychological Association's Annual Conference, Toronto, Ontario, August 9, 2009.

Jones. S. L., & Yarhouse, M. A. (2011). A longitudinal study of attempted religiously-mediated sexual orientation change. *Journal of Sex and Marital Therapy, 37,* 404-27.

Långström, N., Rahman, Q., Carlström, E., & Lichtenstein, P. (2008). Genetic and environmental effects on same-sex sexual behavior: A population study of twins in Sweden. *Archives of Sexual Behavior, 39,* 75-80.

Laumann, E. O., Gagnon, J. H., Michael, R. T., & Michaels, S. (1994). *The social organization of sexuality.* Chicago: University of Chicago Press.

Lewis, R. J., Derlega, V. J., Griffin, J. L., & Krowinski, A. C. (2003). Stressors for gay men and lesbians: Life stress, gay-related stress, stigma consciousness, and depressive symptoms. *Journal of Social and Clinical Psychology, 22,* 716-29.

MacCulloch, M. J., & Feldman, M. P. (1967). Aversion therapy in management of 43 homosexuals. *British Medical Journal, 2,* 594-97.

MacIntosh, H. (1994). Attitudes and experiences of psychoanalysts. *Journal of the American Psychoanalytic Association, 42*(4), 1183-1207.

Matthews, C. R. (2007). Affirmative LGB counseling. In K. J. Bieschke, R. M. Perez & K. A. Debord (Eds.), *Handbook of counseling and psychotherapy with lesbian, gay, bisexual, and transgender clients.* Washington, DC: American Psychological Association.

McConaghy, N. (1970). Subjective and penile plethysmograph responses to aversion therapy for homosexuality: A follow-up study. *British Journal of Psychiatry, 117,* 555-60.

Munzer, J. (1965). Treatment of the homosexual in group psychotherapy. *Topical Problems of Psychotherapy, 5,* 164-69.

Mustanski, B. S., DuPress, M. G., Nievergelt, C. M., Bocklandt, S., Schork, N. J., &

Hamer, D. H. (2005). A genomewide scan of male sexual orientation. *Human Genetics, 116,* 272-78.

Nicolosi, J. (1991). *Reparative therapy of male homosexuality.* Northvale, NJ: Jason Aronson.

Nicolosi, J., Byrd, A. D., & Potts, R. W. (2000). Retrospective self-reports of changes in homosexual orientation: A consumer survey of conversion therapy clients. *Psychological Reports, 86,* 1071-88.

Pittman, F., & DeYoung, C. (1971). The treatment of homosexuals in heterogeneous groups. *International Journal of Group Psychotherapy, 21,* 62-73.

Rosenfeld, B. (2002). The psychology of competence and informed consent: understanding decision-making with regard to clinical research. *Fordham Urban Law Journal, 30,* 173-85.

Savic, I., & Lindström, P. (2008). PET and MRI show differences in cerebral asymmetry and functional connectivity between homo- and heterosexual subjects. *Proceedings of the National Academy of Sciences of the United States of America,* 1-6.

Schaeffer, K. W., Hyde, R. A., Kroencke, T., McCormick, B., & Nottebaum, L. (2000). Religiously motivated sexual orientation change. *Journal of Psychology & Christianity, 19,* 61-70.

Schaeffer, K. W., Nottebaum, L., Smith, P., Dech, K., & Krawczyk, J. (1999). Religiously-motivated sexual orientation change: A follow-up study. *Journal of Psychology and Theology, 27,* 329-37.

Schwartz, M. F., & Masters, W. H. (1984). The Masters and Johnson treatment program for dissatisfied homosexual men. *American Journal of Psychiatry, 141,* 173-81.

Shidlo, A., & Schroeder, M. (2002). Changing sexual orientation: A consumer's report. *Professional Psychology: Research and Practice, 33,* 249-59.

Spitzer, R. L. (2003). Can some gay men and lesbians change their sexual orientation? 200 participants reporting a change from homosexual to heterosexual orientation. *Archives of Sexual Behavior, 32,* 403-17.

Throckmorton, W., & Yarhouse, M. A. (2006). *Sexual identity therapy: Practice guidelines for managing sexual identity conflicts.* Unpublished paper. Retrieved August 21, 2008, from http://wthrockmorton.com/wp-content/uploads/2007/04/sexualidentitytherapyframeworkfinal.pdf.

Truax, R. A., & Tourney, G. (1971). Male homosexuals in group psychotherapy. *Diseases of the Nervous System, 32,* 707-11.

Whitman, J. S., Glosoff, H. L., Kocet, M. M., & Tarvydas, V. (2006, May). Ethical issues related to conversion or reparative therapy. *ACA in the News*. www.coun seling.org/pressroom/newsreleases.aspx?aguid=b68aba97-2f08-40c2-a400-0630765f72f4.

Yarhouse, M. A., & Kays, J. L. (2008). Homosexuality and sexual identity: An update. In D. Rosenau, M. Sytsma & D. Taylor (Eds.), *Basic issues in sex therapy*. [Reading packet]. Suwanee, GA: Institute for Sexual Wholeness.

Yarhouse, M. A., & Tan, E. S. N. (2004). *Sexual identity synthesis: Attributions, meaning-making, and the search for congruence*. Lanham, MD: University Press of America.

Yarhouse, M. A. (1998). When clients seek treatment for same-sex attraction: Ethical issues in the "right to choose" debate. *Psychotherapy: Theory, Research, Practice, Training, 35*, 248-59.

Yarhouse, M. A. (2008). Narrative sexual identity therapy. *Psychotherapy, 36*, 196-210.

Yarhouse, M. A. (2010a). *Homosexuality and the Christian: A guide for parents, pastors, and friends*. Minneapolis, MN: Bethany House.

Yarhouse, M. A. (2010b). *The sexual identity clinic*. Virginia Beach, VA: Institute for the Study of Sexual Identity.

Yarhouse, M. A., Stratton, S. P., Dean, J. B., & Brooke, H. L. (2009). Listening to sexual minorities on Christian college campuses. *Journal of Psychology and Theology, 37*(2), 96-113.

Yelland, C., & Tiggeman, M. (2003). Muscularity and the gay ideal: Body dissatisfaction and disordered eating in homosexual men. *Eating Behaviors, 4*, 107-16.

Clients with Chronic Conditions

James H. Jennison

Many Christian counselors and mental health professionals approach patients who have chronic conditions with the same presuppositions that they might hold regarding patients who present with other, more transient life problems. Models that work well for simple emotional problems may not be as useful for dealing with chronic problems based on organic conditions or psychological disorders that are, by definition, chronic and intractable. This chapter will examine the professional ethical principles that are most pertinent to the evaluation and treatment of chronic conditions, and will discuss in particular the conditions of schizophrenia, major depression, character disorders, Alzheimer's disease, traumatic brain injury and chronic pain.

Christian mental health workers may be trained in a variety of academic disciplines and may hold differing professional licenses and certifications. In this chapter the terms *mental health professional* and *counselor* will refer primarily to the professions of psychiatry, psychology, clinical social work, licensed or certified mental health counseling, and licensed marriage and family therapy. Parts of the discussion may also be helpful to pastoral counselors and paraprofessionals who will undoubtedly encounter some of these individuals in the course of their work and may need to know how to recognize and refer them to other mental health professionals. Some of the information should also be helpful to chaplains who work in hospital settings.

Presuppositions regarding illness and health influence the thinking of the Christian mental health worker. Scriptural accounts of miraculous healing of what appeared to be chronic, intractable conditions (blindness, paralysis, etc.) may contribute to a presupposition that all conditions are subject to the patient's choice of emotional and spiritual health. We run the risk of spiritualizing the physiological or psychological condition of the patient and in so doing may frustrate and harm rather than help. We must avoid the example of Job's friends, who interpreted his malady as symptomatic of some spiritual lapse and thus contributed to his suffering rather than comforting or helping. Job's response to their exhortations was "Now you too have proved to be of no help" (Job 6:21 NIV).

The apostle Paul in 2 Corinthians 12:7-10 refers to his "thorn in the flesh," which appears to be some type of physical or emotional malady. The Scriptures do not give any further clue as to the nature of his condition, and to specify it is merely speculative. Rather than discuss his condition or its physical ramifications, Paul proceeds with a discussion of the spiritual impact and meaning of the *thorn* in his life. He describes how it served to foster humility and a dependence on God. But the text also indicates that he truly suffered, wished to be delivered from it and asked God for deliverance from it, but apparently did not receive the deliverance that he hoped for. Therefore he resigned himself to having the condition chronically. Scripture does not indicate that his condition was resolved or that he ceased to suffer—even though he was able to recognize a spiritual value in the experience.

The role of the Christian mental health worker is to address not only the spiritual significance of the patient's condition but the ongoing human experience as well. In the case of chronic conditions this may pose not only difficult and unanswered questions (e.g., Why do the righteous suffer?) but may challenge the theoretical presuppositions on which the counselor bases his or her work.

PROFESSIONAL CODES OF ETHICS

The ethical principles or standards referred to in this chapter—most notably the "Ethical Principles of Psychologists and Code of Conduct" as adopted and published by the American Psychological Association (2002)—have applicability to other mental heath professions as well as psychologists. The ethical principles or standards chosen for discussion here are those that address particular issues that arise with regard to chronic patients. This is not to imply that the many other principles and ethical codes do not apply or are less important. It is assumed that mental health professionals will follow the full ethical standards of their profession as applicable to all types of practice.

The most basic principle of the American Psychological Association code is contained in the preamble: "Psychologists are committed to increasing scientific and professional knowledge of behavior and people's understanding of themselves and others and to the use of such knowledge to improve the condition of individuals, organizations and society" (2002, p. 1062). A psychologist identifies with a profession that is based on scientific method or on information that is professionally derived. Professionally derived information is that which is held by consensus based on the collective experience of others in the profession, based on generally accepted theory within the profession, and information which may be extrapolated from known scientific data. While mental health professionals other than psychologists or psychiatrists may place differing relative emphasis on the scientific inquiry, all of them rely on a body of knowledge held by consensus within the profession. That body of knowledge is central to the professional identity of that group. While there may be considerable diversity of viewpoints within a professional group, there is an expectation that those who identify themselves as professionals (i.e., psychologist, social worker, psychiatrist, etc.) work responsibly within the scope of the knowledge of that profession. Thus it is inappropriate, for example, for a Christian to present him- or herself as a psychologist, but summarily reject the body of principles and concepts held by consensus within the profession of psychology.

There is a growing body of knowledge about various chronic conditions and the unique aspects of various conditions, as well as aspects shared in common. Within the mental health professions we see a proliferation of subspecialties. As knowledge grows, it becomes impossible for the "general practitioner" model to serve the mental health professions as it has in the past. The Christian mental health professional has an opportunity and a responsibility to those with chronic conditions to contribute to the knowledge base. Careful research and writing that adds to knowledge and dispels misconceptions not only helps the chronically afflicted individual but helps to shape the profession as well. There may be no better way for the Christian to be sure that Christian principles are accepted and integrated by both Christian and non-Christian mental health professionals.

A second standard is competence. Psychologists are expected to recognize the boundaries and the limitations of their competence and expertise, "based on their education, training, supervised experience, consultation, study or professional experience" (APA, 2002, p. 1063). There is an expectation that the psychologist will keep up to date with new information as it becomes available. As we consider various chronic conditions, it will become clear that dealing with particular diagnostic groups may require specialized knowledge and experience. An experienced, competent mental health professional, when beginning to practice with an unfamiliar type of patient, must learn new information, and will need consultation and perhaps supervision by other professionals who are experienced with that diagnostic group or type of treatment. Continuing education, whether formal or informal, is also a necessity. New information becomes available constantly, at an ever-increasing rate. Keeping current is hard but necessary work in order to practice ethically.

A third general standard is integrity. "Psychologists seek to promote accuracy, honesty, and truthfulness in the science, teaching, and practice of psychology" (APA, 2002, p. 1062). Further, "Psychologists are aware of and respect cultural, individual, and role differences, including those based on age, gender, gender identity, race, ethnicity, culture, national origin, religion, sexual orientation, disability, language, and socioeconomic status and consider these factors when working with members of such groups. Psychologists try to eliminate the effect on their work of biases based on those factors and they do not knowingly participate in or condone activities of others based upon such prejudices" (APA, 2002, p. 1063). The Christian mental health worker must not only consider the beliefs, values, needs and limitations of his or her own personality and experience, but must specifically be aware of the implication of Christian beliefs and worldview, and the effect those have on his or her work. This includes respecting the rights of others who hold beliefs that differ from their own, whether Christian or non-Christian. The issue at stake is the well-being of the patient and the administration of professional services consistent with one's profession. The professional may need to think of the spiritual condition of his patient as a variable, much as one might consider ethnic group membership or level of education as a variable. Providing the best mental health services to a Christian patient may include the use of Christian terms, concepts and Scriptures, while to do so for the non-Christian patient would be inappropriate. The Christian mental health professional must carefully define his or her role. While it is not appropriate for Christian psychologists to evangelize patients, their role with the chronic patient may extend over many years and may include repeated demonstration of Christian principles in the life and behavior of the psychologist.

A fourth general standard is directly related to the preceding discussion. The psychologist is to refrain

> from entering into a multiple relationship if the multiple relationship could reasonably be expected to impair the psychologist's objectivity, competence, or effectiveness in performing his or her functions as a psychologist, or otherwise risks exploitation or harm to the person with whom the professional relationship exists. Multiple relationships that would not reasonably be expected to cause impairment or risk exploitation or harm are not unethical. (APA, 2002, p. 1065)

In some cases, it is not possible to prevent contact with patients in other, nonprofessional settings. This is particularly true in small towns, and may also be true in the Christian community within a larger city. The issue, however, is to carefully evaluate the influence of some other relationship or role the professional has with the patient, and to consider what impact it may have on the professional's ability to perform competently, and what impact it may have on the patient's ability to benefit from the professional's services. For those with chronic conditions, the relationship with the mental health professional may extend, at least intermittently, over decades. The patient, and the significant others, may begin to perceive the therapist as "a friend of the family." Involvement in organizations that promote the welfare of specific chronic groups may bring the therapist into contact with the patient outside of the treatment setting. In small towns there may be other nonprofessional contacts that are inevitable, including attending the same church. Subtle issues arise in such cases and may require considerable thought and consultation with other professionals to avoid unethical conduct. The power differential between patient and therapist, and the need for objectivity on the part of the professional, can make these multiple contacts problematic. The length of the ongoing professional involvement compounds the difficulty, whereas in cases of more brief professional service, multiple roles may be much easier to avoid. The overriding issue is to maintain the competence and integrity of the psychologist's professional actions and to protect the patient from exploitation or harm.

The fifth general standard that we will specifically address is the issue of confidentiality. The APA ethics code does not specify what the limits of confidentiality may be, but clearly indicates the importance of the issue and that the psychologist clearly informs the patient with regard to those limits. Confidentiality is described as a "primary obligation," and the interface of law and professional practice and the issues of technology, electronic transmission and recording are addressed. The psychologist is expected to be in compliance with current laws and regulations such as the Health Insurance Portability and Accountability Act (HIPAA).

With patients who have chronic conditions such as those discussed in this chapter, the circle of confidentiality may include a multidisciplinary treatment team, family or personal caregivers, social service systems or legal systems, depending on the issues or situations involved. The circle of confidentiality may also need to change, as the severity of the chronic condition may wax and wane, or as degenerative conditions progress. Any change in the limits of confidentiality should also be specifically discussed with the patient or the patient's guardian or conservator in cases where the patient cannot give informed consent.

CHRONIC CLINICAL CONDITIONS

There are many chronic conditions that may be presented to the professional mental health worker. As the provision of health care has broadened from a traditional medical model, mental health workers are increasingly involved in nonpsychiatric treatment settings. The chronic clinical conditions chosen for discussion here are only a sampling of the wide variety that may be encountered and are chosen simply to provide a context for the understanding of the ethical issues involved. As each chronic condition is presented, a brief discussion will relate particular ethical concerns that may arise with regard to that patient group. Again, this discussion is not exhaustive but designed to highlight the ethical concerns discussed previously in this chapter.

Schizophrenia. Scientific knowledge about schizophrenia is advancing rapidly. Recent editions of well-respected psychiatric texts such as Sadock, Kaplan & Sadock (2007) review the current state of knowledge. Studies indicate that as many as two to three million Americans may be afflicted directly, with many others suffering as family members and loved ones. While there have been significant advances in pharmacological management of the disease, there is no cure. Although about one-third of those afflicted will have some social adjustment, the majority will live unproductive lives, dependent on others for support. Aimlessness, alienation, frequent hospitalizations, homelessness and poverty are more often than not characteristic of the life of the chronic schizophrenic. The prognosis for the schizophrenic is not positive. Five to ten years after the first hospitalization only 10-20% can be said to have a good outcome. More than half have a poor outcome. The probability of readmission within two years of the first hospital discharge is 40-60%. Lack of knowledge about this disease and the limitations of effective management have multiplied the suffering not only for the identified schizophrenic individual but for the parents, siblings and loved ones as well.

Major advances in brain imaging, introduction of new medications and an increased interest in psychosocial factors relevant to the onset, relapse and treatment outcome have increased understanding of this disorder and improved clinical management. Brain imaging studies, together with post-mortem studies, have provided increasing evidence of a biological basis for schizophrenia. A wide range of studies support a genetic component in the etiology of the disorder.

It is equally important to consider what has not been demonstrated by research studies. There is no well-controlled evidence of any specific pattern of family interpersonal relationships that play a causative role in schizophrenia. This misconception, which was strongly held by many professional mental health workers, has caused great suffering for many parents of schizophrenics and has resulted in a lingering anger toward the mental health community.

There have been significant advances in pharmacological management of schizophrenia, particularly the introduction of Clozapine (Clozaril), and promising research on other atypical antipsychotic medications that do not have the devastating neurological side-effects of previous antipsychotics. It is important for nonmedical mental health professionals to be informed and assist their patients in getting whatever help may be available via medication. At the same time it is usually the case that optimal clinical improvement is based on a combination of pharmacological, psychological and social interventions.

As the biological basis of schizophrenia has become better established, there has been an increase in interest in psychosocial factors that may affect the onset of symptoms, relapse or treatment outcomes. The unexplained fact that nearly half of monozygotic twins do not become schizophrenic, even when the other twin has the disorder, suggests that the interaction between the biological and environmental factors is not well understood. While part of the answer may lie in the complexities of the genetic predisposition or physiological development of the individual, it is also reasonable to assume that the course of the disease may be affected by psychosocial stress, much like other diseases such as diabetes or heart disease. While it is important not to "blame" such psychosocial factors for the etiology of schizophrenia, careful management of psychosocial stresses may be important in delaying onset, preventing relapses or obtaining best treatment outcomes.

The mental health worker who works with schizophrenic patients must be careful to keep informed of advances in knowledge regarding this disorder. Theoretical approaches that emphasize family or psychosocial factors as the cause of the disorder are inconsistent with recent evidence. There are very specific criteria for diagnosis outlined in the *Diagnostic and Statistical Manual of Mental Disorders*, 4th ed., text revision (American Psychiatric Association, 2000), as well as reputable psychiatric textbooks. Knowing these criteria will help the worker in understanding the disorder and will help to prevent misdiagnosis or mislabeling of symptoms. Knowledge of resources for the patient and family is also important in making appropriate referrals and assisting the family or caregivers in obtaining the support they may need.

The importance of addressing both biological and psychosocial factors increases the need for the involvement of multiple professional disciplines in effective treatment. It is highly unlikely that optimal treatment will be rendered by a single professional dealing only with the identified patient, as was often the case in the past. This raises issues of confidentiality, as effective treatment will be likely to require information sharing between several treating professionals, caregivers and others. The limits of this "circle of confidentiality" need to be defined and made explicit to all involved. There may also be occasion to modify the limits based on the current mental status of the identified patient. The patient who is actively psychotic may be unable to give consent to information sharing, in which case the issue falls to the responsible guardian or caregiver.

Ethical issues pertaining to professional integrity may arise in the case of schizophrenia. There continues to be significant stigma with regard to schizophrenia, both in the Christian and non-Christian communities. Bizarre behavior raises levels of discomfort, and attempts to explain the disorder in terms of spiritual concepts, such as demon possession, may serve to increase stigma by adding a moral quality to it. Christian mental health professionals must carefully consider the current knowledge of schizophrenia in relation to their own beliefs and worldview. Such a devastating illness inevitably leaves unanswered questions in the mind of the careful Christian thinker.

Major depression. Major depression is a mood disorder with a lifetime prevalence of 15% of the population—maybe as high as 25% in the female population. This gender discrepancy is found in all cultures. Since it is relatively common, it is the subject of countless popular books and articles as well as volumes of scientific literature. As with all subjects in the popular literature there is a maze of differing opinions and "cures" being promoted. The popular literature often treats all depressed mood as if it were a single disorder.

There is increasing evidence of a biological etiology for this disorder, as with schizophrenia. The strongest evidence is biochemical, with a number of studies showing abnormalities of biogenic amine metabolites or neuroendocrine regulation in patients with a diagnosis of major depressive disorder. Brain imaging studies are less conclusive. Genetic factors are strongly implicated in the etiology as family studies show that first-degree relatives of those with major depressive disorder are two to three times more likely to develop the disorder than are those in the general population. Data from twin studies provides "compelling evidence" that genes explain 50-70% of the etiology of mood disorders (Sadock, Kaplan & Sadock, 2007).

Many nonpsychiatric medical conditions and treatments can produce symptoms of a major depression. Medications that the patient is taking for other reasons, for instance, should always be considered possible causes of depressive complaints.

Psychosocial factors are also often important in the onset of a major depression. Clinical observations indicate that the first episode is more often preceded by stressful life events than are subsequent episodes. Some clinicians believe strongly that life events play the primary role in the etiology of depression, while others lean toward a more limited role. Personality studies have failed to identify any single personality trait or type that predisposes one to depression.

The role of psychosocial stressors in the etiology of major depression is an example of a situation where scientific knowledge is not definitive, and professionally derived knowledge has not reached strong consensus. Such differences of professional opinion provide the motivation to continue to investigate, gather data and seek understanding.

Issues of differential diagnosis in the patient with depressive complaints draw our attention to the fact that not all depressions fit the criteria for major depressive disorder. Other diagnoses are provided by the DSM-IV-TR (American Psychiatric Association, 2000), including dysthymic disorder and depressive disorder not otherwise specified, mood disorder due to a general medical condition, and substance-induced mood disorder. Other disorders with primarily depressive symptoms include adjustment disorder with depressed mood and bereavement (which is not considered a disorder but rather a condition that may be a focus of clinical attention).

This wide array of diagnoses may indicate that there are several different conditions or processes that might be popularly labeled "depression." In fact depressive states range from normal to serious psychopathology. Concepts or presuppositions that may serve one diagnosis well may be limited or ineffective for another. The Christian mental health professional may struggle with the relative salience of biological factors as he or she considers the issue of patient responsibility or the contribution of spiritual, religious or philosophical issues to the patient's condition. While spiritual struggles may result in symptoms of depressed mood, it is also true that clinical depression of other etiology may keep an individual from a full appreciation of spiritual truth or a full participation in the church.

Major depressive disorder becomes chronic or recurrent in a significant portion of cases. For that group the general conclusion of most studies indicates a long course with many relapses. Most studies show that a combination of medications and psychotherapy is most effective in treating this disorder. The duration and recurrence of the disorder can be problematic for the clinician who emphasizes the patient's responsibility for his or her own condition. Whether or not patients are seen as responsible for their condition affects the clinician's behavior toward the patient, as will be discussed later.

Personality disorders. Personality disorders have a broad range of presentation, including a variety of behavioral patterns and encompassing a range of pathology from mild to serious. Behaviors associated with some manifestations of personality disorder are particularly distasteful or may violate Christian moral standards. These types of personality disorder are likely to create the most tension for the Christian mental health professional. The ethical principle of integrity must be applied here. The counselor's need to preserve and advance Christian moral principles must not stand in the way of an objective appraisal of the patient. Negative feelings and biases with regard to the patient's behavior may at times result in early termination of the patient or a lower level of service due to the therapist's discomfort.

On the positive side, the Christian counselor may have the advantage of a well-ordered set of moral and behavioral values which may be communicated both directly and indirectly to the character-disordered client. Lacking internal controls, these individuals can profit from external structuring and limit setting. In the Christian perspective there is an external moral reality that transcends the operation of conscience or human will. Philosophies that rely on looking within oneself for guidance are not likely to be helpful to these patients. The application of Christian moral principles must be made openly, with consent of the patient, taking care not to confuse the role of therapist with that of evangelist.

All personality disorders are chronic by definition: "The essential feature of a Personality Disorder is an enduring pattern of inner experience and behavior that deviates markedly from the expectations of the individual's culture" (DSM IV-TR, 2000, p. 686). The pattern is most often lifelong, though some types ease with maturity and aging. Some types are somewhat available to therapeutic modification, while other types are extremely resistant. Persons with personality disorders often do not feel anxiety about their behavior, and in the absence of discomfort lack motivation to change. Their maladaptive pattern of perceiving themselves and the world makes it unlikely that they will understand or recognize the problem as do others. While some modification may result from therapeutic intervention, the change may be small and slow. Concepts of spiritual regeneration and rebirth that are central to Christian belief may predispose the therapist to expect more change and more rapid change than is often seen in personality disorder patients.

The ethical consideration of multiple relationships also is pertinent to the character-disordered patient. Some types of personality disordered patients fail to distinguish clear boundaries between themselves and others. The setting and clarifying of such boundaries is central to the therapeutic task. The therapist must be especially careful regarding dual relationships with these patients. Relationships that might be inconsequential with another type of patient may disrupt the therapeutic process with the character-disordered patient.

Traumatic brain injury. Improved neurosurgical management techniques and the availability of emergency medical services have resulted in a significant increase in the survival rate for individuals that sustain traumatic brain injury. Penetrating injuries, such as gunshot wounds, often result in focal brain lesions—areas of brain tissue that are destroyed by the penetrating object. Closed-head injuries, as often occur in automobile accidents, usually result in more diffuse brain damage. Loss of function based on damage to brain tissue is addressed in rehabilitation services from acute hospitalization to outpatient services to long-term chronic care facilities.

Impairments from penetrating injuries may be dramatic and specific, with areas of functioning left quite intact. Closed-head injury, on the other hand, may result in a tremendous variety of neurobehavioral deficits.

While traumatic brain injury may be seen as a single diagnostic category, treatment must address a wide range of medical, surgical, perceptual, cognitive, emotional, behavioral and social problems. Rehabilitation efforts typically include physicians of multiple specialties, nurses, physical and occupational therapists, speech and language therapists, neuropsychologists, clinical psychologists, social workers, vocational counselors, chaplains and others. Despite the best efforts of all these professionals and the huge expenditure of resources in rehabilitation, long-term studies of the brain-injured suggest that neurobehavioral deficits often become permanent barriers to the total restoration of function (Tellier, Adams, Walker & Rourke, 1990).

The mental health professional is most likely to be asked to address some of the specific behavioral deficits that are often seen in the brain-injured patient. These include altered expression of emotion, decreased initiative and behavioral directedness, impulsivity and disinhibition, denial, depression, and social and family consequences. While the condition and functioning of the injured person's brain is a major causal factor, the effects of learning and conditioning, interpersonal interactions, intrapsychic factors, and environmental contexts must be considered as well.

Patients with injuries to the prefrontal cortex often display flattened or dull affect, and those with right-hemisphere lesions may be unable to accurately perceive the emotional cues from other persons or situations. Emotional lability may also be based on brain damage. Decreased initiative and lack of goal-directed behavior are classic symptoms of frontal lobe damage. Diffuse cortical damage often results in decreased inhibition and increased impulsivity. Denial may be organic, as seen in the condition of anosagnosia (the failure to see or appreciate one's deficits), or psychological. Depression is common and appropriate in those who have suffered disability due to traumatic brain injury. It is usually a transient phase of adjustment but can become more chronic and problematic. Though seen as a "normal" response, it must receive proper attention as a focus of treatment to minimize the negative impact it may have on the patient's recovery and rehabilitation.

Denial is a normal phase in the adjustment to disability after physical trauma. Both the patient and family may fail to appreciate the reality of the situation and the prognosis. In similar fashion, patients or family members may have a religious conversion experience, a sudden flight into religious faith or may appeal to miraculous healing. The needs of the Christian mental health professional to see others expressing faith in God may prompt reinforcement of these behaviors in the patient. This may be counterproductive therapeutically and may later be disruptive of the relationship of the patient and the therapist, as most patients reject their former statements of faith as they become more aware of the permanence of their disability. An understanding of the typical course of recovery and adjustment is essential to avoiding these pitfalls. For example, understanding the "bargaining" phase of adjustment to the losses of the traumatic brain injury patient will allow the counselor to lay the groundwork for a more mature and broadly based faith, and help the patient to see the importance of the resource of faith, regardless of his physical condition.

The issue of confidentiality must also be considered for these patients. Since there are typically multiple professionals involved, particularly in rehabilitation settings, effective treatment requires sharing of information and coordination of efforts among all professionals involved, as well as the family members or significant others. The extent to which information will be shared must be discussed with the patient, though some patients at some times may be unable cognitively to understand the issue. There may be certain information shared with the mental health counselor that is very personal and may not be essential information for the treatment team. This can be held in confidence. At times the high-functioning patient may want to have the option of selectively sharing some information that will be kept confidential.

Issues of confidentiality also are important in the forensic arena as well. Patients with traumatic brain injury are sometimes involved in civil or criminal litigation, and the mental health professional may be required to testify. As early as possible in the treatment this possibility should be discussed with the patient and/or guardians.

Alzheimer's Disease. Alzheimer's-type dementia (AD) is the most common type of dementia, affecting about 5% of persons at age sixty-five and increasing in percentage with increasing age. The prevalence is higher in women than men. Patients with Alzheimer's-type dementia have been estimated to occupy half of all nursing home beds in the United States.

The onset of the disease is insidious, and the cause is unknown. The hallmarks of AD include impaired intellectual functioning, memory loss, dysnomia and visuospatial deficits, though patients may not show all of these in early stages. A useful guideline for the early presentation is memory impairment plus one other area of impaired cognitive functioning. The disease is degenerative, with a mean survival time of eight years. It can progress rapidly (death in one year) or slowly (death in twenty years). There is no known cure.

The psychosocial difficulties presented by the AD patient are substantial. Often, family members become the major caretakers. The burden of the caretaking role may precipitate breakdown in the physical and emotional health of the caretaker. As the patient becomes more impaired, the resources of the family caretaker may become exhausted and institutionalization is required.

In addition to cognitive deterioration, there are behavioral and affective disturbances associated with AD. A consideration of these is equally important for the mental health professional, since they are common presenting complaints and may affect decisions regarding institutionalization. Unlike the cognitive aspects of the disease, which do not respond to treatment, the behavioral disturbances and agitation may sometimes be managed pharmacologically.

Depression in an elderly patient may masquerade as a dementia but is potentially reversible. But symptoms of depression are also common in those clinically diagnosed with AD. The mental health professional must be aware of the potential for misdiagnosis, which may result in effective treatments being denied to the elderly depressed person.

Psychotic symptoms of hallucinations and delusions may also be seen in the AD patient. Frequently persecutory delusions may cause the patient to become suspicious of loved ones and caregivers, and this may precipitate early institutionalization. Pharmacological intervention is often effective in managing these symptoms.

Other behavioral disturbances, including apathy, agitation, irritability and inappropriate patterns of activity, may complicate the management of the AD patient. These are areas in which the mental health counselor can be of assistance. A combination of behavior modification, environmental modifications and community support services may allow the AD patient to remain in the home setting much longer than would otherwise be possible.

As the disease progresses, the mental health professional may need to give more direct attention to support of the caregivers. Support groups are often available, as well as temporary respite care for the patient, allowing the caregivers a break. The physical and emotional demands of taking care of the AD patient are substantial and can overwhelm even the strongest caregiver. The caregiver may feel that he or she has failed the loved one, and the sense of guilt may require psychotherapeutic intervention. There may be need for grief counseling for the spouse or child as they see their loved one slipping away.

One of the difficult ethical issues the counselor may face is to provide accurate, timely information to the AD patient early in the course of the illness. At that time, there may be symptoms of depression, and the patient may be aware that their mental faculties are deteriorating. Diagnosis is an important issue as other treatable conditions may present with the same symptoms as early Alzheimer's disease. If diagnostic examination indicates probable Alzheimer's disease, the patient and family may need to make preparations for what lies ahead by estate planning and modification of living arrangements. It is important to include family members or significant others in the circle of confidentiality, even at early stages, since the disease will have a profound effect on them as well. In some cases the patient may want to "protect" his or her loved one from the pain of knowing, or the family member who brought the patient to the doctor may want to protect the patient. Both patient and family have a right to know the diagnosis, and it is in the best interest of both to be informed.

Chronic pain. Chronic pain is defined as pain that persists beyond normal healing time for a disease or injury (usually longer than six months) and is often associated with functional disability. Distinctions between acute and chronic pain are not always clear, and some diseases (such as malignant cancers) pose special cases of chronic pain that do not necessarily fit the pattern discussed here. Chronic pain patients typically exhibit pain symptoms and disability in excess of that which can be explained by physical pathology, so the mental health professional is often involved in their treatment. Multidisciplinary pain centers, often in hospital settings, have proliferated in recent years due to the large numbers of such patients and the substantial problem they present to health care systems. Effective treatment often depends on the communication and cooperation of multiple professionals of various specialties in a carefully designed treatment regimen.

Wilbert Fordyce and his colleagues at the University of Washington were pioneers in what is now commonly recognized as an operant conditioning model of chronic pain (Fordyce, Fowler & Delateur, 1968; Fordyce, 1976). Understanding that the clinician is dependent on patient behaviors (including verbal behavior) to determine the frequency, intensity, duration and locus of pain, they proceeded to analyze "pain behaviors" in terms of conditioning. Pain behaviors are subject to both classical and operant conditioning. The interaction of learning factors, emotional state and situational circumstances was found to produce a wide variety of pain behaviors. Pain behaviors could often be modified by manipulation of external contingencies. As pain behaviors were modified, subjective distress and functional disability often diminished as well.

In the operant conditioning model of chronic pain, "secondary gain" was seen as reinforcement of pain behaviors. There was no need to attribute blame or intention to the patient or the caregivers, but there was rather a simple recognition that all persons are subject to the effects of reinforcement. The frustration of health care personnel with chronic pain patients had often led to a derogatory labeling and to an effort to simply quiet their complaints by offering some intervention, even if it was known to be ineffective. Iatrogenic problems often resulted, including dysfunction from multiple surgeries and addiction to narcotic analgesics.

In the treatment of the chronic pain patient the counselor must be extremely aware of the reinforcing quality of his or her interaction with the patient. Professional attention can be among the most powerful of reinforcers. Physicians must be aware of the conditioning factors at work in medication regimens. Family members and significant others must be part of the treatment team for effective outcome and generalization of therapeutic gains to the natural environment.

While chronic pain may occur in conjunction with a variety of physiological conditions, it also often coexists with psychopathology, particularly anxiety, depression and personality disorders. Typical approaches to these disorders must be integrated with a broader consideration of the pain problem for successful treatment.

Ethical issues surrounding confidentiality are important in these cases, in which multidisciplinary treatment with the cooperation of many professionals is often necessary. The issues here are similar to those discussed for the traumatic brain injury patient.

The problem of pain has been discussed in many contexts by Christian writers and theologians. A familiarity with works such as *The Problem of Pain* (C. S. Lewis, 1961) may benefit the Christian mental health professional in dealing with patients' philosophical and spiritual questions regarding their condition. Anger is a frequent companion of many of these patients and their families. The counselor must be prepared to discuss issues of meaning without losing focus on concrete and behavioral therapeutic goals.

SOURCES OF BIAS

There are hundreds of types of psychotherapy, each with its own set of beliefs regarding psychopathology, causes of particular diagnoses and the efficacy of various approaches to treatment. Such beliefs may be a function of academic training and support of one's professional peers, published information about a particular form of therapy, or personal clinical experience. Snyder and Thomsen (1988) discuss how bias may develop and operate in the clinical context from an information-processing perspective by using hypothesis testing and confirmation as a model to understand therapist-client interactions. Therapist beliefs and theoretical orientations not only affect the hypotheses they generate, but the outcome of the hypothesis testing. Behavioral confirmation is often the outcome of hypothesis testing in the clinical context. The process is similar to that demonstrated by Rosenthal and Jacobsen (1968) in their now-famous experiments in classroom settings. There is extensive research demonstrating that people treat others in ways that serve to cause behavioral responses consistent with their beliefs and expectations (self-fulfilling prophecy).

Consider the clinical functions of diagnosis, causation and treatment. The therapist forms a working hypothesis regarding diagnosis, often within the first few minutes of contact. This initial diagnosis may be influenced by the client's own presenting statements, previous diagnoses or information from the referring party. Chronic patients of all types accumulate a legacy of diagnostic opinions and labels from professionals they have seen. The counselor must guard against simply going along with previous diagnoses without thinking through the patient's symptoms and presentation. All sources of data, including previous records, need to be considered. The therapist's habits and experience are reflected in a tendency to make diagnoses that are frequently utilized or have been recently utilized by that therapist. This initial diagnosis influences the questions that the therapist may then pose to the client, and by selective questioning, influences the data provided by the client. This process may account in part for the wide differences in symptoms reported by a client, depending on the therapist conducting the interview.

In similar fashion the hypothesis-testing-and-confirmation process may introduce bias into the determination of the cause of a disorder, and the selection, utilization and evaluation of treatment procedures and outcomes.

The issue of bias can also be conceptualized within the framework of attribution theory (Jordan, Harvey & Weary, 1988). Attributions are inferences about people, events, behaviors and causal relationships. The inferences regarding the patient or client made by the mental health worker may be biased by differences of perspective (actor versus observer), theoretical perspective or aspects of the patient's behavior. Bias may also be based on the needs or wishes of the clinician. For example, treatment failures may be attributed to resistance, secondary gain or character defects, while successes are attributed to the positive influence of the therapist or the efficacy of a favored intervention.

Of particular importance for chronic conditions is the issue of the patient's responsibility for his or her own predicament. Jordan et al. (1988) cite research indicating that the clinician's willingness to offer help is influenced by the perception of the "controllability" of the life events of the patient. Other research suggests that clinicians who perceive the patient as more similar to themselves are more apt to attribute the negative life events of the patient to external rather than internal factors. Weiner (1993) discusses the relationship of the attribution of controllability to that of responsibility. Persons who are suffering conditions thought to be brought on by their own actions are more likely to be treated with anger and withholding of help, while those perceived as "innocent victims" are treated with empathy and helping behaviors. These attributions are not unique to the health care arena but are common to all aspects of the human experience. Many patients encountered by the mental health professional are stigmatized by association with the diagnosis of their condition. Weiner describes research of attributions made with regard to a number of diagnoses (such as Alzheimer's disease, heart disease, AIDS, drug addiction, etc.). He concludes that "stigmatized persons were generally not held responsible for uncontrollable physical problems, whereas stigmas for which individuals were held responsible were primarily behavioral and mental problems, which are typically regarded as controllable" (Weiner, 1993, p. 960). In the absence of mitigating information regarding causation, certain conditions may evoke attributions regarding personal responsibility.

Certain chronic conditions are most likely to be seen as uncontrollable, and their sufferers as not responsible for their plight. Dementia of the Alzheimer's type is one of these. The AD patient is not likely to be seen as responsible even though the cause of the disease is unknown. In other conditions, attributions of personal responsibility may be made. In the absence of specific causal information the chronically depressed person may be seen as responsible for the condition. If information is available to link the condition to a neuroendocrine imbalance, the patient is more likely to be seen as a victim. In response to the traumatic brain injury patient, there is a natural tendency to inquire about the circumstances of the injury. Was the gunshot a hunting accident, a war casualty, a gang-related shooting or a wound from a police officer as the patient was attempting a holdup? Do we see the patient as responsible for, and perhaps even deserving of, the pain now suffered? As we observe the chronic pain patient, do we observe increases of pain behaviors in the presence of family members, while the patient appears quite comfortable when no one is watching? Do we attribute personal responsibility to that patient?

The Christian counselor must be aware of all sources of bias and attempt to maintain objectivity. If there are conditions that the counselor is unable to consider in an objective manner, the most ethical course of action may be to refer that patient to some other professional.

ETHICAL ISSUES AND THE CHRONIC PATIENT

Scientific and professional basis for treatment. Scientific and professional basis for treatment pertains specifically to the professional mental health worker. All recognized mental health professions have similar codes of ethics, and each has a body of knowledge, part of which is scientifically derived and part of which has been derived by consensus within that profession.

At the beginning of this chapter we discussed how the profession of psychology relies on scientifically and professionally derived knowledge. In his thought-provoking book *The Scandal of Psychotherapy*, McLemore (1982) states, "While it is patently clear that Christian beliefs are not scientific (using the word in its modern sense), it is less obvious that much of what psychotherapists believe, and do, is equally nonscientific." He further argues that "a psychiatrist, psychologist, psychiatric social worker, or marriage counselor has no special qualification for dispensing opinions about the meaning of life, the nature of the universe, or what is ethically good" (p. 48). The Christian mental health professional is faced with a task of carefully delineating his or her role and making clear to both patients and the professional community the limits of that role. While an integration of one's beliefs as a Christian with one's psychological thought is desirable, neither Christian belief or professional knowledge should be obliterated by the other.

In the varieties of chronic conditions discussed throughout this chapter I have attempted to draw attention to the need of the mental health professional for knowledge and information. Typical psychotherapeutic models may or may not be applicable to specific chronic conditions, and in some cases recent evidence has shown previous assumptions to be false. For example, previous theories regarding the role of parenting in the etiology of schizophrenia have proved untrue as research has demonstrated a biological basis of the disorder. To continue to base one's professional work on theories now disproved only causes unwarranted pain for the "accused" parents and fails to meet ethical standards for a professional.

Competence. It is incumbent upon all professionals to recognize the limits of their own expertise and limit their practice to areas of competence. Some global approaches to Christian counseling have minimized the need for competence with regard to areas of mental health practice, emphasizing spiritual principles that transcend diagnostic categories. Lacking knowledge, the counselor may act in ways that are harmful to the patient. An approach that is appropriate for the borderline personality disorder may not be appropriate for the Alzheimer's patient. A misunderstanding of the emotional lability or disinhibition of the patient with traumatic brain injury may lead to expectations for change that are sure to lead to failure.

Integrity. To maintain integrity, Christian mental health professionals must be aware of the effect of their own beliefs, values, needs and limitations on their work. In our discussion of sources of bias, the importance of attributions regarding the causation of a condition was noted. Based on causal attributions, further attributions are made regarding the controllability of the condition. Whether or not the patient is seen as personally responsible for his or her condition often depends on whether it is seen as controllable. Studies have shown differences in responses of health care professionals to patients perceived as responsible for their condition versus those seen as innocent victims.

Theological beliefs may influence the viewpoint of the Christian mental health worker's view of personal responsibility. But Christian mental health professionals are subject to all the same human failings as non-Christians. As McLemore (1982) observes, "The doctrinal assertion that we are all imperfect sinners has not deterred Christians from hiding their psychological hurts and struggles, out of the fear that these imperfections would reveal moral failings and thus lead to social censure" (pp. 36-37).

Confidentiality. All mental health professionals, regardless of faith, encounter the same issues with regard to confidentiality and the chronic patient. All must make the boundaries of confidence explicit and be careful to indicate when those boundaries must change in order to effectively treat the patient. Multidisciplinary settings such as rehabilitation services or pain clinics require communication between professionals and cooperation on implementation of the treatment plan. The sharing of information must always be done carefully and purposefully, and only information pertinent to the treatment should be shared. On occasion the mental health professional may have information from the patient that is very personal and has little bearing on the treatment program or the rest of the treatment team. Such information should be held in confidence.

CHRISTIAN PERSPECTIVE ON THE CHRONIC PATIENT

The chronic patient often requires professional intervention over a period of many years. An appropriate professional relationship can provide significant service both to the patient and to family members and loved ones yielding a lifelong impact. While it may require an enduring commitment and the exercise of patience on the part of the professional, working with chronic patients provides a unique opportunity to communicate God's love in a very tangible way.

Counseling the chronic patient addresses three broad goals: restoration of function, environmental modification, and maintenance. The first goal is to increase the patient's functional abilities by either retraining and strengthening of preexisting ability or by teaching coping and compensatory mechanisms to circumvent areas of deficit. The second goal is to assist in the modification of the patient's natural environment to maximize the "fit" between the patient's preserved or retrained abilities and compensatory strategies and the demands of the environment. The third goal is to provide support, comfort and encouragement, to prevent isolation, and to assist in the adjustment to disability.

Direct intervention to increase the patient's functional ability may include such diverse activities as insight-oriented psychotherapy, behavior modification, medication management, social skills training, cognitive rehabilitation and education.

The counselor's role in the modification of the patient's environment also encompasses diverse functions. Family members or significant others are perhaps the most important environmental context to be addressed. Education of these caregivers is essential. They must have a clear understanding of the strengths and limitations of the patient and how they can best assist the patient. They often must learn new roles and expectations. Vocational counseling may also be involved and may even extend to the counselor's involvement on behalf of the patient in the workplace. An interface with community agencies may also be part of the counselor's role. The counselor may be an important source of information regarding social programs, and reports from the counselor often are essential for establishing the patient's eligibility for certain social resources.

The chronic patient and counselor may establish a long-term, even lifelong professional relationship, unlike most traditional mental health counseling relationships. This is similar to the relationship of a patient to a family physician, which may extend over decades. The support of the counselor may be key to successful maintenance.

In many cases the counselor will need to be actively involved with family members or significant others in order to achieve these goals. The efforts of even the most well-meaning and highly motivated significant others can be counterproductive and can increase disability. Particularly in the early stages of a chronic disabling condition, the counselor may need to provide instruction and modeling for family members in providing the proper level of care while encouraging the patient to function as independently as possible. It is difficult to watch a loved one struggle to perform a task that could be accomplished so easily by the caregiver. But it is the struggle and the achievement that serves to enhance self-esteem and a proper sense of independence in the patient.

CONCLUSION

The suffering of chronic disabling conditions is not exclusively that of the identified patient but extends to family members and significant others as well. The greatest indignity of all may be the apparent meaninglessness of the suffering. The counselor's role in helping to identify meaning for both patient and family members may serve to make the suffering more "bearable" and to prevent the additional suffering of deepened depression.

Contemporary models of grief and loss typically describe stages or levels of adjustment that may be encountered by the patient. For the chronic patient, adjustment to the loss of function and its meaning at the present may resemble stages of death and dying as described by Elizabeth Kubler-Ross (1969). The phases of adjustment include denial, anger, bargaining, depression and acceptance. Faced with a lifetime of permanent loss, the chronic patient has an adjustment task similar to that of the dying patient. With a model to assist in understanding, both patient and family members will be more able to move toward an experience of meaningful suffering rather than despair. The movement toward acceptance requires a clear view of reality, an understanding of one's finite limitations, a sense of compassion for others and relationships that include a balance of necessary dependency and separateness. If the experience of suffering engenders compassion, true humility and a deeper appreciation for life and relationships, the suffering has not been useless or meaningless.

References

American Psychiatric Association. (2000). *Diagnostic and statistical manual of mental disorders* (4th ed., Text Revision). Washington, DC: American Psychiatric Association.

American Psychological Association. (2002). Ethical principles of psychologists and code of conduct. *American Psychologist, 57,* 1060-1073. Also available (with 2010 amendments) from www.apa.org/ethics/code/index.aspx.

Fordyce, W. E. (1976). *Behavioral methods for chronic pain and illness.* St. Louis, MO: Mosby.

Fordyce, W. E., Fowler, R. S., & Delateur, B. J. (1968). An application of behavior modification technique to a problem of chronic pain. *Behavior Research and Therapy, 6,* 105-7.

Jordan, J. S., Harvey, J. H., & Weary, G. (1988). Attributional biases in clinical decision making. In D. C. Turk & P. Salovey (Eds.), *Reasoning, inference and judgment in clinical psychology* (pp. 90-106). New York: Macmillan.

Kubler-Ross, E. (1969). *On death and dying.* New York: Macmillan.

Lewis, C. S. (1961). *The problem of pain.* London: Collins.

McLemore, C. W. (1982). *The scandal of psychotherapy.* Wheaton, IL: Tyndale House.

Rosenthal, R., & Jacobsen, L. (1968). *Pygmalion in the classroom.* New York: Holt, Rinehart & Winston.

Sadock, B. J., Kaplan, H. I., & Sadock, V. A. (2007). *Synopsis of modern psychiatry* (10th ed.). Philadelphia: Lippencott, Williams & Wilkins.

Snider, M., & Thomsen, C. (1988). Interactions between therapists and clients: Hypothesis testing and behavioral confirmation. In D. C. Turk & P. Salovey (Eds.), *Reasoning, inference and judgment in clinical psychology* (pp. 124-52). New York: Macmillan.

Tellier, A., Adams, K. M., Walker, E. A., & Rourke, B. P. (1990). Long-term effects of severe penetration head injury on psychosocial adjustment. *Journal of Consulting and Clinical Psychology, 58,* 531-37.

Weiner, B. (1993). On sin versus sickness. *American Psychologist, 48,* 957-65.

12

Ethical Concerns in Culturally Sensitive Practice

Sally Schwer Canning, Iryna Shturba Arute,
Andrea M. Librado and Anta F. Yu

The African American mothers sitting around me (Canning) were speaking calmly, but with considerable animation. They had just viewed a tape of a well-trained mental health professional giving a workshop on pre-school child development. Her topic included strategies for parents faced with a public temper tantrum. As a Caucasian graduate student, single and childless at the time, I was talking with parents in urban, low-income, pre-dominantly African American schools as part of my research. I wanted to understand what kind of parent training experiences would be most likely to engage and communicate respect to the parents in this context (Canning & Fantuzzo, 2000). My African American research partner from the community and I asked the mothers to give us their honest opinions about the workshop they had just seen. Just a few of their responses were:

- I don't mean to be racist, but she sounds white.

- She doesn't understand why children have temper tantrums.

- I don't really think she's a parent.

- It doesn't seem like she really wants to be there, more like she's being paid to be there.

- What she's recommending . . . that's the Bill Cosby way [of parenting].

    In that conversation, and in others like it, parents' perceptions of both the content and format of professionally designed and implemented interventions were shot through with a cultural critique. First, parents were unconvinced of the presenter's authenticity, genuine concern and relevance to them. Her more formal, versus conversational, communication style and format (though quite typical for a professional) did little to foster credibility in their eyes, thus undermining parents' receptiveness to her teaching. Second, content in the workshop reinforced parents' sense of cultural dissonance. In response to the workshop leader's recommendations for handling the temper tantrums, parents first agreed that "their children" did not tantrum in public in the manner presented on the tape; "their children" had been taught such behavior was unacceptable. Third, these parents respectfully but firmly took issue with the "ignore and take your child to a quiet place to calm down" strategy advocated by the professional, all the while affirming a high premium on children's respect for parents and a confidence in the effectiveness and suitability of their own, firmer parenting strategy. Parents started to name the differences in outlook in racial terms. Humor often surfaced as parents started getting honest about their perceptions of "black" versus "white" parenting. One parent recounted a grocery store anecdote in which a white mother pushed not one but two shopping carts by herself while her son ambled blithely alongside, offering no assistance, even after the mother requested help. The group erupted into laughter at the point in the story when the storyteller ended with her recommendations for handling the situation. The message was clear: this mother had not commanded respect. They assigned her no small measure of responsibility for her son's disrespect and indolence.

The tutelage I received from these parents dramatically shaped my identity and approach as a psychologist practicing in cross-class, cross-ethnic contexts. These and many experiences like them over the years have left me with a few simple convictions about ethics and diversity that make for a suitable introduction to this chapter. The first is an essential truth for all of us in the helping professions: *culture makes an impact*. In this case culture was a powerful force in shaping the way parents envisioned and carried out their roles, and in the clash between parent and professional perspectives and rapport. But regardless of clinical setting, psychological phenomenon, domain of functioning, presenting problem or professional task, culture will be in the room with us wherever and with whomever we practice, influencing our clients' perspectives, processes and outcomes as well as our own.

The second lesson seems almost paradoxical on the heels of the first: *culture can be missed.* Perhaps not by everyone, nor in every situation, nor in every respect, but I had surely been at risk of missing important aspects of culture in my interactions with these parents. As a person with the privileges of education and middle-class opportunities, a member of the majority culture with respect to my ethnicity, and who had limited experiences across class and culture, my understanding of what these parents experienced and valued was seriously underdeveloped. It was not lost on me that I had seen these and many other parents like them, sitting respectfully, if not always interestedly, in workshops like the one I had just showed them, sometimes nodding at the information, often participating politely. Had we not created a context for parents to give us honest and specific feedback, we may never have known their real impressions, nor learned how seriously we could miss the mark in our interventions.

Third, *culture is complicated.* If, while you read the scenario, you imagined the workshop leader to be white you would be mistaken. She was African American. Despite racial similarities, the participants rejected the advice giver along with her advice, and did so in racial terms. They were apparently responding to something much richer than skin color or "race." The combined effects of socioeconomic status, religious and spiritual influences, along with regional, local and even school values and traditions were being played out in these interactions, and no single aspect of identity can adequately account for their response. Nor can we content ourselves with becoming aware of or skillful regarding one dimension of those with whom we work.

Fourth, *crossing cultures can change us.* As a young trainee, the parenting styles I saw in this community often appeared stricter than the ones I was accustomed to. I had entered psychology training in order to work with children, for whom I had a strong and loving affinity, and I periodically recoiled in response to what I perceived as harsh tones or potentially abusive methods. In addition, much of what I had learned about parenting in professional contexts included a rejection of physical discipline of any kind. As my exposure to the community increased, however, I saw the conditions parents faced firsthand and saw more intimately the richness and nuances of parenting in this community, my judgments about what I saw began to change. In other words, rather than starting from the admonitions of my discipline and working from there, two kinds of knowledge—cultural (my own and those of the parents) and disciplinary—together informed my views.

Finally, *culture has consequences.* These parents knew very well that they themselves were likely to be viewed by whites in general and professionals in particular as deficient in parenting. Still they were confident in their own abilities and were clear about their rationale for taking a different tack: the harsh economic and social realities of their community shaped their views of the kinds of character traits they wanted to foster in their children, which, in turn, shaped how they parented. Beyond preference or tradition, parents in these high crime communities knew that the stakes were high, even life and death: children had to survive if they were going to thrive (Stevenson, Davis & Abdul-Kabir, 2001).

In our contribution to this volume, we hope to honor the many individuals and families who have shared their lives with us, and with those of you reading, by highlighting the importance of cultural considerations in counseling. The interaction of ethics and culture in the helping professions is a sizeable topic. In this chapter we define culturally sensitive practice and discuss the following questions that arise when culture and practice meet:

- How might we think biblically about a rationale for culturally sensitive practice?

- What ethical obligations related to culture are we faced with as professionals?

- What considerations are important for culturally sensitive assessment?

- How can religious and spiritual matters be understood and engaged as another aspect of culture?

CULTURALLY SENSITIVE PRACTICE

In this chapter we draw upon a wide range of concepts related to our topic, including counseling with diverse clients, crosscultural or multicultural therapy, and culture-centered or culturally competent practice. We have chosen the term *culturally sensitive practice* (CSP) as a unifying concept in order to present information from across these interrelated literatures.

The majority of early articles and books written on "culture" for practitioners focused primarily upon racial/ethnic aspects of client identity or on racial/ethnic differences between counselor and counselee. Experts are now moving away from a predominant focus on racial/ethnic identity to describe culture and are incorporating a much broader array of human dimensions in their definitions, such as age, gender, social class, sexual orientation, religion/spirituality, ability status and sometimes nationality and region (Vontress, 2009). Additionally, our understanding of culture has evolved to become increasingly multidimensional. Cultural considerations in practice require attention to various aspects of any one cultural factor, multiple cultural factors and the interaction of these identities within individuals, families and systems. The task for the clinician is to understand that the people he or she serves "simultaneously experience the world on a number of cultural dimensions" (Burnhill et al., 2009, p. 246).

The selection of "sensitivity" rather than "competence" is not meant to dismiss the importance of developing competence. Rather, sensitivity seems to us to be both a broader concept than competence as well as a precursor to it. The clinician must first recognize, or be sensitive to the fact, that culture operates in a clinical context and value it as an important feature of that context. Only then can he or she employ the kinds of knowledge and skills that constitute or foster competent practice. Furthermore, the notion of sensitivity may evoke more of a sense of process than outcome. Cultural "competence," on the other hand, calls to mind a finished product. We hope to convey a firm belief that ethical, culturally sensitive practice represents a complex, demanding, dynamic set of obligations, activities and qualities that will require monitoring and development for as long as we practice.

Our choice of the word *practice* rather than *counseling* or *psychotherapy* is an acknowledgement that cultural sensitivity will be needed in all aspects of our work, whether rapport building, case formulation, psychological assessment, intervention, supervision or consultation. And while our emphasis in this chapter is on interactions with clients and patients, we ask you to keep in mind other kinds of professional interactions and relationships that introduce difference across roles (trainees and supervisors), professions (pastor and psychologist) or disciplines (psychiatrist and social worker) (Fields, 2010).

CULTURE, DIVERSITY AND THE BIBLICAL NARRATIVE

Calls for cultural sensitivity and clinical competence in professional and public spheres vary as to whether a rationale for this sensitivity is explicitly provided. Often, one is not, but the assumptions underlying many of the calls for sensitivity to culture and acceptance of diversity can be traced to humanistic and postmodern ideas about human nature, with an emphasis on what Elliott (2003) calls "authenticity as a moral ideal: the idea that we each have a way of living that is uniquely our own, and that we are each called to live in our own way rather than that of someone else" (p. 29). The kind of relativism often implicit in the broader conversations about diversity is often consistent with the accompanying assumption that differences and diversity are inherently and uniformly good, or at least that they are insulated from the judgment of others outside of the person or group.

Does the Christian helping professional considering a commitment to culturally sensitive practice need to embrace these underlying values, presuppositions and worldviews at the heart of much of the broader conversation? In a word, no. Christians may differ with parts or all of the underlying frameworks in this dialogue without having to abandon a commitment to sensitivity and competence in diversity relationships and contexts. In fact, we hope to show how our faith tradition can provide a compelling framework for considering this commitment as well as a surer foundation upon which to build ethical decision-making and practice.

Reflection on the biblical narrative provides a framework for thinking about the nature of human beings. It can also give us a way to think about diversity through the lens of our faith. The Christian narrative has a dramatic arc that unfolds in at least four important stages: creation, fall, redemption and resurrection. Without intending to reduce the Christian faith to a story about diversity, we will make some observations based upon it.

A Christian understanding of persons may begin with God as Creator and humans as created by him, and bearing his image. While theologians differ about just what constitutes our imaging of God, we may agree that it is one aspect of our identity. These qualities of human nature are established at creation: that we were created by God, and created as good; that we are related to God, to one another and to the rest of creation; and that somehow we bear the image of our Creator. One way the image of God has been understood beyond that of the individual points to ways the community of believers can image God in ways that individuals cannot. This aspect of our imaging has been linked to the triune nature of God's character.

A second aspect of our created nature is that we were deemed to be good, along with all that God made. In the Garden, Adam enjoyed communion with God, with Eve and with the other creatures, even as each remained distinct from the others. Smith & Cahill (2000) examine the creation narrative and conclude that diversity was part of God's good creation from the very beginning. They highlight the process of differentiation, or separation, in the creative process, stating that "the biblical narrative parades the acts of separation that turn creation from a formless void into a spectacularly diverse cosmos" (p. 5). This interpretation differs from the view that diversity was not really present in human experience prior to the introduction of sin.

And only too soon does sin arrive in all its destructive power. In what we refer to as the fall, all the dimensions of human life (spiritual, physical, psychological, relational), though created as good, become marked by separation, distortion and degradation. Central to our discussion are the effects on relationships and society. The fall changes everything:

> The development of all human cultures now knows both good and evil, and it is no longer possible to declare that all that is different is very good. In this new situation, no culture can assume that everything it has to offer, or that everything that comes to it from strangers, is a gift. Diversity is not a good in itself. (Smith & Cahill, 2000, p. 7)

For those who view the introduction of cultural, ethnic and other kinds of diversity as originating in our fallen state, the story of Babel has sometimes been invoked to make this point. In this account the interpretation of God's actions falls along the lines of punishment of sinful humans, thwarting their prideful attempts to be godlike by dividing them through language.

Smith and Cahill's (2000) and McNeil's (2005) alternative accounts present a different interpretation. Both emphasize God's redemptive intention at Babel—putting a stop to man's rejection of God's plan for them and setting them back on the track of obedience. Smith and Cahill locate the people's rebellion in their resistance to God's instruction to spread throughout the earth, choosing instead to entrench themselves where they are, building a city that will broadcast their reputation across the earth. God's intervention, the introduction of linguistic diversity,

> not only judges and disrupts the empire-building project, but also pushes the builders back onto the path God had originally set before them. The close of the Babel story twice underlines the fact that people are once more spreading out over the earth, suggesting that a more final judgment is being averted, that humankind is being returned to a path where there is the possibility of blessing. Whether the confusion spoken of in the narrative is taken to refer to a miraculous multiplying of dialects or simply to the disruption of the conspiratorial consensus of the builders, it is oppressive uniformity rather than diversity that seems to be associated with sin. (p. 8)

What are we to make of diversity at this point in the narrative—good or marred by sin? McNeil (2005) answers yes to both:

> To view culture and ethnicity as simply the consequences of sin may obscure the larger purpose of God and distort the role of diversity in human relations. While we cannot view language and ethnicity outside of the context of fallen humanity, it would be inappropriate to view human diversity as antithetical to the nature and intent of God. (p. 157)

The coming of the Messiah into the world, and the atoning sacrifice of Jesus on the cross, constitutes the next, joyous part of the story. His victorious resurrection and ascension to the Father, along with the coming of the Holy Spirit at Pentecost, bring hope to our fallen states, forgiveness to sinners and transformation in our relationships with God and one another. The separation between human beings and their Creator has found a remedy, and enmity and self-centeredness in human relationships and society can be renewed and replaced with unity, love and shalom.

Of interest to this discussion is how the image of a gathered people, speaking in diverse languages at the action of God, is reintroduced at Pentecost, when the Holy Spirit descends upon believers after the resurrection of the Messiah. Babel and Pentecost are linked in a number of ways relevant to this discussion. McNeil (2005) highlights the impact on the hearers as

God ushers in a new era of membership together in the family of God, even as the distinctiveness of those gathered is preserved. Smith and Cahill (2000) see the introduction of many languages as a reaffirmation of the goodness of diversity.

> If the more pessimistic readings of the Babel story were correct, we would expect to see a return to linguistic uniformity when healing comes, an undoing of the curse of difference. It is not hard to imagine a miracle whereby the hearers are enabled to understand a single language, restoring a taste of lost linguistic oneness. . . . [Pentecost] gives a promissory glimpse of God's plans for the world, . . . a tantalizing preview in the here and now of a promised future. . . . [O]ur solutions to the fragmentation we face will not be genuinely redemptive if they underestimate or trample on human diversity. (p. 15)

We can see in both accounts the in-betweenness of human existence at this point in the narrative. We are redeemed and beloved members of a divine family, an identity that supersedes all other identities, and one that cannot be earned or lost through any of the usual markers of human status or membership, whether nationality, racial/ethnic identification, ability status, gender or class. At the same time, this superseding aspect of our identity does not negate the particularities of our individual or group identities. Paul's reference in Ephesians to the dividing walls in the temple being torn down provides another powerful image of the unity in diversity made possible by Jesus through the work of the Holy Spirit after Pentecost.

The "promissory glimpse of God's plan for the world" points forward to what the whole story is heading toward, the final fulfillment when there is a new heaven and a new earth, and sin no longer holds any sway. The vision of who we will be and how we will relate is certainly veiled. However, there is some reason to think that our identities will preserve some particularities. Smith and Cahill (2000) refer to Zephaniah's vision of the nations "not fused into one, but serving God shoulder to shoulder (Zeph. 3:9)" (p. 15). The description in Revelation of the heavenly city also includes language that appears to acknowledge the idea of particular peoples or nations. Although our understanding of the world to come is shrouded in mystery, our lives together appear to be characterized by both distinctiveness and unity. And if that is to be our destiny, unity in diversity, then what God is doing in his kingdom now will be a part of bringing about that shalom in the days ahead.

So what conclusions may be drawn from our reflection on the biblical narrative? We offer five observations about the way human diversity is portrayed:

1. Diversity is a reflection of the goodness of creation and a partial expression of the image of God.

2. Diversity is a medium for divine correction and restoration in the context of rebellion toward God.

3. Diversity is one arena in which sin is still visibly expressed.

4. Diversity is a context for redemption and restoration in our lives now.

5. Diversity is a characteristic of God's reign both now and in the world to come.

These assertions, taken together if they are to maintain fidelity to the biblical account of our lives, represent an alternative vision to more simplistic characterizations of diversity as either all good or all bad. We hope they can be a useful part of the foundational considerations clinicians bring to their practice in diverse contexts. Certainly, they do not directly tell us what tests to choose, how to strengthen a relationship with a client or when to bring up the subject of sexual orientation. They may, however, inform our own attitudes and approaches, guide our evaluations of recommended culturally sensitive practices and contribute to the many ethical and clinical decisions we make in the course of our work.

ETHICAL CODES, CLINICAL GUIDELINES AND PRACTITIONER COMPETENCIES

Within a biblical framework, Christian counselors must navigate the ethical obligations related to cultural diversity presented to us within our disciplines. Counselors, pastors, psychologists and students alike need to be aware of and respond to the recommendations and requirements of our disciplines related to this aspect of our practice. In this section we consider the guidance contained within existing professional ethics codes, clinical guidelines and lists of practitioner competencies that have been generated regarding practice with diverse populations.

Rationale for culture-related ethical guidance. The biblical examination of diversity just presented begins and ends with the work of God. Along these lines at least one faith-based organization for helping professionals, the American Association of Christian Counselors (AACC, 2004), refers to "the God-given dignity of all persons" (p. 6) as foundational. Other professional ethics codes build upon the idea of human dignity, but as an inherent characteristic or right. The American Psychological Association (APA, 2002, with 2010 amendments), for example, maintains a general presumption of respect for the rights and dignity of all people (see General Principle E).

One of the most elaborated rationales for attending to diversity is contained in the Universal Declaration of Ethical Principles for Psychologists (2008). Beginning with a statement of the inherent worth of all human beings, the International Union of Psychological Science claims:

> This inherent worth means that all human beings are worthy of equal moral consideration. All human beings, as well as being individuals, are interdependent social beings that are born into, live in, and are a part of the history and ongoing evolution of their peoples. The different cultures, ethnicities, religions, histories, social structures and other such characteristics of peoples are integral to the identity of their members and give meaning to their lives. ... As such, respect for the dignity of persons includes moral consideration of and respect for the dignity of peoples. (pp. 1-2)

Extent and specificity of coverage. While individual or cultural differences are referenced in all nine of the ethical codes we examined for this chapter, the scope and specificity of coverage varies greatly. Some codes stand out for their extensive attention to matters of culture and individual differences such as the codes issued by the American Counseling Association (ACA) and the Commission on Rehabilitation Counselor Certification (CRCC). Both include explicit commitments to respecting diversity in the preambles to their ethical codes. The ACA's (2005) standards are introduced by their mission statement, which identifies a central aspect of their organization's purpose as "using the profession and practice of counseling to promote respect for human dignity and diversity" (p. 2).

As a result of their extensive coverage, the ACA and CRCC also included greater specificity in diversity-related guidelines than some others. Diversity-related guidelines are present not only in general principles such as nondiscrimination or competency, but are applied to specific practice situations such as the ACA's inclusion of the need to "understand the challenges of accepting gifts from clients and recognize that in some cultures, small gifts are a token of respect and showing gratitude" (p. 6).

At the other end of the spectrum were the codes adopted by the American Psychiatric Association, the American Association of Marriage and Family Therapists (AAMFT), and the American Association of Pastoral Counselors (AAPC). These included only a single reference to diversity: a standard of nondiscrimination in the provision of services. The Christian Association for Psychological Studies (CAPS) included a similar standard as well, but added guidelines related to professional competence and assessment. The APA and AACC's codes fall somewhere in between, including additional standards relevant to values, therapy, educational and research contexts.

Certain ethical concerns were more likely to be addressed than others. All contained repudiations of discrimination based on individual characteristics such as age, race, national origin and so forth. The uniform inclusion of this particular standard is not surprising given that discriminatory practices have legal as well as ethical implications. Other significant emphases include practitioner competence and the exploration of one's own cultural identity and its effect on the counseling process (ACA, 2005; CRCC, 2010; IUPC, 2008) as well as cultural considerations in the process of informed consent and client confidentiality. Less common was integration of diversity-related issues into the realms of training, supervision, research, therapy termination and referral, the use of technology, bartering or receiving gifts and relationships with other professionals.

Clinical guidelines. In addition to the ethical codes generated by professional organizations, a number of clinical guidelines for practice have been developed. One important example is the APA's (2003) "Guidelines on Multicultural Education, Training, Research, Practice, and Organizational Change for Psychologists." This comprehensive document includes six sets of guidelines on cultural awareness and knowledge of self and others, education, research, practice, and organizational change/policy development. The guidelines are set in historical context and include supporting data, resources for ongoing education and models for multicultural organizational development.

Guidelines that are narrower in scope have been designed to inform practice with specific populations. Current examples target practice with lesbian, gay and bisexual clients (APA, 2005), women and girls (APA, 2007), and older adults (APA, 2004). While tailoring recommendations to their respective population of interest, all three of these guidelines set the needs and concerns of the targeted population in a larger social context, encourage practitioner self-awareness of attitudes toward these populations, offer specific practice recommendations and identify the need for professionals to engage in ongoing education. APA's division 36 (psychology of religion) has also crafted guidelines for engaging the religious and spiritual aspects of clients' identities, although these recommendations have yet to be formally adopted (Hathaway, 2005; Hathaway & Ripley, 2009).

Practitioner competencies. Attempts to identify practitioner competencies constitute a second approach to encouraging ethical practice with diverse populations. Several comprehensive efforts along these lines have been undertaken by the National Council of Schools and Programs in Professional Psychology (NCSPP, 2007), Association for Multicultural Counseling and Development (Arredondo et al., 1996) and the Council of Chairs of Training Councils (CCTC, 2007). The CCTC, for example, compiled a wide-ranging set of foundational and functional competencies for professional psychologists in the areas of self-awareness and applied knowledge. Each competency is expressed in the form of its essential components and is assigned behavioral anchors. Methods suitable to assess each competency are included. Competencies are developmentally formulated, with an eye toward identifying readiness for various stages of training, including practicum, internship and entry into practice.

As in the case of emerging clinical guidelines, some efforts to articulate cultural practice competencies have focused upon specific populations. Examples include the APA's Committee on Aging (2009) publication "Multicultural Competency in Geropsychology," the Association of Lesbian, Gay, Bisexual, and Transgender Issues in Counseling's (ALGBTIC, 2009) recommended competencies for work with LGBT clients, and the Association of Spiritual, Ethical and Religious Values in Counseling's (ASERVIC, 2009) "Competencies for Addressing Spiritual and Religious Issues in Counseling."

Needs and considerations. We anticipate that the numbers of culturally focused clinical guidelines and competency compilations will continue to increase in the coming years. If this occurs, it will likely be in response to both a positive pull from practitioners to have additional, practical guidance in this area (Leach & Aten, 2010), as well as to dissatisfaction about the current state of our resources.

At least five kinds of dissatisfactions have been voiced. The first is simply a call for more guidance, with more specificity, for more populations (Artman & Daniels, 2010; Schwartz, Rodriguez, Santiago-Rivera, Arredondo & Field, 2010). Practicing professionals will need to develop means of staying current with developments in clinical guidelines and in less formal broader literature. Real commitment will be needed in order to do this, given the demands of practice and the rest of life, and the expense and effort involved in continuing education.

A second criticism calls for approaches to go beyond identification and training of discrete skills and pieces of information toward a "narrative, vision, or meaning system" (McNeil & Pozzi, 2007, p. 83) that is paradigmatic in nature (see also Dueck & Reimer, 2009, for one important example).

Third, additional empirical research has been called for that would both inform the development of clinical guidelines and test existing guidelines through an evidence-based approach (Schwartz, Rodriguez, Santiago-Rivera, Arredondo & Field, 2010; Whaley & Davis, 2007). Evaluating our claims by testing them can help to increase accountability, assist us in avoiding harm and help to foster effective outcomes within and across various cultural contexts.

Additionally, there has been a concern that although cultural competence has been receiving considerable attention by professional governing bodies and scholars, the fruit of this attention has not been as extensive in clinical practice (Sue & Sue, 2009; Whaley & Davis, 2007). One investigation reported significant discrepancies between "what [therapists] knew to be important to competent multicultural practice and what they actually did when working with such clients" (Hansen et al., 2006, p. 71). Work remains in our ability to translate ethical obligations and clinical recommendations into actual practice.

Finally, our motivations have come under scrutiny. A recent conversation in the literature led by Gallardo et al. (2009) pointedly asks "Are we invested in [multiculturalism] because we *should be* or because we have a *genuine interest* in understanding the 'other'?" (p. 428, emphasis added). Will we adhere to ethical standards out of self-interest or obligation, or because we authentically value the well-being of our clients and colleagues who differ from us in significant ways? Gallardo pulls no punches:

> The ethical lens that many practicing psychologists rely upon is the assumption that we need to do what we can to protect our own professional and personal livelihood rather than assume that our primary intent is to respond in a culturally, and clinically, consistent manner for the betterment of our clients. A resultant outcome of this underlying premise is that most psychotherapists find themselves practicing on the defense. (p. 427)

He contends that "our minimum standard of competence is insufficient, if not culturally insensitive at times. It is not enough for practicing psychologists to simply 'follow' the ethics codes by meeting the minimum standards of care" (p. 427). As one evidence of genuine concern for the welfare of our clients, he calls for the field to begin with a cultural framework as the lens through which we view our clients and our discipline. Christian counselors may differ with Gallardo on a number of points. But we may find common ground with him in our shared commitment to place the welfare of others ahead of our own self-interest, and by acknowledging that while ethical accountability is necessary, it is not sufficient apart from genuine concern and compassion for the other.

SPECIAL CONSIDERATIONS IN ASSESSMENT

When most people envision counseling, they are likely to think of intervention, but the process also invariably involves assessment. Whether we are formulating a case, assigning a formal diagnosis, conducting psychological testing or listening for the needs of a supervisee, helping professionals regularly engage in assessment. Not surprisingly, cultural considerations are also needed in this context (Sandhu, 1995; Paniagua, 2010). The specific mention of assessment in a number of our ethical codes highlights our responsibility to competently respond to culture in the process (see the codes issued by APA, 2003; AACC, 2004; ACA, 2005; AAMFT, 2001).

Here we consider how culture affects various aspects of assessment, including client identity, presenting problems, the assessment context and psychological testing, offering recommendations along the way.

Culture and Identity Assessment

We have already discussed the general importance of cultural factors in a client's identity. Seeking to understand a person's or family's multiple cultural identities is also critical to the formulation of the person and his or her concerns. Hays (2001) devised a simple but comprehensive means of exploring aspects of a person's cultural identity that counselors might find useful in assessing both their client's cultural identities and their own. Part of a larger framework, the ADDRESSING model, an acronym, leads the clinician to observe and explore the following features of a person's identity: Age and generational influences, Developmental and acquired Disabilities, Religion and spiritual orientation, Ethnicity, Socioeconomic status, Sexual orientation, Indigenous heritage, National origin, and Gender.

Understanding levels of acculturation is often an important aspect of understanding identity. Acculturation refers to the degree to which individuals and families adopt elements from the new culture (e.g., values and social behaviors) and maintain elements from their culture of origin (Sattler, 2008). Formulations and diagnoses made without adequate consideration of levels of acculturation are likely to be incomplete at best and may lead to inaccurate diagnoses and ineffective interventions (Paniagua, 2010).

Culture and the Presenting Problem

Understanding the presenting concern is one of the important emphases of our earliest interactions with clients, whether in intake interviews, first sessions of counseling or the interview portion of a psychological assessment. Even beginning counselors are usually aware that the process is much richer and more complicated than a simple, verbal transmission of information. All sorts of factors determine what clients will share, how they will share it, what they will mean by what they say and what they will be expecting in response. Characteristics of the client and their concerns, of the clinician and their orientation and expertise, of the helping relationship and broader context all come to bear. Cultural influences are at play in all these aspects of the process.

Communication across cultural differences necessarily involves uncertainty and ambiguity, complicating our ability to code and decode the messages we send and receive (Matsumoto, 2000). When a client discloses the reasons for his or her visit, this ambiguity introduces challenges into the process of understanding the meaning attached to this information (Bhui, 2008). It can affect the directness or indirectness of what is communicated as well as the form this reporting takes, such as listing symptoms versus telling a story. Our interpretations of both nonverbal communication and social interactions that surround the telling of the problem are also complicated. Consider the Korean adolescent who does not make eye contact with the professional when describing her school experience. Is her behavior influenced by shyness or depression, or is it a sign of respect? These kinds of judgments are challenging. We can, on the one hand, mistakenly underestimate problematic phenomena or, on the other, pathologize features of a person or relationship that are harmless, simply different or even resourceful (Fontes, 2010; Sattler, 2008). Professionals will want to exercise caution in formulation when cultural features are unfamiliar, seeking ongoing education, exposure and consultation to assist in their assessment.

Clinicians should be attentive, as well, to the ways in which a highly individualized orientation can restrict their view of systemic factors influencing a particular client's presenting problem. Socioeconomic status, racism and other forms of injustice, language, power and privilege, and immigration experiences are examples of systemic influences on functioning that can be missed by practitioners (Fontes, 2010). Indeed clients may also overpersonalize problems that are significantly influenced by context (Constantine, Miville, Kindaichi & Owens 2010).

In the process of assessment, clients and clinicians may differ in the ways they experience attention in counseling to such aspects as problems versus strengths and resources, cognitions versus emotions, or individually focused information versus relationally based content. Exploring resiliency and identifying protective factors in the person's life and context can be helpful strategies for broadening the focus of our evaluations and improving the validity of our outcomes (Eukland & Johnson, 2007; Rogers & Lopez, 2002; Sue et al., 1998).

Culturally sensitive practice also requires that professionals be aware of differences in the prevalence rates of some disorders by gender, ethnicity and other variables and in the ways bias can result in over- or underdiagnosis. For example, fewer African American children are diagnosed and treated for ADHD although the prevalence is likely similar to that of the general population (Baily et al., 2010). To temper the threat of cultural bias in diagnosis, Hays (2001) recommends completing Axis VI first (using the previously mentioned ADDRESSING acronym), followed by Axis IV and Axis III (and then the subsequent axes) to encourage a more complete, strength-focused process, potentially lessening the possibility of misdiagnosis on Axes I or II.

Finally, clinicians should be aware of the existence of culture-bound syndromes or "locality-specific troubling experiences that are limited to certain societies or cultural areas" (APA, 2000, p. 898). *Boufée délirante,* observed in West Africa and Haiti, which refers to "sudden outbursts of aggression, agitation associated with confusion etc" (APA, 2000, p. 899) is one example. While some clinicians will never encounter this kind of syndrome, awareness of their existence is foundational to our capacity to recognize one should the situation arise.

Culture and the Assessment Context

Assessments take place in physical and interpersonal contexts, both of which affect the process and outcome. The physical environment itself can enhance or detract from clients' understanding of the task demands or their sense of trust or welcome (Fontes, 2010). For example, consider what might be communicated to the parent who comes for a clinical interview as part of their child's assessment and is asked to sit at a small desk and chair in a room typically used for child therapy, toys piled in the corner. If power differences between parent and assessor are great, the furniture built for children will not enhance the parent's sense that he or she is an important resource. If the parent's culture has shaped an expectation that the professional's role and behavior will be formal, in line with an expert, the assessor's credibility may be diminished.

Interpersonal aspects of the assessment context also deserve ongoing consideration in light of culture. Typical practitioner approaches of direct eye contact, forward-leaning posture indicating interest, physical proximity between client and therapist, and use of self disclosure may all need to be adjusted (Hays, 2001). Alterations in verbal and nonverbal communication, especially in light of status, power, gender roles and other differences that may exist between professional and client, can foster rapport and facilitate validity in assessment (Hofstede, 1984). While there is debate about the degree of impact of individual characteristics of the examiner on test performance (Sattler, 2008; Marx & Goff, 2005), the assessor should consider how he or she may be perceived as the "other" (Hays, 2001). Considerable evidence suggests that the relationship, not merely the age or race of the person conducting the assessment, is important (Pope-Davis, Toporek & Ortega-Villalobos, 2002; Greenfield, 1997).

PSYCHOLOGICAL TESTING

Psychological testing, as a special form of assessment, involves the measurement of intelligence, personality, social behaviors and a variety of other aspects of functioning. Most commonly, norm-referenced measures are used in which a person's performance is compared to a representative group (Sattler, 2008). This method typically involves the individual directly, but often incorporates information gathered from other sources, such as teachers and parents in the case of children.

Psychological testing arose out of a historical context that did not consider diverse cultural factors to any great extent (Sattler, 2008). Now there is widespread agreement that culture must receive serious consideration in the assessment process.

When psychological tests and procedures are not culturally appropriate, results can be inaccurate and the impact harmful. This is especially the case in high-stakes testing situations such as school or residential placement decisions, custody or employment recommendations or disability determinations.

Psychological tests can have a variety of limitations with respect to culture. *Cultural loading* refers to the degree to which a test requires culture-dependent knowledge such as "language and facts embedded in the geography or history of the culture" in order to perform well on the test (Sattler, 2008, p. 169). *Test bias*, when used in a technical, psychometric sense, is said to be present when tests are differentially valid, or to have different meanings for different subgroups (Gregory, 2007). For example, the MMPI-2 (Minnesota Multiphasic Personality Inventory—a personality test) has been found to overpathologize individuals of Asian heritage (Hays, 2001; Okazaki & Sue, 1995). Beyond psychometrics, *test fairness* has to do with the social consequences when psychological test results are applied such that a test can be free of test bias but still be considered unfair (Gregory, 2007). In this way "the proper application of psychological tests is essentially an ethical conclusion that cannot be established on objective grounds alone" (Gregory, 2007, p. 254). (See Paniagua, 2010, for a helpful summary of tests recommended with culturally diverse groups.)

Finally, professionals should be aware that receiving a referral for psychological testing can bring with it significant cultural baggage for certain individuals and groups. I (Canning) saw this firsthand in my role as a psychologist in a faith-based school serving an African American, low-income, urban neighborhood. The service provided prevention, assessment and intervention services, and parents typically welcomed anyone who genuinely wanted to support their child and help him or her succeed academically. Psychological tests, however, along with the formal diagnoses they were often linked to, were objects of great suspicion. This form of assessment was seen as a tool for labeling that would lead to stigma and exclusion, a view rooted in the legacies of mistrust as a result of oppressive and unethical treatment by professionals or for the "good of science" such as in evidence in events like the Tuskegee Syphilis Study.

So while psychological tests can provide critical information, they can be misused. Whether helping professionals conduct psychological assessment or use their results in treatment planning, it is wise to consider the appropriateness and potential impacts of specific tests and methods before engaging in or applying the results of this form of assessment.

RELIGION, SPIRITUALITY AND CULTURE

As the emphasis on culture has grown in the helping professions and our understanding of culture has broadened, religion and spirituality have begun to be included among the important dimensions of culture or diversity (Hage, Hopson, Siegel, Payton & DeFanti, 2006; Watts, 2001). Practice-focused literature on religion and spirituality is growing, and numerous ethics codes, clinical guidelines and lists of practitioner competencies include this feature of human functioning. (Note: Considerable attention has been paid to defining and distinguishing between religion and spirituality as separate terms with overlapping meanings [Aten & Leach, 2009; Hage, Hopson, Siegel,

Payton & DeFanti, 2006; Post & Wade, 2009; Richards & Bergin, 2005]. We cannot adequately cover these considerations here and use the combined designation "R/S" in many instances for brevity's sake.)

The inclusion of R/S in discussions of culturally sensitive practice is notable given the long history of tensions between religious and psychological traditions. Several influential figures, such as Freud, Skinner and Ellis, expressed their scorn for religion and spirituality as a source of psychopathology (Aten & Leach, 2009). Furthermore, mental health professionals tend to be less religious compared to their clients (Delaney, Miller & Bisonó, 2007) and receive limited training in religious and spiritual issues in graduate programs and predoctoral internships (Brawer, Handal, Fabricatore, Roberts & Wajda-Johnstone, 2002; Russell & Yarhouse, 2006; Saunders, Miller & Bright, 2010; Walker, Gorsuch & Tan, 2004). As a result, practitioners may feel unfamiliar and unprepared to engage these aspects in clinical practice.

Recently, however, a majority of mental health professionals indicate they view religion as beneficial to mental health (Delaney et al., 2007) and believe that the use of R/S interventions can be effective (Morrison, Clutter, Pritchett & Demmitt, 2009). Recent scholarship paints a more nuanced picture of R/S that is multidimensional and recognizes the staggering diversity of beliefs and practices, wide variations in religious salience, and the multiple pathways and outcomes that relate R/S to the promotion or erosion of adaptive coping and health (Hill & Pargament, 2003).

The question now being posed is not whether R/S should be addressed in the clinical context but how (Post & Wade, 2009). In this section we present guidance for practice that is sensitive to the R/S aspect of culture, using the awareness-knowledge-skills model for fostering counselor competence (Sue, Arrendondo & McDavis, 1992). Additional resources may be found in chapter nine of this volume.

Awareness. In R/S, as in other aspects of culture, practice is influenced by the clinician's attitudes, experiences and attention to what is important. Therefore, it is critical for practitioners to be self-aware as a first step in preventing harm and unethical conduct (Savage & Armstrong, 2010), especially when religious/spiritual worldviews of the counselor and client conflict with one another (Bergin, 1980; Jones, 1994). Therapists for whom R/S has low or no salience in their own life or who view R/S in a negative light may inadvertently overlook or downplay the religious/spiritual elements in a client's presentation or even view and respond to them in a critical manner (Gonsiorek, Richards, Pargament & McMinn, 2009). Counselors with high R/S salience, on the other hand, run the risk of overestimating the importance of R/S in their client's life or applying their own framework of belief in a way that could violate client autonomy (APA, Principle E) and damage rapport or worse (Post & Wade, 2009). Helping professionals must also be aware of a tendency to overpathologize unfamiliar religions (O'Connor & Vandenberg, 2005). In addressing these impediments, Wiggins (2009) devotes an entire chapter on the possible counter-transference issues therapists may experience with their religious/spiritual clients and how to increase self-awareness through the use of specific practices such as spiritual autobiographies and genograms, journaling and mindfulness exercises.

Likewise with other dimensions of human diversity, personal membership or identification on the part of the counselor does not automatically translate into competence in this area. This point has been well made in the area of racial/ethnic diversity. Similarly, a therapist's personal faith or religious experience (or lack thereof) is insufficient for competent practice related to R/S, and the sorts of active reflection, course work, experiences and training that are needed in other areas are just as relevant here (Gonsiorek et al., 2009).

Knowledge. The number of religious and spiritual groups in our society continues to grow and diversify (Milstein, Manierre & Yali, 2010). Even with respect to religious traditions that are well embedded in our culture and at least superficially familiar to many, the role of R/S matters in private and public life changes over time. Given the prevalence and importance of religious and spiritual matters to the U.S. population and globally, as well as their evolving nature, counselors are likely to encounter them in therapy (Hook et al., 2010) and will need to be prepared to understand and engage this aspect of their clients' lives.

Schlosser and Safran (2009) recommend that practitioners take an inventory of their R/S knowledge and work to increase it where needed by taking courses, reading texts, interacting with religious leaders and examining one's own views. Savage and Armstrong (2010) recommend having a working knowledge of major Western and Eastern traditions, along with their normative elements, vocabulary and concepts. Counselors need to be aware that members of a particular religion can vary greatly as to their degree of religious participation and adherence to aspects of that religion's beliefs and practices. Most religions are not monolithic, and knowledge of subgroups, sects or denominations within a particular religion is important.

Other aspects of culture will interact with R/S factors. For example, the larger sociocultural context can influence both how clients experience religion and how they are experienced by others (Savage & Armstrong, 2010), how individuals and families make meaning of and cope with their psychopathology, and whether they differentiate between psychological and religious problems (Knox, Catlin, Casper & Schlosser, 2005; Suzuki, Alexander, Lin & Duffy, 2006).

Skills. Thorough coverage of the skills involved in carrying out interventions sensitive to R/S is not possible here. The APA has published several books on this topic that extensively address this area (Aten & Leach, 2009; Aten, McMinn & Worthington, 2011; Plante, 2009; Sperry & Shafranske, 2005). Additionally, Savage and Armstrong (2010) recommend *The Therapist's Notebook for Integrating Spirituality into Counseling: Homework, Handouts and Activities for Use in Psychotherapy* by Helmeke and Sori (2006), as well as reviews of common spiritual interventions by Richards and Bergin (2000), and Eck (2002).

Increasing emphases on evidence-based practices (APA, 2006) means that the ethical clinician will need to stay current with this literature and consider using evidence-based approaches in practice. Post and Wade (2009) review empirical studies that address religious/spiritual issues. Compared to the abundance of literature describing religious interventions, studies of their effectiveness are lagging behind (Richards, Berrett, Hardman & Eggett, 2006). To date, evidence for R/S interventions' effectiveness are mixed, including limited evidence suggesting that they outperform secular approaches, leaving the choice of whether or not to use them to depend upon client preference or therapist comfort (Hook et al., 2010).

Additional skills in crosscultural and cross-disciplinary collaboration will be needed depending upon the communities in which helping professionals serve. Religion and spirituality, as well as other aspects of culture, can influence clients' conceptions of the origins of their problems (a supernatural versus a medical cause, for example), as well as perceptions of the nature and source of help they will seek. Individuals in some cultural communities are more likely to turn to primary care providers, clergy, traditional healers or family and friends than to professionals (Mathews, 2008; DHHS, 2001). For religiously committed clients, practitioners may increase accessibility and acceptability of help by collaborating with indigenous healers or spiritual leaders for referral, consultation or integrated care (APA, 2002; APA, 2003; Johnson & Sandhu, 2010; Savage & Armstrong, 2010). Collaborating with clergy has its unique challenges and rewards (McMinn, Chaddock, Edwards, Lim & Campbell, 1998). Practitioners are advised to be aware of these challenges and to develop relationships with informal gatekeepers and natural helpers within the community, work at establishing credibility (Aten, Mangis & Campbell, 2010) and seek training to build needed competencies (McMinn, Aikins & Lish, 2003; McMinn, Meek, Canning & Pozzi, 2001). Clergy who counsel are valuable resources in communities in which R/S are important and frequently encountered aspects of culture. They too, however, need to attend to culture. The expectations of pastoral and other religious counselors and those of their congregants may differ regarding how roles are defined, who is involved in counseling, how confidentiality is configured and counseling is conducted. The religious leader who counsels is responsible to clarify these aspects of the experience.

ETHICAL, CULTURALLY SENSITIVE PRACTICE: STARTING OR CONTINUING THE JOURNEY

Two of the counselors in an urban community center where one of us (Librado) worked before coming to graduate school, greeted their clients warmly when showing them into the office. The first, a Hispanic woman, offered a kiss on the cheek. The second, a Vietnamese professional, shook hands or bowed slightly. The greetings appeared to be well received and appropriate for the fit between professional and client. Undoubtedly, these salutations would have been poorly received (and the kiss ethically questionable) had the players been interchanged. A student struggling with depression welcomed another of us (Yu) into her home in Japan. Despite constant monitoring of her nonverbal cues and a direct question to see if she was tired, the young woman denied fatigue and continued a dialogue until suddenly asking "You're going home soon, right?" Even an awareness of subtlety in communication style and an active attempt to take culture into account did not prevent a misstep in this interaction.

In preparing this chapter we were struck by the power and complexity of culture in the process and outcome of the helping enterprise so well conveyed by these two illustrations. Our disciplines' understanding of the construct of culture, the extent of demands on practitioner development and the amount of resources now available to inform our practice all seem somehow, simultaneously, overwhelming yet inadequate. We conclude that ethical, culturally sensitive practice is a journey rather than a destination. Whether at the beginning or far down the road, we will never fully arrive. The process will continue to be challenging, but those we accompany need us to accept the exertions of this journey. As we seek to create hospitable spaces for our clients, we may do well to remember that we are also guests and recipients of their hospitality as they invite us into their personal and cultural worlds. We hope and expect to be expanded and exhilarated as we discover that we too are blessed along the way.

REFERENCES

American Association for Marriage and Family Therapy. (2012). *AAMFT code of ethics.* Alexandria, VA: American Association for Marriage and Family Therapy. Retrieved October 24, 2012, from www.aamft.org/imis15/content/legal_ethics/code_of_ethics.aspx.

American Association of Christian Counselors. (2004). *AACC Code of ethics: The Y2004 final code.* Forest, VA: American Association of Christian Counselors. Retrieved January 24, 2011, from www.aacc.net/about-us/code-of-ethics.

American Association of Pastoral Counselors. (2010). *AAPC code of ethics.* Retrieved October 19, 2012, from www.aapc.org/about-us/code-of-ethics.aspx.

American Counseling Association. (2005). *ACA code of ethics.* Alexandria, VA: American Counseling Association. Retrieved January 24, 2011, from www.counseling.org/Resources/CodeOfEthics/TP/Home/CT2.aspx.

American Psychiatric Association. (2000). *Diagnostic and statistical manual of mental disorders* (4th ed.). Washington, DC: American Psychiatric Association.

American Psychiatric Association. (2009). *The principles of medical ethics with annotations especially applicable to psychiatry.* Arlington, VA: Author. Retrieved

January 17, 2011, from www.psych.org/mainmenu/psychiatricpractice/ethics/ resourcesstandards/principlesofmedicalethics.aspx.

American Psychological Association. (2002, with 2010 amendments). Ethical principles of psychologists and code of conduct. *American Psychologist, 57,* 1060-73. Retrieved January 17, 2011, from www.apa.org/ethics/code.

American Psychological Association. (2003). Guidelines on multicultural education, training, research, practice, and organizational change for psychologists. *American Psychologist, 58,* 377-402.

American Psychological Association. (2004). Guidelines for psychological practice with older adults. *American Psychologist, 59,* 236-60.

American Psychological Association. (2005). The professional practice guidelines for psychotherapy with lesbian, gay, and bisexual clients. *American Psychologist, 55,* 1440-51.

American Psychological Association. (2007). Guidelines for psychological practice with girls and women. *American Psychologist, 62*(9), 949-79.

American Psychological Association, Committee on Aging. (2009). *Multicultural competency in geropsychology.* Washington, DC: American Psychological Association.

American Psychological Association, Presidential Task Force on Evidence-Based Practice. (2006). Evidence-based practice in psychology. *American Psychologist, 61,* 271-85.

Arredondo, P., Toporek, M. S., Brown, S., Jones, J., Locke, D. C., Sanchez, J., & Stadler, H. (1996). *AMCD multicultural counseling competencies.* Alexandria, VA: AMCD. Retrieved January 19, 2011, from www.amcdaca.org/amcd/compe tencies.pdf.

Artman, L. K., & Daniels, J. A. (2010). Disability and psychotherapy practice: Cultural competence and practical tips. *Professional Psychology: Research and Practice, 41*(5), 442-48. doi:10.1037/a0020864.

Association of Lesbian, Gay, Bisexual, and Transgender Issues in Counseling. (2009). *Competencies for counseling with transgender clients.* Alexandria, VA: Association of Lesbian, Gay, Bisexual, and Transgender Issues in Counseling.

Association of Spiritual, Ethical and Religious Values in Counseling (ASERVIC). (2009, rev.). *Competencies for addressing spiritual and religious issues in counseling.* Retrieved January 19, 2011, from www.aservic.org/resources/spiritual-competencies.

Aten, J. D., & Leach, M. L. (Eds.). (2009). *Spirituality and the therapeutic process: A comprehensive resource from intake through termination.* Washington, DC: American Psychological Association.

Aten, J. D., Mangis, M. W., & Campbell, C. (2010). Psychotherapy with rural religious fundamentalist clients. *Journal of Clinical Psychology, 66,* 513-23.

Aten, J. D., McMinn, M. R., & Worthington, E. L. (Eds.). (2011). *Spiritually oriented interventions for counseling and psychotherapy.* Washington, DC: American Psychological Association Books.

Baily, R. K., Ali, S., Jabeen, S., Akpudo, H., Avenido, J. U., Bailey, T., et al. (2010). Attention-deficit/hyperactivity disorder in African American youth. *Current Psychiatry Report, 12,* 396-402.

Bergin, A. E. (1980). Psychotherapy and religious values. *Journal of Consulting and Clinical Psychology, 48*(1), 95-105.

Bhui, K., & Dinos, S. (2008). Health beliefs and culture: Essential considerations for outcome measurement. *Disease Management & Health Outcomes, 16*(6), 411-19.

Brawer, P. A., Handal, P. J., Fabricatore, A. N., Roberts, R., & Wajda-Johnston, V. A. (2002). Training and education in religion/spirituality within APA-accredited clinical psychology programs. *Professional Psychology: Research and Practice, 33*(2), 203-6.

Burnhill, D. A., Butler, A. L., Hipolito-Delgado, C. P., Humphrey, M., Lee, C. C., Munoz, O., & Shin, H. (2009). In C. C. Lee, D. A. Burnhill, A. L. Butler, C. P. Hipolito-Delgado, M. Humphrey, O. Munoz & H. Shin (Eds.), *Elements of culture in counseling* (pp. 245-47). Upper Saddle River, NJ: Pearson.

Canning, S. S., & Fantuzzo, J. W. (2000). Competent families, collaborative professionals: Empowered parent education for low-income African-American families. *Journal of Prevention and Intervention in the Community, 20*(1/2), 179-96.

Christian Association for Psychological Studies. (2005). *Ethics statement of the Christian Association for Psychological Studies.* Batavia, IL: Christian Association for Psychological Studies. Retrieved January 17, 2011, from http://caps.net/about-us/statement-of-ethical-guidelines.

Commission on Rehabilitation Counselor Certification. (2010). *Code of professional ethics for rehabilitation counselors.* Schaumburg, IL: Commission on Rehabilitation Counselor Certification. Retrieved January 20, 2011, from www.crc certification.com/pages/crc_ccrc_code_of_ethics/10.php.

Constantine, M. G., Miville, M. L., Kindaichi, M. M., & Owens, D. (2010). Case conceptualizations of mental health counselors: Implications for the delivery of culturally competent care. In J. D. Aten & M. M. Leach (Eds.), *Culture and the therapeutic process: A guide for mental health professionals* (pp. 99-115). New York: Routledge/Taylor & Francis Group.

Council of Chairs of Training Councils. (2007). Assessment of competency benchmarks work group: A developmental model for the defining and measuring competence in professional psychology. Proceedings of the Benchmark Conference. Retrieved October 19, 2012, from www.psychtrainingcouncils.org/pubs/ Comptency%20Benchmarks.pdf.

Delaney, H. D., Miller, W. R., & Bisonó, A. M. (2007). Religiosity and spirituality among psychologists: A survey of clinician members of the American Psychological Association. *Professional Psychology: Research and Practice, 38*(5), 538-46.

Dueck, A., & Reimer, K. (2009). *A peaceable psychology.* Grand Rapids: Brazos Press.

Eck, B. E. (2002). An exploration of the therapeutic use of spiritual disciplines in clinical practice. *Journal of Psychology and Christianity, 21*(3), 266-80.

Elliott, C. (2003). *Better than well: American medicine meets the American dream.* New York: Norton.

Eukland, K., & Johnson, W. B. (2007). Toward cultural competence in child intake assessments. *Professional Psychology: Research and Practice, 38*(4), 356-62.

Fields, A. J. (2010). Multicultural research and practice: Theoretical issues and maximizing cultural exchange. *Professional Psychology: Research and Practice, 4*(3), 196-201.

Fontes, L. A. (2010). Considering culture in the clinical intake interview and report. In J. D. Aten & M. M. Leach (Eds.), *Culture and the therapeutic process: A guide for mental health professionals* (pp. 37-64). New York: Routledge/Taylor & Francis Group.

Gallardo, M. E., Johnson, J., Parham, T. A., & Carter, J. A. (2009). Ethics and multiculturalism: Advancing cultural and clinical responsiveness. *Professional Psychology: Research and Practice, 40*(5), 425-35. doi:10.1037/a0016871.

Gonsiorek, J. C., Richards, P., Pargament, K. I., & McMinn, M. R. (2009). Ethical challenges and opportunities at the edge: Incorporating spirituality and religion into psychotherapy. *Professional Psychology: Research and Practice, 40*(4), 385-95.

Greenfield, P. M. (1997). You can't take it with you: Why ability assessments don't cross cultures. *American Psychologist, 52*(10), 1115-24.

Gregory, R. J. (2007). *Psychological testing: History, principles, and applications* (5th ed.). Boston, MA: Allyn & Bacon.

Hage, S. M., Hopson, A., Siegel, M., Payton, G., & Defanti, E. (2006). Multicultural training in spirituality: An interdisciplinary review. *Counseling & Values, 50*(3), 217-34.

Hansen, N. D., Randazzo, K. V., Schwartz, A., Marshall, M., Kalis, D., Frazier, R., et al. (2006). Do we practice what we preach? An exploratory survey of multicultural psychotherapy competencies. *Professional Psychology: Research and Practice, 37*(1), 66-74. doi:10.1037/0735-7028.37.1.66.

Hathaway, W. L. (2005). *Preliminary practice guidelines for religious/spiritual issues.* Paper presented at the 113th Annual Convention of the American Psychological Association, Washington, DC.

Hathaway, W. L., & Ripley, J. S. (2009). Ethical concerns around spirituality and religion in practice. In J. D. Aten & M. L. Leach (Eds.), *Spirituality and the therapeutic process: A comprehensive resource from intake through termination* (pp. 25-52). Washington, DC: American Psychological Association.

Hays, P. A. (2001). *Addressing cultural complexities in practice: A framework for clinicians and counselors.* Washington, DC: American Psychological Association.

Helmeke, K. B., & Ford Sori, C. (2006). *The therapist's notebook for integrating spirituality into counseling: Homework, handouts and activities for use in psychotherapy* (Vols. 1-2). New York: Haworth Press.

Hill, P. C., & Pargament, K. I. (2003). Advances in the conceptualization and measurement of religion and spirituality: Implications for physical and mental health research. *American Psychologist, 58*(1), 64-74.

Hook, J. N., Worthington, E. L., Jr., Davis, D. E., Jennings II, D. J., Gartner, A. L., & Hook, J. P. (2010). Empirically supported religious and spiritual therapies. *Journal of Clinical Psychology, 66*(1), 46-72.

International Union of Psychological Science. (2008). *Universal declaration of ethical principles for psychologists.* Retrieved January 17, 2011, from http://am.org/iupsys/resources/ethics/univdecl2008.html.

Johnson, L. R., & Sandhu, D. S. (2010). Treatment planning in a multicultural context: Some suggestions for counselors and psychotherapists. In M. M. Leach & J. D. Aten (Eds.), *Culture and the therapeutic process: A clinician's guide* (pp. 117-56). New York: Routledge.

Jones, S. L. (1994). A constructive relationship for religion with the science and profession of psychology: Perhaps the boldest model yet. *American Psychologist, 49*(3), 184-99.

Knox, S., Catlin, L., Casper, M., & Schlosser, L. Z. (2005). Addressing religion and spirituality in psychotherapy: Clients' perspectives. *Psychotherapy Research, 15,* 287-303.

Leach, M. M., & Aten, J. D. (2010). An introduction to the practical incorporation of culture into practice. In M. M. Leach & J. D. Aten (Eds.), *Culture and the therapeutic process: A guide for mental health professionals* (pp. 1-12). New York: Routledge.

Marx, D. M., & Goff, P. A. (2005). Clearing the air: The effect of experimenter race on target's test performance and subjective experience. *British Journal of Social Psychology, 44*, 645-57.

Mastumoto, D. (2000). *Culture and psychology: People around the world* (2nd ed.). Stamford, CT: Wadsworth/Thomson Learning.

Mathews, M. (2008). Explanatory models for mental illness endorsed by Christian clergymen: The development and use of an instrument in Singapore. *Mental Health, Religion & Culture, 11*(3), 287-300.

McMinn, M. R., Aikins, D. C., & Lish, R. (2003). Basic and advanced competence in collaborating with clergy. *Professional Psychology: Research and Practice, 34*(2), 197-202.

McMinn, M. R., Chaddock, T. P., Edwards, L. C., Lim, B. B., & Campbell, C. D. (1998). Psychologists collaborating with clergy. *Professional Psychology: Research and Practice, 29*(6), 564-70.

McMinn, M. R., Meek, K., Canning, S., & Pozzi, C. F. (2001). Training psychologists to work with religious organizations: The center for church-psychology collaboration. *Professional Psychology: Research and Practice, 32*(3), 324-28.

McNeil, J. D. (2005). Unequally yoked? The role of culture in the relationship between theology and psychology. In A. Dueck & C. Lee (Eds.), *Why Psychology Needs Theology* (pp. 140-60). Grand Rapids: Eerdmans.

McNeil, J. D., & Pozzi, C. F. (2007). Developing multicultural competencies. In R. Priest & A. Nieves (Eds.), *This side of heaven: Race, ethnicity and Christian faith* (pp. 81-94). New York: Oxford University Press.

Milstein, G., Manierre, A., & Yali, A. (2010). Psychological care for persons of diverse religions: A collaborative continuum. *Professional Psychology: Research and Practice, 41*(5), 371-81.

Morrison, J. Q., Clutter, S. M., Pritchett, E. M., & Demmitt, A. (2009). Perceptions of clients and counseling professionals regarding spirituality in counseling. *Counseling and Values, 53*(3), 183-94.

National Council of Schools and Programs in Professional Psychology. (2007). *Competency developmental achievement levels (DALs) of the National Council of Schools and Programs in Professional Psychology.* Retrieved June 24, 2011, from www.ncspp.info/DALof NCSPP 9-21-07.pdf.

O'Connor, S., & Vandenberg, B. (2005). Psychosis or faith? Clinicians' assessment of religious beliefs. *Journal of Consulting and Clinical Psychology, 73*(4), 610-16.

Okazaki, S., & Sue, S. (1995). Cultural considerations in psychological assessment of Asian Americans. In J. N. Butcher (Ed.), *Clinical personality assessment: Practical approaches* (pp. 107-19). New York: Oxford University Press.

Paniagua, F. A. (2010). Assessment and Diagnosis in a Cultural Context. In J. D. Aten & M. M. Leach (Eds.), *Culture and the therapeutic process: A guide for mental health professionals* (pp. 65-98). New York: Routledge/Taylor & Francis Group.

Plante, T. G. (2009). *Spiritual practices in psychotherapy*. Washington, DC: American Psychological Association.

Pope-Davis, D. B., Toporek, R. L., & Ortega-Villalobos, L. (2002). Client perspectives of multicultural counseling competence: A qualitative examination. *Counseling Psychologist, 30*(3), 355-93.

Post, B. C., & Wade, N. G. (2009). Religion and spirituality in psychotherapy: A practice-friendly review of research. *Journal of Clinical Psychology, 65*(2), 131-46.

Richards, P. S., & Bergin, A. E. (2000). *Handbook of psychotherapy and religious diversity*. Washington, DC: American Psychological Association.

Richards, P. S., & Bergin, A. E. (2005). *A spiritual strategy for counseling and psychotherapy* (2nd ed.). Washington, DC: American Psychological Association.

Richards, P., Berrett, M. E., Hardman, R. K., & Eggett, D. L. (2006). Comparative efficacy of spirituality, cognitive, and emotional support groups for treating eating disorder inpatients. *Eating Disorders: The Journal of Treatment & Prevention, 14*(5), 401-15.

Rogers, M. R., & Lopez, E. C. (2002). Identifying critical cross-cultural school psychology competencies. *Journal of School Psychology, 40*, 115-41.

Russell, S. R., & Yarhouse, M. A. (2006). Training in religion/spirituality within APA-accredited psychology predoctoral internships. *Professional Psychology: Research and Practice, 37*(4), 430-36.

Sandhu, D. S. (1995). Pioneers of multicultural counseling: An interview with Paul B. Pedersen. *Journal of Multicultural Counseling and Development, 23*, 198-211.

Sattler, J. M. (2008). *Assessment of children: Cognitive foundations* (5th ed.). San Diego: Jerome M. Sattler.

Saunders, S. M., Miller, M. L., & Bright, M. M. (2010). Spiritually conscious psychological care. *Professional Psychology: Research and Practice, 41*(5), 355-62.

Savage, J., & Armstrong, S. (2010). Developing competency in spiritual and religious aspects of counseling. In J. A. E. Cornish, B. A. Schreier, L. I. Nadkarni, L. H. Metzger & E. R. Rodolfa (Eds.), *Handbook of multicultural counseling competencies* (pp. 379-414). Hoboken, NJ: John Wiley.

Schlosser, L. Z., & Safran, D. A. (2009). Implementing treatments that incorporate clients' spirituality. In J. D. Aten & M. L. Leach (Eds.), *Spirituality and the therapeutic process: A comprehensive resource from intake through termination* (pp.

193-216). Washington, DC: American Psychological Association.

Schwartz, A., Rodríguez, M., Santiago-Rivera, A. L., Arredondo, P., & Field, L. D. (2010). Cultural and linguistic competence: Welcome challenges from successful diversification. *Professional Psychology: Research and Practice, 41*(3), 210-20. doi:10.1037/a0019447.

Smith, D. I., & Cahill, B. (2000). *The gift of the stranger: Faith, hospitality, and foreign language learning.* Grand Rapids: Eerdmans.

Sperry, L., & Shafranske, E. P. (Eds.). (2005). *Spiritually oriented psychotherapy.* Washington, DC: American Psychological Association.

Stevenson, H. C., Davis, G., & Abdul-Kabir, S. (2001). *Stickin' to, watchin' over, and gettin' with: An African American parent's guide to discipline.* San Francisco, CA: Jossey-Bass.

Sue, D. W., Arredondo, P., & McDavis, R. J. (1992). Multicultural counseling competencies and standards: A call to the profession. *Journal of Multicultural Counseling and Development, 20*(2), 64-88.

Sue, D. W., Carter, R. T., Casas, J. M., Fouad, N. A., Ivey, A. E., Jensen, M., et al. (1998). *Multicultural counseling competencies: Individual and organizational development.* Thousand Oaks, CA: Sage.

Sue, D., & Sue, D. M. (2007). *Foundations of counseling and psychotherapy: Evidence-based practices for a diverse society.* Hoboken, NJ: Wiley.

Suzuki, L. A., Alexander, C. M., Lin, P., & Duffy, K. M. (2006). Psychopathology in the schools: Multicultural factors that impact assessment and intervention. *Psychology in the Schools, 43*(4), 429-38.

U. S. Department of Health and Human Services. (2001). *Mental health culture, race, and ethnicity: A supplement to mental health: A report of the surgeon general.* Rockville, MD: U.S. Department of Health and Human Services, Substance Abuse and Mental Health Services Administration, Center for Mental Health Services.

Vontress, C. E. (2009). A conceptual approach to counseling across cultures. In C. C. Lee, D. A. Burnhill, A. L. Butler, C. P. Hipolito-Delgado, M. Humphrey, O. Munoz & H. Shin (Eds.), *Elements of culture in counseling* (pp. 19-30). Upper Saddle River, NJ: Pearson.

Walker, D. F., Gorsuch, R. L., & Tan, S. (2004). Therapists' integration of religion and spirituality in counseling: A meta-analysis. *Counseling and Values, 49*(1), 69-80.

Watts, R. E. (2001). Addressing spiritual issues in secular counseling and psychotherapy: Response to Helminiak's (2001) views. *Counseling and Values, 45*(3), 207-17.

Whaley, A. L., & Davis, K. E. (2007). Cultural competence and evidence-based practice in mental health services: A complementary perspective. *American Psychologist, 62*(6), 563-74. doi:10.1037/0003-066X.62.6.563.

Wiggins, M. I. (2009). Therapist self-awareness of spirituality. In J. D. Aten & M. L. Leach (Eds.), *Spirituality and the therapeutic process: A comprehensive resource from intake through termination* (pp. 53-74). Washington, DC: American Psychological Association.

13

Business Ethics in Mental Health Services

Randolph K. Sanders

Imagine you are a young psychotherapist fresh out of graduate school. After several years of the graduate-school grind you assume naively that Christian counseling clinics will be standing in line to hire you, anxious to make use of the outstanding skills in talk therapy you have developed in school. Instead, you struggle to find a position, eventually landing a decent job as a beginning case manager at a new psychiatric hospital with a Christian therapy unit. One month after you arrive, the hospital decides to hold a depression-screening day. Advertisements will be listed encouraging people from the community to come to the hospital and be evaluated for depression. As one of the new case managers, you draw the responsibility of being one of the screeners. At the orientation meeting for the screeners, the hospital administrator announces that it is his goal that 35% of the people who are assessed to be depressed should be admitted to the hospital, and he promises bonuses to all screeners who are able to get at least 35% of their interviewees to enter the hospital. In addition, the administrator promises a vacation to the screener who obtains the highest number of admissions.

THE BUSINESS OF MENTAL HEALTH

Idealistic young psychotherapists seldom think, at least at first, about their work as business. We go to graduate school with the primary purpose of "helping people," but time and the realities of our world cause even the most idealistic to consider the "business" of what they are doing before long.

It's not just young psychotherapists who fail to think about the business ethics of psychotherapy. Seasoned professionals also neglect these issues. Much of our professional thinking about ethics is focused on issues in the therapy room such as confidentiality and multiple relationships. Comparatively little thought is given to the ethical issues of the business office and the boardroom. Unfortunately, when business matters are considered, ethical decisions may be driven as an afterthought (e.g., "Whoops, I should have told the client he would be responsible for the fee if his insurance did not pay") or by expediency (e.g., "What must I do to survive financially?") rather than with prudent moral and ethical consideration.

What would you do if you were the therapist in the example? Would you raise questions about the legitimacy of a screening day whose primary purpose is to find patients to fill empty beds in a new hospital? Or would you look the other way, concerned that to say anything would be to endanger your fledgling career? Perhaps you would tell yourself that many facilities do screenings like this and that it will surely help the lay public in some ways, even if the motivations are not entirely noble.

At their lowest common denominator many of the ethical issues surrounding the business of counseling involve issues of money or power or both. There is a natural tension inherent to providing psychotherapy and other forms of professional mental health services. The tension is in the fact that psychotherapy is at once a service to a hurting individual and at the same time a way of producing income for the professional person. On the one hand, the professional is sworn to attend to the welfare of the client or patient. On the other, professionals are also engaged in an occupation, seeking to provide an income for themselves and their families. Some radical critics who oppose psychotherapy altogether see this conflict as an indictment of psychotherapy, clear proof that psychotherapy is inherently unethical because it allows so-called professionals to profit from the pain and suffering of others (Masson, 1994). Most people would not go that far. Many professions make their income by providing special services to people with needs, whether physical, emotional, legal or financial.

We must not miss the critics' warning, however. Whenever one is providing special services to someone in some type of pain or distress, whether it be providing food and water to victims of a hurricane, providing emergency surgery, giving legal counsel, managing health care or counseling someone through a depression, there is the danger that providers of the service will take advantage of their position, manipulating or unfairly profiting from their clients or patients. It should concern us all that Scripture most clearly highlights Jesus' righteous rage when he threw the traders out of the temple, a definitive indictment of those who would "merchandise" the faith or, in the context of our present discussion, who would "use" Christian counseling for selfish personal gain (Mt 21:12-14; Mk 11:15-18; Lk 19:45-47; Jn 2:13-16).

This chapter focuses on the ethical issues attached to the business of service provision. We will discuss the more obvious issues: advertising, fee setting and third-party payments. But we will also review other less discussed but no less important issues such as the ethics of managed care and the unique issues that face clinicians in for-profit and nonprofit settings.

Truth in Advertising

The fundamental rule when advertising mental health services is, *tell the truth*. Many of the problems in advertising could be avoided if this rule were considered before public statements were made.

Advertising covers a broad range of activities. It can include brochures and newspaper ads, broadcast media announcements, directory listings, resumés, testimonials or information presented by others, book and tape announcements, and so forth. Taken broadly, advertising could even be construed to mean any statement we make that gives information about our services to the public. When therapists and mental health clinics advertise, they should be particularly careful about certain areas.

Training and experience. Prospective clients have a right to know about therapists' background, degrees and experience. Therapists must be truthful about their training, providing the facts and not giving misinformation either by stating things about their training that aren't true or by omitting certain facts that mislead the client into thinking they have training they don't have.

Case 1. A counselor with an M.A. in counseling and a Th.D. in biblical studies advertises himself as Dr. Z, professional counselor, but nowhere in his brochure does it explain that his doctorate is in biblical studies. In fact, throughout the brochure he is always referred to as Dr. Z. This counselor was not being entirely clear, leaving potential counselees with the distinct possibility of assuming he had a doctorate in counseling.

Case 2. Dr. Y had obtained a doctorate and certificate in counseling from a mail-order school of Christian counseling not accredited by any recognized credentialing body. Her training consisted of several brief correspondence courses in "counseling from the Bible" and the payment of a tuition and processing fee. She told counselees she had her doctorate in counseling.

Case 3. Dr. X advertised in the phone book that he had been trained by a well-known Christian therapist, and he named the therapist in his ad. In fact Dr. X had only attended a weekend seminar given by the famous therapist.

Therapists should be clear and avoid misunderstanding when stating their degrees, licensing or certification, and training experiences. They should not imply that membership in certain organizations such as the APA or CAPS implies special competency or training unless the organization specifically makes it clear that it is appropriate to advertise in this way (APA, 2002; Sec. 5; CAPS, 2005, Sec. 8b).

Services. Therapists and clinics have an obligation to be clear and truthful about the services they offer. They should not suggest that they provide a certain service when they are, for whatever reason, not equipped to provide the services in a manner which matches the prevailing standard of care.

Case 4. Mrs. A, a psychotherapist, announced that she was opening a pain-management clinic. A solo practitioner, Mrs. A had no medical consultant for her clinic and had no ready referral network in the medical community. Her pain management treatment program consisted solely of trying to help patients restructure their cognitions about their pain. While Mrs. A's treatment approach might be considered part of an appropriate treatment program, she was implying that she had a comprehensive pain-management program when in fact she did not. Mental health professionals should also avoid making exaggerated claims about the services they provide.

Case 5. Dr. Q's telephone advertisement contained the slogan "You've tried the rest, now counsel with the best." Her colleague reported her to the state board, complaining that Dr. Q could not possibly substantiate her claim that she was the best therapist. The state board ruled against Dr. Q, stating that "a small unscientific sample of happy clients was hardly proof of superior skill." They required her to receive additional education and supervision (APA, 2002, Sec. 5.01b; CAPS, 2005, Sec. 8a, b).

When advertising in the phone book, newspaper or other media, it is best to first study carefully the ethical code of one's professional group to clarify what is considered appropriate and what is not. Rules vary from one professional group to another and from one jurisdiction to another.

Defining appropriate advertising has been complicated in recent years with the entry of government regulations into the process. Until the mid-1970s one could assume that moderation and conservatism in advertising were basic givens. Therapists were usually encouraged by their professional guilds to use very simple ads that gave basic information with no bells or whistles.

Then the Federal Trade Commission and the U.S. Department of Justice issued rulings indicating that guild rules on advertising that were too stringent might in some cases inappropriately limit competition (Keith-Spiegel & Koocher, 1985; Koocher, 1977, 1994). The government rulings were supposedly intended to encourage healthy competition and were not intended to endorse flamboyant, sideshow advertising. However, it could be argued that at the least such rulings make deciding what constitutes appropriate advertising more difficult and thus increase the probability that inappropriate advertising will go unregulated.

Surely Christian therapists should err in the direction of conservatism in advertising. They should not hesitate to state their credentials and training in a clear, forthright manner that helps the consumer understand their skills and be able to make an informed choice about their services. But they should avoid statements that could mislead a layperson and should eschew statements that smack of self-aggrandizement. Most of all they should realize that some things that are fairly acceptable by commercial standards and by the culture at large may not necessarily be acceptable by Christian standards, which encourage care and concern for the welfare of others. They should check state or professional guild standards for advertising and do their best to remain in compliance. They should ask for consultation from fellow professionals when they are in doubt.

Advertising Christian counseling. "Christian" counseling has become very popular. Indeed, laypeople request Christian counseling frequently enough that some managed care and other referral networks now specifically ask therapists to indicate in their applications for provider privileges whether they provide Christian counseling services. In this environment it is not surprising that a few professionals use these terms as much for financial gain as for anything else.

Case 6. A private, for-profit Christian psychiatric therapy unit operating out of several hospitals advertised itself as "a ministry to the emotional needs of God's people." However, the program routinely turned away individuals with severe or chronic mental disorders as well as those lacking the financial means to pay for services. Upon being told that his schizophrenic son was "not appropriate" for the unit and referred to a state hospital, a father questioned the program director regarding whether this program was indeed a ministry to God's people if his son, a Christian and a schizophrenic, was not acceptable.

This case should not be taken to suggest that Christian mental health institutions must be capable of dealing with every type of mental disorder presented to them. But they must be sensitive to the way in which Christian language used too broadly, too carelessly or too simply in an effort to sell services may be misunderstood by their public.

Care also must be taken in the use of Christian language because such terms mean different things to different people. Though there is a huge evangelical population in this country, great individual differences exist between Christians of different denominations in such matters as religious practice, religious knowledge, beliefs and opinions. "Christian counselor" also may mean different things to different people and could imply everything from a Ph.D.-level Christian psychologist to an inquirer's counselor at an evangelistic crusade. The mental health professional should be clear enough to allow the average person to understand who he or she is and the nature of the Christian services provided.

Advertising by third parties. Not only do therapists have a responsibility to manage their own advertising, they also bear ultimate responsibility for statements made for them by others. Today many therapists and agencies hire public-relations professionals to advertise their clinical services, their continuing education programs and so forth. Other therapists write popular books that are advertised by publishers. Ad agencies, book publishers and the like may not know what is appropriate and may use advertising practices that are unacceptable by the therapist's ethical standards. Therapists must assist these persons in knowing what is acceptable. Most will be responsive, a few, however, may view the therapist as impeding their ability to "sell" the therapist's work, and in such cases the therapist will have to be appropriately assertive about what constitutes ethical advertising or will have to find another public-relations service. Therapists must also gently correct well-meaning but mistaken individuals in the community who advertise incorrectly or give misinformation.

Case 7. Mrs. D was doing a weekly marriage seminar at a local church. Each week the associate pastor, who served as emcee, introduced her as Dr. D, psychiatrist, even though Mrs. D was a marriage and family therapist and not an M.D. The incorrect announcement likely represented simple misunderstanding on the part of the pastor. Nevertheless, the therapist should gently correct the pastor and explain or model an appropriate response.

Celebrity endorsements of professional services are a questionable practice. Actors or sports stars, particularly those who have little or no knowledge about professional counseling, are likely to attract potential clients with their name rather than with their understanding of counseling.

Using counselee's testimonials in advertising is also debatable, and in fact, the CAPS guidelines prohibit soliciting testimonials from current counselees (CAPS, 2005, Sec. 8d). Potential counselees under stress may have special difficulty evaluating a testimony and generalizing it to their own circumstances. What's more, single-case successes do not necessarily suggest a pattern of success across a number of cases.

Case 8. A client with a history of bipolar disorder received help from Dr. R. The client then spoke at several of Dr. R's seminars and in the ebullient, expansive style of someone in a hypomanic state explained in glowing terms how Dr. R had changed his life and told the groups that if Dr. R could help him, he could help anybody.

Potential clients could not know the extent to which the person's bipolar disorder could affect his style of testimony, nor could they gauge how the treatment of bipolar might involve skills different from those needed to

treat other disorders. To be sure, one of the best ways that seasoned therapists receive new clients is through word of mouth from former clients.
However, these recommendations typically occur in the context of more
personal one-on-one relationships in which the prospective client may be
better able to judge the veracity of the testimonial and its applicability to his
or her own needs.

In addition, one must be concerned about the welfare of the clients who
give testimonials. In case 8, if the client is in a hypomanic or manic state
when he gives his testimony, is the therapist guilty of using his mental disorder for selfish gain? Even if the therapist is not guilty of manipulating the
situation, what if the client reveals something in his testimonial that causes
significant problems for him in the days ahead? For example, what if he
shares something that causes him to be ostracized by friends, family or
community?

Testimonials are considered appropriate for such things as books, workshops and seminars, and tests or other products. But even here testimonies
should not take the place of objective data, nor should they be used in a
misleading manner.

Endorsements. Occasionally mental health professionals are asked to endorse a product. These requests may be based on the assumption that the
therapist's professional credentials will enhance the perception of the
product and increase the purchaser's willingness to buy. Therapists must
take care about allowing their status to be used in this way. If the product has
nothing to do with mental health, the therapist's professional credentials
may create a halo effect for the product where none exists. If the product is
of a mental health nature, the therapist must take care that the endorsement
not substitute for objective data about the efficacy of the product.

Therapists and clinics must avoid misleading the public about their services. They shouldn't make statements that sound positive but can easily be
misinterpreted or leave false impressions in the mind of the listener.

PAYMENT FOR SERVICES

Fees. Fees are a significant aspect of psychotherapy whether the therapist
(or the client) chooses to think of it that way or not (Knapp & Vandecreek,
1993). The therapist who avoids discussing money matters is likely to be

unclear with clients about the procedures of payment or billing, and perhaps even about the amount to be charged, and may confuse the client or create the mistaken impression in the client's mind that the fee is not particularly important.

For other therapists the business of therapy seems to clearly take precedence over the service of therapy. Every billable hour is accounted for down to the second, and no exceptions are made. Occasionally therapists inflate their fees over those of comparably trained professionals and implicitly or explicitly assert that their high fees are proof of the high quality of their services. Fees should not be misrepresented and should not be exploitive. They should be consistent with the law.

The APA ethics code and CAPS guidelines state that psychologists should clarify fee and billing arrangements as early as is feasible in the therapeutic relationship (APA, 2002, Sec. 6.04; CAPS, 2005, Sec. 4.2). Basic information about fees and billing arrangements may be discussed in the first phone contact between the client and the therapist's office. Therapists should do their best to ensure that their office staff has a clear understanding of the office financial policies so that both staff and therapist will be able to communicate these clearly and consistently to the client. More extensive written information about fees can be provided at the first visit as part of the written informed-consent procedures (see chap. 4). If the therapist reserves the right to charge for missed appointments with less than twenty-four-hour notice (except in cases of emergency), this information should be included also. The therapist or staff should encourage the client to ask questions about anything that is not clear to the client.

Many patients use some kind of health insurance to help pay the cost of certain types of mental health treatment. Will the patient be required to pay at the time service is rendered, or will the practice bill the insurance company on the patient's behalf? It is up to the practitioner to set the policy by which third-party payments are handled, and practitioners must understand that if they are seeing the client under the auspices of managed care, then the managed-care contract will likely dictate much of how the payment procedure is handled.

If the counselor is to contact the insurance provider directly for any reason having to do with the billing, he or she should have a signed release from the patient. Above all, therapists need to inform patients at the outset of treatment that in the event insurance does not pay, for any reason, they (the patients) are ultimately responsible for the bill.

Some therapists and agencies have been known to tell clients that they will accept "insurance only." Under this arrangement the therapist bills the insurance company the customary fee for a session, say, $110. The managed-care company might allow a maximum fee of $80, with the insurance company picking up $40 of this amount (50%) and the client required to pick up the other $40. But suppose the therapist accepts the $40 from the insurance company as the full payment and then asks the client to pay nothing.

While the therapist who does this might see it as a kind gesture toward the client, it constitutes fraud toward the insurance company. The insurance company assumes that the allowable is the fee and pays their part of the claim, expecting that the client will be required to pay the other 50%.

Another fraudulent practice occurs when a practitioner who is eligible to receive third-party payments bills for sessions actually conducted by a practitioner who is ineligible. For example, a board-certified psychiatrist might "sign off" for therapy sessions conducted by a professional counselor in her office who was not on the insurance company's provider list. Or a licensed psychologist might bill the insurance for sessions that were actually conducted by his unlicensed trainee without informing the insurance company that this was what he was doing. Such practices are not only wrong but could expose the therapist to legal prosecution as well.

When fees and billing arrangements have been established and the client does not pay the bill, the therapist should first attempt to come to terms with this issue directly with the client. Therapists should learn to anticipate those clients who, for psychological or other reasons, display a high potential for not paying their obligations, and where appropriate, the therapist should respond to these issues in session.

Case 9. During his first session Mr. P told his therapist that he had bill collectors at his door "all the time" and that he had had problems throughout his life with procrastination. Near the end of the session, Mr. P mentioned that he needed to work out a "time payment plan" with the therapist for his sessions.

Some therapists will use a collection agency or legal measures to obtain compensation for services rendered and that are long past due. However, the therapist or the agency should inform the client ahead of time that such measures may be taken if no response to a bill is forthcoming (APA, 2002, Sec. 6.04e). When obtaining informed consent at the onset of therapy, the therapist should tell clients that he or she reserves the right to utilize a collection agency for unpaid accounts. Furthermore, therapists whose services are regulated by HIPAA must have a HIPAA-compliant business associate agreement with the collection agency prior to releasing any client information to them. Even with such matters in place, therapists need to realize that using collection agencies or legal measures to obtain uncollected fees is a factor that triggers some clients to file malpractice suits against their therapists (Knapp & VandeCreek, 1993). In general, therapists do much better when they have clear and understandable policies and procedures that encourage clients to pay their portion of the charge in a timely manner, preferably at the time services are rendered.

Fees and persons of limited means. There is an undeniable biblical mandate for helping the poor. The poor may be with us always, but we have a responsibility to open ourselves to them (Deut 15:11). Jesus and the early church expressed a solidarity with the poor that is clear and unmistakable. Christ announced that he came to set free the poor and downcast (Lk 4:16-21). He gave strong warnings about not being sensitive to the needs of the poor (Lk 16:19-31). We who have are encouraged to share with those who have not (1 Tim 6:17-18; Heb 13:16) and to avoid favoring the rich over the poor (Jas 2:1-5).

Mental health ethics usually encourage therapists to donate some measure of their services pro bono or on a sliding scale (APA, 2002, Principle B). This is easier to do in some settings than in others. The clinician who works in a community mental health setting may have the fees of poor clients subsidized by the state, foundations or charitable gifts. The private practitioner usually has no such subsidies and must carefully balance services to those with limited means against the financial survival of the practice. Fee scales should be set up carefully, balancing the needs of the community against the real costs of providing quality service (Hinkle, 1981).

In truth, Christian mental health professionals possess a responsibility at two levels when providing services to those of limited means. The first is at the *microlevel*: being concerned about the way they respond to the needs of individual clients who come before them. Christian therapists, whether they work in nonprofit or for-profit settings, need to contemplate carefully any conscious or unconscious prejudices they make between people of various socioeconomic groups who come for counseling. They should develop policies that are realistic and compassionate. If a therapist sincerely feels that he or she cannot by virtue of personal skill or financial stability provide services to a person of limited means, he or she should develop a network of competent resources to which such persons can be referred.

Professionals must also be concerned about their responsibility to address or be a prophetic voice at the *macrolevel* (e.g., at the level of public policy). Professionals need to be concerned about the poor who in some jurisdictions have access only to the most marginal care. They need to be concerned about poor or middle-class individuals who are impeded from accessing care because of current health care policies (e.g., persons who have been priced out of having insurance coverage or persons prohibited from having coverage because of preexisting conditions). What responsibility does the Christian mental health professional have to be an advocate for a more humane mental health system for all people, not just the affluent?

To cut costs some states have severely restricted the services they provide to the chronically and acutely mentally ill, who, coincidentally, are often poor and without means. These people, who at one time would have been provided for through the state hospital or community mental health systems, are often relegated to skid-row tenements, bus stations and other places where they try to survive with minimal assistance.

On the other side of the proverbial tracks, some of the "haves" in the health industry have structured systems that threaten to drive the wedge between services to rich and poor even deeper. Eisenberg (1986) has described the process of "cream skimming" in the medical world, in which some hospitals provide only those services that are the most profitable and leave more costly services and the care of the indigent to public hospitals. This practice increased rapidly during the 1980s, severely taxing the country's already-burdened public hospitals. According to Eisenberg some for-profit institutions structure their entire program, from choosing hospital sites in economically advantaged areas to avoiding certain disorders that are more costly to treat, in such a way as to exclude certain patients. In these settings, losing money on a patient is only "profitable" if it leads to some type of public-relations gain for the hospital.

"Cream-skimming" takes place in mental health settings as well. Some institutions actively avoid patients with conditions that may be more intractable or patients who for various reasons have little in the way of financial resources.

From a Christian prospective, profits should not take precedent over patients. People, whatever their means, need care, and a system that rewards great profits partly by rejecting certain people is not humane. There is the issue of balance, however. On the one side is the need to provide effective, caring service to as many as possible whatever their means. On the other side is the need to have financially sound agencies, institutions and practices to provide the services. Each individual Christian practitioner needs to be willing to look at the bigger picture of how his or her treatment patterns do or don't integrate with other service delivery systems in the community in order to provide for the needs of the total population.

Fee splitting and kickbacks. No one would argue that therapists should not refer clients to those whose skills and integrity they know and trust. Likewise teachers, physicians, pastors, attorneys and other referral persons should feel comfortable with the persons they refer to. However, when money changes hands between referral sources and professionals, there is always the danger that money is more the issue in the referral than is treatment excellence and the needs of the client (APA, 2002, Sec. 6.07).

Case 10. A counselor in a Christian high school referred adolescents with serious problems to a Christian ranch for adolescents four hundred miles away, even though there was another well-respected Christian program within fifty miles. The counselor received $175 for each person she referred. Ostensibly, the payment was for a brief "background report" on the patient.

In this case we must question whether the counselor is referring to the far-removed facility because she really believes its program is far superior or because she is receiving cash payments for sending them there.

Third-party payers and managed care. Insurance companies and other third-party payers have detailed stipulations in their policies specifying what conditions are covered and the financial amount of coverage. It is unethical for a practitioner to misstate or mislead a third-party payer with the intention of extracting additional insurance benefits. In general, misleading the insurance carrier can occur in at least two different ways.

First, the practitioner might bill one amount and actually accept a lesser amount so as to maximize the amount received from the insurance.

Case 11. A therapist uses a sliding scale for clients with financial hardship. The usual fee is $100, but the therapist offers an $80 fee to a client whose income has dropped. However, when billing the client's insurance company the therapist states that the bill was $100.

In such a case, the therapist should note on the billing to the insurance company that the patient was charged a rate based on financial hardship and that the total amount of the charges was $80, not $100.

The practitioner might also mislead the insurance carrier by misstating the diagnosis in order to obtain payment. Third-party payers may reimburse more for certain diagnostic conditions than others (e.g., "severe" mental illness more than "nonsevere"), and may not pay at all for other diagnoses (e.g., V-codes in the DSM). By misstating the diagnosis the practitioner might improperly receive payment for a condition that the patient does not have. Both of these behaviors constitute fraud, and a person found guilty of this behavior can face serious penalties. The fact that, strangely enough, claim representatives for insurance and managed-care companies sometimes advise practitioners to change a diagnosis in order to receive payment should never be taken as official approval to bend the rules. If audited in such a situation, the practitioner would likely pay the price, despite the fact that a representative of the insurance company tacitly gave approval.

The rise of managed care has ushered in a whole new set of ethical dilemmas for the mental health profession (Sanders, 1998a). Managed care can be defined as an organized effort "to regulate the utilization of health care" by the "prospective or concurrent review of care provided to individual patients, with the power to deny payment for care thought to be unnecessary or not cost effective" (Appelbaum, 1993). Mental health care, for example, will be covered by insurance only where it can demonstrated that there is *medical necessity* (Thurston, 1998).

According to its proponents the purpose of managed care is to use case review "to control price and service use, while maintaining quality and assuring that care is rendered in the most appropriate setting" (*NASW News*, cited in Dworkin & Hirsch, 1994, p. 2). They feel that managed care is the best way for the private insurance industry to respond to the escalating cost of health care in most specialties, including the mental health field where costs increased significantly in the late 1980s and early 1990s (Throck-morton, 1998).

To its critics, managed care is just another for-profit industry inserted into an American health care system that is already the least cost-efficient in the industrialized world (Reid, 2009). Contrary to the notion that it assures that patients get good care at fair costs; it often impedes people from getting the care they need in a quality, efficient manner. It does this by placing mountains of resistances, limitations and obfuscation in front of prospective patients seeking care and professionals trying to offer it. While steadily decreasing reimbursements to providers, it at the same time forces providers to spend more and more on staff whose primary jobs are often to spend countless hours wading through managed-care requirements as well as correcting managed-care mistakes in reimbursement or authorization. Managed care also keeps the balance of power in the American health care system weighted in favor of private insurers, their CEOs and their stockholders.

Indeed, many questions have been raised about the quality of care that can be provided under managed care and the reality that managed care is largely about cost savings to the insurance provider and not about service to the patient (Landerman et al., 1994). For these reasons and others, some therapists choose not to be on managed-care panels, and find jobs in settings where they do not have to be reliant on these types of third-party payers. In most settings however, serving on at least some panels is a necessity for economic survival.

Serving on a managed-care panel entails signing a contract with the insurance company that makes certain stipulations on how the therapist will practice (see Polonsky [1993] for an annotated list of typical contract provisions). Therapists should read the fine print carefully before signing any contract to provide managed-care services, being careful to ensure that the terms of the contract are in keeping with the therapist's code of ethical practice (Dworkin & Hirsch, 1994). Therapists should not participate on a managed-care panel where the contract stipulations run counter to their ethics code (Higuchi, 1994). The contract will also set forth limits on how much the insurance company will pay for various categories of assessment or treatment, and how much the patient will pay. In some contracts these "allowables" are low, often much lower than the therapist's customary fee. In signing the contract therapists must understand that they are binding themselves to accept the allowable and that they are forbidden from billing the patient extra amounts to recover more of whatever the therapist's usual and customary fee is. Therapists who do participate in managed care need to be aware of the kinds of ethical issues they may face as network providers.

Case 12. Mrs. B suffered a major depression. Her psychiatrist tried several different antidepressant medications, all of which were ineffective and produced negative side-effects. Finally, the doctor found a medication that successfully lifted Mrs. B's depression. Mrs. B was pleased, but eight weeks into taking the new medication, which was a name brand and thus expensive, her insurance company notified her that they would not cover the more expensive medication and that she would have to go back to a less-costly generic. Mrs. B became distraught after being told by an insurance representative that there "was no other option." She began to have trouble sleeping, worrying about her situation and started to become quite depressed again.

Case 13. Mr. J, a young adult male, entered psychotherapy for treatment of a severe depression that was complicated by the abuse he suffered at the hands of his parents growing up. Moreover, his parents, now aging, had become a serious stress to him in adult life. With Mr. J's permission, his psychologist contacted the patient's insurance company and sought authorization for Mr. J to receive psychotherapy. After several delays, the insurance company authorized fifteen sessions of psychotherapy and provided the doctor with a form to complete, should Mr. J require more treatment. At the end of the fifteen sessions, Mr. J had shown some improvement, but his progress was slowed by his problematic history and several very stressful episodes precipitated by the parents. The doctor filed the form seeking authorization for more sessions, and the insurance company authorized fifteen more sessions. However, after only ten more sessions, Mr. J's insurance refused to pay for any more sessions, and when questioned, they revealed that Mr. J's policy contained a clause that restricted outpatient mental health therapy to twenty-five sessions per year.

When the doctor questioned why the insurance company had authorized fifteen more sessions when in fact only ten were available, the managed-care representative reminded him that in the language of the authorization they had sent him there was a disclaimer barring the insurance company from any responsibility should they misstate any terms of an authorization. Mr. J's reaction upon hearing what his insurance company had done was, "Well, this is just like what my parents did when I was a child, they'd promise me one thing and then do something else if that suited them better."

Case 14. After the eighth session of psychotherapy with Mrs. A, the managed-care company required that her therapist fill out a form that requested various pieces of information such as diagnosis, symptoms and their current severity, and an outline of the therapist's treatment plan. In the therapist's opinion the form was consistent with HIPAA regulations regarding the type of information that could be released; so the therapist completed and submitted the form, and the managed care company authorized eight more sessions. At the end of the next eight sessions, the managed-care company requested a telephone interview with the therapist before any additional sessions would be authorized. During the interview the managed-care reviewer began to ask very personal questions about the life issues precipitating the patient's symptoms. The therapist declined to answer these questions citing HIPAA regulations, which provide a greater level of privacy for the client's most personal information (i.e., material in psychotherapy notes). In response, the managed-care reviewer refused to authorize additional sessions.

Case 15. Mrs. X presented to therapy with panic disorder. After ten sessions of treatment she was symptom free and remained symptom free. One year later, Mrs. X left her employment at a large company, and was hired in a small, nonprofit Christian ministry that offered no health insurance benefit. When she sought to purchase an individual health policy, she was rejected for coverage because she had been previously diagnosed as having a panic disorder.

These cases raise some of the salient issues about providing mental health treatment in the age of managed care and modern health insurance. With managed care, new responsibilities arise both for therapists and for managed-care reviewers. Some of these have been reviewed elsewhere

(Applebaum, 1993; Sanders, 1998a). First, clinicians need to appeal the decisions of a managed-care company when they feel the decisions adversely affect their patients. As never before, therapists are being called on to be *advocates* on behalf of their patients, asserting the necessity of care when it is needed (Sanders, 1998a). Therapists may feel rightly frustrated that they are called on not only to carefully assess and treat troubled clients to the best of their ability, but also to jump bureaucratic hurdles and deal with encumbrances to care placed on them and their patients by the insurance companies themselves.

Yet as difficult (and occasionally as fruitless) as it may be, Christian therapists do bear an ethical responsibility to serve in an advocacy role, asserting for the needs of the patient, where appropriate. Indeed, we not only should be advocates for the patient, we must with diplomacy call managed-care representatives to abide by their own stated mission, ensuring that the human beings who have entrusted their companies with their premium dollars will be properly cared for (Sanders, 1998a). Likewise, Christian therapists have a responsibility to self-regulate and assure that the level of care their patients are receiving is appropriate and is accurately stated in claims documentation.

To the extent possible therapists may also need to educate patients at the beginning of therapy about the potential limitations managed care may place on therapy. Arguably, this is the managed-care company's responsibility, but seldom do they provide this information in ways that are easily understandable to patients. Many patients (as well as employers who subsidize the premiums of the health insurance policies) are frequently clueless about the limitations the insurance may place on payment for care. For patients with problems that may not remit quickly, such as chronic mental disturbances or problems of character, there may be hard choices to face about how much treatment is enough. This is an issue which therapist and patient may have to discuss candidly in therapy.

For some patients, therapists have to try to project contingency plans should their patient's managed-care plan deny or severely limit further coverage but the patient still needs therapy and does not have the financial resources to pay for it. The therapist's goal in such circumstances is to do what he or she can to help the patient continue to get help either with him or her or a competent referral therapist, and in the case of the latter circumstance, to avoid any suspicion of patient abandonment.

Therapists also have to struggle with issues of confidentiality in dealing with managed-care companies. How much detail does the insurance company need to have about a client's case in order to authorize treatment? The Health Insurance Portability an Accountability Act (HIPAA) limits the amount of information that therapists must provide to insurers to justify treatment, but as case 14 illustrates this does not necessarily stop insurers from seeking it anyway. With regard to confidential information appropriate for transmission to the insurers, how confident can therapists and patients be that data entrusted to the insurance company will remain confidential? What if a managed-care reviewer is closely allied to the patient's workplace and the information revealed in therapy could have negative consequences for the client if it were known in the work setting? Higuchi (1994) suggested that therapists consider developing written information to be included in their informed-consent documents outlining the risks and benefits of providing confidential information to managed-care companies. Her article includes a sample document, and a portion of this document can also be found in Sanders (1998a).

As case 15 points out, the sad fact is that sometimes when people receive mental health treatment, it limits them from obtaining insurance later, even when their treatment was successful. The Affordable Care Act, passed by Congress and signed by the president, is designed to increase the pool of Americans who have insurance and prevent people with preexisting conditions from being refused insurance beginning in 2014, but it remains to be seen what type of coverage private insurers will offer and at what price.

Of course, there are some mental health professionals who work not as therapists but as case reviewers for managed-care companies. From an ethical standpoint these individuals bear a responsibility to review cases with care and to contemplate carefully the often contradictory values of saving money for the insurance company and allowing appropriate care for policyholders. Reviewers must also ensure that they have the appropriate training necessary when judging a particular therapist's treatment plan. For example, is it appropriate for a nurse practitioner reviewer with little or no training in cognitive behavior therapy to judge a treatment plan consisting of cognitive therapy for depression? Or consider the psychologist who contacts a managed-care reviewer to pre-certify psychological testing for the client. Suppose that the reviewer refuses to certify the testing but has no training in testing. Clearly the reviewer is working outside his or her area of competence.

Before concluding this section it is important to highlight the fact that not all ethical issues surrounding managed care and third-party payers exist at the level of practice. There are numerous other issues that exist at the level of mental health care policy (Sanders, 1998b; Tjeltveit, 1999). A Christian social justice perspective would call Christian therapists to learn more about the problems that exist in the larger health care system, and then to utilize one's talents and circles of influence to try and make the system more just and humane. For example, some therapists might choose to meet with benefit coordinators at major employers in their area, helping them understand how to choose the best benefit packages for their employees while holding company costs down as much as is possible. Other therapists might speak to community leaders or use different types of media to communicate and educate the public at large about the problems. Some might get involved in the political process or in a professional organization that communicates concerns to politicians and other policy makers.

INTERACTIONS INSIDE AND OUTSIDE THE WORKPLACE

Mental health professionals have the obligation to treat colleagues, employees, employers and students with respect. The business of mental health is seriously impeded by professionals who do not try to conduct themselves well in these relationships (APA, 2002, sects. 2.05, 3.01-3.04, 3.08-3.09).

Relationships with colleagues, staff and students. Every workplace needs clear policies and procedures governing the conduct of the workplace: terms of employment, the manner for handling conflicts and difficulties, and the manner for handling hiring and promotions. Professionals working together in a practice need to strive to have respect for one another. Professionals in charge of the office need to provide basic ethics training for clerical and administrative staff so that everyone understands how to deal with such basic things as confidentiality, clarity regarding fees and who on staff to refer to when in doubt. Written policy and procedure manuals that include basic information about handling ethical issues do much to clarify the rules of the workplace, and it can be important to have employees sign documentation indicating their understanding of and willingness to comply with the rules.

Case 16. An associate minister called the therapist's office to inquire about one of his parishioners, a twenty-year-old woman. He assured the office manager that his motivations were pure and that he was calling because the church was thinking about paying for the woman's counseling out of the benevolence fund. He asked the office manager when the young woman started counseling, who she was seeing, how long she had been coming to therapy and what her diagnosis was.

It is the therapist's responsibility to train his or her staff to be on guard for such situations and not to provide confidential information or even to acknowledge that the individual is a patient. Suppose that the patient in the preceding example had just revealed in therapy that the associate minister in question had recently tried to be inappropriate with her sexually and she was afraid of him?

In considering matters of confidentiality in the workplace, therapists must also give consideration to dealing with contract consultants who may periodically have access to confidential information such as patient names and addresses or billing information. For example, most therapists have a computer consultant who may from time to time be retained to repair the office computers, set up new billing programs and so forth. HIPAA requires that therapists have such individuals read and sign documentation agreeing to maintain and protect the confidentiality of all information they become privy to in the process of their duties at the therapist's office. Therapists must also have a policy in place describing how they maintain the security of private information in their offices, both paper files and computer files.

Interprofessional relationships. Therapists should seek as much as possible to work collegially with fellow professionals outside the immediate workplace. This not only benefits the therapist but may indirectly benefit clients as well. Mental health professionals should avoid "guild wars" and to the extent possible recognize the contribution of each of the therapeutic professions. Therapists need to be able to work closely with other allied professionals in mental health, medicine or ministry who may be able to add their unique talents to help the patient. In this age of intense competition over health care dollars there is an increasing tendency to engage in unethical turf wars with other practitioners. Therapists should avoid such practices as "patient stealing" and should clarify the circumstances carefully with clients who see them during or after they have seen another mental health professional (APA, 2002, Sect. 4.04).

Case 17. Dr. C was seeing a female patient in therapy. It soon became clear that the patient's husband required treatment also, but for various reasons Dr. C felt that the patient's husband might have a better outcome if he referred him to another therapist. He sent the patient's husband to another clinic, explaining his concerns to the therapist there. After one visit the therapist there told the patient's husband that he should see both husband and wife individually and that for the wife to see Dr. C was unethical. The new therapist did not communicate at all with Dr. C about this recommendation, and it was several weeks before Dr. C learned that the other therapist had "stolen" his patient.

The keys to good interprofessional relationships are integrity and communication. Professionals, like other groups, build relationships and trust, which can only be solidified when the people involved talk to one another.

Relationships with employers and boards. Seemingly forgotten in the modern workplace is the virtue of loyalty, whether loyalty of employee to employer or vice versa. Without loyalty, workplace relationships take on a transient quality. But loyalty, particularly the loyalty of employee to employer, does not grow in a vacuum. Loyalty springs up where there is legitimate authority.

Where there is legitimate authority employees have the responsibility to work toward the advancement of the organization and to keep its standards. When there is conflict between the organization and the needs of clients or the requirements of one's ethical standards, the employee works to try to resolve these conflicts.

Nonprofit counseling agencies have active boards to which the mental health professionals in the agencies answer. Interaction with boards raises some unique ethical questions. First is the issue of honesty with the board. Boards frequently consist of bright, caring individuals who nevertheless know a limited amount about the daily work of a counseling center. Counselors have a responsibility to educate board members honestly about their work, giving the board the knowledge it needs to intelligently direct the center. This doesn't mean that board members become amateur mental health professionals; it means they have enough information to use the special talents they each bring to the board effectively in the development of the agency's work.

Second, the integrity of relationships between mental health professionals and the board must be sufficiently strong to withstand the fact that it is inappropriate for boards to know everything about what transpires in the agency each day. Sometimes board members may unknowingly ask therapists to breach confidentiality. It is, of course, inappropriate to breach confidentiality, even with board members, but if the relationship between agency leadership and the board is strong, it is likely to withstand such conflicts.

Mental health administrators must also be careful about potential dual relationships with board members. These may include but are not limited to accepting board members as clients and entering into outside financial liaisons with board members.

Case 18. Mr. F, an accountant, was asked to join the board of a counseling center and become its treasurer. Soon, after joining the board Mr. F approached the director, telling him that he was glad he was on the board because it reminded him of something he had known for years: he really needed to get some marriage counseling. Mr. F asked the director to provide marriage counseling for him in exchange for Mr. F's serving on the board and doing the agency's bookkeeping.

Finally, since boards and their committees often serve in a fundraising capacity for agencies, mental health administrators should promote appropriate fundraising. To do this, boards must be appropriately educated about what the agency does as well as what funds are used for. Boards must be honestly apprised of the financial status of the organization through regular financial reports, which should be verified through regular audits or official financial review.

CONCLUSION

Ethical problems in conducting the business of counseling frequently arise because therapists and administrators often fail to consider consciously the potential problems that might arise. Many of the worst problems stem from a failure to deal well with the inherent tension that exists between mental health as a service to people in pain and mental health as a vocation providing professionals a means for making a living. To avoid problems and build good will, therapists need to develop honest relationships with others about the business of running the counseling center. They must set clear standards that allow them to serve clients' best interests first and still maintain and run their businesses and agencies efficiently and effectively.

REFERENCES

American Psychological Association. (2002). Ethical principles of psychologists and code of conduct. *American Psychologist, 57,* 1060-73. Also available (with 2010 amendments) from www.apa.org/ethics/code/index.aspx.

Appelbaum, P. S. (1993). Legal liability and managed care. *American Psychologist 48,* 251-57.

Christian Association for Psychological Studies. (2005). *Ethics statement of the Christian Association for Psychological Studies.* Batavia, IL: Christian Association for Psychological Studies. Retrieved from http://caps.net/about-us/statement-of-ethical-guidelines.

Dworkin, M., & Hirsch, G. (1994). Responding to managed care: A roadmap for the therapist. *Psychotherapy in Private Practice. 13,* 1-21.

Eisenberg, L. (1986). Health care: For patients or for profits. *American Journal of Psychiatry, 143,* 1015-19.

Higuchi, S. A. (1994). Recent managed-care legislative and legal issues. In R. L. Lowman & R. J. Resnick (Eds.), *The mental health professional's guide to managed care* (pp. 83-117). Washington, DC: American Psychological Association.

Hinkle, J. E., Jr. (1981). Central issues related to the use of fee scales. In J. C. Carr, J. E. Hinkle & D. M. Moss III (Eds.), *The organization and administration of pastoral counseling centers.* (pp. 123-30). Nashville: Abingdon.

Keith-Spiegel, P., & Koocher, G. P. (1985). *Ethics in psychology.* New York: Random House.

Knapp, S., & VandeCreek, L. E. (1993). Legal and ethical issues in billing patients and collecting fees. *Psychotherapy, 30,* 25-31.

Koocher, G. P. (1977). Advertising for psychologists: Pride and prejudice or sense and sensibility? *Professional Psychology, 8,* 149-60.

Koocher, G. P. (1994). APA and FTC: New adventures in consumer protection. *American Psychologist, 49,* 322-28.

Landerman, L. R., Burns, B. J., Swartz, M. S., Wagner, H. R., & George, L. K. (1994). The relationship between insurance coverage and psychiatric disorder in predicting use of mental health services. *American Journal of Psychiatry, 151,* 1785-90.

Masson, J. M. (1994). *Against therapy.* Monroe, ME: Common Courage.

Polonsky, I. (1993, May-June). How to write treatment reports for managed care. *The California Therapist,* 29-32.

Reid, T. R. (2009). *The healing of America: A global quest for better, cheaper, and fairer health care.* New York: Penguin.

Sanders, R. K. (1998a). Integrity in the age of managed care. *Journal of Psychology & Christianity, 17,* 101-9.

Sanders, R. K. (1998b). Integrity: The micro and the macro issues. *Journal of Psychology & Christianity, 17,* 175-76.

Throckmorton, W. (1998). Managed care: "It's like déjà-vu, all over again." *Journal of Psychology & Christianity, 17,* 131-41.

Thurston, R. (1998). An apologetic for managed care. *Journal of Psychology & Christianity, 17,* 142-47.

Tjeltveit, A. C. (1999). *Ethics and values in psychotherapy.* New York: Routledge.

14

Pastors Who Counsel

Bill Blackburn

Pastor, can I talk with you sometime this week? I need some help." "I am so torn up about what I need to do with my mother. Can you see me this week?" "Bill, I lost my job, and I need to talk." "Pastor, my wife told me that she wants a divorce and that she hasn't loved me for a long time. I don't know what to do. Can we get together?" "I think the Lord may be calling me into the ministry, but I'm not sure. I just need to talk with you." "I've never felt anything like this before. I don't feel like doing anything or seeing anyone. Somebody told me I might be depressed. Can you help me?"

Before I retired as a pastor I received numerous requests such as these, many of which resulted in pastoral counseling sessions. Each story is different, and new dimensions of the original request are found once the story unfolds. But what is similar in each instance? Here are people who are hurting and reaching out for help, and they are reaching out to a pastor of a church, implying a recognition that there are spiritual dimensions to their dilemmas.

This chapter will address the major ethical issues involved in pastoral counseling. These issues center around how a pastor sees his or her role as pastor and the particular dimensions of that role when he or she is doing pastoral counseling. The kinds of questions this article will address include: How is pastoral counseling understood in light of the total work of the pastor? Considering the biblical image of the pastor as shepherd, how does that affect the understanding and practice of pastoral counseling? What about the common tendency in pastoral counseling that "uses" God as a means to the end of personal peace? What are some of the limits of what a pastor can or should do in the area of pastoral counseling? What are the ethical dimensions of referral? What are some basic guidelines for pastors who counsel? Searching for answers to these and other questions will, I hope, aid pastors and others who counsel to explore some of the ethical dimensions of counseling.

PASTORAL COUNSELING IN CONTEXT

Many pastors divide their work as pastor into three main areas: (1) preaching/ teaching, (2) pastoral care, and (3) leadership/administration. Obviously, the three areas overlap and are intertwined.

I include pastoral counseling in the area of pastoral care. Whereas pastoral care would include such things as hospital visitation; telephone calls expressing concern or reassurance; and informal, brief conversations about people's needs; pastoral counseling, as used in this chapter, refers to those times when an appointment is made and a parishioner comes asking for help, guidance or perspective on a problem she or he is facing.

It is important for a pastor to set guidelines and limits as to the amount of time he or she will spend on various duties. In my own case, I explained to my church when I became their pastor that I would do only three to four hours per week of pastoral counseling, and that I would see persons for no more than three sessions.

Why did I set these guidelines and hold to them? I do not believe that a pastor can do more than three to four hours a week of counseling and get the rest of the pastor's job done. My major thrust as pastor of a church was as preacher/teacher. My mornings were spent in my study at home and given to prayer, study, and preparation of sermons and Bible studies. My major focus as a pastor was not on counseling, though I did much pastoral care work. But I do not believe a pastor can lead and build a church with an emphasis on pastoral counseling. And as a fellow pastor noted, "When the body of Christ functions as it should, a lot of problems will be resolved at a 'grass roots' level, the first level where counseling ought to take place" (Getz, 1980, p. 132).

Second, I set these guidelines to protect myself and my parishioners. Ministers can get into trouble in sexual relationships with persons they

were first counseling. It is striking how dangerously intimate and even seductive a counseling session can become when a woman is "pouring out her
heart" to a male minister, especially if she is in a bad marriage or is unmarried. He can be providing with his listening and acceptance something
no other male is giving her, and the issues of transference and counter-
transference loom large (Seat, Trent & Kim, 1993).

Additionally, if there is not a general guideline about the number of sessions, it can be easy to start selecting who will have more sessions and who
will have fewer. Often those decisions are made even unconsciously by such
needs as affirmation, dependence or sexual desire.

Third, research has concluded that many parishioners who do in-depth,
long-term counseling with their minister will end up leaving the church.
The parishioners can end up feeling exposed and that the accepted veneer of
social contact has been removed. They can also believe that the pastor is
singling them out from the pulpit in his sermon examples when in fact the
pastor is speaking more generally.

Finally, by following these guidelines, the pastor can limit the counseling
to brief, supportive counseling and to referral counseling. I believe that
these are the forms of counseling most appropriate for pastors (Stone, 1994).
Although I have the educational requirements and experience necessary to
do counseling, I never felt that long-term counseling was what I should
have been doing as pastor of a local congregation.

THE PASTOR AS SHEPHERD

The most basic image of the pastor in the New Testament is shepherd. That
is, of course, what the word literally means. And what is the role of the
shepherd? Looking at the key passages of Ezekiel 34 and John 10, as well as
Matthew 18:10-14 and Luke 15:3-6, we see that the shepherd (1) provides for
the sheep, (2) protects the sheep, and (3) guides the sheep.

What does this tell us about the pastor as counselor? Counseling is an
extension or different dimension of the pastor's total work. In the context of
counseling, the pastor *provides* scriptural and spiritual insight as well as
perspective on what is happening in the counselee's life, given the pastor's
training, experience and the exercise of the gifts of wisdom, discernment
and teaching.

The pastor provides *protection* in several ways. In the trusting and confidential counseling relationship, the individual or couple or family can pour out what is being felt or report what has happened, knowing that what is heard is listened to with openness, concern, confidentiality and prayer. Protection is provided when a couple or family has come and the pastor serves as interpreter/mediator. The pastor acts in this role as one who helps the counselees deal with conflict but also keeps the conflict in bounds.

The pastor provides protection another way. The pastor can warn the counselee(s) about the destructive ways other persons have dealt with the same kinds of problems. And the pastor can caution the counselee from seeking help in either destructive or inappropriate ways such as abusing alcohol or drugs, "looking for love in all the wrong places," or wrongful sexual encounters. It is important to discuss the danger of major decisions made during a crisis, which can sometimes include suicide.

A pastor also provides *guidance*, which can include various ways of listening, responding and offering observations and possible suggestions. For example, I was initially trained in the somewhat stereotypical Rogerian nondirective approach of counseling. Although I benefitted greatly from that training, which taught me to listen carefully and to let counselees know by some form of reflection that they were being heard, I moved to a more directive stance in counseling, which I believe is thoroughly biblical.

In the more directive approach to guidance, a pastor listens carefully and explores through questions and clarification what the client's issues are, how they are viewed by him or her, how they have been responded to, and what the person sees as the options. Then the counselor shares what he or she has heard from the counselee, some perspective on what is happening, and initial guidelines or suggestions about how to deal with the issues. Here the pastor can deal with biblical principles that seem pertinent and can point to particular Scripture passages. Here the pastor may also discuss with the counselee the importance of taking care of him- or herself in regard to diet, exercise, sleep, hobbies, social contact and the spiritual disciplines.

INTEGRITY OF THE PASTOR

In any discussion of ethics, integrity is central. Integrity implies soundness, adherence to principle and completeness in the sense of being undivided.

What shape does integrity take for pastors who counsel?

First, integrity is seen as faithfulness to the Lord. As a pastor who counsels, it must be understood that whatever problems are presented in a counseling session, the ultimate issue is this person's relationship to the Lord. Oates, a pioneer in the fields of pastoral counseling and psychology of religion, deeply desires to help pastoral counselors see "the difference it can make if you and I make the presence of the Eternal God the central dynamic in our dialogue with counselees." He adds, "In essence, I want to move *from dialogue to trialogue* in pastoral counseling" (1986, p. 23).

This does not mean that every counseling session becomes a mini-sermon. But when pastoral counseling is understood in this way, it can dramatically change the counseling event. How the counselee presents him- or herself, what issues the counselee raises, what the counselee does not want to talk about, what history he or she reports—all become facets of the deepest issue of life, the counselee's relationship to the Lord.

In a classic work in the field of pastoral care, *The Minister and the Care of Souls*, Williams writes, "To bring salvation to the human spirit is the goal of all Christian ministry and pastoral care" (1961, p. 23). He goes on to observe, "The key to pastoral care lies in the Christological center of our faith, for we understand Christ as bringing the disclosure of our full humanity in its destiny under God" (p. 13).

God is not just a utility player called in as one among others to help the counselee. In a prophetic message to pastors and other Christian leaders at a conference titled "The Church in the 21st Century," Crabb detailed how easy it is to so focus on the needs of people that God is then used to meet a need. God becomes part of the recipe given to people to help them feel better. Crabb suggests that a central question to ask as a counselee presents symptoms is "What are the obstacles in the soul of this person that are blocking them from God?" (Crabb, 1993).

Consider a distinction made by Oates between the teachings of Jesus and psychoanalysis concerning the issue of leaving one's father and mother. Oates observes that psychoanalysis

> dwells on the fixation and looks to the individual to use the insight to manage his or her life better by a courageous act of will. The New Testament, to the contrary, says that "in the beginning it was not so," i.e., the Creator intended

that a person leave father and mother. He or she is empowered to do so by reason of the larger love of God and neighbor. (1986, p. 47)

This is another illustration of the importance of faithfulness to God in pastoral counseling. When God is at the center of the counseling session, he is never to be among those "things" trotted out to help someone.

A second facet is integrity of role. A continuity exists between who you are as pastor of the church and who you are in the counseling session. Who you are, your perspective and how you present yourself has unity, completeness. In the pastoral counseling session you are still pastor; you are not now junior psychologist or psychiatrist. You are not now a counselor applying the latest technique learned in the last workshop you attended. You are a pastor seeking to be faithful to the Lord and to your calling as you listen and address a person who is seeking help.

Third, there is integrity in regard to the Scripture. The person seeking out the pastor may not be directly asking, as did King Zedekiah, "Is there any word from the LORD?" (Jer 37:17 NIV), but that question is certainly at the background of the whole session. Therefore, what is shared and advised must have integrity with Scripture and not be in violation of scriptural principles.

Fourth, there is an integrity with the congregation. In the pastoral counseling setting the pastor represents the congregation. Pastoral counseling occurs within the body of Christ. The pastor acts as agent for the congregation in the sense that he or she symbolizes the care of the congregation, speaks as the leader of the congregation and represents the congregation's further resources to help deal with what is raised in counseling. What happens in the counseling session should not be in conflict with the pastor's role as representative of the congregation.

Fifth, integrity must be kept in regard to what has been promised. The pastor must take opportunities directly and indirectly to interpret and reinterpret his or her role in the counseling setting. Care must be taken not to promise too much or to hold out unrealistic hope. My mentor and professor of pastoral counseling, Wayne Oates, used to tell students of pastoral counseling, "It's the promises I make that keep me awake. It's the promises I keep that let me sleep."

Sixth, integrity can concern the limits of the pastor's training, experience or responsibility. Many laypeople do not understand what pastors have been trained to do and what their training did not include. I have found, however, that when this is discussed, most persons appreciate the pastor being honest in confessing a lack of training, background or time to deal with the particular issue being faced. In regard to such things as substance abuse, unrelenting depression, sexual abuse, bulimia or the serious threat of suicide, for instance, I am careful to explain why I cannot provide all of the help that is needed and why another professional needs to be called on.

Sullender and Malony state in an article in *The Journal of Pastoral Care*, "Clergy must be mature enough and professional enough to know their limits when it comes to counseling troubled persons. These limits may involve training, available time, conflict of interest, or just available energy" (1990, p. 206).

All pastors and other Christian ministers would do well to meditate on this verse describing King David and his leadership of the people of Israel:

> David shepherded them with integrity of heart;
>   with skillful hands he led them. (Ps 78:72 NIV)

THE ETHICS OF REFERRAL

It is important for pastors who counsel to be willing to refer their counselees to other professionals and to be knowledgeable about when and to whom a counselee should be referred. Following are some guidelines that can be used in this regard.

First, a minister has a responsibility to know the variety of professionals to whom she or he might refer. If you are going to refer a parishioner to another professional, you will want to know his or her (1) reputation, (2) training, (3) experience, (4) professional supervision, (5) network of other professionals/hospitals he or she may call on, and (6) faith commitment or appreciation of such a commitment in the client. The first three points are self-explanatory, but the last three may require some explanation.

It is very important that the professional, whether a pastoral counselor, clinical social worker, psychologist or psychiatrist is receiving some form of supervision or consultation on his or her work. This indicates the person's professional ethics and desire to keep perspective in the midst of helping people in need. What is the extent of the professional's network of consultation and referral? And if hospitalization is a possibility, what arrangements can he or she make for the client?

Should a pastor refer parishioners only to Christian counselors? No. One should do so whenever one can, and the pastor is fortunate when there are many choices for referral. However, I will refer to a non-Christian if I know she or he has the best skills and background in dealing with this particular need and that the counselor would neither demean religious faith nor suggest that the person do something in violation of his or her faith commitment.

Second, a pastor has the responsibility to appropriately present the referral to the counselee. The pastor must interpret carefully why he or she is making this referral and why it is being made to the particular professional. The pastor should explain his or her own limitations of time or training, and the qualifications of the other professional, while being careful not to promise what the other professional will do. It is a good idea to reassure the counselee when needed that he or she isn't crazy (and it may be appropriate to use that word sometimes) or about to lose his or her mind. This is something many counselees are afraid of, and that fear is sometimes inadvertently reinforced with a referral to a mental health professional.

Next, the pastor should explain how to get in touch with the person referred to and something of what the counselee can expect from the sessions. If the cost is raised, provide what information is available and let the person know if the church has a fund to help with these sorts of costs (if it does). In some situations the pastor can make the call to the professional and help set up the first appointment.

Fourth, the pastor should reassure the counselee about their relationship together. The person needs to know that in making the referral, the pastor is not rejecting him or her. Explain that you will be in touch with the person and that along the way you can get back together to talk things over and to pray. One should be careful, of course, not to slip into serving as another therapist, but as pastor.

Fifth, in addition to reassuring the counselee about their relationship, the pastor has the responsibility to maintain that relationship. You can do this by having the person on your prayer list so that you are reminded regularly to pray for him or her and to maintain contact through phone calls, notes and visits.

Finally, it is appropriate for the pastor to keep proper contact with the professional to whom the counselee has been referred. Some professionals want information prior to the first visit and others do not. As the pastor, you probably do not need to get a report on the sessions, but with appropriate consent from the counselee, you may wish to know in a general way how things are going and what you can do to be of further help. And because of the continuing relationship through the church, you may sometimes consult with the professional on any church relationship issues that may arise relative to the person(s) referred.

BOUNDARY ISSUES

How should pastors decide how much they counsel, whom to see, appropriate boundaries in counseling and how available to be to persons in need? These boundary issues are crucial because if they are not decided in some reasonable manner, the pastor can risk his or her effectiveness, mental health, family life and leadership of the congregation.

Some of these issues have been dealt with directly and indirectly in the preceding pages, but they are of such importance that they should be made more specific.

In the guidelines outlined earlier, I noted that I only did three to four hours a week of counseling. Obviously, that varied from week by week, but that is still almost half a day per week of pastoral counseling, and depending on the size of the church even that can be too much time for this facet of pastoral ministry. In order to hold to a limited amount of counseling it is important that the pastor not communicate an unlimited availability to the congregation. One of my professors of preaching, George A. Buttrick, used to tell us, "Many pastors are a quivering mass of availability." I cannot be the husband, father and pastor I need to be and also be constantly available.

Most pastors could end up counseling twelve hours a day if it were allowed. But a failure to draw boundaries and deal with the limits of what one can do often implies other issues.

Is there such a need to please that the pastor cannot say "no" or "later"? Is there a feeling of impotence in other areas of ministry that leads the minister to do an inordinate amount of counseling and thereby feel the power and helpfulness and adulation that often comes from counseling? Is there a

problem in the pastor's marriage or family that encourages getting emotional needs met inappropriately in counseling? Does the pastor have a
messiah complex seen in rescuing persons in trouble? Is there withdrawal
from other duties and relationships and into counseling? In looking at who
is seen for counseling and who is not, is there a clue to the underlying issues
related to too much counseling?

On this last question of who is seen, a troubling issue for many pastors
is whether or not to do counseling with persons who are not members of
the congregation. I generally do not recommend that pastors see persons
for counseling who are from outside the congregation. The pastor might
see someone who is attending and not a member, and could on occasion
see someone known in the community who is in crisis and has requested
to see the pastor. In this latter instance, it should almost always be for one
session, in which time a referral is made if that is needed. One of the
issues for pastors today is that there is a greater possibility of legal liability
when counseling persons who are not members of your congregation
(ABA, 1989).

Concerning boundaries, in looking at the Gospels, did Jesus see every
troubled soul in each village he visited? Did he stay in one place until every
sick person was healed? Was Bartimaeus the only blind person in Jericho?
Didn't Jesus in fact retreat either with the disciples or by himself when he
needed to? And when he retreated, were there not still persons who could
have been helped who were left behind? And didn't Jesus in his ministry
move more toward preaching and training of the disciples and less toward
healing and other miracles?

From the time of Satan's testing in the wilderness at the beginning of
Jesus' public ministry, to how Jesus presented himself to the crowds and the
authorities in his last days in Jerusalem, to his resurrection appearances and
final discourses prior to the ascension, Jesus was setting boundaries and
defining limits according to who he was and what his mission was. Look
again at the repeated "I am" statements of Jesus and you will see boundaries,
limits and possibilities.

As a contemporary pastor, how does one deal with these boundary
issues? The wise pastor will find it necessary to continue interpreting to the
congregation what his or her role is as pastor, how time should be spent,

and what the guidelines should be for counseling. It is important to set aside time for the various parts of pastoring such as preparation for preaching, teaching and administration as well as for pastoral care. The pastor's secretary can help by keeping the schedule and setting appointments within the time that is allotted to certain things. Time is protected for sermon preparation, worship planning, administrative matters, meetings with staff and other key leaders, and pastoral visitation. The wise pastor will also protect time for family and for personal renewal and rest.

GENERAL GUIDELINES FOR PASTORAL COUNSELING

Following are some general guidelines to keep in mind for pastors who counsel. Some of these have been discussed earlier but bear repeating here.

1. Maintain confidentiality. The exception to maintaining confidence would be if there are ethical or legal reasons dictating the breaking of a confidence. It is imperative that pastors familiarize themselves with the laws in their state pertaining to privileged communications with the clergy and to the exceptions to confidentiality. Usually these exceptions will include such things as suspicion of child abuse. These kinds of situations point to the necessity of not making a blanket promise that nothing will be shared out of the counseling session.

2. Avoid manipulating the counselee/parishioner. It almost goes without saying that we must avoid manipulating the counselee, but because there is such a risk due to the vulnerability of many persons in crisis who seek pastors out, it needs to be stated.

3. Avoid making decisions for the person seeking help. Because the pastor is an authority figure who is knowledgeable in the Bible and is assumed to have a strong prayer life, many persons come to him or her expecting a divinely revealed answer to the problem at hand. As indicated earlier, I believe the pastor is often to be directive in his or her approach in counseling but a disservice can be done to the counselee by simply making the decision for him or her.

4. Do not inappropriately carry messages. There are times in the ministry of reconciliation when interpreting the behavior or words of one person to another can be appropriate and healing. However, because the pastor has contact with the entire family or group that the person may be in conflict with or alienated from, sometimes there is a desire or expectation that the pastor will be like a Western Union messenger boy. This is inappropriate.

5. Do not be a voyeur. Particularly in the area of sexuality the pastor must be careful not to seek directly or indirectly information that is not germane to the issue at hand. Seeking information for sexual titillation is inappropriate, unfair and counterproductive.

6. Never become romantically or sexually involved with a counselee. It is assumed, of course, that the pastor must not be romantically or sexually involved with a counselee, but this needs to be stated because it is such an important and pervasive issue. Recent research by Chaves and Garland (2009) indicated that in a large survey, 2.2% of women who attended religious services at least monthly reported that they had been the object of a sexual advance by a married clergyperson or religious leader in their own congregational group since they had turned eighteen. When they were polled about advances by both married and unmarried clergypersons, the percentage increased to 3.1%. The women polled were from a wide variety of religious backgrounds. The researchers estimate that these percentages suggest that somewhere between 1 in 30 and 1 in 50 churchgoing women have been the object of sexual advances by a clergyperson. Clergy sexual misconduct is a serious problem, and clergy affairs can set off a devastating cascade of effects not only on the victim but also on the perpetrating clergyperson's family and the church (Hopkins & Laaser, 1995). In a study done of Southern Baptist ministers through the Baptist Sunday School Board, it was found that among ministers who became involved in adulterous affairs, 71% of those affairs started through counseling sessions (Booth, 1994). A one-on-one counseling relationship with a person of the opposite sex can be powerfully seductive, and a pastor should never assume that he or she is immune from the kinds of sexual feelings that all human beings have at times. This is part of the reason that I have maintained a guideline of seeing a person for only three sessions. It is also why, when seeing a female counselee, I follow the first guideline of making sure someone else is in the office area where I am counseling.

Concerning this last guideline, Wayne Oates used to tell his students that he knew he was beginning to cross over a dangerous line when he woke up in the morning and began thinking about a female counselee he would see that day. If, in anticipation of seeing her, he was careful to select which tie he wore, he knew danger was lurking.

CONCLUSION

The opportunity, responsibility and calling to be a shepherd is awesome and ought to be so intimidating that we go to our knees before the Lord knowing that we cannot do what needs to be done and be who we need to be without God's help. I firmly believe that in the years ahead the task of the pastor will grow more difficult because of the needs of the people, the expectations that grow into demands and the confusion and deterioration of our society. Only by prayer, wisdom and much discipline will pastors be able to carry out their God-given assignment and maintain their spiritual, mental, physical, family and social health.

My deep conviction, borne of experience as a pastor, is that time management that grows out of faith and a clear understanding of the mission of the church and the work of the pastor is crucial to maintaining this health. In that regard I highly commend two books that have proved invaluable to me in this area. The first is *First Things First* by Stephen R. Covey, A. Roger Merrill and Rebecca R. Merrill (New York: Simon & Schuster, 1994). The second is *The Management of Ministry* by James D. Anderson and Ezra Earl Jones (San Francisco: Harper & Row, 1978).

Finally, my prayer for those reading this article, as it has been throughout its research and writing, is that God will use it to help you be a shepherd with integrity of heart and skillful hands (Ps 78:72 NIV).

REFERENCES

American Bar Association. (1990). Tort and religion. Cited in R. S. Sullender & H. N. Malony. Should clergy counsel suicidal persons? *Journal of Pastoral Care, 44,* 206.

Booth, G. (1994, spring). *The Baylor Messenger,* p. 4.

Chaves, M., & Garland, D. (2009). The prevalence of clergy sexual advances toward adults in their congregations. *Journal for the Scientific Study of Religion, 48,* 817-24.

Crabb, L. (1993, June). Vision v. community. Presentation made at the Church in the 21st Century Conference, Orlando, FL (sponsored by Leadership Network).

Getz, G. (1980). Leadership forum: The demands, dilemmas, and dangers of pastoral counseling. *Leadership, 1,* 132.

Hopkins, N. M., & Laaser, M. (Eds.). (1995). *Restoring the soul of a church: Healing congregations wounded by clergy sexual misconduct.* Collegeville, MN: Alban Institute.

Oates, W. E. (1986). *The presence of God in pastoral counseling.* Dallas, TX: Word.

Seats, J. T., Trent, J. T., & Kim, J. K. (1993). The prevalence and contributing factors of sexual misconduct among Southern Baptist pastors in six southern states. *Journal of Pastoral Care, 47,* 363-70.

Stone, H. W. (1994). Brief pastoral counseling. *Journal of Pastoral Care, 48,* 33-43.

Sullender, R. S., & Malony, H. N. (1990). Should clergy counsel suicidal persons? *Journal of Pastoral Care, 44,* 206.

Williams, D. D. (1961). *The minister and the care of souls.* New York: Harper.

15

Lay Counselor Training

Siang-Yang Tan

The field of lay counseling, or the provision of people-helping services by nonprofessionals or paraprofessionals with little or no training in mental health counseling, has mushroomed in recent years, both in secular and in Christian contexts (e.g., see Tan, 1990, 1991a, 1991b, 1994b, 1997, 2002, 2011). Increasingly, churches are training laypeople to minister as lay counselors or lay caregivers to facilitate support and recovery groups, do grief counseling, and provide a number of other helping services to hurting people in need. Often Christian mental health professionals are called on to develop and oversee or supervise lay counselor training programs and lay counseling services. Ethical issues in lay counselor training include the appropriate selection of lay counselors, the adequacy of the training provided for them, the types of counseling they should be trained for and the responsibility of professionals or pastoral staff to properly supervise such lay counselors. Many of these issues have been covered elsewhere (see Tan, 1991a, pp. 212-26) but will be briefly summarized and updated here (see also Tan, 2002, 2011).

Lay counseling is a biblically based ministry that has received much support from the research literature for its effectiveness (see Tan, 1991a, 1997, 2002, 2011). Lay counselors in general have often been found to be as effective therapeutically as professional therapists (Atkins & Christensen, 2001; Berman & Norton, 1985; Bickman, 1999; Christensen & Jacobson, 1994; Durlak, 1979, 1981; Hattie, Sharpley & Rogers, 1984; Nietzel & Fisher, 1981; see also Ali, Rahbar, Naeem & Gul, 2003; Neuner et al; 2008). More controlled outcome research is needed to evaluate the specific effectiveness of lay *Christian* counselors, especially in the local church context (see Toh et al., 1994; Toh & Tan, 1997; see also Garzon & Tilley, 2009; Garzon, Worthington, Tan & Worthington, 2009).

ETHICAL AND LEGAL ISSUES

A number of important and helpful books have been published on legal issues and Christian counseling (Levicoff, 1991; Ohlschlager & Mosgofian, 1992). The literature on ethical issues and Christian counseling has also grown significantly in recent years (Collins, 1991; Ohlschlager & Clinton, 2002; Tan, 1994a, 2003; see also Browning, 2006; Tjeltveit, 1999). However the literature on ethical and legal issues related specifically to lay counselor training and ministry is more limited, and I will briefly review it here (see Tan, 1991a, 1997, 2002, 2011).

Becker (1987) has written a helpful article covering the main legal and ethical considerations pertinent to the paraprofessional or lay counselor in the church context. He emphasizes the need to develop trust in the counseling relationship in three major areas: the *confidentiality* of the relationship, the *competence* of the counselor, and the client's freedom of *choice*.

Confidentiality. In the area of confidentiality Becker notes that lay counselors should follow the legal and ethical standards of professional counselors, which usually require professional counselors to report incidents of child or elder abuse, or situations involving potential danger to self or to others. There are therefore limits to confidentiality that lay counselors should explain to their clients or counselees at the beginning of counseling as they obtain informed consent from them, preferably in writing (or at least verbally, in more informal contexts of lay helping). Even if lay counselors are not mandated by law in some states to report such situations, I agree with Becker (1987) that it is wiser that they do. They definitely should abide by such reporting laws if they are being supervised by a licensed mental health professional. Apart from such limits to confidentiality, lay counselors need to ethically preserve confidentiality with the greatest of care.

A related issue in this regard has to do with whether lay counselors should also be directly involved in church discipline of clients who have broken the moral codes subscribed to by church members, and therefore whether confidentiality can be broken for the sake of church discipline. Becker (1987) has specifically recommended that lay counselors *not* act as agents of church discipline, although they can encourage clients to confess their transgressions to appropriate church leaders. They should *not* break confidentiality for the purpose of church discipline. Some churches may not agree with such a recommendation, especially those using a nouthetic counseling approach that emphasizes providing scriptural direction, including appropriate church discipline. In such churches lay counselors should inform their clients of this further limit to confidentiality for the sake of necessary church discipline as part of obtaining informed consent before starting counseling. The implementation of church discipline, however, still requires much sensitivity, love and wisdom (see Southard, 1986; White & Blue, 1985).

There are also some limits to confidentiality when counseling with minors (see Berryhill & Sabates, in this volume). Becker (1987) especially stresses the need to maintain confidentiality in the context of group counseling and the necessity of keeping records on clients safe and secure, preferably by putting them in the care of a licensed professional supervisor.

Competence. Becker (1987) notes the need to adequately and carefully select, train and supervise lay counselors so that they can function effectively within the limits of their competence or helping abilities and training, and so they can learn to refer more difficult clients to appropriate mental health professionals. I have written a text on lay Christian counseling that describes in detail how to do this (see Tan, 1991a). Briefly, lay counselors should be carefully selected, using criteria such as (1) spiritual maturity; (2) psychological or emotional stability; (3) love for and interest in people; (4) appropriate spiritual gifts for helping ministries (e.g., encouragement or exhortation, healing, knowledge, wisdom, discerning of spirits and mercy); (5) some life experience; (6) previous training or experience in people helping (if possible, but not essential); (7) age, sex and ethnic/cultural background appropriate to the needs of the clients served; (8) teachability and availability; and (9) ability to maintain confidentiality. Potential lay counselors should be interviewed either individually or in a group context as an essential part of the screening process, which can also include other requirements such as letters of recommendation (see Collins, 1980). The use of measures of spiritual gifts, spiritual well-being and spiritual maturity may also be helpful (see Tan, 1991a). Collins (1980) has suggested the use of psychological tests or measures such as the 16 PF in the selection of lay counselors. However, psychological testing in this context is controversial because of issues such as the lack of predictive validity and reliability of particular tests with lay counselors, and the ethical problems associated with testing potential lay counselors who may be friends with the qualified person administering the tests (unless they are administered by an outside licensed psychologist or therapist). It is therefore recommended that psychological tests not be used in the selection of lay counselors.

When it comes to training lay counselors, I have noted elsewhere (Tan, 1991a) that while a systematic training program is essential, there is great variety in the *length* of training and the *counseling approaches* (e.g., Rogerian, psychodynamic, cognitive-behavioral or systems) or *modalities* (e.g., individual, couple, family or group) covered. Usually a minimum of twenty-four to fifty or more hours of basic training in listening and helping skills over a period of several weeks to several months are provided for the lay counselors. However, it should not be assumed that longer and more complicated training programs are necessarily better or more effective than shorter and simpler ones, as Collins (1987) has pointed out.

Collins has raised a further question as to whether professionals are always the best people to provide training for lay counselors. The following are some components of a good training program: (1) practical and clear lectures, (2) homework reading, (3) watching good counseling skills modeled by the trainer or other more experienced counselors (live or through videotapes or DVDs), and (4) experiential practice through role playing, or the use of an "experimental client" or friend, or even real-life cases (with informed consent obtained). Collins (1980) has suggested that the content of a training curriculum for lay counselors should include (1) basic Bible knowledge, particularly that which is pertinent to people-helping ministries (see Collins, 1993); (2) knowledge of counseling skills (including experiential practice or role-plays); (3) understanding of common problems like depression, anxiety, stress and spiritual dryness; (4) awareness of ethics and dangers in counseling; and (5) awareness of the importance of referral and knowledge of referral techniques. While lay counselors can help people who are experiencing a broad range of problems, they should be taught their limits and the need to refer clients to appropriate professionals in difficult situations, such as when the clients or counselees are severely depressed and suicidal, show extremely aggressive behavior, make excessive use of alcohol or drugs, seem to be severely disturbed, have great financial needs, are in legal difficulties, require medical attention, want to switch to another counselor, will need more time than the lay counselor can provide, or arouse strong feelings of dislike, sexual stimulation, or threat in the lay counselor (Collins, 1976, p. 113). The lay counselor should make referrals sensitively and supportively, for example by pointing out that the client deserves help from better trained or more qualified professionals than the lay counselor, not by disparaging or putting down the client.

With regard to the supervision of lay counselors, it is usually recommended that they be supervised by a licensed mental health professional (see Adair, 1992; Lukens, 1987). However, I have noted that although this is ideal or preferable, it is *not* essential. In some churches in rural areas of the country, for example, it may not even be possible because such a professional may not be available. Nevertheless, the supervisor of lay counselors should at least have some basic training and experience in pastoral care or counseling, and also have a licensed mental health professional nearby as a consultant (Tan, 1991a). Lay counselors should receive ongoing, regular supervision of the counseling services they are providing. Usually such supervision is conducted weekly for an hour, whether individually, in pairs or in small groups. The supervision can also occur in small groups on a biweekly basis (meeting for about two hours once every two weeks) or monthly basis (meeting for two to four hours once a month), with individual supervision provided as needed. As Worthington (1987) has pointed out, there should be some observation of the lay counselor's actual counseling work as far as possible. This can be done through audiotapes or videotapes of actual counseling sessions, direct observation through a one-way mirror, or cocounseling, in which the lay counselor and supervisor conduct the counseling session together.

Lay counseling can be provided through a formal, organized model, like a lay counseling center in the church or community, or through an informal, organized model, in which the counseling is provided in more informal settings like homes, hospitals, nursing homes, restaurants and so forth (Tan, 1991a). In such informal contexts cocounseling appears to be the most practical and ethical way of observing lay counselors in action.

Worthington (1987) has also emphasized the need for supervisors to stress what friends and laypeople do well in helping one another, including providing excellent emotional support and empathy for people in crisis, giving good advice after careful empathic listening and understanding, and making available daily, multisituational support. Supervisors should also provide the best supervision they can, making use of the latest developments in the supervision literature (e.g., Aten & Hernandez, 2004; Bernard & Goodyear, 2004; Falender & Shafranske, 2004; Polanski, 2003; see also Tan, 1991a, pp. 135-58, 2007b, 2009; and Worthington, 1987).

There are ethical and legal issues pertaining specifically to the supervision of counselors (see Harrar, VandeCreek & Knapp, 1990; Stoltenberg & Delworth, 1987), including lay counselors. These issues include the need for lay counselors to obtain clients' permission to share information from their counseling sessions with supervisors and other lay counselors if group supervision is used. Such information, of course, is to be kept confidential by those present at supervision sessions. Clients or counselees should be informed regarding who will be providing the supervision, how often it will take place and who else will be present.

Adair (1992) has also stressed the need for lay counselors to take and keep good records as part of the supervision process, and she agrees with Becker (1987) that such records should be kept safe and confidential, preferably with a licensed professional supervisor, or at least separate from other church member records. Clients should also be informed before counseling is started that records on them will be kept. Most churches with formal, organized lay counseling centers require their counselors to keep brief notes or records on their clients. However, there are other churches, especially those involved in more informal but organized models of lay counseling and caregiving, that do not require their counselors or caregivers to keep records on clients. Each lay counseling service or center must decide clearly about record keeping. It is probably wisest to keep some brief records on clients, especially if a formal, organized model of lay counseling is used.

Adair (1992) also noted that the Christian Counselors of Texas added the requirement that lay counselors obtain malpractice insurance as part of their guidelines for supervision (see also Sandy, 2009). However, not all churches have obtained malpractice insurance for their lay counselors, because in some states it is very expensive to do so (see Tan, 1991a), and some churches may not be able to afford it. In some states such malpractice insurance may be very difficult, if not impossible to obtain. Licensed mental health professionals who supervise lay counselors do have some potential liability if lay counselors under their supervision commit ethical or legal violations. Sandy (2009) has therefore recommended that lay counselors obtain malpractice insurance, just as licensed mental health professionals have such insurance.

In summary, Scanish and McMinn (1996) suggest the following guidelines for assessing the competence of lay Christian counselors (p. 29): (1) They are not living in blatant sin. (2) They and their families are spiritually and emotionally healthy. (3) They understand and use Scripture wisely. (4) They represent themselves accurately. (5) They refer where appropriate. (6) They practice within their level of training. (7) They request help for their own problems. (8) They maintain current awareness of pertinent new developments. (9) They use care when speaking in public. (10) They are sensitive to human diversity.

Choice. In the area of choice, Becker (1987) emphasizes that freedom of client choice or informed consent requires the lay counselor to provide accurate and sufficient information on his or her qualifications, training and values, as well as the process, goals and possible consequences of counseling so that the client can make educated choices, including whether to stay with a particular lay counselor or to switch to another. Lay counselors must be particularly careful not to misrepresent themselves as being professionally trained, and they should not use terms like *psychologist* or *psychotherapy* to refer to who they are and what they do. In some states even the term *counselor* cannot be used by lay counselors because of licensing laws, and therefore other alternative titles such as *lay helper, lay minister, lay caregiver* or *lay shepherd* may need to be used instead.

Becker (1987) also recommends that lay counselors follow the ethical standards and guidelines of professional counseling or psychological organizations like the American Counseling Association, the American Association of Marriage and Family Therapists (AAMFT), and the APA. As I have noted elsewhere (Tan, 1991a), it is not as easy or clear-cut a task as Becker suggests for lay counselors to follow all of the professional ethical guidelines. Most of them do apply, but one particular guideline having to do with avoiding dual relationships cannot be applied as clearly to lay counselors, since many of them are involved in peer or friendship counseling. I believe that it is appropriate for lay counselors to help peers or friends, especially in church contexts, but they still need to be careful to refer clients to other lay or professional counselors when their objective judgment is in danger of being impaired. Good supervision is crucial to help lay counselors keep appropriate limits or boundaries, even if these are somewhat different from those that professional counselors need to maintain.

Lay counselors should follow other ethical guidelines for professionals that may clearly apply to them as well—for example, avoiding sexual or romantic relationships with clients, and helping within the limits of their competence. There are at least three codes of ethics written from a Christian perspective that can be helpful for Christian mental health professionals as well as lay Christian counselors to follow: a code of ethics for Christian counselors (Beck & Mathews, 1986), the ethical guidelines for the Christian Association for Psychological Studies or CAPS (2005; see Christian Association for Psychological Studies or see also King, 1986), and the American Association of Christian Counselors (AACC) code of ethics (AACC, 2004).

POSSIBLE HAZARDS FACED BY THE LAY COUNSELOR

Becker (1987) warns lay counselors to avoid the following high-risk situations, partly to reduce the possibility of being sued for malpractice: charging fees or asking for "donations"; using psychological tests without adequate training or supervision; having simplistic beliefs that can lead to superficial intervention, misdiagnosis or harm (e.g., believing that all problems are spiritual); counseling clients with severe problems that require professional help; giving advice against psychological or medical treatment; ignoring client statements regarding intent to harm or signs of violent behavior; counseling with an employee or relative; and developing a romantic or sexual relationship with the client.

Needham (1986) has also written a helpful chapter in a book on clergy malpractice (Malony, Needham & Southard, 1986). He stresses the need to care carefully, and in so doing lists twenty high-risk situations that pastors and lay counselors would do well to avoid, many of which are unethical or illegal, and which overlap with those mentioned by Becker (1987). Needham also suggests the following steps in caring for others while reducing the risks of litigation: (1) develop a formal counseling policy, covering a number of important areas (e.g., determining target needs, assessing resources, determining organizational channels and accountability, establishing selection procedures, setting up training and supervision standards, formulating guidelines on issues like fees or contributions, checking malpractice insurance coverage, and developing a feedback loop); (2) develop adequate selection, training and supervision; (3) avoid misleading claims; (4) conduct a thorough evaluation of the problem(s) presented by a client; (5) learn to benefit from testing (where appropriate and using properly trained and qualified persons); (6) determine the level of intervention (appropriate to the competence of the lay counselor); (7) make use of consultation and referrals; (8) take advantage of continuing education; (9) keep records and information confidential and secure; and (10) provide follow-up care.

Collins (1988), in his well-known text on Christian counseling, has a good chapter on the counselor and counseling in which he describes the potential problems or hazards a Christian counselor, including a lay Christian counselor, may experience. The areas covered include the counselor's motivation, effectiveness, role, vulnerability, sexuality, ethics and burnout (see also Collins, 2007). I have summarized elsewhere these potential problem areas and stressed the need to minimize or avoid them (see Tan, 1991a, pp. 213-15).

Adair (1992), in a paper on ethical considerations of a professional supervising lay counselors, also pointed out that lay counselors do a significant amount of religious counseling, usually without any remuneration. It is my recommendation that fees should not be charged or donations requested by lay counselors in a lay counseling ministry (Tan, 1991a). In providing explicitly religious or Christian counseling, lay counselors often use spiritual resources like prayer, Scripture and referrals to church or parachurch groups where appropriate (see Tan, 1991b). Sensitivity and competence in dealing with religion as a crucial dimension of human diversity are mandated by the APA's "Ethical Principles of Psychologists and Code of Conduct" (2002). However, explicitly religious counseling should still be conducted in an ethical and competent way (Tan, 1994a, 1996, 2007a), because there are potential ethical pitfalls in religious counseling that should be avoided (see Younggren, 1993). For example, Nelson and Wilson (1984) have suggested that it is ethical for counselors to share or use their religious faith in counseling contexts if they are dealing with problems that would be helped by spiritual interventions, if they are working within the client's belief system (and therefore avoid forcing their own religious beliefs on the client), and if they have clearly defined the counseling contract to include the use of religious or spiritual resources or interventions, thereby obtaining the informed consent of the client. Lay Christian counselors need to follow these guidelines in order to do lay counseling that is explicitly Christian or religious in an ethical and helpful way. They can share openly or expose their Christian values without imposing them on their clients and can give the clients the freedom to ultimately choose their own values and courses of action.

Richard (1987) briefly described a number of potential perils that the professional counselor may face in being involved with local paraprofessional mental health organizations, lay counselor training or lay counseling ministries (see also Tan, 1997). They include the following scenarios: (1) other professionals may feel threatened by the work of lay counselors and may therefore need to be educated about the effectiveness of lay counselors as well as the cooperative way in which lay counselors usually work together with professionals, making referrals to them where necessary and serving constituencies not currently being served adequately by the existing mental health system; (2) some churches or Christian organizations may still be antipsychology and anticounseling, and this attitude may be difficult, but not impossible, to change; (3) there is the danger of burnout and exhaustion for the professional counselor who overcommits to a lay organization, and therefore the work should be shared with others; (4) there could be a conflict of interest for a professional counselor in private practice, so he or she should avoid using a lay counseling organization to further private endeavors.

PROPER EVALUATION OF LAY COUNSELORS

One final ethical guideline that has not been sufficiently emphasized is the need for evaluating lay counselors. Both the effectiveness of lay counselor training programs and the efficacy of the counseling provided by lay counselors should be comprehensively evaluated in better controlled studies, particularly for lay Christian counselors (see Toh et al., 1994; Toh & Tan, 1997; see also Garzon & Tilley, 2009). I have elsewhere made detailed suggestions as to how such careful evaluation research can be conducted (see Tan, 1991a, pp. 159-87). There is also a need for further research that more closely examines the skills, deficiencies and limitations of lay counselors (Durlak, 1979). A particularly important area in need of more research and data has to do with the question of how ethical is the actual practice of lay counselors. More specifically, we do not yet know how many lay counselors actually obtain informed consent from their clients prior to counseling with them, keep confidentiality appropriately and follow the other ethical guidelines discussed in this chapter. Although lay counselors have been found generally to be as effective therapeutically as professional therapists, some may question whether lay counselors are as ethical as professional therapists. Only further research can answer this crucial question more adequately. Evaluation is important in adding to and furthering the knowledge we already possess.

CONCLUSION

Lay counselor training and lay counseling ministries are significant areas of service for Christian mental health professionals to be involved in (see Tan, 1997). It is hoped that the ethical and related legal issues discussed in this chapter, as well as recommendations or suggestions provided, will help such professionals to develop and supervise lay counselors effectively and ethically, so that the lay counselors can learn themselves how to function effectively and ethically in people-helping ministries.

REFERENCES

Adair, J. (1992, November). *Ethical considerations of a professional supervising lay counselors.* Paper presented at the meeting of the Second International Congress on Christian Counseling. Atlanta, GA.

Ali, B. S., Rahbar, M. H., Naeem, S., & Gul, A. (2003). The effectiveness of counseling on anxiety and depression by minimally trained counselors: A randomized controlled trial. *American Journal of Psychotherapy, 57,* 324-36.

American Association of Christian Counselors. (2004). *AACC code of ethics: The Y2004 final code.* Forest, VA: American Association of Christian Counselors.

American Psychological Association. (2002). Ethical principles of psychologists and code of conduct. *American Psychologist, 57,* 1060-73. Also available (with 2010 amendments) from www.apa.org/ethics/code/index.aspx.

Atkins, D. C., & Christensen, A. (2001). Is professional training worth the bother? A review of the impact of psychological training on client outcome. *Australian Psychologist, 36*(2), 1-9.

Aten, J. D., & Hernandez, B. C. (2004). Addressing religion in clinical supervision: A model. *Psychotherapy: Theory, Research, Practice, Training, 4,* 152-60.

Beck, J. R., & Mathews, R. K. (1986). A code of ethics for Christian counselors. *Journal of Psychology and Christianity, 5,* 78-84.

Becker, W. W. (1987). The paraprofessional counselor in the church: Legal and ethical considerations. *Journal of Psychology and Christianity, 6,* 78-82.

Berman, J. S., & Norton, N. C. (1985). Does professional training make a therapist more effective? *Psychological Bulletin, 98,* 401-7.

Bernard, J. M., & Goodyear, R. K. (2004). *Fundamentals of clinical supervision* (3rd ed.). Boston: Allyn & Bacon.

Bickman, L. (1999). Practice makes perfect and other myths about mental health services. *American Psychologist, 54,* 965-78.

Browning, D. S. (2006). *Christian ethics and the moral psychologies.* Grand Rapids: Eerdmans.

Christensen, A., & Jacobson, N. S. (1994). Who (or what) can do psychotherapy: The status and challenge of nonprofessional therapies. *Psychological Science, 5,* 8-14.

Christian Association for Psychological Studies. (2005). *Ethics statement of the Christian Association for Psychological Studies.* Retrieved November 4, 2010, from http://caps.net/about-us/statement-of-ethical-guidelines.

Collins, G. R. (1976). *How to be a people helper.* Santa Ana, CA: Vision House.

Collins, G. R. (1980). Lay counseling within the local church. *Leadership, 7*(4), 78-86.

Collins, G. R. (1987). Lay counseling: Some lingering questions for professionals. *Journal of Psychology and Christianity, 6,* 7-9.

Collins, G. R. (1988.) *Christian counseling: A comprehensive guide.* (Rev. ed.). Waco, TX: Word.

Collins, G. R. (1991). *Excellence and ethics in counseling.* Dallas: Word.

Collins, G. R. (1993). *The biblical basis of Christian counseling for people helpers.* Colorado Springs: NavPress.

Collins, G. R. (2007). *Christian counseling: A comprehensive guide* (3rd ed.). Nashville: Thomas Nelson.

Durlak, J. A. (1979). Comparative effectiveness of paraprofessional and professional helpers. *Psychological Bulletin, 86,* 80-92.

Durlak, J. A. (1981). Evaluating comparative studies of paraprofessional and professional helpers: A reply to Nietzel and Fisher. *Psychological Bulletin, 89,* 566-69.

Falender, C. A., & Shafranske, E. P. (2004). *Clinical supervision: A competency-based approach.* Washington, DC: American Psychological Association.

Garzon, F., & Tilley, K. A. (2009). Do lay Christian counseling approaches work? What we currently know. *Journal of Psychology and Christianity, 28,* 130-40.

Garzon, F., Worthington, E. L., Jr., Tan, S.-Y., & Worthington, R. K. (2009). Lay Christian counseling and client expectations for integration in therapy. *Journal of Psychology and Christianity, 28,* 113-20.

Harrar, W. R., VandeCreek, L., & Knapp, S. (1990). Ethical and legal aspects of clinical supervision. *Professional Psychology: Research and Practice, 21,* 37-41.

Hattie, A., Sharpley, C. F., & Rogers, H. J. (1984). Comparative effectiveness of professional and paraprofessional helpers. *Psychological Bulletin, 95,* 534-41.

King, R. R., Jr. (1986). Developing a proposed code of ethics for the Christian association for psychological studies. *Journal of Psychology and Christianity, 5,* 85-90.

Levicoff, S. (1991). *Christian counseling and the law.* Chicago: Moody Press.

Lukens, H. C., Jr. (1987). Lay counselor training revisited: Reflections of a trainer. *Journal of Psychology and Christianity, 6,* 10-13.

Malony, H. N., Needham, T. L., & Southard, S. (1986). *Clergy malpractice.* Philadelphia: Westminster Press.

Needham, T. L. (1986). Helping when the risks are great. In H. N. Malony, T. L. Needham, & S. Southard (Eds.), *Clergy malpractice* (pp. 88-109). Philadelphia: Westminster Press.

Nelson, A. A., & Wilson, W. P. (1984). The ethics of sharing religious faith in psychotherapy. *Journal of Psychology and Theology, 12,* 15-23.

Neuner, F., Onyut, P. L., Ertl, V., Odenwald, M., Schauer, E., & Elbert, T. (2008). Treatment of posttraumatic stress disorder by trained lay counselors in an African refugee settlement: A randomized controlled trial. *Journal of Consulting and Clinical Psychology, 76,* 686-94.

Nietzel, N. T., and Fisher, S. G. (1981). Effectiveness of professional and paraprofessional helpers: A comment on Durlak. *Psychological Bulletin, 89,* 555-65.

Ohlschlager, G. W., & Clinton, T. E. (2002). The ethical helping relationship: ethical conformation and spiritual transformation. In T. E. Clinton & G. W. Ohlschlager (Eds.), *Competent Christian counseling* (pp. 24-293, 750-51). Colorado Springs: Waterbrook.

Polanski, P. J. (2003). Spirituality in supervision. *Counseling and Values, 47,* 131-41.

Richard, R. C. (1987). The professional counselor and local paraprofessional mental health organizations. *Journal of Psychology and Christianity, 6,* 35-38.

Sandy, J. L. (2009). *Church lay counseling risk management guidebook.* Fort Wayne, IN: Brotherhood Mutual Insurance.

Scanish, J. D., & McMinn, M. R. (1996). The competent lay Christian counselor. *Journal of Psychology and Christianity, 15,* 29-37.

Southard, S. (1986). Church discipline: Handle with care. In H. N. Malony, T. L. Needham & S. Southard (Eds.), *Clergy malpractice* (pp. 74-87). Philadelphia: Westminster Press.

Tan, S. Y. (1990). Lay counseling: The next decade. *Journal of Psychology and Christianity, 9,* 59-65.

Tan, S. Y. (1991a). *Lay counseling: Equipping Christians for a helping ministry.* Grand Rapids: Zondervan.

Tan, S. Y. (1991b). Religious values and interventions in lay Christian counseling. *Journal of Psychology and Christianity,* 10, 173-82.

Tan, S. Y. (1994a). Ethical considerations in religious psychotherapy: Potential pitfalls and unique resources. *Journal of Psychology and Theology, 22,* 389-94.

Tan, S. Y. (1994b). Lay counseling: A Christian approach. *Journal of Psychology and Christianity, 13,* 264-69.

Tan, S. Y. (1996). Religion in clinical practice: Implicit and explicit integration. In E. Shafranske (Ed.), *Religion and the clinical practice of psychology* (pp. 365-87). Washington, DC: American Psychological Association.

Tan, S. Y. (1997). The role of the psychologist in paraprofessional helping. *Professional Psychology: Research and Practice, 28,* 368-72.

Tan, S. Y. (2002). Lay helping: The whole church in soul care ministry. In T. E. Clinton and G. W. Ohlschlager (Eds.), *Competent Christian counseling* (Vol. 1, pp. 424-36, 759-62). Colorado Springs: Waterbrook.

Tan, S. Y. (2003). Integrating spiritual direction into psychotherapy: Ethical Issues and guidelines. *Journal of Psychology and Theology, 31,* 14-23.

Tan, S. Y. (2007a). Use of prayer and scripture in cognitive-behavioral therapy. *Journal of Psychology and Christianity, 26,* 101-11.

Tan, S. Y. (2007b). Using spiritual disciplines in clinical supervision. *Journal of Psychology and Christianity, 26,* 328-35.

Tan, S. Y. (2009). Developing integration skills: The role of clinical supervision. *Journal of Psychology and Theology, 37,* 54-61.

Tan, S. Y. (2011). *Counseling and psychotherapy: A Christian perspective.* Grand Rapids: Baker Academic.

Tjeltveit, A. C. (1999). *Ethics and values in psychotherapy.* New York: Routledge.

Toh, Y. M., Tan, S. Y., Osburn, C. D., & Faber, D. E. (1994). The evaluation of a church-based lay counseling program: Some preliminary data. *Journal of Psychology and Christianity, 13,* 270-75.

Toh, Y. M., & Tan, S. Y. (1997). The effectiveness of church-based lay counselors: A controlled outcome study. *Journal of Psychology and Christianity, 16,* 260-67.

White. J., & Blue, K. (1985). *Healing the wounded: The costly love of church discipline.* Downers Grove, IL: InterVarsity Press.

Worthington, E. L., Jr. (1987). Issues in supervision of lay Christian counseling. *Journal of Psychology and Christianity, 6,* 70-77.

Younggren, J. N. (1993). Ethical issues in religious psychotherapy. *Register Report, 19,* 1, 7-8.

16

Mixed Agency Dilemmas for Professionals in the Military and Other Government Agencies

W. Brad Johnson

[The views expressed in this chapter are those of the author and do not reflect the official policy or position of the Department of the Navy, Department of Defense or the United States Government.]

Many mental health professionals (MHPs) are employed by organizations such as government agencies, schools, correctional facilities, medical centers, universities and churches. At times, these organizations may promulgate regulations, policies or even less formal implicit expectations about the MHP's role. Frequently, MHPs may encounter *mixed-agency* ethical dilemmas involving the simultaneous commitment to two or more entities; most often, there is a conflict between the MHP's loyalty to an individual client and the organization (Howe, 2003; Johnson & Koocher, 2012; Kennedy & Johnson, 2009). Mixed-agency situations require ethical practitioners to carefully sort out the sometimes competing ethical obligations to clients, organizations and society while working to resolve the dilemmas responsibly and without causing harm (Koocher & Keith-Spiegel, 2008).

Professionals may encounter mixed-agency dilemmas in many work contexts. In fact, any MHP employed by an organization, agency or institution will likely discover situations in which client needs or best interests are not congruent with or, worse, diametrically opposed to the interests of the organization. For instance, psychiatrists, psychologists, social workers and counselors employed by religious schools, hospitals, managed care groups and the Veteran's Administration (VA) often face ethical predicaments centering on dual obligations to the interests of clients and the larger agency (Johnson & Koocher, 2012; Koocher & Keith-Spiegel, 2008).

This chapter will specifically consider mixed-agency dilemmas that manifest in military and other national security agencies. Military MHPs must carefully balance their sometimes competing obligations to their clients (e.g., military service members) and the United States Department of Defense (DOD). Moreover, military MHPs are commissioned officers and, as such, legally obligated to adhere to a range of federal regulations that may occasionally conflict with salient elements of the MHPs' professional ethics code (Jeffrey, Rankin & Jeffrey, 1992; Kennedy & Johnson, 2009). A survey of U.S. Air Force psychologists revealed that the most common ethical conflict experienced by that group were conflicts between ethics and organizational demands (Orme & Doerman, 2001). Nearly half of those surveyed had experienced conflict abiding by their ethical obligations while also doing what was expected of them as USAF officers.

In addition to the mixed-agency dilemmas generated by MHPs' dual allegiance to clients and the organization, this chapter will consider the added complexity occurring when the Christian MHP's religious commitments come into play. I use the term *three-dimensional mixed-agency dilemmas* to describe those situations in which a professional experiences incongruence or tension between obligations to clients, organizations and personal faith commitment.

UNIQUE ELEMENTS OF MENTAL HEALTH PRACTICE IN THE MILITARY

Military MHPs have a long and distinguished history of service to military members, their families and the nation (Driskell & Olmstead, 1989; Kennedy & McNeil, 2006; Kennedy & Zillmer, 2006; Kraft, 2007; Page, 1996). Military clinicians are often ordered to isolated duty stations or combat theaters in which they are the only MHP. As such, they must be excellent generalists and prepared to provide emergency or triage services for combat-related stress disorders. Further, military MHPs are often *embedded* providers, meaning that they are frequently deployed as part of a military unit or force. In this context the MHP is simultaneously a member of the unit and legally bound to place the unit's mission foremost. There are several distinctive features of practice in embedded military and other government service environments. Each of these features is prone to create specific ethical tensions for the MHP; each of them may also exacerbate mixed-agency dilemmas.

The military MHP has (at least) two distinct professional identities. Military MHPs may struggle with the simultaneous and sometimes competing identities of licensed MHP and commissioned military officer (Jeffery et al., 1992; Johnson, 1995; 2008; Moore & Reger, 2006). As a licensed practitioner the MHP is clearly obligated to uphold and abide by the relevant professional code of ethics as well as the jurisdictional requirements in the state of his or her licensure. But the MHP is simultaneously obligated to abide by DOD regulations and lawful orders from military superiors. Particularly in deployed contexts when the MHP is embedded with a military unit, the immediate military mission is often the most salient obligation. For instance, maintaining clear boundaries and avoiding multiple relationships—a clear-cut ethical obligation—may be exceptionally difficult if not impossible when one must eat, sleep and travel with clients. Moreover, an MHP may experience conflict when required to discipline or sanction a military subordinate who is also a client. Camp (1993) described military MHPs as having "double agent" status; at times MHPs must choose between client-centered therapeutic interests and organization-centered administrative interests.

At times, ethical standards and DOD regulations are incongruent. Military MHPs may occasionally discover subtle incongruities or glaring discord between ethical standards (e.g., American Psychological Association [APA] 2010) and DOD statutes and regulations (Jeffrey et al., 1992). Common conflicts are evident in the areas of confidentiality, multiple relationships, informed consent and serving the individual's best interests (Johnson, 2008). Ethical-legal incongruities related to confidentiality in the military offer a prime example of this conflict. While ethical guidelines are unequivocal regarding the MHP's obligation to take reasonable precautions to protect client confidentiality—including clinical material stored in client records—the military culture may be disinterested in or even hostile to the concept of service member confidentiality (Jeffrey et al., 1992; Johnson,

1995; Orme & Doerman, 2001). Further, DOD statutes specify that a legitimate military authority may have access to a service member's mental health record when that authority has a "need to know" for the purpose of determining fitness and capacity for deployment. Military MHPs may experience quandaries related to determining which entities in the military chain-of-command have a legitimate need to know. It is important to note that uniformed MHPs have been censured by professional organizations for abiding by DOD regulations, and by the DOD for adhering to ethical obligations (Jeffrey et al., 1992).

In military settings, it is often difficult to identify "the client." One feature of government service settings that may be challenging for the MHP is the difficulty inherent in determining the identity of the MHP's primary "client." Although most civilian practitioners can easily point to their individual client as the primary recipient of their services and therefore the one to whom they owe primary consideration from an ethical perspective, this is not always the case in the military. For instance, because many fitness-for-duty evaluations are ordered by a service member's commanding officer, the MHP may experience competing obligations to the individual service member, the commanding officer and the DOD more broadly. When evaluating service members as a combat unit prepares for a sensitive mission, is the military MHP's primary client the commanding officer or the individual soldier or sailor?

The military MHP cannot always anticipate significant role shifts with clients. Another factor that may intensify mixed-agency dilemmas in military settings involves the phenomenon of unanticipated role shifts with clients. Military MHPs rarely get to choose whether to enter or exit clinical relationships with clients (Johnson, Ralph & Johnson, 2005). As solo providers in isolated duty stations, uniformed MHPs must provide services to any member of the community; as such, military MHPs hold multiple roles with many clients. To make matters worse, military clinicians are often required to change roles with clients with little warning. For instance, a military MHP may be asked to perform a commander-directed security clearance evaluation with an ongoing client. The outcome of the evaluation may have serious implications for the service member's career, and the MHP may be legally unable to refuse this secondary role even though the client was not informed about this eventuality when clinical work began.

Military service is a high-risk profession. Uniformed MHPs occupy high-risk roles in comparison to most civilian practitioners. To the extent that MHPs are embedded with deployed military units, they may be required to travel with their unit in active combat theaters. In rare circumstances uniformed MHPs may take up arms against an enemy, either in self-defense or to protect a patient or subordinate (Johnson & Kennedy, 2010). In addition to the stress inherent in combat-proximal settings, military MHPs are very likely to be both directly and vicariously exposed to traumatic events and disturbing images. Environments characterized by risk of physical injury, psychological trauma and ongoing emotional distress may diminish good ethical decision making when mixed-agency dilemmas occur. Wartime demands may cause the MHP to favor organizational—mission-essential—considerations over individual client considerations.

DOD policy and federal regulations may conflict with an MHP's religious convictions. On occasion Christian and other religious practitioners may discover that an organizational (DOD) requirement is at odds with important religious beliefs and commitments. For instance, a Quaker military psychologist who joined the Army to care for psychologically wounded warriors may object on religious grounds to being asked to help a special forces team become more cohesive and efficient when their primary mission is assassinating insurgent leaders far behind enemy lines. As another example, a conservative Christian social worker may object to the recent repeal of "Don't Ask Don't Tell," the federal legislation that prevented gay, lesbian and bisexual service members from open service in the military. As the only MHP at a small military base, the social worker may object to requirements that he provide services—including couples therapy—to LGB service members. Perhaps the most common conflict for religious MHPs in military settings involves the prohibition against sectarian counseling or psychotherapy techniques in DOD facilities. Christian or other religious approaches to intervention are largely considered the purview of military chaplains. In light of the rather clear commitment to church-state separation in government agencies, religious practitioners may encounter resistance from colleagues and supervisors to overtly religious interventions with a client.

MIXED AGENCY DILEMMAS AND THE APA ETHICS CODE

Although each of the primary mental health organizations promulgate a code of ethics relevant to professional practice, in the interests of space, I will focus on the American Psychological Association's (APA) guidance on the topic of mixed-agency dilemmas. APA's recently amended "Ethical Principles of Psychologists and Code of Conduct" (APA, 2010) is similar in many respects to other ethics codes and instructive for MHPs who might find themselves struggling with mixed-agency dilemmas in military and other government settings.

1.03 Conflicts Between Ethics and Organizational Demands

> If the demands of an organization with which psychologists are affiliated or for whom they are working are in conflict with this Ethics Code, psychologists clarify the nature of the conflict, make known their commitment to the Ethics Code, and take reasonable steps to resolve the conflict consistent with the General Principles and Ethical Standards of the Ethics Code. Under no circumstances may this standard be used to justify or defend violating human rights.

Standard 1.03 of the APA Code places responsibility for addressing mixed-agency dilemmas squarely on the shoulders of the military MHP (Johnson, Grasso & Maslowski, 2010; Kennedy & Johnson, 2009). Thus, a military psychologist who becomes aware that a DOD "need to know" policy is being interpreted erroneously so that client confidentiality is seriously and needlessly compromised has a clear ethical obligation to bring this conflict to the attention of the appropriate authorities in the chain of command while continuing to adhere to the ethics code. Similarly, when the uniformed MHP with no training in the diagnosis or treatment of children is ordered by his commanding officer to fill a gap in the children's clinic caused by the deployment of another professional, that MHP owns a duty to object on the basis of inadequate competence. The MHP should be firm but respectful in refusing to engage in unethical practice (e.g., seeing child clients without appropriate training or at least temporary supervision) while helping the organization to understand the ethical problem.

1.02 Conflicts Between Ethics and Law, Regulations, or Other Governing Legal Authority

If psychologists' ethical responsibilities conflict with law, regulations, or other governing legal authority, psychologists clarify the nature of the conflict, make known their commitment to the Ethics Code, and take reasonable steps to resolve the conflict consistent with the General Principles and Ethical Standards of the Ethics Code. Under no circumstances may this standard be used to justify or defend violating human rights.

Perhaps no ethical quandary creates more anxiety for the military MHP than situations in which he or she feels caught between an ethical obligation and a legal statute or lawful regulation (Howe, 2003; Johnson, 1995; Johnson et al., 2010; Orme & Doerman, 2001). MHPs are most likely to encounter ethical-legal conflicts in areas such as confidentiality, informed consent, or participating in nontraditional roles such as detainee interrogations. In most instances ethical and legal requirements are discrepant, creating tension for the MHP, but the discrepancy can be easily resolved. In cases of genuine conflict, the provider discovers that fulfilling legal obligations will necessarily entail violating his or her code of ethics. For instance, an Army psychologist stationed in Iraq feels pressured by a medical command directive to diagnose Posttraumatic Stress Disorder (PTSD) only in the most dire and extreme circumstances (e.g., when there are coexisting psychotic features). Otherwise, soldiers are to be briefly treated and returned to the front lines (Moore & Reger, 2006). When the psychologist complains that it is unethical to alter clinical diagnoses simply to accommodate an organizational policy, the commanding officer orders the MHP to abide by the command policy and refrain from diagnosing PTSD even when it is clearly evident. This psychologist has an ethical obligation to clearly articulate the ethical-legal conflict, continue to adhere to sound ethical practice and persist in raising the concern higher up the chain-of-command until a solution can be found. In the military this might involve a psychologist going to his or her supervisor—perhaps a physician in charge of the medical unit—at a remote operating base and explaining the incongruity between professional obligations and a commander's orders or a implementation of a DOD policy. If the supervisor is not responsive and the conflict persists, the psychologist would then be obligated to raise the concern at a higher level. In this military scenario, this might involve the base commander or the senior medical officer in the region.

It is important to note that although the 2010 revision of the APA "Code of Ethics" (APA, 2010) makes adhering to the ethics code in cases of ethical-legal conflict a clear obligation, Standard 1.02 does not state that psychologists *must* break the law in order to adhere to an ethical principle or standard. Rather, the Code leaves it to the good judgment of the MHP to deliberately resolve the conflict in the most appropriate manner considering a range of context-specific variables such as obligations to clients and the potential for harm. At times a military MHP may decide to violate a lawful order or legal statute as a matter of conscience or commitment to professional ethics, but such disobedience is *required* only when following a law or order would lead to a violation of human rights. In other circumstances an MHP may continue to abide by a law, even though it conflicts with an ethical obligation, while he or she works diligently to resolve the conflict by collaborating respectfully with supervisors or other organizational leaders.

3.04 Avoiding Harm

Psychologists take reasonable steps to avoid harming their clients/patients, students, supervisees, research participants, organizational clients, and others with whom they work, and to minimize harm where it is foreseeable and unavoidable.

At times MHPs employed by government agencies may feel compelled to limit the freedom or overlook the best interests of one person to promote or safeguard the best interests of a larger group or even society at large (Howe, 1986; Kennedy & Johnson, 2009; Koocher & Keith-Spiegel, 2008). At times military MHPs struggle with the decision about when or whether to return a service member to combat (Howe, 1986). Whether the objections are humanitarian, religious or clinical, providers may wrestle with the ethics of sending a service member—especially one who has already suffered significant trauma—back into harm's way. On one hand it is true that all service members are volunteers who have pledged to protect and defend the country. On the other hand, a clinician may interpret the ethical obligation to avoid harm to clients in such a way that his or her recommendations regarding clients' return to combat are incongruent with the needs of the military and the pressing military mission.

3.10 Informed Consent

(a) When psychologists conduct research or provide assessment, therapy, counseling, or consulting services in person or via electronic transmission or other forms of communication, they obtain the informed consent of the individual or individuals using language that is reasonably understandable to that person or persons except when conducting such activities without consent is mandated by law or governmental regulation or as otherwise provided in this Ethics Code.

3.11 Psychological Services Delivered to or Through Organizations

(a) Psychologists delivering services to or through organizations provide information beforehand to clients and when appropriate those directly affected by the services about (1) the nature and objectives of the services, (2) the intended recipients, (3) which of the individuals are clients, (4) the relationship the psychologist will have with each person and the organization, (5) the probable uses of services provided and information obtained, (6) who will have access to the information, and (7) limits of confidentiality. As soon as feasible, they provide information about the results and conclusions of such services to appropriate persons.

The unassailable ethical obligation to provide clear and ongoing informed consent to clients lies at the heart of many mixed-agency ethical dilemmas in government settings. A thoughtful and ethical MHP embedded with a military unit as the only mental health provider could help to diminish the potential for misunderstanding and harm to clients by providing rigorous informed consent procedures (Jeffery et al., 1992; Johnson, 2008; Staal & King, 2000). Specifically, the MHP should carefully inform individual clients about the potential uses of the MHP's work by commanding officers or the DOD broadly, potential role shifts from clinical to forensic or administrative roles, and the likely career outcomes of specific diagnoses and treatments. Of course, mixed-agency dilemmas will also be tempered if MHPs work hard to remind clients that confidentiality is difficult to ensure in military contexts and that the MHP does not control the client's health records. In addition to informing clients of these facts, the

MHP must also work diligently to protect client confidentiality and privacy whenever possible. For instance, when a commanding officer requests information about a client's mental health status, the MHP should employ stringent criteria regarding what information is germane and likely covered under DOD's need to know policy (DOD, 1993). Typically, this will include reason for referral, diagnosis and fitness for continued duty, including combat deployment.

STRATEGIES AND RECOMMENDATIONS FOR MANAGING MIXED-AGENCY DILEMMAS

When MHPs employed by the military or other government agencies encounter conflicts between their loyalties and obligations to clients and the larger military organization, there are three broad approaches to managing the conflict (Johnson & Wilson, 1993). Although all three approaches are employed by military practitioners at times, the first two are likely to be both self-defeating for the MHP and prone to increasing risk of negative outcomes for clients and the organization. Using the *military manual approach*, an MHP adheres strictly to DOD regulations, federal statutes and organizational interpretations of those requirements. In essence, DOD requirements trump ethical principles and standards. This approach is problematic because the military MHP appears to engage in no deliberate process of ethical analysis when making decisions about a specific client and situation (Kennedy & Johnson, 2009). Using this approach, an MHP may answer all questions from a client's commanding officer without careful consideration of the client's right to privacy or the commanding officer's legitimate need to know specific information about a service member.

A second strategy, *the stealth approach*, involves attempting to resolve mixed-agency quandaries by quietly thwarting ethically problematic legal requirements or organizational policies in favor of full adherence to one's code of ethics (Johnson & Wilson, 1993). Kennedy and Johnson (2009) noted that an MHP operating with this approach may make cryptic and incomplete notes in the medical record and omit documentation of activities that violate the Uniformed Code of Military Justice (UCMJ) such as specific sexual behaviors or minor drug use that do not require intervention and do not put anyone at risk. The stealth approach clearly favors the psychologist's clinician role at the expense of his or her officer role.

Most military MHPs employ a third approach to managing and resolving mixed-agency dilemmas. Termed the *best-interests approach* (Johnson & Wilson, 1993), this approach involves a concerted effort to simultaneously promote the best interests of the service member, DOD and society. This approach affords the MHP the greatest hope of protecting client interests, avoiding harm to a client and helping the organization achieve its goals without compromising salient ethical principles and standards. Although the best-interests approach has not been codified or recommended by any organization, it is the approach most often adopted by ethical MHPs who wish to serve the best interests of clients in organizational settings. The ethical principles of promoting client interests and avoiding harm, justice and respect for people's rights and dignity are well-served by a best-interests approach. When an MHP employed by an organization utilizes the best-interests approach, he or she stands the greatest chance of effectively balancing obligations to both the ethics codes and federal regulations.

To illustrate this approach, Kennedy and Johnson (2009) present the case of a Navy parachute rigger who arrived to work one day smelling of alcohol. During a subsequent substance abuse screening, a Navy psychologist found evidence of alcohol dependence. During the course of the evaluation the service member also revealed that he had received numerous and unwanted romantic and sexual advances from a person higher in the chain of command. In this case the psychologist reasoned that a period of required alcohol treatment while the service member worked away from the aviation community was in the best interests of both the DOD (e.g., the safety of other service members would be protected by removing an impaired parachute rigger) and the individual client (e.g., the service member clearly suffered from a substance disorder; successfully completing treatment and maintaining sobriety might be the only thing that would save his career). Although military personnel are required to report sexual harassment whenever it comes to light, the psychologist in this case—after discussing all options with the service member—decided not to file a mandatory report regarding the harassment. Because the report would certainly come to the attention of the service member's chain of command, including the offending officer, because the service member did not wish to deal with the fallout of a formal complaint at the present time and because the psychologist wanted to honor the client's wishes and avoid further damage to the client's career, the psychologist agreed not to report the harassment if the service member would participate in both substance abuse treatment and subsequent outpatient psychotherapy, during which one of the foci of treatment would be the client's response to the harassment. In this case, the psychologist worked to balance the service member's privacy and individual interests with the organization's interests in the safety and well-functioning of its members.

Beyond working to balance the best interests of individual clients and the larger organization, MHPs will be well served by considering each of the following recommendations for ameliorating the negative impact of mixed-agency tensions in military settings.

Government service, even as a Commissioned Officer, does not trump one's obligations as a health care professional. Psychiatrists, psychologists, counselors and other health care providers serving in uniform must be very careful not to lose sight of their ongoing obligation to adhere to their professional code of ethics (Annas, 2008). When serving in embedded military units, when engaging in highly operational (nonclinical) work, and when serving for an extended period of time in combat environments far from other providers, military and other government MHPs should be careful to guard against "drift" in the direction of primary allegiance to military tradition and regulation at the expense of adherence to professional ethics (Johnson et al., 2010). It is often important for MHPs in organizational settings to work hard at maintaining involvement with professional organizations and engagement with colleagues in order to remain sensitive to one's ethical duties and professional identity.

Provide rigorous and ongoing informed consent to all clients. Because serving in organizational settings often poses threats to client confidentiality and privacy, unanticipated role shifts and other unintended outcomes, MHPs should be attentive to achieving detailed and explicit informed consent with all clients (Jeffrey et al., 1992; Johnson et al., 2005). In the military and other organizations, seeking mental health care may be highly stigmatized (Porter & Johnson, 1994) such that even seriously traumatized and impaired service members may avoid seeking or accepting necessary care (Hoge et al., 2004). Clients in these settings should understand that many people beyond the MHP will likely have access to his or her medical record, that specific diagnoses may have dramatically adverse career consequences, and that the MHP may be called upon to engage the client in an unanticipated new role, such as security clearance evaluator. Further, in embedded contexts, MHPs should clarify the range of multiple roles they may have with respect to clients and how the client would prefer to handle potentially uncomfortable encounters.

Assume that every member of the organization is a potential client. One hallmark of service in the military or other government settings is the isolated nature of the community. As is sometimes the case in rural communities and even some small religious organizations or churches, military units constitute cloistered communities in which every member of the organization should be viewed as a prospective client from the first day the MHP arrives. For instance, an MHP serving on an aircraft carrier should assume that everyone onboard, including high-ranking officers and close personal friends may eventually require the MHP to engage them in a formal clinical relationship (Johnson et al., 2005). Alternatively, a small-town MHP who worships in a local church should assume that any fellow parishioner will soon become a client. Mixed-agency dilemmas might be softened if the MHP has maintained a reasonably neutral role in the organization and avoided becoming too personally enmeshed with other members; maintaining strong personal and consultative relationships outside the organization is highly recommended.

Recognize the distinction between mixed-agency tensions and conflicts. When a military MHP encounters an apparent tension or incongruence between a lawful order or DOD regulation and an ethical standard, it need not mean that an ethical and a legal response are mutually exclusive (Johnson et al., 2010). Acute mixed-agency conflicts—occurring when abiding by the law will automatically violate the code of ethics or vice versa—are probably far less common than mixed-agency tensions. For instance, if a military MHP were ordered to provide a client's mental health record under the DOD need-to-know statute (DOD, 1993), a skilled clinician would recognize the mixed-agency tension and work collegially with the requesting source to determine the specific information of interest to the command (e.g., is this service member fit for deployment to a combat zone?). A general fitness-for-duty comment or recommendation may suffice, thereby avoiding escalation of a tension to an intractable conflict.

Establish positive working relationships with senior members of the organization. In concert with the foregoing recommendation, MHPs in government settings will find that they can frequently avert mixed-agency conflicts by working closely and consultatively with leaders in the local chain of command. This requires MHPs to develop positive working relationships with leaders in their own medical command and leaders in the military units that use the MHP's services (Kennedy & Johnson, 2009). So, the military MHP who spends considerable time interfacing with commanders, providing psycho-education such as stress-prevention workshops to local military personnel, and remaining available to provide informal consultation with commanders will have a considerably easier time preventing tensions from becoming conflicts. Collaborative working relationships instill trust between leaders and MHPs such that commanding officers will often defer to the MHPs judgment about a service member's disposition without intruding on the service member's privacy or forcing the MHP to violate confidentiality.

Develop and abide by an ethical decision-making process. Although mixed-agency dilemmas can naturally provoke anxiety in the MHP, it is imperative that professionals avoid rapid or impulsive responses to either clients or organizational leaders. Beginning with a *best-interests* mindset, the military MHP will be well served to avoid deciding quickly that a lawful order or federal statue trumps an ethical standard, or that a federal regulation is inappropriate and therefore should be ignored in favor of ethical considerations. MHPs should adopt one of several deliberate processes for making careful and reasoned ethical decisions (e.g., Barnett & Johnson, 2008; Koocher & Keith-Spiegel, 2008). At the least, these decision-making models will encourage the MHP to clearly define the situation, determine whom will be affected by the decision, consider guidance from relevant ethical guidelines and legal statutes, seek appropriate consultation, formulate alternative courses of action considering the consequences of each, and most important, the MHP's obligations to each party involved in the mixed-agency dilemma.

Emphasize evidence-supported spiritual or religious interventions. The United States military and other government institutions are generally secular in character and mission. Although military service members occupy the full spectrum in terms of personal religious commitment, there is a strong tradition of distinguishing the role of chaplain from that of mental health provider in military psychology and psychiatry. Of course, this does not imply that Christian MHPs must avoid discussion of religious faith or refrain from engaging in competent religiously accommodative practice in government settings (Worthington & Sandage, 2002). William Hathaway (2006) offered several excellent examples of cases in which he provided spiritually sensitive and religiously accommodative interventions in an Air Force medical clinic. In several instances Hathaway's understanding of clients' religious traditions and his expertise with accommodating elements of client faith with clinical interventions proved invaluable in promoting good outcomes. In at least one case, his ability to work within the client's religious framework proved essential to understanding the diagnosis and making an accurate recommendation to the commanding officer.

There are two caveats for Christian MHPs to consider when engaging in religiously accommodative interventions in government contexts. First, religious clinicians in secular contexts should be prepared to show evidence supporting their approach (Worthington & Sandage, 2002). By now, several sectarian approaches to counseling and psychotherapy enjoy at least preliminary empirical support. Christian providers should be ready to nondefensively discuss their rationale and supporting evidence for religious assessment and intervention strategies when questioned by supervisors or other health care colleagues.

A second caveat has to do with tolerance and acceptance of divergent religious traditions. When an MHP accepts employment in the military or other branch of government service, he or she accepts an obligation to be open, respectful and maximally helpful to every client he or she encounters. Christian MHPs should expect to encounter clients from every imaginable religious background as well as clients that are overtly and vocally hostile toward religion. Because military MHPs are often solo providers in small and isolated military bases, they cannot elect to refer clients or refuse to offer treatment. Thus, an MHP who was uncomfortable with not including spirituality or religion as a component of his or her work would not be a good fit in this context. Hathaway (2006), a Christian psychologist working in an Air Force clinic, modeled the kind of Christlike openness I am referring to here when he described working sensitively and helpfully with a twenty-five-year-old Wiccan (witch) Staff Sergeant who was suffering depression.

CONCLUSION

Sooner or later most mental health professionals will encounter an ethical dilemma born of the simultaneous commitment to two or more entities; most often, this will involve a conflict between the MHP's loyalty to a client and obligations to a larger organization. Such mixed-agency quandaries require ethical practitioners to proceed thoughtfully in sorting out competing obligations to each entity without causing harm and while honoring relevant ethical principles and standards. Mixed-agency dilemmas are most prevalent in government agencies such as the military, but MHPs in other settings such as medical centers, correctional facilities, schools and churches should be equally alert for client-organization conflicts. Christian MHPs must additionally remain sensitive to three-dimensional mixed-agency dilemmas that occur when personal faith and religious beliefs increase tension between obligations to clients or organizations.

When, not if, mixed-agency dilemmas arise, MHPs are encouraged to adopt a best-interests mindset, asking, In this context, how can I work to reduce the apparent conflict between my obligations to an individual client and the larger organization while promoting the best interests of each? Better outcomes will be achieved when MHPs provide rigorous and ongoing informed consent to all clients in organizational settings, assume that each member of the community may ultimately become a client, abide by a clear ethical decision-making process, establish positive working relationships with senior members of the organization, and seek consultation as needed from seasoned MHPs with expertise in organizational practice.

REFERENCES

American Psychological Association. (2010). *Ethical principles of psychologists and code of conduct: 2010 Amendments*. Retrieved on April 2, 2010, from www.apa .org/news/press/releases/2010/02/ethics-code.aspx.

Annas, G. J. (2008). Military medical ethics: Physician first, last, and always. *New England Journal of Medicine, 359,* 1087-90.

Barnett, J. E., & Johnson, W. B. (2008). *The ethics desk reference for psychologists.* Washington, DC: American Psychological Association.

Camp, N. M. (1993). The Vietnam War and the ethics of combat psychiatry. *American Journal of Psychiatry, 150,* 1000-1010.

Department of Defense (1993). National Defense Authorization Act for Fiscal Year 1994 (Pub L., 1-3-160, 107 Stat. 1547). Washington, DC: Department of Defense.

Driskell, J. E., & Olmstead, B. (1989). Psychology and the military: Research applications and trends. *American Psychologist, 44,* 43-54.

Hathaway, W. L. (2006). Religious diversity in the military clinic: Four cases. *Military Psychology, 18,* 247-57.

Hoge, C. W., Castro, C. A., Messer, S. C., McGurk, D., Cotting, D. I., & Koffman, R. L. (2004). Combat duty in Iraq and Afghanistan, mental health problems, and barriers to care. *New England Journal of Medicine, 351,* 13-22.

Howe, E. G. (1986). Ethical issues regarding mixed agency of military physicians. *Social Science & Medicine, 23,* 803-15.

Howe, E. G. (2003). Mixed agency in military medicine: Ethical roles in conflict. In D. E. Lounsbury & R. F. Bellamy (Eds.), *Military Medical Ethics,* vol. 1 (pp. 331-65). Falls Church, VA: Office of the Surgeon General, U.S. Department of the Army.

Jeffrey, T. B., Rankin, R. J., & Jeffrey, L. K. (1992). In service of two masters: The ethical-legal dilemma faced by military psychologists. *Professional Psychology: Research and Practice, 23,* 91-95.

Johnson, W. B. (1995). Perennial ethical quandaries in military psychology: Toward American Psychological Association-Department of Defense collaboration. *Professional Psychology: Research and Practice, 26,* 281-87.

Johnson, W. B. (2008). Top ethical challenges for military clinical psychologists. *Military Psychology, 20,* 49-62.

Johnson, W. B., Grasso, I., & Maslowski, K. (2010). Conflicts between ethics and law for military mental health providers. *Military Medicine, 175,* 548-53.

Johnson, W. B., & Kennedy, C. H. (2010). Preparing psychologists for high-risk jobs: Key ethical considerations for military clinical supervisors. *Professional Psychology: Research and Practice, 41,* 298-304.

Johnson, W. B., & Koocher, G. P. (2012). *Ethical conundrums, quandaries, and predicaments in mental health practice: Cases from the files of experts.* New York: Oxford University Press.

Johnson, W. B., Ralph, J., & Johnson, S. J. (2005). Managing multiple roles in embedded environments: The case of aircraft carrier psychology. *Professional Psychology: Research and Practice, 36,* 73-81.

Johnson, W. B., & Wilson, K. (1993). The military internship: A retrospective analysis. *Professional Psychology: Research and Practice,* 24, 312-18.

Kennedy, C. H., & Johnson, W. B. (2009). Mixed agency in military psychology: Applying the American Psychological Association Ethics Code. *Psychological Services, 6,* 22-31.

Kennedy, C. H., & McNeil, J. A. (2006). A history of military psychology. In C. H. Kennedy & E. A. Zillmer (Eds.), *Military psychology: Clinical and operational applications.* New York: Guilford Press.

Kennedy, C. H., & Zillmer, E. A. (2006). *Military psychology: Clinical and operational applications.* New York: Guilford Press.

Koocher, G. P., & Keith-Spiegel, P. (2008). *Ethics in psychology: Professional standards and cases* (3rd ed.). New York: Oxford University Press.

Kraft, H. S. (2007). *Rule number two: Lessons I learned in a combat hospital.* New York: Little Brown.

Moore, B. A., & Reger, G. M. (2006). Clinician as frontline soldier: A look at the roles and challenges of Army clinical psychologists in Iraq. *Journal of Clinical Psychology, 62,* 395-403.

Orme, D. R., & Doerman, A. L. (2001). Ethical dilemmas and U. S. Air Force clinical psychologists: A survey. *Professional Psychology: Research and Practice, 32,* 305-11.

Page, G. D. (1996). Clinical psychology in the military: Developments and issues. *Clinical Psychology Review, 16,* 383-96.

Porter, T. L., & Johnson, W. B. (1994). Psychiatric stigma in the military. *Military Medicine, 159,* 602-5.

Stall, M. A., & King, R. E. (2000). Managing a dual relationship environment: The ethics of military psychology. *Professional Psychology: Research and Practice, 31,* 698-705.

Worthington, E., Jr., & Sandage, S. (2002). Religion and spirituality. In J. C. Norcross (Ed.), *Psychotherapy relationships that work: Therapist contributions and responsiveness to patients* (pp. 383-99). New York: Oxford University Press.

17

Ethical Issues in University Counseling Centers

Roderick D. Hetzel, Cassie Kendrick
and Susan Matlock-Hetzel

This chapter discusses ethical issues commonly encountered by university counseling center (UCC) clinicians. The specific issues covered in this chapter include, among others, those related to privacy and confidentiality, which have received increased attention in the wake of campuswide crises such as the mass killing at Virginia Tech, areas of potential conflict between professional ethical standards and the policies and procedures of the university, ethical issues related to multiple relationships, ethical issues related to competence and integrating religion and spirituality in the delivery of clinical services. Although the specific issues will likely differ from one institution to the next, it is hoped that this chapter will address the needs of clinicians who serve in Christian universities as well as Christian clinicians who work in secular settings.

To provide a foundation for understanding privacy and confidentiality in the university setting, this chapter begins with a discussion of the Federal Educational Rights and Privacy Act (FERPA) and the implications for UCCs. With this foundation established, the chapter then addresses specific ethical issues commonly encountered by UCC clinicians. Each ethical issue will be discussed using the following format: (1) case study to illustrate the ethical issue, (2) review of salient ethical principles and standards, and (3) guidance and suggestions for responding to the ethical issue. This section is meant to provide a brief overview and application of ethical issues commonly encountered in UCC settings. Readers interested in a more thorough discussion of these principles and standards are encouraged to consult the other chapters in this book. This chapter concludes by offering some general guidelines for the UCC clinician to consider in responding to ethical dilemmas that may arise in UCC settings.

Throughout this chapter we will use the general term *clinician* to refer to psychologists, counselors and other mental health professionals working in a UCC setting. When referencing professional ethical principles or standards, we will use the "Ethical Principles of Psychologists and Code of Conduct" published by the American Psychological Association (APA, 2002). Clinicians who are not affiliated with the APA should refer to the ethical standards published by their respective professional associations.

FERPA AND UNIVERSITY COUNSELING CENTERS

The ethics of student privacy and confidentiality have received increasing public attention and scrutiny, particularly in the wake of campus tragedies such as the mass killing at Virginia Tech in 2007. International news coverage and widespread criticism of U.S. gun laws as well as university policies and procedures for responding to students who pose a risk of harm to others followed in the wake of this tragic story. In two separate incidents that occurred approximately two hours apart, student Seung-Hui Cho killed thirty-two people and wounded many others before eventually committing suicide. This mass killing is one of the deadliest shooting incidents by a single gunman in U.S. history, either on or off a college campus. Although Cho's mental status and psychological diagnosis at the time of the shooting are unknown, it is now known that Cho had a history of mental health treatment, was involved in university disciplinary action after stalking two female students, and had drawn the concern of at least one of his professors. After this tragedy, questions arose about whether university personnel should have shared information about Cho's behavior and, by extension, the behavior of any potentially troubled student with other university personnel, family members or other mental health or law enforcement agencies.

In discussing privacy and confidentiality in the university setting, it is important to understand FERPA (U.S. Department of Education, 2008). First created in 1974, FERPA contains information about federal laws pertaining to the release of and access to student educational records. FERPA regulations establish that educational agencies and institutions that receive funding from programs administered by the U.S. Department of Education have a legal obligation to provide students with access to their education records, opportunities to have their records amended and some degree of control over the disclosure of information from the records. In this context the term *educational records* refers to all records containing information directly related to a student and maintained by an educational agency or institution or by a party acting on its behalf. This includes information recorded in handwriting, print, tape, film, microfilm, microfiche and digital image.

With few exceptions, universities must have a student's consent prior to the disclosure of education records. One authorized exception is allowing faculty and staff to share information with one another when there is a "legitimate educational interest" (99 CFR 31). As an example, a university professor who is concerned about a student's disturbing classroom behavior would be allowed, under FERPA regulations, to consult with other faculty and staff, such as the department chair or a UCC clinician, as this would be construed as a "legitimate educational interest." In the Virginia Tech situation, it would have been permissible for the English professor who witnessed Cho's disturbing classroom behavior to share this information and consult with her Chair or other university personnel who may have been able to provide Cho needed assistance or help the professor respond to his behavior. It is a misinterpretation of FERPA to assume that faculty and staff are not able to share information with each other about potentially troubled students.

A recent modification of FERPA that occurred after Virginia Tech includes exceptions for health and safety emergencies that allow universities to share information with family members or other individuals. As stated in 34 CFR 99.36:

> An educational agency or institution may take into account the totality of the circumstances pertaining to a threat to the health or safety of a student or other individuals. If the educational agency or institution determines that there is an articulable and significant threat to the health or safety of a student

or other individuals, it may disclose information from education records to any person whose knowledge of the information is necessary to protect the health or safety of the student or other individuals. If, based on the information available at the time of the determination, there is a rational basis for the determination, the Department will not substitute its judgment for that of the educational agency or institution in evaluating the circumstances and making its determination.

Because FERPA deals with student educational records, it does not apply to observations and oral communications, so university personnel may share these with law enforcement, parents or other parties as needed.

How does FERPA apply to UCCs and mental health records? FERPA (34 CFR 99.3) states that the term *education records* does not apply to those documents or records

> made or maintained by a physician, psychiatrist, psychologist, or other recognized professional or paraprofessional acting in his or her professional capacity or assisting in a paraprofessional capacity; made, maintained or used only in connection with treatment of the student; and disclosed only to individuals providing the treatment.

To clarify this definition, it is noted that the term *treatment* does not include remedial educational activities or activities that are part of the instructional program of the university. As such, any information that is included in the UCC's medical or clinical record cannot be released under FERPA regulations. Although FERPA allows university personnel to share information about students under certain conditions, licensed mental health professionals must act in accordance with their profession's ethical standards and state mental health law. For university personnel who also provide mental health services under a state license, the higher standard is not FERPA but their profession's ethical standards and state mental health law. In most cases this means that UCC clinicians may not release information about a student who is receiving mental health treatment, unless it falls under the standard ethical and legal exceptions to confidentiality (e.g., imminent threat of harm to self or others).

To investigate the problem of school violence, the U.S. Secret Service and U.S. Department of Education (2004) published their final report and findings of the "Safe School Initiative," which was the culmination of an extensive examination of thirty-seven incidents of targeted school violence that occurred in the United States from December 1974 through May 2000. This initiative was searching for answers to two pressing questions: "Could we have known that these attacks were being planned?" and, if so, "What could we have done to prevent these attacks from occurring?" The report concluded that the majority of targeted school attacks are the individual's first violent incident. They discovered that violent acts are neither sudden nor impulsive, but the

> end result of a comprehensible process of thinking and behavior: behavior that typically began with an idea, progressed to the development of a plan, moved on to securing the means to carry out the plan and culminated in an attack. This is a process that potentially may be knowable or discernible from the attacker's behaviors and communications. (p. 32)

They discovered some association between mental illness (most notably having difficulty coping with significant losses or personal failures, or feeling bullied, persecuted, or injured by others) and violence, but reported that most attackers had not received a mental health evaluation, been diagnosed with a mental health disorder or been involved in substance abuse. The report concluded that there is no accurate or useful profile of students who engaged in target school violence.

In the aftermath of Virginia Tech, there has been a push in university settings to identify students who pose a potential risk of harm to themselves or others. All universities should have some process or system to manage the mental health, discipline and judicial problems of students, and a challenge for university administration is to balance the individual rights of the student with the protection of the larger community. One approach for identifying students at risk is to use a campus intervention team or "students of concern" team. Delworth (2009) stated that a campus intervention team should consist, at a minimum, of staff from the UCC, campus police or security, student services administration, student services judicial or disciplinary office, and legal counsel. Delworth (2009) further noted the primary responsibilities of such campus intervention teams:

> First, the team should help develop (or at least approve) policies and proce-

dures to assess students and assign them to specific systems within the institution. Second, the team should be kept apprised of such assignments. The third and most time-consuming function of the team is to develop and implement assessment and intervention programs for students who are either initially assessed as disturbed/disturbing or do not profit from initial assignments. (p. 17)

Because of their training and experience in college student mental health, UCC clinicians may be asked to participate on campus intervention teams. The role of the UCC representative on such teams can vary, depending on the needs and culture of the university, but likely will include helping university officials to develop policies or procedures for identifying at-risk students in the hopes of preventing or more quickly responding to campus emergencies. Participation in a campus intervention team can pose unique challenges for the UCC representative. For example, the UCC representative must maintain the confidentiality of students who are either past or current clients, even when the names of such students are raised during team meeting. Other university staff may not have knowledge about state mental health laws and ethical obligations regarding confidentiality, so it is incumbent for the UCC representative to explain his or her legal and ethical obligations to the team upon its formation. The UCC representative could function as a "silent member" on the team, to receive information from the team about particular students and as needed to communicate information from the team to other UCC clinicians for the purposes of facilitating and coordinating effective treatment.

The UCC representative on a campus intervention team is also cautioned about making diagnoses about students who are discussed during team meetings. Psychological diagnoses can only be made after an appropriate psychological assessment (which requires, at a very minimum, a clinical interview with the student and may also require psychological testing). Along similar lines it is important for university personnel to remember the findings of the Safe School Initiative. The mental health profession is limited in its ability to accurately predict violence. As a result, more emphasis should be given to the development of campuswide threat assessment teams that are more idiographic in their approach. Instead of relying on predetermined profiles, which have limited validity, threat assessment teams are able to look at individual patterns of thought and behaviors in an effort to determine whether a particular student is progressing in the direction of violence.

The Safe School Initiative outlines the reasons for using idiographic data rather than predetermined profiles:

> The use of profiles in this way likewise is not an effective approach to identifying students who may pose a risk for targeted school violence at school or for assessing the risk that a particular student may pose for a school-based attack, once a particular student has been identified. Reliance on profiles to predict future school attacks carries two substantial risks: (1) the great majority of students who fit any given profile of a "school shooter" will not actually pose a risk of targeted violence; and, (2) using profiles will fail to identify some students who in fact pose a risk of violence but share few if any characteristics with prior attackers.
>
> Rather than trying to determine the "type" of student who may engage in targeted school violence, an inquiry should focus instead on a student's behaviors and communications to determine if that student appears to be planning or preparing for an attack. Rather than asking whether a particular student "looks like" those who have launched school-based attacks before, it is more productive to ask whether the student is engaging in behaviors that suggest preparations for an attack, if so how fast the student is moving toward attack, and where intervention may be possible. (p. 34)

The interested reader should consult Reddy et al (2001), who provide additional information and resources on assessment strategies for schools.

ETHICAL ISSUES COMMON TO UNIVERSITY COUNSELING CENTERS

Informed consent. Case 1. A seventeen-year-old undergraduate student presents to the UCC with symptoms of depression. The UCC serves as a training site for a clinical psychology doctoral program, and the client is assigned to an initial intake appointment with a practicum student who is being supervised by a licensed psychologist. The client lives in a campus residential hall. What are the ethical issues involved with this case?

This case highlights two ethical issues related to informed consent that commonly occur in UCC settings: services provided by nonlicensed trainees and services provided to minors. Informed consent is addressed under Standards 3.10 (Informed Consent), 8.02 (Informed Consent to Research), 9.03 (Informed Consent in Assessments), and 10.01 (Informed Consent to Therapy). In summary, these ethical standards mandate that psychologists providing professional services (i.e., research, assessment, therapy, counseling or consulting) must obtain informed consent from the persons who are receiving services, using language that is understandable by such persons. In other words, clients must be fully informed of the professional services they will receive and give their consent to receive or participate in the services.

Before discussing the specific issues regarding informed consent in this case, it is important to remember some key points. First, informed consent is best understood as a process that involves an ongoing discussion between therapist and client, rather than a one-time event occurring only at the start of treatment. Second, informed consent cannot be retroactively given after treatment has started. UCC clinicians should describe clinical services prior to initiation of the professional relationship using language that is accessible to the client. The clinician should continue this discussion as needed over the course of treatment. Third, the informed consent process should provide clear information about the treatment plan, changes in treatment plan if necessary and the potential risks and benefits of treatment. Finally, informed consent must be documented in the medical record. This generally means written documentation (typically in the form of an informed consent form signed and dated by the client, with accompanying documentation by the clinician in a separate clinical note), but could include documentation through audiotape or videotape.

The first issue raised in the present case is the provision of professional services by nonlicensed trainees. Many UCCs serve as training sites for graduate students in psychology, counseling and other mental health professions. Standard 10.01(c) states: "When the therapist is a trainee and the legal responsibility for the treatment provided resides with the supervisor, the client/patient, as part of the informed consent procedure, is informed that the therapist is in training and is being supervised and is given the name of the supervisor." In this case, as part of the informed consent process, the trainee is required to inform the client of his or her trainee status and the name of the trainee's supervisor. It is recommended that this information be included on a written consent form that the client would read and sign, but also discussed with the client as early as is feasible in the process. Good clinical practice also would involve the trainee discussing any concerns or questions the client might have about how the trainee's status might impact the proposed treatment.

Additionally, it is important to note that some states require nonlicensed trainees to audiotape or videotape their sessions for the purposes of clinical supervision. If sessions are recorded, trainees are required to obtain the written (and, preferably, verbal) consent from clients to record the sessions. This issue is addressed in Standard 4.03. This process would include informing clients that sessions are being recorded, explaining the reasons for recording, providing information about how the recordings will be used and how long they will be maintained, and discussing any questions or concerns the client may have about being recorded. If a client is not willing to consent to recording, then the client should be assigned to a licensed clinician.

The second issue in the present case involved providing services to minors. It is not uncommon for UCC clinicians to work with students, most often first-year students, who have not reached the age of majority. In this situation, are minors able to provide their own informed consent, or are clinicians required to obtain parental consent before starting treatment? This issue is not directly addressed in the ethical standards, so UCC clinicians are advised to consult their state's mental health laws. For example, the Texas Family Code (sec. 32.003) states that minors are legally permitted to provide their own informed consent, without parental consent, under the following conditions:

- the minor is active duty with the Armed Services
- the minor is sixteen years old or older and lives apart from parents, with or without their consent, regardless of duration, and manages their own financial affairs regardless of income
- the minor is unmarried and pregnant and seeking medical services for purposes other than abortion
- the minor presents with drug or chemical use, abuse, addiction, suicidal ideation or sexual, physical, or emotional abuse

In the present case the client would be able to consent to treatment because she is sixteen years or older and lives in campus housing, apart from her parents. It is assumed, but not directly mentioned in the present case, that the client manages her own financial resources. In other words, she is responsible for how she spends her money, regardless of whether she receives money from employment, university or federal financial assistance, or her family. In this case, in addition to obtaining informed consent from the client, it is recommended that clinicians document the specific conditions that allow the minor client to consent to treatment. This is most easily done by having a second consent form for minors (in addition to the UCC's standard consent form) that clinicians provide to their minor clients to read and sign.

Although some states permit clinicians to rely on the minor's written statement containing the grounds by which they can consent for treatment, states may also allow clinicians to release information, with or without consent of the minor, to the parents of the minor. In Texas, mental health professionals may release information to parents regarding treatment provided or needed under the following circumstances: sexual, physical or emotional abuse; suicidal ideation; or chemical or drug addiction or dependency. This possibility should be addressed during the informed consent process and discussed with the client if the need arises to disclose this information to parents. In these situations parents have the *right to request access* to their minor student's medical record, but this is not the same as having a *legal right to the record*. The mental health professional and minor student still decide whether to release the information. Again, clinicians are advised to consult their state mental health laws and legal counsel for more information.

Confidentiality. Case 2. A student was referred to the UCC by his residence hall director, who discovered that he has been drinking alcohol on campus. Although this is a violation of official university policy clearly stated in the student handbook, the residence hall director decided not to pursue disciplinary action against the student because he knows the student has been depressed since the recent death of a close friend. After the fifth session of counseling, the residence hall director calls the clinician asking for an update on the student's progress, stating he is concerned because the student has not been attending classes. Later that week the clinician receives an angry phone call from the student's mother. She states that she is paying a lot of money for her son's education and demands to know what the clinician is doing to help her son. What are the ethical issues involved with this case?

This case highlights the often troubling ethical issues of privacy and confidentiality commonly encountered in UCC settings. How can the clinician protect the privacy and confidentiality of his or her clients, and under what circumstances can the clinician release information about clients to other university personnel and family members? In these situations UCC clinicians may find themselves facing a conflict between their profession's ethical standards and the demands of the institution. For example, some student affairs administrators may mandate counseling as an alternative to dismissal for university policy violations. Moreover, some Christian colleges (and some parents) may subscribe to a form of *in loco parentis*, believing that the college (and, by extension, the UCC) have a responsibility to serve as surrogate parents. Thus, clinicians may experience pressure to loosen confidentiality restrictions beyond mandates set forth by professional ethical standards and state law.

In responding to the ethical issues in this case, it is important to understand the distinctions between privacy, confidentiality and privilege. Privacy is considered a basic right granted by the Fourth Amendment to the U.S. Constitution. It is a broad concept that applies to all people and not just clients. Privacy is considered essential to ensure human dignity, which is outlined in Principle E, and forms the basis for the concepts of confidentiality and privilege. Confidentiality is a standard of professional conduct to protect and not reveal any information about a client. It is both an ethical standard (outlined in Standard 4) and a legal status. As such, any breach of confidentiality is subject to both ethical and legal action. Privilege, according to Koocher and Keith-Spiegel (1998), is a "legal term describing certain specific types of relationships that enjoy protection from disclosure in legal proceedings" (p. 58). Legally, the client is considered to own the privilege, although the clinician can claim privilege on behalf of the client.

According to Standard 4.05, clinicians are permitted to disclose information only if the client consents to release the information, or if the clinician is mandated or permitted by law to release information regardless of client consent. In general, confidentiality does not apply if any of the following conditions occur: (1) the client poses a risk of imminent harm to self or others, (2) the client reports abuse or neglect of a child, disabled person or elderly person, or (3) the client reports sexual misconduct by another mental health professional. The specific conditions in which clinicians are mandated to release information and the manner in which they are to release the information may vary from state to state. Thus, clinicians are advised to consult their state mental health laws and state professional associations for more information.

In the present case the clinician is not permitted to disclose information about the client—either to the concerned residence hall director or the client's angry mother—unless the client provides his consent. UCC clinicians may find themselves repeating that state laws prevent them from "either confirming or denying" that a particular student is a client. This might involve some difficult conversations with the third party, but it is important that the privacy and confidentiality of the client be maintained. One approach for responding to this situation would be for the clinician to listen attentively and respond with empathy to the concerns of the third party, but also to educate the third party about ethical standards and state laws. It can be hard for parents to balance their need for communication and assurance that their children are safe with their desire to help their children become autonomous adults. A little empathy from the clinician can go a long way and ultimately help both the client and the client's parents cope with the demands of individuation.

In responding to requests for information, it is permissible for the clinician to refer the third party to other university personnel (e.g., dean of students, university chaplain, vice-president of student affairs, or other personnel designated as resources for concerned staff or parents) who may be able to share more information about the student. Remember, clinicians are prohibited by state law from releasing information about clients, but other university personnel have more latitude under FERPA. When clinicians deny a request to release information, some third parties may appeal to higher administrative authorities at the university by asking to speak with the UCC director, dean, vice-president or even the president. In these situations it is important that the clinician use the opportunity to inform the other university personnel about relevant requirements of ethical standards and state law. Standards 3.07 and 3.11 state that psychologists should inform all parties as soon as possible about the role of the psychologist and the client, the probable uses of the services provided or the information obtained, and the potential limits to confidentiality. In the context of UCCs, this means clarifying the limits of confidentiality with clients during the informed consent process, but also informing university personnel about potential limits to confidentiality. In the current age of litigation, most university personnel understand the need to adhere to ethics and law, although in high-pressure crisis situations they may need a gentle reminder.

Of course, there may be some situations in which it would be clinically indicated for the clinician to release information to parents or other university personnel (e.g., to ensure social support, secure needed resources or obtain other assistance), but this disclosure would need to be incorporated into the treatment plan and therapy process. If such disclosure involved a modification of the treatment plan that was agreed upon at the start of treatment, then the client would need to provide informed consent to modify the treatment plan as well as to release information to a third party. In these situations the clinician is advised to obtain the client's consent about (1) what type of information is to be released, (2) to which third-party individuals, and (3) for which purpose(s). Clients also should be informed about the process for revoking their consent to release information.

There are other situations regarding privacy and confidentiality that are common to UCC settings. As e-mail, text messages and other forms of electronic communication are becoming more common, students should be informed that e-mail is neither a private nor confidential form of communication. E-mail is retained in the logs of service providers and may be stored on personal computers that send and receive the e-mail. As with other unsecured electronic communication, e-mail is vulnerable to third-party interference and potentially could be accessed by unauthorized persons without the sender's or receiver's permission. UCCs are advised to develop a procedure or policy for responding to student e-mails or using electronic communication. UCC clinicians may also encounter privacy and confidentiality issues when students apply for positions as they near graduation. Applications for medical boards, state bars, military and federal agencies, and religious denominations may require students to report if they have ever received mental health services, and in some cases may require applicants to provide consent to release information. This possibility should be discussed with students during the informed consent process.

Multiple relationships. Case 3. A UCC clinician delivers the first part of a two-part outreach presentation on stress management to undergraduate students at a residence hall. At the end of the presentation a female student approaches her, tells her that she feels overwhelmed by stress and asks if she could begin counseling with her. What are the ethical issues involved with this case?

UCC clinicians, particularly those who are employed at smaller colleges, are often faced with situations in which they must interact with students in multiple settings. A key ethical issue in this case is multiple relationships. Standard 3.05(a) states: "A multiple relationship occurs when a psychologist is in a professional role with a person and (1) at the same time is in another role with the same person, (2) at the same time is in a relationship with a person closely associated with or related to the person with whom the psychologist has the professional relationship, or (3) promises to enter into another relationship in the future with the person or a person closely associated with or related to the person."

This standard also refrains a psychologist from entering into a multiple relationship if it could reasonably be expected to either "impair the psychologist's objectivity, competence, or effectiveness in performing his or her functions as a psychologist," or if there is any risk of "exploitation or harm to the person with whom the professional relationship exists."

The ethical standards further state that multiple relationships are not unethical if they would not be expected to cause impairment of the clinician or risk exploitation or harm to the client. In case 3, the UCC clinician would need to determine if providing clinical services to the student while she is also providing outreach services to the student would constitute risk of impairment or exploitation/harm. At first glance it would appear that there are no reasonable expectations for impairment or exploitation/harm, and that the clinician could proceed with the student's request. This depends, however, on the specifics of the situation. If the UCC clinician were assigned to provide ongoing outreach services to that particular residence hall, then she would need to consider the type of future contact she might have with the student. How likely would the clinician's future contact with the student impair her objectivity either in providing outreach or counseling? In providing outreach to the residence hall, does the clinician have any administrative or disciplinary responsibilities that could harm the client (which could also fall under 3.06 Conflicts of Interest and 3.08 Exploitative Relationships)?

UCC clinicians are likely to experience other types of multiple relationships in the regular course of their work. For example, if a clinician is also teaching a class at the university, should she accept one of her current students as a counseling client? Most clinicians would agree that this would constitute a multiple relationship that could potentially impair the clinician's objectivity or risk exploitation or harm to the student. Thus, accepting the student as a client would not be considered ethical. What if the specifics of the situation were changed? If the class were a large undergraduate class and were taught by a graduate teaching assistant who was supervised by the clinician, would the clinician be able to accept the student as a client? If the student had been enrolled in the clinician's class during a previous semester but was not currently enrolled in one of her classes, how would that change the ethical decision-making process? In making such decisions, which at times can be complex, clinicians are urged to return to these two core questions: What is the likelihood of impairment in objectivity or competence? What is the risk of exploitation or harm to the client?

Competence. Case 4. A student presents to the UCC for assistance with a depressed mood following the breakup of a romantic relationship. The clinician diagnoses him with Adjustment Disorder with Depressed Mood and recommends short-term supportive counseling. The client consents to this treatment plan, but also states that his Christian faith is important to him and he would like "Christian counseling" that integrates spiritual issues into therapy. What are the ethical issues involved with this case?

As with the other examples in this chapter, this case represents a familiar situation, not only for UCC clinicians working at Christian universities but also to clinicians working at universities with no religious affiliation. One key ethical issue in this case is the issue of competence. What does the client mean by "Christian counseling?" Does he want a biblically based counseling approach to help him discover areas in which he may be disobedient to the principles and commands outlined in Scripture and to help him learn how to lovingly submit to God's will? Does he want pastoral counseling that can weave spiritual and religious themes throughout therapy and offer advice and guidance within a broader Christian context? Does he want the clinician to pray with him and read verses from the Bible or other sacred texts? Does he want the clinician to hold a Christian faith? Or does he simply want a clinician who will be sensitive to spiritual issues and affirmative of his Christian faith, should he choose to discuss it? The term *Christian counseling* can mean many things, and it is important for the clinician to discover what it means for his individual client.

It is important for clinicians to address these often complex questions about how to integrate religion and spirituality into treatment. Gallup and Lindsay (1999) reported survey results from U.S. respondents showing the following:

- 96% believe in God

- 90% pray to God

- 87% say religion is important in their life

- 82% report a need to experience spiritual growth

- 71% report interest in developing a relationship with God

- 80% value prayer in response to a crisis

- 64% value Bible reading in response to a crisis

- Over 100 million are involved in faith-based small groups

Although these results suggest that many Americans believe in a supreme being and report that religion and spirituality are important to them, many clinicians have not received adequate training in how to address religious and spiritual issues in therapy. Discussing the content of ethics and diversity courses, Yarhouse (2005) noted that most training programs overlook religion and spirituality, placing greater emphasis on other underserved populations and diversity issues related to gender, ethnicity and sexual orientation.

Yet clinicians have an ethical mandate to address issues of religion and spirituality in therapy. Principle E states that psychologists must be "aware of and respect cultural, individual, and role differences, including those based on . . . religion . . . and consider these factors when working with members of such groups." Principle E further states that psychologist seek to "eliminate the effect on their work of biases based on those factors, and do not knowingly participate in or condone activities of others based upon such prejudices." Additionally, Standard 2.01 states that "psychologists provide services, teach, and conduct research with populations and in areas only within the boundaries of their competence, based on their education, training, supervised experience, consultation, study, or professional experience." This standard also states that psychologists obtain training and experience in those areas "where scientific or professional knowledge in the discipline of psychology establishes that an understanding of factors associated with . . . religion . . . is essential for effective implementation of their service." Shafranske and Malony (1996) affirmed this ethical mandate by stating that a client's religious or spiritual worldview is an important aspect of culture and is a central focus for many clients who seek psychological treatment. They further stated that clinicians "should keep an open mind and be willing to explore religious and spiritual concerns as an important component of cultural diversity."

In addition to an ethical mandate, clinicians also have an empirical mandate to address issues of religion and spirituality with their clients. Although empirical results are complex and have found both harmful and helpful expressions of religiosity, research has demonstrated that positive expressions of religion and spirituality are related to improved health outcomes on measures of coronary disease, emphysema, cirrhosis (Comstock & Partridge, 1972), depression (Catipovic-Veselica et al., 1995) and anxiety (Richards & Bergin, 2000). It is beyond the scope of the present chapter to provide a comprehensive review of this literature on religion, spirituality and health outcomes, so the interested reader is referred to these original sources and other reviews of the literature.

Affirming this empirical mandate, Watts (2001) reported that there is sufficient empirical support to indicate that "to ignore, discount, or pathologize the religious and spiritual beliefs of clients is unwise, unethical, and clinically irresponsible," and that clinicians working within the religious or spiritual framework of the client indeed "can practice both ethically and effectively." Sperry and Shafranske (2004) stated that religion and spirituality always must be considered in the clinical encounter. Even in those situations in which religion may appear to be less central to the client's worldview, it nonetheless may contribute to the process and outcome of therapy. They further stated that clinicians who are more attuned to religious and spiritual issues will "recognize the potential contribution of spirituality within a holistic understanding of the patient's presenting concerns, symptoms, resources, and life narrative and history."

In case 4, how should the clinician respond? The first recommendation would be for the clinician to clarify the client's request for "Christian counseling" and his desire to integrate spiritual issues into therapy. If the client is seeking a particular type of biblically based or Christian counseling, then the ethical course of action for the clinician would be to determine if she possessed the competence—that is, the professional knowledge, skills and training—to provide this treatment. If she is competent to provide this treatment, it would also be important for the clinician to determine if providing these services is consistent with the mission and goals of her department and university (e.g., can a clinician trained in a specific Christian counseling model offer those services in a secular university setting). If the clinician determines she is not competent to provide services, then a referral to another provider, such as another mental health professional or (depending on the needs of the client) a religious professional, is warranted. If a referral is made, the clinician should consider meeting with the client for a follow-up consultation appointment to ensure that he has made contact with potential referrals and, if needed, to help him resolve any problems that might have arisen in the referral process.

If the clinician determines that the client is not seeking a specific religiously based treatment modality but rather wishes to have the freedom to discuss religious and spiritual issues in a safe and supportive environment, then the clinician may determine that it would be ethical to provide services. Still, it would be important for the clinician to obtain the needed knowledge and skills to ensure she provides services that are both spiritually sensitive and faith affirmative, just as she would seek training for issues regarding gender, ethnicity, sexual orientation and other expressions of diversity. Fortunately, there are numerous opportunities for mental health professionals to obtain continuing education and training in this area, including workshops, online courses, books and journals.

In the present case example, if the clinician decides to provide services to the client, it is recommended that she conduct a brief assessment or screening to determine the role of religion and spirituality in the client's life. Sperry and Shafranske (2004) offered a helpful screening model, which included salience ("How important is faith in your life?"), integration into orienting system ("Tell me about your faith. How often do you practice your faith? What form does your faith take?"), role in coping ("Think of a time in your life when you experienced real distress. What were you facing? How did you cope with the distress? What was the role of faith?"), presenting complaints related to faith ("How are your concerns related to your faith?"), and resources and strain related to faith ("What resources does your faith offer to you? What sustains you? What stress or stressors stem from your faith?"). If the screening indicates that faith is salient for the client, Sperry and Shafranske recommended an in-depth interview for a more thorough assessment of religious and spiritual variables, including beliefs, affiliations, practices and rituals, moral prescriptions and proscriptions, family and community contexts, religious training and milestones, values-lifestyle congruence, religious motivation (e.g., intrinsic versus extrinsic), attachment style to God, God image (e.g., compensatory versus complementary), and religious coping style.

Aten and Leach (2009) provided useful guidelines for working with religious and spiritual issues. Their guidelines emphasized the importance of trusting the client's view of the therapeutic alliance, using relational experiences of the spiritual perspective as a potential point of connection, respecting clients' spiritual ideals (as they noted, "spiritual beliefs, practices, doubts, and victories are often woven together with most important events of one's life"), taking time to nonjudgmentally explore how clients conceptualize their beliefs, and exploring client resistance about openly discussing spiritual beliefs. They emphasized that clinicians should not underestimate the need to use therapeutically-supportive interventions to help clients understand the connection between their spiritual perspective and psychological difficulties. As Stanford (2008) noted, people of faith, particularly those who are diagnosed with mental disorders, often have received mixed messages about the links between their mental health and their faith, and many are told that they need to pray more and repent of their sin. When clients arrive at the UCC, they may be hesitant to discuss and fully explore the role of their faith. Clinicians should seek to empathically understand the ambivalence experienced by clients in such situations, but nonetheless should invite the client to discuss and explore the connection between their faith and presenting problems.

Plante (2009) provided a list of religious and spiritual tools that some clients might find to be a helpful component of therapy. Internal tools included prayer (described as an "ongoing conversation with the sacred"), meditation (including concentrative approaches that involve focused attention on an external object, mindfulness approaches that involve a detached observation of experiences, and transcendental meditation which involves the repetition of a mantra or sacred word to focus attention), and bibliotherapy. External tools, many of which would be practiced outside of therapy sessions, included attending community services and rituals, volunteering and charity work, cultivating ethical values and behaviors, facilitating forgiveness, gratitude and kindness, involvement with social justice causes, learning from spiritual models and teachers, acceptance of self and others, involvement with something larger than oneself, and appreciating the sacredness of life.

When integrating religious and spiritual issues in treatment within a Christian UCC, the question may arise about how UCC clinicians should address a client's moral behavior when that behavior is grossly inconsistent with the moral values supported or mandated by the university. For instance, does the UCC clinician have a moral or institutional responsibility to promote behavioral standards or expectation regarding substance use, sexual behavior or classroom cheating? Again, as licensed professionals our clinical work should be guided by state mental health laws and professional ethical standards. It also is important to remember that, unless otherwise stated, our client is the student, not the university. Our goal is not to help clients become the kind of persons the university believes they should become, but rather to help them to gain greater awareness of themselves, to develop and achieve their own life goals, and to structure their lives in ways that are congruent with their own beliefs and values. If a client's behavior is inconsistent with the behavioral standards of the Christian university, but it is not clinically relevant, then it should not be targeted for intervention.

This does not mean that behaviors inconsistent with the values of the university should not be discussed in counseling. The majority of traditional-age college students are working through issues of individuation, a normal developmental process which can involve questioning, challenging and even abandoning their prior religious beliefs and behaviors. This can lead some students to explore new beliefs and behaviors that may seem contradictory to the university's mission or behavioral standards. Although such behaviors might be interpreted by some merely as violations to university policy or evidence of declining morality, they may be more usefully understood as reflecting the "liminality" of a normal individuation process. From the Latin word *limen*, meaning threshold, *liminality* is a term that applies to those confusing and often painful stages of life when we stand in the "threshold," somewhere between leaving our "old life" and arriving at our "new life." Burleson (2011) offers this description of liminal space for college students:

> You've left one space but haven't quite yet entered another, which is always an odd place to be. In this space, you don't know where things are just yet . . . or exactly how things work. We are typically off balance, standing in these threshold places and most often uncomfortable. So, our response is to rush . . . either to rush backwards or forwards . . . just so that we can feel comfortable and balanced and in control again.

Understood from the perspective of liminality, clients who are expressing new beliefs or behaviors may be seen as attempting to navigate through a complex developmental process. They may know who they were, but they don't quite yet know who they are or who they will be. When these issues can be openly and honestly addressed in counseling, students will have the potential for tremendous growth, clarity and perspective.

In all clinical encounters involving religion and spirituality, the clinician should strive to build a strong therapeutic alliance in which the client feels heard and understood. It is important for clinicians to be aware of their own beliefs and values (and their countertransference) regarding religion and spirituality, thereby enabling them to be more fully present with and able to learn directly from the client. As Watts (2001) noted, "by taking a 'not-knowing' position and allowing clients to be the experts regarding their spiritual beliefs and values, counselors may open space for clients to thoughtfully reflect on the unique meanings they give their spirituality, both growth-enhancing and potentially growth-inhibiting meanings." The late Catholic priest Henri Nouwen (2000) offered an instructive metaphor for therapists working with religious and spiritual issues in treatment: "A friend once gave me a beautiful photograph of a water lily. I asked him how he had been able to take such a splendid picture. With a smile, he said, 'Well, I had to be very patient and very attentive. It was only after a few hours of compliments that the lily was willing to let me take her picture.'" Given patience and attention, clients will teach clinicians the inner meaning and significance of their faith.

GENERAL GUIDANCE FOR RESPONDING TO ETHICAL DILEMMAS

Even the most well-trained and well-informed clinician will encounter complex and, at times, troubling ethical dilemmas. The experienced UCC clinician will recognize that the issues discussed in this chapter represent a sample of the various ethical dilemmas that are likely to be encountered in UCC settings. In responding to ethical dilemmas, it should be remembered that the Preamble and General Principles are aspirational principles, whereas the Ethical Standards are enforceable rules. Clinicians should also remember that the same behavior that can lead to sanctions from an ethics committee can also produce criminal and civil charges, and this may differ from state to state. A misunderstanding or lack of awareness is not considered a viable defense to a charge of unethical conduct.

When making decisions, clinicians should consider their profession's ethics code, applicable laws (including FERPA, HIPAA and state mental health law), professional licensing board regulations and the policies of the university in which they work. Consultation and supervision with colleagues are important in responding to ethical dilemmas, but UCC clinicians should also consider consulting their university's legal counsel. National and state professional associations may also have consultation services for ethical dilemmas. Finally, it is recommended that all clinicians familiarize themselves with models of ethical decision making, such as the model proposed by Pope and Vasquez (2011). Another model for ethical decision making can be found in chapter twenty-one of this text. If clinicians discover that the demands of their university conflict with their ethical standards, they should discuss this conflict with the appropriate university administrators. As stated in Standard 1.03, psychologists should "clarify the nature of the conflict, make known their commitment to the Ethics Code and take reasonable steps to resolve the conflict consistent with the General Principles and Ethical Standards of the Ethics Code."

REFERENCES

American Psychological Association (2002). Ethical principles of psychologists and code of conduct. *American Psychologist, 57*, 1060-73. Also available (with 2010 amendments) from www.apa.org/ethics/code/index.aspx.

Aten, J. D., & Leach, M. M. (Eds.). (2009). *Spirituality and the therapeutic process: A comprehensive resource from intake through termination.* Washington, DC: American Psychological Association.

Burleson, B. (2011). In between: Responses to new student orientation readings. [Web Log post]. Retrieved from http://buspirituallife.wordpress.com.

Catipovic-Veselica, K.; Ilakovac, V.; Durjancek, J.; & Amidzc, V. (1995). Relationship of eight basic emotions with age, sex, education, satisfaction of life needs, and religion. *Psychological Reports, 77*, 115-21.

Comstock, G. W., & Partridge, K. B. (1972). Church attendance and health. *Journal of Chronic Disease, 25*, 665-72.

Delworth, U. (2009). Dealing with the behavioral and psychological problems of students. In J. H. Dunkle (Ed.), *New Directions for student services, 128*, 11-21. San Francisco: Jossey-Bass.

Gallup, G., & Lindsay, D. M. (1999). *Surveying the religious landscape: Trends in U.S. beliefs.* Harrisburg, PA: Morehouse.

Koocher, G. P., & Keith-Spiegel, P. (1998). *Ethics in psychology* (2nd ed.). New York: Oxford University Press.

Nouwen, H. J. M. (2000). *Clowning in Rome: Reflections on solitude, celibacy, prayer, and contemplation.* New York: Image.

Plante, T. G. (2009). *Spiritual practices in psychotherapy: Thirteen tools for enhancing psychological health.* Washington, DC: American Psychological Association.

Pope, K. S., & Vasquez, M. J. T. (2011). *Ethics in psychotherapy and counseling: A practical guide* (4th ed.). New York: John Wiley.

Reddy, M., Borum, R., Berglund, J., Vossekuil, B., Fein, R., & Modzeleski, W. (2001).

Evaluating risk for targeted violence in schools: Comparing risk assessment, threat assessment, and other approaches. *Psychology in the Schools, 38*, 157-72.

Richards, P. S., & Bergin, A. E. (Eds.). (2000). *Handbook of psychotherapy and religious diversity.* Washington, DC: American Psychological Association.

Shafranske, E. P., & Malony, H. N. (1990). Clinical psychologists' religious and spiritual orientations and their practice of psychotherapy. *Psychotherapy, 27*, 72-78.

Sperry, L., & Shafranske, E. P. (Eds.). (2004). *Spiritually oriented psychotherapy.* Washington, DC: American Psychological Association.

Stanford, M. S. (2008). *Grace for the afflicted: A clinical and biblical perspective on mental illness.* Downers Grove, IL: InterVarsity Press.

U.S. Department of Education. (2008). 34 CFR Part 99: Family Educational Rights and Privacy; final rule. Retrieved from www2.ed.gov/legislation/FedRegister/finrule/2008-4/120908a.pdf.

U.S. Secret Service and U.S. Department of Education. (2004). *The final report and findings of the Safe School Initiative: Implications for the prevention of school attacks in the United States.* Retrieved from www2.ed.gov/admins/lead/safety/preventingattacksreport.pdf.

Watts, R. E. (2001). Addressing spiritual issues in secular counseling and psychotherapy: Response to Helminiak's view. *Counseling and Values, 45*, 207-17.

Yarhouse, M. A. (2005). Constructive relationships between religion and the scientific study of sexuality. *Journal of Psychology and Christianity, 24*, 29-35.

18

Ethics in Member Care

Toward an International Framework

Kelly O'Donnell

I will prescribe *regimens for the good of my patients according to my ability and my judgment and* never do harm *to anyone.*
—Hippocratic Oath, 4th century BC

Darts hit their mark when carefully thrown.
Words travel far when skilfully sown.
—Sem Tob, 14th century AD

All human beings are born free and equal in dignity and rights . . . and should act towards one another in a spirit of brotherhood.
—Universal Declaration of Human Rights, 1948

This chapter outlines important considerations for providing ethical "member care" to the diversity of mission/aid workers around the world.[1] Responsible ethics in international settings must reflect principles that complement, yet go beyond, our usual professional codes. What are some of the main issues, and what are some of the helpful guidelines that can be used by the different types of member care workers (MCWs), including

[1] Many thanks to Dr. Steve Allison for his input and encouragement regarding this chapter. Much of the material is excerpted/adapted from *Global Member Care: The Pearls and Perils of Good Practice* (2011), William Carey Library. Used by permission. For more discussion of member care ethics see the four chapters in part three ("Ethics and Human Rights in Member Care: Developing Guidelines in Mission/Aid"). Some of the material is also available in a video/audio format, recorded from the 2009 Integration Symposium at Fuller School of Psychology, Pasadena, California: www.fuller.edu/academics/school-of-psychology/integration-symposium-2009.aspx.

Challenges for Mission/Aid Workers

1. *A single medical worker in Asia working with refugees.* During times of stress this year I find myself struggling to maintain a balanced eating pattern. It seems we are always on call, and it is hard to turn away such needy people. There are days when I go to the refrigerator and look for things to eat and yet I am aware that I am not even hungry. This really bothers me because I hate to see myself falling into the trap of eating to cope with stress. I wish our base had a person with a pastor's heart who was willing to listen to our concerns and offer advice and encouragement.

2. *An organizational leader in India coaching first-term staff.* Culture shock is the biggest struggle as our new staff pursue learning a different language and culture. This usually is hard on their sense of identity and sifts through those who can stay on long-term from those who cannot. Loneliness and isolation are two words to describe the first year. Depression is frequently a part of the stress they feel as they try to cope with their new and demanding work.

3. *A couple teaching in the Middle East.* As Westerners, we must fight the fear of being unfairly labeled as politically subversive or as en-

mental health professionals and pastoral counselors? We'll explore some foundational values and premises, along with three sets of guidelines. Together these materials point us toward an international framework for good member care practice in the mission/aid community.

Life is awesome—but as we all know it can also be hellish. Just think of some of the misery that confronts the world daily, the "problems without passports" that require the cooperative interventions of people in the faith-based, government, health care and civil society sectors: natural disasters (earthquakes and tsunamis), environmental catastrophes (oil spills and pollution), poverty (one billion slum dwellers), HIV-AIDS (over 33 million infected), malaria (about 250 million cases and one million deaths per year) internecine war (with currently some 125,000 UN personnel serving in 15 peacekeeping operations), and the estimated 450 million people who cur-

emies of the established religion, and consequently be deported from the country. Paranoia is something that can keep one from sharing and helping. We often feel forced to lead divided and overly busy lives. Our "free time" is spent making visits, doing studies and housing visitors. Faith compels us to be people-oriented and compassionate, willing to "waste time" on individuals. The problem is there isn't enough time!

4. *A middle-aged administrator in Europe.* What are the issues that led my wife and me to resign? First, I had labored here for over three years without having the slightest contact from other leaders from our organization in this country. No one asked how I was doing, what I was doing or why. The isolation from full-time workers, from fellowship, and from avenues of dealing with the problems here, were the primary factors. Oddly, in discussing these issues with another leader, he seemed perplexed that they would even be issues. Such mentality prompted a letter to our international director in which I expressed my concern for more in-depth and comprehensive pastoral oversight of staff and leaders. Too little is understood and too much is presumed!

rently struggle with mental, neurological or substance use conditions.[2] For the mission/aid community, helping can often involve staying sane—and alive—in unstable, insane places.[3] Mission/aid work does not always deal with life-threatening experiences, of course. However, helping to relieve the "maims and moans" of creation takes its toll. Mission/aid workers, like the people they are helping, have some special challenges. Consider some of these examples.

---

[2] For a quick and poignant overview of some of the major challenges facing humanity, see (1) the multimedia material for the United Nations Year in Review for 2012, 2011, etc. (www.unmultimedia.org/tv/webcast/2011/12/un-year-in-review-2011.html), and (2) the overview and updates for the Millennium Development Goals (www.un.org/millenniumgoals).

[3] *Mission/aid* is a broad, inclusive term that represents the increasing focus and contributions of faith-based, Christian work around the world. By *mission* I refer to the efforts of both Christian workers serving in crosscultural settings and national Christian workers located in their home/passport countries. By *aid* I refer to the extensive area of humanitarian assistance. This area, or sector, encompasses relief and development operations by civil society, NGOs, the United Nations, faith-based groups and so forth. Mission and aid overlap with each other and using the term mission/aid reflects this practical reality.

MEMBER CARE BACKGROUND

Over the last twenty years, a special ministry, really a movement, within the Christian mission/aid community has developed around the world that is called *member care*. At the core of member care is a commitment to provide ongoing, supportive resources to further *develop* mission/aid personnel. Currently there are an estimated 417,000 full-time "foreign missionaries" and over 12 million national Christian workers from all denominations (Johnson, Barrett & Crossing, 2012). Our member care catchment area is huge! But these figures do not even begin to reflect the number of Christians involved in the overlapping area of humanitarian aid, nor do they reflect the unknown number of "tentmakers"—Christians who intentionally work in different countries while also sharing their good works and faith. Sending organizations and churches, colleagues and friends, specialist providers, and also locals who are befriended are key sources of such care.

Historically, the member care ministry and movement did not develop easily. It was often through crises, mistakes and failure that people began to realize that Christian workers needed quality support in order to help them in their challenging tasks. One of the first books written to help with this need was written by Marjorie Collins in 1974, providing many ideas for how churches and friends could better support mission personnel (*Who Cares About the Missionary?*). Previously in 1970 Joseph Stringham, a psychiatrist and missionary working in South Asia published two landmark articles in *Evangelical Missions Quarterly* on the mental health of missionaries. Stringham identified a number of external and internal challenges, including culture shock, being disillusioned with others, children and medical care (external), and resentment, sexual issues, marital struggles, dishonesty, guilt, spirituality, trauma/deprivation in earlier life and motivation (internal).

Mental health practitioners in particular who ventured into mission/aid were frequently faced with a belief that the desire for special/additional support might mean that Christian workers were being unspiritual or weak, and not trusting the Lord enough. As Tucker and Andrews point out in their article "Historical Notes on Missionary Care" (1992): "Mission societies held high the ideal of sacrifice. Strong faith in God, it was reasoned, was the prescription for a healthy mind and spirit. . . . Self-reliance was the mark of a missionary—tempered only by dependence on God through prayer" (p. 24). But in retrospect, and at the expense of overgeneralizing a bit, we (speaking inclusively) were overlooking our own *humanness*, sometimes trying to be something that we were not created or called to be. We in the mission/aid community began to better appreciate our biblical need for

Connecting and Contributing: Mental Health Professionals and Pastoral Counselors

There are many materials that can help orient and equip mental health professionals and pastoral counselors to member care. These examples are on the Member Caravan website (Training for Member Care section): https://sites.google.com/site/membercaravan/training-for-mc.

1. "Field Counseling: Sifting the Wheat from the Chaff" (Cerny & Smith, 2002) is one of fifty articles in *Doing Member Care Well: Perspectives and Practices from Around the World*. It includes five principles for ethical field care (reaching out, crosscultural issues, dual relationships, responsibilities to counselees and organizations, use of e-mail), a sample confidentiality statement, and eight short case vignettes with analyses.

2. "Training and Using Member Care Workers" (Gardner & Gardner, 1992) is part of the twenty-five chapter compendium, *Missionary Care*, and offers several suggestions for in-house and outside mental health professionals who provide services to mission agencies and mission settings.

3. "What Mission CEOs Want from Mental Health Professionals" (McKaughan, 2002) is in Enhancing Missionary Vitality: Mental Health Professions Serving Global Mission (56 articles). Two of the main suggestions from CEOs (based on a survey) were understandable language and thinking corporately.

4. "Highlights from a One-Week Field Consult" (Member Care Associates, Inc., 2012) is a day-by-day brief description of a member care trip to work with an organization's mission staff. It involves a variety of services and learning too: leadership consultation, brief counseling, debriefing, conference speaking and training.

one another—as seen in the dozens of "one another" verses in the New Testament. We began to understand that the issue was not so much our having a lack of faith but rather our need to clearly see God's plan and his provision of care.

The development of member care really has its origins in the biblical admonitions to "love one another" (Jn 13:34), "bear one another's burdens" (Gal 6:2), "be kind and compassionate to one another" (Eph 4:32), "teach and admonish one another" (Col 3:16), "encourage one another day after day" (Heb 3:13) and scores of similar "one another" verses that fill the New Testament. Member care, in this sense, is nothing new. Christians and Christian workers, for better or for worse, have been trying to practice these relationship principles down through the centuries. Yet what is new are the more organized attempts all over the world to develop comprehensive, sustainable member care approaches to support crosscultural Christian workers. These attempts have drawn on the contributions of practitioners from diverse health care fields like travel/tropical medicine, psychology/psychiatry, intercultural and transition studies, pastoral care and coaching, personnel and human resource development, and recovery and trauma care.

Member care began to be defined more formally in the early 1990s. It was and continues to be seen as the ongoing *investment of resources* by sending groups, service organizations and workers themselves for the *nurture and development* of personnel. It focuses on *every member* of the organization, including children and home office staff. It includes preventative, developmental, supportive and restorative care. A core part of member care is the *mutual care* that workers provide each other. Workers receive it and they give it. Connecting with resources and people in *the local/host community* is also key. Member care seeks to implement an adequate *flow of care* from *recruitment through retirement*. The goal is to develop resilience, skills and virtue, which are key to helping personnel stay *healthy and effective* in their work. Member care thus involves both developing *inner resources* (e.g., perseverance, stress tolerance) and providing *external resources* (e.g., team building, logistical support, skill training).

The term *member care* was especially useful since it also connoted the mutual responsibility that people (members) in a group had to each other. So member care from the start was conceived as a "two-way street," as both senders and goers had responsibilities to each other. It also implied *belonging*: the sense of community between members who are part of a group. Finally, *member care* was a neutral term, which could be more readily used in settings where surveillance and security were an issue. The term has continued to take root over the last two decades internationally, primarily within the Christian mission/aid community. Similar terms that have been used are *personnel development, human resource management, psychosocial support, staff care and development, member health and well-being,* and *people care.*

DOING ETHICS WELL

Member care practitioners are part of quite a diverse group. They come from so many countries, training backgrounds and organizations. We thus need to consider ethical care in light of our diversity (Gauthier and Pettifor, 2011; Sinclair, 2012). In this article I would like to offer three sets of guidelines that can help us chart a course toward an international framework for member care ethics. This framework includes core commitments for member care workers, a set of principles to help mission/aid organizations support/manage their staff, and a grid to review ethical rationalizations. The emphasis on a broad-based ethical framework is a more recent contribution to the development of the member care field. Colleagues are encouraged to utilize this framework along with the professional ethics code(s) they are committed to. They are also encouraged to keep abreast with the major trends in global health, especially in the domain of global mental health (O'Donnell, 2011b).

Underlying this framework are the core values of *beneficence* and *nonmaleficence,* two sides of the same ethics coin. These values impel us to intentionally seek *to do good* and *to do no harm,* respectively, within our spheres of practice and influence. They are embedded in the Hippocratic Oath from the fifth century BC and explicitly mentioned or reflected in many of the ethical codes in human health areas (e.g., American Psychological Association, "Ethical Principles of Psychologists" and "Code of Conduct," 2002, p. 3); Council of Collaboration (six associations), "Common Code of Ethics for Chaplains, Pastoral Counselors, Pastoral Educators and Students" (2004); International Union of Psychological Science and Inter-

Five Premises for Ethical Member Care

- First, staff are humans with intrinsic worth and not just resources with strategic worth. We appreciate staff for who they are as well as for what they do.

- Second, ethical care is concerned with the well-being of everyone involved in mission/aid. This includes the well-being of the organization, its purposes, and its personnel.

- Third, sacrifice and suffering are normal parts of mission/aid work. We acknowledge yet try to mitigate against the serious negative consequences that accompany work in risky places.

- Fourth, we encourage balancing the demands of professional work with the desires for personal growth. Personnel need to find a good work-life balance so they can both run well and rest well.

- Fifth, how we provide services to staff is as significant as the actual services themselves. We respect the dignity and rights of all people and thus provide quality care carefully.

national Association of Applied Psychology, "Universal Declaration of Ethical Principles for Psychologists" (2008). For more information on the applications of the Hippocratic Oath to member care, see the weblog entries from June through September 2009 at www.COREmembercare.blogspot.com.

Those who want to provide quality care in mission/aid settings need to embrace and articulate these following five foundational premises. These premises build upon the *beneficence* and *nonmaleficence* values. They *positively influence* the ethical decisions necessary for good member care practice. They also are *protective factors* to safeguard the purposes and personnel of sending groups in mission/aid.

Consider the following three examples of some common ethical challenges in mission/aid. As you will see, applying these premises is not always a straightforward process. How would you apply these five premises in light of the commitment to do good and to do no harm?

COMMON ETHICAL CHALLENGES

- *Competence.* An experienced consultant makes recommendations to a humanitarian organization based in Africa. The consultant is addressing the care of their emergency staff working in a mass disaster area, rampant with cholera and malaria. The consultant is vaguely familiar with that cultural context and the organization itself. To what extent does the consultant need to inform the agency about limitations in his or her background? When is it OK to "stretch" beyond one's areas of training and experience? What if no one else is readily available to offer advice? So is the consultant acting competently?

- *Confidentiality.* A compassionate leader informally exchanges a few e-mails with a man in their organization who has marital struggles. The man tells the leader that he and his wife have frequent fights that can be overheard by their Asian neighbors. He is also drinking a local alcoholic beverage most nights. Later, the leader prays with his own wife about the other couple's struggles. Is it OK for one's spouse to know such things? Is the disclosure of "significant problems" protected information? Would asking the leader to not share be "secretive"? So what type of confidentiality is appropriate?

- *Responsibility.* A reputable sending organization shortens a family's field preparation from three months to one month. The reason is so that the husband, a medical doctor, can cover a crucial and vacant position in a refugee clinic in the Middle East. To what extent does making such "adjustments" simply reflect the realities of mission/aid work? What if lives or a large funding grant are at stake? So to what extent is the organization acting responsibly toward the family and toward the refugee patients?

Many other types of ethical issues get stirred up in mission/aid settings, not the least of which are jurisdiction issues and managing multiple roles

More Ethical Issues in Mission/Aid

- Assessing physical/mental disabilities during selection, including those of children (e.g., whether hiring, locating or promoting staff is based on such disabilities)

- Determining who has access to personnel files (e.g., if team leaders have access to team members personnel files, especially "negative" information)

- Working in stressful settings with limited supervision, contingency plans and personal debriefing (e.g., whether senders can support staff adequately in isolated settings or with extreme stressors)

- Consulting with people with whom one has many types of social/ work relationships (e.g., whether to do conflict mediation for an interagency group that includes folks from your agency)

- Confronting the unhealthy and harmful practices of leaders and other staff (e.g., how to protect staff that point out problems; whether certain lifestyle choices are private affairs)

and different types of relationships with sending groups/workers (Barber & Hall, 1996). Just a few of the many examples are listed in the box below. It is important for sending groups and MCWs to anticipate and discuss such issues together. We thus need to be very conversant with the values, ethical principles and guidelines that shape our decisions.

THREE SETS OF GUIDELINES

Many types of professional ethical codes exist that can relate to the practice of member care. For some practitioners, these codes are essential and are a good fit. But one size does not fit all! For example, a skilled Nigerian pastor providing trauma training/care in Sudan may not find a North American "code for counselors" so helpful. Such ethical codes are primarily relevant for specific disciplines and countries. Yet many member care workers (MCWs) enter the member care field via a combination of their life experiences and informal training, and are not part of a professional association with a written ethics code. So appealing to another country or discipline's ethical code can result in a rather cumbersome mismatch between the person and the code.[4]

We thus want to carefully identify *relevant ethical guidelines* that fit into as well as transcend our cultural and experiential backgrounds. In other words, MCWs and sending groups must develop an international framework that can further shape their ethical mentality and guide their member care practice. This framework would emphasize: *quality services* by MCWs and senders, *ongoing development* for senders and MCWs, *recognized standards* for those who are using or providing MCW services, and *protection* for service receivers via safeguards. We now consider three core guidelines that help form an international framework for ethical member care.[5]

1. COMMITMENTS FOR MCWs

The following guidelines—"Commitments for Member Care Workers"—include ten basic *commitments* for all types of MCWs. They focus on the personal characteristics, backgrounds and relationships needed to practice member care ethically (qualities and qualifications). Like all three sets of guidelines, they are intended to be referred to regularly, discussed with colleagues and applied in light of the variations in our backgrounds. Sending groups that solicit and receive MCW services for their staff are responsible to carefully choose both internal and external MCWs. Understanding these

---

[4]For examples of various issues and ethical challenges in Christian mission in general see (1) *Serving Jesus with Integrity* and (2) *Ethics and Accountability in Christian Mission* (2010), Dwight Baker and Douglas Hayward (Eds.), William Carey Library; and *Christian Mission: A Case Study Approach* (1995), Alan Neely, Orbis. For additional material on training for international ethics and cultural competence, see the article "Internationalizing the Professional Ethics Curriculum" (Leach & Gauthier, 2012) and the book *Cultural Competence Training in a Global Society* (Dana & Allen, 2008), both part of Springer's extensive series on International and Cultural Psychology.

[5]We refer to the three sets of guidelines as reflecting an international framework for ethical member care. The "MCW Commitments and Sender Principles" have been developed and reviewed by colleagues from many different countries over the past ten years, including colleagues from the Global South(s) and Global North(s). The Rationalization Grid is broadly relevant in that its foundational perspective—the inherent capacity of humans for prevarication or self-deception—is seen clearly throughout Scripture, mental health literature and history. Another international framework relevant for mission/aid is the World Association of Non-Governmental Organization's *Code of Ethics and Conduct for NGOs* (2004).

Commitments for Member Care Workers

1. Ongoing training, personal growth and self-care

2. Ongoing accountability for my personal and work life, including consultation and supervision

3. Recognizing my strengths and limits and representing my skills and background accurately

4. Understanding and respecting felt needs, culture and diversity of those with whom I work

5. Working with other colleagues and making referrals when needed

6. Preventing problems and offering supportive or restorative and at times pro bono services

7. Having high standards in my services and embracing specific ethical guidelines

8. Acknowledging different disciplinary and regulatory norms for different MCWs

9. Abiding by any legal requirements for offering member care where I reside and practice

10. Growing in my relationship to Christ, the Good Practitioner

ten commitments in combination with reviewing references and educational/experiential backgrounds can thus help to evaluate prospective service providers.

Application 1: Finding your ethical niche. Some MCWs are specialists and have advanced degrees or certification in their respective disciplines. For example, for those whose main emphasis and professional identity is pastoral counseling, clinical psychology or human resource management, the codes of professional associations they belong to would be appropriate. Other MCWs have less formal or less systematic training routes (e.g., workshops, life experience). Currently there is no generic accreditation or professional association for MCWs in this category. In view of commitment 7 in this first set of guidelines, MCWs are strongly encouraged to practice member care in light of the specific code of ethics that fits them. It could be a code developed by a national or international organization or discipline, such as codes for Christian counselors, coaches, spiritual directors or ombudsmen. They are also encouraged to have a written endorsement from their organization that attests to their competence and accountability. Note also that many field leaders and team leaders regularly function in member care roles—it is part of their job description in many cases. These leaders may not need a specific code per se, but at the very least they need to be thoroughly informed by ethical guidelines such as those described in this article.

Application 2: Self-care and character. MCWs, like anyone else, can experience serious problems, including emotional, family or moral struggles. In such cases, the quality of MCWs' services can decrease, and MCWs will need help, accountability and often a break for restoration. If MCWs cannot manage their own life well, how will they manage the mission/aid "household" (1 Tim 3:4-5)? Member care receivers expect Christian MCWs to model a healthy, godly lifestyle, and to maintain a close relationship with the Lord. Commitments 1, 2 and 10 are the most relevant for MCW character. These include personal growth, accountability and relationship with Christ.

Application 3: Training and competence. Christian workers in South Asia are being trained to provide pastoral care for staff in their organizations. Most do not have backgrounds in the health sciences. But they are mature people who have been chosen by their leaders to receive special training twice a year in areas like basic counseling, crisis care, running a personnel office and team building. They also have access to the trainers for case consultation via the Internet or telephone. These MCWs reflect a growing number of caregivers who are recognized within their organizations as being able to offer helpful services. Another example is the "peer debriefers" being trained in Africa as a first line of help when critical incidents occur. Commitments 1, 2, 3, 8 and 9 are especially important for MCW competence. These include ongoing training, getting consultation or supervision, knowing strengths and limits, acknowledging different MCW norms, and abiding by legal requirements.

Application 4: Sacrifice and compassion. MCWs often sacrificially give of themselves. They do so not to compensate for personal deficits but rather from a compassionate commitment to help others grow. Compassion has limits, and MCWs need to be aware of their boundaries and practice self-care. Nonetheless, there are times and even seasons when serving others is costly—and helping may be done out of a sense of duty and obedience, and it may temporarily interrupt our commitment to self-care (e.g., the tired disciples being asked to serve the crowds [Lk 9:10-17]). Commitments 1, 5 and 10 are key for maintaining MCW compassion. These include self-care, respecting felt needs and relationship with Christ.

2. PRINCIPLES FOR SENDERS

This set of guidelines focuses on the crucial role of sending groups to respon-

Principles for Senders

1. *Human resources strategy.* Human resources are an integral part of our strategic and operational plans.
   - The organization allocates sufficient human and financial resources to achieve the objectives of the human resources strategy.

2. *Staff policies and practices.* Our human resources policies aim to be effective, fair and transparent.
   - Policies and practices that relate to staff employment are in writing, monitored and reviewed. Staff are familiarized with policies and practices that affect them.

3. *Managing people.* Good support, management and leadership of our staff is key to our effectiveness.
   - Staff have clear work objectives and performance standards, know whom they report to and what management support they will receive. All staff are aware of grievance and disciplinary procedures.

4. *Consultation and communication.* Dialogue with staff on matters likely to affect their employment enhances the quality and effectiveness of our policies and p°ractices.
   - Staff are informed and adequately consulted when we develop or review human resources policies or practices that affect them.

5. *Recruitment and selection.* Our policies and practices aim to attract and select a diverse workforce with the skills and capabilities to fulfill our requirements.

sibly support and manage their staff well: international staff, local/national staff, home office staff and family members of their staff. It also considers the big picture of member care from recruitment through retirement and the commitment to nurture both organizational health and staff health. We have taken these guidelines from the "Code of Good Practice in the Management and Support of Aid Personnel" (2003) developed by People In Aid in the United Kingdom. They include seven principles and several key indicators (specific criteria to demonstrate how the principles are practiced). Sending groups can use the code to help them monitor how their member care (human resources) policies are integrated into their overall goals. These

- Written policies and procedures outline how staff are recruited and selected to positions in our organization. Our selection process is fair, transparent, and consistent.

6. *Learning, training and development.* Learning, training and staff development are promoted throughout the organization.
   - Adequate induction and briefing specific to each role is given to all staff. Written policies outline the training, development and learning opportunities staff can expect from the organization.

7. *Health, safety and security.* The security, good health and safety of our staff are a prime responsibility of our organization.
   - Written policies are available to staff on security, individual health, care and support, health and safety. Program plans include written assessment of security, travel and health risks specific to the country or region, reviewed at appropriate intervals.
   - Before an international assignment, all staff receive health clearance. In addition, they and accompanying dependents receive verbal and written briefing on all risks relevant to the role to be undertaken, and the measures in place to mitigate those risks, including insurance. . . . Briefings are updated when new equipment, procedures or risks are identified. All staff have a debriefing or exit interview at the end of any contract or assignment. Health checks, personal counseling and career advice are available. Managers are trained to ensure these services are provided.

principles are effective when they are understood and embraced at all levels of the sending group and implemented by skilled managers with integrity. The complete code and related documents can be found at www.peopleinaid .org/code. See also Global Connection's (United Kingdom) "Guidelines for Good Practice for Mission Member Care" (2009), one of the most detailed codes for sending groups to date, organized into several core values with detailed guidelines for putting each value into practice.

Application 1: Where there are no (well-resourced) senders. There are a couple important counterpoints for the guidelines suggested here. First, not all mission/aid workers actually have "senders." At least many may not have an ongoing long-term sender; they may work from contract to contract and from agency to agency. Others workers do things much more on their own without a sending group per se. Their charitable work and Christian witness are done as part of their lifestyle in a host culture. Many mission/aid workers surely wish that a sender would be able to support and manage them in ways that are recommended here!

Second, for some sending groups themselves, these guidelines may seem overly idealistic at best and inappropriately constrictive at worst. Senders coming from philosophically different or less-experienced or financially limited settings may not be on the same page about what is needed to do mission/aid and member care well. For instance, some senders may default to the practice of sending out "naked" mission workers who have no apparent resources other than to follow the biblical injunction Christ gave his disciples to go without an extra coat, staff or money. These folks embody that commitment, without an expectation of returning to their home country for furlough or retirement. This may seem extreme, but it does reflect the other end point of the sender's continuum for providing "comprehensive" member care. On a related note, in her concluding chapter in *Sharing the Front Line and Back Hills* (2002), Danieli describes how some potential contributors to her edited work dismissed her work as "preposterous or obscene." The reason was that she was focusing on aid workers themselves—the protectors and providers—rather than on what was perceived to be the far more needy victims who needed help (p. 388).

Application 2: Good versus poor practice. A sending church in Europe helps support ten mission/aid workers. The workers are part of separate agencies and work on four different continents. The agencies' biggest issues are maintaining communication with these workers and feeling connected with each other. Most of the responsibilities for "managing and supporting staff" are assumed to lie with the sending agency rather than the church. During the past year one of the workers was severely injured in a car crash and needs months of intensive physiotherapy, while another suffers from recurrent malaria. What to do?

Good practice. Each worker is assigned a volunteer advocate from church who stays in monthly contact with the worker. The mission coordinator reviews the seven good practice principles with the church pastors and elders. They agree to adopt these principles, and send copies of the "Code of Good Practice" to the volunteer advocates, the workers and the sending agencies. Over the next two months the mission coordinator talks with each personnel director from the sending agencies. They review how best to support the respective workers, taking special note of principles 4, 6 and 7 (communication with staff, learning opportunities and health/safety issues).

Poor practice. The sending church agrees to help send three more mission workers. The addition of three more photos looks pretty good on their world map in the entrance to the church. The mission coordinator gets a copy of the "Code of Good Practice," reads it with appreciation and dutifully files it—until a new crisis hits one of their thirteen mission/aid workers. Rest in pieces.

3. GRID TO REVIEW RATIONALIZATIONS

The "Grid for Rationalizations" consist of ten common rationalizations for our *faux pas* as practitioners. They are coverups. And coverups, of course, can be just as bad or even worse than the ethical mistakes themselves. These rationalizations can be seen as substandards that we can unfortunately all-too-easily tolerate or even adopt. The prefix *sub* here refers to standards that are both inferior and wrong. Sending organizations and MCWs would benefit by adding to these ten items in light of one's own preferred rationalizations. But beware: we can rationalize our rationalizations with meta-rationalizations. One of the prime examples of a meta-rationalization is the self-serving belief that we do not in fact rationalize. Or a corollary meta-rationalization is to believe that even if we do rationalize, we do so for a very

ethical or noble reason. I have drawn upon the work of Ken Pope and Melba
Vasquez (1999) by adding to and adapting some of the rationalizations that

Grid for Rationalizations

- It is ethical as long as you don't know a Bible verse, law or ethical principle that prohibits it.

- It is ethical as long as your colleagues or service receivers do not complain about it, or as long as no one else knows or wants to know, or as long as you can convince others that it is OK.

- It is ethical as long as you or your telecommunications technology were having a "bad day," thus affecting your usual quality of work, or as long as the circumstances and decision were difficult, or as long as you are busy, rushed or multitasking.

- It is ethical as long as you follow the majority of your ethical guidelines, or as long as you only intend to do it one time.

- It is ethical as long as there is no intent to do harm, you are being sincere, "your heart is in the right place" and you are trying to do the best that you can.

- It is ethical as long as you are a moral person, or a nice, competent, or respected person, or as long as you provide free services.

- It is ethical as long as you "take responsibility" for your decision or behavior, or as long as you were acting with "integrity," or as long as it does not seem to negatively impact your behavior or emotions.

- It is ethical as long as the matter is not completely black and white, or as long as someone else is also "wrong or more wrong" than you are, or as long as others do it, or as long as someone in authority over you reassures you or pressures you and asks you to do it.

- It is ethical as long as you believe or feel it is not unethical or as long as you think God is on your side.

- It is ethical as long as you are an important person or the most powerful person.

they have identified in the practice of psychology.

Application 1: Rationalization or reflection. Using the "Grid for Rationalizations" is part of a larger process for both sending groups and MCWs to regularly look in the mirror of our hearts. We do this individually and with others in order to scrutinize both our motives and the ethical quality of our member care work. Our own capacity for self-deception and self-justifying revisions of our personal and work-related history give cause for much concern. In addition to reviewing the copious amount of Scriptures that expose our prevarication-prone human nature (e.g., Jer 17:9), see the compelling work of Tavris and Aronson (2007) on how we distort reality: *Mistakes Were Made (But Not by Me): Why We Justify Foolish Beliefs, Bad Decisions, and Hurtful Acts.* So we have to trust ourselves surely, yet we also must have a healthy respect for the possibility of our own distortions.

Consider this situation. At an international health care conference, a group of mission leaders and MCWs discuss member care issues during a special interest group. The facilitator uses the ten items in this grid as a springboard to discuss how quality services can be compromised. Many tricky examples are voiced: "I needed to do what I thought was best as there was no opportunity to consult a book or colleague." "I do prayer ministry for depression and professional ethics are not relevant." "I am a good person and my good intentions guide how I run the personnel department." The participants then break into small groups to relate these ten rationalizations with sayings from the book of Proverbs. They also identify a couple of safeguards from the "Commitments for MCWs and the Principles for Senders" to help prevent them from lapsing into ethical substandards.

FINAL THOUGHTS

We have explored some of the ethical terrain in the diverse field of member care in mission/aid.[6] I have suggested some important values and premises

---

[6]For additional materials regarding member care in mission/aid as well as ideas for involvement, see (1) CORE Member Care blogsite: www.COREmembercare.blogspot.com (e.g., the entries on global integration of mental health-member care, July 13 to December 15, 2011; and culture and diversity in member care-international health, February 15 to May 12, 2010); (2) the Member Caravan web site: http://sites.google.com/site/membercaravan (e.g., Resource Updates, MC Library); and (3) the PowerPoint, "God in the Global Office" (2009): www.slideshare.net/MCAresources/god-in-the-global-office.

to help shape ethical practice. I have offered three sets of guidelines that I believe helpfully point us toward an international framework for member care. These guidelines are seen as being complementary to one's own professional code of ethics.

Our quest for ethical member care has a destination. It ultimately leads us to the doorsteps of the world in need as we seek to positively impact the major challenges facing humanity (Grand Challenges, 2011; Johnstone, 2011). Our quality, ethical care can significantly bolster the well-being of the hundreds of thousands of workers within the mission/aid community. Our member care work is thus a strategic support for those who in turn reach out in so many noble ways to help this struggling world.

The Case of Philip Faithful and Family

I conclude this chapter with a case study in two parts. It pulls together some of the member care issues and ethical challenges that we are likely to face in international mission/aid settings. This fictitious account includes at least twenty-five poor practices, including many unethical ones (part one), as well as good, ethical ones (part two). An analysis of a similar case (chap. 19 of *Missionary Care*, 1992) is available at Member Caravan's website: http://sites.google.com/site/member caravan/test/mc-counting-the-cost-book-.

Review 1: Good intentions. Read through this study and identify several of the ethical issues. Keep in mind these three broad areas in your analysis: (1) the organization's policies and procedures for staff care, (2) where and with whom the actual "problems" reside, and (3) the involvement of well-meaning people in helping roles. All of these areas are intertwined with the crosscultural context of this case.[a] How are the three sets of guidelines in this chapter (MCW commit-

---

[a]For more perspective on cultural issues relevant for helping professionals, see (1) Anthony Marsella, (2011, October), "Twelve Critical Issues for Mental Health Professionals Working with Ethno-Culturally Diverse Populations," *Psychology International*, 22(3), 7-10: www.apa.org/international/pi/2011/10/index.aspx; (2) World Federation for Mental Health, (2001, October 10), "Mental Health in a Changing World: The Impact of Culture and Diversity," www.wfmh.org/PDF/Englishversion2007.pdf; and (3) Jenifer Erickson et al. (Eds.), (2010), *Handbook of Multicultural Counseling Competencies* (Hoboken, NJ: John Wiley & Sons).

ments, sender principles, rationalization grid) being utilized or not utilized?

Review 2: Good interventions. Describe what you would do to help in terms of these five areas for ethical care: organizational responsibility, confidentiality, MCW competence, testing, and personal values/legal standards. Based on the epilogue, list some of the main ways that the pastoral counselor, mental health professional and senior leader intervened appropriately. Make a summary recommendation to this organization for improving its member care program. List some key ethical challenges for mental health professionals and pastoral counselors who work in international settings like this.

■ ■ ■

The Faithful Family

Phillip, Anne (parents); Fatima, Jerome (children)

Part 1. Phillip Faithful is a twenty-eight-year-old staff member of a large Christian humanitarian organization in Southeast Asia. On the average he works ten hour days and is almost always available to help out when there is a need in the office. He is the type of person who exudes goodness and doesn't say no to those over him, sometimes at the expense of his own needs. He often uses part of his three weeks of annual vacation for helping others.

Phillip was raised in Singapore and went to a university in England for two years, where he met his wife, Anne. He married at age twenty-four and has two healthy children, Fatima (age 3) and Jerome (age six months). Currently he and his family live in Jakarta, Indonesia, and are involved in work locally and in Asia.

During the last three months Phillip, who is usually very friendly, has become increasingly irritable with his colleagues and somewhat withdrawn with his family. His supervisor noticed these changes and talked to Phillip's wife about what he viewed as "pride and independence" in Phillip. She confided in him that they both feel apathetic and that she has little energy to take care of her home and work responsibilities.

The supervisor shares some Scripture with her. He then encourages her to talk to Phillip about taking time off to "get back into work shape," and that he talk to someone about his problems. She follows his advice.

Phillip was too busy to take time off but he did agree to contact the director of training, Ms. North, for counseling. She is a North American woman who has taken some counseling courses at a Christian university and is recognized for her ability to listen and offer appropriate advice. She also provides counseling to Christians from some of the local churches to supplement her income.

Ms. North works on a fundraising committee in a local church with Phillip that meets once a month. Phillip approaches her after a meeting and schedules a time with her to talk and pray about his problems. She also begins to pray regularly for Phillip with the pastoral care committee in the church.

Ms. North obtained Phillips personnel files from the temporary secretary in the personnel department to better acquaint herself with his background. Phillip had taken two personality tests as part of the screening process to be accepted on staff. He scored high on the "depression" scale, so she wondered if he had tendencies toward a serious emotional disorder.

Ms. North also decided to speak to Phillip's wife and supervisor to better understand his struggles. The supervisor recommended that Ms. North borrow a "temperament analysis" test and administer it to Phillip in order to further explore his personality. She administered the test along with an inventory to assess stress and then spoke with the supervisor, suggesting that Phillip be put in a department with less paperwork and more people contact.[b]

Phillip and Ms. North meet for four counseling sessions. They spend most of their time talking about the challenges of raising his two

---

[b]Examples of other self-assessment tools for stress management and work-life balance are listed on the Reality DOSE website (from Member Care Associates, Headington Institute, International Federation of the Red Cross and the like): https://sites.google .com/site/mcaresources/giantsfoxeswolvesandflies.

children, his past relationship with his father and his apprehension to openly talk about his work frustrations with leaders. Ms. North spends time listening for what might be the root of his problems, and subsequently advises him to work fewer hours, spend more time with his family and be more assertive with colleagues.

After the fourth session Ms. North tells Phillip that she would like to recommend that he see a visiting leader from a Christian charity from Europe. She feels this person can encourage him and possibly give him more insights into his current situation. Phillip gives her a small honorarium for her services, and a few days later approaches the visiting leader. The leader has never heard anything about Phillip.

■ ■ ■

Part 2. One week later, with no changes in Phillip's situation, the supervisor updates a senior leader in the organization. The leader arranges a meeting the next day with the supervisor, Ms. North and a certified pastoral counselor living in Jakarta. The counselor trained in Australia and receives regular referrals from several humanitarian organizations.

During the meeting everyone compares notes and agrees that Phillip has fallen through the member care cracks and that he needs professional help. Ms. North briefly shares how this has been difficult for her. The pastoral counselor points out that other family members will likely need support too and agrees to meet with Phillip and his wife, Anne, if they are willing. He points out that a physical exam, an assessment tool for depression symptoms and a review of the overall work environment and relationships would be helpful. The counselor clarifies his fees for service (to be paid for by the organization) and confidentiality policy (stipulating that a general progress report can be given only with Philip and Anne's permission).

Later that day the supervisor meets with both Philip and Anne to see how they are doing, informs them of the meeting earlier that day and asks for their perspectives and what they think is best. The couple expresses their willingness to meet with the pastoral counselor, especially as they know of his reputation and are comfortable that he is not part of their organization.

Later that night the organization leader talks informally with his sister-in-law about the situation (via Internet webcam). She is a mental health professional (MHP) in the United States who is part of a member care network and consults regularly with member care situations internationally. The MHP is glad to give some general input with the caveat that there is only partial information available and that the local pastoral counselor should be the main person being consulted regarding member care for Philip and Anne. Because of their good relationship and similar backgrounds, the MHP is able to talk candidly with the leader, asking what he believes has and has not been done well so far. She then decides to focus the conversation on the bigger picture regarding the impact of the organization's ethos on work and member care, and explores the overall human resource system (HR) that is in place.

Based on the MHP's suggestions and prompted by the near crisis with Philip, the leader is very interested in improving HR and member care. They brainstorm together about ways to do so. In the process the leader confides with the MHP that Philip's situation bears some similarity to his own, with major work pressures and time commitments beginning to wear him out. The MHP suggests that the leader and his wife take an online work-life balance inventory and discuss it together as a couple, identifying both challenges and supports in their lives. The MHP also agrees to send an HR assessment resource to help the leader better understand the main components of HR and also gives a referral for a colleague who works in HR with international organizations. Their conversation ends with the leader recalling People In Aid's "Code of Good Practice" (2003) and committing to review it with fellow leaders.

REFERENCES

American Psychological Association. (2002). *Ethical principles for psychologists and code of conduct.* Washington, DC: American Psychological Association. Retrieved from www.apa.org/ethics/code2002.html.

Cerny, L., & Smith, D. (2002). Field counseling: Shifting the wheat from the chaff. In K. O'Donnell (Ed.), *Doing member care well: Perspectives and practices from around the world* (pp. 489-99). Pasadena, CA: William Carey Library.

Collins, M. (1974). *Who cares about the missionary?* Chicago: Moody.

Council of Collaboration (2004). *Common code of ethics for chaplains, pastoral counselors, pastoral educators and students.* Retrieved from www.acpe.edu /acroread/Common%20Code%20of%20Ethics%20Revised%20March%202005.pdf.

Dana, R., & Allen, J. (2008). (Eds). *Cultural competence training in a global society.* New York: Springer.

Danieli, Y. (2002). (Ed.). *Sharing the front line and the back hills: Peacekeepers, humanitarian aid workers, and the media in the midst of crises.* New York: Baywood Press.

Gardner, L., & Gardner, R. (1992). Training and using member care workers. In K. O'Donnell (Ed.), *Missionary care: Counting the cost for world evangelization* (pp. 315-31). Pasadena, CA: William Carey Library.

Global Connections (2009). *Guidelines for good practice for mission member care.* London: Global Connections. Retrieved from http://www.globalconnections .co.uk/forums/TCKForum/membercareguidelines.

Grand Challenges in Global Health (2011). Retrieved from www.grandchallenges .org/about/Pages/Overview.aspx.

Hall, M., & Barber, B. (1996). The therapist in a missions context: Avoiding dual role conflicts. *Journal of Psychology and Theology, 24*, 212-19.

Hippocratic oath. Retrieved from www.bbc.co.uk/dna/h2g2/A1103798.

International Union of Psychological Science, and International Association of Applied Psychology (2008). *Universal declaration of ethical principles for psychologists.* Retrieved from www.cpa.ca/cpasite/userfiles/Documents/Universal _Declaration_asADOPTEDbyIUPsySIAAP_July2008.pdf.

Johnson, T., Barrett, D., & Crossing, P. (2012). Christianity 2012: The 200th anniversary of American foreign missions. *International Bulletin of Missionary Research, 36*, 28-29.

Johnstone, P. (2011). *The future of the global church.* Downers Grove, IL: InterVarsity Press.

Leach, M., & Gauthier, J. (2012). Internationalizing the professional ethics curriculum. In F. Leong, W. Pickren, M. Leach & A. Marsella (Eds.), *Internationalizing the psychology curriculum in the United States: Meeting the challenges and opportunities in a global age* (pp. 29-50). New York: Springer. doi:10.1007/978-1-4614-0073-8_3.

McKaughan, P. (2002). What mission CEOs want from mental health professionals. In J. Powell & J. Bowers (Eds.), *Enhancing missionary vitality: Mental health professions serving global mission*. Palmer Lake, CO: Mission Training International.

O'Donnell, K. (2002). (Ed.). *Doing member care well: Perspectives and practices from around the world*. Pasadena, CA: William Carey Library.

O'Donnell, K. (2011a). *Global member care: The pearls and perils of good practice*. Pasadena, CA: William Carey Library.

O'Donnell, K. (2011b). Global mental health: A resource map for connecting and contributing. *Psychology International, 22*(2), 4-6. Retrieved from www.apa.org/international/pi/2011/07/global-health.aspx.

O'Donnell, K., & O'Donnell, M. (1992). Ethical concerns in providing member care services. In K. O'Donnell (Ed.), *Missionary care: Counting the cost for world evangelization* (pp. 260-68). Pasadena, CA: William Carey Library.

People in Aid. (2003). *Code of good practice in the management and support of aid personnel*. London: People in Aid.

Pope, K., & Vasquez, M. (1999, May). On violating the ethical standards. *California Board of Psychology Update*, 1-2. (Excerpted from *Ethics in psychotherapy and counseling: A practical guide*. [2nd ed.]. San Francisco, Jossey-Bass, 1998).

Stringham, J. (1970). Likely causes of emotional difficulties among missionaries. *Evangelical Missions Quarterly, 6*, 193-203.

Stringham, J. (1970). The missionary's mental health. *Evangelical Missions Quarterly, 7*, 1-9.

Tavris, C., & Aronson, E. (2007). *Mistakes were made (but not by me): Why we justify foolish beliefs, bad decisions, and hurtful acts*. Orlando: Harcourt.

Tob, S. (1985/c. 1355). *Proverbios morales*. Madrid: Editorial Castalia.

Tucker, R., & Andrews, L. (1992). Historical notes on missionary care. In K. O'Donnell (Ed.), *Missionary care: Counting the cost for world evangelization* (pp. 24-36). Pasadena, CA: William Carey.

United Nations. (1948). *Universal declaration of human rights*. United Nations. Retrieved from www.un.org/en/documents/udhr/index.shtml.

World Organization of Non-Governmental Organizations (2004). *Code of ethics and conduct for NGOs*. Retrieved from www.wango.org/codeofethics.aspx.

19

Ethics in Providing Psychological First Aid

Cynthia B. Eriksson and
Thomas C. Duke

Love your neighbor as yourself" is a command in the Torah that Jesus referred to as part of the Greatest Commandment (Lev 19:18; Mk 12:28-31). However, an expert in Jewish law challenged Jesus by asking, "And who is my neighbor?" (Lk 10:29 NRSV). Jesus responded with what is now known as the parable of the good Samaritan, a story of a man who is in desperate need of help, and after being overlooked by two different religious leaders is finally aided unexpectedly by a Samaritan, a person outside of the traditional Jewish religion. After telling this story Jesus asked, "Which of these three, do you think, was a neighbor to the man who fell into the hands of the robbers?" (Lk 10:36). The expert in the law replied, "The one who showed him mercy," to which Jesus responded, "Go and do likewise" (Lk 10:37).

If we are to follow the command, "Love your neighbor as yourself," then we too should "Go and do likewise." In this parable "the Samaritan shows us a compassion unrestricted by national, racial, or religious barriers" (Nolland, 1993, p. 597). The way the Samaritan loved his neighbor was simply to show mercy, to tend to his most basic needs and to help him get to a place of safety and stability where further needs could be met. As mental health professionals, learning and implementing psychological first aid is a unique opportunity to follow the Samaritan's example and Jesus' instructions to "Go and do likewise."

In order to aid the Christian counselor in the attempt to follow this call to compassion, this chapter will present a basic description of current evidence-supported methods of immediate response to large-scale disaster and tragedy. Understanding what psychological first aid *is* and *is not* will then allow for an overview of ethical dimensions of this work including issues of competency, responsibility, integrity and diversity. Particular challenges for Christian counselors or religious professionals will be identified, and finally, the authors will introduce the ethical dimensions of providing psychological aid in international contexts.

WHAT IS PSYCHOLOGICAL FIRST AID?

In the vacuum of little empirical evidence to dictate best practices for post-emergency interventions, two general approaches emerged: (1) provide care for everyone (e.g., a debriefing model) or (2) do not do anything until the immediate crisis is passed and those with clinical disorders can be identified. However, the hard work of several agencies and individuals has created an evidence-supported alternative (Watson & Ruzek, 2009; Watson & Shalev, 2005). Psychological First Aid (PFA) is a set of practices based on the current mental health literature that have the goals of lessening the immediate distress of populations affected by disasters or mass violence, and helping to bolster their ongoing functioning and effective coping. (Brymer et al., 2006a). The development of this set of practices has come out of a steadily evolving attention to the effects of trauma and the benefits of early intervention. In the United States, the National Child Traumatic Stress Network (NCTSN) and the National Center for PTSD (NCPTSD) combined their efforts with several other individuals knowledgeable in disaster response (Watston & Ruzek, 2009), in order to create the "Field Operations Guide for Psychological First Aid" (Brymer et al., 2006a). This guide has now become widely used among organizations involved in disaster and mass violence relief, and is available without cost at the National Child Traumatic Stress Network website, http://www.nctsnet.org/content/psychological -first-aid.

PFA is offered with respect and dignity to the emergency survivors. It assumes that community members vary in their response to overwhelming events and that they have strengths and resources they can draw upon.

There are eight components of PFA:

1. contact and engagement

2. safety and comfort

3. stabilization

4. information gathering: current needs and concerns

5. practical assistance

6. connection with social supports

7. information on coping

8. linkage with collaborative services (Brymer et al., 2006a, p. 19).

These components are meant to be clear, practical and accessible. They are not intended to only be implemented by mental health professionals. A PFA worker can be any individual working as part of a disaster or emergency response unit, organization or team, including community religious professionals (Brymer et al., 2006b). The components of PFA are designed to help caregivers prioritize the needs of survivors and to meet those needs in a caring, non-intrusive manner.

Once caregivers have been oriented and trained to serve in the particular disaster context and particular service location (shelters, food distribution centers, emergency room or hospital settings, etc.), they begin by initiating contact with survivors and then following up with requests for practical supports. Because the time period immediately following a disaster is often extremely chaotic, a key step is to assist survivors by calmly getting them to places of safety and helping meet their most essential needs. This could include helping to connect victims with needed immediate relief services, helping victims find missing family or helping victims who are in grief over the loss of loved ones due to the incident. PFA workers are instructed to especially attend to and help stabilize those survivors who are particularly "emotionally overwhelmed and disoriented" (Brymer et al., 2006a, p. 49).

After basic safety and stabilization are established, the caregiver then ascertains as much information about necessary relief and recovery services as possible, helps survivors assess their most pressing needs and empowers them to connect with service providers. This is a process that can help restore a sense of self-efficacy and hope. PFA workers also pay special attention to those with potential risk factors that could lead to the onset of stress disorder symptoms, harm to one's self or harm to others. Once pressing needs have been addressed, caregivers can then assist survivors by helping them reconnect with supportive members of their community, teaching them positive coping skills and informing them about common reactions to trauma and distress (Brymer et al., 2006a).

Finally, there may be several who still need additional services such as further medical help, mental health services, faith-based services or help related to problems with substance abuse. Caregivers can then help the individual access needed services and facilitate the transition from one professional to another. The caregiver should especially attend to the needs of those most at risk during this time, such as children, the elderly or the disabled (Brymer et al., 2006a).

PFA fits within a framework of community services and interventions. First, preventive training and disaster preparedness are valuable prior to an event even happening. Then, once an event occurs, rescue and survival takes first priority. It is within the early aftermath that PFA workers can provide initial safety, support and connection to key resources. As the response to the emergency continues, community-oriented interventions of training, providing accurate information, needs assessments and triage to more intensive care become important (Watson & Ruzek, 2009). Finally, individuals with indicators of high risk can be referred for specific early interventions such as adapted cognitive behavioral therapies, pharmacological therapies and other brief interventions with evidence for mitigating the effects of trauma (Bryant, 2007; Gray & Litz, 2005; McNally, Bryant & Ehlers, 2003).

ETHICAL ISSUES RELATED TO PROVIDING PSYCHOLOGICAL FIRST AID

Integrity and competence. "Psychologists seek to promote accuracy, honesty, and truthfulness in the science, teaching, and practice of psychology" (APA, 2010, p. 2). The APA ethical principle of integrity is closely linked to the ethical standard of competence. "Accuracy" and "truthfulness" demand a clarification of efficacy, benefit and competence in practice. In the unique context of emergency response, one can delineate issues of competence and efficacy by considering *who* can provide PFA, *what* exactly they do, and *why* they do it?

The *who* of PFA providers can be any mental health professional, community clergy member or other worker who is working within a structured disaster response effort. Each professional background has its own standards of competence, and within the framework of the eight components of PFA there may be times when each professional is pushed to consider his or her own limits and training. For example, a pastoral counselor may be asked to assess whether a survivor's lack of response or disorientation requires medical attention, or a psychologist may be approached by a wife desperate for advice regarding traditional burial rites for her husband.

The APA ethics code does include a specific statement regarding competence in the provision of services during emergencies (APA, 2010). It allows psychologists to perform services for those who do not have access to other mental health services, even when the psychologist does not have the specific training for that service. It is the expectation that this assistance would be shifted to appropriate providers when the services become available. During emergencies, this caveat allows for psychologists to step into roles that may not be specifically part of their training or stated competency. However, the PFA manual emphasizes that workers should stay within the boundaries of their own skills and their role on the PFA team (Brymer et al., 2006a). Working within a structured multidisciplinary response allows for a team response and consultation, but each professional must balance their own competency and the risks inherent in providing emergency care (Rosser, 2008).

In order to increase the competency of clergy in disaster settings, several groups have created training modules specific to community clergy covering disaster mental health, assessment of trauma reactions and spiritual distress (McCabe et al., 2007; Suite, Rollin, Bowman & La Bril, 2007). In addition, the developers of the PFA manual have also created web-based training available at http://learn.nctsn.org/course/category.php?id=11.

Competency and integrity in practice are also linked to the actual *what* of PFA. Researchers have identified five key components of early response to emergencies based on an exhaustive review of the recent literature: "1) a sense of safety, 2) calming, 3) a sense of self—and community efficacy, 4)

connectedness, and 5) hope" (Hobfoll et al., 2007, p. 284). The eight components of PFA follow closely in this model of support and empowerment.
The components are also based on the assumption that individuals and
communities can demonstrate a range of responses to disasters and emergencies, and that they have social networks, personal strengths and coping
strategies that can be supported or augmented to benefit adjustment.

It is also important to note what PFA *is not*, in order to define competent
practice in emergency settings. As mentioned earlier, PFA is an alternative
to a debriefing model. Contemporary practices in early posttraumatic psychological interventions first came about as a response to the needs of soldiers in World War I and World War II. The U.S. military began utilizing
postcombat debriefing sessions as a means for soldiers to process the
trauma they had experienced and then prepare to reenter battle as soon as
possible (Litz & Gray, 2004). More recently, variations of debriefing became
popular among a variety of first responder organizations because of their
brevity and supposed effectiveness, and then they began to be used in community settings (Litz & Gray, 2004).

In general, a debriefing model uses a single session, encourages a re-
telling of the trauma experience, processes emotional reactions and nor-
malizes the experience of the survivor (Rose, Bisson, Churchill & Wessely,
2002). However, systematic review of the empirical literature testing the
debriefing model suggests that there is little evidence that this method of
early intervention produces positive results, and there is evidence to suggest
that these practices are related to negative outcomes among some individuals (Litz & Gray, 2004; Rose & Bisson, 1998). In fact, Rose and colleagues
(2002) make the statement that "Compulsory debriefing of victims of
trauma should cease" (p. 1). While disaster and emergency survivors may
naturally share their experiences with a PFA worker, the PFA model clearly
states that workers "do not 'debrief' by asking for details of what happened"
(Brymer et al., 2006a, p. 8).

Finally, the principle of integrity also applies to the motivation of a
worker or *why* one participates in emergency response. While many counselors, therapists or clergy provide their services as volunteers, there are
groups and individuals that depend on grants and other humanitarian
funding for their livelihoods. As research on PFA and other early interven-

tions for tragedy continues, practitioners need to maintain integrity in their report of the outcomes, even if it means that certain interventions cannot be supported (McNally, Bryant & Ehlers, 2003).

Do no harm. Not doing detailed debriefing of survivors in the midst of immediate response is certainly one way to avoid harm. However, there are more subtle ways that a well-intentioned worker might cause harm. For example, a particularly unique aspect of PFA work is the recognition that the community is made up of survivors, and workers need to respect (and not subvert) the process of resilience that is naturally occurring. This must also be balanced with the fact that many survivors are in vulnerable positions due to recent losses, uncertainties and the chaos of the emergency environment. The counselor, therapist or pastor then walks a fine line in the PFA setting; both bringing professional understanding, but carrying the power dynamic of being a mental health or religious professional. In particular, Principle A of the APA Code states that the psychologist should "guard against . . . factors that might lead to misuse of their influence" (APA, 2010, p. 1). The PFA worker needs to be mindful of the ways that his or her comments might be seen as a diagnosis, a spiritual conviction or a judgment of behaviors. PFA workers do not assume that every person has been traumatized, and they treat survivors with dignity and respect (Brymer et al., 2006a).

For religious professionals responding with PFA it is important to note that there may be a variety of responses simply because of one's title or religious affiliation (Brymer et al., 2006b). Some survivors may be comforted by the presence of a religious professional simply because of his or her title, while others may have a more neutral stance, and some may have a negative reaction toward the religion or role that the professional represents. Regardless of the reaction of the individual it is important to remember that in this setting of immediate response, maintaining a calm, nonintrusive and compassionate demeanor is of the utmost importance.

At a very basic level one of the dimensions of what is "ethical practice" of counseling, pastoral care or therapy is defined by a relationship, or as Principle A states: "those with whom they work" (APA, 2010, p. 1). This raises a question: Is PFA therapy or counseling? Professionals agree that it is not intended to be a psychological intervention or a context to emotionally process traumatic events (Litz & Gray, 2004), but it is a relationship that is established in the context of crisis. A unique aspect of providing psychological first aid is that often the contact happens at the initiation of the PFA worker, rather than the survivor seeking out the worker. The developers of PFA have addressed questions of informed consent in the sense that the PFA worker is instructed to introduce him- or herself with a clear statement of identity, professional role and purpose in the crisis setting. It is the survivor's choice as to whether he or she is interested or care to respond to the outreach of the worker. The worker is also encouraged to first connect with a parent or responsible adult and ask permission to talk with a child. Or, if a child is in crisis and an adult is not nearby, the worker can introduce him- or herself to the child and ask if there are things the child needs, and then follow up that conversation by seeking out the responsible adult and letting her or him know about the interaction (see pages 23-24 of "PFA Field Operations Guide," Brymer et al., 2006a).

In regards to confidentiality, the PFA manual makes it very clear that once an individual or family has chosen to talk with the PFA worker, ethics regarding confidentiality remain similar to typical professional practice, even if the context for the conversation has limited privacy. For example, if the worker is a mandated reporter of child abuse and neglect, she or he must follow the expectations of state laws of reporting that information to the proper authorities. In addition, peer consultation can be an important form of support for PFA workers as they share about their experiences at the site, but maintaining confidentiality is expected in those dialogues (Brymer et al., 2006a). While a set of HIPAA regulations for health care settings may be waived by the Secretary of Health and Human Services in the case of declared emergencies, even without that official waiver the HIPAA Privacy Rule allows for the disclosure of certain identifying information to aid or emergency agencies in order to facilitate treatment or to assist in situations such as locating family members (Department of Health and Human Services, 2008).

Often PFA workers are participating in response in areas away from their home or work due to a deployment by a relief agency, the Red Cross or other structured emergency teams. However, a Christian counselor may find him- or herself part of a response happening within the counselor's own home community from the service of his or her own church or faith community or another local service organization. It is these various locations a PFA worker comes from that lead to more or less challenge in the area of dual relationships. A local worker may hold other roles in the community, and these could impact the opportunity to offer support. In many cases one's role as a mental health or religious leader in the local community may be seen as a benefit—there may be an added sense of credibility or trustworthiness. However, a local counselor or therapist who will be in the community beyond the initial aftermath needs to be intentional in the boundaries about expectations for care or mental health intervention that goes beyond the PFA support model. For example, Scurfield (2006) describes working as psychologist in an academic setting badly affected by Hurricane Katrina. He remarks on the natural dialogue that happens within the clean-up and postcrisis environment, but he also identifies that as a professor he needed to remain attentive to possible dual relationships in offering care to students and fellow faculty.

The APA "Code of Ethics" Principle A also states that psychologists should "strive to be aware of the possible effect of their own physical and mental health on their ability to help those with whom they work" (APA, 2010, p. 1). In the emergency setting it is important for the counselor, therapist and pastor to consider her or his own response and current well-being in the context of providing PFA. Rosser (2008) noted that many of the mental health professionals in the local areas impacted by Hurricane Katrina needed to be focused on the basic needs of their own survival, suggesting both that these professionals were not available for consultation and that they should not be expected to fill in as service providers. He also noted that his own decision to volunteer for emergency mental health service rested on the consideration of three factors: his current family responsibilities, his professional obligations and his competency and motivation to contribute to the efforts (Rosser, 2008). Community religious professionals are also encouraged to consider the ways that their own religious community is responding to any disaster or tragedy, and their responsibility to that community (Brymer et al., 2006b).

Dignity and diversity. The work of disaster support requires respect of and provision of care to those from diverse cultural, racial, socioeconomic, age, ability, sexual orientation and political backgrounds (Brymer, et al., 2006a; Church World Service, n.d.). Intentional awareness of this diversity has not always been the case, and accounts regarding the religious and ethnic diversity of those affected by Hurricane Katrina (African American, Native American, Mexican, Vietnamese, Caucasian, Protestant, Pentecostal, Catholic, Buddhist, etc.) drive home the necessity of both awareness of and access to diversity in resources and response (Dass-Braislford, 2006; Bourne, 2006). The PFA worker needs to be mindful of ways that immigration status, language, stigma regarding mental health service and socioeconomic differences may contribute to the difficulty of accessing resources or feeling welcome and safe in an emergency shelter. An introduction to general cultural issues and sensitivities in disaster settings for several specific populations can be found in a volume edited by Marsella, Johnson, Watson and Gryczynski (2008).

PFA also acknowledges that individuals may experience a variety of spiritual distress or painful reactions related to religious beliefs. The PFA manual has been adapted for use by community religious professionals, and there are sections that describe possibilities of the types of painful reactions (e.g., anger at God, fears about divine retribution, personal guilt, anxiety related to difficulty following religious rituals [Brymer et al., 2006b]). A Christian PFA worker can offer a supportive listening ear, but also needs to respect the place the individual is in at that moment. Workers are instructed not to "contradict or try to 'correct' what a person says about his/her religious beliefs" (Brymer et al., 2006a, p. 39), even if that belief seems to be contributing to the person's emotional pain. The immediate crisis response is not the context for theological debate or lessons. Listening with understanding allows for openness, and then the worker can ask if the disaster survivor would like to connect with a religious professional from her or his own background (Church World Service, n.d.).

Our hope is that this is a standard understanding, but it may be important to state upfront that the aftermath of a disaster or tragedy is not the context for evangelism (Church World Service, n.d.). We are certainly called to care, sacrifice and help, and 1 Peter states that we should be ready to give an answer for the hope that we have (1 Pet 3:15). But it is not ethical or moral to link access to services to doctrinal alliance, and it is not ethical to use the devastation of a trauma to convince people of their need for Christianity.

Other organizations have recognized both the reality of spiritual distress and the ethical concerns regarding providing care across religious or doctrinal boundaries. These agencies have created points of consensus and codes of conduct for spiritual care (Church World Service, n.d.; National Voluntary Organizations Active in Disaster, 2009). The first point of agreement for the Church World Service Standard of Care communicates the boundary well:

> We are called to this ministry by our common commitment to Christ and our desire to be faithful to scripture in showing mercy, doing justice, and walking humbly with our Lord. While we will refrain from using disaster as an opportunity for evangelization and proselytizing, we are nonetheless compelled to do this work out of our love for God, one another, and those we serve. (Church World Service, n.d., p. 1)

ETHICAL ISSUES IN PROVIDING PFA IN INTERNATIONAL SETTINGS

A Christian counselor or group of Christian professionals may decide to travel to a completely different cultural setting in order to offer aid and support to a community after a disaster or crisis. It is important to note that the ethical dimensions of offering psychological first aid can become even more complicated in international efforts. An international version of PFA that reflects general principles for crisis care within low and middle income countries is now available online (World Health Organization, War Trauma Foundation and World Vision, 2011). In addition, a primary source for standards of good practice and professional guidance is the Inter-Agency Standing Committee (IASC) "Guidelines on Mental Health and Psychosocial Support in Emergency Settings" (IASC, 2007); these guidelines are a *must read* for any individual or group interested in providing psychosocial or mental health care in international settings.

One of the unique factors in providing care in an international emergency setting is that there may not be an organized infrastructure to support the general PFA model. But even without formal structure, the local culture, leaders and faith community need to be at the center of efforts for support and recovery. In fact, it is critical that any individual or group intending to offer support in an international setting have an official invitation to participate in these efforts (IASC, 2007).

As a general overlay, the responsibility to "do no harm" is a critical concern in international emergency settings where power dynamics between the effected community and the service providers may create unintentional harm (see Anderson, 1999; Corbett & Fikkert, 2009). For example, a survivor may expect that participation in early psychosocial programs is linked to the availability of financial resources. The rush to get programs going with local workers may also put frontline staff in positions of intense crisis response with little supervision or support. In addition, donor funding designated only for "counseling" can also drive a humanitarian aid program to provide "counseling" offered by local workers with limited or no training in counseling skills. It may even be that simple financial support, rather than counseling, is a greater need (Gilbert, 2009).

The initial chaos of an international emergency may limit participation in immediate crisis response. In fact, the early efforts may need to be undertaken by international first responders and those whose primary work is international relief. Following the initial impact of the disaster, workers can begin to design interventions, and there are steps that can be taken to reduce the possibility of faulty or harmful programmatic decisions. First, workers should approach the task of mental health and psychosocial care with an overall commitment to human rights and dignity. Second, workers should make certain to coordinate efforts with local and international agencies that allow for mutual learning, avoidance of overlapping services and attention to services that are missing. Also, valuing competency and ongoing evaluation of services helps to avoid harm. Workers need to have sufficient cultural sensitivity to the particular context and build intervention plans based on assessments (which involve the participation of the community) of perceived needs, context, resources and available support structures. The program development must also take into account current and relevant evidence, and there should be transparency in the evaluation and ongoing review of the program's effectiveness (IASC, 2007). In addition to these general principles, the IASC Guidelines emphasize that each organization or program should have a clear code of conduct and ethical standards that have been communicated to volunteers and staff. The local community should also know what these standards are and how to confidentially make a complaint.

The possibility of spiritual and religious distress is recognized within the international community as well. The IASC guidelines highlight a number of aspects of psychosocial and mental health care that are directly related to the involvement of local religious leaders and religious rituals. For example, Action Sheet 5.3 states that workers should "Approach local religious and spiritual leaders and other cultural guides to learn their views on how people have been affected and on practices that would support the affected population" (IASC, 2007, p. 107). Workers are cautioned that "ethical sensitivity" (p. 107) must be used as some religious practices may cause physical harm and actually be counter to the expectations of human rights. It is critical to carefully assess and communicate with religious leaders with respect and concern if issues are raised. For example, during a humanitarian project in Liberia, an orphanage leader told one of the authors that during a time of prayer, God had revealed that the war orphans should fast if they wet the bed. This created a complicated conversation with the aim to support the leader's reliance on God, while also talking about the risks of fasting with a group of children who were already in jeopardy of malnourishment. Ultimately, there was a meaningful dialogue with orphanage staff regarding children's regressive behavior as a response to trauma and stress.

The IASC guidelines also outline the process and benefits of learning from local leaders about the traditional methods of healing in the cultural context. These traditional interventions may be assessed to be "potentially beneficial, harmful, or neutral" (IASC, 2007, p. 137). These conversations about benefit or harm can be complicated for a Christian worker, especially if the local religious practice does not fit what a worker would consider orthodox, or if the worker is concerned that facilitating certain practices would be against their own faith. The worker must be very conscious of his or her own expectations about spiritual struggles and spiritual support, and it may mean that a worker chooses not to engage in certain practices.

And finally, similar to the domestic emergency, it is unethical to use international disaster or crisis response as an effort to proselytize or "further a particular . . . religious standpoint" (International Federation of the Red Cross and Red Crescent Societies, 2010, p. 1). While an agency can work as a faith-based organization, the relief aid needs to be offered without discrimination toward others of different faiths. There are few guidelines for these international psychosocial or mental health interventions that target specific spiritual struggles or religious resources, and this can create an ethical challenge for agencies trying to address spiritual needs in a unique cultural context, while avoiding unintentionally limiting access of care to others (Schafer, 2010). Further research and dialogue is needed, and in the meantime first aid workers in international contexts must be mindful of this complex balance of power as an outside agency, provision of needed resources and meaningful collaboration with local religious leaders.

CONCLUSION

Unfortunately, there will always be disasters, violence and other emergencies in our world. Whether these events happen in our backyards or thousands of miles away, we need to ask whether we are being invited to "Go and do likewise." The model of psychological first aid provides a unique framework for service of mercy and compassion that is based on what empirical evidence suggests are the things that most promote resilience and recovery for affected individual, families and communities: comfort, resources, personal or communal sense of mastery, social connection, and hope (Hobfoll, et al., 2007). Ethical practice requires that Christian counselors seek to enact these principles and skills in ways that prioritize competence, integrity in service, responsibility to those with whom they work and recognition of the diverse cultural, religious and emergency contexts.

REFERENCES

American Psychological Association. (2010). *Ethical principles of psychologists and code of conduct: 2010 Amendments*. Retrieved from www.apa.org/ethics/code/index.aspx.

Anderson, M. B. (1999). *Do no harm: How aid can support peace—or war*. Boulder, CO: Lynne Reinner.

Bourne, D. R. (2006). Evacuation patterns of ethnic minority populations affected by Hurricane Katrina. In *Hurricane Katrina: A Multicultural Disaster* [Special Section] (pp. xiii-xvi) *Communiqué*. Washington, DC: Office of Ethnic Minority Affairs, Public Interest Directorate, American Psychological Association.

Bryant, R. A. (2007). Early intervention for post-traumatic stress disorder. *Early Intervention in Psychiatry, 1,* 19-26. doi:10.1111/j.1751-7893.2007.00006.x.

Brymer, M. J., Layne, C. M., Jacobs, A. K., Pynoos, R. S., Ruzek, J. I., Steinberg, A. M., et al. (2006a). *Psychological first aid: Field operations guide* (2nd ed.). Los Angeles: National Child Traumatic Stress Network and National Center for PTSD. Retrieved from www.nctsnet.org/nccts/nav.do?pid=typ_terr_resources_pfa.

Brymer, M. J., Layne, C. M., Jacobs, A. K., Pynoos, R. S., Ruzek, J. I., Steinberg, A. M., et al. (2006b). *Psychological first aid: Field operations guide for community religious professionals.* Los Angeles: National Child Traumatic Stress Network and National Center for PTSD. Retrieved from www.nctsnet.org/nccts/nav. do?pid=typ_terr_resources_pfa.

Church World Service. (n.d.). *Church World Service standard of care for disaster spiritual care ministries.* Retrieved from www.churchpandemicresources.ca/files/SpiritualCareStandards.pdf.

Corbett, S., & Fikkert, B. (2009). *When helping hurts: How to alleviate poverty without hurting the poor . . . and yourself.* Chicago: Moody Publishers.

Dass-Brailsford, P. P. (2006). Eye witness report: Ignore the dead! We want the living! Helping after the storm. In *Hurricane Katrina: A Multicultural Disaster* [Special Section] (pp. vi-viii) *Communiqué.* Washington, DC: Office of Ethnic Minority Affairs, Public Interest Directorate, American Psychological Association.

Gauthier, J., & Pettifor, J. (2011). The evolution of ethics in psychology: Going international and global. In P. R. Martin, F. M. Cheung, M. C. Knowles, M. Kyrios, L. Littlefield, J. B. Overmier & J. Prieto (Eds.), *IAAP handbook of applied psychology* (pp. 700-714). Hoboken, NJ: Wiley-Blackwell.

Gilbert, J. (2009). Power and ethics in psychosocial counseling: Reflections on the experience of an international NGO providing services for Iraqi refugees in Jordan. *Intervention, 7,* 50-60. doi:10.1097/WTF.0b013e32832ad355.

Gray, M. G., & Litz, B. T. (2005). Behavioral interventions for recent trauma: Empirically informed practice guidelines. *Behavioral Modification, 29,* 189-215. doi:10.1177/0145445504270884.

Hobfoll, S. E., Watson, P., Bell, C. C., Bryant, R. A., Brymer, M. J., Friedman, M. J., et al. (2007). Five essential elements of immediate and mid-term mass trauma intervention: empirical evidence. *Psychiatry, 70,* 283-315. doi:10.1521/psyc.2007.70.4.283.

Inter-Agency Standing Committee. (2007). *IASC Guidelines on Mental Health and Psychosocial Support in Emergency Settings.* Geneva: IASC. Retrieved from www

.who.int/mental_health/emergencies/guidelines_iasc_mental_health_psycho social_june_2007.pdf.

International Federation of the Red Cross and Red Crescent Societies. (2010). *The code of conduct: Principles of conduct for The International Red Cross and Red Crescent Movement and NGOs in disaster response programmes.* Retrieved from www.ifrc.org/publicat/conduct/code.asp.

Litz, B. T., & Gray, M. J. (2004). Early intervention for trauma in adults: A framework for first aid and secondary prevention. In B. T. Litz (Ed.), *Early intervention for trauma and traumatic loss* (pp. 87-111). New York: Guilford.

Marsella, A. J., Johnson, J. L., Watson, P., & Gryszynski, J. (Eds.). (2008). *Ethnocultural perspectives on disaster and trauma: Foundations, issues, and applications.* New York: Springer.

McCabe, O. L., Lating, J. M., Everly, G. S., Mosley, A. M., Teague, P. J., Links, J. M., & Kaminsky, M. J. (2007). Psychological First Aid training for the faith community: A model curriculum. *International Journal of Emergency Mental Health, 9,* 181-92.

McNally, R. J., Bryant, R. A., & Ehlers, A. (2003). Does early psychological intervention promote recovery from posttraumatic stress? *Psychological Science in the Public Interest, 4,* 45-79. doi:10.1111/1529-1006.01421.

National Voluntary Organizations Active in Disaster. (2009). *Points of consensus: Disaster spiritual care.* Retrieved from http://march2recovery.org/wp-content/uploads/2012/05/Points-of-Consensus-Spiritual-Care.pdf.

Nolland, J. (1993). Luke 9:21–18:34. In D. A. Hubbard & G. W. Barker (Eds.), *Word biblical commentary, 35b* (pp. 586-98). Dallas: Word.

Rose, S., & Bisson, J. (1998). Brief early psychological interventions following trauma: A systematic review of the literature. *Journal of Traumatic Stress, 11*(4), 697-712. doi:10.1023/A:1024441315913.

Rose, S. C., Bisson, J., Churchill, R., & Wessely, S. (2002). Psychological debriefing for preventing post-traumatic stress disorder (PTSD). *Cochrane Database of Systematic Reviews, 2,* no. CD000560. doi:10.1002/14651858.CD000560.

Rosser, B. R. S. (2008). Working as a psychologist in the Medical Reserve Corps: Providing emergency mental health relief services in Hurricanes Katrina and Rita. *Professional Psychology: Research and Practice, 39,* 37-44. doi:10.1037/0735-7028.39.1.37.

Schafer, A. (2010). Spirituality and mental health in humanitarian contexts: An exploration based on World Vision's Haiti earthquake response. *Intervention, 8,* 121-30. doi:10.1097/WTF.0b013e32833c1f57.

Scurfield, R. M. (2006). Post-Katrina aftermath and helpful interventions on the Mississippi Gulf coast. *Traumatology, 12*, 104-20. doi:10.1177/1534765606295924.

Sinclair, C. (2012). Ethical principles, values and codes for psychologists: An historical journey. In M. M. Leach, M. J. Stevens, G. Lindsay, A. Ferrero & Y. Korkut (Eds.), *The Oxford handbook of international psychological ethics* (pp. 3-18). Oxford: Oxford University Press.

Suite, D. H., Rollin, S. A., Bowman, J. C., La Bril, R. D. (2007). From fear to faith: Efficacy of trauma assessment training for New York-based Southern Baptist church groups. *Research on Social Work Practice, 17*, 258-63. doi:10.1177/10497315 06296678.

Watson, P. J., & Ruzek, J. I. (2009). Academic/state/federal collaborations and the improvement of practices in disaster mental health services and evaluation. *Administration and Policy in Mental Health and Mental Services Research, 36*, 215-20. doi:10.1007/s10488-009-0212-4.

Watson, P. J., & Shalev, A. Y. (2005). Assessment and treatment of adult acute responses to traumatic stress following mass traumatic events [Electronic version]. *CNS Spectrums, 10*, 123-31.

World Health Organization, War Trauma Foundation and World Vision International. (2011). *Psychological first aid: Guide for field workers.* WHO: Geneva, Switzerland. Retrieved from http://whqlibdoc.who.int/publications/2011/97892 41548205_eng.pdf.

U.S. Department of Health and Human Services. (October, 2008). *Is the HIPAA Privacy Rule suspended during a national or public health emergency?* Retrieved on October 17, 2010, from www.hhs.gov/hipaafaq/providers/hipaa-1068.html.

20

Training Programs

Tamara L. Anderson, Gregory R. Schneller
and John Eric Swenson III

To educate a person in mind and not in morals is to educate
a menace to society.
—Theodore Roosevelt

Education in professional ethics begins with an understanding of expected behavior for practitioners in their given field. In psychology, the "Ethical Principles of Psychologists and Code of Conduct" (APA, 2002) provide aspirational and enforceable standards by which psychologists are meant to practice (these standards are mirrored in other codes governing counselors). What is not widely known, and worth noting, is that the development of the APA professional code is unique in that it was originally derived from what is called the "critical incident method." As twentieth-century psychologists moved increasingly into providing psychotherapy as part of their primary duties, it became apparent that a code of behavior was necessary to provide guidelines and expectations for practitioners. In 1947 the first Committee on Ethical Standards for Psychologists was formed to work toward devising a code of conduct. The first code was developed utilizing a process whereby the committee asked practicing psychologists to describe what ethical dilemmas they themselves had faced in their practices or any that they knew their colleagues had encountered. Approximately seven thousand psychologists were contacted with a return rate of over two thousand (APA, 1953). From these stories the ethics code was born.

Subsequently, the role of the ethics committee continued to develop and include consultation and, later, sanction in the case of incompetent practitioners. The unique factor in the development of the psychology ethics code is in the polling of the constituency *before* rendering professional guidelines. A more typical approach for the development of professional codes is to elect a committee to write the code and then to present it to their particular constituency. In doing so the actual dilemmas faced are limited to the committee's thoughts and unique experiences. Understanding the genesis of the psychology ethics code puts in perspective the intent to develop a code that addressed real-life dilemmas from a broad range of practitioners. Given this history, and the thoughtful revisions based on changes in the field, the psychology ethics code provides practical guidelines that are important for psychologists functioning in many different roles. In training graduate students in psychology there is no substitute for requiring students to digest this code and understand the important role it plays in providing a helpful and necessary frame for good client care and research.

As is often the case, when students begin their training in ethics they expect that their time will consist of just memorizing (and parroting) a list of rules regarding how to handle various aspects of clinical practice. Therefore, given this predisposition it is imperative that educators help students understand the history of the psychology ethics code (as well as other codes of conduct specific to client care) and the value of learning the code. After this foundation has been laid, it is particularly satisfying for educators to watch their graduate students come to embrace the reality that ethical decision making is much more nuanced and layered than previously thought. In fact, successful training in how to effectively handle ethical dilemmas is accomplished by helping students develop an ability to look at the broader context of the dilemma, rather than to only focus on whether ethical rules were broken. The hope of the educator is that students will over time develop discernment regarding the many facets that are present in most ethical dilemmas. In this chapter we will identify what we believe are necessary components of robust training in ethics, highlight the relevant research on what therapists of faith report regarding their training in ethics, and present areas of focus that we believe should be included in the training of ethics.

THE IMPORTANCE OF TEACHING ETHICAL THEORY: ENHANCING DECISION MAKING

In 1979 the APA mandated that all programs accredited by the APA include ethics training for graduate students. This decision was based on the belief that students needed not only to read the ethics code and understand their professional responsibilities, but to also spend time in discussion regarding ethical decision making and what constitutes ethical behavior. As professors and students engage in these discussions, it quickly becomes clear that training in moral theories is important for framing any discussion of ethics (Cottone & Claus, 2000; Welfel, 2000).

Miner (2005) suggests that "training students in philosophical bases of ethics allows students to recognize their implicit moral theories, develop an appreciation of other ways of conceptualizing the good and present and explicit, informed ethical justification of their decisions" (p. 54). She proposes that training in ethics should move beyond the enforceable standards, based on recorded therapeutic dilemmas and require students to engage their decision-making process at a deeper level. Miner states that "moral theory provides a basis for acting ethically in novel or extreme situations" (p. 55), which are those situations that require a higher level of critical thinking. In fact, Davidson, Garton, and Joyce (2003) felt so strongly about the need for students to develop a fully informed ethical decision-making process that they made the following recommendations for training psychologists in ethics: Years 1-3, teach moral theory; year 4, teach ethical decision making; years 5-7, teach applied ethics. All of these authors advocate for a deep knowledge of ethical theory, and for good reason. The ethical dilemmas that counselors encounter in today's sophisticated technological world are even more complex than in previous years (Foreman, 2010). Questions that face today's therapists include whether to Google or not Google clients, or whether to friend or not friend a client on Facebook. Greggo (2010) poses another example of a modern dilemma in his discussion of bioethics and the expectation on the part of clients that Christian counselors are equipped to provide wisdom to help them with difficult health dilemmas. Greggo makes the point that Christian counselors are indeed uniquely poised to fill the gap between medical professional and patient. However, traditional training in ethics does not necessarily prepare these counselors to step into such difficult situations.

Secular moral theories offer valuable insights regarding the complexities of human behavior. However, there is a rich literature base in the area of Christian ethics to which trainees would certainly benefit. Obviously, Christian ethics is germane to clinicians of faith and the Christian clients they treat, but in fact even those who do not endorse Judeo-Christian tenets can appreciate "Christian ethics as a valuable set of guidelines and ideals for society" (Rae, 2009, p. 24). So how do Christian ethics inform the professional ethics of the faith-based clinician? It begins with how the clinician views the human condition. Christian ethics help trainees grasp the human condition from the perspective of the Creator and the created: "So God created human beings in his own image" (Gen 1:27) and "then God looked over all he had made, and he saw that it was very good" (Gen 1:31 NLT). Being created in God's image is central to a Christian's identity, and understanding that God deemed humans "good" provides a context in which to understand human beliefs, thoughts, feelings and behaviors.

Christian ethicists endorse the basic idea that morality is grounded in the person of God; that the ultimate source for morality is not God's law but God's *character*. God's character is *displayed* through his law and spiritual disciplines, as in the Old Testament, and in the person of Christ and the indwelling of the Spirit as presented in the New Testament (Browning, 2006; Geisler, 1989; Rae, 2009). God is perfect and therefore his character is perfect, and "morality is ultimately grounded in the Character of God" (Rae, 2009, p. 24). God is also unchanging and manifests his character in humanity through special (scriptural) and general (natural law) revelation. These revelations are the foundation on which Christian faith is lived out. Concepts such as social justice, care for the poor, virtue, love and transformational change are central to Christian ethics and have direct bearing on clinical work.

In summary, it becomes imperative to provide clinicians in training with a grounding in Christian ethics, moral theory, exposure to their given profession's ethical standards as well as facilitation of growth through practice and attention to current issues. However, rather than beginning the educational process with information on various moral theories, we suggest that the educational process begin with the activation into awareness of each student's ethical/moral history, for it is on this scaffolding that all the training in theory and practical dilemmas will rest and on which all ethical decisions will be made.

Understanding our individual decision-making heritage

In Dr. Anderson's graduate course in ethics (taught the spring of second year to Ph.D. and Psy.D. doctoral students), she begins the semester with an assignment in which students are asked to create what is called an ethics genogram. Basically, she takes the principles and process of creating a genogram outlined in *Genograms: Assessment and Intervention* (Mc-Goldrick, Gerson & Shellenberger, 1999) and asks students to map out their ethical heritage. Students map out their history based on prompt questions such as: Who has spoken into your life regarding ethical thinking? Who modeled ethical decision making for you? Who are those people you do *not* want to emulate, and why? Students are asked to be creative in producing their project, using artistic techniques, color and form. She has required this assignment for over thirteen years and has seen some beautiful artwork and poignant declarations regarding impactful people and moments in students' lives. To discuss these assignments students are broken up into a group of four or five and are asked to describe their experience of creating their ethical genogram as they share with each other the finished product. Students are then asked to voluntarily share with the larger group their observations of the process of mapping their heritage on paper. It is these comments that encourage the assignment of this project each year. Students share observations such as, "I was so amazed to see how alike my grandfather, my dad, and I are in how we approach right and wrong." Or "I had never really thought about it before, but I learned how *not* to treat people from my maternal grandmother. She was extremely judgmental and overly concerned with the appearance of doing the right thing, instead of the action of doing the right thing."

This exercise teaches students that they carry a heritage of decision making within them. Beliefs and behaviors they observed, or that were tacitly passed down to them, may predispose them to view professional, ethical situations in a unique way. The project allows them to identify these influences, reflect on them and understand their place in how the student approaches and thinks through ethical dilemmas in general. Given that this assignment is required in a faith-based institution, there are often references to spiritual mentors and leaders who are identified as examples to follow or avoid.

In educational theory there is a term, *transformative learning*, that captures this same concept on which the ethics genogram is based. The term is derived from Mezirow's (2000) transformative learning theory and describes a process by which the learner becomes aware of tacit beliefs. After these beliefs and experiences are brought into awareness, the learner is then able to evaluate whether they still hold relevance.

It is important to acknowledge where we come from and what familial, cultural and experiential factors inform our decision-making process. Furthermore, and from a broader perspective, how do we view the world? Do we have more of a deontological or teleological perspective (Nagy, 2011)? Deontological decision making is based on consistency. Basically, it stresses the obligation or duty to always do what is right. This view was first conceptualized and articulated by Immanuel Kant (1724-1804), who proposed that we take a similar course of action that we have taken in the past regardless of present circumstances.

A teleological perspective evaluates the likelihood of an outcome for the greater good, and so takes into account individual circumstances. This approach, developed by Jeremy Bentham (1748-1832) and elaborated by John Stuart Mill (1806-1873), provides an allowance for cause-and-effect relationships and inconsistency for the benefit of the many (Callan & Callan, 2005; Nagy, 2011).

As an example of how one might approach a common clinical dilemma from these two points of view, let's pose the following question: Should a therapist ever hug a client? If the majority opinion from the counseling community is no, then from a deontological view a therapist should never hug a client, regardless of the situation. From a teleological point of view the answer would be "maybe." The therapist would take into account the client's history, what the circumstances are at the given moment the hug is being contemplated and a myriad of other considerations. As therapists we may find ourselves automatically responding from a deontological viewpoint, which tends to be more inherent and reactive, instead of from a teleological position, which is a more considered view. This tendency often mirrors the developmental level of clinicians in training. Early on in their training students feel more comfortable with absolutes, whereas students farther along in their training can exist more comfortably in the gray areas.

Teaching students to attend to and understand their automatic responses will make it much more likely that they will take nuances into account in a given ethical situation and will be less likely to respond from a place of safety or rigidity. So how do we train and assess students' abilities in decision making and practice? What responsibilities do training programs have in ensuring competence, both ethically and across domains?

ISSUES OF CLINICAL APPLICATION AND COMPETENCY

In 1992 Welfel conducted a review of the literature relevant to ethics education from the previous forty years. In her conclusions she noted three particular areas in training that were systematically lacking: "(a) the need for more attention to clinical applications of the APA's Ethical Code; (b) interns' understanding of competence; and (c) the need for more formal evaluations regarding the outcomes of ethics education" (p. 188) (see also Callan & Bucky, 2005).

In this chapter we would like to address her first two suggestions. Regarding her first suggestion, the need for more clinical application of the ethics code has been a concern echoed by other educators, authors and researchers of graduate training in ethics (e.g., Callan & Callan, 2005; Knapp & VandeCreek, 2003; McMinn & Meek, 1997; Nagy, 2005). There is a necessary practice component to teaching ethical decision making that allows students to "try on" various responses and discuss the likely outcomes. The use of case vignettes in presenting various ethical dilemmas, with ample time for discussion, is a useful tool. To begin with a particular scenario and then change the facts, places or timeframes is one method that seems particularly effective. Not only does it hone the student's knowledge base in a given area, it teaches flexibility in thinking that more accurately mirrors what is expected in the real-world clinical experiences students will face. An example is the following case:

> A local pastor refers Susie, a single twenty-four-year-old Caucasian woman, for therapy. In the first session Susie states that she is seeing another therapist, but that it isn't working out. As you inquire further, Susie reports that this

other therapist wanted her to see a psychiatrist due to some unusual thoughts she was having about some painful and embarrassing events from her childhood that have caused her to "make poor decisions." When you inquire further, Susie states that it really is no big deal and changes the subject. How do you proceed?

This case raises many ethical and legal issues for discussion. To name a few, Susie states that she is currently in a therapeutic relationship with another therapist. Standard 10.04 of "Providing Therapy to Those Served by Others" requires that psychologists dialogue with clients about their reasons for seeking services from an additional clinician. The charge to the therapist is to "minimize the risk for confusion and conflict" (APA, 2002, p. 4). However, Susie is entitled to self-determination regarding her own care. So how do you proceed?

Does Susie have a thought disorder, and if so, how impaired might she be? Do you have an ethical and legal responsibility to make sure she is cared for? Furthermore, what painful and embarrassing events is Susie referring to? What if Susie discloses that these events involved childhood abuse? Susie is now over eighteen and therefore you may or may not be obligated to report the abuse to authorities. It could be that children are still at risk. Given that reporting laws differ based on state law, do you maintain or breach confidentiality? Standard 4.01, "Privacy and Confidentiality," cautions practitioners on breaching confidentiality without clear cause.

Now let's change the details. What if Susie were a Mexican American seventeen-year-old? Age and ethnicity now affect decision making. Are you familiar with Mexican culture? What generation immigrant is Susie? Principle E, of the APA Ethics Code, while not an enforceable standard, calls clinicians to be *aware* of cultural differences. Susie is a minor; can she consent to therapy on her own? Since she is a minor, will your state law allow you to withhold information that she does decide to reveal to you from her parents should they desire that information? What if it turns out that the "embarrassing event" is that her father molested her when she was a girl? The exercise of having students rethink the case based on various scenario and demographic changes allows them to practice the behavior of quickly assessing a situation and handling the unexpected twists that often present in the therapeutic environment.

Welfel's second suggestion involves teaching students about what clinical competence means. In the years subsequent to Welfel's suggestion, competencies across clinical domains have become a focus of the American Psychological Association, as well as other groups such as the National Counsel of Schools and Programs in Professional Psychology (NCSPP). In fact, both groups have developed specific documents defining competencies in professional psychology. In 2006 the American Psychological Association Board of Educational Affairs in collaboration with the Council of Chairs of Training Councils convened a work group whose task it was to produce a detailed document outlining the various areas of competency viewed as necessary for practicing clinicians, and to go beyond just defining competencies to measuring those competencies. The result is the "Assessment of Competency Benchmarks Work Group: A Developmental Model for Defining and Measuring Competence in Professional Psychology" (Fouad et al., 2009).

In addition to several key areas of professional practice (e.g., assessment, supervision, intervention), the document is broken down into core competency domains of the cube model (Rodolfa et al., 2005), and more specifically into foundational competencies and functional competencies. "Foundational competencies refer to the knowledge, skills, attitudes, and values that serve as the foundation for the functions a psychologist is expected to carry out (e.g., an understanding of ethics, awareness and understanding of individual and cultural diversity issues)" (p. 5), while functional competencies encompass the major functions of a psychologist such as assessment, intervention and research.

The core competencies of the cube model are broken down into the following categories, which allow for achievement of the competency based on developmental level: readiness for practicum, readiness for internship, readiness for entry to practice, and readiness for advanced practice and specialization. Assessing students based on their developmental level allows for a more accurate expectation of performance as well as expected incremental gains in each area over time. One particular foundational competency listed in the Benchmark document that seems particularly important is called reflective practice self-assessment. This area highlights the need for trainees to understand the boundaries of their competence, to engage in critical thinking and to commit to lifelong learning. Training programs that adopt this language and expectation can emphasize that self-reflection is a very important area of growth for their students, a traditionally difficult area to define and assess, yet essential to acting ethically.

One way to encourage self-assessment and reflection is to require psychotherapy for all therapists in training. The benefits to students are numerous; however, we will only mention two here. First, when sitting with their therapists, students engage in an experiential didactic of what being a therapist is like. The modeling of the therapeutic experience by the student's therapist is impactful, as it teaches students how to engage in introspection, as well as helps shape their identity as a therapist. While self-assessment of one's own emotional issues is hoped for as a career habit, many therapists in training have difficulty identifying growth areas in themselves that may negatively affect client care (Schwartz-Mette, 2009). Therefore, ensuring a therapeutic experience for each therapist in training provides a safe and confidential environment in which introspection can take place. Since its inception forty years ago, Rosemead School of Psychology at Biola University has required that all its students complete fifty hours of individual therapy while in the program. Not only do students typically attend on average eighty sessions but yearly program-outcome data gathered for APA purposes show that alums of Rosemead continue to rank this experience as the most impactful of their training years.

Second, during their own therapy students are able to process stress typical of graduate training in psychotherapy, specifically the pressures they experience as a novice therapist. Schwartz-Mette (2009) discusses the need for academic training programs, supervisors and peers of therapists in training to be alert to the increased risk of emotional impairment these students face. Whereas mandating personal therapy after a student has experienced impairment is complicated by the tension between confidentiality and accountability (Elman & Forrest, 2004), students who choose to enter therapy as part of their doctoral program are able to utilize their therapeutic experience to alleviate stress as they encounter it. Furthermore, students who enter a graduate program with the understanding that personal psychotherapy is a requirement are more likely to be individuals who are open to introspection and change. It may also be that students who are willing to engage in an introspective process are more likely to handle potential boundary issues with clients, such as sexual feelings in psychotherapy and dual roles, more effectively.

SEXUAL FEELINGS IN PSYCHOTHERAPY

According to Pope, Sonne, and Holroyd (1993), one area of discussion that has traditionally been lacking in ethics training is that of sexual feelings of the therapist toward a client. When therapists experience sexual feelings in psychotherapy, they typically keep it to themselves and omit any details of their experience related to these feelings from supervisors, professors and peers. In a survey McMinn and Meek (1996, 1997) found that Christian therapists in particular are more likely to report never having experienced sexual attraction to a client. Perhaps Christian therapists tend to approach ethical dilemmas involving sexual issues from either a position of transcendent protection or shame. The former is encapsulated for me (Anderson) in one discussion I had with a student during an ethics class some years back. As I was lecturing on my "it's not if but when" concept, which acknowledges that at some point in their career, every clinician will experience some instance of sexual *attraction* to a client, I had a student comment, "Oh, but Dr. Anderson, I am a Christian married man, so I really don't believe I will experience this situation." I must say I was truly dumbfounded at this very bright, affable, well-meaning young man's naiveté. My response to him was that if he truly believed that he was immune given his marital status and faith commitment, he had already taken his first step down the road of having sex with a client. My response is predicated on the belief that therapists who deny the possibility of an inappropriate relationship with a client are unable to be thoughtful about recognizing the precursors and preventing it. It is important for students to understand that the overwhelming majority of therapists do not enter the field of counseling with the intent to engage in sexual relationships with clients (Pope, 1994). However, results of one survey indicate that at least 87% of therapists admitted to sexual attraction toward a client at least once in their careers (Pope, Tabachnick & Keith-Spiegel, 1987). The incremental steps that lead to such a relationship are subtle and usually take place over a long period of time. Therefore, armed with this knowledge it behooves educators to ensure that therapists in training understand what unmet needs may move them into an inappropriate relationship with a client.

Pope, in his book *Sexual Feelings in Psychotherapy*, discusses various warning signs to an impending inappropriate therapeutic relationship. Dressing for a client, moving a client to the end of the day so you can spend more time with him or her, finding yourself unwilling to honestly evaluate a client because it is unacceptable for you to think you could be attracted to someone with psychopathology are just a few examples of how our feelings about or for a client can cloud our judgment and affect our actions (Pope et al., 1993).

A Christian clinician may also contend with feelings of shame and guilt perpetuated by the Christian subculture regarding issues of sexuality. As these feelings are left unprocessed, the likelihood that a therapist will act out may increase. Educators who can approach this idea of sexual attraction in a direct and open manner have a wonderful opportunity to model for their students that discussion of attraction is healthy and appropriate, and will help them guard against any sexual action with clients. Furthermore, becoming comfortable consulting with trusted colleagues regarding sexual feelings in psychotherapy positions the therapist to more easily consult on other situations regarding clients that are by comparison benign yet still impactful.

DUAL ROLES PARTICULAR TO THE CHRISTIAN THERAPIST

There are many types of dual roles that therapists encounter throughout their career, and some dual roles are unique to therapists of faith. Examples include worshiping at the same church, serving on the worship team and attending the same Bible study as your client. These types of dilemmas are discussed in chapter six of this book (see also research on dual roles by Sanders, Swenson & Schneller, 2011). However, it is worth emphasizing that educators who take time to discuss these unique and nuanced dilemmas that often arise make it possible for students to rehearse their actions and reactions prior to the actual occurrence. This rehearsal allows for the therapist in training to gain experience in problem-solving behavior, as well as work through the emotions that might arise in these situations. For example, if a therapist is enjoying the experience of attending the Wednesday morning women's Bible study, which meets for lecture and break out groups, it is understandable that she might experience feelings of resentment if her client begins attending the same study.

These are but a few examples of how clinicians might encounter clients in their faith communities. In the next section research is presented concerning ethical dilemmas that arise in the Christian counseling arena and how well therapists of faith believe they have been prepared to handle these dilemmas.

TRAINING FOR ETHICAL DILEMMAS ARISING IN CHRISTIAN COUNSELING: WHAT THE RESEARCH SAYS

Since the 1950s there has been an increasing emphasis on ethics education in psychology training programs, and by 1990 100% of APA-approved programs provided ethics training (Vanek, 1990). Empirical research on the effectiveness of ethics training has accompanied this trend. Surveys of faculty members about the effectiveness of their ethics training programs have generally found that instructors believe that their programs effectively instill ethical competencies in their students (Urofsky & Sowa, 2004; Vanek, 1990; Welfel, 1992). However, student ratings do not always parallel the ratings of their instructors. For example, Housman and Stake (1999) surveyed both student and faculty members' opinions of the sexual ethics training in their graduate programs and found that faculty tended to provide significantly more positive ratings than students.

Clearly, asking trainees (or former trainees) about the scope and depth of their graduate ethics training is necessary. Moreover, it should be noted that most of the previous research on ethics training has focused on secular training sites. However, what about programs that integrate religious faith into clinical training? Although the number of doctoral programs that integrate faith and professional training has grown steadily during the past three decades (Johnson & McMinn, 2003), only a few studies have investigated ethics training in these types of programs. The earliest of these was a survey of religiously oriented counselor-education programs regarding the multicultural training they provided (Kanitz, Mendoza & Ridley, 1992). The authors reported that 88% provided such training. Although the authors identified their study as investigating ethics training, its contribution is limited because developing multicultural competencies is only one facet of sound, ethical practice.

McMinn and Meek (1997) surveyed ethical beliefs and behaviors of nine hundred members of the American Association of Christian Counselors. Among other questions, AACC respondents were asked to rate the adequacy of their graduate training programs. McMinn and Meek reported that 79% of their sample rated their graduate programs as at least adequate; 60% of these said their programs were either "good" or "excellent" in preparing them for "effective, appropriate, and ethical practice" (p. 279). Only 6% of these Christian counselors rated their training programs as "less than adequate." The researchers' conclusion was that the majority of these Christian mental health professionals do see their graduate training in professional ethical issues as meaningful.

Because McMinn and Meek's study obtained from participants a single, global rating of graduate ethics training, several questions remained. What types of specific ethical dilemmas do Christian therapists encounter? Do they receive graduate training for how to handle those dilemmas? Is training for ethical issues that arise in explicitly Christian therapy as thorough as for ethical dilemmas that may arise in any therapy context (secular or Christian)? Two of the present authors attempted to answer these questions in a recent study (Schneller, Swenson & Sanders, 2010). The remainder of this section will discuss our findings.

The population of interest in our study was Christian mental health practitioners. We asked 1,279 clinicians who were members of the Christian Association for Psychological Studies (CAPS) to complete an ethics survey and demographic sheet. We received 362 completed surveys. Research method and participant demographics have been reported elsewhere (Swenson, Schneller & Sanders, 2009). Our ethics survey consisted of eighty specific ethical dilemmas. Twenty-three of the items were adopted from previous large-scale ethics surveys (Helbok, Marinelli & Walls, 2006; McMinn & Meek, 1996; Pope et al., 1987). These items consisted of situations that require an ethical decision (e.g., "Lend money to a client") but they did not include content specific to faith-based therapy settings. We added fifty-seven new items—forty-two of which covered ethical situations specific to faith-based therapy (e.g., "Pray with a client upon request of the client") and fifteen pertaining to multiple relationship issues. For each of the eighty ethical behavior situations, participants were asked to indicate, "Yes, I have received ethics training related to this behavior" or "No, I have received *no* ethics training related to this behavior."

The focus of our study was to explore and compare "general" ethical dilemmas which may arise in most therapy contexts with ethical dilemmas more specific to therapy in a Christian context. For sake of convenience, we will refer to survey items assessing these dilemmas as "general items" and "Christian items," respectively. Respondents reported significantly more training for general items than for Christian items. The ethical dilemmas for which the highest number of respondents had received training were all general items. The greatest amount of training was reported for items such as "Discuss with a client the limits of confidentiality at the beginning of therapy" (98.3% respondents reported receiving training), "Obtain some form of written informed consent from your clients (or their guardians)" (97.5%), and "Consult with peers/colleagues on difficult cases" (97.5%). The ethical dilemmas for which the lowest number of respondents had received training were almost exclusively Christian items. Examples of ethical dilemmas for which the least number of respondents reported training were: "Hesitate to refer to other therapists who may not adhere to Christian values" (45.2% respondents reported receiving training), "Without explicitly saying so, use stories in therapy that are patterned after the Bible" (41.6%), and "Use exorcism as a technique in your therapy practice" (35.3%).

Two related factors appear to have influenced the amount of ethics training in our sample of respondents. The first had to do with respondents' age and how recently they attended graduate school. Younger, more recently trained clinicians indicated they had received broader, more thorough ethics training. This was true for both general and Christian ethical dilemmas. Specifically, those trained in the past ten years reported the most extensive training. The second factor affecting the amount of ethics training respondents reported had to do with integration training. We asked our participants to indicate whether their graduate training included how to integrate Christian faith into psychotherapy. Most respondents (62.5%) indicated they had received such training, with more recent graduates being significantly more likely to have received integration training. It appeared that such training conferred an advantage regarding training for ethical dilemmas. Clinicians who had received integration training reported receiving more ethics training overall than those who did not. As would be expected, they reported significantly more training for ethical dilemmas specific to faith-based settings. Additionally, those who received graduate training in integration also reported significantly more training for general items. This suggests that their integration programs had also more thoroughly prepared them to face generic ethical issues that may arise in any psychotherapy setting.

Interestingly, the apparent advantage of receiving integration training was specific to the graduate school setting. Participants were also asked to indicate whether they had received integration training in continuing education (CE) settings, but the number of hours of integration CE credits was unrelated to amount of ethics training for either Christian or general items. It may be that most integration CE workshops are focused on topics other than professional ethics. Nearly half of state licensing boards in the United States require that CE credits include ethics training (APA, 2006). However, no formal studies have compared the impact of CE education with graduate training in ethics. This is an important topic for future research.

The results of our research provide hopeful news for integration training programs. It is encouraging that our sample of Christian therapists, especially those who attended integration graduate programs, were well trained in general ethical issues. It is also a positive trend that more recent graduates report having broader training in faith-based ethical dilemmas. Several other studies have also found better ethics training in more recent graduates (Glaser & Thorpe, 1986; Pope & Feldman-Summers, 1992). The present results also lay down a challenge for integration training programs. Some ethical issues, especially those related to practice in a Christian context, may need to be covered more thoroughly in graduate ethics training. We encourage faith-based graduate training programs to examine the breadth of issues covered in their ethics training and ensure that they are addressing ethical issues which will be relevant to working in a Christian counseling context.

Effective Methods in the Teaching of Ethics

Based in part on the research presented in the previous section, information garnered from the authors' experiences and other sources, three teaching methods have been identified as particularly helpful in training students in the area of ethics. Also mentioned are integrative approaches made possible in a faith-based program.

Professors sharing their own experiences. Surveys of graduate students and professionals revealed that mentored students enjoyed their doctoral programs more, were more likely to publish their research and showed more involvement with professional organizations (Cameron & Blackburn, 1981; Clark, Hardin & Johnson, 2000; Reskin, 1979). This research shows that students who are mentored experience obvious and substantial benefits above what their nonmentored peers experience.

Johnson (2002) provides a broad definition of mentoring: Mentoring is a personal relationship in which a more experienced (usually older) faculty member or professional acts as a guide, role model, teacher and sponsor of a less experienced (usually younger) graduate student or junior professional. A mentor provides the protégé with knowledge, advice, challenge, counsel and support in the protégé's pursuit of becoming a full member of a particular profession (p. 88). These mentoring relationships take place in and out of the classroom. Typically, students are eager to learn from the experiences of their mentors/professors and often remember the stories (and lessons taught) shared by these important people. If therapists in training learn from the thoughtful decisions and positive interventions made by their professors, then even more so do they learn through the sharing of past mistakes, poor judgment and difficult ethical challenges faced by these same professors. The trainee can project him- or herself into these stories. The experience instills in students that they too will encounter difficult decisions, which they will not always handle well, provides for them examples of best and worst practices, and allows them to experience less anxiety as they take on their new roles as therapists. There is likely no book, or video that can match the stories of the professor.

Why then are some professors hesitant to share? It may be that the professor is not comfortable being cast in a negative light or is concerned that the student will somehow ascertain some kind of "permission granted" to make similar poor decisions. We suggest that withholding all less-flattering information about the professor's experiences is not helpful as compared to the great benefit to the student from the judicious use of carefully chosen examples of successes and failures.

Practice consulting on difficult issues. Another area of particular importance in training therapists is to help them become accustomed to consulting. Providing repeated opportunities for students to consult with peers regarding ethical dilemmas helps them to develop an internal rubric that can (and hopefully will) be referenced again and again when facing new dilemmas. We make the suggestion that each ethics class session include time for the students to break into groups to consult on a vignette. Other exercises include encouraging students to read a book such as *Sexual Feelings in Psychotherapy* by Pope (1993) and meet weekly with a few other students to discuss the readings, or write their own vignettes including consultation questions which the class can take turns discussing. Learning to consult throughout one's career, and thereby preventing dangerous isolation, is a habit that must be highly encouraged and practiced. Fisher (2009) states that, "Consultation with colleagues is an important means of ensuring and maintaining the competence of one's work and the ethical conduct of psychology" (p. 148).

Addressing training in issues unique to therapists of faith. In their research on the ethical training of Christian therapists, Schneller et al. (2010) found that Christian therapists experienced a lack of attention in their training to situations unique to their work with clients of faith. Earlier it was briefly mentioned that therapists of faith might encounter unique dual-role situations given their involvement in their local faith communities, of which their clients may be a part. Schneller et al. found that even when attending a faith-based graduate institution, Christian therapists in training did not always engage in meaningful and pointed dialogue regarding issues germane to them. We suggest here that faith-based institutions are uniquely poised to engage in these conversations. The ethics professor can model his or her own experiences managing these issues and engage students in opportunities to consult with Christian peers as to their opinions and suggestions regarding circumstances specific to a faith-based clientele. While heartening to find that Christian therapists felt very prepared in secular ethics, it is in working through situations unique to being a Christian therapist (e.g., praying with or for clients; providing counseling as part of the church staff) that the faith-based institutions can provide much-needed knowledge and experience.

TRENDS IN CONTINUING EDUCATION: SPECIALTY AREAS

It is naive to think that sufficient training in ethical decision making can be accomplished in graduate school. Regardless of the creativeness, intensity and varied exposure to both ethical theory and ethical dilemmas that may be present in instruction, the field is too varied (and specialized) to allow for every contingency to be dissected and discussed. Also, as new dilemmas emerge, such as those related to new technology, they challenge us to think in new ways and entertain new ethical considerations and outcomes. Therefore, continuing education (CE) in ethical decision making is necessary. In fact, most states now require CE credits, and many have further designated a certain number of continuing education hours be spent on ethics review (e.g., California Psychologists are required to take four out of every thirty-six continuing education hours in the subject of ethics).

In addition to seminars discussing professional ethics from certain models of training or specific codes of ethics (e.g., counseling psychologists, clinical psychologists, marriage and family therapists), some groups have developed their own thoughtful discourse and training in ethics from a specific theoretical modality. For example, members of the American Psychoanalytic Association have written specifically on how ethics is viewed (and should be trained) from their perspective (Dewald & Clark, 2008; Ransohoff, 2010; Sandler & Godley, 2004). These various approaches to continuing education seem to be heralding a positive trend in broadening the sometimes redundant and pedantic review of ethical matters, which may seem like a rehash of the same dilemmas that were discussed in graduate school.

In keeping with this trend toward specific CE coursework, we suggest that ethical dilemmas specific to therapists of faith would be an appropriate and helpful subject matter to introduce into CE offerings. For example, the Christian Association for Psychological Studies frequently offers approved CE of this kind as part of their conference programs (see www.caps.net). Faith-based graduate programs could also sponsor such courses and feature professors and practitioners from various faith-based settings around the country to co-lead these sessions, thereby providing a range of points of view and discussion.

CONCLUSION

It seems fitting to revisit the word *discernment* as an overarching trait necessary for success in managing ethical situations and working in the helping profession. Training programs shoulder the burden of teaching their students how to handle ethical dilemmas from a place of knowledge regarding the individual student's ethical decision-making process, a specific clinical code of conduct and logical process, all the while modeling flexibility in thought and action. These two seemingly incompatible processes must learn to coexist if students are to engage in full-assessment of ethical dilemmas. Approaching ethical dilemmas from a place of rigidity only guarantees a course of action that leads to missed nuances and subtleties present with each client and situation.

For therapists of faith, to understand that we, not being God, have a finite grasp of the facts at any given time should lead us to pray for his wisdom as we seek to combine our earthly knowledge of moral theory and appropriate ethical behavior with the undeniable truth that God is the "All-knowing One." As educators and students alike, if we are ever under the impression that in any given clinical or ethical situation we have it *all* figured out, then we can be certain we've missed something. We agree with Benjamin Franklin who said, "For having lived long, I have experienced many instances of being obliged, by better information or fuller consideration, to change opinions, even on important subjects, which I once thought right but found to be otherwise."

As educators the onus is on us to teach and model for our students the ongoing quest for wisdom and discernment in ethical matters in hopes that it would aid them as they seek to care for their clients and as they seek to live out their own lives.

REFERENCES

American Psychological Association. (1953). *Ethical standards of psychologists.* Washington, DC: American Psychological Association.
American Psychological Association. (2002). Ethical principles of psychologists

and code of conduct. *American Psychologist, 57,* 1060-73. Also available (with 2010 amendments) from www.apa.org/ethics/code/index.aspx.

American Psychological Association. (2009). *Guidelines and principles for accreditation of programs in professional psychology.* Retrieved July 15, 2010, from www.apa.org/ed/accreditation/about/policies/guiding-principles.pdf.

American Psychological Association. (2006). Results of State Provincial Mandatory Continuing Education in Psychology (MCEP) Requirements Survey—2006 Results. Retrieved July 15, 2010, from www.apa.org/ed/sponsor/resources/requirements.aspx.

Browning, D. S. (2006). *Christian ethics and the moral psychologies.* Grand Rapids: Eerdmans.

Callan, J. E., & Bucky, S. F. (2005). Ethics in the teaching of mental health professionals. *Journal of Aggression, Maltreatment & Trauma, 11*(3), 287-309.

Callan, J., & Callan, M. (2005). An historic overview of basic approaches and issues in ethical and moral philosophy and principles: A foundation for understanding ethics in psychology. In S. Bucky, J. Callan & G. Stricker (Eds), *Ethical and legal issues for mental health professionals* (pp. 11-26). Binghamton, NY: Haworth Maltreatment & Trauma Press.

Cameron, S. W., & Blackburn, R. T. (1981). Sponsorship and academic career success. *Journal of Higher Education, 52,* 369-77.

Clark, R. A., Harden, S. L., & Johnson, W. B. (2000). Mentor relationships in clinical psychology doctoral training: Results of a national survey. *Teaching of Psychology, 27,* 262-68.

Cottone, R. R., & Claus, R. E. (2000). Ethical decision-making models: A review of the literature. *Journal of Counseling and Development, 78,* 275-83.

Davidson, G., Garton, A., & Joyce, M. (2003). Survey of ethics education in Australian university schools and departments of psychology. *Australian Psychologist, 38,* 216-22.

Dewald, P. A., & Clark, R. W. (Eds.). (2008). *Ethics case book of the American Psychoanalytic Association.* New York: American Psychoanalytic Association.

Elman, N., & Forrest, L. (2004). Psychotherapy in the remediation of psychology trainees: Exploratory interviews with training directors. *Professional Psychology: Research and Practice, 35,* 123-30.

Fisher, C. B. (2009). *Decoding the ethics code: A practical guide for psychologists.* Thousand Oaks, CA: SAGE Publications.

Foreman, J. (2010, April 12). Think before you click: In a 21st-century twist on medical ethics, internet search engines and social networking sites test traditional boundaries between patients and doctors. *Boston Globe.*

Fouad, N. A., Grus, C. L., Hatcher, R. L., Kaslow, N. J., Hutchings, P. S., Madson, M., Collins, F. L., Jr., & Crossman, R. E. (2009). Competency benchmarks: A developmental model for understanding and measuring competence in professional psychology. *Training and Education in Professional Psychology.* Vol. 3(4, Suppl.), November 2009, S5-S26. doi:10.1037/a0015832.

Geisler, N. L. (1989). *Christian ethics: Options and issues.* Grand Rapids: Baker.

Glaser, R. D., & Thorpe, J. S. (1986). Unethical intimacy: A survey of sexual contact and advances between psychology educators and female graduate students. *American Psychologist, 41,* 43-51.

Greggo, S. P. (2010). Applied Christian bioethics: Counseling on the moral edge. *Journal of Psychology and Christianity, 29,* 252-62.

Helbok, C. M., Marinelli, R. P., & Walls, R. T. (2006). National survey of ethical practices across rural and urban communities. *Professional Psychology: Research and Practice, 37,* 36-44.

Housman, L. M., & Stake, J. E. (1999). The current state of sexual ethics training in clinical psychology: Issues of quantity, quality, and effectiveness. *Professional Psychology: Research and Practice, 30,* 302-11.

Johnson, W. B., & McMinn, M. R. (2003). Thirty years of integrative doctoral training: Historic developments, assessment of outcomes, and recommendations for the future. *Journal of Psychology and Theology, 31,* 83-96.

Kanitz, B. E., Mendoza, D. W., & Ridley, C. R. (1992). Multicultural training in religiously-oriented counselor education programs: A survey. *Journal of Psychology and Christianity, 11,* 337-44.

Knapp, S., & VandeCreek, L. (2003). Legal and ethical issues in billing patients and collecting fees. *Psychotherapy: Theory, Research, Practice, Training, 30,* 25-31.

McGoldrick, M., Gerson, R., & Shellenberger, S. (1999). *Genograms: Assessment and intervention.* New York: Norton.

McMinn, M. R., & Meek, K. R. (1996). Ethics among Christian counselors: A survey of beliefs and behaviors. *Journal of Psychology and Theology, 24,* 26-37.

McMinn, M. R., & Meek, K. R. (1997). Training programs. In R. K. Sanders (Ed.), *Christian counseling ethics: A handbook for therapists, pastors, and counselors* (pp. 277-96). Downers Grove, IL: InterVarsity Press.

Mezirow, J. (2000). *Learning as transformation: Critical perspectives on a theory in progress.* San Francisco: Jossey-Bass.

Minor, M. H. (2005). Ethics education: Further reasons why a grounding in ethical theory is essential. Comment on Davidson, Garton and Joyce (2003). *Australian Psychologist, 40*(1), 54-56.

Nagy, T. (2005). *Ethics in plain English: An illustrative casebook for psychologists.* Washington, DC: American Psychological Association.

Nagy, T. F. (2011). *Essential ethics for psychologists: A primer for understanding and mastering core issues.* Washington, DC: American Psychological Association.

Pope, K. S., Tabachnick, B. G., & Keith-Spiegel, P. (1987). Ethics of practice: The beliefs and behaviors of psychologists as therapists. *American Psychologist, 47,* 993-1006.

Pope, K. S., & Feldman-Summers, S. (1992). National survey of psychologists' sexual and physical abuse history and their evaluation of training and competence in these areas. *Professional Psychology: Research and Practice, 23,* 353-61.

Pope, K. S., Sonne, J. L., & Holroyd, J. (1993). *Sexual feelings in psychotherapy: Explorations for therapists and therapists-in-training.* Washington, DC: American Psychological Association.

Pope, K. S. (1994). *Sexual involvement with therapists: Patient Assessment, subsequent therapy, forensics.* Washington, DC: American Psychological Association.

Rae, S. B. (2009). *Moral choices: An introduction to ethics* (Rev. ed.). Grand Rapids: Zondervan.

Ransohoff, P. M. (2010). Ethics education in psychoanalytic training: A survey. *Journal of the American Psychoanalytic Association, 58,* 83-99.

Reskin, B. F. (1979). Academic sponsorship and scientists' careers. *Sociology of Education, 52,* 129-46.

Rodolfa, E. R., Bent, R. J., Eisman, E., Nelson, P. D., Rehm, L., & Ritchie, P. (2005). A cube model for competency development: Implications for psychology educators and regulators. *Professional Psychology: Research and Practice, 36,* 347-54.

Sanders, R. K., Swenson, J. E., & Schneller, G. R. (2011). Beliefs and practices of Christian psychotherapists regarding non-sexual multiple relationships. *Journal of Psychology & Theology, 39,* 330-44.

Sandler, A. M., & Godley, W. (2004). Institutional responses to boundary violations: The case of Masud Khan. *International Journal of Psychoanalysis, 85,* 27-42.

Schneller, G. R., Swenson, J. E., & Sanders, R. K. (2010). Training for ethical dilemmas arising in Christian counseling: A survey of CAPS members. *Journal of Psychology & Christianity, 29,* 343-53.

Schwartz-Mette, R. A. (2009). Challenges in addressing graduate student impairment in academic professional psychology programs. *Ethics & Behavior, 19*(2), 91-102.

Swenson, J. E., Schneller, G. R., & Sanders, R. K. (2009). Ethical issues in integrating Christian faith and psychotherapy: Beliefs and behaviors among CAPS members.

Journal of Psychology and Christianity, 28, 302-14.

Urofsky, R., & Sowa, C. (2004). Ethics education in CACREP-accredited counselor education programs. *Counseling and Values, 49,* 37-47.

Vanek, C. A. (1990). Survey of ethics education in clinical and counseling psychology. *Dissertation Abstracts International, 52,* 5797B. (University Microfilms No. 91-14, 449).

Welfel, E. R. (1992). Psychologist as ethics educator: Successes, failures, and unanswered questions. *Professional Psychology: Research and Practice, 23,* 182-89.

Welfel, E. R. (2000). *Ethics in counseling & psychotherapy: Standards, research, & emerging issues* (3rd ed.). Belmont, CA: Thomson, Brooks/Cole.

21

A Model for Ethical Decision Making

Randolph K. Sanders

Learning to act with integrity in the everyday world of the therapy room, the classroom and the boardroom is imperative for the Christian therapist who would aspire to excellence. Familiarity with one's ethics codes, guidelines and laws is absolutely essential to this task and provides a superstructure for ethical practice. However, the ethical dilemmas faced in everyday practice are frequently more complicated than a code can hope to adequately address (Barnett, Behnke, Rosenthal & Koocher, 2007). Situations arise in which therapists are faced with the competing claims of two or more ethical requirements, and have to make the best choice they can in a far from ideal situation. Sometimes the codes do not clearly address a specific problem that arises. Sometimes there are conflicts between legal requirements and ethical requirements.

What's more, psychotherapists, like other human beings, have frailties. Seen through a broad theological lens, we understand that sin has an enduring presence in every one of our lives and in the natural world (Cooper, 2003; Niebuhr, 1964). From a scientific perspective the fields of social psychology, genetics, neuroscience, moral development and education all have something to say about the reality of human imperfections. Emotions such as anxiety, depression, exhaustion and anger can trump the therapist's objectivity and cause him or her to be less than objective when dealing with ethical matters. Or consider the human tendency to rationalize, which in the case of therapists, can cause them to create self-justifying reasons for doing differently than the ethics code would require. Specialists in moral development have described what is known as a "moral judgment-action gap." By this they refer to the discrepancy that arises between what a person knows is right and what they actually end up doing (Blasi, 1980; Walker, 2004). Human beings sometimes make choices based more on expediency and opportunism than on being consistent. Indeed, research by Smith et al. (1991) pointed out that mental health professionals, when faced with an ethical conflict, sometimes do less than they believe the codes require them to do, particularly when the codes are not especially clear or when there is a lack of legal statute or legal precedent to back up the code.

To find their way through the complicated and sometimes confusing world of ethical dilemmas, Christian therapists need models for ethical decision making. These models, while not perfect, can assist therapists in dealing with the difficult ethical issues that face them in the real world. They can help therapists maintain their objectivity in the face of stress, give them more tools for working through problems and help them avoid the disillusionment that sometimes comes when one is confronted by dilemmas for which there is no one clear answer.

DESIGNING A MODEL FOR ETHICAL DECISION MAKING

What follows is a model for making ethical decisions along with two case studies that demonstrate the use of the model in practice. Several models of ethical decision making have informed the present model (Eberlein, 1987; Forester-Miller & Davis, 1995; Kitchener, 1986; Koocher & Keith-Spiegel, 2008; Pope & Vasquez, 2011; Sileo & Kopala, 1993; Tymchuk, 1982; Welfel & Kitchener, 1995). To be useful, any model must start with the expectation that the clinician will familiarize him- or herself with the ethics codes, rules of practice, legal standards, as well as the aspirational ideals we discussed in chapter one. Knowledge of these standards is fundamental to ethical practice.

Beyond that, an effective decision-making model must seek to help therapists overcome the things that cause them to respond less ethically than they should. Koocher and Keith-Spiegel (2008) list a number of reasons that therapists behave unethically. Their list may be summarized as follows:

1. ignorance and misinformation

2. incompetence

3. insensitivity

4. exploitativeness

5. irresponsible behavior

6. vengefulness

7. emotional impairment or burnout

8. lack of or distorted view of interpersonal boundaries

9. self-serving rationalization

10. "slips" caused by momentarily losing sight of goals or by distraction (pp. 9-16)

While all of these reasons are potentially important, I believe that "insensitivity" may be one of the more important and inclusive, particularly if part of what is meant by insensitivity is the therapist's *lack of empathy*. It seems strange to suggest that therapists lack empathy since empathy training is one of the foundational building blocks in virtually any graduate training program for mental health professionals. Yet not infrequently ethical infractions are committed by therapists who at the time of the infraction showed an inability to see things from the standpoint of the client's greatest good. There are a number of reasons why a therapist might fail to empathize in this way, and the rest of Koocher and Keith-Spiegel's list illustrates a number of causes that could trigger a failure to empathize with the client's greater good. Implied in several of the items on Koocher and Keith-Spiegel's list seems to be the presence of acute or chronic emotional issues present in the therapist. The therapist who is not self-aware of his or her own present or ongoing susceptibilities to stress or anxiety is at risk for poor ethical decision making. The therapist who is struggling with depression or is bipolar or has any one of several disorders may be compromised in his or her ability to reason ethically. Therapists with narcissistic, antisocial or borderline tendencies can be expected to have difficulty with ethical decision making.

In presenting their list, Koocher and Keith-Spiegel (2008) point out that practitioners may fail for more than one reason at once. We should also not assume that their list exhausts the possibilities. However, such a list can help us as we devise an effective decision-making model. For example, a model that encourages the therapist to seek consultation from colleagues can help the therapist overcome the blind spots evident in the Koocher and Keith-Spiegel list. A model that urges the therapist to consider the potential impact of an ethical decision on the client can be helpful to the therapist in overcoming self-serving biases.

DILEMMA PREPAREDNESS

Any ethical decision-making model presupposes that the therapist is *prepared* to use it. By this I mean that the therapist has taken proactive steps in advance to make him- or herself a more effective ethical decision maker when dilemmas arise (Crowley & Gottlieb, 2012; see also the chapter on ethics training by Anderson, Schneller & Swenson elsewhere in this volume). The optimally prepared therapist will:

- Be thoroughly acquainted with the fundamentals of ethics codes, laws and guidelines that apply to the scope of his or her practice

- Have preset procedures, forms and other materials that help alert him or her to possible ethical dilemmas in advance

- Learn to predict clinical or diagnostic situations likely to present ethical dilemmas or high risk

- Have referral and consultative networks in place in the event that he or she needs additional help

- Be self-aware regarding his or her own personal ethics, beliefs, values, vulnerabilities and how these might impact his or her ethical reasoning

- Be self-aware of his or her own emotional vulnerabilities, both acute and ongoing, and how these might impact his or her reasoning

- Be mindful of positive resources that may help him or her with his or her ethical reasoning and judgment. Contemplative prayer, meditative prayer, stress management and cognitive restructuring each have their place in helping the therapist work through his or her own thoughts and feelings about an ethical dilemma.

By being prepared for dilemmas in advance, the therapists should be able to deal more prudently and objectively with problems when they arise.

ETHICAL DECISION-MAKING MODEL

The ethical decision-making model that follows is not intended to be exhaustive in scope. It does not provide a canned program by which one can solve every ethical dilemma. The sequence in which the steps are listed may fit many dilemmas. Certainly the first two steps should occur as early as possible in the decision process. However, the exact sequence in which the steps are taken is not as important as making sure each step is given its due. Not all steps are equally important in each individual case, but one should not ignore steps that are truly necessary.

The model does not take the place of the development of personal character and virtue, which are learned from significant others through a life of commitment to Christian discipleship. Christian maturity is a process gained through a combination of making oneself vulnerable to God's nurture and acting out the principles one learns, allowing them to become deeply imbedded in one's being so that they become a natural outflow of one's everyday behavior. This speaks to the importance of the kind of learning that begins long before one enters formal training to become a mental health professional or counselor, and hopefully continues throughout life. If moral reasoning takes place at both an *intuitive* and a *critical-evaluative level* as Kitchener (1984) says, then the development of character and virtue may be expected to predispose one to better ethical reasoning at the intuitive, or what might be termed the *prereflective level*.

Still, a model can assist in piercing through much of the confusion that often surrounds ethical decision making. It can help one make the decision at hand and gain skill for making future decisions. An outline of the model follows:

1. Assess a situation for its ethical dimensions.

2. Seek to define the problem using codes and principles.

3. Understand and process your emotional reaction to the problem.

4. Seek consultation as needed. (This step may actually be enacted at any point during the decision-making process.)

5. Determine whom you should be considering in making an ethical decision and why you should consider them.

6. Determine if there is precedent in other cases that would help you in making your decision.

7. Consider the options you could take.

8. Consider the possible consequences of each option.

9. Make the decision and be prepared to take appropriate responsibility for the consequences of your action.

Each step in this decision process should assume that at *any* point the therapist has the option of seeking consultation with other professionals who may be able to offer perception and insight that may, in the midst of the ethical dilemma, be difficult to see by oneself. Indeed, the ethical therapist should never work too long in relative isolation from peers. Each of us needs developing relationships with God and with other therapists that offer consultation, support and accountability. Ideally these relationships allow us to see beyond the unconscious blind spots and frailties in our own thinking which can make us susceptible to ethical lapses.

1. Assess a situation for its ethical dimensions. Potential ethical dilemmas are often first experienced as a vague uncomfortableness felt in response to something that has just occurred: the affable and persuasive client who asks you to code her bill some other way so she can obtain insurance payments, the friendly pastor who innocently asks you to tell him about his teen daughter's counseling session with you, the attorney in a divorce case who assures you that he has both parties' welfare at heart and just needs to see their marital therapy records in order to help them settle their divorce as amicably as possible. Prior to ever defining the problem, you often experience the affective sensation that there might be a problem. Such recognition is not automatic, especially in situations in which the emerging dilemma is less than clear. It requires ethical sensitivity, which is more likely when the practitioner is well acquainted with the ethical codes and the principles that underlie them.

At this stage the therapist gathers information in an effort to add definition to the situation and decide if there are indeed ethical dimensions to the problem. This requires a deliberateness on the part of the therapist, first to be conscious that some difficulty exists, and then to investigate its meaning. Sometimes making a list of the facts and problematic circumstances can help to organize one's thinking. Consultation (see step 4) may also be beneficial.

2. *Seek to define the problem using codes and principles.* Once information has been gathered, turn to the codes, laws and other guidelines. Are there standards that apply directly to the matter at hand? Keep in mind that codes, laws and institutional policies do not always agree. Ultimately, it is the therapist's responsibility to review all applicable laws and guidelines. In many cases the guidelines speak directly to the issue at hand with clarity, and contradictory or complicating concerns do not arise. When the guidelines are clear, following the rules should lead to resolution (Forester-Miller & Davis, 1995). When resolution does not occur or when the application of specific standards, laws or guidelines are unclear, contradictory or competing, it may be helpful to review the aspirational ideals in the code. Kitchener (1984) pointed out that the aspirational ideals of client autonomy, nonmaleficence, beneficence, justice and fidelity are at a more abstract level than the ethical rules, and can be applied effectively to many situations in which specific ethical rules are contradictory or are otherwise difficult to clearly apply. The Christian ethical ideals described in chapter one may also be helpful to the therapist seeking to make a rational ethical decision. These aspirational ideals are likely to add insight as one attempts to apply the rules.

3. *Understand and process your emotional reaction to the problem.* Traditional training in mental health ethics has focused on studying cases in the classroom at an intellectual level, applying codes of conduct to cases in an analytical or logical manner. Real clinical dilemmas do not take place in that kind of environment. Most are emotionally charged, and a few take place under crisis conditions (Rogerson et al., 2011; Sanders, 1997).

If the ethical problem triggers an emotional reaction, it is important to develop means for being mindful of that reaction, because those emotions may affect one's judgment and the decisions one makes about the problem (Loewenstein, Weber, Hsee & Welch, 2001). Research indicates that when faced with an ethical conflict, therapists tend to rely on the ethical codes when defining what they should do, but also rely on personal values, intuition and expediency when deciding what they actually will do (Smith et al., 1991). While generally overlooked by most models for ethical decision making, the ability to address one's emotional response to an ethical dilemma turns out to be a key component in responding well.

When faced with an ethical dilemma, the therapist may *fear* the possible legal consequences that could occur if the wrong decision is made. For instance, suppose a therapist believes that a client is not abusing his children, but he is. The therapist could be held accountable. When a client expresses suicidal thoughts, particularly when the client's intentions are ambiguous, the therapist will be worried about the client's safety, but will also worry about the prospect of breaking the client's confidentiality. The therapist may feel *angry* about an ethical dilemma. The dilemma may have arisen at the same time he or she is dealing with other clinical or personal stressors. The therapist may feel *frustrated* because he or she feels the dilemma will complicate or slow the client's speedy progress in therapy. In other cases the therapist may already be experiencing negative counter-transference feelings toward the client when the unwelcome dilemma arises. And, of course, s*exual or affectionate feelings* can also blur objectivity and empathy.

If the ethical dilemma involves business issues in your clinical practice, other types of feelings could emerge. You may feel *threatened* by new competitors who move into the "catchment area" of your clinical practice, or you may experience *greed* as you consider moving into someone else's territory.

The problem may raise issues from the therapist's own past. If you were abused as a child, your client's report of abuse may trigger feelings of *hatred*, *bitterness* or *anger* that make it difficult for you to look objectively at your responsibility. If you are under a great deal of stress in your personal life, you may find the ethical dilemma deeply frustrating. You may have difficulty focusing objectively on the issues at hand or may allow your own difficulties to distract you from following a carefully thought out decision path in dealing with the issues.

Whatever the case, accepting your emotional state and then taking steps to deal with it is a prerequisite to being able to deal conscientiously with the ethical issue before you. Outlining the problem on paper may help objectify the situation and lead to effective problem solving. Psychophysiological methods such as diaphragmatic breathing or progressive relaxation may help calm anxiety both inside and outside the therapy room. Contemplative prayer may help you to see the problems from a different perspective and redeem the negative emotions to more positive ends. The help and support of a trusted colleague may also do much to help you deal with the feelings and move on to responsibly dealing with the ethical dilemma. Occasionally the added stress of an ethical dilemma accents other problems in the personal life of the psychotherapist and triggers the realization of the need for professional help for oneself.

4. Seek consultation as needed. Consultation may actually be considered at any point in the decision-making process. It may be considered as soon as the therapist experiences the uncomfortable feeling signaling that a situation is emerging. Indeed, consultation with another professional may even help define exactly what the problem is. Seeking consultation with valued colleagues is one of the most important things a therapist can do at any time during the process of decision making.

Ideally the consultant should be mature, experienced and have good ethical decision-making skills. The consultant may be a colleague or a supervisor or someone with special skill in ethical matters. If dealing with a particular type of clinical case (i.e., an issue of abuse, family confidentiality, drugs or alcohol, borderline personality), it is helpful if the person has expertise in that area. In fact, if the consultant has little or no experience in the area in question, consultation could actually be unhelpful, no matter how wise the consultant is in general. If the case includes legal ramifications, consultation with an attorney experienced in mental health matters may be needed.

There are several reasons why consultation is important. The consultant will add a measure of *objectivity* that a clinician who is personally involved in the case will not have. The consultant can often help the therapist define the problem more accurately and, in the decision-making phase, can help the therapist evaluate competing courses of action and choose the course of greatest integrity.

The consultant also multiplies the amount of *experience* available to consider the ethical problem. At the very least the consultant will have a different history of clinical experiences than the clinician directly involved in the case. In many cases the consultant will have more experience, and in the best-case scenario will have had specialty training in the areas that pertain to the case at hand.

If a consultant is more experienced and has known or worked with the clinician for some time, then he or she may serve as an effective *mentor* and *model* for the clinician (see chap. 20). The clinician may already have benefitted from observing the consultant's model in similar cases. In a more general way the consultant's model of key virtues, sound thinking and measured actions may motivate the clinician to imitate such behaviors, thus providing a solid foundation from which good decision making can develop.

An effective consultant will encourage *accountability* on the part of the clinician. The best consulting relationship is one in which the two parties feel comfortable enough with each other that the clinician will be completely truthful regarding the case and his or her thinking about it. Likewise, the consultant will be able to lovingly confront and hold accountable the clinician without this impairing the effectiveness of the relationship.

Documenting the consultation is important and may help the clinician keep focus; it may also be helpful from a risk-management standpoint. If the clinician is ever called to defend his or her behavior, it will be important to show that the clinician recognized that there was a dilemma and sought help. In one legal case the court recognized that while therapists admittedly do sometimes encounter conflicting ethical dilemmas that are not easily solved, they have a responsibility to seek appropriate consultation (Rost v. State Board, 1995).

5. Determine whom you should be considering in making an ethical decision and why you should consider them. Obviously a clinician's first and foremost concern should be for the client or patient. The client's welfare, autonomy and right of self-determination are extremely important.

However, as Eberlein (1987) has pointed out, respect for the client does not absolve the clinician from considering others as well. In fact it can be argued that some ethical dilemmas are difficult because they place the therapist in the uncomfortable position of trying to consider the needs and rights of more than one person. Therapists should never assume that commitment to the patient releases them from considering others.

This can be most apparent in family therapy, group therapy or any other setting where there is more than one client involved. If a therapist promises a child client complete confidentiality, what will he or she do if the child's father decides that, as guardian, he wants to know the details of what the child has disclosed? Moreover, even in traditional individual adult therapy, the therapist must be mindful that ethical decisions may impact not only the client but also the family system and perhaps the client's larger social sphere.

Considering the competing ethical claims of different people and groups is extremely important if the practitioner is to proceed beyond the tendency to simply apply ethical rules legalistically and impulsively to clinical situations. Suppose a client who has a history of bipolar disorder enters therapy. The client has recently married, and his wife knows nothing of his condition and what the ramifications of it are. The client refuses to have his new wife come with him to a session to understand more about his condition and discuss things they might both do to maintain his health. What are the responsibilities of the therapist to the different people involved?

At the simplest level the therapist has a duty to accept the client's autonomy and right to privacy. But does the therapist also have any duties to the client at other levels or to the client's wife, family or to him- or herself as a therapist attempting to behave responsibly and appropriately? How should the therapist proceed in a case like this? What are the potential risks and benefits to each of the parties involved, both immediate and long-term, of any action the therapist might take?

6. Determine if there is precedent in other cases that would help you in making your decision. Previous case material may help in discovering possible courses of action for the present dilemma. Past cases may help clarify more clearly the potential outcomes of various decisions the therapist might make to solve the dilemma.

The APA periodically publishes articles that include case material presented by the APA Ethics Committee, and a number of books on ethics in psychology and counseling contain good case illustrations (APA, 1987; Bennet et al., 1990; Bersoff, 2008; Corey, Corey & Callanan, 2010; Ford, 2006; Koocher & Keith-Spiegel, 2008). Previous legal cases such as *Tarasoff* (1974, 1976), allow the clinician a chance to view how the courts have evaluated problem situations and may assist the therapist in building a defensible course of action. Research studies of ethical behavior and journal articles on ethical decision making may also help.

A therapist's own past cases or those of colleagues may also help. In addition to having a host of his or her own clinical experiences, a trusted colleague can help a therapist view the dilemma from a different perspective. This illustrates again why consultation with an experienced colleague can be so important. However, it must be added that each ethical dilemma one faces usually has its own unique nuances that can sometimes make blanket comparison to one's own or other's previous cases risky.

7. Consider the options you could take. Here the therapist considers all the possible options to take to deal with the ethical dilemma. All options are considered before critically evaluating or discarding any. Sometimes more than one option may have merit, and no option may be perfect. In considering options, ask yourself whether discussing the dilemma with the client and getting input from him or her would be useful. For example, this is sometimes helpful in situations where there is a present or emerging nonsexual multiple relationship, and the question of whether to engage or not engage is a gray area. However, there are other situations where it would not be appropriate to collaborate with the client on a decision, and furthermore, the therapist must also always remember that in the final analysis, he or she is expected to be the responsible party (the fiduciary) who has the most knowledge about what is and is not ethically appropriate in therapeutic relationships.

8. Consider the possible consequences of each option. What effect will each decision likely have on each of the people considered in step 5? The clinician should consider both costs and benefits, whether these are of a psychological, social or economic nature, as well as long-term and short term consequences (Tymchuk, 1982).

9. Make the decision and be prepared to take appropriate responsibility for the consequences. At this point the clinician makes a decision and documents it, including the rationale for the decision. Taking appropriate responsibility acts as an additional check, encouraging the therapist to consider again the potential consequences to all parties involved of any action he or she might take to solve the dilemma. It encourages those therapists who would decide impulsively to reconsider their actions. If seen correctly, it can also encourage the reticent therapist to move toward the response of greatest integrity. And though it might not immediately seem like it, accepting one's own measure of responsibility for actions one takes can actually empower the therapist to move forward with courage, recognizing that in the most difficult decisions, selecting a course of action is sometimes a matter of trying to choose the best from among several less-than-satisfactory alternatives and courageously hoping for a positive outcome while preparing for negative consequences. It will not always mean that the therapist will *feel* fully satisfied with the choice he or she has had to make (Gladding, Remley & Huber, 2000). For instance, a therapist may feel bad about having to call law enforcement to protect a person who is openly suicidal, even though the action is necessary.

CASE ONE

Dr. Sally Vernon begins counseling Jack Burns for depression and job stress.[1] Jack is also taking antidepressant medication, which is prescribed by his internist. Several weeks into therapy Jack reveals that he has been drinking quite a bit, especially in the evenings. He started drinking prior to beginning the antidepressant as a way of trying to help himself sleep, but he has continued the practice in spite of the fact that his physician told him to limit his use of alcohol with this particular medication.

With some probing, Dr. Vernon learns from Jack that he has not informed his physician of his drinking. She first seeks to help Jack understand that alcohol will actually counteract the effectiveness of the antidepressant he is taking, and in larger amounts could pose serious danger. She reminds Jack that the physician has warned him against drinking and taking medication, and recommends that Jack contact his physician prior to the next session, inform him of what he is doing and request detailed instruction. Dr. Vernon also suggests that Jack tell the physician that he is now in therapy.

When Jack returns for his next session, he admits that he has not contacted his physician and that he is still mixing medication and alcohol. Dr. Vernon asks Jack to sign a release so that she can talk to the physician herself, but Jack refuses. He says he doesn't want his physician to know because he and the physician attend the same church, and he thinks the internist will

---

[1]The case studies and the names of all characters in the chapter are fictitious.

think less of him if he knows. He tells Dr. Vernon that he'll just stop drinking and that will "take care of the problem." Dr. Vernon acknowledges his concerns but she believes it unlikely that Jack will stop drinking, and she feels an ethical as well as a therapeutic conflict growing in the relationship (step 1). She is sworn to confidentiality (step 2) and should not release information without her client's signed release. However, she believes that Jack's course of action is not healthy, and she has promised to be concerned about his welfare (step 2).

She becomes more aware of her conflicting feelings about the case—wanting to help, feeling trapped in her efforts to properly serve the client and somewhat anxious about the potential risks of continuing service to Jack (step 3). She realizes that part of her anxiety is brought on by the fact that as a nonmedical therapist, she is not well versed in how harmful the client's medication mixed with alcohol actually is. She decides to contact her clinic's medical consultant (step 4) and get additional information about the medication her client is taking and its interaction with alcohol. The consultant confirms that mixing alcohol with this medication is not recommended, and the therapist documents this in her chart.

She thinks carefully about the persons she should consider in this case (step 5). Of course there is Jack, who obviously needs treatment but seems tenuously committed at this point. There is some concern about Jack's physician, who apparently is trying to treat Jack without needed facts about the case. Finally, Dr. Vernon is concerned about herself in her efforts to serve Jack appropriately.

She is also concerned about the denial apparent in Jack's behavior, and she wants to foster a therapeutic relationship of honesty. She is concerned about Jack as one of God's people struggling, albeit haphazardly, to deal with many problems. She considers past cases where people have wanted her or other therapists to tacitly condone their misuse of medication or their involvement in other risky behaviors (step 6).

She considers her options and their possible consequences (steps 7, 8). She could decline to continue to be Jack's therapist, indicating her inability to work with him based on his refusal to follow appropriate professional advice and offering him alternative referrals. She could continue to discuss the matter with him, reviewing carefully the therapeutic problems of continuing his current actions, discussing the bind she is in, considering the alternatives available to him and discussing his perspective (see step 7). She might talk to him about his denial. She considers these and other options as well as the possible consequences of pursuing any one of them.

What would you do if you were Dr. Vernon? Is there one best solution?

CASE TWO

After the second session with Martha Riley, Dr. Anthony Case was completing his progress note. He was surprised that he and this new client had developed rapport so easily. When he first received information about the referral, he wondered if the pleasant first impression often needed for a positive therapeutic outcome to occur would be present.

As it turned out Martha was a likable woman who opened up quickly and seemed motivated for therapy. By the second session she was talking about how much his counsel had helped already, and though Dr. Case was usually skeptical of success that arrived too quickly, he thought he sensed that Martha's improvements were genuine.

He hoped things continued to progress. He was looking forward to his third session with her, and he found himself spending extra time thinking about and preparing for the session.

Once again, the session went well. It seemed as though every interpretation he made was on target and all his suggestions and recommendations were gladly received. Martha was sitting near the window today, and he couldn't help but notice how pretty she looked with the light cast across her face. He thought she reminded him of someone out of his past but couldn't quite remember who it was. He found it difficult to end the session that day. One insight led to another, and both of them seemed to want to stretch the session longer. When they rose and walked toward the door, Martha paused to ask him something and he realized that she was standing rather close, closer than most clients in similar situations. A moment later, the question answered, the session was over.

In the days ahead he thought about Martha a number of times. He knew their rapport seemed excellent. He knew she seemed to have excellent insight. He wasn't allowing himself to know what else was building in their relationship.

But by the end of session four the truth was difficult to ignore (step 1). As they walked to the door, Martha was too close again. She lingered and smiled as she spoke appreciatively about his help and lightly touched his arm as she moved out the door. He felt paralyzed by a contradictory mixture of feelings within himself.

In a way, he knew what the problem was (step 2), and he knew he should get consultation (step 4), but to give the problem a name and share it with a wiser colleague was to admit the problem and shed the light of day on it.

He resisted, even rationalized at first, but his extensive knowledge of the rules combined with spiritual and character values developed over a number of years, along with some fear and guilt pushed him to call his mentor. He and the mentor discussed the fact that however therapeutic the relationship might be, a dual relationship was developing (step 2). They also talked openly about Case's emotional reactions to what was happening (step 3). Case began to realize more clearly the confusing array of emotions he had been feeling: relieved that rapport was easily established, empathetic toward Martha's problems, encouraged by her appreciation, exhilarated that she seemed to find him attractive, aware that he was attracted to her, embarrassed about revealing his feelings to a colleague and anxious about the entire situation.

His mentor asked him to consider each person in this situation and what their needs were (step 5). He also encouraged him to consider some Christian principles that applied to the problem. The two brainstormed some concerns, realizing that their list was not all-inclusive.

- Concern for Martha as one of God's people and the importance of trust in *the therapeutic relationship.* Martha had told Dr. Case that she had been seriously hurt in her relationship with her own father. Now she was beginning a therapeutic relationship with another male that if handled poorly could further harm her.

- Concern for honesty. The longer the present situation continued, the less likely that what was occurring in the office could properly be defined as therapy.

- Stewardship of talents. Dr. Case's career and personal integrity could be in jeopardy if he made poor decisions about his present circumstances.

- Christian responsibility. Since Dr. Case believed that God's kingdom does extend to the therapy room, he knew he had a responsibility to be honest with God about his feelings and deal responsibly and with agape love toward Martha.

Dr. Case also thought about other therapists who had "fallen from grace" and of the difficulties it had caused for all concerned (step 6). Case agreed that over the next several days he would make a list of possible ways to respond appropriately to his situation and would go over these with his mentor prior to Martha's next session (steps 7, 4). He would consider possible consequences to any option he might choose (step 8). The mentor reminded Case of evidence in the literature suggesting that telling a client about one's attraction for them is usually not helpful and can lead to serious problems (Fisher, 2004). Consequently, they decided they would not consider this as a viable option.

How would you deal with this situation if you were in Dr. Case's position? What would be the potential positive and negative consequences of your course of action?

CONCLUSION

Therapists, no matter how well trained, face ethical situations that defy easy solutions. However, it is imperative that Christian professionals endeavor to do the best they can to discern and practice what is right and what is good in the real world of the therapy room, the classroom and the boardroom. Familiarity with ethics codes helps, but they may lack the nuance necessary in very complicated situations. Moreover, the frailties embedded in human nature work against the successful use of an ethical strategy solely dependent on following rules. Good models for ethical decision making can help the Christian professional manage his or her own emotions in ethically stressful situations and arrive at better reasoned decisions. Any good model will include among other things, the use of consultation where necessary. Relationships with others within the profession marked by support and accountability will help the Christian counselor avoid the biases and blind spots that lead to ethical errors and lapses. These personal relationships, which can take place at a local level as well as through one's relationships in professional organizations, mirror the intimate relationship of love, support and account-ability the Christian counselor or therapist should endeavor to develop with God.

REFERENCES

American Psychological Association. (1987). *Casebook on ethical principles of psy-chologists*. Washington, DC: American Psychological Association.

American Psychological Association. (2002). Ethical principles of psychologists and code of conduct. *American Psychologist, 57,* 1060-73. Also available (with 2010 amendments) from www.apa.org/ethics/code/index.aspx.

Barnett, J. E., Behnke, S. H., Rosenthal, S. L., & Koocher, G. P. (2007). In case of ethical dilemma break glass: Commentary on ethical decision making in practice. *Professional Psychology: Research and Practice, 38,* 7-12.

Bennett, B. E., Bryant, B. K., VandenBos, G. R., & Greenwood, A. (1990). *Profes-sional liability and risk management.* Washington, DC: American Psychological Association.

Bersoff, D. N. (Ed.). (2008). *Ethical conflicts in psychology* (4th ed.). Washington, DC: American Psychological Association.

Blasi, A. (1980). Bridging moral cognition and moral action: A critical review of the literature. *Psychological Bulletin, 88,* 1-41.

Christian Association for Psychological Studies. (2005). *Ethics statement of the Christian Association for Psychological Studies* (Available from www.caps.net).

Cooper, T. D. (2003). *Sin, pride and self-acceptance.* Downers Grove, IL: InterVarsity Press.

Corey, G., Corey, M. S., & Callanan, P. (2010). *Issues and ethics in the counseling Professions* (8th ed.). Monterey, CA: Brooks/Cole.

Crowley, J. D., & Gottlieb, M. C. (2012). Objects in the mirror are closer than they appear: A primary prevention model for ethical decision making. *Professional Psychology: Research and Practice, 43,* 65-72.

Eberlein, L. (1987). Introducing ethics to beginning psychologists: A problem-approach. *Professional Psychology: Research and Practice, 18,* 353-59.

Fisher, C. D. (2004). Ethical issues in therapy: Therapist self-disclosure of sexual feelings. *Ethics and Behavior, 14,* 105-21.

Ford, G. G. (2006). *Ethical reasoning for mental health professionals.* Thousand Oaks, CA: Sage.

Forester-Miller, H., & Davis, T. E. (1995). *A practitioner's guide to ethical decision-making.* Annapolis Junction, MD: American Counseling Association.

Gladding, S. T., Remley, T. P., & Huber, C. H. (2000). *Ethical, legal, and professional issues in the practice of marriage and family therapy* (3rd ed.). Upper Saddle River, NJ: Prentice-Hall.

Kitchener, K. S. (1984). Intuition, critical evaluation and ethical principles: The foundation for ethical decisions in counseling psychology. *Counseling Psychologist, 12,* 43-55.

Kitchener, K. S. (1986). Teaching applied ethics in counselor education: An integration of psychological processes and philosophical analysis. *Journal of Counseling and Development, 64,* 306-10.

Koocher, G. P., & Keith-Spiegel, P. (2008). *Ethics in psychology and the mental health professions: Standards and cases* (3rd ed.). New York: Oxford.

Loewenstein, G. F., Weber, E. U., Hsee, C. K., & Welch, N. (2001). Risk as feelings. *Psychological Bulletin, 127,* 267-86.

McMinn, M. R. (2004). *Why sin matters.* Wheaton, IL: Tyndale.

Miller, D. J. (1991). The necessity of principles in virtue ethics. *Professional Psychology: Research and Practice, 22,* 107.

Niebuhr, R. (1964). *The nature and destiny of man.* (Vols. 1-2). New York: Scribner's.

Pope, K. S., & Vasquez, M. J. T. (2011). *Ethics in psychotherapy and counseling* (4th ed.). New York: Wiley.

Rogerson, M. D., Gottlieb, M. C., Handelsman, M. M., Knapp, S., & Younggren, J. (2011). Non-rational processes in ethical decision making. *American Psychologist, 66,* 614-23.

Rost v. State Board, (1995). Cited in "Legal Briefs." *Register Report,* 22(1996): 18-19.

Sanders, R. K. (1997). A model for ethical decision making. In R. K. Sanders (Ed.), *Christian counseling ethics: A handbook for therapists, pastors and counselors* (pp. 297-312). Downers Grove, IL: InterVarsity Press.

Sileo, F. J., & Kopala, M. (1993). An A-B-C-D-E worksheet for promoting beneficence when considering ethical issues. *Counseling and Values, 37,* 89-95.

Smith, T. S., McGuire, J. M., Abbott, D. W., & Blau, B. I. (1991). Clinical ethical decision-making: An investigation of the rationales used to justify doing less than one believes one should. *Professional Psychology: Research and Practice, 22,* 235-39.

Tarasoff v. Board of Regents of the University of California, 13 Cal. 3d 177, 529 P. 2d 533 (1974), *Vacated,* 17 Cal. 3d 425, 551 P. 2d 334 (1976).

Tymchuk, A. J. (1982). Strategies for resolving value dilemmas. *American Behavioral Scientist, 26,* 159-75.

Walker, L. J. (2004). Gus in the gap: Bridging the judgment-action gap in moral functioning. In D. K. Lapsley & D. Narvaez (Eds.), *Moral development, self, and identity* (pp. 1-20). Mahwah, NJ: Erlbaum.

Welfel, E. R., & Kitchener, K. S. (1995). Introduction to the special section: Ethics education—an agenda for the '90s. In D. N. Bersoff (Ed.), *Ethical conflicts in psychology*. Washington, DC: American Psychological Association.

Ethical Codes
and Guidelines

In the appendix that follows, we highlight several of the frequently used ethics codes including ones that have a Christian or religious orientation. It is impossible in this space to do justice to the nuances present in each code, whether in describing their interpretation of ethical principles or their presentation of Christian foundations. The reader is urged to use the URLs supplied to access the full codes via the Internet. Moreover, this list of codes is not exhaustive. A number of other codes exist, both nationally and internationally. The reader will note that there is substantial overlap between codes in the subject matter covered.

In addition to the codes of ethics established by their own professional guilds, therapists should also be familiar with the laws pertaining to counseling in their states as well as the rules of practice established by the state boards of the professional groups with which they are affiliated.

American Psychological Association (APA)
Ethical Principles of Psychologists and Code of Conduct (2010)
http://www.apa.org/ethics/code/index.aspx
The APA Code of Ethics was the first ethics code devised for the mental health professions. The latest revision was published in 2002 and amended in 2010. The code contains two major parts: the General Principles and the Ethical Standards. The General Principles are aspirational ideals, over-arching ethical themes and principles that psychologists should endeavor to reach. They include such things as striving to benefit those they serve (beneficence), striving to do no harm (nonmaleficence), maintaining in-

tegrity and respecting the rights of those they serve. The Ethical Standards, on the other hand, are enforceable rules, which the APA and other bodies may use to sanction psychologists when necessary. There are 89 standards in all, organized into 10 subject areas. The subject areas are: (1) Resolving Ethical Issues, (2) Competence, (3) Human Relations (including multiple relationships, informed consent, harassment, etc.), (4) Privacy and Confidentiality, (5) Advertising and Other Public Statements, (6) Record Keeping and Fees, (7) Education and Training, (8) Research and Publication, (9) Assessment and (10) Therapy. In addition to the Code of Ethics, the APA also publishes guideline statements from time to time. While not enforceable, these guidelines provide recommendations to psychologists on different areas of practice and treatment such as record keeping and psychological testing.

American Counseling Association (ACA)
Code of Ethics (2005)
http://www.counseling.org/ethics/feedback/aca2005code.pdf
The ACA Code contains eight major sections. They are (1) The Counseling Relationship (which covers a wide range of topics including respect for client welfare, record keeping, counseling clients seeking employment, informed consent, avoiding harm and imposing values, multiple relationships, group work, end-of-life care, fees and bartering, termination and referral, and technology), (2) Confidentiality, Privileged Communication and Privacy, (3) Professional Responsibility (which covers such topics as competence, advertising and public responsibility), (4) Relationships with Other Professionals, (5) Evaluation, Assessment and Interpretation, (6) Supervision, Training and Teaching, (7) Research and Publication, and (8) Resolving Ethical Issues. The ACA Code is very detailed with numerous individual rules within each of the eight sections.

American Association for Marriage and Family Therapy (AAMFT)
Code of Ethics (2012)
http://www.aamft.org/imis15/content/legal_ethics/code_of_ethics.aspx
The AAMFT Code contains eight principles. They are (1) Responsibility to Clients (which covers topics such as informed consent and multiple rela-

tionships), (2) Confidentiality (including in couple or family therapy), (3) Professional Competence and Integrity, (4) Responsibility to Students and Supervisees, (5) Responsibility to Research Participants, (6) Responsibility to the Profession, (7) Financial Arrangements, and (8) Advertising.

Christian Association for Psychological Studies (CAPS)
Ethics Statement (2005)
http://caps.net/about-us/statement-of-ethical-guidelines
The Preamble to the CAPS Ethics Statement states that "As Christian leaders, we are called to be ethical, not as a legalistic obligation, but as part of an ever deepening intimate and covenantal relationship with God in Christ." The 2005 version of the statement contains two parts: Biblical Principles and Ethical Principles. The Biblical Principles serve as a foundation for the Ethical Principles and cover such areas as the image of God in humanity, the reality of sin and the responsibilities of servant-leaders. The Ethical Principles cover nine topics. They are (1) personal commitment as a Christian, (2) competence, (3) confidentiality, (4) counseling and psychotherapy (including informed consent, financial arrangements, treatment of couples and families, documentation, group therapy, multiple relationships and nondiscrimination), (5) assessment and testing, (6) education and training, (7) publication and research, (8) advertising and public statements, and (9) resolving ethical issues.

American Association of Christian Counselors (AACC)
Code of Ethics (2004)
http://aacc.net/wp-images/fammed/aacc_code_of_ethics.doc
The AACC code contains a Biblical-Ethical Foundations section, an Ethical Standards section and a Procedural Rules Section covering the adjudication process. The Biblical-Ethical section contains seven foundations, the first one being that "Jesus Christ—and His revelation in the Old and New Testaments of the Bible—is the pre-eminent model for Christian counseling practice, ethics, and caregiving activities." The Ethical Standards contain five subsections: (1) ethical standards for Christian counselors, (2) ethical standards for supervisors, educators, researchers and writers, (3) standards and exemptions for ordained ministers and pastoral counselors, (4) standards

and exemptions for lay helpers and other ministers, and (5) standards for resolving legal-ethical conflicts. The subsection on standards for Christian counselors contains most of the rules applicable to professional counselors. The rules are organized under eight different topic areas: (1) first, do no harm, (2) competence in Christian counseling, (3) informed consent in Christian counseling, (4) confidentiality, privacy and privileged communication, (5) ethical practice in Christian counseling and evaluation, (6) ethical relations in the professional workplace, (7) ethics in advertising and public relations, and (8) ethical relations with the state and other social systems. This is a very detailed code with numerous rules under each topic area.

American Association of Pastoral Counselors (AAPC)
Code of Ethics (2010)

http://www.aapc.org/about-us/code-of-ethics.aspx

The AAPC Code contains nine principles titled as follows: (1) Prologue, (2) Professional Practices, (3) Client Relationships, (4) Confidentiality, (5) Supervisee, Student and Employee Relationships, (6) Interprofessional Relationships, (7) Advertising, (8) Research, and (9) Procedures (which includes the methods for dealing with complaints). The prologue notes that AAPC members "are respectful of the various theologies, traditions and values of our faith communities and committed to the dignity and worth of each individual," and "are dedicated to advancing the welfare of those who seek our assistance and to the maintenance of high standards of professional conduct and competence."

OTHER SOURCES FOR CODES OF ETHICS

American Psychiatric Association. (2006). *Principles of medical ethics with annotations especially applicable to psychiatry.* Available at http://www.psychiatry.org/practice/ethics.

National Association of Social Workers. (2008). *Code of ethics.* Available at http://www.naswdc.org/pubs/code/code.asp.

Canadian Psychological Association. (2000). *Canadian code of ethics for psychologists.* Available at http://www.cpa.ca/cpasite/userfiles/Documents/Canadian%20Code%20of%20Ethics%20for%20Psycho.pdf.

APPENDIX 2

Sample Forms

The forms included on the pages that follow are samples of the types of forms that may be used for release of information and informed consent. Information included in such forms will necessarily vary according to the type of counseling services provided (e.g., counseling centers that serve certain treatment populations or conditions) or the counseling setting (church-based center, private practice, hospital, agency, school, etc.). It should also be understood that laws regarding what must be incorporated in such forms, treatment of minors, exceptions to confidentiality, etc. may vary from state to state. Samples of HIPAA notice of privacy forms are not included here for that reason (For further information on state-specific HIPAA privacy forms, readers may wish to obtain forms through the APA [www.apait.org/apait/resources/hipaa/faq.aspx] or other professional groups.) A sample of a service agreement that might be used when a collateral is involved in the treatment process can be found at www.apait.org/apait/resources/riskmanagement/cinf.aspx. Readers may also need to consult with other professional leaders in their state or seek legal consultation before constructing their own forms.

Mail _____ Fax _____ File _____

AUTHORIZATION FOR RELEASE OF CONFIDENTIAL INFORMATION AND FOR USE OR DISCLOSURE OF PROTECTED HEALTH INFORMATION

I authorize _____ and/or his/her staff _____ to

release to _____ to obtain from _____

Person (s) _____

Organization _____

Address _____

City _____ State _____ Zip Code _____

Phone _____   Fax _____

the following information:

__ Protected Health Information   __ All Medical Records   __ Verbal Communication

__ Initial Evaluation   __ Progress Notes/Report   __ Psychosocial History

__ Psychological Testing Report   __ Psychiatric Evaluation   __ Discharge or Treatment Summary

__ List of Medications   __ Other (specify) _____

This information is to be released for the purpose of continued treatment or (specify)

_____

This authorization shall remain in effect until (fill in expiration date) _____

You may revoke this authorization, in writing, at any time, by sending written notification to Dr. _____'s office address. However, your revocation will not be effective if Dr._____ or his/her staff have already taken action on your authorization, or if the authorization was obtained as a condition of obtaining insurance coverage and the insurer has a legal right to contest a claim.

I also understand that information used or disclosed pursuant to the authorization may be subject to redisclosure by the recipient of your information and no longer protected by the HIPAA Privacy Rule.

Patient _____ Date of Birth _____

Signature of Patient _____Date _____

Parent/Guardian Signature _____ Date _____

(if patient is a minor)

Mail _____ Fax _____ File _____

AUTHORIZATION TO RELEASE PSYCHOTHERAPY NOTES

Psychotherapy Notes are defined as notes I may have made about our conversation during a private, group, joint or family counseling session which I have kept separate from the rest of your medical record. These records are given a greater degree of protection than other Protected Health Information under HIPAA (Health Insurance Portability and Accountability Act).

I authorize _____ and/or his/her staff _____ to release to; _____ to obtain from

Person (s) _____

Organization _____

Address _____

City _____ State _____ Zip Code _____

Phone _____ Fax _____

the following information: Psychotherapy Notes.

This information is to be released for the purpose of continued treatment or (specify)

_____

This authorization shall remain in effect until (fill in expiration date)

_____

You may revoke this authorization, in writing, at any time, by sending written notification to Dr. _____'s office address. However, your revocation will not be effective if Dr._____ or his/her staff have already taken action on your authorization, or if the authorization was obtained as a condition of obtaining insurance coverage and the insurer has a legal right to contest a claim.

I also understand that information used or disclosed pursuant to the authorization may be subject to redisclosure by the recipient of your information and no longer protected by the HIPAA Privacy Rule.

Patient _____ Date of Birth _____

Signature of Patient _____ Date _____

Parent/Guardian Signature _____ Date _____
(if patient is a minor)

Insurance/Payment Information

Responsible Party

Last Name _____ First Name _____ M.I. ____

Address _____

City _____ State _____ Zip _____

Home Phone (____)_____

Date of Birth _____SSN _____ Relationship to Patient _____

Employer _____ Address _____

Occupation_____Business Phone(____)_____

Spouse Name _____ SSN _____

Primary Insurance Co_____Effective Date _____

Insured's Name_____ DOB _____SSN _____

Address (if different) _____

Policy No. _____ Group No. _____ Relationship to patient _____

Secondary Insurance Co _____Effective Date _____

Insured's Name_____DOB _____SSN _____

Address (if different) _____

Policy No. _____ Group No _____ Relationship to patient _____

I (we) authorize payment of medical benefits to the provider herein for all medical/psychological services rendered. I (we) authorize the provider to release any information required to process my insurance claims. I (we) authorize my insurance benefits to be paid directly to _____. I (we) understand that I (we) am (are) financially responsible for payment of any insurance deductible, copayments, and non-covered charges or services. A photocopy of this signature is valid as the original.

Signature of Responsible Party_____ Date _____

Signature of Spouse _____ Date _____

(required if marital treatment)

Please provide us with your insurance card in order to have a copy on file. Please notify us of any changes to your insurance.

Consent for Psychological Services to Child

Child's Name _____ Date of Birth _____

Name of person requesting services _____

Your relationship to child: Parent Stepparent Grandparent Guardian Other _____

Are you the legal parent or custodian of the above-named child ? Yes _____ No _____

In instances of divorce, it is essential that the legal custodian of the child grant permission for the services.

If you are a divorced parent, a stepparent, a grandparent, a guardian or other, you will be asked to provide a copy of the court order which names you the legal custodian of the above-named child. Are you willing to do so? Yes _____ No _____

If you are unwilling or unable to provide such documentation, psychological services cannot be provided to the above-named child until a copy of the court order is received by this office.

By my signature below, I consent for the minor child named above to receive psychological services which may include _____ clinical interviews, _____ psychological testing, _____ counseling/psychotherapy, other services: _____

I acknowledge that both natural parents, even though divorced, may have a right to obtain from the provider named below information regarding the nature and course of treatment of the child.

Printed name of person giving consent _____

Signature of person giving consent _____

Date _____

Important Information for New Clients of Dr. _____

Welcome!

This sheet has been prepared to help you know more about me and the psychological services I provide. If at any time during our work together, you have questions, please don't hesitate to let me know. I welcome your questions and believe that they help the therapeutic process.

Dr._____

Services

Dr. _____'s services include the following:

- Individual psychotherapy for adults, adolescents and children
- Marital therapy
- Psychological testing
- Pastoral psychotherapy
- Health psychology

For more information about specific problems or other services, please contact Dr. _____'s office.

About Psychotherapy

Dr. _____ uses a variety of accepted psychotherapeutic treatments depending on the nature of the problems presented. His primary objective is to use treatment methods that have been validated by research or clinical experience. Some of the more frequently used treatments he employs are cognitive behavior therapy, dialectical behavior therapy, and client-centered therapy.

His primary concern at the beginning is to understand as fully as possible the things that have brought you to therapy and the background factors behind them. On occasion, Dr. _____ may suggest psychological testing as a way of understanding your needs more fully.

Psychotherapy itself is best viewed as an individualized educational process. You and Dr. _____ work together to understand what brought you to this point in your life and to fashion ways that you can improve and grow. At times, Dr. _____ will give you homework assignments to complete between sessions. Like any educational process, therapy takes time. The exact amount of time depends on the nature of the problems presented, your personality traits and background, and your active participation in the therapeutic process. Psychotherapy is a positive overall experience for most people. The process of psychotherapy is not always easy, however, and at times a person may experience intense emotions or distress while he or she is participating in therapy. Also, while psychotherapy can lead to positive growth and increased understanding, there can be no guarantee that this will be true for everyone.

Each session is usually scheduled for 45 minutes. Sessions are most often scheduled weekly or once every two weeks, at least at first. The exact frequency of sessions depends on the individual circumstances. The overall length of therapy depends on several factors, including the nature of the problems being treated. If at any time you have questions about the length, frequency and number of sessions, or the nature or direction of the psychotherapy, do not hesitate to ask.

Confidentiality

Psychotherapy sessions are confidential. Information about you will not be released without your permission. You need to know, however, that there are limited circumstances under which, by law, Dr. _____ would be required to share information with appropriate third parties without your permission. Examples of such situations include, but are not limited to, when a person could be a danger to themselves or someone else, when there is concern about possible child abuse or in certain court proceedings. These situations are further discussed in our HIPAA Notice Form, which accompanies this document. If you are using insurance to help cover your treatment, you will be asked to sign a release form allowing us to provide information to your insurance company regarding your treatment. If you have any questions regarding confidentiality, please do not hesitate to ask.

Your Freedom & Responsibility

Dr. _____ will encourage you to remain in therapy long enough to improve and reach goals. In working to achieve goals, firm effort may be required on your part and some aspects of changing may be difficult. Dr. _____ will assist you as you work toward your goals, but you have the ultimate responsibility for the growth and change you make in psychotherapy. You do have the right to terminate or quit therapy if you desire.

Personal Values

The personal beliefs and values of the therapist and the client may have an effect on the therapy, even though they may not always be an explicit part of the therapy. Dr. _____ is a Christian and his personal values emanate from that tradition. While he will not attempt to impose his beliefs on anyone, these values are a significant part of Dr. _____'s life and work. If you have personal beliefs, spiritual issues or values concerns that you wish to discuss in therapy, please do not hesitate to let Dr. _____ know.

Fees and Insurance

Dr. _____'s standard fees are as follows:

Initial Evaluation (first interview)	$_____
Standard Psychotherapy Session (45 minute session)	$_____

Charges for psychological testing or other services that you may require are made separately and vary according to the procedure. Payment is expected at the time services are rendered and may be made by check or in cash.

As a licensed psychologist, the services Dr. _____ provides are often covered in whole or in part by health insurance companies and other third-party payers. If you choose to use your insurance, we will be happy to assist you in attempting to verify your benefits and, with your permission, in filing for your insurance. However, please understand that you are ultimately responsible for the payment of services rendered, if for any reason your insurance decides not to provide reimbursement. It is in your best interest to study your insurance plan coverage yourself and contact your insurance company for more details if necessary. As noted previously, you should also be aware that insurance companies usually require that we provide them with information about you and your treatment in order to reimburse for services rendered. If you have any questions about any matter related to payment of services or insurance, please ask.

Cancelled Appointments

Your appointments are held exclusively for you. If you must cancel your appointment please do so at least 24 hours in advance. You will be billed a fee of $___ for any appointment that is missed or cancelled without 24-hour notification. The fee cannot be billed to your insurance company.

Life-threatening Emergencies

If you have a life-threatening psychological emergency you should call our answering service at XXX-XXX-XXXX and request the therapist on call. If you do not receive a call back within a reasonable period, please go to your nearest hospital emergency room for care or contact 911.

Other Services

Dr. _____'s practice is one of several options for receiving mental health services in this community. If you have not already, you are welcome to compare the different options that are available to you. Also, if at any point in our work together, we need to consider a referral to another professional, I will be glad to assist you in any way that I can.

About Dr. _____
Dr. _____ is a licensed psychologist in _____.
Ph.D. (psychology) _____University
M.A. (psychology) _____ University
B.A. (psychology) _____ College
Dr. _____'s clinical training was taken in a variety of settings, including _____
_____.

Please Ask Questions

You are encouraged to discuss openly and freely with Dr. _____any question or concern you might have about your counseling and therapy program. We welcome your questions.

Consent

I have read and understand the information in the paragraphs above. I give my consent to enter treatment with Dr. _____.
Signature of Patient _____
Signature of Responsible Party (if different) _____
Date _____ Dr. _____

Confidential Client Information

Today's date _____   Case no. _____

Client's name _____ M___ F___ Date of birth _____ Age_____

Address _____ City _____State ___ Zip _____

Social Security no.: _____ Occupation _____

Employer _____

Telephone: Home _____ OK to call? Y N Work _____ OK to call? Y N

Cell _____ OK to call? Y N Pager _____ OK to call? Y N

Education _____

Marital status: Single ____ Married ____ Separated ____ Divorced ____ Widowed ____

Previous marriages: Yes ___ No ___ Dates: 1. _____ 2: _____ 3: _____

Spouse's name _____ Date of birth _____ Age _____

Spouse's Employer _____ Tel _____

Children

_____ Age ___ Date of birth _____ Grade ___ Living with _____

_____ Age ___ Date of birth _____ Grade ___ Living with _____

_____ Age ___ Date of birth _____ Grade ___ Living with _____

_____ Age ___ Date of birth _____ Grade ___ Living with _____

Emergency Contact Person (other than household member):

Name _____ Address _____

Relationship _____ Telephone (H) _____ (W) _____

Please describe any current/recent medical problems _____

_____

Please list all current medications you are taking _____

_____

Family Physician _____ Phone _____

Referred by _____

Have you or any family member received previous counseling or psychotherapy?

Outpatient?   Yes   No   Providers and dates: _____

Inpatient?   Yes   No   Facility and dates: _____

In what way(s) would you like me to assist you? _____

_____

_____

_____

_____

Please rate each of the following concerns as they apply to you *at the present time* on a scale of 1-5 (1 = not a problem, no concern; 5 = a very strong or severe concern or problem)

Feelings of sadness, crying, being "down"	1	2	3	4	5
My mind feels like it's racing	1	2	3	4	5
Unwanted thoughts in my mind	1	2	3	4	5
Sometimes I can't control what I do	1	2	3	4	5
Sleep problems..	1	2	3	4	5
Feeling worthless.	1	2	3	4	5
Problems with anger/temper	1	2	3	4	5
Feeling like things aren't real.	1	2	3	4	5
Problems with my eating.	1	2	3	4	5
There are things too painful to talk about.	1	2	3	4	5
Concerns about my sexuality	1	2	3	4	5
Use of alcohol and/or drugs.	1	2	3	4	5
Doing things over and over.	1	2	3	4	5
Seeing or hearing things that others don't	1	2	3	4	5
Feeling anxious/nervous	1	2	3	4	5
Being close to people	1	2	3	4	5
Spiritual concerns.	1	2	3	4	5
Pain and/or health concerns.	1	2	3	4	5

Are there current or past relationships that are a particular concern for you? Please describe briefly. _____

_____

_____

_____

What are the most significant stresses that you are currently dealing with? _____

_____

_____

_____

_____

_____

What do you consider to be your most important strengths? _____

_____

_____

_____

_____

_____

Are there other areas of concern (emotional, physical, spiritual, relational, educational or vocational) that you would like to let me know about that have not been covered in this form? _____

_____

_____

_____

_____

_____

I appreciate your taking the time to give me this important information. I hope that this visit and future visits will be of service to you. Please feel free to ask any questions or raise any concerns that you might have at any time.

Contributors

Tamara L. Anderson (Ph.D., California School of Professional Psychology at Los Angeles) is professor of psychology and associate dean of graduate students at the Rosemead School of Psychology, Biola University. Her special interests include gender issues, attachment, and ethics and law.

Iryna Shturba Arute, M.A., is a doctoral student in the clinical psychology program at Wheaton College. Born and raised in Ukraine, she is especially interested in service to culturally diverse populations through scholarship and clinical work.

Jeffrey S. Berryhill (Ph.D., Graduate School of Psychology, Fuller Theological Seminary) is a psychologist in private practice in St. Paul, Minnesota. He is also an adjunct professor of psychology at Bethel University, where his graduate teaching includes child and adolescent assessment and psychopathology, as well as ethics and professional issues.

Bill Blackburn (Ph.D., Southern Seminary) recently retired as executive director of Partners in Ministry in Kerrville, Texas. Prior to that, he served as pastor of Trinity Baptist Church in Kerrville for many years. He is the author of five books, including *What You Should Know About Suicide*, and has done postdoctoral work at Oxford University in biblical studies and medical ethics.

Richard E. Butman (Ph.D., Graduate School of Psychology, Fuller Theological Seminary) is professor of psychology at Wheaton College. He is co-author (with Stanton Jones) of *Modern Psychotherapies: A Christian Ap-*

praisal (InterVarsity Press) and is also coauthor (with Mark Yarhouse and Barrett McRay) of *Modern Psychopathologies: A Comprehensive Christian Appraisal* (InterVarsity Press). His current interests include bereavement and psychopathology, and he is involved in ministries in Africa, Asia, Chicago and Latin America.

Sally Schwer Canning (Ph.D., University of Pennsylvania) is professor of psychology at Wheaton College and a behavioral health provider at Lawndale Christian Health Center. A licensed clinical psychologist and active scholar, Dr. Canning has 25 years of experience practicing, consulting and doing research aimed at understanding and promoting the well-being of children and families in poor urban contexts. She trains future psychologists for culturally competent practice and research with underserved populations and in community-based organizations. She teaches ethics, community psychology, and child/adolescent practice courses and is a faculty cochair of the Psy.D. program's diversity committee.

Thomas C. Duke, M.A., is a doctoral student in clinical psychology at the Fuller Theological Seminary Graduate School of Psychology. He participates in research pertaining to the mental health needs of humanitarian aid workers, and he has worked internationally with aid organizations in Azerbaijan, Swaziland, Uganda, Guatemala and Mexico.

Cynthia B. Eriksson (Ph.D., Graduate School of Psychology, Fuller Theological Seminary) is an associate professor of psychology and director of the Headington Program Research Lab at the Fuller Theological Seminary Graduate School of Psychology. She conducts research and teaches in the area of psychological trauma. She was a collaborator with the National Child Traumatic Stress Network in the adaptation of the *Psychological First Aid Manual for Community Religious Professionals*.

Roderick D. Hetzel (Ph.D., Texas A&M University) is a licensed psychologist in independent practice at Waco Psychological Associates, PC. He is an adjunct professor in the Department of Educational Psychology and the George W. Truett Theological Seminary at Baylor University. Dr. Hetzel is a former senior psychologist and coordinator of clinical training at the Baylor University Counseling Center.

James H. Jennison (Ph.D., Graduate School of Psychology, Fuller Theological Seminary) is a psychologist in private practice providing medical legal evaluations for injured workers in Southern California. He is a member of the American Psychological Association, the National Academy of Neuropsychology, and the California Society of Industrial Medicine and Surgery, and is a Fellow of the American College of Forensic Examiners.

W. Brad Johnson (Ph.D., Graduate School of Psychology, Fuller Theological Seminary) is professor in the Department of Leadership, Ethics, & Law at the United States Naval Academy, and is also a faculty associate in the Graduate School of Education at Johns Hopkins University. His research interests include mentor relationships, professional ethics and leadership.

Stanton L. Jones (Ph.D., Arizona State University) is provost and professor of psychology at Wheaton College and an academic clinical psychologist. He has written widely on psychological theory and theology, and on human sexuality.

Jill L. Kays (Psy.D., Regent University) is a licensed psychologist in Charlotte, North Carolina. She currently works as a clinical psychologist in the public sector. She is a member of the American Psychological Association.

Cassie Kendrick (Psy.D., Baylor University) is a postdoctoral fellow at Baylor's Mind-Body Medicine Research Laboratory.

Andrea M. Librado, M.A., is a doctoral student in the clinical psychology program at Wheaton College. Her special interests include working with low-income urban populations and understanding culture through a variety of lenses, including but also extending beyond those of ethnicity, race and geography.

Horace C. Lukens Jr. (Ph.D., University of Maine) is a licensed psychologist serving as a medical consultant with the Massachusetts Social Security Disability Administration. He is retired from full-time clinical practice and served two terms as president of the board of CAPS but continues to maintain an active interest in the integration of faith and psychology.

Susan Matlock-Hetzel (Ph.D., Texas A&M University) is a clinical psychologist in the Department of Mental Health and Behavior Medicine at the Waco VA Medical Center. She is a former staff psychologist and coordinator of outreach at the Baylor University Counseling Center.

Kelly O'Donnell (Psy.D., Rosemead School of Psychology, Biola University) is a consulting psychologist living in Europe and serving as CEO of Member Care Associates, Inc. His member care emphases include staff well-being, crisis care, ethics, team development and practitioner affiliations. He is also the coordinator of the Mental Health-Psychosocial Working Group for the Geneva-based NGO Forum for Health. He has published widely on member care, including *Doing Member Care Well: Perspective and Practices from Around the World* and *Global Member Care: The Pearls and Perils of Good Practice* (both published by William Carey Library).

Jennifer S. Ripley (Ph.D., Virginia Commonwealth University) is professor of psychology and director of the doctor of psychology program at Regent University. She is also director of the Marriage and Ministry Assessment, Training and Empowerment (MMATE) Center.

Angela M. Sabates (Ph.D., Northwestern University) is associate professor of psychology at Bethel University in St. Paul, Minnesota. Her background is in child clinical psychology and in social psychology, and she recently published *Social Psychology in Christian Perspective: Exploring the Human Condition* (InterVarsity Press).

Steven J. Sandage (Ph.D., Virginia Commonwealth University) is professor of marriage and family studies at Bethel University in St. Paul, Minnesota, and a licensed psychologist in practice with Arden Woods Psychological Services, PA, in New Brighton, Minnesota.

Randolph K. Sanders (Ph.D., Graduate School of Psychology, Fuller Theological Seminary) is a clinical psychologist in independent practice in New Braunfels, Texas. He is the former executive director of the Christian Association for Psychological Studies (CAPS) and served as an ex-officio member of the committee that revised the CAPS Statement of Ethical Guidelines. He is a noted writer and speaker on ethical matters in psychotherapy, and he also serves on the board of consultants of his denomination's state ethics and social concerns agency.

Gregory R. Schneller (Ph.D., Southern Illinois University) is associate professor of psychology at McMurry University. His interest areas include ethics and the integration of psychology and Christianity.

John F. Shackelford (Psy.D., Rosemead School of Psychology, Biola University) is a clinical psychologist in private practice in Richardson and Glen Rose, Texas. His special interests include the integration of the psychological concepts of self and ego with Christian spirituality, personality assessment and ADHD assessment.

John Eric Swenson III (Ph.D., University of Memphis) is associate professor of psychology at Hardin-Simmons University. He also provides psychological services at the Ministry of Counseling and Enrichment in Abilene, Texas. His special interests include psychotherapy ethics and the integration of Christian faith and psychology.

Siang-Yang Tan (Ph.D., McGill University) is professor of psychology at Fuller Theological Seminary and senior pastor of First Evangelical Church of Glendale in Southern California. He is a fellow of the American Psychological Association, and has authored or coauthored thirteen books, including *Lay Counseling* and *Counseling and Psychotherapy: A Christian Perspective*.

Alan C. Tjeltveit (Ph.D. in clinical psychology, Graduate School of Psychology, Fuller Theological Seminary) is professor of psychology at Muhlenberg College and the author of *Ethics and Values in Psychotherapy* (Routledge).

Everett L. Worthington Jr. (Ph.D., University of Missouri) is professor of psychology at Virginia Commonwealth University. He has published numerous books and articles including *Marriage Counseling: A Christian Approach to Counseling Couples, Hope-Focused Marriage Counseling* and *Forgiving and Reconciling* (InterVarsity Press).

Mark A. Yarhouse (Psy.D., Wheaton College) is the Rosemarie S. Hughes Endowed Chair and Professor of Psychology at Regent University. He is a clinical psychologist in private practice in Virginia Beach, Virginia.

Anta F. Yu is a doctoral student in the clinical psychology program at Wheaton College and a student representative on the Diversity and Justice Committee there. Her interests include methods for providing ethical, empowering and culturally honoring services to diverse populations.

Subject Index

abandonment of clients, 107-8

abortion, 162

absolutism, 21

abuse, 91, 162, 176-77, 177-78, 199-201

access to records, 100

accountability, therapist, 38-39

advertising, 10, 345-50

    government regulations concerning, 347

Alzheimer's disease, 298-300

aspirational ethics, 12-16, 45-49

assessment and testing (psychological), 255-56, 324-29, 385, 420-21, 433

autonomy, client, 15, 37, 95-98, 207, 228-31, 234-35, 239, 268-75, 331

beneficence and nonmaleficence, 12, 24, 237, 239, 263, 344-45, 404-5, 445-47, 471, 476

bias in evaluation, 324-29

Bible and counseling ethics, 14, 26-28, 43, 49, 65, 66, 76-77, 81, 160, 162, 177, 180-81, 289, 315-19, 345, 353, 370, 373, 377, 388, 444, 528

    See also Christian ethics

boundaries, 79, 104, 142, 369-70, 376-78, 399, 473

brain injury, 296

burnout, therapist, 64-65, 75, 80-82, 390-91, 508

business ethics and counseling, 22-23, 343-66

character, therapist's, 43, 60, 510

    See also virtue ethics

children, 186-214, 312-13, 472

    abuse of, 91, 199-201

    as clients, 186-214

    and confidentiality, 93, 194-99, 204, 210-11

    custody of, 190-91

    documentation for, 204-5

    faith of, 206-9

    involuntary treatment for, 193

    multiple relationships, 201-4

Christian counseling and therapy, 8-10, 20-21, 24-25, 96, 298, 307-8, 348, 429-36

    as calling, 13, 28

    outcome studies, 52-53, 411

    in secular settings, 25, 397-412

    See also evangelizing in therapy

Christian counselors and therapists, 82-83

    education of, 65-67, 482-501

Christian ethics

    counseling and, 8-10, 28, 33-53, 160, 164, 173-80

    ethical theory and, 49-50, 485

    marriage and, 160

    See also Bible and counseling ethics

chronic conditions, ethics of counseling for, 285-309

chronic pain, 300-302

church discipline, 383-84

client

    definition of, 167-69, 187, 400, 515-16

    participation in ethical decisions, 153, 179, 407

codes of ethics, 10-13, 17, 24-25, 35-39, 45, 139-42, 163, 286-90, 319-24, 402-6, 436, 445-46, 506-7

    clinical application of, 483, 488-89

    decision making, use of in, 512

    development of, 482-83

    ignorance of, 19, 436

    lay counselors and, 389

    See also appendix 1

colleagues, relationships with, 362-64

collection agencies, use of, 352-53

community, responsibility to, 15-16, 28, 515-16

competence, professional, 10, 17, 37,